RALPH WALDO EMERSON

Christopher Pearse Cranch's drawing of Emerson's "transparent eye-ball" from *Nature*.

Ralph Waldo Emerson

The Major Prose

EDITED BY

RONALD A. BOSCO

AND JOEL MYERSON

THE BELKNAP PRESS *of* HARVARD UNIVERSITY PRESS

Cambridge, Massachusetts ⬩ London, England

2015

Library of Congress Cataloging-in-Publication Data
Emerson, Ralph Waldo, 1803–1882.
[Works. Selections]
Ralph Waldo Emerson : the major prose / edited by Ronald A. Bosco
and Joel Myerson.
pages cm
Includes bibliographical references and index.
ISBN 978-0-674-41706-9 (alk. paper)
I. Bosco, Ronald A., editor.   II. Myerson, Joel, editor.   III. Title.
PS1602.B68 2015
814′.3—dc23   2014032666

Contents

Preface

   Ralph Waldo Emerson: The Major Prose is the only anthology of his writings that draws from the three predominant sources of his prose: the pulpit, the lecture hall, and print. The completion of *The Collected Works of Ralph Waldo Emerson* (1971–2013), published by the Belknap Press of Harvard University Press, along with the preparation of both *The Complete Sermons of Ralph Waldo Emerson* (1989–1992) and *The Later Lectures of Ralph Waldo Emerson* (2001), in scholarly editions based on Emerson's original manuscripts, have made this volume possible. At the outset, we gratefully acknowledge our debt to the many editors of volumes in those editions; their names will be found in the Abbreviations list that follows. Additionally, we gratefully acknowledge the care that the Emerson family, through the Ralph Waldo Emerson Memorial Association, and the Houghton Library of Harvard University have invested in the preservation of Emerson's manuscripts and significant portions of his personal library, and made both available to scholars. Here, we wish to recognize Margaret Emerson Bancroft, president of the Association, and Leslie A. Morris, Curator of Modern Books and Manuscripts at the Houghton Library.

Mr. Bosco is grateful to President Robert J. Jones, Dean of Arts and Sciences Edelgard Wulfert, and Chair of English Randall Craig at the University at Albany, State University of New York, for providing him with the intellectual space to work on this project. Mr. Myerson thanks for their support William Rivers and Nina Levine, Chairs of the English Department, Dean of Arts and Sciences Mary Anne Fitzpatrick of the University of South Carolina at Columbia, and Michael Weisenburg for his assistance with the texts. Mr. Bosco and Mr. Myerson both acknowledge John Gregory Kulka, Alexander Morgan, and Heather Hughes of the Harvard University Press for their consistent encouragement and support of our work over the years.

Abbreviations

CEC   *The Correspondence of Emerson and Carlyle.* Edited by Joseph Slater. New York: Columbia University Press, 1964.

CS   *The Complete Sermons of Ralph Waldo Emerson.* Albert J. von Frank, chief editor; Ronald A. Bosco, Andrew Delbanco, Teresa Toulouse, and Wesley T. Mott, editors. 4 vols. Columbia: University of Missouri Press, 1989–1992.

CW   *The Collected Works of Ralph Waldo Emerson.* Alfred R. Ferguson, Joseph Slater, Douglas Emory Wilson, and Ronald A. Bosco, general editors; Robert E. Burkholder, Jean Ferguson Carr, Glen M. Johnson, Joel Myerson, Philip Nicoloff, Barbara L. Packer, Robert E. Spiller, Albert J. von Frank, Wallace E. Williams, and Thomas Wortham, editors. 10 vols. Cambridge, Mass.: The Belknap Press of Harvard University Press, 1971–2013.

EAW   *Emerson's Antislavery Writings.* Edited by Len Gougeon and Joel Myerson. New Haven: Yale University Press, 1995.

EL   *The Early Lectures of Ralph Waldo Emerson.* Edited by Stephen E. Whicher, Robert E. Spiller, and Wallace E. Williams. 3 vols. Cambridge, Mass.: The Belknap Press of Harvard University Press, 1959–1972.

JMN   *The Journals and Miscellaneous Notebooks of Ralph Waldo Emerson.* William H. Gilman and Ralph H. Orth, chief editors; Linda Allardt, Ronald A. Bosco, George P. Clark, Merrell R. Davis, Harrison Hayford, David W. Hill, Glen M. Johnson, J. E. Parsons, A. W. Plumstead, Merton M. Sealts, Jr., and Susan Sutton Smith, editors; Ruth H. Bennett, associate editor. 16 vols. Cambridge, Mass.: The Belknap Press of Harvard University Press, 1960–1982.

L   *The Letters of Ralph Waldo Emerson.* Edited by Ralph L. Rusk (vols. 1–6) and Eleanor M. Tilton (vols. 7–10). New York: Columbia University Press, 1939, 1990–1995.

LL   *The Later Lectures of Ralph Waldo Emerson, 1843–1871.* Edited by Ronald A. Bosco and Joel Myerson. 2 vols. Athens: University of Georgia Press, 2001.

PN   *The Poetry Notebooks of Ralph Waldo Emerson.* Edited by Ralph H. Orth, Albert J. von Frank, Linda Allardt, and David W. Hill. Columbia: University of Missouri Press, 1986.

SelL   *Selected Lectures of Ralph Waldo Emerson.* Edited by Ronald A. Bosco and Joel Myerson. Athens: University of Georgia Press, 2005.

TN   *The Topical Notebooks of Ralph Waldo Emerson.* Ralph H. Orth, chief editor; Ronald A. Bosco, Glen M. Johnson, and Susan Sutton Smith, editors. 3 vols. Columbia: University of Missouri Press, 1990–1994.

W   *The Complete Works of Ralph Waldo Emerson.* Edited by Edward Waldo Emerson. Centenary Edition. 12 vols. Boston: Houghton, Mifflin, 1903–1904.

Introduction

> Do not set the least value on what I do, or the least discredit on what
> I do not, as if I pretended to settle anything as true or false. I unsettle
> all things. No facts are to me sacred; none are profane; I simply ex-
> periment, an endless seeker, with no Past at my back.
>
> —"Circles," para 27[1]

Ralph Waldo Emerson's life spanned nearly the entire nineteenth century. He was born on 23 May 1803, the year when there were seventeen states in the young Republic and President Thomas Jefferson completed
the Louisiana Purchase, and he died on 27 April 1882, the year that Franklin
Delano Roosevelt, Virginia Woolf, and James Joyce were born, Oscar Wilde
came to America as the young British apostle of Aestheticism, the Standard
Oil Trust was organized, and the country had grown to thirty-eight states.
His life began when slavery was legal, he did his part to bring about its abolition,[2] and he died after the South reversed the clock by repudiating Reconstruction. He began his schooling when John Locke and the sensationalist
philosophy of the Scottish philosophers were ascendant, was essential in
turning the tide towards the idealistic philosophy of Immanuel Kant, and was
able to see the rise of pragmatism as his writings influenced John Dewey and
William James. The recipient of a traditional Harvard education, Emerson
revolted against its strictures and influenced President Charles W. Eliot's cur-
ricular revisions at Harvard.[3] Emerson's literary career opened just as British
Romanticism had finally gained traction with a general audience in America,
and he died just as realism and naturalism emerged as significant literary
forces both in America and abroad.

Although Emerson's personal life moved in a straightforward, linear fashion, the man himself contained many opposites. He was a peripatetic speaker at a time when the lyceum movement flourished in America, delivering some 1,500 lectures over the course of his career throughout the Eastern United States and newly designated Midwestern states and territories; yet even as his reputation spread through his lectures and publications, from the time he made Concord, Massachusetts, his permanent home in 1834, he was rooted in the life and scenery of the town his ancestors had settled in the seventeenth century. He was considered a dreamy mystic by many who heard his lectures or read his books, yet he was wise about his monetary dealings and, in his relations with publishers, was one of the century's canniest authors. He was a careful literary stylist whose writings struck readers as opaque and assembled in a slipshod fashion. He wrote about nature, but unlike Henry Thoreau, who preferred only that technology that was immediately useful to him—advances in pencil-making techniques and surveying equipment, for instance—Emerson was fascinated by all advancements in science and technology, including the advent of the steam engine, the telegraph, and photography, the use of anesthesia in dentistry, the prospect of hot-air balloon flight, and the building of the Transcontinental Railroad and the laying of the Atlantic telegraph cable.[4] He desired no disciples, but still they came, even if for a short time: Thoreau served a mentorship with him, Walt Whitman was cheered when Emerson wrote to say, "I greet you at the beginning of a great career," and Emily Dickinson had his books in her library, beginning with his *Poems* (1847).[5]

Emerson's life spanned the last decades of New England's Calvinist tradition to the establishment of the Free Religious Association in Boston in 1867. He emerged from an American Puritan past—which held that humankind had been corrupted by original sin, that we lived in a hostile and unknowable world, and that individual salvation had been determined by chance before birth—to embrace a Unitarian world view that humankind had inherited an ordered universe in which one could progress through good works while living in a benevolent environment and that the quality of the life lived would be taken into consideration on judgment day. Soon even Unitarianism proved insufficiently liberal for Emerson, who eventually characterized it as "corpse-cold."[6]

The son and grandson of ministers, Emerson preached some 160 sermons before and after his ordination in 1829. Even though he left the established church, first by resigning his ministry in 1832, and then by signing off from his parish in Concord in 1852 (see *L*, 4:289), Emerson's thought is infused with religious belief. For him, all humankind and nature are emanations of the creative power of a larger force (sometimes called the "over-soul") and, as a result, both humans and nature contain divinity within them ("one mind is everywhere").[7] In one of his more controversial statements, Emerson declares: "Good is positive. Evil is merely privative, not absolute. It is like cold, which is the privation of heat."[8] Departing from the prevailing Manichean view of the world as an everlasting battleground between the forces of good and evil, Emerson believed that we are all born good and become bad only by straying from the right path.

Emerson resigned his pulpit because he rejected the observance of the Lord's Supper, arguing that the ritualistic administration of it distanced Christ from humankind as someone to be "commemorated" not, as Emerson wished, to be seen as a living force so that "men might be filled with his spirit." As he comments on the doctrine of transubstantiation (that the bread and wine at Communion become the body and blood of Christ), "To eat bread is one thing; to love the precepts of Christ and resolve to obey them is quite another."[9] Years after leaving his pulpit, Emerson continued to make a powerful case for what, in slightly different terms, the minister Theodore Parker saw as the distinction between the transient and the permanent in Christianity.[10] Emerson makes this clear in "The Divinity School Address," where he complains "that the divine nature is attributed to one or two persons, and denied to all the rest, and denied with fury," with the result that the "doctrine of inspiration is lost." What Christ said to us in a "jubilee of sublime emotion, 'I am divine. Through me, God acts; through me, speaks. Would you see God, see me; or, see thee, when thou also thinkest as I now think,'" becomes subverted into worship of the person, not the teachings, and the "idioms of his language, and the figures of his rhetoric, have usurped the place of his truth; and churches are not built on his principles, but on his tropes." This is, said Emerson, "Historical Christianity": "it is not the doctrine of the soul, but an exaggeration of the personal, the positive, the ritual. It has dwelt, it dwells, with noxious exaggeration about the *person* of Jesus." Emerson returns to this theme as late as 1866, when he declares the "excellence of Jesus" is "that he affirms the Divinity in him and in us."[11]

Because the figure of Christ has been divorced from his teachings, Emerson complains, the clergy focus on supernatural events to convert parishioners and not on the moral suasion of Christ's teachings ("He teaches us how to become like God"), and nowhere is this more apparent than in the argument for the validity of miracles. To the religious conservatives of his day, miracles, which by their very nature cannot be explained by humans, must be taken on faith as manifestations of God's work, while to the liberals, such supernatural worship separates God from humankind. Drawing on the Higher Biblical Criticism (or comparative religion) prevalent in early nineteenth-century Germany, Emerson argues that, because Christian miracles were drawn from the religious texts of other cultures, to "aim to convert a man by miracles, is a profanation of the soul," for "by his holy thoughts, Jesus serves us, and thus only." And in one of his most compelling images, he states "the very word Miracle, as pronounced by Christian churches, gives a false impression; it is Monster. It is not one with the blowing clover and the falling rain."[12] Connecting "Miracle" to "Monster" with capital M's, and contrasting the supernatural miracles that we cannot prove with the naturalistic clover and rain that we can observe, Emerson employs literary devices to make his theological point.

Emerson offers a twofold solution to humankind's sense of separation from God: first and foremost, prayer, and second, confidence in the fact that life itself is an ongoing miracle in which all share. In his first sermon, "Pray without Ceasing" (1826), Emerson defines "true prayers" as the "daily, hourly, momentary desires, that come without impediment, without fear, into the soul" and recognizes *"every desire of the human mind"* as *"a prayer uttered to God and registered in heaven"*; and if, he continues, "Every secret wish is a prayer," then it follows that "Every house is a church."[13] Prayer thus becomes an individual's means of direct communication with God and, at the same time, elevates the individual into partnership with a class of persons Emerson would define a decade after "Pray without Ceasing" as

> natural preachers, men of inward light, whose eye is opened upon the laws of duty, and the beauty of holiness[,] . . . who feel and . . . make us feel that the Revelation is not closed and sealed, but times of refreshment and words of power are evermore coming from the presence of the Lord; that neither is the age of mira-

cles over and forever gone; that the Creation is an endless miracle as new at this hour as when Adam awoke in the garden.[14]

Philosophically, Emerson rejects the view of the world held by his parents' generation that, according to John Locke, all knowledge must be verified by the senses. To Locke, the mind is a blank tablet *(tabula rasa)* or sheet of blank paper on which is inscribed the sum of an individual's experiences. It is as if we are a blank book at birth, and as we proceed through life we write down our experiences, so that our existence ultimately is experientially inscribed in our book of life. Emerson adapts the ideas of Immanuel Kant that there are categories of preexisting knowledge that can be grasped intuitively. To Emerson, the book individuals are handed at birth is not blank, but contains within it certain universally acknowledged truths, and from the start one instinctively reads this book rather than inscribes one's self in it. If universal truths exist, then each of us becomes an independent reader capable of discerning those truths in whatever texts we choose to read, be they secular (for example, literary texts), religious (the Bible), or the natural world. Emerson uses terms that had wide circulation in his day, "Understanding" and "Reason," to distinguish between, respectively, Lockean empiricism or sensationalism and Kantian intuition, once writing, "Reason is the highest faculty of the soul—what we mean often by the soul itself; it never *reasons,* never proves, it simply perceives; it is vision. The Understanding toils all the time, compares, contrives, adds, argues, near sighted but strong-sighted, dwelling in the present the expedient the customary."[15]

If Emerson distinguishes between the world of humans and the world of spirit in religion, he also does so in his philosophical thinking. In "Pray without Ceasing," Emerson foretold his beliefs: "It ought to be distinctly felt by us that we stand in the midst of two worlds, the world of matter and the world of spirit"; our bodies belong to matter, our thoughts to spirit.[16] Given a choice between the sensationalism of Locke and the idealism of Kant, Emerson always chooses Kant. In fact, one reason for Emerson's continued popularity is his ability to state such philosophical dichotomies in language the average reader can comprehend: "Idealism saith: matter is a phenomenon, not a substance." Rather than cite at length Kant or Samuel Taylor Coleridge on the difference between spirit and matter, Emerson concludes with surprising brevity that "Idealism is a hypothesis to account for nature by other principles than those of carpentry and chemistry." But a world of phenomena without spirit is not good, for it "leaves God out of me," and Emerson would be doomed to eternity in "the splendid labyrinth of my perceptions, to wander without end." Importantly, once we become followers of Kant, there is no going back: "Every materialist will be an idealist; but an idealist can never go backward to be a materialist." And in a passage that contains one of his most memorable images, Emerson argues that the Idealist sees "things as the reverse side of the tapestry," thus conjuring up an image of a woven tapestry in which the picture being viewed on the front (matter) is composed of numerous interconnected fibers on the back (spirit), and it is the invisible action of those fibers that makes the object on the front visible.[17]

Emerson's philosophy—his approach to everyday experiences and how they reflect or contribute to a life of the mind—has remained popular for nearly two centuries because he offers his readers a process philosophy, or ontology of being, that can be profitably pursued throughout one's life rather than a set of static precepts to be memorized and tucked away. "Our life," Emerson believes, "is an apprenticeship to the truth."[18] Neither life nor truth is static or circumscribed. Nor is the road traveled a dull one: "Life is a series of surprises" and it "would not be worth taking or keeping, if it were not." Emerson distinguishes between stasis and process by changing verb tenses in his examples: "Life only avails, not the having lived"; "It is the office of a true teacher to show us that God is, not was; that He speaketh, not spake"; and the goal of the "American Scholar" is to be "Man Thinking." Even when we see a great person, we should not try to pattern ourselves solely on them, because "Imitation cannot go above its model" and the "imitator dooms himself to hopeless mediocrity." Indeed, "great men exist that there may be greater men." Although Emerson often names people he admires in his writings, he does not wish to hold up any one of them as a fixed example, because then his process philosophy would come to a halt. Emerson is always in search of better models, ready to discard old ones: "I look in vain for the poet whom I describe" or "there is no pure Transcendentalist; . . . we know of none but the prophets and heralds of such a philosophy." In short, "every action admits of being outdone." At the same time, though, new actions often cause us to lose as well as gain: while the "civilized man has built a coach," he has "lost the use of his feet," and the invention of the watch was followed by our losing "the skill to tell the hour by the sun."[19]

Some readers may register discomfort with Emerson's philosophy, because they prefer to believe that knowledge is something acquired and built up, like a glass being filled, rather than a series of explorations, each one leading to another. Emerson anticipated such readers' discomfort when he wrote of his contemporaries, "Man is timid and apologetic. . . . He dares not say 'I think,' 'I am,'[20] but quotes some saint or sage."[21] For such readers during Emerson's time or in our own, the most challenging aspect of his process philosophy to grasp is that it never ends—there will always be something else to learn, and the "only sin is limitation." Emerson approves of this, because the alternative to humankind's moving forward is either its stasis or its entropy. This path can be hard, because people like concrete evidence of their advancement, such as school grades and approval from peers. To these doubters, Emerson expresses his personal preference for "imperfect theories, and sentences, which contain glimpses of truth," over "digested systems which have no one valuable suggestion."[22] For Emerson, an individual's intuitive glimpse of the infinite is far better than a seemingly comprehensive but dead theory that may be learned from a book.

The distinction between spirit and matter also underlies Emerson's approaches in other areas. In philosophy, as we have seen, it finds its analogy in the difference between Reason and Understanding. In literature, it informs Emerson's distinction between genius and talent; the former, associated with the poet, signifies inspiration or originality, as when Isaac Newton watches an apple fall and declares, "'I see the law of all nature,'" while the latter, by contrast, involves a process of collecting and "slow observation" that "makes good this bold word." Late in life, Emerson describes the difference thus: "when the wit is totally surrendered to intellectual truth,—that is genius. Talent for talent's sake is a bauble and a show." Emerson's own adherence to this concept of genius is clear: "I have followed my inclination rather than consulted my ability." It is the poet or man of pure genius who dwells in the realm of Reason: "The sensual man conforms thoughts to things; the poet conforms things to his thoughts. The one esteems nature as rooted and fast; the other, as fluid, and impresses his being thereon."[23]

How humankind applies spirit to the natural world is the subject of Emerson's first book, *Nature* (1836), published anonymously (though Emerson's authorship was well known). In *Nature*, Emerson brought together a number of intellectual strands that had been in the air: from Germany, the philosophy of Kant; from England, the Romantic sense of the importance of the natural world; from America, the emphasis on the common man embodied in the presidency of Andrew Jackson and a spirit of revolt against the restrictions of the past evidenced in the religious transitions from Calvinism to Unitarianism to Transcendentalism. He accomplished this in down-to-earth language (especially relative to the weighty tomes and journal articles of the time) that developed naturalistic examples as opposed to historical precedents. And his readership encompassed some who would become major figures in the Transcendentalist movement and/or American literature: Thoreau, Margaret Fuller, Emily Dickinson, and Walt Whitman.

Throughout his long life, Emerson attempts to answer the question he first poses in 1836: "Let us inquire, to what end is nature?," something he structures as tripartite query, "What is matter? Whence is it? and Whereto?" Rather than engaging in an extended philosophical debate, Emerson, relying on his idealistic beliefs, quickly comes to the point: "matter is a phenomenon, not a substance." And while there is a "noble doubt" as to "whether nature outwardly exists," Emerson cuts the Gordian knot by asking what difference it makes: "Whether nature enjoy a substantial existence without, or is only in the apocalypse of the mind, it is alike useful and alike venerable to me. Be it what it may, it is ideal to me, so long as I cannot try the accuracy of my senses." That is, if the question cannot be answered definitively, Emerson in any case prefers the ideal theory and the use of intuition over intellectualization, of Reason over Understanding. Or, to place this in a religious context, "These laws refuse to be adequately stated. They will not by us or for us be written out on paper, or spoken by the tongue."[24]

If, as Emerson says, nature is significant and instructive—"The beauty of the world is a perpetual invitation to the study of the world" and "Nature is thoroughly mediate" because it "is made to serve"—then we must discover its lessons so that it may serve us. These lessons are, of course, divine ones. Nature and humankind are both emanations of the godhead, so that "the ancient precept, 'Know thyself,' and the modern precept, 'Study nature,' become at last one maxim." When Emerson visited the cabinets of curiosity in the Jardin des Plantes in Paris's Muséum d'Histoire Naturelle in 1833, he saw there for the first time a means of classifying organisms that suggested "a grammar of botany—where the plants rise, each in its class, its order, and its genus"; then and there he decided, "I will be a naturalist."[25]

The interrelations among humankind, nature, and God also underpin Emerson's belief in a microcosm/macrocosm theory of nature.[26] To him, "every atom" is "a miniature of the world," and a "drop is a small ocean." By studying something small we can make generalizations about something large. Emerson gives Thoreau as the example of the ideal student of nature, calling him a "genius" who "swiftly inferred universal law from the single fact." Emerson occasionally expresses concern that we focus too much on details rather than on the larger picture, resulting in "this tyrannizing unity" that "evermore separates and classifies things" and fails "to explain the relation between things and thoughts," and he also warns that once something is removed from its larger context—a seashell from the beach, humankind from God, nature from humankind—it loses the value it had by association: "A single object is only so far beautiful as it suggests this universal grace."[27]

These beliefs led to the concepts of organicism and compensation. Organicism holds that form follows function, and form is derived from nature. The American architect Frank Lloyd Wright, an admirer of Emerson, is an excellent example of an artist who consistently applied organicism to his designs. Compensation, by contrast, is a type of moral Newtonianism, stipulating that for every action there is an equal and opposite reaction, as when Emerson writes "that nature's dice are always loaded; that in her heaps and rubbish are concealed sure and useful results," or when he points out that "Good is a good doctor, but Bad is sometimes a better," giving as examples how the "oppressions of William the Norman, savage forest laws, and crushing despotism" made the Magna Carta possible, or how the "cruel wars" fought by Alexander "introduced the civility, language, and arts of Greece into the savage East."[28]

Nature's lessons can be applied to various spheres. The study of "natural history," for instance, becomes a "translation into an universal cipher applicable to the Intellect" for Emerson. In language, "Particular natural facts are symbols of particular spiritual facts," as in using "the *heart* to express emotion, the *head* to denote thought." In legal terms, "law was not an opinion . . . but a transcript of natural right. . . . an immoral law is void," a principle that later serves Emerson as a justification for supporting abolition, even though he felt that planters should be reimbursed for the loss of their property.[29] Just as studying nature results in a direct connection to divinity, so too does humankind deserve a direct connection to God, through prayer without the interference of a mediating class—the clergy—or the bible, which is the work of men and can be interpreted only by the ministerial class.

Still, as he so often does, Emerson warns that our direct observation of nature and learning of its lessons is not easy. One must, first of all, be in the right frame of mind: "Whosoever would gain anything of her, must submit to the essential condition of all learning, must go in the spirit of a little child," just as a child firmly believes that it can catch a squirrel or a bird while the adult knows, through experience, that this is impossible. Nevertheless, the successful adult is one "who has retained the spirit of infancy even into the era of manhood." Because of this, Emerson always argues for a sense of wonder when approaching nature, and he recognizes that our moods can prejudice our judgment: "Nature always wears the colors of the spirit," because life "is a train of moods like a string of beads" that "prove to be many-colored lenses which paint the world their own hue," and it "depends on the mood of the man, whether he shall see the sunset or the fine poem." Even weather influences readers and the books they read: "One author is good for winter, and one for the dog-days." In short, the responsibility of correctly interpreting nature, and God, and humankind itself, is up to us and the manner in which we view the natural world: "'Every scripture is to be interpreted by the same spirit which gave it forth,'—is the fundamental law of criticism." If we live a "life in harmony with nature," and gain "the love of truth and of virtue," then we will "understand her text." Emerson also recognizes that viewing the world from different perspectives brings us a different vision of the whole, depending upon the point of view, or, as he describes the situation, "Turn the eyes upside down, by looking at the landscape through your legs, and how agreeable is the picture, though you have seen it any time these twenty years!"[30] But before we can see, we need to clear away the fog of the past and its influences in the present.

If we all partake of divinity, and if we are all born good and can go astray only by deviating from the path before us, then it necessarily follows that what Emerson calls "self-reliance" is in fact "god-reliance." His concept of self-reliance came about at a time described by one historian as "the rise of the common man"[31] and by many others as "Jacksonian democracy," reflecting the way in which Andrew Jackson's presidency led to a surge in democratic participation to offset special interests. At the same time, British Romanticism took root in America, showing that the everyday—not just elevated subjects—can be the subject of verse, which is why Emerson complains of the "discord" between man and nature: "you cannot freely admire a noble landscape, if laborers are digging in the field hard by." All of these are greeted by Emerson as a "sign of our times" showing "the new importance given to the single person."[32] Emerson fully articulates his views on self-reliance in his eponymously titled signature essay and elsewhere, dealing with three main subjects: how self-reliance is achieved, how the public will react to it, and how the self-reliant person should act.

If the "main enterprise of the world for splendor, for extent, is the up-building of a man," then individuals have a corresponding duty to raise themselves up: "To believe your own thought, to believe that what is true for you in your private heart, is true for all men,—that is genius." In a seeming contradiction, Emerson states the way to find yourself is to lose yourself: "To go into solitude, a man needs to retire as much from his chamber as from society. . . . if a man would be alone, let him look at the stars."[33] (Or in the words of the popular song, "Freedom's just another word for nothing left to lose.")[34] We must leave society and its influences and distractions to discover who we really are. Loss of selfhood and recognition of the God-nature-human triad are best expressed in the words of Emerson's famous epiphany as he walked across Boston Common: "Standing on the bare ground,—my head bathed by the blithe air, and uplifted into infinite space,—all mean egotism vanishes. I become a transparent eye-ball. I am nothing. I see all. The currents of the Universal Being circulate through me; I am part or particle of God"[35] (see the frontispiece).

For Emerson, then, insight into our natural and religious relations, into the interconnectedness of all things, makes for the self-reliant person. Believing the educational establishment actually unfits us to be self-reliant, he rejects it as well as the sort of persons it typically produces: "we are shut up in schools, and colleges, . . . and come out at last with a bag of wind." Because our education encourages us to align with a particular political party, religious group, or system of beliefs, Emerson warns, if "I know your sect, I anticipate your argument." The Anglophilic and continental biases of the educational system mean that we "have listened too long to the courtly muses of

Europe," suggesting the elegance of these siren-like muses as well as their undemocratic principles. As late as 1860, Emerson is still hoping that one day "we shall cast out the passion for Europe, by the passion for America."[36]

Put bluntly, the public does not like self-reliance: "Society everywhere is in conspiracy against the manhood of every one of its members" because it is "a joint-stock company in which the members agree for the better securing of his bread to each shareholder, to surrender the liberty and culture of the eater." As a result, the "virtue in most request is conformity" and "Self-reliance is its aversion." Society knows that whenever "God lets loose a thinker on this planet," suddenly "all things are at risk" as it is "when a conflagration has broken out in a great city, and no man knows what is safe, or where it will end." Elsewhere, Emerson likens the power of "one wise man in a company" to that of a rapid "contagion" which, in this instance, increases the wisdom of others in the company. But society is afraid of the conflagration or contagion caused by an individual's challenge to the established order—be it in society, politics, or religion—and thus turns on that person for being different. "For non-conformity the world whips you with its displeasure," because "it saith, Whoso goes to walk alone, accuses the whole world; . . . it is very uncivil, nay, insulting; Society will retaliate."[37]

In risking society's wrath, we "must know how to estimate a sour face," and Emerson cautions that these sour faces, "like their sweet faces, have no deep cause,—disguise no god, but are put on and off as the wind blows, and a newspaper directs." The self-reliant person cannot be concerned by how their actions will be received and, especially, about changing one's mind, for, as Emerson asks, "Suppose you should contradict yourself; what then?" Thoreau understood this because he "lived for the day, not cumbered and mortified by his memory." And Emerson continues in another famous statement: "A foolish consistency is the hobgoblin of little minds." Here, Emerson is not arguing against "consistency," only a "foolish" one that fails to recognize how our views do change over time. He believes that "Everything in the universe goes by indirection. There are no straight lines." Emerson's analogy is a ship's voyage that "is a zigzag line of a hundred tacks," but when the line is seen from a distance, it appears to be straight, much as a pixilated image appears as a series of dots up close and as a fully-drawn picture from a distance.[38]

The actions and responsibilities of the self-reliant person are many. One must spurn influence and be original, Emerson says, arguing that "Genius is always sufficiently the enemy of genius by over-influence." We must find our own way, regardless of the perceived chances of success, because nothing is worse "than this idolatry of success, this fear to fail." If we do not push forward, but hold back out of fear, then we fall into this trap: "In every work of genius we recognise our own rejected thoughts." If we do not follow our instincts and "abide by our spontaneous impression[s]" with "good humored inflexibility," then tomorrow a stranger will say "what we have thought and felt all the time" and "we shall be forced to take with shame our own opinion from another."[39] But once we have achieved something original, it is time to move on, because, while "it was excellent when it was done the first time, . . . [it] loses all value when it is copied."[40] Emerson is blunt in his advice:

> Unless the action is necessary, unless it is adequate, I do not wish to perform it. I do not wish to do one thing but once. I do not love routine. Once possessed of the principle, it is equally easy to make four or forty thousand applications of it. A great man will be content to have indicated in any the slightest manner his perception of the reigning Idea of his time, and will leave to those who like it the multiplication of examples.[41]

This is not to say that self-reliant people should hold themselves aloof from society: "Action is with the scholar subordinate, but it is essential," and "the good and wise must learn to act, and carry salvation to the combatants and demagogues in the dusty arena below." Eschewing the role of hermit, Emerson encourages involvement in the world, while at the same time assessing the risks involved: "It is easy in the world to live after the world's opinion; it is easy in solitude to live after our own; but the great man is he who in the midst of the crowd keeps with perfect sweetness the independence of solitude." Emerson believed that Thoreau had failed in this aspect of the "great man" test: "I cannot help counting it a fault in him that he had no ambition. . . . instead of engineering for all America, he was the captain of a huckleberry party."[42]

But society also owes something to the self-reliant person. Emerson recommends a type of spiritual research-and-development model that encourages research (the search for self-reliance) with a down-to-earth Yankee argument that one day all this would pay off in material ways that will aid society.

Self-reliant people may be outliers, but possibly "some benefit may yet accrue from them to the state." Emerson himself recognizes that not all spiritual seekers are successful, for with some of them there "will be cant and pretension" and "subtilty and moonshine"; these people "are of unequal strength, and do not all prosper." Still, on occasion we all mostly fail the test of correctly choosing between talent and genius: "Works and days were offered us, and we took works."[43]

Among his many encouragements to those whose courage falters at the prospect of what genuine self-reliance requires of them, Emerson offers these hard-hitting three: "Trust thyself: every heart vibrates to that iron string"; "Insist on yourself; never imitate. . . . Where is the master who could have taught Shakspeare?"; and "Nothing is at last sacred but the integrity of your own mind." And to those who expect a pat on the back for exercising self-reliance, Emerson also offers three blunt cautions: "A man is fed, not that he may be fed, but that he may work"; "The reward of a thing well done, is to have done it"; and "You would compliment a coxcomb doing a good act, but you would not praise an angel. The silence that accepts merit as the most natural thing in the world, is the highest applause."[44]

For all the appeal of his optimism and candor, there is another, less appealing side of Emerson. For instance, his concepts of self-reliance and process come together somewhat harshly in his comments about friendship, which he considers to be "a serious and majestic affair, like a royal presence, or a religion," and not a "dinner to be eaten on the run." Relations between friends must have a purpose: "it is not instruction, but provocation, that I can receive from another soul." As a result, men who know "the same things are not long the best company for each other," and once "a friend has supplied us with a standard of excellence," when "he has, moreover, become an object of thought," then his presence "is a sign to us that his office is closing, and he is commonly withdrawn from our sight in a short time." In other words, "Men cease to interest us when we find their limitations." Even in his own life, there is a bit of chill to Emerson. This is how he describes his reaction to the death of his son, Waldo, in 1842:

> In the death of my son, now more than two years ago, I seem to have lost a beautiful estate,—no more. . . . it does not touch me: something which I fancied was a part of me, which could not be

torn away without tearing me, nor enlarged without enriching me, falls off from me, and leaves no scar. . . . I grieve that grief can teach me nothing.[45]

Emerson's acknowledgement of his inability to fathom intellectually and thus control the emotional trauma from young Waldo's death is a sad confession from one who believes in the life of the mind.

Occasionally, Emerson's comments on the role of women in American life can rise to the level of those of a radical reformer, but, more often, they stay within the boundaries of contemporary generalization. He can astutely echo Margaret Fuller's "There is no wholly masculine man, no purely feminine woman" with "we often meet masculine minds in many women, and feminine minds in men." In chastising the South over slavery, he calls upon women to dissent, noting that women "always carry the conscience of a people"; elsewhere, he expresses his belief that "a sufficient definition of civilization" is "the influence of good women." In his most extended comment on the subject, "Address at the Woman's Rights Convention," he states common objections to women voting before demolishing them: "first, a want of practical wisdom; second, a too purely ideal view; and third, a danger of contamination." He even takes woman's so-called "delicacy" and turns it into a virtue: "They are more delicate than men, and, as thus more impressionable, they are the best index of the coming hour." But, he also takes some steps backwards, as when he describes how women "are victims of their finer temperament": "They have tears, and gaieties, and faintings, and glooms, and devotion to trifles," and as a result, they are "[m]ore vulnerable, more infirm, more mortal than men." Comparatively, then, "Man is the will, and woman the sentiment." And in one of his statements about granting women the vote, it is unclear whether he is being ironic or providing a backhanded compliment: "they would give, I suppose, as intelligent a vote as the five thousand Irish voters of Boston or New York."[46]

Like many of his contemporaries, Emerson generalizes about racial characteristics, even though he claims that "[n]ational characteristics . . . give way to individual ones." In America, the "Southerner lives for the moment, relies on himself, and conquers by personal address," while the "Northerner lives for the year, and does not rely on himself, but on the whole apparatus of means he is wont to employ." As a result, the "Southerner is haughty, wilful, generous, unscrupulous, . . . [and] will have his way," in contrast to the "Northerner [who] must think the thing over, and his conscience and his commonsense throw a thousand obstacles between him and his wishes, which perplex his decision and unsettle his behaviour." On the eve of the Civil War, Emerson notes that the Southerner will welcome the war because it will be "a chivalrous sport to him, like hunting, and suits his semi-civilized condition," whereas the Northerner will fight it for a righteous cause, even though he has otherwise "advanced some ages on the war-state,—to trade, art, and general cultivation." In contrasting Americans and Englishmen, Emerson describes the former as "demonstrative," and the latter as "shy and reserved"; and Americans have "a certain versatility" that allows them to "more readily and genially" entertain "more speculative, more contemplative" thoughts, while "the Englishman seems mortgaged to the past."[47]

With respect to his style, Emerson has often been criticized for the apparent opaqueness of his prose. Bronson Alcott's wily description is better than most: "It makes no difference," he says,

> whether you begin at the last paragraph and read backwards, or begin at what he meant for the beginning. There is some principle in that. There is, nevertheless, a thread running through all his writings; it takes a very subtle, fluent, and ingenious reader to find that thread; but be assured there is a thread on which he strings all his pearls; it is not accidental.[48]

Those who complain of the lack of topic sentences in his paragraphs might consider that, in the often irregular rhythms and development of Emerson's prose, we can see parallels to the way our own minds work in thinking through a problem; indeed, as we search for the topic sentences, we are forced to think through the work at hand as if we are in dialogue with its author and sharing in his process of intellection.

Style was important to Emerson because of his belief that the author, like a friend, should provoke thought. Poets, he declares, are "liberating gods." Emerson had numerous chances to perfect his style. A typical work started as a journal entry, which over time was combined with other journal entries and connective prose to form a lecture, which was then performed numerous times and made better with each delivery, and, finally, was written as an essay for publication—and works received multiple revisions at every stage of composition, delivery, and eventual publication. Emerson looked at published works as extensions of the lecture room, the latter being "the true Church of the coming time." All he asks of those who came to hear his lectures is "a convertible audience,—an audience coming up to the house, not knowing what shall befall them there, but uncommitted and willing victims to reason and love," and an audience that accepted that in the lecture hall "everything is admissible, philosophy, ethics, divinity, criticism, poetry, humor, anecdote, mimicry,—ventriloquism almost."[49]

A lecturer turned author, Emerson did not refrain from provoking his audience in print as well as in speech. Sometimes complementing the intellectual quality of his work is a confrontational aspect, as bears notice in his earlier pieces. When invited to speak before Harvard's Phi Beta Kappa Society in 1837, he warns that we "have listened too long to the courtly muses of Europe," and one can almost imagine him looking directly at his audience when, three lines later, he adds, "See already the tragic consequence." The following year, when asked to address the Harvard Divinity School graduating class, he begins by stating, "I shall endeavor to discharge my duty to you, on this occasion, by pointing out two errors" in the church. When he compares the "man on whom the soul descends, through whom the soul speaks," with "the man who aims to speak as books enable, as synods use, as the fashion guides, and as interest commands," he decides the latter "babbles. Let him hush"; and in the very next sentence we can again imagine Emerson talking directly to his audience as he refers to the immediate antecedent: "To this holy office, you propose to devote yourselves."[50]

The difficulty some modern readers have with Emerson's prose is largely a function of the distance between the respective literary practices of his time and ours. He often uses archaic and British spellings (especially "our" for "or" words). Many words he uses have changed meaning over time: for example, "Reason" no longer means intuition, and "Understanding" is not a pejorative term. He will sometimes give definitions that puzzle as much as they define: "Transcendentalism is the Saturnalia or excess of Faith."[51] And, like most of his contemporaries, he punctuated according to either rhetorical or grammatical practice by employing punctuation marks in order to affect rhetorically the meaning conveyed by the sentence or to follow a set pattern of grammatical rules. The following examples illustrate that principle in practice:

> This which I think and feel, underlay that former state of life and circumstances, as it does underlie my present, and will always all circumstance, and what is called life, and what is called death.

> The chief value of the new fact, is to enhance the great and constant fact of Life, which can dwarf any and every circumstance, and to which the belt of wampum, and the commerce of America, are alike.

> But, granting the truth, rightly read, of the historical aphorism, that "the people always conquer," it is to be noted, that, in the Southern States, the tenure of land, and the local laws, with slavery, give the social system not a democratic, but an aristocratic complexion; and those States have shown every year a more hostile and aggressive temper, until the instinct of self-preservation forced us into the war.[52]

Each of these sentences appears overpunctuated by modern standards, but reading them aloud will demonstrate that the commas are there either as breath marks or as a stop to add emphasis for what follows. This is no accident, given Emerson's background in the pulpit and on the lecture platform, and it was also a natural way to punctuate in an era when reading aloud was common practice in the home as well as in the larger community.

Many modern readers are put off by the numerous quotations Emerson uses from his readings.[53] He has a reason for this: if he remembers some writers' words "so well that I must often use them to express my thought" it is "because I perceive that we have heard the same truth, but they have heard it better." Too many readers miss the way in which Emerson balances numerous quotations from his sources with proverbs drawn from daily life. Also, Emerson can be humorous. His humor can be based in the natural world, as when, in talking of reformers, he states that even "the insect world was to be defended,—that had been too long neglected, and a society for the protection of ground-worms, slugs, and mosquitos was to be incorporated without delay," or in making his point about how everything in nature fits together: "A *man* in the rocks under the sea, would indeed be a monster; but a lobster is a most handy and happy fellow there." He can be jocular, too, as when he describes how "The people [of the American Midwest] are all kings,—if the sceptre is a cattledealer's driving-whip," or, when talking about the expensive library purchased by a new university in New York for its students, he adds that it is "now triumphantly mounted on the shelves at Rochester, to be explored, at leisure, as soon as they have learned enough to read it." And, in a vein similar to the American tall tale story, he presents this grotesque imagery: "The state of society is one in which the members have suffered amputation from the trunk, and strut about so many walking monsters,—a good finger, a neck, a stomach, an elbow, but never a man."[54]

Ralph Waldo Emerson: The Major Prose is the only anthology of his writings that draws from the three predominant sources of his prose: the pulpit, the lecture hall, and print.[55] Together, they justify Bronson Alcott's assertion that "Emerson has certainly been a university to our people."[56] We trust that by presenting such a broad spectrum of Emerson's works, the vitality of his prose—from his most important sermon, which effectively announced his decision to resign from his pastorate, to some of his last essays—can been seen as a continual search for answers by one of America's greatest questioners. Readers of this volume will witness how Emerson did, indeed, "unsettle all things," for the questions he raises in the works that follow about our place in the world are as valid today as they were to his contemporaries.

Notes

1. In the notes to this Introduction, as well as in the notes to all writings by Emerson printed in this volume, cross-references are uniformly cited by titles of works and paragraph number(s) provided for each Emerson text in this volume.
2. Emerson's writings on abolition are gathered in *Emerson's Antislavery Writings,* ed. Len Gougeon and Joel Myerson (New Haven: Yale University Press, 1995).
3. Emerson's major contribution to this endeavor was his participation in the University Lectures, a series of graduate-level courses that Eliot arranged for delivery in academic years 1869–1870 and 1870–1871 as forerunners to the establishment of Harvard's graduate school. In the spring terms of 1870 and 1871, Emerson delivered a course on "Natural History of the Intellect"; see Ronald A. Bosco, "'His

Lectures Were Poetry, His Teaching the Music of the Spheres': Annie Adams Fields and Francis Greenwood Peabody on Emerson's Natural History of the Intellect University Lectures at Harvard in 1870," *Harvard Library Bulletin,* Special Issue, n.s. 8 (1997): 1–79.

4. See Emerson's excitement at these and many other examples of human progress throughout "Works and Days," printed in this volume. In "The Adirondacs," he went so far as to celebrate the initial attempt at laying the Atlantic Cable in verse: "Two of our mates returning with swift oars. / One held a printed journal waving high. . . . / Big with great news, and shouted the report / For which the world had waited, now firm fact, / Of the wire-cable laid beneath the sea, / And landed on our coast, and pulsating / With ductile fire" (ll. 237–244, *CW,* 9:350).

5. *L,* 8:446; Jack L. Capps, *Emily Dickinson's Reading 1836–1886* (Cambridge: Harvard University Press, 1966), p. 173; available at http://pds.lib.harvard.edu/pds/view/17582837 (viewed 19 November 2013).

6. *JMN,* 9:381.

7. For Emerson's discussion of the "over-soul" concept, see "The Over-Soul," *CW,* 2:159; "one mind": "The Divinity School Address," para 7.

8. "Good is": "The Divinity School Address," para 7.

9. "commemorated" and "filled with his spirit": "The Lord's Supper," para 33; "To eat bread": para 32.

10. See Parker, *A Discourse of the Transient and Permanent in Christianity* (1841), in *Transcendentalism: A Reader,* ed. Myerson (New York: Oxford University Press, 2000), pp. 340–366.

11. "the divine nature" and "doctrine of inspiration": "The Divinity School Address," para 11; "jubilee" and "idioms": para 13; "historical Christianity": para 15. "excellence of Jesus": "Character," para 13.

12. "He teaches": "The Lord's Supper," para 31. "aim to convert": "The Divinity School Address," para 17; "very word Miracle": para 13.

13. "Pray without Ceasing," *CS,* 1:57, 56.

14. Sermon CLXXI, *CS,* 4:246. Although he formally left the pulpit in 1832, Emerson continued to serve as a "supply preacher" when asked to fill temporarily a vacant pulpit or deliver a lecture that also might serve as a funeral sermon. This sermon, preached on 17 July 1836, served both purposes, and it is worth noting that the sentiment Emerson expresses in this passage anticipates themes associated with *Nature,* which at the time he was readying for publication in September.

15. *L,* 1:412–413.

16. "Pray without Ceasing," *CS,* 1:55.

17. "Idealism saith" through "the splendid labyrinth": *Nature,* para 91. "Every materialist": "The Transcendentalist," para 1; "tapestry," para 2.

18. As Emerson writes in "Circles": "Our life is an apprenticeship to the truth, that around every circle another can be drawn; that there is no end in nature, but every

end is a beginning; that there is always another dawn risen on mid-noon, and under every deep a lower deep opens" (para 1).

19. "Life is a series": "Experience," para 16. "Life only avails": "Self-Reliance," para 29. "It is the office": "The Divinity School Address," para 30. "Man Thinking": "The American Scholar," para 8. "Imitation" and "imitator": "The Divinity School Address," para 31. "great men": "Uses of Great Men," para 35. "I look in vain": "The Poet," para 32. "there is no pure": "The Transcendentalist," para 10. "every action": "Circles," para 1. "civilized man": "Self-Reliance," para 49.

20. Possibly Emerson's play on "cogito ergo sum" ("I think, therefore I am"), René Descartes's 1644 statement that the very act of thinking about our existence proves our existence.

21. "Man is timid": "Self-Reliance," para 26.

22. "only sin': "Circles," para 12. "imperfect theories": *Nature,* para 97.

23. "'I see" and "slow observation": "Humanity of Science," para 6. "when the wit": "The Scholar," para 50. "I have followed": "The Uses of Natural History," para 1. "The sensual man": *Nature,* para 74.

24. "Let us inquire": *Nature,* para 3; "What is matter?": para 91; "noble doubt" to "accuracy of my senses," para 67. "These laws": "The Divinity School Address," para 4.

25. "The beauty": "The Uses of Natural History," para 3. "Nature is thoroughly mediate": *Nature,* para 57; "the present expositor": para 94. "the ancient precept": "The American Scholar," para 10. "a grammar of botany": "The Uses of Natural History," para 9. "I will be a naturalist," *JMN,* 4:200.

26. In the poem "Each and All," Emerson expresses the theme of interrelation this way: "All are needed by each one; / Nothing is fair or good alone" (ll. 11–12, *CW,* 9:14).

27. "every atom": "The Natural Method of Mental Philosophy," para 54. "drop is a small ocean": "The American Scholar," para 44. "genius": "Thoreau," para 26. "this tyrannizing unity": *Nature,* para 96; "a single object:" para 28.

28. "that nature's dice": *Nature,* para 53. "Good is": "Considerations by the Way," *CW,* 6:134.

29. "natural history": "The Natural Method of Mental Philosophy," para 10. "Particular natural facts": *Nature,* para 32; "the *heart,*" para 34. "law was not": "American Slavery," para 37. For planters being reimbursed, see "American Civilization," para 37.

30. "Whosoever would gain": "The Uses of Natural History," para 45. "the spirit of infancy": *Nature,* para 9; "Nature always wears": para 11. "a train of moods": "Experience," para 6. "One author is good": "Works and Days," para 24. "'Every scripture": *Nature,* para 45; "Turn the eyes": para 72.

31. See Carl Russell Fish, *The Rise of the Common Man, 1830–1850* (New York: Macmillan, 1927).

32. "discord" and "you cannot freely": *Nature*, para 94. "sign of our times": "The American Scholar," para 46.

33. "main enterprise": "The American Scholar," para 37. "To believe": "Self-Reliance," para 4. "To go into solitude": *Nature*, para 6.

34. Kris Kristofferson and Fred Foster, "Me and Bobby McGee" (1969).

35. "Standing on the bare ground": *Nature*, para 9.

36. "we are shut": "New England Reformers," *CW*, 3:152. "I know your sect": "Self-Reliance," para 13. "we have listened": "The American Scholar," para 46. "we shall cast out": "Considerations by the Way," *CW*, 6:141.

37. "Society everywhere" and "virtue in most request": "Self-Reliance," para 9. "God lets loose": "Circles," para 14. "one wise man": "Uses of Great Men," para 25. "For non-conformity": "Self-Reliance," para 14. "it saith, Whoso goes": "The Transcendentalist," para 17.

38. "must know how": "Self-Reliance," para 14; "Suppose you should contradict": para 16. "lived for the day": "Thoreau," para 13. "A foolish consistency": "Self-Reliance," para 17. "Everything in the universe": "Works and Days," para 41. "a zigzag line": "Self-Reliance," para 19. In "Song of Myself," Whitman echoes Emerson's position here when he writes in part 51, "Do I contradict myself? / Very well then I contradict myself, / (I am large, I contain multitudes)."

39. "Genius is always": "The American Scholar," para 17. "idolatry of success": "New England," para 44. "In every work of genius": "Self-Reliance," para 4.

40. "New England Reformers," *CW*, 3:151. Emerson recognized this quality in Thoreau, who, after being complimented for making excellent pencils, "replied that he should never make another pencil. 'Why should I? I would not do again what I have done once'" ("Thoreau," para 2).

41. "Unless the action is necessary": "The Transcendentalist," para 22.

42. "Action is": "The American Scholar," para 22. "the good and wise": "The Transcendentalist," para 20. "It is easy": "Self-Reliance," para 12. "I cannot help": "Thoreau," para 34.

43. "some benefit": "The Transcendentalist," para 37; "cant and pretension": para 35. "Works and days": "Works and Days," para 19.

44. "Trust thyself": "Self-Reliance," para 6; "Insist on yourself": para 46; "Nothing is at last sacred": para 10. "A man is fed": *Nature*, para 16. "The reward": "New England Reformers," *CW*, 3:166. "You would compliment": "The Divinity School Address," para 34.

45. "a serious and majestic affair": "Considerations by the Way," *CW*, 6:145. "it is not instruction": "The Divinity School Address," para 11. "the same things": "Uses of Great Men," para 32. "a friend has supplied us": *Nature*, para 65. "Men cease to interest": "Circles," para 12. "In the death": "Experience," para 4.

46. Fuller, "The Great Lawsuit" (her precursor to *Woman in the Nineteenth Century*

[1845]), in *Transcendentalism: A Reader,* ed. Myerson, p. 418. "we often meet": "The Natural Method of Mental Philosophy," para 43. "always carry the conscience": "Remarks at the Kansas Relief Meeting," para 10. "a sufficient definition of civilization": "American Civilization," para 7. "first, a want of practical": "Address at the Woman's Rights Convention," para 35; "They are more delicate": para 2; "victims of their finer temperament": para 27; "[m]ore vulnerable": para 15; "Man is the will": para 4; "they would give": para 32.

Caroline Healey Dall praised Emerson for the "beautiful address" at the Woman's Rights Convention, though she also noted that "some of the papers thought it doubtful whether you were for us or against us" (7 October 1855, quoted in Helen R. Deese, "'A Liberal Education': Caroline Healey Dall and Emerson," *Emersonian Circles: Essays in Honor of Joel Myerson,* ed. Wesley T. Mott and Robert E. Burkholder [Rochester: University of Rochester Press, 1997], p. 248).

47. "[n]ational characteristics": "New England," para 1; "Southerner lives for" through "unsettle his behaviour": para 5. "a chivalrous sport": "American Civilization," para 36. "demonstrative" and "shy and reserved": "The Anglo-American," para 61. "a certain versatility": "England," para 40.

48. Quoted in *Emerson in His Own Time,* ed. Ronald A. Bosco and Joel Myerson (Iowa City: University of Iowa Press, 2003), p. 59.

49. "liberating gods": "The Poet," paras 25, 26. "the true Church" through "ventriloquism almost": "New England," para 26.

50. "See already the tragic": "The American Scholar," para 46. "I shall endeavor to": "The Divinity School Address," para 12; "man on whom" through "you propose to devote yourselves," paras 21, 22.

51. "Transcendentalism is the Saturnalia": "The Transcendentalist," para 11.

52. "This which I think": "Self-Reliance," para 28. "The chief value": "The Poet," para 17. "But, granting the truth": "The President's Proclamation," para 10.

53. In presenting quotations, Emerson once stated that he distinguished in his writings between using double quotation marks whenever he made "a *bona fide* quotation from any person" and single quotation marks "when the quotation is only rhetorical" or when he quotes himself (*L,* 8:17). For the most part, he adhered to the distinction in his practices, but readers should also note that he was quite adept at paraphrase and allusion, as indicated by any number of footnotes accompanying the writings that follow.

54. "so well that": "Character," para 17. Emerson balances his numerous quotations from his sources with proverbs from daily life: see, especially, *Nature,* para 34, and "The Uses of Natural History," para 58. "the insect world": "New England Reformers," *CW,* 3:150. "A *man* in the rocks": "The Uses of Natural History," para 33. "The people": "The Anglo-American," para 36; "now triumphantly mounted": para 8. "The state of society": "The American Scholar," para 5.

55. Selections from Emerson's writings on politics and social reform are collected in both *The Political Emerson,* ed. David M. Robinson (Boston: Beacon Press, 2004), and *Political Writings,* ed. Kenneth M. Sacks (New York: Cambridge University Press, 2008), and selections from his writings on religion are collected in *The Spiritual Emerson,* ed. David M. Robinson (Boston: Beacon Press, 2003).

56. Quoted in *Emerson in His Own Time,* ed. Bosco and Myerson, p. 61.

Textual Policies

An imaginative book renders us much more service at first, by stimulating us through its tropes, than afterward, when we arrive at the precise sense of the author.

—"The Poet," para 26

To-day, I am full of thoughts, and can write what I please. . . . What I write, whilst I write it, seems the most natural thing in the world: but, yesterday, I saw a dreary vacuity in this direction in which now I see so much; and a month hence, I doubt not, I shall wonder who he was that wrote so many continuous pages.

—"Circles," para 10

Ralph Waldo Emerson: The Major Prose employs an editorial policy that publishes a text as close as possible to the one that contemporary audiences heard or read.

We have reprinted previously unpublished texts edited from manuscript in modern scholarly editions. "The Lord's Supper" is from *The Complete Sermons of Ralph Waldo Emerson,* edited by Albert J. von Frank et al., 4 vols. (Columbia: University of Missouri Press, 1989–1992). "The Uses of Natural History" and "Humanity of Science" are from *Selected Lectures of Ralph Waldo Emerson,* edited by Ronald A. Bosco and Joel Myerson (Athens: University of Georgia Press, 2005). "New England: Genius, Manners, and Customs," "England," "The Anglo-American," "American Slavery," "Address at the Woman's Rights Convention," "The Natural Method of Mental Philosophy," and "The Scholar" are from *The Later Lectures of Ralph Waldo Emerson,* edited by Bosco and Myerson, 2 vols. (Athens: University of Georgia Press, 2001).[1] The editorial principles on which these editions are based may be found on the following pages, respectively: 1:33–39; pp. xxix–xxxiii; and 1:xliv–lxii.

Because different textual policies were used at various periods in the preparation and publication of *The Collected Works of Ralph Waldo Emerson (CW),*[2] we have re-edited some texts and reprinted others.

The first volume of *CW, Nature, Addresses, and Lectures* (1971), presents the most complicated textual issues. Published in 1849, it includes Emerson's first book, *Nature* (1836), four addresses published as pamphlets between 1837 and 1841, and five lectures, two of which had first appeared in the *Dial* in 1841 and 1843. In addition, new editions appeared in 1856 (as *Miscellanies*), 1870, 1876, 1883, and 1903. In their section on "The Text," the editors rightly state that they use as the basis for their edition (or copy-text) "the earliest printed form of the text, since no manuscript forms have survived."[3] Their thinking, in line with modern editorial theory, is that the more times a text is printed, the greater the chances for printers' or compositors' errors to enter into it. But what about texts that were revised between six and thirteen years after their original publication? The editors do acknowledge that Emerson's revisions "left us a retouched version of his first philosophy in which the sharp edges are softened and blurred. . . . [and] impelled him toward tightening diction and cutting illustration, aiming toward language for the eye rather than the flow of sound for the ear,"[4] resulting in an Emerson that was "somewhat muted and moderated." Faced with a choice between printing the earlier Emerson, that his initial audience read, or the later Emerson, versions of which were read by different audiences at different times, the editors chose to present a text that never existed: "Our principle is to present the fullest version of the early writings. . . . Broadly speaking, then, revisions in later editions which increased the original or clarified it without excision are accepted; revisions which reduced the original are refused."[5]

In order to present "the fullest version of the early writings," the editors created a farrago of a text, adding any changes they deemed to be by Emerson but automatically rejecting changes, even those possibly by Emerson, if they reduced the text. This arbitrary and unacceptable editorial policy was abandoned in the next volume of *CW, Essays: First Series* (1979), with this statement: "all revisions identifiable as Emerson's will ordinarily be accepted."[6] But here, too, changes in the text made decades later were accepted as revisions in the original text and, again, the editors created a procrustean text that stretched over several decades, beginning three years later with a new edition in 1847. Describing the "some 500 verbal changes" in the latter, Paul Lauter shows how Emerson deleted "unnecessary rhetorical baggage like formal introductions, wordy links, and hortatory phrases," as well as many "contrasts, similes, [and] illustrations" that reiterated his point. Stylistically, the revisions concentrate Emerson's prose into "a plainer, more concrete, more vivid style" by eliminating "structural devices like repetition and inversion which he had perhaps carried into his writing from platform and pulpit experience." Philosophically, the revisions "reflect the development of Emerson's conception of man's relation to deity" from "mere *passivity* . . . before an omnipotent and dominating (and to some extent external) 'Eternal,' and toward an *acceptance* of one's 'place.'"[7]

This editorial policy of producing eclectic texts drawn from many sources over many decades (1850, 1865, 1870, and 1876) continued to be followed in the next volume of *CW, Essays: Second Series* (1983), which also relied on what the editors called Emerson's "correction" copy, an 1844 edition in which he made changes in the text as well as in a list of "Consideranda." Unfortunately, they never adequately considered that the changes made in this copy were entered over a long period of time and that "Consideranda" are not the same as "errata," and rather than adopting all these readings, as they did, they should have evaluated them, as did Emerson, as revisions to be considered or evaluated. The editors of *Poems* in *CW* have rightly described similar "correction copies" of Emerson's poetry as volumes he maintained to "record potential emendations in advance of new printings or editions" as "from time to time" they occurred to him; in other words, for Emerson these "potential emendations" amounted to "nothing more than memoranda to be acted upon or not at such time" as the work might be reprinted.[8]

Because the aim of the present volume is to publish a text as close as possible to what contemporary audiences read, we have printed first edition texts, conservatively emended to correct errors. Thus, we have re-edited, according to this principle, the following texts from the first three volumes of *CW: Nature,* "The Divinity School Address," "Self-Reliance," "Circles," "The Transcendentalist," "The Poet," "Experience," and "Nominalist and Realist." By the fourth volume of *CW* (1987), the editorial policy had become more conservative and we reprint from this and the sixth volume "Uses of Great Men" and "Fate." The textual policy of the present collection is the same as that employed in the final three prose volumes of *CW* edited by Ronald A. Bosco and/or Joel Myerson, from which we reprint these texts: *An Address . . . on the Emancipation of the Negroes in the British West Indies,*" "Mr. R. W. Emerson's Remarks at the Kansas Relief Meeting in Cambridge," "American

Civilization," "Thoreau," "The President's Proclamation," "Character," and "Works and Days."

The text of "The American Scholar" presents a special case. When it was published in volume one of *CW* using the 1837 first edition as copy-text, the editors did not know at that time of a partial set of revised page proofs for the second, 1838 edition,[9] which include changes in some two hundred instances of punctuation and of fifteen words from the 1837 edition. While we have used the 1837 edition as our copy-text, we have emended it to reflect the changes in punctuation and wording from the 1838 edition, which was carefully proofread by Emerson and by the compositors, something the earlier editors of *CW* could not do. The result is the first text of "The American Scholar" edited according to modern textual practices.[10]

Our brief annotations to Emerson's texts are derived from more extensive ones, which may be consulted in the appropriate editions of Emerson's *Complete Sermons, Early Lectures, Later Lectures, Selected Lectures,* and *Collected Works.*

Notes

1. We have chosen the lecture "England" to include in this volume rather than a selection from *English Traits* (1856; *CW,* 5), because we believe the lecture has a more immediate connection to Emerson's experiences there than the later book, in which his comments were abridged and filtered for the larger public.

2. For a discussion of the evolving editorial theories of *CW,* see Robert N. Hudspeth's magisterial *"The Collected Works of Ralph Waldo Emerson," Nineteenth-Century Prose* 40:2 (Fall 2013): 1–104.

3. *CW,* 1:xxix.

4. Nineteenth-century authors punctuated according to either rhetorical or grammatical practice by employing punctuation marks "either to affect the meaning conveyed by the sentence (rhetorical) or to follow a set pattern of formal rules (grammatical)"; see *Transcendentalism: A Reader,* ed. Joel Myerson (New York: Oxford University Press, 2000), pp. xix–xx, for examples.

5. *CW,* 1:xxxi–xxxiii.

6. *CW,* 2:xxxv n.

7. Paul Lauter, "Emerson's Revisions of *Essays* (First Series)," *American Literature* 33 (May 1961): 143–158.

8. See *CW,* 9:cxiii–cxiv.

9. The proofs are in the Joel Myerson Collection of Nineteenth-Century American Literature, University of South Carolina.

10. For an extended discussion of the role of the 1838 proof sheets in determining Emerson's text, see Joel Myerson, "Re-editing Emerson's 'American Scholar' Address," *Manuscripts* 65 (Fall 2013): 297–303.

Sermon CLXII
["The Lord's Supper"][1]

The kingdom of God is not meat and drink;
but righteousness and peace and joy in the holy ghost.

—Romans 14:17

In the history of the Church no subject has been more   1
fruitful of controversy than the Lord's Supper. There never has been any unanimity in the understanding of its nature nor any uniformity in the mode of
celebrating it. Without considering the frivolous questions which have been
hotly debated as to the posture in which men should partake or whether
mixed or unmixed wine should be served, whether leavened or unleavened
bread should be broken, the questions have been settled differently in every
church, who should be admitted to partake, and how often it should be prepared. In the Catholic Church once infants were permitted and then forbidden to partake. Since the ninth Century, bread only is given to the laity and
the cup is reserved to the priesthood. So as to the time. In the fourth Lateran
Council it was decreed that every believer should communicate once in a
year at Easter.[2] Afterwards three times—But more important have been the
controversies respecting its nature. The great question of the Real Presence
was the main controversy between the Church of England and Church of
Rome. The doctrine of the Consubstantiation maintained by Luther was denied by Calvin.[3] In the Church of England Archbishops Laud and Wake maintained that that it was a Eucharist or sacrifice of thanksgiving to God, Cud-

worth and Warburton that it was not a sacrifice but a feast after a sacrifice, and Bishop Hoadly that it was a simple commemoration.[4]

2   If there seem to you an agreement in this last opinion among our churches it is only but of yesterday and within narrow limits.

3   And finally it is now near 200 years since the Society of Quakers denied the authority of the Supper altogether and gave good reasons for disusing it.

4   I allude to these facts only to show that so far from the Supper being a tradition in which all are fully agreed, there has always been the widest room for difference of opinion upon this particular.

5   Having recently paid particular attention to this subject, I was led to the conclusion that Jesus did not intend to establish an institution for perpetual observance when he ate the passover with his disciples; and further, to the opinion that it is not expedient to celebrate it as we do. I shall now endeavour to state distinctly my reasons for these two opinions.

6   An account of the last Supper of Christ with his disciples is given by the four Evangelists, Matthew, Mark, Luke and John.

7   In St. Matthew's Gospel (26:26) are recorded the words of Jesus in giving bread and wine on that occasion to his disciples but no expression occurs intimating that this feast was hereafter to be commemorated.

8   In St. Mark the same words are recorded and still with no intimation that the occasion was to be remembered (14:22).

9   St. Luke, after relating the breaking of the bread, has these words: 'This do in remembrance of me' (22:19).

10   In St. John, although other occurrences of the same evening are related, this whole transaction is passed over without notice.

11   Now observe the facts. Two of the evangelists (namely, Matthew and John) were of the twelve disciples and were present on that occasion. Neither of them drops the slightest intimation of any intention on the part of Jesus to set up any thing permanent. John especially, the beloved disciple, who has recorded with minuteness the conversation and the transactions of that memorable evening has quite omitted such a notice.[5]

12   Neither did it come to the knowledge of St. Mark, who relates the other facts. It is found in Luke alone, who was not present. There is no reason, however, that we know for rejecting the account of Luke. I doubt not that the expression was used by Jesus. I shall presently consider its meaning. I have only brought these accounts together that you may judge whether it is likely

that a solemn institution to be continued to the end of time, by all mankind, as they should come, nation after nation, within the influence of the Christian religion, was to be established in this slight manner, in a manner so slight that the intention of remembering it should not have caught the ear or dwelt in the mind of the only two among the twelve, who wrote down what happened!

Still we must suppose that expression—This do in remembrance of me— 13 had come to the ear of Luke from some disciple present. What did it really signify? It is a prophetic and an affectionate expression. Jesus is a Jew sitting with his countrymen celebrating their national feast. He thinks of his own impending death and wishes the minds of his disciples to be prepared for it and says to them, "When hereafter you shall keep the passover it will have an altered aspect in your eyes. It is now a historical covenant of God with the Jewish nation. Hereafter it will remind you of a new covenant sealed with my blood. In years to come, as long as your people shall come up to Jerusalem to keep this feast (forty years) the connexion which has subsisted between us will give a new meaning in your eyes to the national festival as the anniversary of my death."—I see natural feeling and beauty in the use of such language from Jesus, a friend to his friends. I can readily imagine that he was willing and desirous that when his disciples met, his memory should hallow their intercourse, but I cannot bring myself to believe that he looked beyond the living generation, beyond the abolition of the festival he was celebrating and the scattering of the nation, and meant to impose a memorial feast upon the whole world.

But though the words *Do this in remembrance,* to which so much meaning 14 has been given, do not occur in Matthew, Mark, or John, yet many persons are apt to imagine that the very striking and formal manner in which this eating and drinking is described intimates a striking and formal purpose to found a festival. This opinion would easily occur to any one reading only the New Testament, but the impression is removed by reading any narrative of the mode in which the ancient or the modern Jews kept the passover. It is then perceived at once that the leading circumstances in the gospel are only a faithful account of that ceremony. Jesus did not celebrate the passover and afterwards the supper, but the supper *was* the passover. He did with his disciples exactly what every master of a family in Jerusalem was doing at the same hour with his household. It appears that the Jews ate the lamb and the unleavened bread and drank wine after a prescribed manner. It was the custom for the Lord or master of the feast to break the bread and to bless it, using this formula, which the Talmudists have preserved to us, 'Blessed be thou O Lord who givest us the fruits of the earth,' and to give it to every one at the table. It was the custom for the master of the family to take the cup which contained the wine and to bless it saying 'Blessed be thou O Lord who givest us the fruit of the vine,' and then to give the cup to all. Among the modern Jews, a hymn is sung after this ceremony, specifying the twelve great works done by God for the deliverance of their fathers out of Egypt. And Jesus did the same thing.

15   But why did he use expressions so extraordinary and emphatic as these: This is my body which is broken for you. Take, Eat. This is my blood which is shed for you. Drink it.[6] They are not extraordinary expressions from him. They were familiar in his mouth. He always taught by parables and symbols. It was the national way of teaching and was largely used by him. Remember the readiness he always showed to spiritualize every occurrence. He stooped and wrote on the sand.[7] He admonished his disciples respecting the leaven of the Pharisees.[8] He instructed the woman of Samaria respecting living water.[9] He permitted himself to be anointed, declaring it was for interment.[10] He washed the feet of his disciples.[11] These are admitted to be symbolical actions and expressions. Here in like manner he calls the bread his body and bids the disciples eat. He had used the same expression repeatedly before. The reason why St. John does not repeat the words here, seems to be that he had narrated a similar discourse of Jesus to the people of Capernaum more at length already (John 6:27). He there tells the Jews—'Except ye eat the flesh of the Son of Man and drink his blood, ye have no life in you.'[12]

16   And when the Jews on that occasion complained that they did not comprehend what he meant, he added for their better understanding, and as if for our understanding, that we might not think that his body was to be actually eaten, that he only meant we should live by his commandment. He closed his discourse with these explanatory expressions: "The flesh profiteth nothing;—the *words* that I speak to you, they are spirit and they are life."[13]

17   Whilst I am upon this topic I cannot help remarking that it is very singular we should have preserved this rite and insisted upon perpetuating one symbolical act of Christ whilst we have totally neglected others, particularly one other which had at least an equal claim to our observance. Jesus washed

the feet of his disciples and told them that 'As he had washed their feet, they ought to wash one another's feet, for he had given them an example that they should do as he had done to them.'[14] I ask any person who believes the Supper to have been designed by Jesus to be commemorated forever, to go and read the account of it in the other gospels, and then compare with it the account of this transaction in St. John and tell me if it is not much more explicitly authorized than the supper. It only differs in this, that we have found the Supper used in New England and the washing of the feet not. If we had found this rite established, it would be much more difficult to show its defective authority. That rite is used by the Church of Rome and the Sandemanians.[15] It has been very properly dropped by other Christians. Why? 1. Because it was a local custom and unsuitable in western countries, and 2. because it was typical and all understand that humility is the thing signified. But the passover was local too and does not concern us; and its bread and wine were typical and do not help us to understand the love which they signified.

These views of the original account of the Lord's Supper lead me to esteem it an occasion full of solemn and prophetic interest but never intended by Jesus to be the foundation of a perpetual institution. 18

It appears however from Paul's Epistle to the Corinthians that the disciples had very early taken advantage of these impressive words of Christ to hold religious meetings where they broke bread as and drank wine as symbols.[16] 19

I look upon this fact as very natural in the circumstances of the Church. The disciples lived together; they threw all their property into a common stock; they were bound together by the memory of Christ and nothing could be more natural than that this eventful evening should be affectionately remembered by them; that they, Jews like Jesus, should adopt his expression and his type, and furthermore that what was done with peculiar propriety by them, by his personal friends, should come to be extended to their companions also. In this way religious feasts grew up among the early Christians. They were readily adopted by the Jewish converts who were familiar with religious feasts, and also by the Pagan converts whose idolatrous worship had been made up of sacred festivals and who very readily abused these to gross riot as appears from the censures of St. Paul. Many persons consider this fact, the observance of such a memorial feast by the early disciples, decisive of the 20 question whether it ought to be observed by us. For my part I see nothing to wonder at in its originating there; all that is surprizing is that it should exist amongst us. It had great propriety for his personal friends to remember their friend and repeat his words. It was but too probable that among the half-converted Pagans and Jews any rite, any form would be cherished whilst yet unable to comprehend the spiritual character of Christianity.

21   The circumstance however that St. Paul favors these views has seemed to many persons conclusive in favor of the institution. I am of opinion that it is wholly on this passage and not upon the gospels that the ordinance stands. A careful examination of that passage will not I think make that evidence so weighty as it seems. That passage, the eleventh chapter I Corinthians, appears to be a reproof to the Corinthian converts of certain gross abuses that had grown up among them, offending against decency not less than against Christianity: accusing their contentiousness; the fanaticism of certain of their women; and the intemperance into which they had fallen at the Lord's supper. The end he has in view, in that Chapter, and this is observable, is not to enjoin upon them to observe the supper, but to censure their abuse of it. *We* quote the passage nowadays as if it enjoined attendance on the supper, but he wrote it merely to chide them for drunkenness. To make their enormity plainer he goes back to the origin of this religious feast to show what that feast was out of which this their riot came and so relates the transactions of the Lord's supper. *I have received of the Lord,* he says.[17] By this expression it is often thought that a miraculous communication is implied, but certainly without good reason if it is remembered that St. Paul was living in the lifetime of all the apostles who could give him an account of the transaction, and it is contrary to all experience to suppose that God should work a miracle to convey information that might be so easily got by natural means. So that the import of the expression is that he had got the account of the Evangelists, which we also possess.

22   But the material circumstance which diminishes our confidence in the correctness of the apostle's view is the observation that his mind had not escaped the prevalent error of the primitive Church, the belief namely that the second coming of Christ would shortly occur, until which time, he tells them, this feast was to be kept. At that time the world would be burnt with fire, and a new government established in which the Saints would sit on thrones; so slow were the disciples during the life and after the ascension of Christ to re-

ceive the idea which we receive that his Second Coming was a spiritual kingdom, the dominion of his religion in the hearts of men to be extended gradually over the whole world.

In this manner I think we may see clearly enough how this ancient ordi-   23
nance got its footing among the early Christians and this single expectation
of a speedy reappearance of a temporal messiah upon earth, which kept its
influence even over so spiritual a man as St. Paul, would naturally tend to
preserve the use of the rite, when once established.

We arrive then at this conclusion: 1. That it does not appear from a care-   24
ful examination of the account of the Last Supper in the Evangelists that it
was designed by Jesus to be perpetual. 2. It does not appear that the opinion
of St. Paul, all things considered, ought to alter our opinion derived from the
Evangelists.

I have not attempted to ascertain precisely the purpose in the mind of Je-   25
sus. But you will see that many opinions may be entertained of his intention
all consistent with the opinion that he did not design the ordinance to be perpetual. He may have foreseen that his disciples would meet together to remember him and seen good in it. It may have crossed his mind that this
would be easily continued a hundred or a thousand years, as men more easily
transmit a form than a virtue, and yet have been altogether out of his purpose to fasten it upon men in all times and all countries.

Admitting that the disciples kept it and admitting Paul's feeling of its per-   26
petuity, that does not settle the question for us. I think it was good for them. I
think it is not suited to this day. We do not take them for guides in other
things. They were, as we know, obstinately attached to their Jewish prejudices. All the intercourse with the most persuasive of teachers seems to have
done very little to enlarge their views. On every subject we have learned to
think differently, and why shall not we form a judgment upon this, more in
accordance with the spirit of Christianity than was the practice of the early
ages?

But it is said, Admit that the rite was not designed to be perpetual. What   27
harm doth it? Here it stands generally accepted under some form by the
Christian world, the undoubted occasion of much good; is it not better it
should remain? This is the question of Expediency.

I proceed to notice a few objections that in my judgment lie against its   28
use in its present form.

29   1. If the view which I have taken of the history of the institution be correct, then the claim of authority should be dropped in administering it. You say, every time you celebrate the rite, that Jesus enjoined it, and the whole language you use conveys that impression. But if you read the New Testament as I do, you do not believe he did.

30   2. It has seemed to me (yet I make the objection with diffidence) that the use of this ordinance tends to produce confusion in our views of the relation of the soul to God. It is the old objection to the doctrine of the Trinity that the true worship was transferred from God to Christ or that such confusion was introduced into the soul that an undivided worship was given nowhere. Is not that the effect of the Lord's Supper? I appeal now to the convictions of communicants and ask such persons whether they have not been occasionally conscious of a painful confusion of thought between the worship due to God and the commemoration due to Christ. For the service does not stand upon the basis of a voluntary act, but is imposed by authority. It is an expression of gratitude to him enjoined by him. There is an endeavour to keep Jesus in mind whilst yet the prayers are addressed to God. I fear it is the effect of this ordinance to clothe Jesus with an authority which he never claimed and which distracts the mind of the worshipper. I know our opinions differ much respecting the nature and offices of Christ and the degree of veneration to which he is entitled. I am so much a Unitarian as this, that I believe the human mind cannot admit but one God, and that every effort to pay religious homage to more than one being goes to take away all right ideas. I appeal, brethren, to your individual experience. In the moment when you make the least petition to God, though it be but a silent wish that he may approve you, or add one moment to your life—do you not—in the very act—necessarily exclude all other beings from your thought? In that act the soul stands alone with God, and Jesus is no more present to the mind than your brother or your child.

31   But is not Jesus called in Scripture the Mediator?[18] He is the Mediator in that only sense in which possibly any being can mediate between God and man, that is an Instructor of Man. He teaches us how to become like God. And a true disciple of Jesus will receive the light he gives most thankfully, but the thanks he offers and which an exalted being will accept are not compliments, commemorations—but the use of that instruction.

3. To pass by other objections, I come to this: that the *use of the elements,* however suitable to the people and the modes of thought in the East where it originated, is foreign and unsuited to affect us. Whatever long usage and strong association may have done in some individuals to deaden this repulsion I apprehend that their use is rather tolerated than loved by any of us. We are not accustomed to express our thoughts or emotions by symbolical actions. Most men find the bread and wine no aid to devotion and to some persons it is an impediment. To eat bread is one thing; to love the precepts of Christ and resolve to obey them is quite another. It is of the greatest importance that whatever forms we use should be animated by our feelings; that our religion through all its acts should be living and operative.

The statement of this objection leads me to say that I think this difficulty, wherever it is felt, to be entitled to the greatest weight. It is alone a sufficient objection to the ordinance. It is my own objection. This mode of commemorating Christ is not suitable to me. That is reason enough why I should abandon it. If I believed that it was enjoined by Jesus on his disciples, and that he even contemplated to make permanent this mode of commemoration every way agreeable to an Eastern mind, and yet on trial it was not agreeable to my own feelings, I should not adopt it. I should choose other ways which he would approve more. For what could he wish to be commemorated for? Only that men might be filled with his spirit. I find that other modes comport with my education and habits of thought. For I chuse that my remembrances of him should be pleasing, affecting, religious. I will love him as a glorious friend after the free way of friendship and not pay him a stiff sign of respect as men do to those whom they fear. A passage read from his discourses, the provoking each other to works like his, any act or meeting which tends to awaken a pure thought, a glow of love, an original design of virtue I call a worthy, a true commemoration.

4. In the last place the importance ascribed to this particular ordinance is not consistent with the spirit of Christianity. The general object and effect of this ordinance is unexceptionable. It has been and is, I doubt not, the occasion of indefinite good, but an importance is given by the friends of the rite to it which never can belong to any form. My friends, the kingdom of God is not meat and drink. Forms are as essential as bodies. It would be foolish to declaim against them, but to adhere to one form a moment after it is outgrown

is foolish. That form only is good and Christian which answers its end. Jesus came to take the load of ceremonies from the shoulders of men and substitute principles. If I understand the distinction of Christianity, the reason why it is to be preferred over all other systems and is divine is this, that it is a moral system; that it presents men with truths which are their own reason, and enjoins practices that are their own justification; that if miracles may be said to have been its evidence to the first Christians they are not its evidence to us, but the doctrines themselves; that every practice is Christian which praises itself and every practice unchristian which condemns itself. I am not engaged to Christianity by decent forms; it is not saving ordinances, it is not usage, it is not what I do not understand that engages me to it—let these be the sandy foundation of falsehoods. What I revere and obey in it is its reality, its boundless charity, its deep interior life, the rest it gives to my mind, the echo it returns to my thoughts, the perfect accord it makes with my reason, the persuasion and courage that come out of it to lead me upward and onward.

35   Freedom is the essence of Christianity. It has for its object simply to make men good and wise. Its institutions should be as flexible as the wants of men. That form out of which the life and suitableness have departed should be as worthless in its eyes as the dead leaves that are falling around us.

36   And therefore, though for the satisfaction of others I have labored to show by the history that it was not intended to be perpetual, though I have gone back to weigh the expressions of Paul, I feel that here is the true way of viewing it. In the midst of considerations as to what Paul thought and why he so thought, I cannot help feeling that it is labor misspent to argue to or from his convictions or those of Luke or John respecting any form. I seem to lose the substance in seeking the shadow. That for which Paul lived and died so gloriously; that for which Jesus was crucified; the end that animated the thousand martyrs and heroes that have followed him, was to redeem us from a formal religion, and teach us to seek our wellbeing in the reformation of the soul. The whole world was full of idols and ordinances. The Jewish was a religion of forms; the Pagan was a religion of forms; it was all body, it had no life,—and the Almighty God was pleased to qualify and send forth a man to teach men that they must serve him with the heart;[19] that only that life was religious which was thoroughly good, that sacrifice was smoke and forms were shadows, and this man lived and died true to this purpose, and now, with his blessed words and life before us, Christians must contend that it is a

matter of vital importance, really a duty, to commemorate him by a certain form whether that form be agreeable to their understandings or not.

Is not this to make vain the gift of God? Is not this to turn back the hands on the dial? Is not this to make men, to make ourselves, forget that not forms but duties, not names but righteousness and love are enjoined and that in the eye of God there is no other measure of the value of any one form than the measure of its use. 37

There remain some practical objections to the ordinance which I need not state. There is one on which I had intended to say a few words, the unfavorable relation in which it puts those persons who abstain from it merely from disinclination to that rite. 38

Influenced by these considerations, I have proposed to the brethren of the church to drop the use of the elements and the claim of authority in the administration of this ordinance, and have suggested a mode in which a meeting for the same purpose might be held, free of objection. 39

They have considered my views with patience and candor, and have recommended unanimously an adherence to the present form. I have therefore been compelled to consider whether it becomes me to administer it. I am clearly of opinion that I ought not. This discourse has already been so far extended that I can only say that the reason of my determination is shortly this—It is my desire, in the office of a Christian minister, to do nothing which I cannot do with my whole heart. Having said this, I have said all. I have no hostility to this institution. I am only stating my want of sympathy with it. Neither should I ever have obtruded this opinion upon other people, had I not been called by my office to administer it. That is the end of my opposition, that I am not interested in it. I am content that it stand to the end of the world if it please men and please heaven, and shall rejoice in all the good it produces. 40

As it is the prevailing opinion and feeling in our religious community that it is an indispensable part of the pastoral office to administer this ordinance, I am about to resign into your hands that office which you have confided to me. It has many duties for which I am feebly qualified. It has some which it will always be my delight to discharge according to my ability wherever I exist. And whilst the thought of its claims oppresses me with a sense of my unworthiness, I am consoled by the hope that no time and no change can deprive me of the satisfaction of pursuing and exercising its highest functions. 41

Notes

1. Although frequently cited as "The Lord's Supper," Emerson never gave this sermon a title other than the biblical text from Romans in the title.

2. The Fourth Council of the Lateran was convened in 1215 by Pope Innocent III (ca. 1160–1216).

3. "Consubstantiation" is the religious doctrine of the real substantial presence of the body and blood of Christ together with the bread and wine in the Eucharist, as distinguished from "Transubstantiation," in which the whole substance of the bread and wine is believed to be changed into the body and blood of Christ. German theologian Martin Luther (1483–1546) and French theologian John Calvin (1509–1564) were leading figures of the Protestant Reformation.

4. The English prelates are William Laud (1573–1645) and William Wake (1657–1737), both holding the position of archbishop of Canterbury; Ralph Cudworth (1617–1688), a prominent Cambridge Platonist; William Warburton (1691–1779), bishop of Gloucester and editor of Shakespeare; and Benjamin Hoadly (1676–1761), bishop of Winchester. Throughout this paragraph, and in paragraphs 2–3, 5–8, 12, 14–15, and 17–18 below, Emerson draws extensively from theological discussions in Thomas Clarkson, *A Portraiture of Quakerism*, 3 vols. (New York, 1806); for additional details, see *CS*, 4:185–186.

5. See John 13–17.

6. With "This is my body . . . Drink it", cf. Matthew 26:26–28, Mark 14:22–24, and Luke 22:19–20.

7. Cf. John 8:6–8.

8. See Matthew 11:6–12, Mark 8:15–21, and Luke 12:1.

9. See John 4:7–15.

10. Mark 14:8.

11. John 13:5.

12. John 6:53.

13. John 6:63.

14. John 13:14–15.

15. Sandemanians are members of a Protestant fundamentalist religious sect descended from the "Glasites," or "Glassites," founded by Scottish minister John Glas, or Glass (1695–1773) during the First Great Awakening; Robert Sandeman (1718–1771), Glas's son-in-law, spread the faith in England and to America.

16. For Paul's account of these practices, see 1 Corinthians 10:1–31 and 11:20–34.

17. 1 Corinthians 11:23.

18. See 1 Timothy 2:5.

19. With "The Jewish was . . . the heart;", cf. Matthew 22:37, Mark 12:30–33, Luke 10:27, and Ephesians 6:6.

The Uses of Natural History

In accepting the invitation with which the Directors of this   1
Society have honored me to introduce the Course, I have followed my inclination rather than consulted my ability.[1] My time has been so preoccupied as
to prevent any particular course of reading or collection of novel illustrations
of the subjects treated, which I should gladly have proposed to myself. I shall
therefore say what I think on the subject of this Lecture according to such
imperfect general information as I already possessed.

It seems to have been designed, if anything was, that men should be stu-   2
dents of Natural History. Man is, by nature, a farmer, a hunter, a shepherd
and a fisherman, who are all practical naturalists and by their observations
the true founders of all societies for the pursuit of science. And even after society has made some progress, so that the division of labor removes men into
cities, and gives rise to sedentary trades and professions, every man who is
fortunate enough to be born in circumstances that require him to make any
exertion to live, is compelled to pick up in his own experience, a considerable
knowledge of natural philosophy,—as, an acquaintance with the properties
of water, of wood, of stone, of light, of heat, and the natural history of many
insects, birds and beasts.

3   And as if to secure this end in the constitution of all men, the eye is so fitted to the face of nature or the face of nature to the eye that the perception
of beauty is continually awakened in all places and under the most ordinary
circumstances. The beauty of the world is a perpetual invitation to the study
of the world. Sunrise and sunset; fire; flowers; shells; the sea—in all its shades,
from indigo to green and gray, by the light of day, and phosphorescent under
the ship's keel at night; the airy inaccessible mountain; the sparry cavern; the
glaring colours of the soil of the volcano; the forms of vegetables; and all the
elegant and majestic figures of the creatures that fly, climb, or creep upon the
earth—all, by their beauty, work upon our curiosity and court our attention.
The earth is a museum, and the five senses a philosophical apparatus of such
perfection, that the pleasure we obtain from the aids with which we arm
them, is trifling, compared with their natural information.

4   It is frequently observed how much power the influence of natural objects gives to the sentiment of love of country which is strongest in the most
wild and picturesque regions. It deserves notice also as it is this which not
only heightens but creates the charm which hunting has for many persons
who would start at being thought to have any poetry in their constitution. If
the running down a fox or hare were performed under cover, or in a street, it
would soon lose its noble name, but great bodily exertion made along the
mountain side, upon fields glittering with a million beads of dew, or in the
shades of a wood—which always seem to say something, we cannot well
make out what;—exhilarated by the fragrant scents, and cheered on by the
trumpet of all the winds,—it is not strange that a man should learn to love
these scenes, though he err in thinking he loves to kill his game.

5   Yielding ourselves to the same pleasant influences, let us inquire what are
the advantages which may be expected to accrue from the greater cultivation
of Natural Science.

6   They are in my judgment great and manifold, and probably more than
can be now enumerated. I do not think we are yet masters of all the reasons
that make this knowledge valuable to us. They will only disclose themselves
by a more advanced state of science. I say this because we have all a presentiment of relations to external nature, which outruns the limits of actual science.

7   I lately had an opportunity of visiting that celebrated Repository of Natural Curiosities, the Garden of Plants in Paris;[2] and except to Naturalists, I

might hesitate to speak of the feelings it excited in me. There is the richest collection in the world of natural curiosities arranged for the most imposing effect. The mountain and morass and prairie and jungle, the ocean, and rivers, the mines and the atmosphere have been ransacked to furnish whatever was rich and rare; the types of each class of beings—Nature's proof impressions;—to render account of her three kingdoms to the keen insatiable eye of French Science.

In spacious grounds skilfully laid out, and shaded with fine groves and shrubberies, you walk among the animals of every country, each in his own paddock with his mates, having his appropriate food before him,—his habits consulted in his accommodation. There towers the camelopard nearly twenty feet high, whose promenade and breakfast attract as much attention as the king's; the lions from Algiers and Asia; the elephants from Siam—whose bath is occasionally performed with great applause from the boys;—our own countrymen, the buffalo and the bear from New Hampshire and Labrador.[3] All sizes and all stripes of tygers, hyenas, leopards, and jackals; a herd of monkeys; not to mention the great numbers of sheep, goats, llamas, and zebras, that sleep, browse, or ruminate in their several country fashions, as much at ease as in their own wilds, for the amusement of the whole world in the heart of the capital of France.

Moving along these pleasant walks, you come to the botanical cabinet, an inclosed garden plot, where grows a grammar of botany—where the plants rise, each in its class, its order, and its genus, as nearly as their habits in reference to soils will permit, arranged by the hand of Jussieu himself.[4] If you have read Decandolle with engravings, or with a *hortus siccus,* conceive how much more exciting and intelligible is this natural alphabet, this green and yellow and crimson dictionary, on which the sun shines, and the winds blow.[5]

The Cabinet of Natural History is contained in a large stone edifice in the centre of the grounds. It is a prodigality to visit in one walk all the various halls in this great gallery of Nature. The ornithological chambers require an entire day: For who would mix and confound so fine and delicate sensations? This house of stuffed birds is a finer picture gallery than the Louvre. The whole air is flushed with the rich plumage and beautiful forms of the birds. The fancy coloured vests of those elegant beings make me as pensive as the hues and forms of a cabinet of shells have done before. They fill the mind with calm and genial thought. Some of the birds have a fabulous beauty that

8

9

10

seems more appropriate to some Sultan's garden in the Arabian Nights Entertainments than to a real tangible Scientific Collection.[6] You see the favourites of nature,—Creatures in whose form and coat seems to have been a design to charm the eye of cultivated taste. Observe that parrot called *Psittacus Erythropterus.* You need not write down his name for he is the beau of all birds and you will find him as you will find a Raffaelle[7] in a gallery. Then the humming birds so little and so gay—from the least of all, the *Trochilus Niger* not so big as a beetle—to the *Trochilus Pella* with his irresistible neck of gold and silver and fire; and the *Trochilus Delalandi* from Brazil whom the French call the magnificent fly or glory in miniature.

11   The birds of Paradise are singularly delicate and picturesque in their plumage. The manucode or royal Paradisaea from New Guinea, the red Paradisaea, and the Paradisaea Apoda, seem each more beautiful than the last and each, if seen alone, would be pronounced a peerless creature. I watched the different groups of people who came in to the gallery, and noticed that they picked out the same birds to point to the admiration of their companions. They all noticed the Veuve à épaulettes—the widow with epaulettes—a grotesque black fowl called Emberiza Longicauda with fine shoulder ornaments and a long mourning tail, and the Ampelis Cotinga. All admired the *Phasianus Argus,* a pheasant that appeared to have made its toilette after the pattern of the peacock, and the *Trogon pavoninus,* called also the Couroucon. But it were vain to enumerate even the conspicuous individuals in the parti-coloured assembly. There were black swans and white peacocks, the famous venerable ibis come hither to Paris out of Egypt,—both the sacred and the rosy; the flamingo with a neck like a snake; the Toucan, rightly denominated the rhinoceros; and a vulture whom to meet in a wilderness would make the flesh creep, so truculent and executioner-like he stood.

12   The Cabinet of birds was a single and even small part of that noble magazine of natural wonders. Not less complete, scarcely less attractive is the collection of stuffed beasts, prepared with the greatest skill to represent the forms and native attitudes of the quadrupeds. Then follow the insects, the reptiles, the fishes, the minerals. In neighboring apartments is contained the collection of comparative anatomy, a perfect series from the skeleton of the *balaena* which reminds everyone of the frame of a schooner, to the upright form and highly developed skull of the Caucasian race of man.[8]

13   The eye is satisfied with seeing and strange thoughts are stirred as you see

more surprizing objects than were known to exist; transparent lumps of amber with gnats and flies within; radiant spars and marbles; huge blocks of quartz; native gold in all its forms of crystallization and combination, gold in threads, in plates, in crystals, in dust; and silver taken from the earth molten as from fire. You are impressed with the inexhaustible gigantic riches of nature. The limits of the possible are enlarged, and the real is stranger than the imaginary. The universe is a more amazing puzzle than ever, as you look along this bewildering series of animated forms, the hazy butterflies, the carved shells, the birds, beasts, insects, snakes, fish, and the upheaving principle of life every where incipient, in the very rock aping organized forms. Whilst I stand there I am impressed with a singular conviction that not a form so grotesque, so savage, or so beautiful, but is an expression of something in man the observer. We feel that there is an occult relation between the very worm, the crawling scorpions, and man. I am moved by strange sympathies. I say I will listen to this invitation. I will be a Naturalist.

Under the influence of such thoughts, I say that I suppose many inducements to the study of Natural History will disclose themselves as its secrets are penetrated. Besides that the general progress of the Science has given it a higher and higher place in the public estimation is there not every now and then some inexplicable fact or new class of relations suggested which for the time seems not so much to invite as to defy scientific solution? For example, what known laws are to classify some of the astounding facts embodied in the Report of the Committee of the French Institute in 1830 upon the subject of Animal Magnetism—a committee too, considering the persons and the circumstances, who might be regarded as a picked jury of the most competent scientific persons on earth?[9] But not to venture upon this dangerous ground, the debateable land of the sublime and the ridiculous, let me confine my attention to the enumeration of certain specific advantages easily marked and understood which may serve as the commendation of the objects of this society.

First. It is the lowest and yet not a bad recommendation of the occupations of the Naturalist that they are serviceable to the health. The ancient Greeks had a fable of the giant Antaeus, that when he wrestled with Hercules, he was suffocated in the gripe of the hero, but every time he touched his mother earth, his strength was renewed. The fable explains itself of the body and the mind. Man is the broken giant, and in all his weakness he is invigo-

14

15

rated by touching his mother earth, that is, by habits of conversation with nature. It is good for the body exhausted by the bad air, and artificial life of cities, to be sent out into the fresh and fragrant fields, and there employed in exploring the laws of the creation. The study of Botany deserves the attention of those interested in Education, for this, if for no other cause. The wild rose will reflect its hues upon the cheek of the lover of nature. It is well known that the celebrated Wilson was led to the study of Ornithology for the benefit of his enfeebled health, and in his enthusiastic rambles in the wilderness his constitution was established whilst he enlarged the domain of science.[10]

16   The mountain minerals will pay their searcher with active limbs and refreshed spirits: And he who wanders along the margin of the sounding sea for shellfish or marine plants, will find strength of limb and sharpness of sight and bounding blood in the same places. Dig your garden, cross your cattle, graft your trees, feed your silkworms, set your hives—in the field is the perfection of the senses to be found, and quiet restoring Sleep,—

His poppy grows among the Corn.[11]

17   Second. In the second place, the main advantage to be proposed from the study of natural history is that which may seem to make all further argument needless; to be itself the manifest ground on which the study stands in the favor of mankind, I mean the direct service which it renders to the cultivator and the world, the amount of useful economical information which it communicates. The proof of this assertion is the history of all discoveries, almost the history of civilization itself. Who is not indebted for the comforts and accommodations of every day to the investigations which have been carried into every kingdom of nature?

18   It is the earth itself and its natural bodies that make the raw material out of which we construct our food, clothing, fuel, furniture, and arms. And it is the Naturalist who discovers the virtues of these bodies and the mode of converting them to use. In the most refined state of society, these are most accumulated; but these are now so numerous and the subdivision of labor has removed each process so far out of sight, that a man, who by pulling a bell can command any luxury the world contains, is in danger of forgetting that iron came out of a mine, and perfume out of a cat.

19   You sit in your parlor surrounded by more proofs of the cultivation of

Natural Science than books or cabinets contain. The water that you drink was pumped up from a well by an application of the air pump. The well ventilated chimney which every mason can build, derived its hint from Franklin and Rumford.[12] The sugar in your dish was refined by the instruction given by a modern chemist on the adjustment of temperature for the crystallization of syrup; the brasses, the silver, the iron, the gold, which enter into the construction of so many indispensable articles, and indeed the glass, the cloth, the paints and dyes, have employed the philosopher as well as the mechanic.

There is scarcely any manufacture whose processes are not assisted or directed by rules and principles derived from the observations of Naturalists, apart from the consideration that all the foreign fabrics, drugs, fruits, and condiments, which are as familiar as salt, were transported hither across the sea by the aid of that map of the stars and the Record of the predicted places of the sun and the earth, which the lovers of nature from the Chaldean Shepherd to Laplace and Bowditch have aided in bringing to perfection.[13]

20

The history of modern times has repeatedly shown that a single man devoted to Science may carry forward the mechanic arts and multiply the products of commerce more than the united population of a country can accomplish in ages wherein no particular devotion to scientific pursuits exists. This is forcibly illustrated by the historical fact of the influence produced in France by the appointment of the celebrated Duhamel to the professorship of the School of Mines.[14] In 1822 it was stated to the Academy by its Secretary

21

that from the appointment of M. Duhamel to the time of his death, the products of iron in France were quadrupled; the mines of this metal opened near the Loire in the region of coal, and in the midst of combustible matter, were about to yield iron at the same price as in England. Antimony, manganese, which we formerly imported, are now exported in considerable quantities. Chrome, discovered by one of our chemists, is also the useful product of one of our mines. Zinc and tin have already been extracted from the mines on the coast of Brittany. Alum and Vitriol, formerly almost unknown in France, are collected in abundance. An immense mass of rock-salt has just been discovered in Lorraine, and all promises that these new creations will not stop here. Doubtless it is not to a single man, nor to the appointment of a single professorship that all this may be attributed but it is not the less true that this one man, this one professorship has been the primary cause of these advantages.

22   But the advantages which Science has presented to human life are in all probability the least part of her possessions. To the powers of science no limit can be assigned. All that has been is only an accumulated force to act upon the future. The prospective power, the armed hand, the learned eye are worth more than the riches they have acquired. It is a maxim in philosophy that a general truth is more valuable than all the particular facts which it has disclosed.

23   The natural history of water is not studied with less diligence or advantage at this moment than when Watt and Fulton made it a day laborer for mankind.[15] It is but the other day that our countryman, Mr. Jacob Perkins, noticed the small bubbles that are formed on the sides and bottom of a vessel in which water is heated, and most rapidly on the hottest parts, and discovered that these bubbles operate as a screen between the fire and the body of water in the vessel, preventing the rise of the temperature within in any proportion to the increase of the temperature on the outside.[16] He found especially that in the boilers of steam engines great inconvenience and danger frequently resulted from this cause because when the engineer quickened his fire it consumed the coats of the boiler more rapidly without making a proportionate expansion of the steam. This observation led to the thought that a strong circulation in the water might be caused which should continually rush against the sides of the vessel and break or remove these air bubbles. This thought he has recently executed in the machine called the Circulators and which has already been adopted in three of the locomotives on the Liverpool and Manchester Railroad with the best success and is about being introduced into all. And this may serve for a hundred examples of the benefit resulting from these observations.

24   Third. But it is high time to enumerate a third reason for the cultivation of natural history which is the *delight which springs from the contemplation of this truth,* independent of all other considerations. I should be ashamed to neglect this good, in too particular a showing what profit was to accrue from

the knowledge of nature. The knowledge itself, is the highest benefit. He must be very young or very sordid who wishes to know what good it will do him to understand the sublime mechanism on which the stability of the Solar System and the faithful return of the seasons depend. What good will it do him? Why, the good of knowing that fact. Is not that good enough?—

Moreover, is it not disgraceful to be served by all the arts and sciences at our tables, and in our chambers and never know who feeds us, nor understand the cunning they employ? I cannot but think it becoming that every gentleman should know why he puts on a white hat in summer, and a woolen coat in winter; and why his shoes cannot be made until the leather is tanned. Better sit still than be borne by steam, and not know how; or guided by the needle and the quadrant through thousands of miles of sea, without a mark in the horizon, and brought to a little dent in the shore on the other half the globe, as truly as if following a clew in the hand—and never ask how that feat is accomplished.

Bias was asked what good, education would do for a boy;—"When he goes there," pointing to the marble seats of the theatre, he replied, "that he might not be a stone sitting upon a stone."[17] Every fact that is disclosed to us in natural history removes one scale more from the eye; makes the face of nature around us so much more significant. How many men have seen it snow twenty or forty winters without a thought being suggested beyond the need of stout boots, the probability of good sleighing, and the country trade; until some kind philosopher has drawn our attention to the singular beauty of that phenomenon, the formation of snow; and shown us the texture of that self-weaving blanket with which the parts of the globe exposed to cold, cover themselves in pile proportioned to their exposure, at the time when the animated creation on the same side of the earth whiten and thicken their fleeces. We cannot see again without new pleasure what the Latin poet calls the thick fleece of silent waters—

densum tacitarum vellus aquarum.[18]

You cannot go out when the snow is falling in a calm still air and catch the little hexagon upon the palm of your hand and measure the invariable angles of the radii of the star without a finer delight than ever sprang from the consideration of the convenience of the general railroad with which it covers the

25
26
27

country for the woodcutter and the farmer. The snowstorm becomes to your eye a philosophical experiment performed in a larger laboratory and on a more magnificent scale than our chemists can command.

28 To the naturalist belongs all that keen gratification which arises from the observation of the singular provision for human wants that in some instances, requiring ages for its completion, was begun ages before the use of it was shown.

29 The science of Geology which treats of the structure of the Earth has ascertained that before the period when God created man upon the earth very considerable changes have taken place in the planet. It is made probable that the various rocks that are now found broken upon it, as granite, slate, chalk, and so forth, covered it as so many concentric crusts or coats, like the coats of the onion, one without the other. But the soils which now cover it are formed by the decomposition of these stones, so that in this position of them that mixture of them which is essential to the production of vegetable life could never have been affected. By internal volcanoes, or other means, these several strata have been broken and raised and are now found lying as may be seen in mountain countries in oblique and perpendicular instead of horizontal layers so as to yield their various treasures to man and to the soil.

30 This is yet more striking in the case of coal, so important to old countries, and recently to this, and has naturally attracted the particular attention of British naturalists.

31 It is well known how vastly the great development of the commerce of Great Britain and thence of the great civilization of that country is indebted to the boundless abundance of coal in its mines. In consequence of the abundance and accessibility of this mineral in that island, and its opportune association with beds of iron ore, and the invariable contiguity of limestone employed to flux the iron, the English have been enabled to surpass all other nations in the cheapness of machinery and thence in the extent of their manufactures.

32 But the discoveries of geologists have shown that the coal which is undoubtedly a vegetable formation is the relic of forests which existed at an unknown antiquity before the era of the creation of mankind, and by the overflowing of the sea and other changes of the surface had been buried below the surface at too great a depth to be reached by man. But before the creation

of our race Earthquakes or other convulsions of enormous force have lifted up these mineral beds into ledges so that they are found extending from one thousand feet above the level of the ocean, to unknown depths below it. And so it happens that these vast beds of fuel so essential to man's comfort and civilization, which would have been covered by the crust of the globe from his knowledge and use, are thus brought up within reach of his little hands; and a great work of Nature in an antiquity that hath no record—namely the deposit and crystallization of Antediluvian forests, is made to contribute to our pleasure and prosperity at this hour.

Thus knowledge will make the face of the earth significant to us: it will make the stones speak and clothe with grace the meanest weed. Indeed it is worth considering in all animated nature what different aspect the same object presents to the ignorant and the instructed eye. It only needs to have the eye informed, to make everything we see, every plant, every spider, every moss, every patch of mould upon the bark of a tree, give us the idea of fitness, as much as the order and accommodation of the most ingeniously packed dressing box. For, every form is a history of the thing. The comparative anatomist can tell at sight whether a skeleton belonged to a carnivorous or herbivorous animal—to a climber, a jumper, a runner, a digger, a builder. The conchologist can tell at sight whether his shell were a river or a sea shell, whether it dwelt in still or in running waters, whether it were an annual or a perennial covering, and many the like particulars. And this takes away the sense of deformity from all objects; for, every thing is a monster till we know what it is for. A ship, a telescope, a surgical instrument, a box of strange tools are puzzles and painful to the eye, until we have been shown successively the use of every part, and then the thing tells its story at sight, and is beautiful. A lobster is monstrous to the eye the first time it is seen, but when we have been shown the use of the case, the color, the tentacula, and the proportion of the claws, and have seen that he has not a scale nor a bristle, nor any part, but fits exactly to some habit and condition of the creature, he then seems as perfect and suitable to his sea-house, as a glove to a hand. A *man* in the rocks under the sea, would indeed be a monster; but a lobster is a most handy and happy fellow there. So there is not an object in nature so mean or loathsome, not a weed, not a toad, not an earwig, but a knowledge of its habits would lessen our disgust, and convert it into an object of some worth; perhaps of

33

admiration. Nothing is indifferent to the wise. If a man should study the economy of a spire of grass—how it sucks up sap, how it imbibes light, how it resists cold, how it repels excess of moisture, it would show him a design in the form, in the color, in the smell, in the very posture of the blade as it bends before the wind.

34   There is an excellent story in one of our children's books called "Eyes and No Eyes."[19] A dull, dumb, unprofitable world is this to many a man that has all his senses in health. But bring under the same arch of day, upon the same green sod, under the shadow of the same hills Linnaeus or Buffon or Cuvier or Humboldt and the sea and the land will break forth into singing, and all the trees of the field will clap their hands.[20] The traveller casts his eye upon a broken mountainside, and sees nothing to detain his attention a moment. Let Cuvier regard the same thing; in the rough ledges, the different shades and superposition of the strata, his eye is reading as in a book the history of the globe, the changes that were effected by fire, by water, by pressure, by friction in ages long prior to the existence of man upon the planet; he is hearkening to the infallible testimony of events whereof is no chronicle but in the memory of God, and taking down minutes of the same for the guidance and confirmation of future inquirers.

35   It has been felt by their contemporaries as a public calamity when such an observer who knew the value of his senses has been deprived of their use. One of the most touching incidents in biography is the affliction that befel Galileo, who, after announcing in rapid succession to the world his splendid discoveries, made by the aid of the telescope, namely, the uneven surface of the moon; the spots on the sun by which the revolution of that body was proved; that Venus was horned like the moon; the satellites, and the belt of Jupiter; the ring of Saturn;—was bereaved of sight. His friend Castelli wrote to one of his correspondents, "The noblest eye is darkened that nature ever made; an eye so priveleged, and gifted with such rare qualities, that it may with truth be said to have seen more than all of those which are gone, and to have opened the eyes of all which are to come."[21]

36   These men have used their senses to such good purpose, led on by the mere pleasure of observation, the high delight which they found in exploring the works of nature.

37   Fourth. There is a fourth good purpose answered by the study of Natural

History which deserves a distinct enumeration. I refer to its salutary effect upon the mind and character of those who cultivate it. It makes the intellect exact, quick to discriminate between the similar and the same, and greedy of truth.

Moreover, I hope it will not be thought undue refinement to suppose that long habits of intimate acquaintance with nature's workmanship, which is always neat, simple, masterly, accustoms her scholars to think and work in her style. All our ideas of sublimity and beauty are got from that source. Our contrivances are good but will not bear comparison with hers. 38

An orrery is esteemed an ingenious and elegant machine to exhibit the relative motions of the bodies of the solar system, but compare it with nature's own orrery, as it would appear to the eye of an observer placed above the plane of the system. He should see the beautiful balls moving on, self-poised in empty space: no rods reaching from them to the sun—no wires fastening the moons to their planets, but all bound by firm but invisible cords, that never entangle, nor crack, nor wear, nor weigh, namely, those threads of attraction, that join every particle in creation to every other particle. 39

Or to take a much lower instance in an object at our feet of the simplicity of the means by which important ends are effected. Who are those that hoe and harrow the surface of the ground to keep it in a state of looseness fit for tillage, and to make the fallow land penetrable to the roots of the grasses, and to the germination of forest trees? The Earthworms. 40

It has been observed by the entomologist that Worms promote vegetation by boring, perforating, and loosening the soil, and rendering it pervious to rains, and to the fibres of plants; by drawing straws and stalks of leaves and twigs into it; and most of all by throwing up such infinite numbers of lumps of earth called Worm-casts which manure the grain and grass.[22] Without the incessant aid of these little gardeners and farmers, the earth would soon become cold, and hardbound, and void of fermentation. 41

Thus Nature keeps the surface of the soil open; but how does she make the soil? Who are the strong and skilful architects that build up the solid land from the bottom of the sea? A little insect, the coralline, the madrepore, almost too small for sight, possessing the power of extracting lime from the sea water, builds up the coral reefs from the bed of the ocean to the surface, and these make in the course of ages the broad floor, on which by the agency of 42 the marine vegetation, and of the birds, and the accidents of drift timber, a coat of soil is gradually laid, and a new land opened for the accommodation of man.

43   There are numberless examples in the economy of bees, the celebrated discovery of Reaumur relative to the angles of the cells, the observations of Huber upon the simplicity of the means by which the hive is ventilated, that are too long and too well known to be detailed.[23]

44   Can the effect be other than most beneficent upon the faculties dedicated to such observations?—upon the man given

> To reverend watching of each still report
> That Nature utters from her rural shrine.[24]

45   Moreover, the state of mind which nature makes indispensable to all such as inquire of her secrets is the best discipline. For she yields no answer to petulance, or dogmatism, or affectation; only to patient, docile observation. Whosoever would gain anything of her, must submit to the essential condition of all learning, must go in the spirit of a little child. The naturalist commands nature by obeying her.

46   And this benign influence passes from the intellect into the affections and makes not only the judgment sound but the manners simple and the whole character amiable and true. Fontenelle, who wrote the lives of the members of the French Academy of Sciences, a society of natural philosophers and mathematicians, takes notice of the amiable simplicity of their manners which rather seemed common to that class of men of letters than peculiar to any individual. D'Alembert, who wrote the lives of the Members of the Academy—a society of poets and fine writers—nowhere pretends to represent this amiable quality as characteristic of this class of men of letters.[25]

47   Indeed I think that a superiority in this respect of truth and simplicity of character extends generally to people resident in the country whose manner of life so nearly resembles that of the professed naturalist. That flippancy which is apt to be so soon learned in cities is not often found in the country. Nor are men *there* all ground down to the same tame and timid mediocrity which results in cities from the fear of offending and the desire of display. But the peculiarities of original genius stand out more strongly which are the results of that framework which the hand of God has laid for each man and which it behoves every man to respect as it constitutes the only plan accord-

ing to which his particular structure can ever rise to greatness. These peculiarities in the resident of the country are the effects no doubt of silence and
solitude, and of constant familiarity with calm and great objects. Though this
influence is often exaggerated, yet I believe none of us are quite insensible to
it, as every man may prove who goes alone into a picturesque country. I apprehend that every man who goes by himself into the woods, not at the time
occupied by any anxiety of mind, but free to surrender himself to the genius
of the place, feels as a boy again without loss of wisdom. In the presence of
nature he is a child.

One thing more under this head of the effect of these studies upon the
mind and character. It generates enthusiasm, the highest quality, say rather,
the highest *state* of the character. It has been the effect of these pursuits and
most conspicuously upon the first class of minds to absorb their attention.
What was sought at first as a secondary object, to satisfy an occasional curiosity, or amuse a rainy day, gradually won upon their interest, excluding every
former occupation, until it possessed itself of the whole man.

They have felt the interest in truth as truth which was revealed to their
inquiries. The story of Archimedes running as a madman, around the streets
of Syracuse, after discovering the mode of determining the specific gravity
of bodies, crying out as he ran, "I have found it," is familiar to children.[26]
Scarce less notorious is that trait recorded of Newton, that, when after the
new measurement of a degree of the earth's surface, he renewed his comparison of the earth's attraction of the moon, to the earth's attraction of a
falling apple,—and saw, in the progress of the calculation, that he was approaching the result he had formerly anticipated, he was so much agitated by
the grandeur of the fact about to be disclosed, that he was unable to go on,
and was obliged to call in a friend to finish the computation.[27] As they say, the
soldier who dies in hot blood never feels the wound, it is remarked of several
physiologists, that they have continued their observations into the very doors
of death. It is recorded of Haller, the celebrated Swiss physiologist, that he
continued his observations in his last illness upon the progress of his disease
with perfect calmness; taking note of the successive alterations in his system,
and keeping his hand upon his own pulse,—until at last he exclaimed to his
physician, "My friend, the artery ceases to beat," and expired.[28]

And it is related of John Hunter that he retained the habit of critical observation to the last pulse, and said to a friend who sat beside him, "I wish I

48

49

50

had power of speaking or writing that I might tell you how pleasant are the sensations of dying."[29]

51   These are the heroes of science who have an instinctive preference of the value of truth, and who think that man has no nobler vocation than to watch and record the wonders that surround him. Hence the high prophetic tone which they have sometimes assumed, speaking as with the voice of time and nature.

52   When Kepler had discovered the three harmonic laws that regulate the motion of the heavenly bodies, he exclaims,

>   At length, after the lapse of eighteen months, the first dawn of light has shone upon me; and on this remarkable day, I have perceived the pure irradiation of sublime truth. Nothing now represses me: I dare yield myself up to my holy ardor; I dare insult mankind by acknowledging, that, I have turned worldly science to advantage; that I have robbed the vessels of Egypt to erect a temple to the living God. If I am pardoned, I shall rejoice; if blamed, I shall endure it. The die is cast; I have written this book:—whether it be read by posterity or by my contemporaries, is of no consequence: it may well wait for a reader during one century since God himself during six thousand years has waited for an observer like myself.[30]

53   The biography of chemists, botanists, physicians, geometers abounds with the narrative of sleepless nights, laborious days and dangerous journeyings. There is no hazard the love of science has not prompted them to brave; no wilderness they have not penetrated; no experiment suggested, which they have not tried. And with all my honour for science, so much greater is my respect for the observer Man, than for any thing he observes, that I esteem this development of character—this high unconditional devotion to their cause, this trampling under foot of every thing pitiful and selfish in the zeal of their pursuit of nature,—to be worth all the stars they have found, all the bugs or crystals or zoophytes they have described, all the laws how sublime soever, which they have deduced and divulged to mankind.

54   Fifth. I have spoken of some of the advantages which may flow from the culture of natural science: health; useful knowledge; delight; and the im-

provement of the mind and character. I should not do the subject the imperfect justice in my power if I did not add a fifth. It is in my judgment the greatest office of natural science, and one which as yet is only begun to be discharged, to explain man to himself. The knowledge of the laws of nature,—how many wild errors—political, philosophical, theological, has it not already corrected. The knowledge of all the facts of all the laws of nature will give man his true place in the system of being. But more than the correction of specific errors by the disclosure of particular facts, there yet remain questions of the highest interest which are unsolved and on which a far more profound knowledge of Nature will throw light.

The most difficult problems are those that lie nearest at hand. I suppose   55 that every philosopher feels that the simple fact of his own existence is the most astonishing of all facts. But I suggest the question, with great humility, to the reason of everyone present, whether, the most mysterious and wonderful fact, after our own existence, with which we are acquainted, be not, the power of *expression* which belongs to external nature; or, that correspondence of the outward world to the inward world of thoughts and emotions, by which it is suited to represent what we think.

There is more beauty in the morning cloud than the prism can render account of. There is something in it which reflects the aspects of mortal life, its   56 epochs, and its fate. Is the face of heaven and earth—this glorious scene always changing—yet always good—fading all around us into fair perspective,—over-hung with the gay awning of the clouds,—floating themselves as scraps of down under the high stars, and the ever lasting vault of space,—is this nothing to us but so much oxygen, azote, and carbon of which what is visible is composed?[31] Is there not a secret sympathy which connects man to all the animate and to all the inanimate beings around him? Where is it these fair creatures, in whom an order and series is so distinctly discernible, find their link, their cement, their keystone, but in the Mind of Man? It is he who marries the visible to the Invisible by uniting thought to Animal Organization.

The strongest distinction of which we have an idea is that between   57 thought and matter. The very existence of thought and speech supposes and is a new nature totally distinct from the material world; yet we find it impossible to speak of it and its laws in any other language than that borrowed from our experience in the material world. We not only speak in continual metaphors of the morn, the noon and the evening of life, of dark and bright thoughts, of sweet and bitter moments, of the healthy mind and the fading memory; but all our most literal and direct modes of speech—as right and wrong, form and substance, honest and dishonest, and so forth, are, when hunted up to their original signification, found to be metaphors also. And this, because the whole of Nature is a metaphor or image of the human Mind. The laws of moral nature answer to those of matter as face to face in a glass. "The visible world," it has been well said, "and the relations of its parts is the dial plate of the invisible one."[32] In the language of the poet,

> For all that meets the bodily sense I deem
> Symbolical, one mighty alphabet
> For infant minds.[33]

58   It is a most curious fact that the axioms of geometry and of mechanics only translate the laws of ethics. Thus,

> A straight line is the shortest distance between two points;
> The whole is greater than its part;
> The smallest weight may be made to lift the greatest, the differ-
>   ence of force being compensated by time;
> Reaction is equal to action;

and a thousand the like propositions which have an ethical as well as a material sense. They are true not only in geometry but in life; they have a much more extensive and universal signification as applied to human nature than when confined to technical use. And every common proverb is only one of these facts in nature used as a picture or parable of a more extensive truth; as when we say, "A bird in the hand is worth two in the bush," "A rolling stone gathers no moss," "'Tis hard to carry a full cup even," "Whilst the grass grows the steed starves."—In themselves these are insignificant facts but we repeat them because they are symbolical of moral truths. These are only trivial instances designed to show the principle. But it will probably be found to hold of all the facts revealed by chemistry or astronomy that they have the same harmony with the human mind.

59   And this undersong, this perfect harmony does not become less with more intimate knowledge of nature's laws but the analogy is felt to be deeper

and more universal for every law that Davy or Cuvier or Laplace has revealed.[34] It almost seems as if according to the idea of Fontenelle, "We seem to recognize a truth the first time we hear it."

I look then to the progress of Natural Science as to that which is to develop new and great lessons of which good men shall understand the moral. Nature is a language and every new fact we learn is a new word, but it is not a language taken to pieces and dead in the dictionary, but the language put together into a most significant and universal sense. I wish to learn this language—not that I may know a new grammar but that I may read the great book which is written in that tongue. A man should feel that the time is not lost and the efforts not misspent that are devoted to the elucidation of these laws; for herein is writ by the Creator his own history. If the opportunity is afforded him he may study the leaves of the lightest flower that opens upon the breast of Summer, in the faith that there is a meaning therein before whose truth and beauty all external grace must vanish, as it may be, that all this outward universe shall one day disappear, when its whole sense hath been comprehended and engraved forever in the eternal thoughts of the human mind.

Notes

1. "The Uses of Natural History" is the first lecture Emerson delivered after leaving the pulpit and deciding upon his new callings of lecturer and naturalist. He read the lecture on 5 November 1833 as the introductory lecture in a course sponsored by the Natural History Society in Boston.
2. Emerson's visit to the Jardin des Plantes at the Muséum d'Histoire Naturelle, Paris, on 13 July 1833, and his exploration of the cabinets of curiosities assembled there, fundamentally changed the way he looked at nature (see *JMN*, 4:187–200, 405–406).
3. A camelopard is a giraffe; Siam was the name of Thailand in Emerson's time.
4. Antoine-Laurent de Jussieu (1748–1836), French botanist who helped devise the modern system for classifying plants.
5. Either Augustin-Pyrame de Candolle (1778–1841) or his son Alphonse-Louis-Pierre-Pyrame de Candolle (1806–1893), Swiss botanists; a *hortus siccus* is a herbarium, or collection of dried plants.

6. A reference to the collection of ancient Persian-Indian-Arabian traditional tales called *The Arabian Nights' Entertainments* or *A Thousand and One Nights* (1450), originally in Arabic.

7. Raphael (1483–1520), Italian painter whose works adorn the Vatican, also called "Raphaelle" or "Raphaello" by Emerson.

8. *Balaena* is the genus of the Greenland whale.

9. Animal magnetism is a type of hypnosis.

10. Alexander Wilson (1766–1813), American ornithologist born in Scotland.

11. Emerson's source is "Of Greatness" (1668) by Alexander Cowley (1618–1667), British poet, in a translation from the Roman poet Horace (65–8 BCE).

12. Benjamin Franklin (1706–1790), American statesman, author, and inventor of, among other things, a stove that held its heat well; Benjamin Thompson, Count Rumford (1753–1814), British scientist and philanthropist born in Massachusetts, developed a type of fireplace that bears his name.

13. The Chaldeans of early Babylon were known for their study of astronomy; Pierre-Simon, marquis de Laplace (1749–1827), French astronomer and mathematician; Nathaniel Bowditch (1773–1838), American mathematician, actuary, and astronomer who translated Laplace's five-volume *Mécanique celeste* (1799–1825).

14. Jean-Pierre-François Guillot Duhamel (1730–1816), French scientist and inspector of mines.

15. James Watt (1736–1819), Scottish engineer who harnessed steam power; Robert Fulton (1765–1849), American civil engineer and inventor of the steamboat.

16. Jacob Perkins (1766–1849), American inventor and mechanical engineer.

17. Bias of Priene, sixth-century BCE Greek writer known for his apothegms.

18. "[T]hickly the still fleecy shower [flows down]" (*JMN*, 4:61n); Emerson's source is *Epigrams*, 4.3, by Martial (ca. 40–ca. 104), Roman poet born in Spain.

19. "Eyes and No Eyes; or, The Art of Seeing" was published in *Evenings at Home* (1792–1796), edited by John Aiken (1747–1822), English essayist and physician, and his sister, Anna Letitia Barbauld (1743–1825), English poet and editor.

20. Carolus Linnaeus (1707–1778), Swedish botanist, is considered one of the founders of modern systematic botany; Georges-Louis Leclerc, Count de Buffon (1707–1788), French naturalist; Georges Cuvier (1769–1832), French naturalist and comparative anatomist; Alexander von Humboldt (1769–1859), German traveler and scientist.

21. Galileo Galilei (1564–1642), Italian physicist and astronomer indicted as a heretic by the Catholic Church; Benedetto Castelli (1578–1643), Galileo's student, Italian mathematician, and Benedictine monk, quoted in J. E. D. Bethune, "Life of Galileo," in *Lives of Eminent Persons* (London, 1833), p. 75.

22. Emerson's source for "It has been . . . and grass" is *The Natural History and Antiquities of Selborne* (1789), by Gilbert White (1720–1793), English naturalist.

23. René Antoine Ferchault de Réaumur (1683–1757), French naturalist and inventor of a thermometer that bears his name; François Huber (1750–1831), French naturalist who specialized in the study of bees.

24. "Written upon a Blank Leaf in 'The Complete Angler'" (1819), ll. 5–6, by William Wordsworth (1770–1850), English poet and, with Samuel Taylor Coleridge (1772–1834)—English poet and philosopher—founder of the Romantic movement.

25. Bernard Le Bovier de Fontenelle (1657–1757), French philosopher and author; Jean Le Rond d'Alembert (1717–1783), French mathematician. In a note in the manuscript, Emerson attributes the contrasting views of the two writers to *The Theory of the Moral Sentiments* (Philadelphia, 1817), p. 213, by Adam Smith (1723–1790), Scottish political economist and moral philosopher.

26. Archimedes (ca. 287–212 BCE), Greek mathematician and engineer born in Siracusa, Sicily.

27. Sir Isaac Newton (1642–1727), English natural philosopher and mathematician, who invented an early form of differential calculus. David Brewster's *The Life of Sir Isaac Newton* (1831) is Emerson's favorite early source for information about Newton's life and ideas.

28. Albrecht von Haller (1708–1777), Swiss scientist and poet.

29. John Hunter (1728–1793), British surgeon and physiologist born in Scotland.

30. Johannes Kepler (1571–1630), German mathematician and astronomer, who articulated Newton's third law of planetary motion, that the force between the earth and the moon must be inversely proportional to the square of the distance between them.

31. Azote, a gas that is fatal when breathed, is another name for nitrogen.

32. Attributed to Samuel Sandels, "Emanuel Swedenborg," *New Jerusalem Magazine* 5 (July 1832): 437, by Emerson (*JMN*, 4:33).

33. Samuel Taylor Coleridge, "The Destiny of Nations: A Vision" (1817), ll. 18–20.

34. Sir Humphry Davy (1778–1829), English chemist who advanced an electrical theory of affinity.

Nature

1   "Nature is but an image or imitation of wisdom, the last thing of the soul; nature being a thing which doth only do, but not know."

—Plotinus.[1]

Introduction.

2   Our age is retrospective. It builds the sepulchres of the fathers. It writes biographies, histories, and criticism. The foregoing generations beheld God and nature face to face; we, through their eyes. Why should not we also enjoy an original relation to the universe? Why should not we have a poetry and philosophy of insight and not of tradition, and a religion by revelation to us, and not the history of theirs? Embosomed for a season in nature, whose floods of life stream around and through us, and invite us by the powers they supply, to action proportioned to nature, why should we grope among the dry bones of the past, or put the living generation into masquerade out of its faded wardrobe? The sun shines to-day also. There is more wool and flax in the fields. There are new lands, new men, new thoughts. Let us demand our own works and laws and worship.

3   Undoubtedly we have no questions to ask which are unanswerable. We must trust the perfection of the creation so far, as to believe that whatever curiosity the order of things has awakened in our minds, the order of things can satisfy. Every man's condition is a solution in hieroglyphic to those inquiries he would put. He acts it as life, before he apprehends it as truth. In like

manner, nature is already, in its forms and tendencies, describing its own design. Let us interrogate the great apparition, that shines so peacefully around us. Let us inquire, to what end is nature?

All science has one aim, namely, to find a theory of nature. We have theories of races and of functions, but scarcely yet a remote approximation to an idea of creation. We are now so far from the road to truth, that religious teachers dispute and hate each other, and speculative men are esteemed unsound and frivolous. But to a sound judgment, the most abstract truth is the most practical. Whenever a true theory appears, it will be its own evidence. Its test is, that it will explain all phenomena. Now many are thought not only unexplained but inexplicable; as language, sleep, dreams, beasts, sex.

Philosophically considered, the universe is composed of Nature and the Soul. Strictly speaking, therefore, all that is separate from us, all which Philosophy distinguishes as the NOT ME, that is, both nature and art, all other men and my own body, must be ranked under this name, NATURE. In enumerating the values of nature and casting up their sum, I shall use the word in both senses;—in its common and in its philosophical import. In inquiries so general as our present one, the inaccuracy is not material; no confusion of thought will occur. *Nature,* in the common sense, refers to essences unchanged by man; space, the air, the river, the leaf. *Art* is applied to the mixture of his will with the same things, as in a house, a canal, a statue, a picture. But his operations taken together are so insignificant, a little chipping, baking, patching, and washing, that in an impression so grand as that of the world on the human mind, they do not vary the result.

Chapter I.

To go into solitude, a man needs to retire as much from his chamber as from society. I am not solitary whilst I read and write, though nobody is with me. But if a man would be alone, let him look at the stars. The rays that come from those heavenly worlds, will separate between him and vulgar things. One might think the atmosphere was made transparent with this design, to give man, in the heavenly bodies, the perpetual presence of the sublime. Seen in the streets of cities, how great they are! If the stars should appear one night in a thousand years, how would men believe and adore; and preserve for many generations the remembrance of the city of God which had been shown!² But every night come out these preachers of beauty, and light the universe with their admonishing smile.

7   The stars awaken a certain reverence, because though always present, they are always inaccessible; but all natural objects make a kindred impression, when the mind is open to their influence. Nature never wears a mean appearance. Neither does the wisest man extort all her secret, and lose his curiosity by finding out all her perfection. Nature never became a toy to a wise spirit. The flowers, the animals, the mountains, reflected all the wisdom of his best hour, as much as they had delighted the simplicity of his childhood.

8   When we speak of nature in this manner, we have a distinct but most poetical sense in the mind. We mean the integrity of impression made by manifold natural objects. It is this which distinguishes the stick of timber of the wood-cutter, from the tree of the poet. The charming landscape which I saw this morning, is indubitably made up of some twenty or thirty farms. Miller owns this field, Locke that, and Manning the woodland beyond. But none of them owns the landscape. There is a property in the horizon which no man has but he whose eye can integrate all the parts, that is, the poet. This is the best part of these men's farms, yet to this their land-deeds give them no title.

9   To speak truly, few adult persons can see nature. Most persons do not see the sun. At least they have a very superficial seeing. The sun illuminates only the eye of the man, but shines into the eye and the heart of the child. The lover of nature is he whose inward and outward senses are still truly adjusted to each other; who has retained the spirit of infancy even into the era of manhood. His intercourse with heaven and earth, becomes part of his daily food. In the presence of nature, a wild delight runs through the man, in spite of real sorrows. Nature says,—he is my creature, and maugre all his impertinent griefs, he shall be glad with me. Not the sun or the summer alone, but every hour and season yields its tribute of delight; for every hour and change corresponds to and authorizes a different state of the mind, from breathless noon to grimmest midnight. Nature is a setting that fits equally well a comic or a mourning piece. In good health, the air is a cordial of incredible virtue. Crossing a bare common, in snow puddles, at twilight, under a clouded sky, without having in my thoughts any occurrence of special good fortune, I have enjoyed a perfect exhilaration. Almost I fear to think how glad I am. In the woods too, a man casts off his years, as the snake his slough, and at what period soever of life, is always a child. In the woods, is perpetual youth.

Within these plantations of God, a decorum and sanctity reign, a perennial festival is dressed, and the guest sees not how he should tire of them in a thousand years. In the woods, we return to reason and faith. There I feel that nothing can befal me in life,—no disgrace, no calamity, (leaving me my eyes,) which nature cannot repair. Standing on the bare ground,—my head bathed by the blithe air, and uplifted into infinite space,—all mean egotism vanishes. I become a transparent eye-ball. I am nothing. I see all. The currents of the Universal Being circulate through me; I am part or particle of God. The name of the nearest friend sounds then foreign and accidental. To be brothers, to be acquaintances,—master or servant, is then a trifle and a disturbance. I am the lover of uncontained and immortal beauty. In the wilderness, I find something more dear and connate than in streets or villages. In the tranquil landscape, and especially in the distant line of the horizon, man beholds somewhat as beautiful as his own nature.

The greatest delight which the fields and woods minister, is the sugges- 10 tion of an occult relation between man and the vegetable. I am not alone and unacknowledged. They nod to me and I to them. The waving of the boughs in the storm, is new to me and old. It takes me by surprise, and yet is not unknown. Its effect is like that of a higher thought or a better emotion coming over me, when I deemed I was thinking justly or doing right.

Yet it is certain that the power to produce this delight, does not reside in 11 nature, but in man, or in a harmony of both. It is necessary to use these pleasures with great temperance. For, nature is not always tricked in holiday attire, but the same scene which yesterday breathed perfume and glittered as for the frolic of the nymphs, is overspread with melancholy today. Nature always wears the colors of the spirit. To a man laboring under calamity, the heat of his own fire hath sadness in it. Then, there is a kind of contempt of the landscape felt by him who has just lost by death a dear friend. The sky is less grand as it shuts down over less worth in the population.

Chapter II.
Commodity.

Whoever considers the final cause of the world, will discern a multitude 12 of uses that enter as parts into that result. They all admit of being thrown into one of the following classes; Commodity; Beauty; Language; and Discipline.

13   Under the general name of Commodity, I rank all those advantages which our senses owe to nature. This, of course, is a benefit which is temporary and mediate, not ultimate, like its service to the soul. Yet although low, it is perfect in its kind, and is the only use of nature which all men apprehend. The misery of man appears like childish petulance, when we explore the steady and prodigal provision that has been made for his support and delight on this green ball which floats him through the heavens. What angels invented these splendid ornaments, these rich conveniences, this ocean of air above, this ocean of water beneath, this firmament of earth between? This zodiac of lights, this tent of dropping clouds, this striped coat of climates, this fourfold year? Beasts, fire, water, stones, and corn serve him. The field is at once his floor, his work-yard, his play-ground, his garden, and his bed.

> "More servants wait on man
> Than he'll take notice of."[3]

14   Nature, in its ministry to man, is not only the material, but is also the process and the result. All the parts incessantly work into each other's hands for the profit of man. The wind sows the seed; the sun evaporates the sea; the wind blows the vapor to the field; the ice, on the other side of the planet, condenses rain on this; the rain feeds the plant; the plant feeds the animal; and thus the endless circulations of the divine charity nourish man.

15   The useful arts are but reproductions or new combinations by the wit of man, of the same natural benefactors. He no longer waits for favoring gales, but by means of steam, he realizes the fable of Æolus's bag, and carries the two and thirty winds in the boiler of his boat.[4] To diminish friction, he paves the road with iron bars, and, mounting a coach with a ship-load of men, animals, and merchandise behind him, he darts through the country, from town to town, like an eagle or a swallow through the air. By the aggregate of these aids, how is the face of the world changed, from the era of Noah to that of Napoleon![5] The private poor man hath cities, ships, canals, bridges, built for him. He goes to the post-office, and the human race run on his errands; to the book-shop, and the human race read and write of all that happens, for him; to the court-house, and nations repair his wrongs. He sets his house upon the road, and the human race go forth every morning, and shovel out the snow, and cut a path for him.

16   But there is no need of specifying particulars in this class of uses. The

catalogue is endless, and the examples so obvious, that I shall leave them to the reader's reflection, with the general remark, that this mercenary benefit is one which has respect to a farther good. A man is fed, not that he may be fed, but that he may work.

Chapter III.
Beauty.

A nobler want of man is served by nature, namely, the love of Beauty.

17

The ancient Greeks called the world κόσμος, beauty.[6] Such is the constitution of all things, or such the plastic power of the human eye, that the primary forms, as the sky, the mountain, the tree, the animal, give us a delight *in and for themselves;* a pleasure arising from outline, color, motion, and grouping. This seems partly owing to the eye itself. The eye is the best of artists. By the mutual action of its structure and of the laws of light, perspective is produced, which integrates every mass of objects, of what character soever, into a well colored and shaded globe, so that where the particular objects are mean and unaffecting, the landscape which they compose, is round and symmetrical. And as the eye is the best composer, so light is the first of painters. There is no object so foul that intense light will not make beautiful. And the stimulus it affords to the sense, and a sort of infinitude which it hath, like space and time, make all matter gay. Even the corpse hath its own beauty. But beside this general grace diffused over nature, almost all the individual forms are agreeable to the eye, as is proved by our endless imitations of some of them, as the acorn, the grape, the pine-cone, the wheat-ear, the egg, the wings and forms of most birds, the lion's claw, the serpent, the butterfly, seashells, flames, clouds, buds, leaves, and the forms of many trees, as the palm.

18

For better consideration, we may distribute the aspects of Beauty in a threefold manner.

19

1. First, the simple perception of natural forms is a delight. The influence of the forms and actions in nature, is so needful to man, that, in its lowest functions, it seems to lie on the confines of commodity and beauty. To the body and mind which have been cramped by noxious work or company, nature is medicinal and restores their tone. The tradesman, the attorney comes out of the din and craft of the street, and sees the sky and the woods, and is a man again. In their eternal calm, he finds himself. The health of the eye

20

seems to demand a horizon. We are never tired, so long as we can see far enough.[7]

21   But in other hours, Nature satisfies the soul purely by its loveliness, and without any mixture of corporeal benefit. I have seen the spectacle of morning from the hill-top over against my house, from day-break to sun-rise, with emotions which an angel might share. The long slender bars of cloud float like fishes in the sea of crimson light. From the earth, as a shore, I look out into that silent sea. I seem to partake its rapid transformations: the active enchantment reaches my dust, and I dilate and conspire with the morning wind. How does Nature deify us with a few and cheap elements! Give me health and a day, and I will make the pomp of emperors ridiculous. The dawn is my Assyria; the sun-set and moon-rise my Paphos, and unimaginable realms of faerie; broad noon shall be my England of the senses and the understanding; the night shall be my Germany of mystic philosophy and dreams.[8]

22   Not less excellent, except for our less susceptibility in the afternoon, was the charm, last evening, of a January sunset. The western clouds divided and subdivided themselves into pink flakes modulated with tints of unspeakable softness; and the air had so much life and sweetness, that it was a pain to come within doors. What was it that nature would say? Was there no meaning in the live repose of the valley behind the mill, and which Homer or Shakspeare could not re-form for me in words?[9] The leafless trees become spires of flame in the sunset, with the blue east for their background, and the stars of the dead calices of flowers, and every withered stem and stubble rimed with frost, contribute something to the mute music.

23   The inhabitants of cities suppose that the country landscape is pleasant only half the year. I please myself with observing the graces of the winter scenery, and believe that we are as much touched by it as by the genial influences of summer. To the attentive eye, each moment of the year has its own beauty, and in the same field, it beholds, every hour, a picture which was never seen before, and which shall never be seen again. The heavens change every moment, and reflect their glory or gloom on the plains beneath. The state of the crop in the surrounding farms alters the expression of the earth from week to week. The succession of native plants in the pastures and road-sides, which make the silent clock by which time tells the summer hours, will make even the divisions of the day sensible to a keen observer. The tribes of birds and insects, like the plants punctual to their time, follow each other, and

the year has room for all. By water-courses, the variety is greater. In July, the blue pontederia or pickerel-weed blooms in large beds in the shallow parts of our pleasant river, and swarms with yellow butterflies in continual motion. Art cannot rival this pomp of purple and gold. Indeed the river is a perpetual gala, and boasts each month a new ornament.

But this beauty of Nature which is seen and felt as beauty, is the least part. The shows of day, the dewy morning, the rainbow, mountains, orchards in blossom, stars, moonlight, shadows in still water, and the like, if too eagerly hunted, become shows merely, and mock us with their unreality. Go out of the house to see the moon, and 't is mere tinsel; it will not please as when its light shines upon your necessary journey. The beauty that shimmers in the yellow afternoons of October, who ever could clutch it? Go forth to find it, and it is gone: 't is only a mirage as you look from the windows of diligence.

2. The presence of a higher, namely, of the spiritual element is essential to its perfection. The high and divine beauty which can be loved without effeminacy, is that which is found in combination with the human will, and never separate. Beauty is the mark God sets upon virtue.[10] Every natural action is graceful. Every heroic act is also decent, and causes the place and the bystanders to shine. We are taught by great actions that the universe is the property of every individual in it. Every rational creature has all nature for his dowry and estate. It is his, if he will. He may divest himself of it; he may creep into a corner, and abdicate his kingdom, as most men do, but he is entitled to the world by his constitution. In proportion to the energy of his thought and will, he takes up the world into himself. "All those things for which men plough, build, or sail, obey virtue;" said an ancient historian.[11] "The winds and waves," said Gibbon, "are always on the side of the ablest navigators."[12] So are the sun and moon and all the stars of heaven. When a noble act is done,—perchance in a scene of great natural beauty; when Leonidas and his three hundred martyrs consume one day in dying, and the sun and moon come each and look at them once in the steep defile of Thermopylæ; when Arnold Winkelried, in the high Alps, under the shadow of the avalanche, gathers in his side a sheaf of Austrian spears to break the line for his comrades; are not these heroes entitled to add the beauty of the scene to the beauty of the deed?[13] When the bark of Columbus nears the shore of America;—before it, the beach lined with savages, fleeing out of all their huts of cane; the sea behind; and the purple mountains of the Indian Archipelago

24

25

around, can we separate the man from the living picture? Does not the New World clothe his form with her palm-groves and savannahs as fit drapery? Ever does natural beauty steal in like air, and envelope great actions. When Sir Harry Vane was dragged up the Tower-hill, sitting on a sled, to suffer death, as the champion of the English laws, one of the multitude cried out to him, "You never sate on so glorious a seat."[14] Charles II., to intimidate the citizens of London, caused the patriot Lord Russell to be drawn in an open coach, through the principal streets of the city, on his way to the scaffold. "But," to use the simple narrative of his biographer, "the multitude imagined they saw liberty and virtue sitting by his side."[15] In private places, among sordid objects, an act of truth or heroism seems at once to draw to itself the sky as its temple, the sun as its candle. Nature stretcheth out her arms to embrace man, only let his thoughts be of equal greatness. Willingly does she follow his steps with the rose and the violet, and bend her lines of grandeur and grace to the decoration of her darling child. Only let his thoughts be of equal scope, and the frame will suit the picture. A virtuous man, is in unison with her works, and makes the central figure of the visible sphere. Homer, Pindar, Socrates, Phocion, associate themselves fitly in our memory with the whole geography and climate of Greece.[16] The visible heavens and earth sympathize with Jesus. And in common life, whosoever has seen a person of powerful character and happy genius, will have remarked how easily he took all things along with him,—the persons, the opinions, and the day, and nature became ancillary to a man.

26   3. There is still another aspect under which the beauty of the world may be viewed, namely, as it becomes an object of the intellect. Beside the relation of things to virtue, they have a relation to thought. The intellect searches out the absolute order of things as they stand in the mind of God, and without the colors of affection. The intellectual and the active powers seem to succeed each other in man, and the exclusive activity of the one, generates the exclusive activity of the other. There is something unfriendly in each to the other, but they are like the alternate periods of feeding and working in animals; each prepares and certainly will be followed by the other. Therefore does beauty, which, in relation to actions, as we have seen comes unsought, and comes because it is unsought, remain for the apprehension and pursuit of the intellect; and then again, in its turn, of the active power. Nothing divine dies. All good is eternally reproductive. The beauty of nature reforms itself in the mind, and not for barren contemplation, but for new creation.

All men are in some degree impressed by the face of the world. Some men even to delight. This love of beauty is Taste. Others have the same love in such excess, that, not content with admiring, they seek to embody it in new forms. The creation of beauty is Art.

The production of a work of art throws a light upon the mystery of humanity. A work of art is an abstract or epitome of the world. It is the result or expression of nature, in miniature. For although the works of nature are innumerable and all different, the result or the expression of them all is similar and single. Nature is a sea of forms radically alike and even unique. A leaf, a sun-beam, a landscape, the ocean, make an analogous impression on the mind. What is common to them all,—that perfectness and harmony, is beauty. Therefore the standard of beauty, is the entire circuit of natural forms,—the totality of nature; which the Italians expressed by defining beauty "il piu nell' uno."[17] Nothing is quite beautiful alone: nothing but is beautiful in the whole. A single object is only so far beautiful as it suggests this universal grace. The poet, the painter, the sculptor, the musician, the architect seek each to concentrate this radiance of the world on one point, and each in his several work to satisfy the love of beauty which stimulates him to produce. Thus is Art, a nature passed through the alembic of man. Thus in art, does nature work through the will of a man filled with the beauty of her first works.

The world thus exists to the soul to satisfy the desire of beauty. Extend this element to the uttermost, and I call it an ultimate end. No reason can be asked or given why the soul seeks beauty. Beauty, in its largest and profoundest sense, is one expression for the universe. God is the all-fair. Truth, and goodness, and beauty, are but different faces of the same All. But beauty in nature is not ultimate. It is the herald of inward and eternal beauty, and is not alone a solid and satisfactory good. It must therefore stand as a part and not as yet the last or highest expression of the final cause of Nature.

Chapter IV.
Language.

A third use which Nature subserves to man is that of Language. Nature is the vehicle of thought, and in a simple, double, and threefold degree.

1. Words are signs of natural facts.

2. Particular natural facts are symbols of particular spiritual facts.

33   3. Nature is the symbol of spirit.

34   1. Words are signs of natural facts. The use of natural history is to give us aid in supernatural history. The use of the outer creation is to give us language for the beings and changes of the inward creation. Every word which is used to express a moral or intellectual fact, if traced to its root, is found to be borrowed from some material appearance. *Right* originally means *straight; wrong* means *twisted. Spirit* primarily means *wind; transgression,* the crossing of a *line; supercilious,* the *raising of the eye-brow.* We say the *heart* to express emotion, the *head* to denote thought; and *thought* and *emotion* are, in their turn, words borrowed from sensible things, and now appropriated to spiritual nature. Most of the process by which this transformation is made, is hidden from us in the remote time when language was framed; but the same tendency may be daily observed in children. Children and savages use only nouns or names of things, which they continually convert into verbs, and apply to analogous mental acts.

35   2. But this origin of all words that convey a spiritual import,—so conspicuous a fact in the history of language,—is our least debt to nature. It is not words only that are emblematic; it is things which are emblematic. Every natural fact is a symbol of some spiritual fact. Every appearance in nature corresponds to some state of the mind, and that state of the mind can only be described by presenting that natural appearance as its picture. An enraged man is a lion, a cunning man is a fox, a firm man is a rock, a learned man is a torch. A lamb is innocence; a snake is subtle spite; flowers express to us the delicate affections. Light and darkness are our familiar expression for knowledge and ignorance; and heat for love. Visible distance behind and before us, is respectively our image of memory and hope.

36   Who looks upon a river in a meditative hour, and is not reminded of the flux of all things? Throw a stone into the stream, and the circles that propagate themselves are the beautiful type of all influence. Man is conscious of a universal soul within or behind his individual life, wherein, as in a firmament, the natures of Justice, Truth, Love, Freedom, arise and shine. This universal soul, he calls Reason: it is not mine or thine or his, but we are its; we are its property and men. And the blue sky in which the private earth is buried, the sky with its eternal calm, and full of everlasting orbs, is the type of Reason. That which, intellectually considered, we call Reason, considered in relation to nature, we call Spirit. Spirit is the Creator. Spirit hath life in itself. And man in all ages and countries, embodies it in his language, as the FATHER.

It is easily seen that there is nothing lucky or capricious in these analogies, but that they are constant, and pervade nature. These are not the dreams of a few poets, here and there, but man is an analogist, and studies relations in all objects. He is placed in the centre of beings, and a ray of relation passes from every other being to him. And neither can man be understood without these objects, nor these objects without man. All the facts in natural history taken by themselves, have no value, but are barren like a single sex. But marry it to human history, and it is full of life. Whole Floras, all Linnæus' and Buffon's volumes, are but dry catalogues of facts; but the most trivial of these facts, the habit of a plant, the organs, or work, or noise of an insect, applied to the illustration of a fact in intellectual philosophy, or, in any way associated to human nature, affects us in the most lively and agreeable manner. The seed of a plant,—to what affecting analogies in the nature of man, is that little fruit made use of, in all discourse, up to the voice of Paul, who calls the human corpse a seed,—"It is sown a natural body; it is raised a spiritual body."[18] The motion of the earth round its axis, and round the sun, makes the day, and the year. These are certain amounts of brute light and heat. But is there no intent of an analogy between man's life and the seasons? And do the seasons gain no grandeur or pathos from that analogy? The instincts of the ant are very unimportant considered as the ant's; but the moment a ray of relation is seen to extend from it to man, and the little drudge is seen to be a monitor, a little body with a mighty heart, then all its habits, even that said to be recently observed, that it never sleeps, become sublime.

Because of this radical correspondence between visible things and human thoughts, savages, who have only what is necessary, converse in figures. As we go back in history, language becomes more picturesque, until its infancy, when it is all poetry; or, all spiritual facts are represented by natural symbols. The same symbols are found to make the original elements of all languages. It has moreover been observed, that the idioms of all languages approach each other in passages of the greatest eloquence and power. And as this is the first language, so is it the last. This immediate dependence of language upon nature, this conversion of an outward phenomenon into a type of somewhat in human life, never loses its power to affect us. It is this which gives that piquancy to the conversation of a strong-natured farmer or backwoodsman, which all men relish.

Thus is nature an interpreter, by whose means man converses with his fellow men. A man's power to connect his thought with its proper symbol, and so utter it, depends on the simplicity of his character, that is, upon his love of truth and his desire to communicate it without loss. The corruption of man is followed by the corruption of language. When simplicity of character and the sovereignty of ideas is broken up by the prevalence of secondary desires, the desire of riches, the desire of pleasure, the desire of power, the desire of praise,—and duplicity and falsehood take place of simplicity and truth, the power over nature as an interpreter of the will, is in a degree lost; new imagery ceases to be created, and old words are perverted to stand for things which are not; a paper currency is employed when there is no bullion in the vaults. In due time, the fraud is manifest, and words lose all power to stimulate the understanding or the affections. Hundreds of writers may be found in every long-civilized nation, who for a short time believe, and make others believe, that they see and utter truths, who do not of themselves clothe one thought in its natural garment, but who feed unconsciously upon the language created by the primary writers of the country, those, namely, who hold primarily on nature.

40   But wise men pierce this rotten diction and fasten words again to visible things; so that picturesque language is at once a commanding certificate that he who employs it, is a man in alliance with truth and God. The moment our discourse rises above the ground line of familiar facts, and is inflamed with passion or exalted by thought, it clothes itself in images. A man conversing in earnest, if he watch his intellectual processes, will find that always a material image, more or less luminous, arises in his mind, cotemporaneous with every thought, which furnishes the vestment of the thought. Hence, good writing and brilliant discourse are perpetual allegories. This imagery is spontaneous. It is the blending of experience with the present action of the mind. It is proper creation. It is the working of the Original Cause through the instruments he has already made.

41   These facts may suggest the advantage which the country-life possesses for a powerful mind, over the artificial and curtailed life of cities. We know more from nature than we can at will communicate. Its light flows into the mind evermore, and we forget its presence. The poet, the orator, bred in the woods, whose senses have been nourished by their fair and appeasing changes, year after year, without design and without heed,—shall not lose their lesson altogether, in the roar of cities or the broil of politics. Long hereafter, amidst agitation and terror in national councils,—in the hour of revolu-

tion,—these solemn images shall reappear in their morning lustre, as fit symbols and words of the thoughts which the passing events shall awaken. At the call of a noble sentiment, again the woods wave, the pines murmur, the river rolls and shines, and the cattle low upon the mountains, as he saw and heard them in his infancy. And with these forms, the spells of persuasion, the keys of power are put into his hands.

3. We are thus assisted by natural objects in the expression of particular meanings. But how great a language to convey such peppercorn informations! Did it need such noble races of creatures, this profusion of forms, this host of orbs in heaven, to furnish man with the dictionary and grammar of his municipal speech? Whilst we use this grand cipher to expedite the affairs of our pot and kettle, we feel that we have not yet put it to its use, neither are able. We are like travellers using the cinders of a volcano to roast their eggs. Whilst we see that it always stands ready to clothe what we would say, we cannot avoid the question, whether the characters are not significant of themselves. Have mountains, and waves, and skies, no significance but what we consciously give them, when we employ them as emblems of our thoughts? The world is emblematic. Parts of speech are metaphors because the whole of nature is a metaphor of the human mind. The laws of moral nature answer to those of matter as face to face in a glass. "The visible world and the relation of its parts, is the dial plate of the invisible."[19] The axioms of physics translate the laws of ethics.[20] Thus, "the whole is greater than its part;" "reaction is equal to action;" "the smallest weight may be made to lift the greatest, the difference of weight being compensated by time;" and many the like propositions, which have an ethical as well as physical sense. These propositions have a much more extensive and universal sense when applied to human life, than when confined to technical use.

In like manner, the memorable words of history, and the proverbs of nations, consist usually of a natural fact, selected as a picture or parable of a moral truth. Thus; A rolling stone gathers no moss; A bird in the hand is worth two in the bush; A cripple in the right way, will beat a racer in the wrong; Make hay whilst the sun shines; 'T is hard to carry a full cup even; Vinegar is the son of wine; The last ounce broke the camel's back; Long-lived trees make roots first;—and the like. In their primary sense these are trivial facts, but we repeat them for the value of their analogical import. What is true of proverbs, is true of all fables, parables, and allegories.

44   This relation between the mind and matter is not fancied by some poet, but stands in the will of God, and so is free to be known by all men. It appears to men, or it does not appear.[21] When in fortunate hours we ponder this miracle, the wise man doubts, if, at all other times, he is not blind and deaf;

> ————"Can these things be,
> And overcome us like a summer's cloud,
> Without our special wonder?"[22]

for the universe becomes transparent, and the light of higher laws than its own, shines through it. It is the standing problem which has exercised the wonder and the study of every fine genius since the world began; from the era of the Egyptians and the Brahmins, to that of Pythagoras, of Plato, of Bacon, of Leibnitz, of Swedenborg.[23] There sits the Sphinx at the road-side, and from age to age, as each prophet comes by, he tries his fortune at reading her riddle.[24] There seems to be a necessity in spirit to manifest itself in material forms; and day and night, river and storm, beast and bird, acid and alkali, preëxist in necessary Ideas in the mind of God, and are what they are by virtue of preceding affections, in the world of spirit. A Fact is the end or last issue of spirit. The visible creation is the terminus or the circumference of the invisible world. "Material objects," said a French philosopher, "are necessarily kinds of *scoriæ* of the substantial thoughts of the Creator, which must always preserve an exact relation to their first origin; in other words, visible nature must have a spiritual and moral side."[25]

45   This doctrine is abstruse, and though the images of "garment," "scoriæ," "mirror," &c., may stimulate the fancy, we must summon the aid of subtler and more vital expositors to make it plain. "Every scripture is to be interpreted by the same spirit which gave it forth,"—is the fundamental law of criticism.[26] A life in harmony with nature, the love of truth and of virtue, will purge the eyes to understand her text. By degrees we may come to know the primitive sense of the permanent objects of nature, so that the world shall be to us an open book, and every form significant of its hidden life and final cause.

46   A new interest surprises us, whilst, under the view now suggested, we contemplate the fearful extent and multitude of objects; since "every object rightly seen, unlocks a new faculty of the soul."[27] That which was uncon-

scious truth, becomes, when interpreted and defined in an object, a part of the domain of knowledge,—a new amount to the magazine of power.

Chapter V.
Discipline.

In view of this significance of nature, we arrive at once at a new fact, that nature is a discipline.[28] This use of the world includes the preceding uses, as parts of itself.

47

Space, time, society, labor, climate, food, locomotion, the animals, the mechanical forces, give us sincerest lessons, day by day, whose meaning is unlimited. They educate both the Understanding and the Reason. Every property of matter is a school for the understanding,—its solidity or resistance, its inertia, its extension, its figure, its divisibility. The understanding adds, divides, combines, measures, and finds everlasting nutriment and room for its activity in this worthy scene. Meantime, Reason transfers all these lessons into its own world of thought, by perceiving the analogy that marries Matter and Mind.

48

1. Nature is a discipline of the understanding in intellectual truths. Our dealing with sensible objects is a constant exercise in the necessary lessons of difference, of likeness, of order, of being and seeming, of progressive arrangement; of ascent from particular to general; of combination to one end of manifold forces. Proportioned to the importance of the organ to be formed, is the extreme care with which its tuition is provided,—a care pretermitted in no single case. What tedious training, day after day, year after year, never ending, to form the common sense; what continual reproduction of annoyances, inconveniences, dilemmas; what rejoicing over us of little men; what disputing of prices, what reckonings of interest,—and all to form the Hand of the mind;—to instruct us that "good thoughts are no better than good dreams, unless they be executed!"[29]

49

The same good office is performed by Property and its filial systems of debt and credit. Debt, grinding debt, whose iron face the widow, the orphan, and the sons of genius fear and hate;—debt, which consumes so much time, which so cripples and disheartens a great spirit with cares that seem so base, is a preceptor whose lessons cannot be foregone, and is needed most by those

50

who suffer from it most. Moreover, property, which has been well compared to snow,—"if it fall level to-day, it will be blown into drifts to-morrow,"—is merely the surface action of internal machinery, like the index on the face of a clock. Whilst now it is the gymnastics of the understanding, it is hiving in the foresight of the spirit, experience in profounder laws.

51   The whole character and fortune of the individual is affected by the least inequalities in the culture of the understanding; for example, in the perception of differences. Therefore is Space, and therefore Time, that man may know that things are not huddled and lumped, but sundered and individual. A bell and a plough have each their use, and neither can do the office of the other. Water is good to drink, coal to burn, wool to wear; but wool cannot be drunk, nor water spun, nor coal eaten. The wise man shows his wisdom in separation, in gradation, and his scale of creatures and of merits, is as wide as nature. The foolish have no range in their scale, but suppose every man is as every other man. What is not good they call the worst, and what is not hateful, they call the best.

52   In like manner, what good heed, nature forms in us! She pardons no mistakes. Her yea is yea, and her nay, nay.

53   The first steps in Agriculture, Astronomy, Zoölogy, (those first steps which the farmer, the hunter, and the sailor take,) teach that nature's dice are always loaded; that in her heaps and rubbish are concealed sure and useful results.

54   How calmly and genially the mind apprehends one after another the laws of physics! What noble emotions dilate the mortal as he enters into the counsels of the creation, and feels by knowledge the privilege to BE! His insight refines him. The beauty of nature shines in his own breast. Man is greater that he can see this, and the universe less, because Time and Space relations vanish as laws are known.

55   Here again we are impressed and even daunted by the immense Universe to be explored. 'What we know, is a point to what we do not know.'[30] Open any recent journal of science, and weigh the problems suggested concerning Light, Heat, Electricity, Magnetism, Physiology, Geology, and judge whether the interest of natural science is likely to be soon exhausted.

56   Passing by many particulars of the discipline of nature we must not omit to specify two.

57   The exercise of the Will or the lesson of power is taught in every event.

From the child's successive possession of his several senses up to the hour when he saith, "thy will be done!" he is learning the secret, that he can reduce under his will, not only particular events, but great classes, nay the whole series of events, and so conform all facts to his character.[31] Nature is thoroughly mediate. It is made to serve. It receives the dominion of man as meekly as the ass on which the Saviour rode. It offers all its kingdoms to man as the raw material which he may mould into what is useful. Man is never weary of working it up. He forges the subtile and delicate air into wise and melodious words, and gives them wing as angels of persuasion and command. More and more, with every thought, does his kingdom stretch over things, until the world becomes, at last, only a realized will,—the double of the man.

2. Sensible objects conform to the premonitions of Reason and reflect the conscience. All things are moral; and in their boundless changes have an unceasing reference to spiritual nature. Therefore is nature glorious with form, color, and motion, that every globe in the remotest heaven; every chemical change from the rudest crystal up to the laws of life; every change of vegetation from the first principle of growth in the eye of a leaf, to the tropical forest and antediluvian coal-mine; every animal function from the sponge up to Hercules, shall hint or thunder to man the laws of right and wrong, and echo the Ten Commandments.[32] Therefore is nature always the ally of Religion: lends all her pomp and riches to the religious sentiment. Prophet and priest, David, Isaiah, Jesus, have drawn deeply from this source.

This ethical character so penetrates the bone and marrow of nature, as to seem the end for which it was made. Whatever private purpose is answered by any member or part, this is its public and universal function, and is never omitted. Nothing in nature is exhausted in its first use. When a thing has served an end to the uttermost, it is wholly new for an ulterior service. In God, every end is converted into a new means. Thus the use of Commodity, regarded by itself, is mean and squalid. But it is to the mind an education in the great doctrine of Use, namely, that a thing is good only so far as it serves; that a conspiring of parts and efforts to the production of an end, is essential to any being. The first and gross manifestation of this truth, is our inevitable and hated training in values and wants, in corn and meat.

It has already been illustrated, in treating of the significance of material things, that every natural process is but a version of a moral sentence. The moral law lies at the centre of nature and radiates to the circumference. It is

58

59

60

the pith and marrow of every substance, every relation, and every process. All things with which we deal, preach to us. What is a farm but a mute gospel? The chaff and the wheat, weeds and plants, blight, rain, insects, sun,—it is a sacred emblem from the first furrow of spring to the last stack which the snow of winter overtakes in the fields. But the sailor, the shepherd, the miner, the merchant, in their several resorts, have each an experience precisely parallel and leading to the same conclusions. Because all organizations are radically alike. Nor can it be doubted that this moral sentiment which thus scents the air, and grows in the grain, and impregnates the waters of the world, is caught by man and sinks into his soul. The moral influence of nature upon every individual is that amount of truth which it illustrates to him. Who can estimate this? Who can guess how much firmness the sea-beaten rock has taught the fisherman? how much tranquillity has been reflected to man from the azure sky, over whose unspotted deeps the winds forevermore drive flocks of stormy clouds, and leave no wrinkle or stain? how much industry and providence and affection we have caught from the pantomime of brutes? What a searching preacher of self-command is the varying phenomenon of Health!

61   Herein is especially apprehended the Unity of Nature,—the Unity in Variety,—which meets us everywhere. All the endless variety of things make a unique, an identical impression. Xenophanes complained in his old age, that, look where he would, all things hastened back to Unity.[33] He was weary of seeing the same entity in the tedious variety of forms. The fable of Proteus has a cordial truth.[34] Every particular in nature, a leaf, a drop, a crystal, a moment of time is related to the whole, and partakes of the perfection of the whole. Each particle is a microcosm, and faithfully renders the likeness of the world.

62   Not only resemblances exist in things whose analogy is obvious, as when we detect the type of the human hand in the flipper of the fossil saurus, but also in objects wherein there is great superficial unlikeness. Thus architecture is called 'frozen music' by De Stael and Goethe.[35] 'A Gothic church' said Coleridge, 'is a petrified religion.' Michael Angelo maintained, that, to an architect, a knowledge of anatomy is essential.[36] In Haydn's oratorios, the notes present to the imagination not only motions, as, of the snake, the stag, and the elephant, but colors also; as the green grass.[37] The granite is differenced in its laws only by the more or less of heat, from the river that wears it away.

The river, as it flows, resembles the air that flows over it; the air resembles the light which traverses it with more subtile currents; the light resembles the heat which rides with it through Space. Each creature is only a modification of the other; the likeness in them is more than the difference, and their radical law is one and the same. Hence it is, that a rule of one art, or a law of one organization, holds true throughout nature. So intimate is this Unity, that, it is easily seen, it lies under the undermost garment of nature, and betrays its source in universal Spirit. For, it pervades Thought also. Every universal truth which we express in words, implies or supposes every other truth. *Omne verum vero consonat.*[38] It is like a great circle on a sphere, comprising all possible circles; which, however, may be drawn, and comprise it, in like manner. Every such truth is the absolute Ens seen from one side.[39] But it has innumerable sides.

The same central Unity is still more conspicuous in actions. Words are finite organs of the infinite mind. They cannot cover the dimensions of what is in truth. They break, chop, and impoverish it. An action is the perfection and publication of thought. A right action seems to fill the eye, and to be related to all nature. "The wise man, in doing one thing, does all; or, in the one thing he does rightly, he sees the likeness of all which is done rightly."[40]

Words and actions are not the attributes of mute and brute nature. They introduce us to that singular form which predominates over all other forms. This is the human. All other organizations appear to be degradations of the human form. When this organization appears among so many that surround it, the spirit prefers it to all others. It says, 'From such as this, have I drawn joy and knowledge. In such as this, have I found and beheld myself. I will speak to it. It can speak again. It can yield me thought already formed and alive.' In fact, the eye,—the mind,—is always accompanied by these forms, male and female; and these are incomparably the richest informations of the power and order that lie at the heart of things. Unfortunately, every one of them bears the marks as of some injury; is marred and superficially defective. Nevertheless, far different from the deaf and dumb nature around them, these all rest like fountain-pipes on the unfathomed sea of thought and virtue whereto they alone, of all organizations, are the entrances.

It were a pleasant inquiry to follow into detail their ministry to our education, but where would it stop? We are associated in adolescent and adult life with some friends, who, like skies and waters, are coextensive with our idea;

63

64

65

who, answering each to a certain affection of the soul, satisfy our desire on that side; whom we lack power to put at such focal distance from us, that we can mend or even analyze them. We can not chuse but love them. When much intercourse with a friend has supplied us with a standard of excellence, and has increased our respect for the resources of God who thus sends a real person to outgo our ideal; when he has, moreover, become an object of thought, and, whilst his character retains all its unconscious effect, is converted in the mind into solid and sweet wisdom,—it is a sign to us that his office is closing, and he is commonly withdrawn from our sight in a short time.

Chapter VI.
Idealism.

66   Thus is the unspeakable but intelligible and practicable meaning of the world conveyed to man, the immortal pupil, in every object of sense. To this one end of Discipline, all parts of nature conspire.

67   A noble doubt perpetually suggests itself, whether this end be not the Final Cause of the Universe; and whether nature outwardly exists. It is a sufficient account of that Appearance we call the World, that God will teach a human mind, and so makes it the receiver of a certain number of congruent sensations, which we call sun and moon, man and woman, house and trade. In my utter impotence to test the authenticity of the report of my senses, to know whether the impressions they make on me correspond with outlying objects, what difference does it make, whether Orion is up there in heaven, or some god paints the image in the firmament of the soul?[41] The relations of parts and the end of the whole remaining the same, what is the difference, whether land and sea interact, and worlds revolve and intermingle without number or end,—deep yawning under deep, and galaxy balancing galaxy, throughout absolute space, or, whether, without relations of time and space, the same appearances are inscribed in the constant faith of man. Whether nature enjoy a substantial existence without, or is only in the apocalypse of the mind, it is alike useful and alike venerable to me. Be it what it may, it is ideal to me, so long as I cannot try the accuracy of my senses.

68   The frivolous make themselves merry with the Ideal theory, as if its consequences were burlesque; as if it affected the stability of nature. It surely does not. God never jests with us, and will not compromise the end of na-

ture, by permitting any inconsequence in its procession. Any distrust of the permanence of laws, would paralyze the faculties of man. Their permanence is sacredly respected, and his faith therein is perfect. The wheels and springs of man are all set to the hypothesis of the permanence of nature. We are not built like a ship to be tossed, but like a house to stand. It is a natural consequence of this structure, that, so long as the active powers predominate over the reflective, we resist with indignation any hint that nature is more short-lived or mutable than spirit. The broker, the wheelwright, the carpenter, the toll-man, are much displeased at the intimation.

But whilst we acquiesce entirely in the permanence of natural laws, the 69 question of the absolute existence of nature, still remains open. It is the uniform effect of culture on the human mind, not to shake our faith in the stability of particular phenomena, as of heat, water, azote; but to lead us to regard nature as a phenomenon, not a substance; to attribute necessary existence to spirit; to esteem nature as an accident and an effect.

To the senses and the unrenewed understanding, belongs a sort of instinctive belief in the absolute existence of nature. In their view, man and nature are indissolubly joined. Things are ultimates, and they never look beyond their sphere. The presence of Reason mars this faith. The first effort of thought tends to relax this despotism of the senses, which binds us to nature as if we were a part of it, and shows us nature aloof, and, as it were, afloat. Until this higher agency intervened, the animal eye sees, with wonderful accuracy, sharp outlines and colored surfaces. When the eye of Reason opens, to outline and surface are at once added, grace and expression. These proceed from imagination and affection, and abate somewhat of the angular distinctness of objects. If the Reason be stimulated to more earnest vision, outlines and surfaces become transparent, and are no longer seen; causes and spirits are seen through them. The best, the happiest moments of life, are these delicious awakenings of the higher powers, and the reverential withdrawing of nature before its God.

Let us proceed to indicate the effects of culture. 1. Our first institution in 71 the Ideal philosophy is a hint from nature herself.

Nature is made to conspire with spirit to emancipate us. Certain mechan- 72 ical changes, a small alteration in our local position apprizes us of a dualism. We are strangely affected by seeing the shore from a moving ship, from a balloon, or through the tints of an unusual sky. The least change in our point of view, gives the whole world a pictorial air. A man who seldom rides, needs only to get into a coach and traverse his own town, to turn the street into a puppet-show. The men, the women,—talking, running, bartering, fighting,— the earnest mechanic, the lounger, the beggar, the boys, the dogs, are unrealized at once, or, at least, wholly detached from all relation to the observer, and seen as apparent, not substantial beings. What new thoughts are suggested by seeing a face of country quite familiar, in the rapid movement of the rail-road car! Nay, the most wonted objects, (make a very slight change in the point of vision,) please us most. In a camera obscura, the butcher's cart, and the figure of one of our own family amuse us.[42] So a portrait of a well-known face gratifies us. Turn the eyes upside down, by looking at the landscape through your legs, and how agreeable is the picture, though you have seen it any time these twenty years!

73   In these cases, by mechanical means, is suggested the difference between the observer and the spectacle,—between man and nature. Hence arises a pleasure mixed with awe; I may say, a low degree of the sublime is felt from the fact, probably, that man is hereby apprized, that, whilst the world is a spectacle, something in himself is stable.

74   2. In a higher manner, the poet communicates the same pleasure. By a few strokes he delineates, as on air, the sun, the mountain, the camp, the city, the hero, the maiden, not different from what we know them, but only lifted from the ground and afloat before the eye. He unfixes the land and the sea, makes them revolve around the axis of his primary thought, and disposes them anew. Possessed himself by a heroic passion, he uses matter as symbols of it. The sensual man conforms thoughts to things; the poet conforms things to his thoughts. The one esteems nature as rooted and fast; the other, as fluid, and impresses his being thereon. To him, the refractory world is ductile and flexible; he invests dust and stones with humanity, and makes them the words of the Reason. The imagination may be defined to be, the use which the Reason makes of the material world. Shakspeare possesses the power of subordinating nature for the purposes of expression, beyond all poets. His imperial muse tosses the creation like a bauble from hand to hand, to embody any capricious shade of thought that is uppermost in his mind. The remotest spaces of nature are visited, and the farthest sundered things are brought together, by a subtile spiritual connexion. We are made aware that magnitude of mate-

rial things is merely relative, and all objects shrink and expand to serve the passion of the poet. Thus, in his sonnets, the lays of birds, the scents and dyes of flowers, he finds to be the *shadow* of his beloved; time, which keeps her from him, is his *chest;* the suspicion she has awakened, is her *ornament;*

> The ornament of beauty is Suspect,
> A crow which flies in heaven's sweetest air.[43]

His passion is not the fruit of chance; it swells, as he speaks, to a city, or a state.

> No, it was builded far from accident;
> It suffers not in smiling pomp, nor falls
> Under the brow of thralling discontent;
> It fears not policy, that heretic,
> That works on leases of short numbered hours,
> But all alone stands hugely politic.[44]

In the strength of his constancy, the Pyramids seem to him recent and transitory. And the freshness of youth and love dazzles him with its resemblance to morning.

> Take those lips away
> Which so sweetly were forsworn;
> And those eyes,—the break of day,
> Lights that do mislead the morn.[45]

The wild beauty of this hyperbole, I may say, in passing, it would not be easy to match in literature.

This transfiguration which all material objects undergo through the passion of the poet,—this power which he exerts, at any moment, to magnify the small, to micrify the great,—might be illustrated by a thousand examples from his Plays. I have before me the Tempest, and will cite only these few lines.

> ARIEL.   The strong based promontory
> Have I made shake, and by the spurs plucked up
> The pine and cedar.

Prospero calls for music to sooth the frantic Alonzo, and his companions;

> A solemn air, and the best comforter
> To an unsettled fancy, cure thy brains
> Now useless, boiled within thy skull.

Again;

> The charm dissolves space
> And, as the morning steals upon the night,
> Melting the darkness, so their rising senses
> Begin to chase the ignorant fumes that mantle
> Their clearer reason.
> Their understanding
> Begins to swell: and the approaching tide
> Will shortly fill the reasonable shores
> That now lie foul and muddy.[46]

79   The perception of real affinities between events, (that is to say, of *ideal* affinities, for those only are real,) enables the poet thus to make free with the most imposing forms and phenomena of the world, and to assert the predominance of the soul.

80   3. Whilst thus the poet delights us by animating nature like a creator, with his own thoughts, he differs from the philosopher only herein, that the one proposes Beauty as his main end; the other Truth. But, the philosopher, not less than the poet, postpones the apparent order and relations of things to the empire of thought. "The problem of philosophy," according to Plato, "is, for all that exists conditionally, to find a ground unconditioned and absolute."[47] It proceeds on the faith that a law determines all phenomena, which being known, the phenomena can be predicted. That law, when in the mind, is an idea. Its beauty is infinite. The true philosopher and the true poet are one, and a beauty, which is truth, and a truth, which is beauty, is the aim of both. Is not the charm of one of Plato's or Aristotle's definitions, strictly like that of the Antigone of Sophocles?[48] It is, in both cases, that a spiritual life has been imparted to nature; that the solid seeming block of matter has been pervaded and dissolved by a thought; that this feeble human being has penetrated the vast masses of nature with an informing soul, and recognised itself in their harmony, that is, seized their law. In physics, when this is attained, the

memory disburthens itself of its cumbrous catalogues of particulars, and carries centuries of observation in a single formula.

Thus even in physics, the material is ever degraded before the spiritual. The astronomer, the geometer, rely on their irrefragable analysis, and disdain the results of observation. The sublime remark of Euler on his law of arches, "This will be found contrary to all experience, yet is true;"[49] had already transferred nature into the mind, and left matter like an outcast corpse. ⁸¹

4. Intellectual science has been observed to beget invariably a doubt of the existence of matter. Turgot said, "He that has never doubted the existence of matter, may be assured he has no aptitude for metaphysical inquiries."[50] It fastens the attention upon immortal necessary uncreated natures, that is, upon Ideas; and in their beautiful and majestic presence, we feel that our outward being is a dream and a shade. Whilst we wait in this Olympus of gods, we think of nature as an appendix to the soul.[51] We ascend into their region, and know that these are the thoughts of the Supreme Being. "These are they who were set up from everlasting, from the beginning, or ever the earth was. When he prepared the heavens, they were there; when he established the clouds above, when he strengthened the fountains of the deep. Then they were by him, as one brought up with him. Of them took he counsel."[52] ⁸²

Their influence is proportionate. As objects of science, they are accessible to few men. Yet all men are capable of being raised by piety or by passion, into their region. And no man touches these divine natures, without becoming, in some degree, himself divine. Like a new soul, they renew the body. We become physically nimble and lightsome; we tread on air; life is no longer irksome, and we think it will never be so. No man fears age or misfortune or death, in their serene company, for he is transported out of the district of change. Whilst we behold unveiled the nature of Justice and Truth, we learn the difference between the absolute and the conditional or relative. We apprehend the absolute. As it were, for the first time, *we exist*. We become immortal, for we learn that time and space are relations of matter; that, with a perception of truth, or a virtuous will, they have no affinity. ⁸³

5. Finally, religion and ethics, which may be fitly called,—the practice of ideas, or the introduction of ideas into life,—have an analogous effect with all lower culture, in degrading nature and suggesting its dependence on spirit. Ethics and religion differ herein; that the one is the system of human duties ⁸⁴

commencing from man; the other, from God. Religion includes the personality of God; Ethics does not. They are one to our present design. They both put nature under foot. The first and last lesson of religion is, "The things that are seen, are temporal; the things that are unseen are eternal."[53] It puts an affront upon nature. It does that for the unschooled, which philosophy does for Berkeley and Viasa.[54] The uniform language that may be heard in the churches of the most ignorant sects, is,—'Contemn the unsubstantial shows of the world; they are vanities, dreams, shadows, unrealities; seek the realities of religion.' The devotee flouts nature. Some theosophists have arrived at a certain hostility and indignation towards matter, as the Manichean and Plotinus.[55] They distrusted in themselves any looking back to these flesh-pots of Egypt. Plotinus was ashamed of his body.[56] In short, they might all better say of matter, what Michael Angelo said of external beauty, "it is the frail and weary weed, in which God dresses the soul, which he has called into time."[57]

85   It appears that motion, poetry, physical and intellectual science, and religion, all tend to affect our convictions of the reality of the external world. But I own there is something ungrateful in expanding too curiously the particulars of the general proposition, that all culture tends to imbue us with idealism. I have no hostility to nature, but a child's love to it. I expand and live in the warm day like corn and melons. Let us speak her fair. I do not wish to fling stones at my beautiful mother, nor soil my gentle nest. I only wish to indicate the true position of nature in regard to man, wherein to establish man, all right education tends; as the ground which to attain is the object of human life, that is, of man's connexion with nature. Culture inverts the vulgar views of nature, and brings the mind to call that apparent, which it uses to call real, and that real, which it uses to call visionary. Children, it is true, believe in the external world. The belief that it appears only, is an afterthought, but with culture, this faith will as surely arise on the mind as did the first.

86   The advantage of the ideal theory over the popular faith, is this, that it presents the world in precisely that view which is most desirable to the mind. It is, in fact, the view which Reason, both speculative and practical, that is, philosophy and virtue, take. For, seen in the light of thought, the world always is phenomenal; and virtue subordinates it to the mind. Idealism sees the world in God. It beholds the whole circle of persons and things, of actions and events, of country and religion, not as painfully accumulated, atom after atom, act after act, in an aged creeping Past, but as one vast picture, which

God paints on the instant eternity, for the contemplation of the soul. Therefore the soul holds itself off from a too trivial and microscopic study of the universal tablet. It respects the end too much, to immerse itself in the means. It sees something more important in Christianity, than the scandals of ecclesiastical history or the niceties of criticism; and, very incurious concerning persons or miracles, and not at all disturbed by chasms of historical evidence, it accepts from God the phenomenon, as it finds it, as the pure and awful form of religion in the world. It is not hot and passionate at the appearance of what it calls its own good or bad fortune, at the union or opposition of other persons. No man is its enemy. It accepts whatsoever befals, as part of its lesson. It is a watcher more than a doer, and it is a doer, only that it may the better watch.

Chapter VII.
Spirit.

It is essential to a true theory of nature and of man, that it should contain somewhat progressive. Uses that are exhausted or that may be, and facts that end in the statement, cannot be all that is true of this brave lodging wherein man is harbored, and wherein all his faculties find appropriate and endless exercise. And all the uses of nature admit of being summed in one, which yields the activity of man an infinite scope. Through all its kingdoms, to the suburbs and outskirts of things, it is faithful to the cause whence it had its origin. It always speaks of Spirit. It suggests the absolute. It is a perpetual effect. It is a great shadow pointing always to the sun behind us.   87

The aspect of nature is devout. Like the figure of Jesus, she stands with bended head, and hands folded upon the breast. The happiest man is he who learns from nature the lesson of worship.   88

Of that ineffable essence which we call Spirit, he that thinks most, will say least. We can foresee God in the coarse and, as it were, distant phenomena of matter; but when we try to define and describe himself, both language and thought desert us, and we are as helpless as fools and savages. That essence refuses to be recorded in propositions, but when man has worshipped him intellectually, the noblest ministry of nature is to stand as the apparition of God. It is the great organ through which the universal spirit speaks to the individual, and strives to lead back the individual to it.   89

When we consider Spirit, we see that the views already presented do   90 not include the whole circumference of man. We must add some related thoughts.

91   Three problems are put by nature to the mind; What is matter? Whence is it? and Whereto? The first of these questions only, the ideal theory answers. Idealism saith: matter is a phenomenon, not a substance. Idealism acquaints us with the total disparity between the evidence of our own being, and the evidence of the world's being. The one is perfect; the other, incapable of any assurance; the mind is a part of the nature of things; the world is a divine dream, from which we may presently awake to the glories and certainties of day. Idealism is a hypothesis to account for nature by other principles than those of carpentry and chemistry. Yet, if it only deny the existence of matter, it does not satisfy the demands of the spirit. It leaves God out of me. It leaves me in the splendid labyrinth of my perceptions, to wander without end. Then the heart resists it, because it baulks the affections in denying substantive being to men and women. Nature is so pervaded with human life, that there is something of humanity in all, and in every particular. But this theory makes nature foreign to me, and does not account for that consanguinity which we acknowledge to it.

92   Let it stand then, in the present state of our knowledge, merely as a useful introductory hypothesis, serving to apprize us of the eternal distinction between the soul and the world.

93   But when, following the invisible steps of thought, we come to inquire, Whence is matter? and Whereto? many truths arise to us out of the recesses of consciousness. We learn that the highest is present to the soul of man, that the dread universal essence, which is not wisdom, or love, or beauty, or power, but all in one, and each entirely, is that for which all things exist, and that by which they are; that spirit creates; that behind nature, throughout nature, spirit is present; that spirit is one and not compound; that spirit does not act upon us from without, that is, in space and time, but spiritually, or through ourselves. Therefore, that spirit, that is, the Supreme Being, does not build up nature around us, but puts it forth through us, as the life of the tree puts forth new branches and leaves through the pores of the old. As a plant upon the earth, so a man rests upon the bosom of God; he is nourished by unfailing fountains, and draws, at his need, inexhaustible power. Who can set bounds to the possibilities of man? Once inspire the infinite, by being admitted to behold the absolute natures of justice and truth, and we learn that man has

access to the entire mind of the Creator, is himself the creator in the finite. This view, which admonishes me where the sources of wisdom and power lie, and points to virtue as to

> "The golden key
> Which opes the palace of eternity,"[58]

carries upon its face the highest certificate of truth, because it animates me to create my own world through the purification of my soul.

The world proceeds from the same spirit as the body of man. It is a re-   94
moter and inferior incarnation of God, a projection of God in the unconscious. But it differs from the body in one important respect. It is not, like
that, now subjected to the human will. Its serene order is inviolable by us. It is
therefore, to us, the present expositor of the divine mind. It is a fixed point
whereby we may measure our departure. As we degenerate, the contrast between us and our house is more evident. We are as much strangers in nature,
as we are aliens from God. We do not understand the notes of birds. The fox
and the deer run away from us; the bear and tiger rend us. We do not know
the uses of more than a few plants, as corn and the apple, the potato and the
vine. Is not the landscape, every glimpse of which hath a grandeur, a face of
him? Yet this may show us what discord is between man and nature, for you
cannot freely admire a noble landscape, if laborers are digging in the field
hard by. The poet finds something ridiculous in his delight, until he is out of
the sight of men.

Chapter VIII.
Prospects.

In inquiries respecting the laws of the world and the frame of things, the   95
highest reason is always the truest. That which seems faintly possible—it is so
refined, is often faint and dim because it is deepest seated in the mind among
the eternal verities. Empirical science is apt to cloud the sight, and, by the
very knowledge of functions and processes, to bereave the student of the
manly contemplation of the whole. The savant becomes unpoetic. But the
best read naturalist who lends an entire and devout attention to truth, will
see that there remains much to learn of his relation to the world, and that it is
not to be learned by any addition or subtraction or other comparison of

known quantities, but is arrived at by untaught sallies of the spirit, by a continual self-recovery, and by entire humility. He will perceive that there are far more excellent qualities in the student than preciseness and infallibility; that a guess is often more fruitful than an indisputable affirmation, and that a dream may let us deeper into the secret of nature than a hundred concerted experiments.

For, the problems to be solved are precisely those which the physiologist and the naturalist omit to state. It is not so pertinent to man to know all the individuals of the animal kingdom, as it is to know whence and whereto is this tyrannizing unity in his constitution, which evermore separates and classifies things, endeavouring to reduce the most diverse to one form. When I behold a rich landscape, it is less to my purpose to recite correctly the order and superposition of the strata, than to know why all thought of multitude is lost in a tranquil sense of unity. I cannot greatly honor minuteness in details, so long as there is no hint to explain the relation between things and thoughts; no ray upon the *metaphysics* of conchology, of botany, of the arts, to show the relation of the forms of flowers, shells, animals, architecture, to the mind, and build science upon ideas. In a cabinet of natural history, we become sensible of a certain occult recognition and sympathy in regard to the most bizarre forms of beast, fish, and insect.[59] The American who has been confined, in his own country, to the sight of buildings designed after foreign models, is surprised on entering York Minster or St. Peter's at Rome, by the feeling that these structures are imitations also,—faint copies of an invisible archetype. Nor has science sufficient humanity, so long as the naturalist overlooks that wonderful congruity which subsists between man and the world; of which he is lord, not because he is the most subtile inhabitant, but because he is its head and heart, and finds something of himself in every great and small thing, in every mountain stratum, in every new law of color, fact of astronomy, or atmospheric influence which observation or analysis lay open. A perception of this mystery inspires the muse of George Herbert, the beautiful psalmist of the seventeenth century. The following lines are part of his little poem on Man.

> "Man is all symmetry,
> Full of proportions, one limb to another,
> And to all the world besides.

Each part may call the farthest, brother;
For head with foot hath private amity,
    And both with moons and tides.

"Nothing hath got so far
But man hath caught and kept it as his prey;
    His eyes dismount the highest star;
    He is in little all the sphere.
Herbs gladly cure our flesh, because that they
    Find their acquaintance there.

"For us, the winds do blow,
The earth doth rest, heaven move, and fountains flow;
    Nothing we see, but means our good,
    As our delight, or as our treasure;
The whole is either our cupboard of food,
    Or cabinet of pleasure.

"The stars have us to bed:
Night draws the curtain; which the sun withdraws.
    Music and light attend our head.
    All things unto our flesh are kind,
In their descent and being; to our mind,
    In their ascent and cause.

"More servants wait on man
Than he'll take notice of. In every path,
    He treads down that which doth befriend him
    When sickness makes him pale and wan.
Oh mighty love! Man is one world, and hath
    Another to attend him."[60]

The perception of this class of truths makes the eternal attraction which draws men to science, but the end is lost sight of in attention to the means. In view of this half-sight of science, we accept the sentence of Plato, that, "poetry comes nearer to vital truth than history."[61] Every surmise and vaticination of the mind is entitled to a certain respect, and we learn to prefer imperfect theories, and sentences, which contain glimpses of truth, to digested systems which have no one valuable suggestion.[62] A wise writer will feel that the ends of study and composition are best answered by announcing undiscovered regions of thought, and so communicating, through hope, new activity to the torpid spirit.

98   I shall therefore conclude this essay with some traditions of man and nature, which a certain poet sang to me; and which, as they have always been in the world, and perhaps reappear to every bard, may be both history and prophecy.

99   'The foundations of man are not in matter, but in spirit. But the element of spirit is eternity. To it, therefore, the longest series of events, the oldest chronologies are young and recent. In the cycle of the universal man, from whom the known individuals proceed, centuries are points, and all history is but the epoch of one degradation.

100   'We distrust and deny inwardly our sympathy with nature. We own and disown our relation to it, by turns. We are, like Nebuchadnezzar, dethroned, bereft of reason, and eating grass like an ox.[63] But who can set limits to the remedial force of spirit?

101   'A man is a god in ruins. When men are innocent, life shall be longer, and shall pass into the immortal, as gently as we awake from dreams. Now, the world would be insane and rabid, if these disorganizations should last for hundreds of years. It is kept in check by death and infancy. Infancy is the perpetual Messiah, which comes into the arms of fallen men, and pleads with them to return to paradise.

102   'Man is the dwarf of himself. Once he was permeated and dissolved by spirit. He filled nature with his overflowing currents. Out from him sprang the sun and moon; from man, the sun; from woman, the moon. The laws of his mind, the periods of his actions externized themselves into day and night, into the year and the seasons. But, having made for himself this huge shell, his waters retired; he no longer fills the veins and veinlets; he is shrunk to a drop. He sees, that the structure still fits him, but fits him colossally. Say, rather, once it fitted him, now it corresponds to him from far and on high. He adores timidly his own work. Now is man the follower of the sun, and woman the follower of the moon. Yet sometimes he starts in his slumber, and wonders at himself and his house, and muses strangely at the resemblance betwixt him and it. He perceives that if his law is still paramount, if still he have elemental power, "if his word is sterling yet in nature,"[64] it is not con-

scious power, it is not inferior but superior to his will. It is Instinct.' Thus my Orphic poet sang.[65]

At present, man applies to nature but half his force. He works on the world with his understanding alone. He lives in it, and masters it by a penny-wisdom; and he that works most in it, is but a half-man, and whilst his arms are strong and his digestion good, his mind is imbruted and he is a selfish savage. His relation to nature, his power over it, is through the understanding; as by manure; the economic use of fire, wind, water, and the mariner's needle; steam, coal, chemical agriculture; the repairs of the human body by the dentist and the surgeon. This is such a resumption of power, as if a banished king should buy his territories inch by inch, instead of vaulting at once into his throne. Meantime, in the thick darkness, there are not wanting gleams of a better light,—occasional examples of the action of man upon nature with his entire force,—with reason as well as understanding. Such examples are; the traditions of miracles in the earliest antiquity of all nations; the history of Jesus Christ; the achievements of a principle, as in religious and political revolutions, and in the abolition of the Slave-trade; the miracles of enthusiasm, as those reported of Swedenborg, Hohenlohe, and the Shakers;[66] many obscure and yet contested facts, now arranged under the name of Animal Magnetism; prayer; eloquence; self-healing; and the wisdom of children. These are examples of Reason's momentary grasp of the sceptre; the exertions of a power which exists not in time or space, but an instantaneous in-streaming causing power. The difference between the actual and the ideal force of man is happily figured by the schoolmen, in saying, that the knowledge of man is an evening knowledge, *vespertina cognitio,* but that of God is a morning knowledge, *matutina cognitio.*[67]

The problem of restoring to the world original and eternal beauty, is solved by the redemption of the soul. The ruin or the blank, that we see when we look at nature, is in our own eye. The axis of vision is not coincident with the axis of things, and so they appear not transparent but opake. The reason why the world lacks unity, and lies broken and in heaps, is, because man is disunited with himself. He cannot be a naturalist, until he satisfies all the demands of the spirit. Love is as much its demand, as perception. Indeed, neither can be perfect without the other. In the uttermost meaning of the words, thought is devout, and devotion is thought. Deep calls unto deep.[68] But in actual life, the marriage is not celebrated. There are innocent men who worship God after the tradition of their fathers, but their sense of duty has not yet extended to the use of all their faculties. And there are patient naturalists, but they freeze their subject under the wintry light of the understanding. Is not prayer also a study of truth,—a sally of the soul into the unfound infinite? No man ever prayed heartily, without learning something. But when a faithful thinker, resolute to detach every object from personal relations, and see it in the light of thought, shall, at the same time, kindle science with the fire of the holiest affections, then will God go forth anew into the creation.

105   It will not need, when the mind is prepared for study, to search for objects. The invariable mark of wisdom is to see the miraculous in the common. What is a day? What is a year? What is summer? What is woman? What is a child? What is sleep? To our blindness, these things seem unaffecting. We make fables to hide the baldness of the fact and conform it, as we say, to the higher law of the mind. But when the fact is seen under the light of an idea, the gaudy fable fades and shrivels. We behold the real higher law. To the wise, therefore, a fact is true poetry, and the most beautiful of fables. These wonders are brought to our own door. You also are a man. Man and woman, and their social life, poverty, labor, sleep, fear, fortune, are known to you. Learn that none of these things is superficial, but that each phenomenon hath its roots in the faculties and affections of the mind. Whilst the abstract question occupies your intellect, nature brings it in the concrete to be solved by your hands. It were a wise inquiry for the closet, to compare, point by point, especially at remarkable crises in life, our daily history, with the rise and progress of ideas in the mind.

106   So shall we come to look at the world with new eyes. It shall answer the endless inquiry of the intellect,—What is truth? and of the affections,—What is good? by yielding itself passive to the educated Will. Then shall come to pass what my poet said; 'Nature is not fixed but fluid. Spirit alters, moulds, makes it. The immobility or bruteness of nature, is the absence of spirit; to pure spirit, it is fluid, it is volatile, it is obedient. Every spirit builds itself a house; and beyond its house, a world; and beyond its world, a heaven. Know then, that the world exists for you. For you is the phenomenon perfect. What we are, that only can we see. All that Adam had, all that Cæsar could, you have and can do.[69] Adam called his house, heaven and earth; Cæsar called his house, Rome; you perhaps call yours, a cobler's trade; a hundred acres of

ploughed land; or a scholar's garret. Yet line for line and point for point, your dominion is as great as theirs, though without fine names. Build, therefore, your own world. As fast as you conform your life to the pure idea in your mind, that will unfold its great proportions. A correspondent revolution in things will attend the influx of the spirit. So fast will disagreeable appearances, swine, spiders, snakes, pests, mad-houses, prisons, enemies, vanish; they are temporary and shall be no more seen. The sordor and filths of nature, the sun shall dry up, and the wind exhale. As when the summer comes from the south, the snow-banks melt, and the face of the earth becomes green before it, so shall the advancing spirit create its ornaments along its path, and carry with it the beauty it visits, and the song which enchants it; it shall draw beautiful faces, and warm hearts, and wise discourse, and heroic acts, around its way, until evil is no more seen. The kingdom of man over nature, which cometh not with observation,—a dominion such as now is beyond his dream of God,—he shall enter without more wonder than the blind man feels who is gradually restored to perfect sight.'

Notes

1. Quoted from Plotinus, third-century Greek philosopher who set out the basic tenets of Neoplatonism. In the 1849 edition of *Nature,* Emerson replaced this motto with lines from his poem "Nature": "A subtle chain of countless rings / The next unto the farthest brings; / The eye reads omens where it goes, / And speaks all languages the rose; / And, striving to be man, the worm / Mounts through all the spires of form" (*CW,* 9:659–660).
2. "If the stars . . . of God" was used as the epigraph to Isaac Asimov's (1920–1992) well-known science-fiction story "Nightfall" (1941).
3. "Man" (1633), ll. 43–44, by George Herbert (1593–1633), English metaphysical poet.
4. Æolus, god of the winds, appears in Homer's *Odyssey.*
5. Napoleon Bonaparte (1769–1821), French general and ruler.
6. Cosmos, in Greek, means primarily "order," secondarily "beauty."
7. Emerson attributes this sentence to his brother Charles Chauncy Emerson (1808–1836).
8. Assyria, a kingdom in northern Mesopotamia, represents power; Paphos, a city on Cyprus, home of the worship of Aphrodite, Greek goddess of love and beauty, represents myth.

9. According to Western tradition, the Greek Homer (fl. ca. 850 BCE) is the author of the *Iliad* and the *Odyssey*. William Shakespeare (1564–1616), famed English poet, playwright, and dramatist.

10. See "Of Love," in *Morals* by Plutarch (ca. 46–ca. 120), Greek historian best known for his series of "lives" of famous Greek and Roman figures arranged in pairs for comparison.

11. Although the 1849 edition attributes this quotation to the first-century BCE Roman historian Sallust, it is more likely from *Apology for Smectymnuus* (1641) by John Milton (1608–1674), English poet and polemicist.

12. From *Decline and Fall of the Roman Empire* (1776–1778) by Edward Gibbon (1737–1794), English historian.

13. Leonidas, king of Sparta (d. 490 BCE), defended the pass of Thermopylae against the Persians in a hopeless, costly sacrifice; according to tradition, Arnold von Winkelried brought victory in the Battle of Sempach (1386) to the Swiss by gathering all the Austrian pikes he could reach into his own body, thus creating a breach in the enemy line.

14. Sir Henry Vane, English Puritan statesman (1613–1662), who after a distinguished political career in both England and America was executed for treason after the Restoration.

15. Charles II (1630–1685) restored the monarchy to England after the Commonwealth was overthrown; William Russell (1639–1683), "Lord Russell" by courtesy title only, was accused by informers of complicity in the Rye House Plot, charged with high treason, and executed.

16. Pindar (ca. 522–443 BCE), the greatest of the Greek lyric poets; Socrates (ca. 470–399 BCE), one of the most famous Greek philosophers, known for his dialogic method of teaching; Phocion (ca. 402–318 BCE), Athenian general, statesman, and student of Plato, ruled Athens after the death of Alexander the Great, or Alexander III of Macedon, fourth century BCE conquerer of the known civilized world, but was executed on a false charge of treason.

17. Emerson drew "il piu nell' uno"—"multitude in unity"—from *Specimens of the Table Talk of the Late Samuel Taylor Coleridge* (1835).

18. 1 Corinthians 15:44.

19. Quoted from Emanuel Swedenborg (1688–1772), Swedish scientist, theologian, and mystic.

20. Emerson's variation on a remark by Madame de Staël (1766–1817), French novelist and social critic, in *Germany* (London, 1813).

21. Plotinus, *Enneads.*

22. Shakespeare, *Macbeth*, III, iv, 110–112.

23. Worshippers of Brahma, Brahmins were of the priestly class and thus in the highest social order in Hinduism. Pythagoras (d. 497 BCE), Greek philosopher and

mathematician; Plato (428/7–348/7 BCE), the most famous of the Greek philosophers; Roger Bacon (ca. 1214–1294), English scientist and philosopher; Gottfried Wilhelm von Leibnitz (1646–1716), German philosopher and mathematician.

24. In his poem "The Sphinx" (1841), Emerson answers the riddle, after which the Sphinx says, "Who telleth one of my meanings / Is Master of all I am" (see *CW*, 9:3–12).

25. From Guillaume Oegger (ca. 1790–ca. 1853), French cleric, linguist, and Swedenborgian, *The True Messiah; or The Old and New Testaments, Examined According to The Principles of the Language of Nature* (1842).

26. George Fox (1624–1691), founder of the Society of Friends (Quakers), quoted from William Sewel, *The History of the Rise, Increase, and Progress of the Christian People Called Quakers* (1823).

27. Attributed to Coleridge, *Aids to Reflection* (1824), by the editors of *CW*, it is an "almost verbatim translation" from Johann Wolfgang von Goethe (1749–1832), Germany's most famous writer (see Gustaaf Van Cromphout, "Goethe, Not Coleridge," *Emerson Society Papers* 13:1 [Spring 2002]: 1, 8).

28. Emerson is using the term "discipline" in the sense of education or instruction.

29. Paraphrased by Emerson from Francis Bacon (1561–1626), English statesman, scientist, and philosopher, "Of Great Place" (1612).

30. Attributed to Joseph Butler (1692–1752), English bishop and philosopher, in the novel *Tremaine* (1825) by Robert Plumer Ward (1765–1845), English politician.

31. With "thy will be done!", cf. Matthew 26:42 and 6:10.

32. In Greek mythology, Hercules is the god of strength.

33. Xenophanes of Elea (570–480 BCE), Greek philosopher who may have been a source of Emerson's repeated concept of "each and all."

34. According to legend, Proteus is the old man of the sea who, in order to avoid prophesying, could assume a variety of forms, but, when forced to tell the truth, resumed his own.

35. This concept is traced by Emerson to Vitruvius, a first-century BCE Roman architect, engineer, and writer on architecture, by way of Madame de Staël and Goethe.

36. Michelangelo Buonarroti (1475–1564), Italian painter, sculptor, and poet.

37. Joseph Haydn (1732–1809), Austrian composer.

38. "All truth accords with the truth."

39. A philosophical term from the Latin, "the absolute Ens" refers to "an abstract being."

40. Quoted from the translation by Thomas Carlyle (1795–1881), prolific Scottish writer and Emerson's correspondent for over forty years, of Goethe's *Wilhelm Meister's Travels* (1821, 1829).

41. Orion, Greek mythological hunter whose name was given to a constellation in

the form of a hunter with a belt and a sword, is named after the giant hunter slain by Artemis, Greek goddess of wild animals.

42. The "camera obscura" is a device that permits images to be reflected through a lens or mirror onto paper in order that they may be traced.

43. Shakespeare, Sonnet LXX, ll. 3–4.

44. Shakespeare, Sonnet CXXIV, ll. 5–7, 9–11.

45. Shakespeare, *Measure for Measure,* IV, i, 1–4.

46. Shakespeare, *The Tempest,* V, i, 46–68; Emerson erroneously ascribes the opening lines to Ariel rather than Prospero.

47. Quoted from Coleridge, *The Friend* (1818).

48. Aristotle, fourth-century BCE Greek philosopher and scientist; *Antigone* is a play by Sophocles, fifth-century BCE Greek dramatist.

49. Leonhard Euler (1707–1783), Swiss mathematician, physicist, and speculative philosopher, quoted from Coleridge, *Aids to Reflection.*

50. Anne Robert Jacques Turgot (1727–1781), French statesman and economist.

51. Olympus is the home of the gods in Greek and Roman mythology.

52. Adapted by Emerson from Proverbs 8:23, 27, 28, 30.

53. 2 Corinthians 4:18.

54. George Berkeley (1685–1753), English idealistic philosopher. Viasa is the reputed arranger of the Indian Vedas, a philosopher even more legendary and synthetic than Homer.

55. Manichean refers to the religious philosophy of the Babylonian Manes, third-century Christian mystic, who regarded the world as the site of constant struggle between good and evil.

56. This statement is the first sentence in the *Life of Plotinus,* by Porphyry of Tyre (234–305).

57. Michelangelo, Sonnet LI, ll. 3–4.

58. Milton, *Comus, a Mask,* ll. 13–14.

59. Emerson is recalling his visit to the Jardin des Plantes at the Muséum d'Histoire Naturelle, Paris, on 13 July 1833, where he discovered "an occult relation between the very scorpions and man" (*JMN,* 4:198–200).

60. George Herbert, "Man," stanzas 3–6, 8.

61. Ideas close to this were ascribed to both Plato and Aristotle in a review of John Knox's *Remarks on . . . Longinus* in the September 1831 *Edinburgh Review.*

62. A "vaticination" is a prediction or prophecy.

63. Nebuchadnezzar II (ca. 630–ca. 561 BCE), king of Babylon, whose dream is interpreted in Daniel 4:25, 32, 33.

64. Emerson's paraphrase of Shakespeare, *King Richard II,* IV, i, 264.

65. There has been much conjecture as to whom Emerson refers here, but his tendency to create an alter ego when he wishes to speak in the voice of the poet as

seer (as Osman, Saadi, etc.) would seem to eliminate the more literal identification with Amos Bronson Alcott (1799–1888), American Transcendentalist, Emerson's longtime friend and Concord neighbor, and the author of a series of "Orphic Sayings."

66. Prince Alexander Leopold of Hohenlohe-Waldenberg-Schillingsfürst (1794–1849), German Roman Catholic bishop and writer; Shakers, an English communal order whose leaders came to America in 1774, known for its pacificism and furniture making.

67. Emerson's source is *An Essay Towards the Theory of the Ideal or Intellectual World*, 2 vols. (London, 1701–1704), 1:159 (*JMN*, 5:141), by John Norris (1657–1711), English cleric and Platonist philosopher, on the scholastic difference between the knowledge of man and the knowledge of God.

68. Cf. Psalms 42:7.

69. Gaius Julius Caesar, first-century BCE Roman general and statesman.

Humanity of Science

1   It is the perpetual effort of the mind to seek relations between the multitude of facts under its eye, by means of which it can reduce them to some order. The mind busies itself in a perpetual comparison of objects to find resemblances by which those resembling may be set apart as a class. Of those resembling it seeks to abstract the common property; which it compares again with another common property of another resembling class, to derive from these two, a still higher common property. This is Method, Classification.

2   The child puts his playthings in a circle or in a row; he builds his blocks into a spire or a house; he aims still at some intelligible arrangement. A man puts his tools in one place; his food in another; his clothes in a third, his ornaments in a fourth. Woman is an angel of system. Her love of order is a proverbial blessing. A house is her classification. The art of bookkeeping is a striking example of the pleasure and the power of arbitrary classification. A state, an army, a shop, a school, a post-office are others.

3   The first process of thought in examining a new object is to compare it with known objects and refer it to a class. The mind is reluctant to make

many classes or to suppose many causes. This reduction to a few laws, to one law, is not a choice of the individual. It is the tyrannical instinct of the mind.

This act of classifying is attended with pleasure, as it is a sort of unlocking the spiritual sight. I am shown a violet, the hearts ease, for example. If I have never seen a plant of the sort, I fasten my attention on the stem, leaves, and petals, of this; and I do not easily believe in the existence of any other sort of violet, than that I see. But another is shown me,—the white; then the round-leaved; then the yellow. I see each with a livelier pleasure, and begin to see that there exists a violet family, after which type all these particular varieties are made. I experience the like delight in being shown each of the tribes in the natural system of Botany, as the liliaceous, the papilionaceous, the mosses, or the grasses.   4

There is great difference between men in this habit or power of classifying. Some men unite things by their superficial resemblances, as if you should arrange a company by the color of their dress, or by their size, or complexion. Others by occult resemblances, which is the habit of wit; others by intrinsic likeness, which is Science. The great moments of scientific history, have been the perception of these relations.   5

Newton sees an apple fall, and cries—"the motion of the moon is but an apple-fall; the motion of the earth is but a larger apple-fall: I see the law of all nature"—and slow observation makes good this bold word. It happened in our time that a German poet beholding a plant and seeing, as we may see in a pond-lily, a petal in transition from a leaf, exclaimed, And why is not every part of a plant a transformed leaf? A petal is a leaf, a fruit is a leaf, a seed is a leaf, metamorphosed, and slow-paced experiment has made good this prophetic vision,[1] that is, it may be demonstrated that a flower is analogous in its structure to a branch covered with leaves,—is a branch of metamorphosed leaves.—This is shown by proving a bract to be a modification of a leaf; a sepal of a bract; a petal of a sepal; a stamen of a petal; the carpel of a leaf; the ovule of a leaf-bud, a view now accepted by the English and French botanists.   6

The same gifted man walking in the Jews' burying ground in the city of Venice saw a sheep's skull on the ground and was struck with the gradation by which the vertebrae passed into the bones of the head. Instantly he said to himself, the vertebra of the spine is the unit of anatomy; all other parts are merely metamorphoses, degradations, abortions, or enlargements of this.   7

The head was only the uppermost vertebra transformed. "The plant goes from knot to knot, closing at last with the flower and the seed. So the tapeworm, the caterpillar, goes from knot to knot, and closes with the head. Man and the higher animals are built up through the vertebrae, the powers being concentrated in the head." He is the author of a beautiful theory of colors beginning to be studied in which the prismatic hues are reckoned simply mixtures of darkness and light.[2]

8   The system of Lamarck aims to find a monad of organic life which shall be common to every animal, and which becomes an animalcule, a poplarworm, a mastiff, or a man, according to circumstances.[3] It says to the caterpillar, "How dost thou, Brother! Please God, you shall yet be a philosopher." In the like spirit of audacious system another physiologist concludes that the monad becomes animal or plant only according to the element of darkness or light in which it unfolds. These are extreme examples of the impatience of the human mind in the presence of a multitude of separate facts, and the energy with which it aims to find some mark on them according to which they can all be set in some order.

9   Classification is one of the main actions of the intellect. A man of great sagacity divides, distributes, with every word he speaks. And we are always at the mercy of a better classifier than ourselves.

10   Every system of faith, every theory of science, every argument of a barrister, is a classification, and gives the mind the sense of power in proportion to the truth or centrality of the traits by which it arranges. Calvinism, Romanism, and the Church of Swedenborg, are three striking examples of coherent systems which each organize the best-known facts of the world's history, and the qualities of character, into an order that reacts directly on the will of the individual.[4] The success of Phrenology is a lively proof of the pleasure which a classification of the most interesting phenomena gives to the unscientific.[5]

11   Whilst we consider this appetite of the mind to arrange its phenomena, there is another fact which makes this useful.

12   There is in nature a parallel unity, which corresponds to this unity in the mind, and makes it available. This methodizing mind meets no resistance in its attempts. The scattered blocks with which it strives to form a symmetrical structure, fit. This design following after, finds with joy that like design went before. Not only man puts things in a row, but things belong in a row. The im-

mense variety of objects is really composed of a few elements. The world is the fulfilment of a few laws.

Hence, the possibility of Science. When one considers the feeble physical nature of man, how disproportionate to the natures which he investigates, he may well ask, How to such an animal, of seventy inches, walking and in the earth, is the solar system measurable and the nature of matter universally? Because a straw shows how the stream runs, and the wind blows; because as falls the apple, so falls the moon; because as grows one inch of one vegetable in a flowerpot, so grow all the forests; and as one animal of one species is formed, so are formed all animals of all species; because in short the wide universe is made up of a few elements and a few laws; perhaps of one element and one law. 13

Nature works unique through many forms. All agents—the most diverse—are pervaded by radical analogies, so that music, optics, mechanics, galvanism, electricity, magnetism are only versions of one law. The study of one natural object is like the study of a book in a foreign language. When he has mastered that one book, the learner finds with joy that he can read with equal facility in ten thousand books. A half inch of vegetable tissue will tell all that can be known on the subject from all the forests; and one skeleton or a fragment of animal fibre intimately known is a zoological cabinet. 14

But whilst the laws of the world coexist in each particle, they cannot be learned by the exclusive study of one creature. A man shall not say, I will dedicate my life to the study of this moss, and through that I will achieve nature. Nature hates cripples and monomaniacs. All her secrets are locked in one plant; but she does not unlock them in any one. She shows one function in a tree, and another function in a seaweed. If the spiral vessels are exposed in a hyacinth, the vesicles are seen in a chara; the stomata in [blank]; the pila in a mullein; and chromule in sage; and to show all the parts of one plant, she leads you round the whole garden.[6] 15

She writes every obscure and minute fact in colossal characters somewhere. Our microscopes are not necessary. They are a pretty toy for chamber philosophers, but nature has brought every fact within reach of the unarmed eye somewhere. It is difficult in the most level country or on the highest mountain to appreciate the outline of the earth, but on the seashore the dark blue sea line reveals at once the true curve of the globe. The question was once vexed whether mineral coal was of vegetable origin. Playfair found the 16 bough of a tree which was perfect wood at one end, and passed through imperceptible gradations to perfect mineral coal at the other.[7]

17   In the old fossil fishes, the earliest creation, the vertebrae of the back are not divided; but an unbroken cord or bone runs from the head to the tail. Modern science has discovered one or two fishes yet existing, in which the vertebral column is still undivided; thus bringing to the eye of the anatomist the reality of this antique and fabulous structure, and connecting it with the living races. Again; the utmost attention has been given by modern physiologists to microscopic observations of the changes of the egg, especially in fishes and reptiles. It is now found that the order of changes in the egg determines the order of the strata containing remains. Each of the temporary states through which the young animal passes in the egg, is the type of a great class of animals which existed in that form on the earth for thousands of years, and when doubt existed as to the priority of two strata, it has been determined by reference to the living egg.

18   A peat bog may show us how the coal mines were formed. A shower of rain in the mountains may explain the diluvial and alluvial formations; the frost shooting on the windowpane, the process of crystallization; the deposit of sediment in a boiling pot, is a small Vesuvius; as Vesuvius is a small Himalaya.[8]

19   Science is the arrangement of the phenomena of the world after their essential relations. It is the reconstruction of nature in the mind. This is at once its ideal and its historical aspect.

20   The most striking trait of modern science is its approximation towards central truths. On all sides it is simplifying its laws and finding one cause for many effects. Unexpected resemblances in the most distant objects betray a common origin. It has been observed in earthquakes that remote countries were shaken at the same hour, showing that the explosion was far within the globe, and the vibrations communicated through vast hollows radiating from a deep centre to equidistant points on the surface, but points very distant from each other. In like manner, from a common law at the foundation of terrestrial natures may spring a great variety of surface actions. This is the theory of comparative anatomy. One grand idea hovers over a wide variety of forms. Look at the skeleton of man, with legs and arms. Then look at the horse or the ox, and you see the same skeleton with some variations. Occasionally, the type comes out conspicuously, when five fingers are severed, usu-

ally bound up in a hoof. In a bird, you see the same radical skeleton, but whilst the legs remain of the same use, the arm is deprived of the hand, is covered with feathers and made a wing. In the whale the forearm is a flipper to swim the sea. By insensible gradations, this one type may be detected in fishes and insects. It is so conspicuous, that Camper, the physiologist, was wont to draw on his blackboard the man, and by a few strokes transform him into a horse, then into an ox, into a bird, into a fish.[9]

In like manner see how the type of a leaf is present and creative in all leaves. It was once supposed that the various forms of leaves required each a new theory for its form. A leaf was a body originally undivided which owing to some unintelligible action became cut into segments in different ways so as to acquire at last a lobed form. But more accurate botanists showed that at a certain distance from the stem the stalk of the leaf follows the analogy of the tree and begins to branch; each branch carrying with it its green coat of parenchyma. If these branches remain distinct we have the simplest form of leaf with many threadlike claws, such as occurs in some species of the ranunculus. If these claws should grow together at their edges, a more entire leaf is formed; if still more, a leaf more perfect like the wild geranium; then a fivefinger like the passion flower; and when the green web quite joins the claws, a round leaf like the plane tree or lime tree is at last produced. 21

The phenomena of sound and of light were observed to be strikingly similar. Both observed the same law of reflection and of radiation. Both were subject to the same law of interference and harmony. That is, two rays of light meeting, cause darkness; two beats of sound meeting, cause silence. Whenever the eye is affected by one prevailing color, it sees at the same time the accidental color; and in music, the ear is sensible at the same time to the fundamental note and its harmonic sounds. 22

It was then observed that the same laws might be translated into the laws of Heat; that all the principal phenomena of heat might be illustrated by a comparison with those of sound. The analogy is followed out, and Light, Heat, Sound, and the Waves of fluids are found to have the same laws of reflection, and are explained as undulations of an elastic medium. 23

This analogy is followed by others of deeper origin. Light and Heat are analogous in their law to Electricity and Magnetism. Magnetism and Electricity are shown to be identical,—the spark has been drawn from the magnet and polarity communicated to the needle by electricity. Then Davy thought 24 that the primary cause of electrical effects and of chemical effects is one and the same,—the one acting on masses, the other on particles. The phenomena of Crystallization resemble electric laws. The famous experiment of Chladni demonstrates a relation between harmonic sounds and proportioned forms.[10] Finally the sublime conjecture sanctioned by the minds of Newton, Hooke, Boscovich, and now of Davy, that the forms of natural bodies depend upon different arrangements of the same particles of matter; that possibly the world shall be found to be composed of oxygen and hydrogen;[11] and that even these two elements are but one matter in different states of electricity;—all these, whether they are premature generalizations or not, indicate the central unity, the common law that pervades nature from the deep centre to the unknown circumference.

25   Chemistry, Geology, Astronomy, surprise all the time, and the appointed way of man from infancy to omniscience, is through an infinite series of pleasant surprises.

26   In a just history, what is the face of science? What lesson does it teach? What wisdom will a philosopher draw from its recent progress?

27   A lesson which science teaches, unanimous in all her discoveries, is the omnipresence of spirit. Life, creation, and final causes meet us everywhere. The world is saturated with law. Beautifully shines a spirit through all the bruteness and toughness of matter. Alone omnipotent it converts all things to its own end. The adamant streams into softest but precise form before it. The same ponderable matter which lay yesterday in a clod of earth, today takes the form of a grain of wheat, and tomorrow, in fine nourishment, enters the stomach of man, replenishes the waste of the day, and sparkles in the humors of the eye, or grasps, pulls, or pushes in the fingers of the hand. Life refuses to be analysed. The best studies of modern naturalists have developed the doctrines of Life and of Presence, of Life conceived as a sort of guardian genius of each animal and vegetable form which overpowers chemical laws, and of Presence whereby in chemistry atoms have a certain restraining atmospheric influence where they do not chemically act. Behind all the processes which the lens can detect, there is a *Life* in a seed, which predominates over all brute matter, and which irresistibly forces carbon, hydrogen, and water, to take shape in a shaft, in leaves, in colors of a lily, which they could never take themselves. More wonderful is it in animal nature. Above every being, over every organ, floats this predetermining law, whose inscrutable secret defies

the microscope and the alembic. The naturalist must presuppose it, or his results are foolish and offensive. As the proverb says, "he counts without his host who leaves God out of his reckoning," so science is bankrupt which attempts to cut the knot which always spirit must untie.

In monsters there is never a new thing, but merely the joining of two normal forms that do not belong together; one being developed, the other not yet developed, as part fish, part man: it is right things out of place. "This we learn if from nothing else from malformations and monsters. If we never saw anything but what followed a known law, we should think there was a necessity for this thing; it could not be otherwise. But deviations, degradations, monsters, teach us that the law is not only firm and eternal, but is also alive; that the creature can turn itself, not indeed out of itself into somewhat else, but, within its own limits, into deformity; always however being holden back as with bit and bridle by the inexorable masterdom of the law."[12]

This spiritual presence which awes us in the phenomena of life is not inactive elsewhere; for every step of Science is to find measures, checks, adaptations. There is no outlaw, no forgotten or useless matter in the globe. Nowhere is death, deformity, immoveableness; but as the ivy creeps over the ruined tower, and grass over the new-made grave, so, over the spoils of a mountain chain, shivered, abraded, and pulverized by frost, rain, and gravity, and brought down in ruins into the sea, a new architecture is commenced and perfected in darkness. Under the ooze of the Atlantic, she builds her basalts and pours melted granite like warm wax into fissures of clay and lime and when the deposits of a thousand rivers have strewn the bed of the ocean with every year a new floor of spoils, she blows her furnaces with a gas and lifts the bed of the ocean above the water and man enters from a boat, kindles a fire in the new world, and worships God thereon, plants a field and builds a school.

The ameliorating presence of spirit, using to great ends what is base and cheap, teaches in a very impressive manner. The order of the world has been wisely called "an open secret."[13] And it is true that Nature's mode of concealing a law is in its very simplicity; she hides facts by putting them next us. Where is that power not present? Where are the crypts in which Nature has deposited her secret and notched every day of her thousand millenniums? In facts that stare at us all day; in the slab of the pavement, the stone of the wall, the side of the hill, the gravel of the brook. In these pages every strong agent

28

29

30

has written his name: the whirlpool, the lake, the volcano, and the wind. The facts are capable of but one interpretation, as the rings on the tree or on the cow's horn record every year of their age. No leaps, no magic, eternal, tranquil procession of old familiar laws, the wildest convulsion never overstepping the calculable powers of the agents; the earthquake and boiling geyser as accurate results of known laws as the rosebud and the hatching of a robin's egg. The irresistible destroyers of the old are all the time strong builders of the new—the irresistible destroyers who have rent and shivered the planet being now as near and potent as ever, nay the beautiful companions and lights of man's daily walk, mountain and stream, cloud and frost, sun and moon. "In the economy of the world," said Hutton, "I can find no traces of a beginning, no prospect of an end."[14]

31   The permanence and at the same time endless variety of spiritual nature finds its fit symbol in the durable world, which never preserves the same face for two moments. All things change; moon and star stand still never a moment. Heaven, earth, sea, air, and man are in a perpetual flux. Yet is all motion circular, so that, whilst all parts move the All is still.

32   The two sciences of astronomy and geology have been explored with wonderful diligence in these times, and have bestowed splendid gifts on men. Astronomy, which seems to be geometry exemplified in the glorious diagrams of the sidereal heavens, is the most appeasing influence to the agitations of human life and is our symbol of material grandeur exhausting in its realities the straining conception of possible power, size, and duration.

33   But in all this extent our little globe and its friendly globes or globules that attend it, farther or nearer, are a sufficient guide and index. Far as we rove in observation or induction, we never come into new laws. We can go nowhere into a foreign country, though we run along the vast diameters of the sidereal spaces.

34   In Geology, again, we have a book of Genesis, wherein we read when and how the worlds were made, and are introduced to periods as portentous as the distances of the sky. But here too, we are never strangers; it is the same functions, slower performed; the wheel of the clock which now revolves in the life of our species, once took the duration of many races of animals on the planet to complete its circle. The world was newer; the blood was colder; life had not yet so fierce a glow; or rather, the vast chart of being which lay in outline already, was to be prospectively and symmetrically consummated; an

immense unity of plan we infer from these old medals of deluges and confla-
grations, which has never been departed from, and can never: a plan successively realized and the now existing types were in view at the beginning.

Yet in all the multitude and range of spawning life, there is no unrelated
creature, and the laws so firm and so apprehensible, that Cuvier not long
since from a fragment of a fossil bone succeeded in restoring correctly the
true skeleton and outline of a saurian; and Agassiz, in these very days, from a
single scale of one fossil fish, undertook to determine the form of the perfect
fish, and when, soon after, a specimen of the fish was found in the strata, it
did not differ materially from the professor's drawing.[15]

The presence and the antecedence of spirit are impressively taught by
modern science. Step by step with these facts, we are apprised of another,
namely, the Humanity of that spirit; or, that nature proceeds from a mind
analogous to our own.

Nature proceeds from a mind congenial with ours. Nature is overflowed
and saturated with humanity. All things solicit us to know them by obscure
attractions which we call the beauty of nature. We explore them and learn
their law; straightway we find the discovery an exalting influence. So that I
may say, we more fully possess ourselves for our new possession. A certain
enthusiasm, as all know, has attended the great naturalists. As we learn more,
we see that it is natural to know. Each discovery takes away some deformity
from things, and gives them beauty; or takes away a less beauty, which hid a
greater. There is nothing in nature disagreeable, which science does not bereave of its offence. Anatomy and Chemistry awake an absorbing interest in
processes and sights the most tedious and revolting to the ignorant, so that it
is observed at universities that of all the liberal professions it is only students
of medicine who work out of study hours.

As we advance in knowledge we learn that all wears this great countenance of wisdom. Nothing is mean. It speaks to the noblest faculties. It conspires with piety: it conspires with poetry. It is the work of a perfect mind but
of one which he can follow and evermore become. The reason which in us is
so dim a ray, is a conflagration of light in Nature. Man sees that it is the measure of his attainments, for so much of nature as he is ignorant of, just so
much of his own mind does he not yet possess.

Reason finds itself at home in nature and everything fits man and is intelligible to him. My mind is not only an inlet into the human mind but into the

35

36

37

38

39

inferior intelligences that surround us in the field and stall. To this point let me quote a passage from the works of an acute observer, the eminent historian of the Anglo-Saxons.

> If I could transfer my own mind divested of all the human knowledge it has acquired, but with its natural faculties unimpaired into the body of any fowl, and could give it the ideas and memory which their organs and habits have acquired—should I in the exercise of my judgment on such sensations as theirs act otherwise than they do? When I have put the question to myself I have not been able to discern that I should. They seem to do all the things they ought, and to act with what may be called a steady common sense in their respective situations. I have never seen a bird do a foolish thing for a creature of its powers, frame, and organs. Each acts with a uniform propriety, nothing fantastic, absurd, inconsistent, maniacal, or contradictory appears in their simple habits or daily conduct. They seem to have mental faculties and feelings like mine up to a certain extent, but to that they are limited. They have not the universality, the diversifying capacity, nor the improvability of the human intellect.[16]

40   Whilst this analogy exists in the animated creation the inanimate is so far pervaded by a homogeneous design that the human reason is its interpreter and its prophet; for in how many instances has the sagacity of men of science anticipated a late discovery.

41   A very curious and sublime subject of speculation is the identity of nature's mind, and man's. We always confide that there is a reason for every fact in the order of nature, which, whenever we hit upon it, will justify the arrangement to our judgment also. I have seen certain fishes found in the waters of the Mammoth Cave of Kentucky, which have no eyes, nor any rudiments of eyes; for they are born in darkness, and live in the dark.[17] It is an example of the eternal relation betwixt power and use, and such as we should expect beforehand. Indeed, man may well be of the same mind as nature, for he too is a part of nature, and is inundated with the same genius or spirit. He lives by some pulsations of her life.

42   Man's wit is secondary to nature's wit. He applies himself to nature to

copy her methods, to imbibe her wisdom. The art of the surgeon limits itself to relieving the dislocated parts from their false position, putting them free;—they fly into place by action of their own muscles. The art of medicine is in removing and withholding causes of irritation. On this art of nature, all our arts rely. The correction of the refraction of glass, was borrowed from the use of two humours in the eye.

> For nature is made better by no mean
> But nature makes that mean.[18]

One can feel that we are brothers of the oak and of the grass, that the vegetable principle pervades human nature also. The old Norsemen represented the power of life by the tree Ygdrasil, which groweth out of Mimir's spring, where knowledge and wit are hidden.[19]

It grows when we sleep. It is observed that our mental processes go forward, even when they seem suspended. Scholars say, that, if they return to the study of a new language, after some interruption, the intelligence of it seems to have grown in their mind. A subject of thought to which we return from month to month, from year to year, has always some ripeness, of which we can give no account. Hence we say, the book grew in the author's mind.

And we are very conscious that this identity extends far wider than we know,—that it has no limits, or none that we can ascertain; as appears in the language men use in regard to men of extraordinary genius. For the signal performances of great men seem only the same art of nature applied to toys or puppets. Thus in Laplace and Napoleon, is the old planetary arithmetic now walking in a man; in the builder of Egyptian or in the designer of Gothic piles a reduction of nature's great aspects in caverns or forests to a scale of human convenience. And there is a conviction in the mind that some such impulse is constant, that if the solar system is good art and architecture, the same achievement is in our brain also, if only we can be kept in height of health, and hindered from any interference with our great instincts. The current knows the way to be realized in some distant future. Something like this is the root of all the great arts; of picture, music, sculpture, architecture, poetry. And the history of the highest genius will warrant the conclusion, that, in proportion as a man's life comes into union with nature, his thoughts run parallel with the creative law.

The history of science in the last and the present age teems with this

43

44

45

46

truth. The multitude of problems; the stimulated curiosity with which they have been pondered and solved, the formation of societies, the expeditions of discovery and the surveys, the gifts which science has made to the domestic arts are signs that the human race is in sympathy with this omnipresent spirit and in a perception of its rights and duties in regard to external nature.

47   Hence arises a corollary which every page of modern history repeats; that is, that science should be humanly studied. It will publish all its plan to a spirit akin to that which framed it. When science shall be studied with piety; when in a soul alive with moral sentiments, the antecedence of spirit is presupposed; then humanity advances, step by step with the opening of the intellect and its command over nature. Shall the problems never be assayed in a feeling of their beauty? Is not the poetic side of science entitled to be felt and presented by its investigators? Is it quite impossible to unite severe science with a poetic vision?

48   Nature's laws are as charming to Taste and as pregnant with moral meaning as they are geometrically exact. Why then must the student freeze his sensibilities and cease to be a man that he may be a chemist and a physiologist?

49   I know the cry which always arises from the learned at this expectation. It is like Bonaparte who charged Lafayette and every lover of freedom with being an ideologist.[20] They tax us directly with enthusiasm and dreamers.

50   It is certainly true that the tendency of imaginative men is to rash generalization and to the confounding of intuitive perception with conjecture. Conscious of good-meaning the poet leaps to a conclusion which is false. Whilst he is thus swift, Nature is not; she holds by herself; and he must be brought back from his error by a faithful comparison of the facts with his premature anticipation.

51   On the other hand, not less dangerous is the tendency of men of detail to distrust final causes, and the generous sovereign glances of the soul over things, and to cling to the cadaverous fact until Science becomes a dead catalogue, and arbitrary classification. Then, when facts are allowed to usurp the throne of the mind, and the naturalist works as the slave of nature, and loses sight of its origin in spirit connate, yea identical with his own, then is wrong done to human nature, science is unhallowed and baneful; as happened signally in philosophic France; and has often befallen individuals.

And just so far as the fear of theory and the idolatry of facts characterises
science, just so far must it lack the sympathy of humanity. The great men, the
heroes of science, are persons who added to their accuracy of study a sympathy with men, a strong common sense, and an earnest nature susceptible of
religion, as Kepler, Galileo, Newton, Linnaeus, and in our days Davy, Cuvier,
Humboldt. For it certainly must be, that not those parts of science which
here and there a virtuoso may love, as the reckoning of logarithms or minute
and merely curious chemical compositions, are the most attractive to the
great naturalist, but those which catch the eye and fire the curiosity of all
men: the discovery of a new planetary system, the discovery of a new analogy uniting great classes of hitherto sundered facts, the decomposition of diamond and the earths.

It is a characteristic of the present day that public education has advanced
so far as to create a great number of books, lectures, and experiments having
for their object to acquaint the people with the elements of the sciences. This
was at first ridiculed, and undoubtedly a large deduction is to be made from
the apparent result. What did it all signify? The Mechanics' Institutes had acquainted a few laboring men with the order of oolitic series or the habits of
the kangaroo.[21] But here is the benefit. It will be the effect of the populariza-
tion of science to keep the eye of scientific men on that human side of nature
wherein lie grandest truths. The poet, the priest must not only receive an inspiration, but they must bring the oracle low down to men in the market-
place. And why not Newton and Laplace? The education of the people forces
the savant to show the people something of his lore which they can comprehend, and he is taught by their taste to look for what humanity yet remains in
his science, and now calls to mind, seeing how it is valued, much that he has
forgotten. It lets in good sense upon it, which is to laboratories and telescopes
what the air of heaven is to dungeons or the hot chamber of the sick.

Any reader of history will see this clearly in comparing the science of antiquity with that of the present day, that the modern science is pervaded with
good sense. In antiquity a great man was allowed to give currency to a silly
opinion; as we read in Plutarch's *Placita Philosophorum* the grave nonsense of
Empedocles and Anaxagoras about astronomy and physics.[22] It could not
happen otherwise; it was the influence of genius when science was confined
to a few. But now the effect of National Education and of the Press is that

great numbers of men are directly or indirectly parties to the experiment of
the philosopher and judges of it; So that the great instincts of mankind, and
indeed the verdict of the Universal mind has an irresistible check upon the
whims and spirit of system of the individual. But it is only the morning of the
day. The philosopher and the philanthropist may forebode the time when an
interest like that which now is felt in scientific circles in the wonders opened
by Faraday, Ampere, and Oersted, in Magnetism and Electricity; a finger-
pointing at laws and powers of unrivalled simplicity and extent,—shall take
the place in the general mind of contemptible questions concerning persons
and interests which now divide men into parties and embitter and degrade
the mind of millions.[23]

55   The highest moral of science is the transference of that trust which is
felt in nature's admired arrangements, light, heat, gravity,—to the social and
moral order. The first effect of science is to stablish the mind, to disclose beneficent arrangements, to remove groundless terrors. Once we thought the
errors of Jupiter's moons were alarming; it was then shown that they were
periodic. More recently mankind have been frighted with news of a resisting
medium in the celestial spaces which threatens to throw all things into a
lump. Men of science conversant with these unerring agents, with stars, with
acids, with plants, with light, heat, gravity, are observed to grow calm and
simple in their manners and tastes, the calm and security of the order of nature steals into their lives, and the contrast between them and the irritability
of poetic genius appears to all and one may easily believe that a man of life-
long habit of observation of nature in the laboratory or the observatory who
should come into politics, or into courts of justice, or into trade, and see the
meanness and the falsehood which are so busy in these places, would conceive an impatience and disgust at this lawless and confused living. Let Newton or Cuvier or Laplace, peaceful with beholding the order of planets and of
strata, come into senates or bureaus, and see some pert boy with some con-
ceited proposition which he wishes to impose as a civil law on the millions of
subjects of an empire: and indeed the whole history of states has been the
uncalled for interference of foolish, selfish persons with the course of events.
They might well wish to fly,—as the old hermits, to their desart and cell;—so
these to their alembic and thermometer. Indeed, if they could entertain the
belief that these rash hands really possessed any power to change the course

of events, men would wish to rush by suicide out of the door of this staggering Temple.

But the survey of nature irresistibly suggests that the world is not a tinderbox left at the mercy of incendiaries. No outlaw, no anomaly, no violation, no impulse of absolute freedom is permitted to exist; that the circles of Law round in every exception and resistance, provide for every exigency, balance every excess. The self-equality in the birth of the sexes is constant; so is the relation of the animal to his food; so is the composition of the air in all places. The same symmetry and security is universal; and the inference is inevitable that the same Law extends into the kingdom of human life, and balances these refractory parties one against the other, and from age to age carries forward by war as well as by peace, by selfishness and ignorance and cheating, as well as by honour and love, the general prosperity and education of souls.

56

Notes

1. Attributed to Goethe by Emerson (*JMN*, 5:20).
2. Goethe published a study of optics in 1810.
3. Jean-Baptiste de Lamarck (1744–1829), French naturalist and forerunner of Darwin in evolutionary theory, classified animals into vertebrates and invertebrates.
4. "Romanism" refers to Roman Catholicism.
5. Phrenology is a way of reading a person's character through the configuration of his or her skull.
6. Between "the stomata in" and the semicolon there occurs a short blank space in the manuscript; as late as 1853 Emerson was undecided as to what word to insert (*JMN*, 13:229).
7. John Playfair (1749–1819), Scottish natural philosopher and geologist.
8. Mount Vesuvius in Italy erupted in 79 CE, burying Pompeii and two other cities.
9. Pieter Camper (1722–1789), Dutch physician and comparative anatomist.
10. Ernst Florens Friedrich Chladni (1756–1824), German physicist and authority on acoustics, invented the euphonium.
11. Robert Hooke (1635–1703), English scientist and experimental philosopher; Ruggiero Guiseppe Boscovich (1711–1787), Croatian Jesuit and mathematician and physicist, defined matter as composed of indivisible and mutually repulsive atoms.

12. Attributed to Goethe by Emerson (*EL*, 2:30n).

13. Attributed to Goethe by Emerson (*JMN*, 5:139).

14. James Hutton (1726–1797), Scottish geologist and naturalist.

15. Louis Agassiz (1807–1873), Swiss-born American naturalist and zoological explorer.

16. Attributed to Sharon Turner (1768–1847), English historian, in Emerson's note in the manuscript.

17. Emerson wrote his wife, Lidian Jackson Emerson (1802–1892), describing Mammoth Cave in Kentucky; see *L*, 4:211–214.

18. William Shakespeare, *The Winter's Tale*, IV, iv, 89–90.

19. Yggdrasil (or Igdrasil or Yggdrasil) in Norse mythology is an ash tree that binds earth, hell, and heaven together; Mimir, a water demon, is the Scandinavian god of wisdom; Mimir's Well (Mimisbrunner) is under the root of Yggdrasil.

20. Marie Joseph Paul Yves Roch Gilbert du Motier, marquis de Lafayette (1757–1834), French military leader and a hero of the American Revolution.

21. An "oolite" is a rock consisting of small grains, typically calcium carbonate, cemented together.

22. Empedocles (ca. 490–430 BCE), Greek poet, statesman, and philosopher who believed that he possessed magic powers; Anaxagoras (ca. 500–428 BCE), Greek philosopher whose work predicts atomic theory.

23. Michael Faraday (1791–1867), English chemist and physicist, known for his experiments with electromagnetism; André-Marie Ampère (1775–1836), French physicist who discovered the relationship between magnetism and electricity; Hans Christian Ørsted (1777–1851), Danish physicist and chemist, founded the study of electromagnetism.

The American Scholar

Mr. President and Gentlemen,[1]

I greet you on the re-commencement of our literary year. Our anniversary is one of hope, and, perhaps, not enough of labor. We do not meet for games of strength or skill, for the recitation of histories, tragedies, and odes, like the ancient Greeks; for parliaments of love and poesy, like the Troubadours; nor for the advancement of science, like our cotemporaries in the British and European capitals. Thus far, our holiday has been simply a friendly sign of the survival of the love of letters amongst a people too busy to give to letters any more. As such, it is precious as the sign of an indestructible instinct. Perhaps the time is already come, when it ought to be, and will be, something else; when the sluggard intellect of this continent will look from under its iron lids, and fill the postponed expectation of the world with something better than the exertions of mechanical skill. Our day of dependence, our long apprenticeship to the learning of other lands, draws to a close. The millions, that around us are rushing into life, cannot always be fed on the sere remains of foreign harvests. Events, actions arise, that must be sung, that will sing themselves. Who can doubt, that poetry will revive and lead in a new age, as the star in the constellation Harp,[2] which now flames in our zenith, astronomers announce, shall one day be the pole-star for a thousand years?

3   In the light of this hope, I accept the topic which not only usage, but the nature of our association, seem to prescribe to this day,—the AMERICAN SCHOLAR. Year by year, we come up hither to read one more chapter of his biography. Let us inquire what new lights, new events and more days have thrown on his character, his duties, and his hopes.

4   It is one of those fables, which, out of an unknown antiquity, convey an unlooked-for wisdom, that the gods, in the beginning, divided Man into men, that he might be more helpful to himself; just as the hand was divided into fingers, the better to answer its end.

5   The old fable covers a doctrine ever new and sublime; that there is One Man,—present to all particular men only partially, or through one faculty; and that you must take the whole society to find the whole man. Man is not a farmer, or a professor, or an engineer, but he is all. Man is priest, and scholar, and statesman, and producer, and soldier. In the *divided* or social state, these functions are parcelled out to individuals, each of whom aims to do his stint of the joint work, whilst each other performs his. The fable implies, that the individual, to possess himself, must sometimes return from his own labor to embrace all the other laborers. But unfortunately, this original unit, this fountain of power, has been so distributed to multitudes, has been so minutely subdivided and peddled out, that it is spilled into drops, and cannot be gathered. The state of society is one in which the members have suffered amputation from the trunk, and strut about so many walking monsters,—a good finger, a neck, a stomach, an elbow, but never a man.

6   Man is thus metamorphosed into a thing, into many things. The planter, who is Man sent out into the field to gather food, is seldom cheered by any idea of the true dignity of his ministry. He sees his bushel and his cart, and nothing beyond, and sinks into the farmer, instead of Man on the farm. The tradesman scarcely ever gives an ideal worth to his work, but is ridden by the routine of his craft, and the soul is subject to dollars. The priest becomes a form; the attorney, a statute-book; the mechanic, a machine; the sailor, a rope of a ship.

7   In this distribution of functions, the scholar is the delegated intellect. In the right state, he is, *Man Thinking.* In the degenerate state, when the victim of society, he tends to become a mere thinker, or, still worse, the parrot of other men's thinking.

8   In this view of him, as Man Thinking, the whole theory of his office is

contained. Him nature solicits with all her placid, all her monitory pictures. Him the past instructs. Him the future invites. Is not, indeed, every man a student, and do not all things exist for the student's behoof? And, finally, is not the true scholar the only true master? But, as the old oracle said, "All things have two handles. Beware of the wrong one."[3] In life, too often, the scholar errs with mankind and forfeits his privilege. Let us see him in his school, and consider him in reference to the main influences he receives.

I. The first in time and the first in importance of the influences upon the mind is that of nature. Every day, the sun; and, after sunset, night and her stars. Ever the winds blow; ever the grass grows. Every day, men and women, conversing, beholding and beholden. The scholar must needs stand wistful and admiring before this great spectacle. He must settle its value in his mind. What is nature to him? There is never a beginning, there is never an end, to the inexplicable continuity of this web of God, but always circular power returning into itself. Therein it resembles his own spirit, whose beginning, whose ending, he never can find,—so entire, so boundless. Far, too, as her splendors shine, system on system shooting like rays, upward, downward, without centre, without circumference,—in the mass and in the particle, nature hastens to render account of herself to the mind. Classification begins. To the young mind, every thing is individual, stands by itself. By and by, it finds how to join two things, and see in them one nature; then three, then three thousand; and so, tyrannized over by its own unifying instinct, it goes on tying things together, diminishing anomalies, discovering roots running under ground, whereby contrary and remote things cohere, and flower out from one stem. It presently learns, that, since the dawn of history, there has been a constant accumulation and classifying of facts. But what is classification but the perceiving that these objects are not chaotic, and are not foreign, but have a law which is also a law of the human mind? The astronomer discovers that geometry, a pure abstraction of the human mind, is the measure of planetary motion. The chemist finds proportions and intelligible method throughout matter; and science is nothing but the finding of analogy, identity, in the most remote parts. The ambitious soul sits down before each refractory fact; one after another, reduces all strange constitutions, all new powers, to their class and their law, and goes on forever to animate the last fibre of organization, the outskirts of nature, by insight.

10   Thus to him, to this school-boy under the bending dome of day, is suggested, that he and it proceed from one root; one is leaf and one is flower; relation, sympathy, stirring in every vein. And what is that Root? Is not that the soul of his soul?—A thought too bold,—a dream too wild. Yet when this spiritual light shall have revealed the law of more earthly natures,—when he has learned to worship the soul, and to see that the natural philosophy that now is, is only the first gropings of its gigantic hand, he shall look forward to an ever expanding knowledge as to a becoming creator. He shall see, that nature is the opposite of the soul, answering to it part for part. One is seal, and one is print. Its beauty is the beauty of his own mind. Its laws are the laws of his own mind. Nature then becomes to him the measure of his attainments. So much of nature as he is ignorant of, so much of his own mind does he not yet possess. And, in fine, the ancient precept, "Know thyself," and the modern precept, "Study nature," become at last one maxim.[4]

11   II. The next great influence into the spirit of the scholar, is, the mind of the Past,—in whatever form, whether of literature, of art, of institutions, that mind is inscribed. Books are the best type of the influence of the past, and perhaps we shall get at the truth,—learn the amount of this influence more conveniently,—by considering their value alone.

12   The theory of books is noble. The scholar of the first age received into him the world around; brooded thereon; gave it the new arrangement of his own mind, and uttered it again. It came into him,—life; it went out from him,—truth. It came to him,—short-lived actions; it went out from him,—immortal thoughts. It came to him,—business; it went from him,—poetry. It was,—dead fact; now, it is quick thought. It can stand, and it can go. It now endures, it now flies, it now inspires. Precisely in proportion to the depth of mind from which it issued, so high does it soar, so long does it sing.

13   Or, I might say, it depends on how far the process had gone, of transmuting life into truth. In proportion to the completeness of the distillation, so will the purity and imperishableness of the product be. But none is quite perfect. As no air-pump can by any means make a perfect vacuum, so neither can any artist entirely exclude the conventional, the local, the perishable from his book, or write a book of pure thought, that shall be as efficient, in all respects, to a remote posterity, as to cotemporaries, or rather to the second age.

Each age, it is found, must write its own books; or rather, each generation for the next succeeding. The books of an older period will not fit this.

Yet hence arises a grave mischief. The sacredness which attaches to the act of creation,—the act of thought,—is instantly transferred to the record. The poet chanting, was felt to be a divine man. Henceforth the chant is divine also. The writer was a just and wise spirit. Henceforward it is settled, the book is perfect; as love of the hero corrupts into worship of his statue. Instantly, the book becomes noxious. The guide is a tyrant. We sought a brother, and lo, a governor. The sluggish and perverted mind of the multitude, always slow to open to the incursions of Reason, having once so opened, having once received this book, stands upon it, and makes an outcry, if it is disparaged.[5] Colleges are built on it. Books are written on it by thinkers, not by Man Thinking; by men of talent, that is, who start wrong, who set out from accepted dogmas, not from their own sight of principles. Meek young men grow up in libraries, believing it their duty to accept the views, which Cicero, which Locke, which Bacon, have given, forgetful that Cicero, Locke, and Bacon were only young men in libraries when they wrote these books.[6]

Hence, instead of Man Thinking, we have the bookworm. Hence, the book-learned class, who value books, as such; not as related to nature and the human constitution, but as making a sort of Third Estate with the world and the soul. Hence, the restorers of readings, the emendators, the bibliomaniacs of all degrees.

This is bad; this is worse than it seems. Books are the best of things, well used; abused, among the worst. What is the right use? What is the one end, which all means go to effect? They are for nothing but to inspire. I had better never see a book than to be warped by its attraction clean out of my own orbit, and made a satellite instead of a system. The one thing in the world of value, is, the active soul,—the soul, free, sovereign, active. This every man is entitled to; this every man contains within him, although, in almost all men, obstructed, and as yet unborn. The soul active sees absolute truth; and utters truth, or creates. In this action, it is genius; not the privilege of here and there a favorite, but the sound estate of every man. In its essence, it is progressive. The book, the college, the school of art, the institution of any kind, stop with some past utterance of genius. This is good, say they,—let us hold by this.

14

15

16

They pin me down. They look backward and not forward. But genius always looks forward. The eyes of man are set in his forehead, not in his hindhead. Man hopes. Genius creates. To create,—to create,—is the proof of a divine presence. Whatever talents may be, if the man create not, the pure efflux of the Deity is not his;—cinders and smoke there may be, but not yet flame. There are creative manners, there are creative actions, and creative words; manners, actions, words, that is, indicative of no custom or authority, but springing spontaneous from the mind's own sense of good and fair.

17   On the other part, instead of being its own seer, let it receive always from another mind its truth, though it were in torrents of light, without periods of solitude, inquest, and self-recovery, and a fatal disservice is done. Genius is always sufficiently the enemy of genius by over-influence. The literature of every nation bear me witness. The English dramatic poets have Shakspearized now for two hundred years.

18   Undoubtedly there is a right way of reading, so it be sternly subordinated. Man Thinking must not be subdued by his instruments. Books are for the scholar's idle times. When he can read God directly, the hour is too precious to be wasted in other men's transcripts of their readings. But when the intervals of darkness come, as come they must,—when the soul seeth not, when the sun is hid, and the stars withdraw their shining,—we repair to the lamps which were kindled by their ray, to guide our steps to the East again, where the dawn is. We hear, that we may speak. The Arabian proverb says, "A fig tree, looking on a fig tree, becometh fruitful."

19   It is remarkable, the character of the pleasure we derive from the best books. They impress us ever with the conviction, that one nature wrote and the same reads. We read the verses of one of the great English poets, of Chaucer, of Marvell, of Dryden, with the most modern joy,—with a pleasure, I mean, which is in great part caused by the abstraction of all *time* from their verses.[7] There is some awe mixed with the joy of our surprise, when this poet, who lived in some past world, two or three hundred years ago, says that which lies close to my own soul, that which I also had wellnigh thought and said. But for the evidence thence afforded to the philosophical doctrine of the identity of all minds, we should suppose some preëstablished harmony, some foresight of souls that were to be, and some preparation of stores for their future wants, like the fact observed in insects, who lay up food before death for the young grub they shall never see.

I would not be hurried by any love of system, by any exaggeration of instincts, to underrate the Book. We all know, that, as the human body can be
nourished on any food, though it were boiled grass and the broth of shoes, so
the human mind can be fed by any knowledge. And great and heroic men
have existed, who had almost no other information than by the printed page.
I only would say, that it needs a strong head to bear that diet. One must be an
inventor to read well. As the proverb says, "He that would bring home the
wealth of the Indies, must carry out the wealth of the Indies."[8] There is then
creative reading as well as creative writing. When the mind is braced by labor
and invention, the page of whatever book we read becomes luminous with
manifold allusion. Every sentence is doubly significant, and the sense of our
author is as broad as the world. We then see, what is always true, that, as the
seer's hour of vision is short and rare among heavy days and months, so is its
record, perchance, the least part of his volume. The discerning will read, in
his Plato or Shakspeare, only that least part,—only the authentic utterances
of the oracle,—and all the rest he rejects, were it never so many times Plato's
and Shakspeare's.

Of course, there is a portion of reading quite indispensable to a wise
man. History and exact science he must learn by laborious reading. Colleges,
in like manner, have their indispensable office,—to teach elements. But they
can only highly serve us, when they aim not to drill, but to create; when they
gather from far every ray of various genius to their hospitable halls, and, by
the concentrated fires, set the hearts of their youth on flame. Thought and
knowledge are natures in which apparatus and pretension avail nothing.
Gowns, and pecuniary foundations, though of towns of gold, can never
countervail the least sentence or syllable of wit. Forget this, and our American colleges will recede in their public importance, whilst they grow richer
every year.

III. There goes in the world a notion, that the scholar should be a recluse,
a valetudinarian,—as unfit for any handiwork or public labor, as a penknife
for an axe.[9] The so-called 'practical men' sneer at speculative men, as if, because they speculate or *see,* they could do nothing. I have heard it said that the
clergy,—who are always, more universally than any other class, the scholars
of their day,—are addressed as women; that the rough, spontaneous conversation of men they do not hear, but only a mincing and diluted speech. They

are often virtually disfranchised; and, indeed, there are advocates for their celibacy. As far as this is true of the studious classes, it is not just and wise. Action is with the scholar subordinate, but it is essential. Without it, he is not yet man. Without it, thought can never ripen into truth. Whilst the world hangs before the eye as a cloud of beauty, we cannot even see its beauty. Inaction is cowardice, but there can be no scholar without the heroic mind. The preamble of thought, the transition through which it passes from the unconscious to the conscious, is action. Only so much do I know, as I have lived. Instantly we know whose words are loaded with life, and whose not.

23 The world,—this shadow of the soul, or *other me,* lies wide around. Its attractions are the keys which unlock my thoughts and make me acquainted with myself. I launch eagerly into this resounding tumult. I grasp the hands of those next me, and take my place in the ring to suffer and to work, taught by an instinct, that so shall the dumb abyss be vocal with speech. I pierce its order; I dissipate its fear; I dispose of it within the circuit of my expanding life. So much only of life as I know by experience, so much of the wilderness have I vanquished and planted, or so far have I extended my being, my dominion. I do not see how any man can afford, for the sake of his nerves and his nap, to spare any action in which he can partake. It is pearls and rubies to his discourse. Drudgery, calamity, exasperation, want, are instructers in eloquence and wisdom. The true scholar grudges every opportunity of action past by, as a loss of power.

24 It is the raw material out of which the intellect moulds her splendid products. A strange process too, this, by which experience is converted into thought, as a mulberry leaf is converted into satin. The manufacture goes forward at all hours.

25 The actions and events of our childhood and youth, are now matters of calmest observation. They lie like fair pictures in the air. Not so with our recent actions,—with the business which we now have in hand. On this we are quite unable to speculate. Our affections as yet circulate through it. We no more feel or know it, than we feel the feet, or the hand, or the brain of our body. The new deed is yet a part of life,—remains for a time immersed in our unconscious life. In some contemplative hour, it detaches itself from the life like a ripe fruit, to become a thought of the mind. Instantly, it is raised, transfigured; the corruptible has put on incorruption. Always now it is an

object of beauty, however base its origin and neighbourhood. Observe, too, the impossibility of antedating this act. In its grub state, it cannot fly, it cannot shine,—it is a dull grub. But suddenly, without observation, the selfsame thing unfurls beautiful wings, and is an angel of wisdom. So is there no fact, no event, in our private history, which shall not, sooner or later, lose its adhesive, inert form, and astonish us by soaring from our body into the empyrean.[10] Cradle and infancy, school and playground, the fear of boys, and dogs, and ferules, the love of little maids and berries, and many another fact that once filled the whole sky, are gone already; friend and relative, profession and party, town and country, nation and world, must also soar and sing.[11]

Of course, he who has put forth his total strength in fit actions, has the richest return of wisdom. I will not shut myself out of this globe of action and transplant an oak into a flower-pot, there to hunger and pine; nor trust the revenue of some single faculty, and exhaust one vein of thought, much like those Savoyards, who, getting their livelihood by carving shepherds, shepherdesses, and smoking Dutchmen, for all Europe, went out one day to the mountain to find stock, and discovered that they had whittled up the last of their pine trees.[12] Authors we have, in numbers, who have written out their vein, and who, moved by a commendable prudence, sail for Greece or Palestine, follow the trapper into the prairie, or ramble round Algiers to replenish their merchantable stock.

If it were only for a vocabulary the scholar would be covetous of action. Life is our dictionary. Years are well spent in country labors; in town,—in the insight into trades and manufactures; in frank intercourse with many men and women; in science; in art; to the one end of mastering in all their facts a language by which to illustrate and embody our perceptions. I learn immediately from any speaker how much he has already lived, through the poverty or the splendor of his speech. Life lies behind us as the quarry from whence we get tiles and copestones for the masonry of to-day. This is the way to learn grammar. Colleges and books only copy the language which the field and the work-yard made.

But the final value of action, like that of books, and better than books, is, that it is a resource. That great principle of Undulation in nature, that shows itself in the inspiring and expiring of the breath; in desire and satiety; in the ebb and flow of the sea; in day and night; in heat and cold; and as yet more

26

27

28

deeply ingrained in every atom and every fluid, is known to us under the name of Polarity,—these 'fits of easy transmission and reflection,' as Newton called them, are the law of nature because they are the law of spirit.

29   The mind now thinks; now acts; and each fit reproduces the other. When the artist has exhausted his materials, when the fancy no longer paints, when thoughts are no longer apprehended, and books are a weariness,—he has always the resource *to live*. Character is higher than intellect. Thinking is the function. Living is the functionary. The stream retreats to its source. A great soul will be strong to live, as well as strong to think. Does he lack organ or medium to impart his truths? He can still fall back on this elemental force of living them. This is a total act. Thinking is a partial act. Let the grandeur of justice shine in his affairs. Let the beauty of affection cheer his lowly roof. Those 'far from fame,' who dwell and act with him, will feel the force of his constitution in the doings and passages of the day better than it can be measured by any public and designed display. Time shall teach him, that the scholar loses no hour which the man lives. Herein he unfolds the sacred germ of his instinct, screened from influence. What is lost in seemliness is gained in strength. Not out of those, on whom systems of education have exhausted their culture, comes the helpful giant to destroy the old or to build the new, but out of unhandselled savage nature, out of terrible Druids and Berserkirs, come at last Alfred and Shakspeare.[13]

30   I hear therefore with joy whatever is beginning to be said of the dignity and necessity of labor to every citizen. There is virtue yet in the hoe and the spade, for learned as well as for unlearned hands. And labor is everywhere welcome; always we are invited to work; only be this limitation observed, that a man shall not for the sake of wider activity sacrifice any opinion to the popular judgments and modes of action.

31   I have now spoken of the education of the scholar by nature, by books, and by action. It remains to say somewhat of his duties.

32   They are such as become Man Thinking. They may all be comprised in self-trust. The office of the scholar is to cheer, to raise, and to guide men by showing them facts amidst appearances. He plies the slow, unhonored, and unpaid task of observation. Flamsteed and Herschel, in their glazed observatories, may catalogue the stars with the praise of all men, and, the results being splendid and useful, honor is sure.[14] But he, in his private observatory,

cataloguing obscure and nebulous stars of the human mind, which as yet no man has thought of as such,—watching days and months, sometimes, for a few facts; correcting still his old records;—must relinquish display and immediate fame. In the long period of his preparation, he must betray often an ignorance and shiftlessness in popular arts, incurring the disdain of the able who shoulder him aside. Long he must stammer in his speech; often forego the living for the dead. Worse yet, he must accept,—how often! poverty and solitude. For the ease and pleasure of treading the old road, accepting the fashions, the education, the religion of society, he takes the cross of making his own, and, of course, the self-accusation, the faint heart, the frequent uncertainty and loss of time, which are the nettles and tangling vines in the way of the self-relying and self-directed; and the state of virtual hostility in which he seems to stand to society, and especially to educated society. For all this loss and scorn, what offset? He is to find consolation in exercising the highest functions of human nature. He is one, who raises himself from private considerations, and breathes and lives on public and illustrious thoughts. He is the world's eye. He is the world's heart. He is to resist the vulgar prosperity that retrogrades ever to barbarism, by preserving and communicating heroic sentiments, noble biographies, melodious verse, and the conclusions of history. Whatsoever oracles the human heart in all emergencies, in all solemn hours, has uttered as its commentary on the world of actions,—these he shall receive and impart. And whatsoever new verdict Reason from her inviolable seat pronounces on the passing men and events of to-day,—this he shall hear and promulgate.

These being his functions, it becomes him to feel all confidence in himself, and to defer never to the popular cry. He and he only knows the world. The world of any moment is the merest appearance. Some great decorum, some fetish of a government, some ephemeral trade, or war, or man, is cried up by half mankind and cried down by the other half, as if all depended on this particular up or down. The odds are that the whole question is not worth the poorest thought which the scholar has lost in listening to the controversy. Let him not quit his belief that a popgun is a popgun, though the ancient and honorable of the earth affirm it to be the crack of doom. In silence, in steadiness, in severe abstraction, let him hold by himself; add observation to observation, patient of neglect, patient of reproach; and bide his own time,— happy enough, if he can satisfy himself alone, that this day he has seen

33

something truly. Success treads on every right step. For the instinct is sure, that prompts him to tell his brother what he thinks. He then learns, that in going down into the secrets of his own mind, he has descended into the secrets of all minds. He learns that he who has mastered any law in his private thoughts, is master to that extent of all men whose language he speaks, and of all into whose language his own can be translated. The poet, in utter solitude remembering his spontaneous thoughts and recording them, is found to have recorded that, which men in 'cities vast' find true for them also. The orator distrusts at first the fitness of his frank confessions,—his want of knowledge of the persons he addresses,—until he finds that he is the complement of his hearers;—that they drink his words because he fulfils for them their own nature; the deeper he dives into his privatest, secretest presentiment, to his wonder he finds, this is the most acceptable, most public, and universally true. The people delight in it; the better part of every man feels, This is my music; this is myself.

34   In self-trust, all the virtues are comprehended. Free should the scholar be,—free and brave. Free even to the definition of freedom, "without any hindrance that does not arise out of his own constitution."[15] Brave; for fear is a thing, which a scholar by his very function puts behind him. Fear always springs from ignorance. It is a shame to him if his tranquillity, amid dangerous times, arise from the presumption, that, like children and women, his is a protected class; or if he seek a temporary peace by the diversion of his thoughts from politics or vexed questions, hiding his head like an ostrich in the flowering bushes, peeping into microscopes, and turning rhymes, as a boy whistles to keep his courage up. So is the danger a danger still; so is the fear worse. Manlike let him turn and face it. Let him look into its eye and search its nature, inspect its origin,—see the whelping of this lion,—which lies no great way back; he will then find in himself a perfect comprehension of its nature and extent; he will have made his hands meet on the other side, and can henceforth defy it, and pass on superior. The world is his, who can see through its pretension. What deafness, what stone-blind custom, what overgrown error you behold, is there only by sufferance,—by your sufferance. See it to be a lie, and you have already dealt it its mortal blow.

35   Yes, we are the cowed,—we the trustless. It is a mischievous notion that we are come late into nature; that the world was finished a long time ago. As the world was plastic and fluid in the hands of God, so it is ever to so much of

his attributes as we bring to it. To ignorance and sin, it is flint. They adapt themselves to it as they may; but in proportion as a man has anything in him divine, the firmament flows before him and takes his signet and form. Not he is great who can alter matter, but he who can alter my state of mind. They are the kings of the world who give the color of their present thought to all nature and all art, and persuade men by the cheerful serenity of their carrying the matter, that this thing which they do, is the apple which the ages have desired to pluck, now at last ripe, and inviting nations to the harvest. The great man makes the great thing. Wherever Macdonald sits, there is the head of the table.[16] Linnæus makes botany the most alluring of studies and wins it from the farmer and the herb-woman. Davy, chemistry; and Cuvier, fossils. The day is always his, who works in it with serenity and great aims. The unstable estimates of men crowd to him whose mind is filled with a truth, as the heaped waves of the Atlantic follow the moon.

For this self-trust, the reason is deeper than can be fathomed,—darker than can be enlightened. I might not carry with me the feeling of my audience in stating my own belief. But I have already shown the ground of my hope, in adverting to the doctrine that man is one. I believe man has been wronged; he has wronged himself. He has almost lost the light, that can lead him back to his prerogatives. Men are become of no account. Men in history, men in the world of to-day are bugs, are spawn, and are called 'the mass' and 'the herd.' In a century, in a millenium, one or two men; that is to say,—one or two approximations to the right state of every man. All the rest behold in the hero or the poet their own green and crude being,—ripened; yes, and are content to be less, so *that* may attain to its full stature. What a testimony,— full of grandeur, full of pity, is borne to the demands of his own nature, by the poor clansman, the poor partisan, who rejoices in the glory of his chief. The poor and the low find some amends to their immense moral capacity, for their acquiescence in a political and social inferiority. They are content to be brushed like flies from the path of a great person, so that justice shall be done by him to that common nature which it is the dearest desire of all to see enlarged and glorified. They sun themselves in the great man's light, and feel it to be their own element. They cast the dignity of man from their downtrod selves upon the shoulders of a hero, and will perish to add one drop of blood to make that great heart beat, those giant sinews combat and conquer. He lives for us, and we live in him.

37   Men such as they are, very naturally seek money or power; and power because it is as good as money,—the 'spoils,' so called, 'of office.' And why not? for they aspire to the highest, and this, in their sleep-walking, they dream is highest. Wake them, and they shall quit the false good and leap to the true, and leave governments to clerks and desks. This revolution is to be wrought by the gradual domestication of the idea of Culture.[17] The main enterprise of the world for splendor, for extent, is the upbuilding of a man. Here are the materials strown along the ground. The private life of one man shall be a more illustrious monarchy,—more formidable to its enemy, more sweet and serene in its influence to its friend, than any kingdom in history. For a man, rightly viewed, comprehendeth the particular natures of all men. Each philosopher, each bard, each actor, has only done for me, as by a delegate, what one day I can do for myself. The books which once we valued more than the apple of the eye, we have quite exhausted. What is that but saying, that we have come up with the point of view which the universal mind took through the eyes of that one scribe; we have been that man, and have passed on. First, one; then, another; we drain all cisterns, and, waxing greater by all these supplies, we crave a better and more abundant food. The man has never lived that can feed us ever. The human mind cannot be enshrined in a person, who shall set a barrier on any one side to this unbounded, unboundable empire. It is one central fire, which, flaming now out of the lips of Etna, lightens the capes of Sicily; and, now out of the throat of Vesuvius, illuminates the towers and vineyards of Naples. It is one light which beams out of a thousand stars. It is one soul which animates all men.

38   But I have dwelt perhaps tediously upon this abstraction of the Scholar. I ought not to delay longer to add what I have to say, of nearer reference to the time and to this country.

39   Historically, there is thought to be a difference in the ideas which predominate over successive epochs, and there are data for marking the genius of the Classic, of the Romantic, and now of the Reflective or Philosophical age. With the views I have intimated of the oneness or the identity of the mind through all individuals, I do not much dwell on these differences. In fact, I believe each individual passes through all three. The boy is a Greek; the youth, romantic; the adult, reflective. I deny not, however, that a revolution in the leading idea may be distinctly enough traced.

Our age is bewailed as the age of Introversion. Must that needs be evil? We, it seems, are critical. We are embarrassed with second thoughts. We cannot enjoy any thing for hankering to know whereof the pleasure consists. We are lined with eyes. We see with our feet. The time is infected with Hamlet's unhappiness,—

    "Sicklied o'er with the pale cast of thought."[18]

Is it so bad then? Sight is the last thing to be pitied. Would we be blind? Do we fear lest we should outsee nature and God, and drink truth dry? I look upon the discontent of the literary class, as a mere announcement of the fact, that they find themselves not in the state of mind of their fathers, and regret the coming state as untried; as a boy dreads the water before he has learned that he can swim. If there is any period one would desire to be born in,—is it not the age of Revolution; when the old and the new stand side by side, and admit of being compared; when the energies of all men are searched by fear and by hope; when the historic glories of the old, can be compensated by the rich possibilities of the new era? This time, like all times, is a very good one, if we but know what to do with it.

I read with joy some of the auspicious signs of the coming days, as they glimmer already through poetry and art, through philosophy and science, through church and state.

One of these signs is the fact, that the same movement which effected the elevation of what was called the lowest class in the state, assumed in literature a very marked and as benign an aspect. Instead of the sublime and beautiful; the near, the low, the common, was explored and poetized. That, which had been negligently trodden under foot by those who were harnessing and provisioning themselves for long journeys into far countries, is suddenly found to be richer than all foreign parts. The literature of the poor, the feelings of the child, the philosophy of the street, the meaning of household life, are the topics of the time. It is a great stride. It is a sign,—is it not? of new vigor, when the extremities are made active, when currents of warm life run into the hands and the feet. I ask not for the great, the remote, the romantic; what is doing in Italy or Arabia; what is Greek art, or Provençal minstrelsy; I embrace the common, I explore and sit at the feet of the familiar, the low. Give me insight into to-day, and you may have the antique and future worlds. What would we really know the meaning of? The meal in the firkin;[19] the

40

41

42

43

milk in the pan; the ballad in the street; the news of the boat; the glance of the eye; the form and the gait of the body;—show me the ultimate reason of these matters; show me the sublime presence of the highest spiritual cause lurking, as always it does lurk, in these suburbs and extremities of nature; let me see every trifle bristling with the polarity that ranges it instantly on an eternal law; and the shop, the plough, and the leger, referred to the like cause by which light undulates and poets sing;—and the world lies no longer a dull miscellany and lumber-room, but has form and order; there is no trifle;[20] there is no puzzle; but one design unites and animates the farthest pinnacle and the lowest trench.

44   This idea has inspired the genius of Goldsmith, Burns, Cowper, and, in a newer time, of Goethe, Wordsworth, and Carlyle.[21] This idea they have differently followed and with various success. In contrast with their writing, the style of Pope, of Johnson, of Gibbon, looks cold and pedantic.[22] This writing is blood-warm. Man is surprised to find that things near are not less beautiful and wondrous than things remote. The near explains the far. The drop is a small ocean. A man is related to all nature. This perception of the worth of the vulgar is fruitful in discoveries. Goethe, in this very thing the most modern of the moderns, has shown us, as none ever did, the genius of the ancients.

45   There is one man of genius, who has done much for this philosophy of life, whose literary value has never yet been rightly estimated;—I mean Emanuel Swedenborg. The most imaginative of men, yet writing with the precision of a mathematician, he endeavoured to engraft a purely philosophical Ethics on the popular Christianity of his time. Such an attempt, of course, must have difficulty, which no genius could surmount. But he saw and showed the connexion between nature and the affections of the soul. He pierced the emblematic or spiritual character of the visible, audible, tangible world. Especially did his shade-loving muse hover over and interpret the lower parts of nature; he showed the mysterious bond that allies moral evil to the foul material forms, and has given in epical parables a theory of insanity, of beasts, of unclean and fearful things.

46   Another sign of our times, also marked by an analogous political movement, is, the new importance given to the single person. Every thing that tends to insulate the individual,—to surround him with barriers of natural respect, so that each man shall feel the world is his, and man shall treat with

man as a sovereign state with a sovereign state;—tends to true union as well as greatness. "I learned," said the melancholy Pestalozzi, "that no man in God's wide earth is either willing or able to help any other man."[23] Help must come from the bosom alone. The scholar is that man who must take up into himself all the ability of the time, all the contributions of the past, all the hopes of the future. He must be an university of knowledges. If there be one lesson more than another, which should pierce his ear, it is, The world is nothing, the man is all; in yourself is the law of all nature, and you know not yet how a globule of sap ascends; in yourself slumbers the whole of Reason; it is for you to know all, it is for you to dare all. Mr. President and Gentlemen, this confidence in the unsearched might of man belongs, by all motives, by all prophecy, by all preparation, to the American Scholar. We have listened too long to the courtly muses of Europe. The spirit of the American freeman is already suspected to be timid, imitative, tame. Public and private avarice make the air we breathe thick and fat. The scholar is decent, indolent, complaisant. See already the tragic consequence. The mind of this country, taught to aim at low objects, eats upon itself. There is no work for any but the decorous and the complaisant. Young men of the fairest promise, who begin life upon our shores, inflated by the mountain winds, shined upon by all the stars of God, find the earth below not in unison with these,—but are hindered from action by the disgust which the principles on which business is managed inspire, and turn drudges, or die of disgust,—some of them suicides. What is the remedy? They did not yet see, and thousands of young men as hopeful now crowding to the barriers for the career, do not yet see, that, if the single man plant himself indomitably on his instincts, and there abide, the huge world will come round to him. Patience,—patience;—with the shades of all the good and great for company; and for solace, the perspective of your own infinite life; and for work, the study and the communication of principles, the making those instincts prevalent, the conversion of the world. Is it not the chief disgrace in the world, not to be an unit;—not to be reckoned one character;—not to yield that peculiar fruit which each man was created to bear, but to be reckoned in the gross, in the hundred, or the thousand, of the party, the section, to which we belong; and our opinion predicted geographically, as the north, or the south. Not so, brothers and friends,— please God, ours shall not be so. We will walk on our own feet; we will work with our own hands; we will speak our own minds. Then shall man be no longer a name for pity, for doubt, and for sensual indulgence. The dread of man and the love of man shall be a wall of defence and a wreath of joy around all. A nation of men will for the first time exist, because each believes himself inspired by the Divine Soul which also inspires all men.

Notes

1. Emerson delivered his address before the Phi Beta Kappa Society of Harvard College on 31 August 1837. It was later titled "The American Scholar."
2. The constellation Lyra, which contains the white star Vega, the fourth brightest star in the heavens.
3. *Encheiridion,* by Epictetus, first-century Greek Stoic philosopher.
4. "Know thyself" is attributed to the Athenian lawgiver Solon (638–558 BCE).
5. When capitalized, as here, "Reason" is used in the special Coleridgean sense of the higher knowledge.
6. Marcus Tullius Cicero (106–43 BCE), Roman orator, philosopher, and statesman; John Locke (1632–1704), English founder of the sensationalist school of philosophy.
7. Geoffrey Chaucer (ca. 1342–1400), English poet best-known for *The Canterbury Tales;* Andrew Marvell (1621–1678), English metaphysical poet and satirist; and John Dryden (1631–1700), English poet and dramatist.
8. Emerson may have found this proverb quoted in James Boswell's *Life of Johnson.* Boswell (1740–1795), Scottish biographer and friend of Samuel Johnson (1709–1784), English lexicographer, editor, and critic.
9. A "valetudinarian" is someone who is weak, sickly, or infirm.
10. "Empyrean" refers to the highest heaven, where pure fire supposedly exists.
11. A "ferule" is a piece of wood used to strike unruly children on their palms.
12. Savoyards are natives of Savoy, an alpine region in eastern France.
13. Druids were ancient Celtic priests of wealth and power. The grandson of the Scandinavian Starkader was called Berserker ("bare of mail") because he fought without armor, hence, anyone who fights wildly and irrationally. Alfred the Great (849–899), king of England from 871 to his death.
14. John Flamsteed (1646–1719) and Sir William Herschel (1738–1822), English pioneers in modern astronomy.
15. Among the definitions of "freedom" in Webster's *Dictionary* (1828), which Emerson may have used, are "A state of exemption from the power or control of another" and "Without impediment or hindrance."
16. Paraphrase of "Where Macgregor sits, there is the head of the table," *Gnomologia,* No. 5122 (1732), by Thomas Fuller (1654–1734), English clergyman and physician.

Popularly attributed to Rob Roy Macgregor (ca. 1720) and said to have been quoted by the Scottish novelist Sir Walter Scott (1771–1832), author of *Rob Roy* (1818).

17. In Emerson's special sense of the word "Culture," "the basis of Culture is that part of human nature which in philosophy is called the ideal" (*EL*, 1:217), and its unfolding in himself "is the chief end of man" (*EL*, 1:215).

18. Shakespeare, *Hamlet,* III, i, 85–87.

19. A "firkin" is a small cask or vessel.

20. Colloquially, a "lumber-room" is a site where unused furniture or other miscellanea may be stored.

21. Oliver Goldsmith (1728–1774), multifaceted English writer born in Ireland; Robert Burns (1759–1796), Scotland's most famous poet; and William Cowper (1731–1806), English poet and satirist.

22. Alexander Pope (1688–1744), English poet who championed the heroic couplet.

23. Johann Heinrich Pestalozzi (1746–1827), Swiss educator, whose organic principles of education were followed by Bronson Alcott.

The Divinity School Address[1]

In this refulgent summer it has been a luxury to draw the breath of life. The grass grows, the buds burst, the meadow is spotted with fire and gold in the tint of flowers. The air is full of birds, and sweet with the breath of the pine, the balm-of-Gilead, and the new hay. Night brings no gloom to the heart with its welcome shade. Through the transparent darkness pour the stars their almost spiritual rays. Man under them seems a young child, and his huge globe a toy. The cool night bathes the world as with a river, and prepares his eyes again for the crimson dawn. The mystery of nature was never displayed more happily. The corn and the wine have been freely dealt to all creatures, and the never-broken silence with which the old bounty goes forward, has not yielded yet one word of explanation. One is constrained to respect the perfection of this world, in which our senses converse. How wide; how rich; what invitation from every property it gives to every faculty of man! In its fruitful soils; in its navigable sea; in its mountains of metal and stone; in its forests of all woods; in its animals; in its chemical ingredients; in the powers and path of light, heat, attraction, and life, is it well worth the pith and heart of great men to subdue and enjoy it. The planters, the mechanics, the inventors, the astronomers, the builders of cities, and the captains, history delights to honor.

But the moment the mind opens, and reveals the laws which traverse the   2
universe, and make things what they are, then shrinks the great world at once
into a mere illustration and fable of this mind. What am I? and What is? asks
the human spirit with a curiosity new-kindled, but never to be quenched. Behold these outrunning laws, which our imperfect apprehension can see tend
this way and that, but not come full circle. Behold these infinite relations, so
like, so unlike; many, yet one. I would study, I would know, I would admire
forever. These works of thought have been the entertainments of the human
spirit in all ages.

A more secret, sweet, and overpowering beauty appears to man when his   3
heart and mind open to the sentiment of virtue. Then instantly he is instructed in what is above him. He learns that his being is without bound; that,
to the good, to the perfect, he is born, low as he now lies in evil and weakness. That which he venerates is still his own, though he has not realized it
yet. *He ought.* He knows the sense of that grand word, though his analysis
fails entirely to render account of it. When in innocency, or when by intellectual perception, he attains to say,—'I love the Right; Truth is beautiful within
and without, forevermore. Virtue, I am thine: save me: use me: thee will I
serve, day and night, in great, in small, that I may be not virtuous, but virtue;'—then is the end of the creation answered, and God is well pleased.

The sentiment of virtue is a reverence and delight in the presence of cer-   4
tain divine laws. It perceives that this homely game of life we play, covers,
under what seem foolish details, principles that astonish. The child amidst his
baubles, is learning the action of light, motion, gravity, muscular force; and in
the game of human life, love, fear, justice, appetite, man, and God, interact.
These laws refuse to be adequately stated. They will not by us or for us be
written out on paper, or spoken by the tongue. They elude, evade our persevering thought, and yet we read them hourly in each other's faces, in each
other's actions, in our own remorse. The moral traits which are all globed
into every virtuous act and thought,—in speech, we must sever, and describe
or suggest by painful enumeration of many particulars. Yet, as this sentiment
is the essence of all religion, let me guide your eye to the precise objects of
the sentiment, by an enumeration of some of those classes of facts in which
this element is conspicuous.

The intuition of the moral sentiment is an insight of the perfection of the   5
laws of the soul. These laws execute themselves. They are out of time, out of
space, and not subject to circumstance. Thus; in the soul of man there is a

justice whose retributions are instant and entire. He who does a good deed, is instantly ennobled himself. He who does a mean deed, is by the action itself contracted. He who puts off impurity, thereby puts on purity. If a man is at heart just, then in so far is he God; the safety of God, the immortality of God, the majesty of God do enter into that man with justice. If a man dissemble, deceive, he deceives himself, and goes out of acquaintance with his own being. A man in the view of absolute goodness, adores, with total humility. Every step so downward, is a step upward. The man who renounces himself, comes to himself by so doing.

6   See how this rapid intrinsic energy worketh everywhere, righting wrongs, correcting appearances, and bringing up facts to a harmony with thoughts. Its operation in life, though slow to the senses, is, at last, as sure as in the soul. By it, a man is made the Providence to himself, dispensing good to his goodness, and evil to his sin. Character is always known. Thefts never enrich; alms never impoverish; murder will speak out of stone walls. The least admixture of a lie,—for example, the smallest mixture of vanity, the least attempt to make a good impression, a favorable appearance,—will instantly vitiate the effect. But speak the truth, and all nature and all spirits help you with unexpected furtherance. Speak the truth, and all things alive or brute are vouchers, and the very roots of the grass underground there, do seem to stir and move to bear you witness. See again the perfection of the Law as it applies itself to the affections, and becomes the law of society. As we are, so we associate. The good, by affinity, seek the good; the vile, by affinity, the vile. Thus of their own volition, souls proceed into heaven, into hell.

7   These facts have always suggested to man the sublime creed, that the world is not the product of manifold power, but of one will, of one mind; and that one mind is everywhere, in each ray of the star, in each wavelet of the pool, active; and whatever opposes that will, is everywhere baulked and baffled, because things are made so, and not otherwise. Good is positive. Evil is merely privative, not absolute. It is like cold, which is the privation of heat. All evil is so much death or nonentity. Benevolence is absolute and real. So much benevolence as a man hath, so much life hath he. For all things proceed out of this same spirit, which is differently named love, justice, temperance, in its different applications, just as the ocean receives different names on the several shores which it washes. All things proceed out of the same spirit, and all things conspire with it. Whilst a man seeks good ends, he is strong by the

whole strength of nature. In so far as he roves from these ends, he bereaves himself of power, of auxiliaries; his being shrinks out of all remote channels, he becomes less and less, a mote, a point, until absolute badness is absolute death.

The perception of this law of laws always awakens in the mind a sentiment which we call the religious sentiment, and which makes our highest happiness. Wonderful is its power to charm and to command. It is a mountain air. It is the embalmer of the world. It is myrrh and storax, and chlorine and rosemary. It makes the sky and the hills sublime, and the silent song of the stars is it. By it, is the universe made safe and habitable, not by science or power. Thought may work cold and intransitive in things, and find no end or unity. But the dawn of the sentiment of virtue on the heart, gives and is the assurance that Law is sovereign over all natures; and the worlds, time, space, eternity, do seem to break out into joy. 8

This sentiment is divine and deifying. It is the beatitude of man. It makes him illimitable. Through it, the soul first knows itself. It corrects the capital mistake of the infant man, who seeks to be great by following the great, and hopes to derive advantages *from another,*—by showing the fountain of all good to be in himself, and that he, equally with every man, is a door into the deeps of Reason. When he says, "I ought;" when love warms him; when he chooses, warned from on high, the good and great deed; then, deep melodies wander through his soul from Supreme Wisdom. Then he can worship, and be enlarged by his worship; for he can never go behind this sentiment. In the sublimest flights of the soul, rectitude is never surmounted, love is never outgrown. 9

This sentiment lies at the foundation of society, and successively creates all forms of worship. The principle of veneration never dies out. Man fallen into superstition, into sensuality, is never wholly without the visions of the moral sentiment. In like manner, all the expressions of this sentiment are sacred and permanent in proportion to their purity. The expressions of this sentiment affect us deeper, greatlier, than all other compositions. The sentences of the oldest time, which ejaculate this piety, are still fresh and fragrant. This thought dwelled always deepest in the minds of men in the devout and contemplative East; not alone in Palestine, where it reached its purest expression, but in Egypt, in Persia, in India, in China. Europe has always owed to oriental genius, its divine impulses. What these holy bards said, all sane men 10 found agreeable and true. And the unique impression of Jesus upon mankind, whose name is not so much written as ploughed into the history of this world, is proof of the subtle virtue of this infusion.

11   Meantime, whilst the doors of the temple stand open, night and day, before every man, and the oracles of this truth cease never, it is guarded by one stern condition; this, namely; It is an intuition. It cannot be received at second hand. Truly speaking, it is not instruction, but provocation, that I can receive from another soul. What he announces, I must find true in me, or wholly reject; and on his word, or as his second, be he who he may, I can accept nothing. On the contrary, the absence of this primary faith is the presence of degradation. As is the flood so is the ebb. Let this faith depart, and the very words it spake, and the things it made, become false and hurtful. Then falls the church, the state, art, letters, life. The doctrine of the divine nature being forgotten, a sickness infects and dwarfs the constitution. Once man was all; now he is an appendage, a nuisance. And because the indwelling Supreme Spirit cannot wholly be got rid of, the doctrine of it suffers this perversion, that the divine nature is attributed to one or two persons, and denied to all the rest, and denied with fury. The doctrine of inspiration is lost; the base doctrine of the majority of voices, usurps the place of the doctrine of the soul. Miracles, prophecy, poetry, the ideal life, the holy life, exist as ancient history merely; they are not in the belief, nor in the aspiration of society; but, when suggested, seem ridiculous. Life is comic or pitiful, as soon as the high ends of being fade out of sight, and man becomes near-sighted, and can only attend to what addresses the senses.

12   These general views, which, whilst they are general, none will contest, find abundant illustration in the history of religion, and especially in the history of the Christian church. In that, all of us have had our birth and nurture. The truth contained in that, you, my young friends, are now setting forth to teach. As the Cultus, or established worship of the civilized world, it has great historical interest for us. Of its blessed words, which have been the consolation of humanity, you need not that I should speak. I shall endeavor to discharge my duty to you, on this occasion, by pointing out two errors in its administration, which daily appear more gross from the point of view we have just now taken.

13   Jesus Christ belonged to the true race of prophets. He saw with open eye the mystery of the soul. Drawn by its severe harmony, ravished with its

beauty, he lived in it, and had his being there. Alone in all history, he estimated the greatness of man. One man was true to what is in you and me. He
saw that God incarnates himself in man, and evermore goes forth anew to
take possession of his world. He said, in this jubilee of sublime emotion, 'I
am divine. Through me, God acts; through me, speaks. Would you see God,
see me; or, see thee, when thou also thinkest as I now think.' But what a dis-
tortion did his doctrine and memory suffer in the same, in the next, and the
following ages! There is no doctrine of the Reason which will bear to be
taught by the Understanding. The understanding caught this high chant from
the poet's lips, and said, in the next age, 'This was Jehovah come down out
of heaven. I will kill you, if you say he was a man.' The idioms of his language, and the figures of his rhetoric, have usurped the place of his truth; and
churches are not built on his principles, but on his tropes. Christianity became a Mythus, as the poetic teaching of Greece and of Egypt, before. He
spoke of miracles; for he felt that man's life was a miracle, and all that man
doth, and he knew that this daily miracle shines, as the man is diviner. But the
very word Miracle, as pronounced by Christian churches, gives a false impression; it is Monster. It is not one with the blowing clover and the falling
rain.

He felt respect for Moses and the prophets; but no unfit tenderness at
postponing their initial revelations, to the hour and the man that now is; to
the eternal revelation in the heart. Thus was he a true man. Having seen that
the law in us is commanding, he would not suffer it to be commanded. Boldly,
with hand, and heart, and life, he declared it was God. Thus was he a true
man. Thus is he, as I think, the only soul in history who has appreciated the
worth of a man.

1. In thus contemplating Jesus, we become very sensible of the first defect
of historical Christianity. Historical Christianity has fallen into the error that
corrupts all attempts to communicate religion. As it appears to us, and as it
has appeared for ages, it is not the doctrine of the soul, but an exaggeration
of the personal, the positive, the ritual. It has dwelt, it dwells, with noxious
exaggeration about the *person* of Jesus. The soul knows no persons. It invites
every man to expand to the full circle of the universe, and will have no prefer-
ences but those of spontaneous love. But by this eastern monarchy of a
Christianity, which indolence and fear have built, the friend of man is made
the injurer of man. The manner in which his name is surrounded with ex-

pressions, which were once sallies of admiration and love, but are now petrified into official titles, kills all generous sympathy and liking. All who hear me, feel, that the language that describes Christ to Europe and America, is not the style of friendship and enthusiasm to a good and noble heart, but is appropriated and formal,—paints a demigod, as the Orientals or the Greeks would describe Osiris or Apollo.[2] Accept the injurious impositions of our early catechetical instruction, and even honesty and self-denial were but splendid sins, if they did not wear the Christian name. One would rather be

"A pagan suckled in a creed outworn,"[3]

than to be defrauded of his manly right in coming into nature, and finding not names and places, not land and professions, but even virtue and truth foreclosed and monopolized. You shall not be a man even. You shall not own the world; you shall not dare, and live after the infinite Law that is in you, and in company with the infinite Beauty which heaven and earth reflect to you in all lovely forms; but you must subordinate your nature to Christ's nature; you must accept our interpretations; and take his portrait as the vulgar draw it.

16   That is always best which gives me to myself. The sublime is excited in me by the great stoical doctrine, Obey thyself. That which shows God in me, fortifies me. That which shows God out of me, makes me a wart and a wen. There is no longer a necessary reason for my being. Already the long shadows of untimely oblivion creep over me, and I shall decease forever.

17   The divine bards are the friends of my virtue, of my intellect, of my strength. They admonish me, that the gleams which flash across my mind, are not mine, but God's; that they had the like, and were not disobedient to the heavenly vision.[4] So I love them. Noble provocations go out from them, inviting me also to emancipate myself; to resist evil; to subdue the world; and to Be. And thus by his holy thoughts, Jesus serves us, and thus only. To aim to convert a man by miracles, is a profanation of the soul. A true conversion, a true Christ, is now, as always, to be made, by the reception of beautiful sentiments. It is true that a great and rich soul, like his, falling among the simple, does so preponderate, that, as his did, it names the world. The world seems to them to exist for him, and they have not yet drunk so deeply of his sense, as to see that only by coming again to themselves, or to God in themselves, can they grow forevermore. It is a low benefit to give me something; it is a high benefit to enable me to do somewhat of myself. The time is coming

when all men will see, that the gift of God to the soul is not a vaunting, over-powering, excluding sanctity, but a sweet, natural goodness, a goodness like thine and mine, and that so invites thine and mine to be and to grow.

The injustice of the vulgar tone of preaching is not less flagrant to Jesus, than it is to the souls which it profanes. The preachers do not see that they make his gospel not glad, and shear him of the locks of beauty and the attri-butes of heaven. When I see a majestic Epaminondas, or Washington;[5] when I see among my contemporaries, a true orator, an upright judge, a dear friend; when I vibrate to the melody and fancy of a poem; I see beauty that is to be desired. And so lovely, and with yet more entire consent of my human being, sounds in my ear the severe music of the bards that have sung of the true God in all ages. Now do not degrade the life and dialogues of Christ out of the circle of this charm, by insulation and peculiarity. Let them lie as they befel, alive and warm, part of human life, and of the landscape, and of the cheerful day.

2. The second defect of the traditionary and limited way of using the mind of Christ is a consequence of the first; this, namely; that the Moral Na-ture, that Law of laws, whose revelations introduce greatness,—yea, God himself, into the open soul, is not explored as the fountain of the established teaching in society. Men have come to speak of the revelation as somewhat long ago given and done, as if God were dead. The injury to faith throttles the preacher; and the goodliest of institutions becomes an uncertain and in-articulate voice.

It is very certain that it is the effect of conversation with the beauty of the soul, to beget a desire and need to impart to others the same knowledge and love. If utterance is denied, the thought lies like a burden on the man. Always the seer is a sayer. Somehow his dream is told. Somehow he publishes it with solemn joy. Sometimes with pencil on canvas; sometimes with chisel on stone; sometimes in towers and aisles of granite, his soul's worship is builded; sometimes in anthems of indefinite music; but clearest and most permanent, in words.

The man enamored of this excellency, becomes its priest or poet. The of-fice is coeval with the world. But observe the condition, the spiritual limita-tion of the office. The spirit only can teach. Not any profane man, not any sensual, not any liar, not any slave can teach, but only he can give, who has; he only can create, who is. The man on whom the soul descends, through

18

19

20

21

whom the soul speaks, alone can teach. Courage, piety, love, wisdom, can teach; and every man can open his door to these angels, and they shall bring him the gift of tongues. But the man who aims to speak as books enable, as synods use, as the fashion guides, and as interest commands, babbles. Let him hush.

22   To this holy office, you propose to devote yourselves. I wish you may feel your call in throbs of desire and hope. The office is the first in the world. It is of that reality, that it cannot suffer the deduction of any falsehood. And it is my duty to say to you, that the need was never greater of new revelation than now. From the views I have already expressed, you will infer the sad conviction, which I share, I believe, with numbers, of the universal decay and now almost death of faith in society. The soul is not preached. The Church seems to totter to its fall, almost all life extinct.[6] On this occasion, any complaisance, would be criminal, which told you, whose hope and commission it is to preach the faith of Christ, that the faith of Christ is preached.

23   It is time that this ill-suppressed murmur of all thoughtful men against the famine of our churches; this moaning of the heart because it is bereaved of the consolation, the hope, the grandeur, that come alone out of the culture of the moral nature; should be heard through the sleep of indolence, and over the din of routine. This great and perpetual office of the preacher is not discharged. Preaching is the expression of the moral sentiment in application to the duties of life. In how many churches, by how many prophets, tell me, is man made sensible that he is an infinite Soul; that the earth and heavens are passing into his mind; that he is drinking forever the soul of God? Where now sounds the persuasion, that by its very melody imparadises my heart, and so affirms its own origin in heaven? Where shall I hear words such as in elder ages drew men to leave all and follow,—father and mother, house and land, wife and child? Where shall I hear these august laws of moral being so pronounced, as to fill my ear, and I feel ennobled by the offer of my uttermost action and passion? The test of the true faith, certainly, should be its power to charm and command the soul, as the laws of nature control the activity of the hands,—so commanding that we find pleasure and honor in obeying. The faith should blend with the light of rising and of setting suns, with the flying cloud, the singing bird, and the breath of flowers. But now the priest's Sabbath has lost the splendor of nature; it is unlovely; we are glad

when it is done; we can make, we do make, even sitting in our pews, a far better, holier, sweeter, for ourselves.

Whenever the pulpit is usurped by a formalist, then is the worshipper defrauded and disconsolate. We shrink as soon as the prayers begin, which do not uplift, but smite and offend us. We are fain to wrap our cloaks about us, and secure, as best we can, a solitude that hears not. I once heard a preacher who sorely tempted me to say, I would go to church no more. Men go, thought I, where they are wont to go, else had no soul entered the temple in the afternoon. A snowstorm was falling around us. The snowstorm was real; the preacher merely spectral; and the eye felt the sad contrast in looking at him, and then out of the window behind him, into the beautiful meteor of the snow.[7] He had lived in vain. He had no one word intimating that he had laughed or wept, was married or in love, had been commended, or cheated, or chagrined. If he had ever lived and acted, we were none the wiser for it. The capital secret of his profession, namely, to convert life into truth, he had not learned. Not one fact in all his experience, had he yet imported into his doctrine. This man had ploughed, and planted, and talked, and bought, and sold; he had read books; he had eaten and drunken; his head aches; his heart throbs; he smiles and suffers; yet was there not a surmise, a hint, in all the discourse, that he had ever lived at all. Not a line did he draw out of real history. The true preacher can always be known by this, that he deals out to the people his life,—life passed through the fire of thought. But of the bad preacher, it could not be told from his sermon, what age of the world he fell in; whether he had a father or a child; whether he was a freeholder or a pauper; whether he was a citizen or a countryman; or any other fact of his biography.

It seemed strange that the people should come to church. It seemed as if their houses were very unentertaining, that they should prefer this thoughtless clamor. It shows that there is a commanding attraction in the moral sentiment, that can lend a faint tint of light to dulness and ignorance, coming in its name and place. The good hearer is sure he has been touched sometimes; is sure there is somewhat to be reached, and some word that can reach it. When he listens to these vain words, he comforts himself by their relation to his remembrance of better hours, and so they clatter and echo unchallenged.

I am not ignorant that when we preach unworthily, it is not always quite

24

25

26

in vain. There is a good ear, in some men, that draws supplies to virtue out of very indifferent nutriment. There is poetic truth concealed in all the common-places of prayer and of sermons, and though foolishly spoken, they may be wisely heard; for, each is some select expression that broke out in a moment of piety from some stricken or jubilant soul, and its excellency made it remembered. The prayers and even the dogmas of our church, are like the zodiac of Denderah, and the astronomical monuments of the Hindoos, wholly insulated from anything now extant in the life and business of the people.[8] They mark the height to which the waters once rose. But this docility is a check upon the mischief from the good and devout. In a large portion of the community, the religious service gives rise to quite other thoughts and emotions. We need not chide the negligent servant. We are struck with pity, rather, at the swift retribution of his sloth. Alas for the unhappy man that is called to stand in the pulpit, and *not* give bread of life. Everything that befals, accuses him. Would he ask contributions for the missions, foreign or domestic? Instantly his face is suffused with shame, to propose to his parish, that they should send money a hundred or a thousand miles, to furnish such poor fare as they have at home, and would do well to go the hundred or the thousand miles, to escape. Would he urge people to a godly way of living;—and can he ask a fellow creature to come to Sabbath meetings, when he and they all know what is the poor uttermost they can hope for therein? Will he invite them privately to the Lord's Supper?[9] He dares not. If no heart warm this rite, the hollow, dry, creaking formality is too plain, than that he can face a man of wit and energy, and put the invitation without terror. In the street, what has he to say to the bold village blasphemer? The village blasphemer sees fear in the face, form, and gait of the minister.

27   Let me not taint the sincerity of this plea by any oversight of the claims of good men. I know and honor the purity and strict conscience of numbers of the clergy. What life the public worship retains, it owes to the scattered company of pious men, who minister here and there in the churches, and who, sometimes accepting with too great tenderness the tenet of the elders, have not accepted from others, but from their own heart, the genuine impulses of virtue, and so still command our love and awe, to the sanctity of character. Moreover, the exceptions are not so much to be found in a few eminent preachers, as in the better hours, the truer inspirations of all,—nay, in the sincere moments of every man. But with whatever exception, it is still

true, that tradition characterizes the preaching of this country; that it comes out of the memory, and not out of the soul; that it aims at what is usual, and not at what is necessary and eternal; that thus, historical Christianity destroys the power of preaching, by withdrawing it from the exploration of the moral nature of man, where the sublime is, where are the resources of astonishment and power. What a cruel injustice it is to that Law, the joy of the whole earth, which alone can make thought dear and rich; that Law whose fatal sureness the astronomical orbits poorly emulate, that it is travestied and depreciated, that it is behooted and behowled, and not a trait, not a word of it articulated. The pulpit in losing sight of this Law, loses all its inspiration, and gropes after it knows not what. And for want of this culture, the soul of the community is sick and faithless. It wants nothing so much as a stern, high, stoical, Christian discipline, to make it know itself and the divinity that speaks through it. Now man is ashamed of himself; he skulks and sneaks through the world, to be tolerated, to be pitied, and scarcely in a thousand years does any man dare to be wise and good, and so draw after him the tears and blessings of his kind.

Certainly there have been periods when, from the inactivity of the intellect on certain truths, a greater faith was possible in names and persons. The Puritans in England and America, found in the Christ of the Catholic Church, and in the dogmas inherited from Rome, scope for their austere piety, and their longings for civil freedom.[10] But their creed is passing away, and none arises in its room. I think no man can go with his thoughts about him, into one of our churches, without feeling that what hold the public worship had on men, is gone or going. It has lost its grasp on the affection of the good, and the fear of the bad. In the country,—neighborhoods, half parishes are *signing off*,—to use the local term. It is already beginning to indicate character and religion to withdraw from the religious meetings. I have heard a devout person, who prized the Sabbath, say in bitterness of heart, "On Sundays, it seems wicked to go to church."[11] And the motive, that holds the best there, is now only a hope and a waiting. What was once a mere circumstance, that the best and the worst men in the parish, the poor and the rich, the learned and the ignorant, young and old, should meet one day as fellows in one house, in sign of an equal right in the soul,—has come to be a paramount motive for going thither.

My friends, in these two errors, I think, I find the causes of that calamity of a decaying church and a wasting unbelief, which are casting malignant influences around us, and making the hearts of good men sad. And what greater calamity can fall upon a nation, than the loss of worship? Then all things go to decay. Genius leaves the temple, to haunt the senate, or the market. Literature becomes frivolous. Science is cold. The eye of youth is not lighted by the hope of other worlds, and age is without honor. Society lives to trifles, and when men die, we do not mention them.

30   And now, my brothers, you will ask, What in these desponding days can be done by us? The remedy is already declared in the ground of our complaint of the Church. We have contrasted the Church with the Soul. In the soul, then, let the redemption be sought. In one soul, in your soul, there are resources for the world. Wherever a man comes, there comes revolution. The old is for slaves. When a man comes, all books are legible, all things transparent, all religions are forms. He is religious. Man is the wonderworker. He is seen amid miracles. All men bless and curse. He saith yea and nay, only. The stationariness of religion; the assumption that the age of inspiration is past, that the Bible is closed; the fear of degrading the character of Jesus by representing him as a man; indicate with sufficient clearness the falsehood of our theology. It is the office of a true teacher to show us that God is, not was; that He speaketh, not spake. The true Christianity,—a faith like Christ's in the infinitude of man,—is lost. None believeth in the soul of man, but only in some man or person old and departed. Ah me! no man goeth alone. All men go in flocks to this saint or that poet, avoiding the God who seeth in secret.[12] They cannot see in secret; they love to be blind in public. They think society wiser than their soul, and know not that one soul, and their soul, is wiser than the whole world. See how nations and races flit by on the sea of time, and leave no ripple to tell where they floated or sunk, and one good soul shall make the name of Moses, or of Zeno, or of Zoroaster, reverend forever.[13] None assayeth the stern ambition to be the Self of the nation, and of nature, but each would be an easy secondary to some Christian scheme, or sectarian connexion, or some eminent man. Once leave your own knowledge of God, your own sentiment, and take secondary knowledge, as St. Paul's, or George Fox's, or Swedenborg's, and you get wide from God with every year this secondary form lasts, and if, as now, for centuries,—the chasm yawns to that breadth, that men can scarcely be convinced there is in them anything divine.

31   Let me admonish you, first of all, to go alone; to refuse the good models,

even those most sacred in the imagination of men, and dare to love God without mediator or veil. Friends enough you shall find who will hold up to your emulation Wesleys and Oberlins, Saints and Prophets.[14] Thank God for these good men, but say, 'I also am a man.' Imitation cannot go above its model. The imitator dooms himself to hopeless mediocrity. The inventor did it, because it was natural to him, and so in him it has a charm. In the imitator, something else is natural, and he bereaves himself of his own beauty, to come short of another man's.

Yourself a newborn bard of the Holy Ghost,—cast behind you all conformity, and acquaint men at first hand with Deity. Be to them a man. Look to it first and only, that you are such; that fashion, custom, authority, pleasure, and money are nothing to you,—are not bandages over your eyes, that you cannot see,—but live with the privilege of the immeasurable mind. Not too anxious to visit periodically all families and each family in your parish connexion,—when you meet one of these men or women, be to them a divine man; be to them thought and virtue; let their timid aspirations find in you a friend; let their trampled instincts be genially tempted out in your atmosphere; let their doubts know that you have doubted, and their wonder feel that you have wondered. By trusting your own soul, you shall gain a greater confidence in other men. For all our penny-wisdom, for all our soul-destroying slavery to habit, it is not to be doubted, that all men have sublime thoughts; that all men do value the few real hours of life; they love to be heard; they love to be caught up into the vision of principles. We mark with light in the memory the few interviews, we have had in the dreary years of routine and of sin, with souls that made our souls wiser; that spoke what we thought; that told us what we knew; that gave us leave to be what we inly were. Discharge to men the priestly office, and, present or absent, you shall be followed with their love as by an angel.

And, to this end, let us not aim at common degrees of merit. Can we not leave, to such as love it, the virtue that glitters for the commendation of society, and ourselves pierce the deep solitudes of absolute ability and worth? We easily come up to the standard of goodness in society. Society's praise can be cheaply secured, and almost all men are content with those easy merits; but the instant effect of conversing with God, will be, to put them away. There are sublime merits; persons who are not actors, not speakers, but influences; persons too great for fame, for display; who disdain eloquence; to whom all we call art and artist, seems too nearly allied to show and by-ends, to the exaggeration of the finite and selfish, and loss of the universal. The orators, the poets, the commanders encroach on us only as fair women do, by our allowance and homage. Slight them by preoccupation of mind, slight them, as you can well afford to do, by high and universal aims, and they instantly feel that you have right, and that it is in lower places that they must shine. They also feel your right; for they with you are open to the influx of the all-knowing Spirit, which annihilates before its broad noon the little shades and gradations of intelligence in the compositions we call wiser and wisest.

34   In such high communion, let us study the grand strokes of rectitude: a bold benevolence, an independence of friends, so that not the unjust wishes of those who love us, shall impair our freedom, but we shall resist for truth's sake the freest flow of kindness, and appeal to sympathies far in advance; and,—what is the highest form in which we know this beautiful element,—a certain solidity of merit, that has nothing to do with opinion, and which is so essentially and manifestly virtue, that it is taken for granted, that the right, the brave, the generous step will be taken by it, and nobody thinks of commending it. You would compliment a coxcomb doing a good act, but you would not praise an angel. The silence that accepts merit as the most natural thing in the world, is the highest applause. Such souls, when they appear, are the Imperial Guard of Virtue, the perpetual reserve, the dictators of fortune. One needs not praise their courage,—they are the heart and soul of nature. O my friends, there are resources in us on which we have not drawn. There are men who rise refreshed on hearing a threat; men to whom a crisis which intimidates and paralyzes the majority—demanding not the faculties of prudence and thrift, but comprehension, immovableness, the readiness of sacrifice,—comes graceful and beloved as a bride. Napoleon said of Massena, that he was not himself until the battle began to go against him; then, when the dead began to fall in ranks around him, awoke his powers of combination, and he put on terror and victory as a robe.[15] So it is in rugged crises, in unweariable endurance, and in aims which put sympathy out of question, that the angel is shown. But these are heights that we can scarce remember and look up to, without contrition and shame. Let us thank God that such things exist.

35   And now let us do what we can to rekindle the smouldering, nigh quenched fire on the altar. The evils of that church that now is, are manifest. The question returns, What shall we do? I confess, all attempts to project and

establish a Cultus with new rites and forms, seem to me vain. Faith makes us, and not we it, and faith makes its own forms. All attempts to contrive a system, are as cold as the new worship introduced by the French to the goddess of Reason,—to-day, pasteboard and fillagree, and ending to-morrow in madness and murder. Rather let the breath of new life be breathed by you through the forms already existing. For, if once you are alive, you shall find they shall become plastic and new. The remedy to their deformity is, first, soul, and second, soul, and evermore, soul. A whole popedom of forms, one pulsation of virtue can uplift and vivify. Two inestimable advantages Christianity has given us; first; the Sabbath, the jubilee of the whole world; whose light dawns welcome alike into the closet of the philosopher, into the garret of toil, and into prison cells, and everywhere suggests, even to the vile, a thought of the dignity of spiritual being. Let it stand forevermore, a temple, which new love, new faith, new sight shall restore to more than its first splendor to mankind. And secondly, the institution of preaching,—the speech of man to men,— essentially the most flexible of all organs, of all forms. What hinders that now, everywhere, in pulpits, in lecture-rooms, in houses, in fields, wherever the invitation of men or your own occasions lead you, you speak the very truth, as your life and conscience teach it, and cheer the waiting, fainting hearts of men with new hope and new revelation.

I look for the hour when that supreme Beauty, which ravished the souls of those Eastern men, and chiefly of those Hebrews, and through their lips spoke oracles to all time, shall speak in the West also. The Hebrew and Greek Scriptures contain immortal sentences, that have been bread of life to millions. But they have no epical integrity; are fragmentary; are not shown in their order to the intellect. I look for the new Teacher, that shall follow so far those shining laws, that he shall see them come full circle; shall see their rounding complete grace; shall see the world to be the mirror of the soul; shall see the identity of the law of gravitation with purity of heart; and shall show that the Ought, that Duty, is one thing with Science, with Beauty, and with Joy.

Notes

1. Emerson delivered this address before the senior class at the Harvard Divinity College on 15 July 1838.
2. Osiris is the Egyptian god of fertility.

3. William Wordsworth, "The World Is Too Much with Us" (1806), l. 10.

4. For the last phrase, see Acts 26:19.

5. Epaminondas (ca. 418–362 BCE), Theban statesman and general; George Washington (1732–1799), first President of the United States and commander-in-chief of the Continental Army during the American Revolution.

6. Emerson is indicting the Unitarian Church, which he once described as "corpse-cold" (*JMN*, 9:381).

7. Emerson refers to his minister in Concord, the appropriately named Barzillai Frost (1804–1858).

8. Denderah is a town on the upper Nile that contains the well-preserved temple of the cow goddess Hathor, where the signs of the zodiac are sculptured on the ceiling.

9. In his sermon on "The Lord's Supper," printed above, Emerson argued, "We are not accustomed to express our thoughts or emotions by symbolical actions. Most men find the bread and wine no aid to devotion and to some persons it is an impediment" (para 32). On this issue he resigned his pastorate.

10. Puritans, some of whom helped settle America, were late sixteenth and early seventeenth-century English reformers noted for religious and moral earnestness.

11. The quoted words are those of Emerson's wife, Lidian Jackson Emerson.

12. With "seeth in secret," cf. Matthew 6:4 and 6:18.

13. Zeno of Citium, late fourth-century BCE Greek philosopher, founder of the Stoic school; Zoroaster was a sixth-century BCE Iranian philosopher and mystic.

14. John Wesley (1703–1791), English clergyman and a founder of Methodism; Jean Frédéric Oberlin (1740–1826), French Protestant clergyman and reformer.

15. André Masséna, duc de Rivoli (ca. 1758–1817), one of Napoleon's field marshals.

Self-Reliance

Ne te quæsiveris extra.[1]
"Man is his own star; and the soul that can

Render an honest and a perfect man,
Commands all light, all influence, all fate;
Nothing to him falls early or too late.
Our acts our angels are, or good or ill,
Our fatal shadows that walk by us still."[2]

> —*Epilogue to Beaumont and Fletcher's*
> *Honest Man's Fortune.*

Cast the bantling on the rocks,

Suckle him with the she-wolf's teat;
Wintered with the hawk and fox,
Power and speed be hands and feet.[3]

I read the other day some verses written by an eminent

painter which were original and not conventional.[4] Always the soul hears an admonition in such lines, let the subject be what it may. The sentiment they instil is of more value than any thought they may contain. To believe your own thought, to believe that what is true for you in your private heart, is true for all men,—that is genius. Speak your latent conviction and it shall be the universal sense; for always the inmost becomes the outmost,—and our first thought is rendered back to us by the trumpets of the Last Judgment. Familiar as the voice of the mind is to each, the highest merit we ascribe to Moses, Plato, and Milton, is that they set at naught books and traditions, and spoke not what men but what they thought. A man should learn to detect and watch that gleam of light which flashes across his mind from within, more than the lustre of the firmament of bards and sages. Yet he dismisses without notice his thought, because it is his. In every work of genius we recognise our own rejected thoughts: they come back to us with a certain alienated majesty.

Great works of art have no more affecting lesson for us than this. They teach us to abide by our spontaneous impression with good humored inflexibility then most when the whole cry of voices is on the other side. Else, to-morrow a stranger will say with masterly good sense precisely what we have thought and felt all the time, and we shall be forced to take with shame our own opinion from another.

5   There is a time in every man's education when he arrives at the conviction that envy is ignorance; that imitation is suicide; that he must take himself for better, for worse, as his portion; that though the wide universe is full of good, no kernel of nourishing corn can come to him but through his toil bestowed on that plot of ground which is given to him to till. The power which resides in him is new in nature, and none but he knows what that is which he can do, nor does he know until he has tried. Not for nothing one face, one character, one fact makes much impression on him, and another none. It is not without preëstablished harmony, this sculpture in the memory. The eye was placed where one ray should fall, that it might testify of that particular ray. Bravely let him speak the utmost syllable of his confession. We but half express ourselves, and are ashamed of that divine idea which each of us represents. It may be safely trusted as proportionate and of good issues, so it be faithfully imparted, but God will not have his work made manifest by cowards. It needs a divine man to exhibit any thing divine. A man is relieved and gay when he has put his heart into his work and done his best; but what he has said or done otherwise, shall give him no peace. It is a deliverance which does not deliver. In the attempt his genius deserts him; no muse befriends; no invention, no hope.

6   Trust thyself: every heart vibrates to that iron string. Accept the place the divine Providence has found for you; the society of your contemporaries, the connexion of events. Great men have always done so and confided themselves childlike to the genius of their age, betraying their perception that the Eternal was stirring at their heart, working through their hands, predominating in all their being. And we are now men, and must accept in the highest mind the same transcendent destiny; and not pinched in a corner, not cowards fleeing before a revolution, but redeemers and benefactors, pious aspirants to be noble clay plastic under the Almighty effort, let us advance and advance on Chaos and the Dark.

What pretty oracles nature yields us on this text in the face and behavior of children, babes and even brutes. That divided and rebel mind, that distrust of a sentiment because our arithmetic has computed the strength and means opposed to our purpose, these have not. Their mind being whole, their eye is as yet unconquered, and when we look in their faces, we are disconcerted. Infancy conforms to nobody: all conform to it, so that one babe commonly makes four or five out of the adults who prattle and play to it. So God has armed youth and puberty and manhood no less with its own piquancy and charm, and made it enviable and gracious and its claims not to be put by, if it will stand by itself. Do not think the youth has no force because he cannot speak to you and me. Hark! in the next room, who spoke so clear and emphatic? Good Heaven! it is he! it is that very lump of bashfulness and phlegm which for weeks has done nothing but eat when you were by, that now rolls out these words like bell-strokes. It seems he knows how to speak to his contemporaries. Bashful or bold, then, he will know how to make us seniors very unnecessary.

The nonchalance of boys who are sure of a dinner, and would disdain as much as a lord to do or say aught to conciliate one, is the healthy attitude of human nature. How is a boy the master of society; independent, irresponsible, looking out from his corner on such people and facts as pass by, he tries and sentences them on their merits, in the swift summary way of boys, as good, bad, interesting, silly, eloquent, troublesome. He cumbers himself never about consequences, about interests: he gives an independent, genuine verdict. You must court him: he does not court you. But the man is, as it were, clapped into jail by his consciousness. As soon as he has once acted or spoken with eclat, he is a committed person, watched by the sympathy or the hatred of hundreds whose affections must now enter into his account. There is no Lethe for this.[5] Ah, that he could pass again into his neutral, godlike independence! Who can thus lose all pledge, and having observed, observe again from the same unaffected, unbiassed, unbribable, unaffrighted innocence, must always be formidable, must always engage the poet's and the man's regards. Of such an immortal youth the force would be felt. He would utter opinions on all passing affairs, which being seen to be not private but necessary, would sink like darts into the ear of men, and put them in fear.

These are the voices which we hear in solitude, but they grow faint and inaudible as we enter into the world. Society everywhere is in conspiracy against the manhood of every one of its members. Society is a joint-stock company in which the members agree for the better securing of his bread to each shareholder, to surrender the liberty and culture of the eater. The virtue in most request is conformity. Self-reliance is its aversion. It loves not realities and creators, but names and customs.

10   Whoso would be a man must be a nonconformist. He who would gather immortal palms must not be hindered by the name of goodness, but must explore if it be goodness. Nothing is at last sacred but the integrity of your own mind. Absolve you to yourself, and you shall have the suffrage of the world. I remember an answer which when quite young I was prompted to make to a valued adviser who was wont to importune me with the dear old doctrines of the church. On my saying, What have I to do with the sacredness of traditions, if I live wholly from within? my friend suggested—"But these impulses may be from below, not from above." I replied, "They do not seem to me to be such; but if I am the Devil's child, I will live then from the Devil." No law can be sacred to me but that of my nature. Good and bad are but names very readily transferable to that or this; the only right is what is after my constitution, the only wrong what is against it. A man is to carry himself in the presence of all opposition as if every thing were titular and ephemeral but he. I am ashamed to think how easily we capitulate to badges and names, to large societies and dead institutions. Every decent and well-spoken individual affects and sways me more than is right. I ought to go upright and vital, and speak the rude truth in all ways. If malice and vanity wear the coat of philanthropy, shall that pass? If an angry bigot assumes this bountiful cause of Abolition, and comes to me with his last news from Barbadoes,[6] why should I not say to him, 'Go love thy infant; love thy wood-chopper: be good-natured and modest: have that grace; and never varnish your hard, uncharitable ambition with this incredible tenderness for black folk a thousand miles off. Thy love afar is spite at home.' Rough and graceless would be such greeting, but truth is handsomer than the affectation of love. Your goodness must have some edge to it—else it is none. The doctrine of hatred must be preached as the counteraction of the doctrine of love when that pules and whines. I shun father and mother and wife and brother, when my genius calls me. I would write on the lintels of the door-post, *Whim.* I hope it is somewhat better than whim at last, but we cannot spend the day in explanation. Expect me not to show cause why I seek or why I exclude company. Then, again, do not tell me, as a good man did to-day, of my obligation to put all

poor men in good situations. Are they *my* poor? I tell thee, thou foolish philanthropist, that I grudge the dollar, the dime, the cent I give to such men as
do not belong to me and to whom I do not belong. There is a class of persons
to whom by all spiritual affinity I am bought and sold; for them I will go to
prison, if need be; but your miscellaneous popular charities; the education at
college of fools; the building of meeting-houses to the vain end to which
many now stand; alms to sots; and the thousandfold Relief Societies;—
though I confess with shame I sometimes succumb and give the dollar, it is a
wicked dollar which by-and-by I shall have the manhood to withhold.

Virtues are in the popular estimate rather the exception than the rule.
There is the man *and* his virtues. Men do what is called a good action, as
some piece of courage or charity, much as they would pay a fine in expiation
of daily non-appearance on parade. Their works are done as an apology or
extenuation of their living in the world,—as invalids and the insane pay a
high board. Their virtues are penances. I do not wish to expiate, but to live.
My life is not an apology, but a life. It is for itself and not for a spectacle. I
much prefer that it should be of a lower strain, so it be genuine and equal,
than that it should be glittering and unsteady. I wish it to be sound and sweet,
and not to need diet and bleeding. My life should be unique; it should be an
alms, a battle, a conquest, a medicine. I ask primary evidence that you are a
man, and refuse this appeal from the man to his actions. I know that for myself it makes no difference whether I do or forbear those actions which are
reckoned excellent. I cannot consent to pay for a privilege where I have intrinsic right. Few and mean as my gifts may be, I actually am, and do not need for
my own assurance or the assurance of my fellows any secondary testimony.

What I must do, is all that concerns me, not what the people think. This
rule, equally arduous in actual and in intellectual life, may serve for the whole
distinction between greatness and meanness. It is the harder, because you
will always find those who think they know what is your duty better than you
know it. It is easy in the world to live after the world's opinion; it is easy in
solitude to live after our own; but the great man is he who in the midst of the
crowd keeps with perfect sweetness the independence of solitude.

The objection to conforming to usages that have become dead to you, is,
that it scatters your force. It loses your time and blurs the impression of your
character. If you maintain a dead church, contribute to a dead Bible-Society,
vote with a great party either for the Government or against it, spread your

11

12

13

table like base housekeepers,—under all these screens, I have difficulty to detect the precise man you are. And, of course, so much force is withdrawn from your proper life. But do your thing, and I shall know you. Do your work, and you shall reinforce yourself. A man must consider what a blindman's-buff is this game of conformity. If I know your sect, I anticipate your argument. I hear a preacher announce for his text and topic the expediency of one of the institutions of his church. Do I not know beforehand that not possibly can he say a new and spontaneous word? Do I not know that with all this ostentation of examining the grounds of the institution, he will do no such thing? Do I not know that he is pledged to himself not to look but at one side;—the permitted side, not as a man, but as a parish minister? He is a retained attorney, and these airs of the bench are the emptiest affectation. Well, most men have bound their eyes with one or another handkerchief, and attached themselves to some one of these communities of opinion. This conformity makes them not false in a few particulars, authors of a few lies, but false in all particulars. Their every truth is not quite true. Their two is not the real two, their four not the real four: so that every word they say chagrins us, and we know not where to begin to set them right. Meantime nature is not slow to equip us in the prison-uniform of the party to which we adhere. We come to wear one cut of face and figure, and acquire by degrees the gentlest asinine expression. There is a mortifying experience in particular which does not fail to wreak itself also in the general history; I mean, "the foolish face of praise," the forced smile which we put on in company where we do not feel at ease in answer to conversation which does not interest us.[7] The muscles, not spontaneously moved, but moved by a low usurping wilfulness, grow tight about the outline of the face and make the most disagreeable sensation, a sensation of rebuke and warning which no brave young man will suffer twice.

For non-conformity the world whips you with its displeasure. And therefore a man must know how to estimate a sour face. The bystanders look askance on him in the public street or in the friend's parlor. If this aversation had its origin in contempt and resistance like his own, he might well go home with a sad countenance; but the sour faces of the multitude, like their sweet faces, have no deep cause,—disguise no god, but are put on and off as the wind blows, and a newspaper directs. Yet is the discontent of the multitude more formidable than that of the senate and the college. It is easy enough for a firm man who knows the world to brook the rage of the cultivated classes.

Their rage is decorous and prudent, for they are timid as being very vulnerable themselves. But when to their feminine rage the indignation of the people is added, when the ignorant and the poor are aroused, when the unintelligent brute force that lies at the bottom of society is made to growl and mow, it needs the habit of magnanimity and religion to treat it godlike as a trifle of no concernment.

The other terror that scares us from self-trust is our consistency; a reverence for our past act or word, because the eyes of others have no other data for computing our orbit than our past acts, and we are loath to disappoint them. 15

But why should you keep your head over your shoulder? Why drag about this monstrous corpse of your memory, lest you contradict somewhat you have stated in this or that public place? Suppose you should contradict yourself; what then? It seems to be a rule of wisdom never to rely on your memory alone, scarcely even in acts of pure memory, but bring the past for judgment into the thousand-eyed present, and live ever in a new day. Trust your emotion. In your metaphysics you have denied personality to the Deity: yet when the devout motions of the soul come, yield to them heart and life, though they should clothe God with shape and color. Leave your theory as Joseph his coat in the hand of the harlot, and flee.[8] 16

A foolish consistency is the hobgoblin of little minds, adored by little statesmen and philosophers and divines. With consistency a great soul has simply nothing to do. He may as well concern himself with his shadow on the wall. Out upon your guarded lips! Sew them up with packthread, do. Else, if you would be a man, speak what you think to-day in words as hard as cannon balls, and to-morrow speak what to-morrow thinks in hard words again, though it contradict every thing you said to-day. Ah, then, exclaim the aged ladies, you shall be sure to be misunderstood. Misunderstood! It is a right fool's word. Is it so bad then to be misunderstood? Pythagoras was misunderstood, and Socrates, and Jesus, and Luther, and Copernicus, and Galileo, and Newton, and every pure and wise spirit that ever took flesh.[9] To be great is to be misunderstood. 17

I suppose no man can violate his nature. All the sallies of his will are rounded in by the law of his being as the inequalities of Andes and Himmaleh are insignificant in the curve of the sphere. Nor does it matter how you gauge and try him. A character is like an acrostic or Alexandrian stanza; 18

—read it forward, backward, or across, it still spells the same thing.[10] In this pleasing contrite wood-life which God allows me, let me record day by day my honest thought without prospect or retrospect, and, I cannot doubt, it will be found symmetrical, though I mean it not, and see it not. My book should smell of pines and resound with the hum of insects. The swallow over my window should interweave that thread or straw he carries in his bill into my web also. We pass for what we are. Character teaches above our wills. Men imagine that they communicate their virtue or vice only by overt actions and do not see that virtue or vice emit a breath every moment.

19   Fear never but you shall be consistent in whatever variety of actions, so they be each honest and natural in their hour. For of one will, the actions will be harmonious, however unlike they seem. These varieties are lost sight of when seen at a little distance, at a little height of thought. One tendency unites them all. The voyage of the best ship is a zigzag line of a hundred tacks. This is only microscopic criticism. See the line from a sufficient distance, and it straightens itself to the average tendency. Your genuine action will explain itself and will explain your other genuine actions. Your conformity explains nothing. Act singly, and what you have already done singly, will justify you now. Greatness always appeals to the future. If I can be great enough now to do right and scorn eyes, I must have done so much right before, as to defend me now. Be it how it will, do right now. Always scorn appearances, and you always may. The force of character is cumulative. All the foregone days of virtue work their health into this. What makes the majesty of the heroes of the senate and the field, which so fills the imagination? The consciousness of a train of great days and victories behind. There they all stand and shed an united light on the advancing actor. He is attended as by a visible escort of angels to every man's eye. That is it which throws thunder into Chatham's voice, and dignity into Washington's port, and America into Adams's eye.[11] Honor is venerable to us because it is no ephemeris. It is always ancient virtue. We worship it to-day, because it is not of to-day. We love it and pay it homage, because it is not a trap for our love and homage, but is self-dependent, self-derived, and therefore of an old immaculate pedigree, even if shown in a young person.

20   I hope in these days we have heard the last of conformity and consistency. Let the words be gazetted and ridiculous henceforward. Instead of the gong for dinner, let us hear a whistle from the Spartan fife.[12] Let us bow and apolo-

gize never more. A great man is coming to eat at my house. I do not wish to
please him: I wish that he should wish to please me. I will stand here for humanity, and though I would make it kind, I would make it true. Let us affront
and reprimand the smooth mediocrity and squalid contentment of the times,
and hurl in the face of custom, and trade, and office, the fact which is the up-
shot of all history, that there is a great responsible Thinker and Actor moving
wherever moves a man; that a true man belongs to no other time or place,
but is the centre of things. Where he is, there is nature. He measures you, and
all men, and all events. You are constrained to accept his standard. Ordinarily
every body in society reminds us of somewhat else or of some other person.
Character, reality, reminds you of nothing else. It takes place of the whole
creation. The man must be so much that he must make all circumstances indifferent,—put all means into the shade. This all great men are and do. Every
true man is a cause, a country, and an age; requires infinite spaces and numbers and time fully to accomplish his thought;—and posterity seem to follow
his steps as a procession. A man Cæsar is born, and for ages after, we have a
Roman Empire. Christ is born, and millions of minds so grow and cleave to
his genius, that he is confounded with virtue and the possible of man. An institution is the lengthened shadow of one man; as, the Reformation, of Luther; Quakerism, of Fox; Methodism, of Wesley; Abolition, of Clarkson.[13]
Scipio, Milton called "the height of Rome;"[14] and all history resolves itself
very easily into the biography of a few stout and earnest persons.

Let a man then know his worth, and keep things under his feet. Let him
not peep or steal, or skulk up and down with the air of a charity-boy, a bas-
tard, or an interloper, in the world which exists for him. But the man in the
street finding no worth in himself which corresponds to the force which built
a tower or sculptured a marble god, feels poor when he looks on these. To
him a palace, a statue, or a costly book have an alien and forbidding air, much
like a gay equipage, and seem to say like that, 'Who are you, sir?' Yet they all
are his, suitors for his notice, petitioners to his faculties that they will come
out and take possession. The picture waits for my verdict: it is not to command me, but I am to settle its claims to praise. That popular fable of the sot
who was picked up dead drunk in the street, carried to the duke's house,
washed and dressed and laid in the duke's bed, and, on his waking, treated
with all obsequious ceremony like the duke, and assured that he had been insane,—[15] owes its popularity to the fact, that it symbolizes so well the state of

21

man, who is in the world a sort of sot, but now and then wakes up, exercises his reason, and finds himself a true prince.

22   Our reading is mendicant and sycophantic. In history, our imagination makes fools of us, plays us false. Kingdom and lordship, power and estate are a gaudier vocabulary than private John and Edward in a small house and common day's work: but the things of life are the same to both: the sum total of both is the same. Why all this deference to Alfred, and Scanderbeg, and Gustavus?[16] Suppose they were virtuous: did they wear out virtue? As great a stake depends on your private act to-day, as followed their public and re-nowned steps. When private men shall act with vast views, the lustre will be transferred from the actions of kings to those of gentlemen.

23   The world has indeed been instructed by its kings, who have so magne-tized the eyes of nations. It has been taught by this colossal symbol the mu-tual reverence that is due from man to man. The joyful loyalty with which men have every where suffered the king, the noble, or the great proprietor to walk among them by a law of his own, make his own scale of men and things, and reverse theirs, pay for benefits not with money but with honor, and rep-resent the Law in his person, was the hieroglyphic by which they obscurely signified their consciousness of their own right and comeliness, the right of every man.

24   The magnetism which all original action exerts is explained when we in-quire the reason of self-trust. Who is the Trustee? What is the aboriginal Self on which a universal reliance may be grounded? What is the nature and power of that science-baffling star, without parallax, without calculable ele-ments, which shoots a ray of beauty even into trivial and impure actions, if the least mark of independence appear?[17] The inquiry leads us to that source, at once the essence of genius, the essence of virtue, and the essence of life, which we call Spontaneity or Instinct. We denote this primary wisdom as In-tuition, whilst all later teachings are tuitions. In that deep force, the last fact behind which analysis cannot go, all things find their common origin. For the sense of being which in calm hours rises, we know not how, in the soul, is not diverse from things, from space, from light, from time, from man, but one with them, and proceedeth obviously from the same source whence their life and being also proceedeth. We first share the life by which things exist, and afterwards see them as appearances in nature, and forget that we have shared their cause. Here is the fountain of action and the fountain of thought. Here

are the lungs of that inspiration which giveth man wisdom, of that inspiration of man which cannot be denied without impiety and atheism. We lie in the lap of immense intelligence, which makes us organs of its activity and receivers of its truth. When we discern justice, when we discern truth, we do nothing of ourselves, but allow a passage to its beams. If we ask whence this comes, if we seek to pry into the soul that causes,—all metaphysics, all philosophy is at fault. Its presence or its absence is all we can affirm. Every man discerns between the voluntary acts of his mind, and his involuntary perceptions. And to his involuntary perceptions, he knows a perfect respect is due. He may err in the expression of them, but he knows that these things are so, like day and night, not to be disputed. All my wilful actions and acquisitions are but roving;—the most trivial reverie, the faintest native emotion are domestic and divine. Thoughtless people contradict as readily the statement of perceptions as of opinions, or rather much more readily; for, they do not distinguish between perception and notion. They fancy that I choose to see this or that thing. But perception is not whimsical, but fatal. If I see a trait, my children will see it after me, and in course of time, all mankind,—although it may chance that no one has seen it before me. For my perception of it is as much a fact as the sun.

The relations of the soul to the divine spirit are so pure that it is profane to seek to interpose helps. It must be that when God speaketh, he should communicate not one thing, but all things; should fill the world with his voice; should scatter forth light, nature, time, souls, from the centre of the present thought; and new date and new create the whole. Whenever a mind is simple, and receives a divine wisdom, then old things pass away,—means, teachers, texts, temples fall; it lives now and absorbs past and future into the present hour. All things are made sacred by relation to it,—one thing as much as another. All things are dissolved to their centre by their cause, and in the universal miracle petty and particular miracles disappear. This is and must be. If, therefore, a man claims to know and speak of God, and carries you backward to the phraseology of some old mouldered nation in another country, in another world, believe him not. Is the acorn better than the oak which is its fulness and completion? Is the parent better than the child into whom he has cast his ripened being? Whence then this worship of the past? The centuries are conspirators against the sanity and majesty of the soul. Time and space are but physiological colors which the eye maketh, but the soul is light; where

25

it is, is day; where it was, is night; and history is an impertinence and an injury, if it be anything more than a cheerful apologue or parable of my being and becoming.[18]

26   Man is timid and apologetic. He is no longer upright. He dares not say 'I think,' 'I am,' but quotes some saint or sage. He is ashamed before the blade of grass or the blowing rose. These roses under my window make no reference to former roses or to better ones; they are for what they are; they exist with God to-day. There is no time to them. There is simply the rose; it is perfect in every moment of its existence. Before a leaf-bud has burst, its whole life acts; in the full-blown flower, there is no more; in the leafless root, there is no less. Its nature is satisfied, and it satisfies nature, in all moments alike. There is no time to it. But man postpones or remembers; he does not live in the present, but with reverted eye laments the past, or, heedless of the riches that surround him, stands on tiptoe to foresee the future. He cannot be happy and strong until he too lives with nature in the present, above time.

27   This should be plain enough. Yet see what strong intellects dare not yet hear God himself, unless he speak the phraseology of I know not what David, or Jeremiah, or Paul. We shall not always set so great a price on a few texts, on a few lives. We are like children who repeat by rote the sentences of grandames and tutors, and, as they grow older, of the men of talents and character they chance to see,—painfully recollecting the exact words they spoke; afterwards, when they come into the point of view which those had who uttered these sayings, they understand them, and are willing to let the words go; for, at any time, they can use words as good, when occasion comes. So was it with us, so will it be, if we proceed. If we live truly, we shall see truly. It is as easy for the strong man to be strong, as it is for the weak to be weak. When we have new perception, we shall gladly disburthen the memory of its hoarded treasures as old rubbish. When a man lives with God, his voice shall be as sweet as the murmur of the brook and the rustle of the corn.

28   And now at last the highest truth on this subject remains unsaid; probably, cannot be said; for all that we say is the far off remembering of the intuition. That thought, by what I can now nearest approach to say it, is this. When good is near you, when you have life in yourself,—it is not by any known or appointed way; you shall not discern the foot-prints of any other; you shall not see the face of man; you shall not hear any name;—the way, the thought, the good shall be wholly strange and new. It shall exclude all other being. You take the way from man not to man. All persons that ever existed

are its fugitive ministers. There shall be no fear in it. Fear and hope are alike beneath it. It asks nothing. There is somewhat low even in hope. We are then in vision. There is nothing that can be called gratitude nor properly joy. The soul is raised over passion. It seeth identity and eternal causation. It is a perceiving that Truth and Right are. Hence it becomes a Tranquillity out of the knowing that all things go well. Vast spaces of nature; the Atlantic Ocean, the South Sea; vast intervals of time, years, centuries, are of no account. This which I think and feel, underlay that former state of life and circumstances, as it does underlie my present, and will always all circumstance, and what is called life, and what is called death.

Life only avails, not the having lived. Power ceases in the instant of re- 29 pose; it resides in the moment of transition from a past to a new state; in the shooting of the gulf; in the darting to an aim. This one fact the world hates, that the soul *becomes;* for, that forever degrades the past; turns all riches to poverty; all reputation to a shame; confounds the saint with the rogue; shoves Jesus and Judas equally aside. Why then do we prate of self-reliance? Inasmuch as the soul is present, there will be power not confident but agent. To talk of reliance, is a poor external way of speaking. Speak rather of that which relies, because it works and is. Who has more soul than I, masters me, though he should not raise his finger. Round him I must revolve by the gravitation of spirits; who has less, I rule with like facility. We fancy it rhetoric when we speak of eminent virtue. We do not yet see that virtue is Height, and that a man or a company of men plastic and permeable to principles, by the law of nature must overpower and ride all cities, nations, kings, rich men, poets, who are not.

This is the ultimate fact which we so quickly reach on this as on every 30 topic, the resolution of all into the ever blessed ONE. Virtue is the governor, the creator, the reality. All things real are so by so much of virtue as they contain. Hardship, husbandry, hunting, whaling, war, eloquence, personal weight, are somewhat, and engage my respect as examples of the soul's presence and impure action. I see the same law working in nature for conservation and growth. The poise of a planet, the bended tree recovering itself from the strong wind, the vital resources of every vegetable and animal, are also demonstrations of the self-sufficing, and therefore self-relying soul. All history from its highest to its trivial passages is the various record of this power.

Thus all concentrates; let us not rove; let us sit at home with the cause. 31 Let us stun and astonish the intruding rabble of men and books and institutions by a simple declaration of the divine fact. Bid them take the shoes from off their feet, for God is here within.[19] Let our simplicity judge them, and our docility to our own law demonstrate the poverty of nature and fortune beside our native riches.

32   But now we are a mob. Man does not stand in awe of man, nor is the soul admonished to stay at home, to put itself in communication with the internal ocean, but it goes abroad to beg a cup of water of the urns of men. We must go alone. Isolation must precede true society. I like the silent church before the service begins, better than any preaching. How far off, how cool, how chaste the persons look, begirt each one with a precinct or sanctuary. So let us always sit. Why should we assume the faults of our friend, or wife, or father, or child, because they sit around our hearth, or are said to have the same blood? All men have my blood, and I have all men's. Not for that will I adopt their petulance or folly, even to the extent of being ashamed of it. But your isolation must not be mechanical, but spiritual, that is, must be elevation. At times the whole world seems to be in conspiracy to importune you with emphatic trifles. Friend, client, child, sickness, fear, want, charity, all knock at once at thy closet door and say, 'Come out unto us.'—[20] Do not spill thy soul; do not all descend; keep thy state; stay at home in thine own heaven; come not for a moment into their facts, into their hubbub of conflicting appearances, but let in the light of thy law on their confusion. The power men possess to annoy me, I give them by a weak curiosity. No man can come near me but through my act. "What we love that we have, but by desire we bereave ourselves of the love."[21]

33   If we cannot at once rise to the sanctities of obedience and faith, let us at least resist our temptations; let us enter into the state of war, and wake Thor and Woden, courage and constancy, in our Saxon breasts.[22] This is to be done in our smooth times by speaking the truth. Check this lying hospitality and lying affection. Live no longer to the expectation of these deceived and deceiving people with whom we converse. Say to them, O father, O mother, O wife, O brother, O friend, I have lived with you after appearances hitherto. Henceforward I am the truth's. Be it known unto you that henceforward I obey no law less than the eternal law. I will have no covenants but proximities. I shall endeavor to nourish my parents, to support my family, to be the chaste husband of one wife,—but these relations I must fill after a new and unprecedented way. I appeal from your customs. I must be myself. I cannot

break myself any longer for you, or you. If you can love me for what I am, we shall be the happier. If you cannot, I will still seek to deserve that you should. I must be myself. I will not hide my tastes or aversions. I will so trust that what is deep is holy, that I will do strongly before the sun and moon whatever inly rejoices me, and the heart appoints. If you are noble, I will love you; if you are not, I will not hurt you and myself by hypocritical attentions. If you are true, but not in the same truth with me, cleave to your companions; I will seek my own. I do this not selfishly, but humbly and truly. It is alike your interest and mine and all men's, however long we have dwelt in lies, to live in truth. Does this sound harsh to-day? You will soon love what is dictated by your nature as well as mine, and if we follow the truth, it will bring us out safe at last.—But so you may give these friends pain. Yes, but I cannot sell my liberty and my power, to save their sensibility. Besides, all persons have their moments of reason when they look out into the region of absolute truth; then will they justify me and do the same thing.

The populace think that your rejection of popular standards is a rejection of all standard, and mere antinomianism; and the bold sensualist will use the name of philosophy to gild his crimes.[23] But the law of consciousness abides. There are two confessionals, in one or the other of which we must be shriven. You may fulfil your round of duties by clearing yourself in the *direct,* or, in the *reflex* way. Consider whether you have satisfied your relations to father, mother, cousin, neighbor, town, cat, and dog; whether any of these can upbraid you. But I may also neglect this reflex standard, and absolve me to myself. I have my own stern claims and perfect circle. It denies the name of duty to many offices that are called duties. But if I can discharge its debts, it enables me to dispense with the popular code. If any one imagines that this law is lax, let him keep its commandment one day. 34

And truly it demands something godlike in him who has cast off the common motives of humanity, and has ventured to trust himself for a taskmaster. High be his heart, faithful his will, clear his sight, that he may in good earnest be doctrine, society, law to himself, that a simple purpose may be to him as strong as iron necessity is to others. 35

If any man consider the present aspects of what is called by distinction *society,* he will see the need of these ethics. The sinew and heart of man seem to be drawn out, and we are become timorous desponding whimperers. We are afraid of truth, afraid of fortune, afraid of death, and afraid of each other. 36

Our age yields no great and perfect persons. We want men and women who shall renovate life and our social state, but we see that most natures are insolvent; cannot satisfy their own wants, have an ambition out of all proportion to their practical force, and so do lean and beg day and night continually. Our housekeeping is mendicant, our arts, our occupations, our marriages, our religion we have not chosen, but society has chosen for us. We are parlor soldiers. The rugged battle of fate, where strength is born, we shun.

37   If our young men miscarry in their first enterprizes, they lose all heart. If the young merchant fails, men say he is *ruined.* If the finest genius studies at one of our colleges, and is not installed in an office within one year afterwards in the cities or suburbs of Boston or New York, it seems to his friends and to himself that he is right in being disheartened and in complaining the rest of his life. A sturdy lad from New Hampshire or Vermont, who in turn tries all the professions, who *teams it, farms it, peddles,* keeps a school, preaches, edits a newspaper, goes to Congress, buys a township, and so forth, in successive years, and always, like a cat, falls on his feet, is worth a hundred of these city dolls. He walks abreast with his days, and feels no shame in not 'studying a profession,' for he does not postpone his life, but lives already. He has not one chance, but a hundred chances. Let a stoic arise who shall reveal the resources of man, and tell men they are not leaning willows, but can and must detach themselves; that with the exercise of self-trust, new powers shall appear; that a man is the word made flesh, born to shed healing to the nations,[24] that he should be ashamed of our compassion, and that the moment he acts from himself, tossing the laws, the books, idolatries, and customs out of the window,—we pity him no more but thank and revere him,—and that teacher shall restore the life of man to splendor, and make his name dear to all History.

38   It is easy to see that a greater self-reliance,—a new respect for the divinity in man,—must work a revolution in all the offices and relations of men; in their religion; in their education; in their pursuits; their modes of living; their association; in their property; in their speculative views.

39   1. In what prayers do men allow themselves! That which they call a holy office, is not so much as brave and manly. Prayer looks abroad and asks for some foreign addition to come through some foreign virtue, and loses itself in endless mazes of natural and supernatural, and mediatorial and miraculous. Prayer that craves a particular commodity—any thing less than all good,

is vicious. Prayer is the contemplation of the facts of life from the highest point of view. It is the soliloquy of a beholding and jubilant soul. It is the spirit of God pronouncing his works good. But prayer as a means to effect a private end, is theft and meanness. It supposes dualism and not unity in nature and consciousness. As soon as the man is at one with God, he will not beg. He will then see prayer in all action. The prayer of the farmer kneeling in his field to weed it, the prayer of the rower kneeling with the stroke of his oar, are true prayers heard throughout nature, though for cheap ends. Caratach, in Fletcher's Bonduca, when admonished to inquire the mind of the god Audate, replies,

> "His hidden meaning lies in our endeavors,
> Our valors are our best gods."[25]

Another sort of false prayers are our regrets. Discontent is the want of self-reliance: it is infirmity of will. Regret calamities, if you can thereby help the sufferer; if not, attend your own work, and already the evil begins to be repaired. Our sympathy is just as base. We come to them who weep foolishly, and sit down and cry for company, instead of imparting to them truth and health in rough electric shocks, putting them once more in communication with the soul. The secret of fortune is joy in our hands. Welcome evermore to gods and men is the self-helping man. For him all doors are flung wide. Him all tongues greet, all honors crown, all eyes follow with desire. Our love goes out to him and embraces him, because he did not need it. We solicitously and apologetically caress and celebrate him, because he held on his way and scorned our disapprobation. The gods love him because men hated him. "To the persevering mortal," said Zoroaster, "the blessed Immortals are swift."[26]

As men's prayers are a disease of the will, so are their creeds a disease of the intellect. They say with those foolish Israelites, 'Let not God speak to us, lest we die. Speak thou, speak any man with us, and we will obey.'[27] Everywhere I am bereaved of meeting God in my brother, because he has shut his own temple doors, and recites fables merely of his brother's, or his brother's brother's God. Every new mind is a new classification. If it prove a mind of uncommon activity and power, a Locke, a Lavoisier, a Hutton, a Bentham, a Spurzheim, it imposes its classification on other men, and lo! a new system.[28] In proportion always to the depth of the thought, and so to the num-

40

41

ber of the objects it touches and brings within reach of the pupil, is his com-
placency. But chiefly is this apparent in creeds and churches, which are also
classifications of some powerful mind acting on the great elemental thought
of Duty, and man's relation to the Highest. Such is Calvinism, Quakerism,
Swedenborgianism. The pupil takes the same delight in subordinating every
thing to the new terminology that a girl does who has just learned botany, in
seeing a new earth and new seasons thereby. It will happen for a time, that
the pupil will feel a real debt to the teacher,—will find his intellectual power
has grown by the study of his writings. This will continue until he has exhausted his master's mind. But in all unbalanced minds, the classification is
idolized, passes for the end, and not for a speedily exhaustible means, so that
the walls of the system blend to their eye in the remote horizon with the
walls of the universe; the luminaries of heaven seem to them hung on the
arch their master built. They cannot imagine how you aliens have any right
to see,—how you can see; 'It must be somehow that you stole the light
from us.' They do not yet perceive, that light, unsystematic, indomitable, will
break into any cabin, even into theirs. Let them chirp awhile and call it their
own. If they are honest and do well, presently their neat new pinfold will be
too strait and low, will crack, will lean, will rot and vanish, and the immortal
light, all young and joyful, million-orbed, million-colored, will beam over the
universe as on the first morning.

42   2. It is for want of self-culture that the idol of Travelling, the idol of Italy,
of England, of Egypt, remains for all educated Americans. They who made
England, Italy, or Greece venerable in the imagination, did so not by rambling round creation as a moth round a lamp, but by sticking fast where they
were, like an axis of the earth. In manly hours, we feel that duty is our place,
and that the merrymen of circumstance should follow as they may. The soul
is no traveller: the wise man stays at home with the soul, and when his necessities, his duties, on any occasion call him from his house, or into foreign
lands, he is at home still, and is not gadding abroad from himself, and shall
make men sensible by the expression of his countenance, that he goes the
missionary of wisdom and virtue, and visits cities and men like a sovereign,
and not like an interloper or a valet.

43   I have no churlish objection to the circumnavigation of the globe, for the
purposes of art, of study, and benevolence, so that the man is first domesticated, or does not go abroad with the hope of finding somewhat greater than

he knows. He who travels to be amused, or to get somewhat which he does not carry, travels away from himself, and grows old even in youth among old things. In Thebes, in Palmyra, his will and mind have become old and dilapidated as they. He carries ruins to ruins.

Travelling is a fool's paradise. We owe to our first journeys the discovery that place is nothing. At home I dream that at Naples, at Rome, I can be intoxicated with beauty, and lose my sadness. I pack my trunk, embrace my friends, embark on the sea, and at last wake up in Naples, and there beside me is the stern Fact, the sad self, unrelenting, identical, that I fled from. I seek the Vatican, and the palaces. I affect to be intoxicated with sights and suggestions, but I am not intoxicated. My giant goes with me wherever I go. 44

3. But the rage of travelling is itself only a symptom of a deeper unsoundness affecting the whole intellectual action. The intellect is vagabond, and the universal system of education fosters restlessness. Our minds travel when our bodies are forced to stay at home. We imitate; and what is imitation but the travelling of the mind? Our houses are built with foreign taste; our shelves are garnished with foreign ornaments; our opinions, our tastes, our whole minds lean, and follow the Past and the Distant, as the eyes of a maid follow her mistress. The soul created the arts wherever they have flourished. It was in his own mind that the artist sought his model. It was an application of his own thought to the thing to be done and the conditions to be observed. And why need we copy the Doric or the Gothic model?[29] Beauty, convenience, grandeur of thought, and quaint expression are as near to us as to any, and if the American artist will study with hope and love the precise thing to be done by him, considering the climate, the soil, the length of the day, the wants of the people, the habit and form of the government, he will create a house in which all these will find themselves fitted, and taste and sentiment will be satisfied also. 45

Insist on yourself; never imitate. Your own gift you can present every moment with the cumulative force of a whole life's cultivation; but of the adopted talent of another, you have only an extemporaneous, half possession. That which each can do best, none but his Maker can teach him. No man yet knows what it is, nor can, till that person has exhibited it. Where is the master who could have taught Shakspeare? Where is the master who could have instructed Franklin, or Washington, or Bacon, or Newton? Every great man is an unique. The Scipionism of Scipio is precisely that part he 46 could not borrow. If any body will tell me whom the great man imitates in the original crisis when he performs a great act, I will tell him who else than himself can teach him. Shakspeare will never be made by the study of Shakspeare. Do that which is assigned thee, and thou canst not hope too much or dare too much. There is at this moment, there is for me an utterance bare and grand as that of the colossal chisel of Phidias, or trowel of the Egyptians, or the pen of Moses, or Dante, but different from all these.[30] Not possibly will the soul all rich, all eloquent, with thousand-cloven tongue, deign to repeat itself;[31] but if I can hear what these patriarchs say, surely I can reply to them in the same pitch of voice: for the ear and the tongue are two organs of one nature. Dwell up there in the simple and noble regions of thy life, obey thy heart, and thou shalt reproduce the Foreworld again.

47   4. As our Religion, our Education, our Art look abroad, so does our spirit of society. All men plume themselves on the improvement of society, and no man improves.

48   Society never advances. It recedes as fast on one side as it gains on the other. Its progress is only apparent, like the workers of a treadmill. It undergoes continual changes: it is barbarous, it is civilized, it is christianized, it is rich, it is scientific; but this change is not amelioration. For every thing that is given, something is taken. Society acquires new arts and loses old instincts. What a contrast between the well-clad, reading, writing, thinking American, with a watch, a pencil, and a bill of exchange in his pocket, and the naked New Zealander, whose property is a club, a spear, a mat, and an undivided twentieth of a shed to sleep under. But compare the health of the two men, and you shall see that his aboriginal strength the white man has lost. If the traveller tell us truly, strike the savage with a broad axe, and in a day or two the flesh shall unite and heal as if you struck the blow into soft pitch, and the same blow shall send the white to his grave.[32]

49   The civilized man has built a coach, but has lost the use of his feet. He is supported on crutches, but loses so much support of muscle. He has got a fine Geneva watch, but he has lost the skill to tell the hour by the sun. A Greenwich nautical almanac he has, and so being sure of the information when he wants it, the man in the street does not know a star in the sky.[33] The solstice he does not observe; the equinox he knows as little; and the whole bright calendar of the year is without a dial in his mind. His note-books impair his memory; his libraries overload his wit; the insurance office increases

the number of accidents; and it may be a question whether machinery does not encumber; whether we have not lost by refinement some energy, by a christianity entrenched in establishments and forms, some vigor of wild virtue. For every stoic was a stoic;[34] but in Christendom where is the Christian?

There is no more deviation in the moral standard than in the standard of height or bulk. No greater men are now than ever were. A singular equality may be observed between the great men of the first and of the last ages; nor can all the science, art, religion and philosophy of the nineteenth century avail to educate greater men than Plutarch's heroes, three or four and twenty centuries ago. Not in time is the race progressive. Phocion, Socrates, Anaxagoras, Diogenes, are great men, but they leave no class.[35] He who is really of their class will not be called by their name, but be wholly his own man, and, in his turn the founder of a sect. The arts and inventions of each period are only its costume, and do not invigorate men. The harm of the improved machinery may compensate its good. Hudson and Behring accomplished so much in their fishing-boats, as to astonish Parry and Franklin, whose equipment exhausted the resources of science and art.[36] Galileo, with an opera-glass, discovered a more splendid series of facts than any one since. Columbus found the New World in an undecked boat. It is curious to see the periodical disuse and perishing of means and machinery which were introduced with loud laudation, a few years or centuries before. The great genius returns to essential man. We reckoned the improvements of the art of war among the triumphs of science, and yet Napoleon conquered Europe by the Bivouac, which consisted of falling back on naked valor, and disencumbering it of all aids.[37] The Emperor held it impossible to make a perfect army, says Las Cases, "without abolishing our arms, magazines, commissaries, and carriages, until in imitation of the Roman custom, the soldier should receive his supply of corn, grind it in his hand-mill, and bake his bread himself."[38]

Society is a wave. The wave moves onward, but the water of which it is composed, does not. The same particle does not rise from the valley to the ridge. Its unity is only phenomenal. The persons who make up a nation to-day, next year die, and their experience with them.

And so the reliance on Property, including the reliance on governments which protect it, is the want of self-reliance. Men have looked away from themselves and at things so long, that they have come to esteem what they call the soul's progress, namely, the religious, learned, and civil institutions,

50

51

52

as guards of property, and they deprecate assaults on these, because they feel them to be assaults on property. They measure their esteem of each other, by what each has, and not by what each is. But a cultivated man becomes ashamed of his property, ashamed of what he has, out of new respect for his being. Especially he hates what he has, if he see that it is accidental,—came to him by inheritance, or gift, or crime; then he feels that it is not having; it does not belong to him, has no root in him, and merely lies there, because no revolution or no robber takes it away. But that which a man is, does always by necessity acquire, and what the man acquires is permanent and living property, which does not wait the beck of rulers, or mobs, or revolutions, or fire, or storm, or bankruptcies, but perpetually renews itself wherever the man is put. "Thy lot or portion of life," said the Caliph Ali, "is seeking after thee; therefore be at rest from seeking after it."[39] Our dependence on these foreign goods leads us to our slavish respect for numbers. The political parties meet in numerous conventions; the greater the concourse, and with each new uproar of announcement, The delegation from Essex! The Democrats from New Hampshire! The Whigs of Maine! the young patriot feels himself stronger than before by a new thousand of eyes and arms. In like manner the reformers summon conventions, and vote and resolve in multitude. But not so, O friends! will the God deign to enter and inhabit you, but by a method precisely the reverse. It is only as a man puts off from himself all external support, and stands alone, that I see him to be strong and to prevail. He is weaker by every recruit to his banner. Is not a man better than a town? Ask nothing of men, and in the endless mutation, thou only firm column must presently appear the upholder of all that surrounds thee. He who knows that power is in the soul, that he is weak only because he has looked for good out of him and elsewhere, and so perceiving, throws himself unhesitatingly on his thought, instantly rights himself, stands in the erect position, commands his limbs, works miracles; just as a man who stands on his feet is stronger than a man who stands on his head.

53 So use all that is called Fortune. Most men gamble with her, and gain all, and lose all, as her wheel rolls. But do thou leave as unlawful these winnings, and deal with Cause and Effect, the chancellors of God. In the Will work and acquire, and thou hast chained the wheel of Chance, and shalt always drag her after thee. A political victory, a rise of rents, the recovery of your sick, or the return of your absent friend, or some other quite external event, raises your spirits, and you think good days are preparing for you. Do not believe it.

It can never be so. Nothing can bring you peace but yourself. Nothing can bring you peace but the triumph of principles.

Notes

1. *Satires*, I, 7: "Look to no one outside yourself," by Persius, first-century Latin moralistic poet.

2. *Honest Man's Fortune* (1647), epilogue, ll. 33–38, by Francis Beaumont (1584–1616) and John Fletcher (1579–1625), English dramatists.

3. These lines by Emerson were published as "Power" in his *May-Day* (1867); see *CW*, 9:531–533.

4. In his journal, Emerson identifies Washington Allston (1779–1843), American historical painter and novelist, as his subject (*JMN*, 5:377); the poem to which he refers is "To the Author of 'The Diary of an Ennuyée,'" published in Allston's posthumous *Lectures on Art, and Poems* (1850).

5. Lethe is the Greek mythological river of oblivion.

6. Slavery was abolished in Barbados in 1834.

7. With "the foolish face of praise," cf. Alexander Pope, *Epistle to Dr. Arbuthnot* (1735), l. 212.

8. The biblical Joseph and his coat of many colors; with the allusion, cf. Genesis 39:7–10.

9. Pythagoras was "misunderstood" possibly because when he returned to Samos at the age of fifty-six after years of study in Egypt, "no one was genuinely desirous of those disciplines which he endeavoured by all means to introduce among the Greeks," or possibly because later "they numbered him with the Gods" (*Iamblichus' Life of Pythagoras . . . translated from the Greek by Thomas Taylor* [London, 1818], pp. 13–14). Nicolaus Copernicus (1473–1543), Polish astronomer who believed the planets revolved around the sun.

10. In acrostics, the initial letter of each line of a poem, when read down, forms a word or words, but to be read forward, backward, or across, the work needs to be a palindrome. Both were used by the Greeks in the Alexandrian period.

11. William Pitt (1708–1778), 1st Earl of Chatham, considered England's best prime minister. John Adams (1735–1826), second president of the United States.

12. Sparta was an ancient Greek state.

13. Thomas Clarkson (1760–1846), English abolitionist.

14. Scipio Africanus the Elder (236–ca. 183 BCE), Roman general referred to in Milton's *Paradise Lost* (1667), IX, 510.

15. With this fable, cf. William Shakespeare, Induction to *The Taming of the Shrew*.

16. Scanderbeg (1403–1468), leader of the Albanian rebellion against the Turks; Gusta-

vus Adolphus (1594–1632), king of Sweden and leader of interventionist forces in the Thirty Years' War.

17. Parallax is the apparent change in the position of a star caused by the earth's motion as it orbits the sun.

18. An "apologue" is an allegorical narrative.

19. With "Bid them take . . . here within," cf. Exodus 3:5.

20. With "'Come out unto us,'" cf. Isaiah 36:16.

21. Emerson's adaptation of a sentiment expressed by Johann Christoph Friedrich von Schiller (1759–1805), German philosopher, in *Select Minor Poems, Translated from the German of Goethe and Schiller,* ed. John S. Dwight, in *Specimens of Foreign Standard Literature,* ed. George Ripley, 14 vols. (Boston, 1838–1842), 3:352 (*JMN,* 7:214).

22. Thor and Woden, or Odin, are Norse gods of war.

23. Antinomians are generally individuals who consciously take a stand against established rules. In Christian tradition, antinomianism refers to those who believe that salvation by grace excuses them from obeying the laws of humankind; in New England, the antinomian "heresy," imported from Germany, was fundamentally a rejection of the doctrine of the Divine authority of moral law and is chiefly associated with the banishment of Anne Hutchinson (1591–1643) from Massachusetts Bay Colony to Rhode Island in 1637. Emerson was an antinomian insofar as he believed that the moral law could be discovered only by the individual, but this belief in its absolute existence, based on Divine authority, kept him from going all the way. See "The Transcendentalist," para 7, below.

24. With "the word made . . . the nations," cf. John 1:14 and Revelation 22:2.

25. With these lines, cf. Fletcher, *Bonduca* (1647), III, 1. Audate was the God of war.

26. This sentence appears among "The Chaldaean Oracles of Zoroaster" in *Ancient Fragments of the Phoenician, Chaldaean . . . and Other Writers* (London, 1832), p. 271, compiled by Isaac Preston Cory (1802–1842), a Cambridge classicist.

27. With "'Let not God . . . will obey,'" cf. Exodus 20:19.

28. Antoine Laurent Lavoisier (1743–1794), French founder of modern chemistry; Jeremy Bentham (1748–1832), English reformer and utilitarian philosopher; Johann Kaspar Spurzheim (1776–1832), a founder of the pseudo-science of phrenology, which held that people's characters could be read through the configuration of their skulls.

29. Doric and Gothic are styles of architecture from, respectively, Greece and twelfth-through fifteenth-century England and France.

30. Phidias, fifth-century BCE Greek sculptor. Dante Alighieri (1265–1321), Italian poet and Christian humanist whose *Divina commedia* (completed in 1321) recounts the poet's journey through Hell *(Inferno),* Purgatory *(Purgatorio),* and Paradise *(Paradisio).*

31. With "thousand-cloven tongue," cf. Acts 2:1–4 and "Circles," para 6, below.

32. Emerson's source is likely the account by English explorer James Cook (1728–1879) of his first visit to New Zealand in *The Three Voyages of Captain James Cook Round the World,* 7 vols. (London, 1821), 2:34–38.

33. Greenwich, England, is the site of the Royal Observatory.

34. Stoicism, a philosophical school known for its belief in submitting to necessity, was founded in 308 BCE.

35. Diogenes (ca. 412–323 BCE), Greek cynic philosopher constantly seeking an honest man.

36. Henry Hudson (ca. 1565–1611), English explorer who attempted to discover the Northwest Passage between Europe and Asia through the Arctic Ocean; Vitus Bering, or Behring (1681–1741), Danish explorer of the strait between what is now Alaska and Russia; Sir William Edward Parry (1790–1855) and Sir John Franklin (1786–1847), English Arctic explorers.

37. To bivouac is to encamp for the night without tents or any coverings.

38. Emerson's source is *Mémorial de Sainte Hélène. Journal of the Private Life and Conversations of the Emperor Napoleon . . .* , 4 vols. (Boston, 1822–1823), 4:vii, 124, by Count Emmanuel Augustin Dieudonne de Las Cases (1766–1842), French historian (*JMN,* 5:508).

39. Emerson's source for this sentence, the fifteenth of the "Sentences of Ali, Son-in-Law of Mahomet, and his Fourth Successor," is the Appendix to Simon Ockley, *The Conquest of Syria, Persia, and Ægypt by the Saracens,* 2 vols. (London, 1708–1709), 2:2 (*JMN,* 6:388).

Circles[1]

1   The eye is the first circle; the horizon which it forms is the second; and throughout nature this primary figure is repeated without end. It is the highest emblem in the cipher of the world. St. Augustine described the nature of God as a circle whose centre was everywhere, and its circumference nowhere.[2] We are all our lifetime reading the copious sense of this first of forms. One moral we have already deduced in considering the circular or compensatory character of every human action. Another analogy we shall now trace; that every action admits of being outdone. Our life is an apprenticeship to the truth, that around every circle another can be drawn; that there is no end in nature, but every end is a beginning; that there is always another dawn risen on mid-noon, and under every deep a lower deep opens.[3]

2   This fact, as far as it symbolizes the moral fact of the Unattainable, the flying Perfect, around which the hands of man can never meet, at once the inspirer and the condemner of every success, may conveniently serve us to connect many illustrations of human power in every department.

3   There are no fixtures in nature. The universe is fluid and volatile. Permanence is but a word of degrees. Our globe seen by God, is a transparent law, not a mass of facts. The law dissolves the fact and holds it fluid. Our culture is

the predominance of an idea which draws after it all this train of cities and institutions. Let us rise into another idea: they will disappear. The Greek sculpture is all melted away, as if it had been statues of ice: here and there a solitary figure or fragment remaining, as we see flecks and scraps of snow left in cold dells and mountain clefts, in June and July. For, the genius that created it, creates now somewhat else. The Greek letters last a little longer, but are already passing under the same sentence, and tumbling into the inevitable pit which the creation of new thought opens for all that is old. The new continents are built out of the ruins of an old planet: the new races fed out of the decomposition of the foregoing. New arts destroy the old. See the investment of capital in aqueducts, made useless by hydraulics; fortifications, by gunpowder; roads and canals, by railways; sails, by steam; steam by electricity.

You admire this tower of granite, weathering the hurts of so many ages. 4 Yet a little waving hand built this huge wall, and that which builds, is better than that which is built. The hand that built, can topple it down much faster. Better than the hand, and nimbler, was the invisible thought which wrought through it, and thus ever behind the coarse effect, is a fine cause, which, being narrowly seen, is itself the effect of a finer cause. Every thing looks permanent until its secret is known. A rich estate appears to women and children, a firm and lasting fact; to a merchant, one easily created out of any materials, and easily lost. An orchard, good tillage, good grounds, seem a fixture, like a gold mine, or a river, to a citizen, but to a large farmer, not much more fixed than the state of the crop. Nature looks provokingly stable and secular, but it has a cause like all the rest; and when once I comprehend that, will these fields stretch so immovably wide, these leaves hang so individually considerable? Permanence is a word of degrees. Every thing is medial. Moons are no more bounds to spiritual power than bat-balls.

The key to every man is his thought. Sturdy and defying though he look, 5 he has a helm which he obeys, which is, the idea after which all his facts are classified. He can only be reformed by showing him a new idea which commands his own. The life of man is a self-evolving circle, which, from a ring imperceptibly small, rushes on all sides outwards to new and larger circles, and that without end. The extent to which this generation of circles, wheel without wheel will go, depends on the force or truth of the individual soul. For, it is the inert effort of each thought having formed itself into a circular

wave of circumstance, as, for instance, an empire, rules of an art, a local usage, a religious rite, to heap itself on that ridge, and to solidify, and hem in
the life. But if the soul is quick and strong, it bursts over that boundary on all
sides, and expands another orbit on the great deep, which also runs up into a
high wave, with attempt again to stop and to bind. But the heart refuses to be
imprisoned; in its first and narrowest pulses, it already tends outward with a
vast force, and to immense and innumerable expansions.

6   Every ultimate fact is only the first of a new series. Every general law
only a particular fact of some more general law presently to disclose itself.
There is no outside, no enclosing wall, no circumference to us. The man fin-
ishes his story,—how good! how final! how it puts a new face on all things! He
fills the sky. Lo, on the other side, rises also a man, and draws a circle around
the circle we had just pronounced the outline of the sphere. Then already is
our first speaker, not man, but only a first speaker. His only redress is forthwith to draw a circle outside of his antagonist. And so men do by themselves.
The result of to-day which haunts the mind and cannot be escaped, will presently be abridged into a word, and the principle that seemed to explain nature, will itself be included as one example of a bolder generalization. In the
thought of to-morrow there is a power to upheave all thy creed, all the creeds,
all the literatures of the nations, and marshal thee to a heaven which no epic
dream has yet depicted. Every man is not so much a workman in the world,
as he is a suggestion of that he should be. Men walk as prophecies of the
next age.

7   Step by step we scale this mysterious ladder: the steps are actions; the
new prospect is power. Every several result is threatened and judged by that
which follows. Every one seems to be contradicted by the new; it is only limited by the new. The new statement is always hated by the old, and, to those
dwelling in the old, comes like an abyss of skepticism. But the eye soon gets
wonted to it, for the eye and it are effects of one cause; then its innocency and
benefit appear, and, presently, all its energy spent, it pales and dwindles before the revelation of the new hour.

8   Fear not the new generalization. Does the fact look crass and material,
threatening to degrade thy theory of spirit? Resist it not; it goes to refine and
raise thy theory of matter just as much.

9   There are no fixtures to men, if we appeal to consciousness. Every man
supposes himself not to be fully understood; and if there is any truth in him,

if he rests at last on the divine soul, I see not how it can be otherwise. The last chamber, the last closet, he must feel, was never opened; there is always a residuum unknown, unanalyzable. That is, every man believes that he has a greater possibility.

Our moods do not believe in each other. To-day, I am full of thoughts, and can write what I please. I see no reason why I should not have the same thought, the same power of expression to-morrow. What I write, whilst I write it, seems the most natural thing in the world: but, yesterday, I saw a dreary vacuity in this direction in which now I see so much; and a month hence, I doubt not, I shall wonder who he was that wrote so many continuous pages. Alas for this infirm faith, this will not strenuous, this vast ebb of a vast flow! I am God in nature; I am a weed by the wall.

The continual effort to raise himself above himself, to work a pitch above his last height, betrays itself in a man's relations.[4] We thirst for approbation, yet cannot forgive the approver. The sweet of nature is love; yet if I have a friend, I am tormented by my imperfections. The love of me accuses the other party. If he were high enough to slight me, then could I love him, and rise by my affection to new heights. A man's growth is seen in the successive choirs of his friends. For every friend whom he loses for truth, he gains a better. I thought, as I walked in the woods and mused on my friends, why should I play with them this game of idolatry? I know and see too well, when not voluntarily blind, the speedy limits of persons called high and worthy. Rich, noble, and great they are by the liberality of our speech, but truth is sad. O blessed Spirit, whom I forsake for these, they are not thee! Every personal consideration that we allow, costs us heavenly state. We sell the thrones of angels for a short and turbulent pleasure.

How often must we learn this lesson? Men cease to interest us when we find their limitations. The only sin is limitation. As soon as you once come up with a man's limitations, it is all over with him. Has he talents? has he enterprises? has he knowledge? it boots not. Infinitely alluring and attractive was he to you yesterday, a great hope, a sea to swim in; now, you have found his shores, found it a pond, and you care not if you never see it again.

Each new step we take in thought reconciles twenty seemingly discordant facts, as expressions of one law. Aristotle and Plato are reckoned the respective heads of two schools. A wise man will see that Aristotle Platonizes. By going one step farther back in thought, discordant opinions are reconciled, by being seen to be two extremes of one principle, and we can never go so far back as to preclude a still higher vision.

14   Beware when the great God lets loose a thinker on this planet. Then all things are at risk. It is as when a conflagration has broken out in a great city, and no man knows what is safe, or where it will end. There is not a piece of science, but its flank may be turned to-morrow; there is not any literary reputation, not the so-called eternal names of fame, that may not be revised and condemned. The very hopes of man, the thoughts of his heart, the religion of nations, the manners and morals of mankind, are all at the mercy of a new generalization. Generalization is always a new influx of the divinity into the mind. Hence the thrill that attends it.

15   Valor consists in the power of self-recovery, so that a man cannot have his flank turned, cannot be outgeneralled, but put him where you will, he stands. This can only be by his preferring truth to his past apprehension of truth; and his alert acceptance of it from whatever quarter; the intrepid conviction that his laws, his relations to society, his christianity, his world, may at any time be superseded and decease.

16   There are degrees in idealism. We learn first to play with it academically, as the magnet was once a toy. Then we see in the heyday of youth and poetry that it may be true, that it is true in gleams and fragments. Then, its countenance waxes stern and grand, and we see that it must be true. It now shows itself ethical and practical. We learn that God IS; that he is in me; and that all things are shadows of him. The idealism of Berkeley is only a crude statement of the idealism of Jesus, and that, again, is a crude statement of the fact that all nature is the rapid efflux of goodness executing and organizing itself. Much more obviously is history and the state of the world at any one time, directly dependent on the intellectual classification then existing in the minds of men. The things which are dear to men at this hour, are so on account of the ideas which have emerged on their mental horizon, and which cause the present order of things as a tree bears its apples. A new degree of culture would instantly revolutionize the entire system of human pursuits.

17   Conversation is a game of circles. In conversation we pluck up the *termini* which bound the common of silence on every side. The parties are not to be judged by the spirit they partake and even express under this Pentecost. To-morrow they will have receded from this high-water mark. To-morrow you shall find them stooping under the old packsaddles. Yet let us enjoy the cloven flame whilst it glows on our walls.[5] When each new speaker strikes a new

light, emancipates us from the oppression of the last speaker, to oppress us with the greatness and exclusiveness of his own thought, then yields us to another redeemer, we seem to recover our rights, to become men. O what truths profound and executable only in ages and orbs, are supposed in the announcement of every truth! In common hours, society sits cold and statuesque. We all stand waiting, empty,—knowing, possibly, that we can be full, surrounded by mighty symbols which are not symbols to us, but prose and trivial toys. Then cometh the god, and converts the statues into fiery men, and by a flash of his eye burns up the veil which shrouded all things, and the meaning of the very furniture, of cup and saucer, of chair and clock and tester, is manifest. The facts which loomed so large in the fogs of yesterday,— property, climate, breeding, personal beauty, and the like, have strangely changed their proportions. All that we reckoned settled, shakes now and rattles; and literatures, cities, climates, religions, leave their foundations, and dance before our eyes. And yet here again see the swift circumscription. Good as is discourse, silence is better, and shames it. The length of the discourse indicates the distance of thought betwixt the speaker and the hearer. If they were at a perfect understanding in any part, no words would be necessary thereon. If at one in all parts, no words would be suffered.

Literature is a point outside of our hodiernal circle, through which a new one may be described.[6] The use of literature is to afford us a platform whence we may command a view of our present life, a purchase by which we may move it. We fill ourselves with ancient learning; install ourselves the best we can in Greek, in Punic, in Roman houses, only that we may wiselier see French, English, and American houses and modes of living.[7] In like manner, we see literature best from the midst of wild nature, or from the din of affairs, or from a high religion. The field cannot be well seen from within the field. The astronomer must have his diameter of the earth's orbit as a base to find the parallax of any star.[8]

Therefore, we value the poet. All the argument, and all the wisdom, is not in the encyclopedia, or the treatise on metaphysics, or the Body of Divinity, but in the sonnet or the play. In my daily work I incline to repeat my old steps, and do not believe in remedial force, in the power of change and reform. But some Petrarch or Ariosto, filled with the new wine of his imagination, writes me an ode, or a brisk romance, full of daring thought and action.[9] He smites and arouses me with his shrill tones, breaks up my whole chain of habits, and I open my eye on my own possibilities. He claps wings to the sides

18

19

of all the solid old lumber of the world, and I am capable once more of choosing a straight path in theory and practice.

20   We have the same need to command a view of the religion of the world. We can never see christianity from the catechism:—from the pastures, from a boat in the pond, from amidst the songs of wood-birds, we possibly may. Cleansed by the elemental light and wind, steeped in the sea of beautiful forms which the field offers us, we may chance to cast a right glance back upon biography. Christianity is rightly dear to the best of mankind; yet was there never a young philosopher whose breeding had fallen into the christian church, by whom that brave text of Paul's, was not specially prized, "Then shall also the Son be subject unto Him who put all things under him, that God may be all in all."[10] Let the claims and virtues of persons be never so great and welcome, the instinct of man presses eagerly onward to the impersonal and illimitable, and gladly arms itself against the dogmatism of bigots with this generous word, out of the book itself.

21   The natural world may be conceived of as a system of concentric circles, and we now and then detect in nature slight dislocations, which apprize us that this surface on which we now stand, is not fixed, but sliding. These manifold tenacious qualities, this chemistry and vegetation, these metals and animals, which seem to stand there for their own sake, are means and methods only, are words of God, and as fugitive as other words. Has the naturalist or chemist learned his craft, who has explored the gravity of atoms and the elective affinities, who has not yet discerned the deeper law whereof this is only a partial or approximate statement, namely, that like draws to like; and that the goods which belong to you, gravitate to you, and need not be pursued with pains and cost? Yet is that statement approximate also, and not final. Omnipresence is a higher fact. Not through subtle, subterranean channels, need friend and fact be drawn to their counterpart, but, rightly considered, these things proceed from the eternal generation of the soul. Cause and effect are two sides of one fact.

22   The same law of eternal procession ranges all that we call the virtues, and extinguishes each in the light of a better. The great man will not be prudent in the popular sense; all his prudence will be so much deduction from his grandeur. But it behoves each to see when he sacrifices prudence, to what god he devotes it; if to ease and pleasure, he had better be prudent still: if to a great trust, he can well spare his mule and panniers, who has a winged chariot instead. Geoffrey draws on his boots to go through the woods, that his

feet may be safer from the bite of snakes; Aaron never thinks of such a peril. In many years, neither is harmed by such an accident. Yet it seems to me that with every precaution you take against such an evil, you put yourself into the power of the evil. I suppose that the highest prudence is the lowest prudence. Is this too sudden a rushing from the centre to the verge of our orbit? Think how many times we shall fall back into pitiful calculations, before we take up our rest in the great sentiment, or make the verge of to-day the new centre. Besides, your bravest sentiment is familiar to the humblest men. The poor and the low have their way of expressing the last facts of philosophy as well as you. "Blessed be nothing," and "the worse things are, the better they are," are proverbs which express the transcendentalism of common life.

One man's justice is another's injustice; one man's beauty, another's ugliness; one man's wisdom, another's folly; as one beholds the same objects from a higher point of view. One man thinks justice consists in paying debts, and has no measure in his abhorrence of another who is very remiss in this duty, and makes the creditor wait tediously. But that second man has his own way of looking at things; asks himself, which debt must I pay first, the debt to the rich, or the debt to the poor? the debt of money, or the debt of thought to mankind, of genius to nature? For you, O broker, there is no other principle but arithmetic. For me, commerce is of trivial import; love, faith, truth of character, the aspiration of man, these are sacred: nor can I detach one duty, like you, from all other duties, and concentrate my forces mechanically on the payment of moneys. Let me live onward: you shall find that, though slower, the progress of any character will liquidate all these debts without injustice to higher claims. If a man should dedicate himself to the payment of notes, would not this be injustice? Owes he no debt but money? And are all claims on him to be postponed to a landlord's or a banker's?

There is no virtue which is final; all are initial. The virtues of society are vices of the saint. The terror of reform is the discovery that we must cast away our virtues, or what we have always esteemed such, into the same pit that has consumed our grosser vices.

> "Forgive his crimes, forgive his virtues too,
> Those smaller faults, half converts to the right."[11]

It is the highest power of divine moments that they abolish our contritions also. I accuse myself of sloth and unprofitableness, day by day; but when these waves of God flow into me, I no longer reckon lost time. I no longer poorly compute my possible achievement by what remains to me of the month or the year; for these moments confer a sort of omnipresence and omnipotence, which asks nothing of duration, but sees that the energy of the mind is commensurate with the work to be done, without time.

26   And thus, O circular philosopher, I hear some reader exclaim, you have arrived at a fine pyrrhonism, at an equivalence and indifferency of all actions, and would fain teach us, that, *if we are true,* forsooth, our crimes may be lively stones out of which we shall construct the temple of the true God.[12]

27   I am not careful to justify myself. I own I am gladdened by seeing the predominance of the saccharine principle throughout vegetable nature, and not less by beholding in morals that unrestrained inundation of the principle of good into every chink and hole that selfishness has left open, yea, into selfishness and sin itself; so that no evil is pure; nor hell itself without its extreme satisfactions.[13] But lest I should mislead any when I have my own head, and obey my whims, let me remind the reader that I am only an experimenter. Do not set the least value on what I do, or the least discredit on what I do not, as if I pretended to settle anything as true or false. I unsettle all things. No facts are to me sacred; none are profane; I simply experiment, an endless seeker, with no Past at my back.

28   Yet this incessant movement and progression, which all things partake, could never become sensible to us, but by contrast to some principle of fixture or stability in the soul. Whilst the eternal generation of circles proceeds, the eternal generator abides. That central life is somewhat superior to creation, superior to knowledge and thought, and contains all its circles. Forever it labors to create a life and thought as large and excellent as itself; but in vain; for that which is made, instructs how to make a better.

29   Thus there is no sleep, no pause, no preservation, but all things renew, germinate, and spring. Why should we import rags and relics into the new hour? Nature abhors the old, and old age seems the only disease: all others run into this one. We call it by many names, fever, intemperance, insanity, stupidity, and crime: they are all forms of old age: they are rest, conservatism, appropriation, inertia, not newness, not the way onward. We grizzle every day. I see no need of it. Whilst we converse with what is above us, we do not grow old, but grow young. Infancy, youth, receptive, aspiring, with religious eye looking upward, counts itself nothing, and abandons itself to the instruction flowing from all sides. But the man and woman of seventy, assume to know all; throw up their hope; renounce aspiration; accept the actual for the

necessary; and talk down to the young. Let them then become organs of the Holy Ghost; let them be lovers; let them behold truth; and their eyes are uplifted, their wrinkles smoothed, they are perfumed again with hope and power. This old age ought not to creep on a human mind. In nature, every moment is new; the past is always swallowed and forgotten; the coming only is sacred. Nothing is secure but life, transition, the energizing spirit. No love can be bound by oath or covenant to secure it against a higher love. No truth so sublime but it may be trivial tomorrow in the light of new thoughts. People wish to be settled: only as far as they are unsettled, is there any hope for them.

Life is a series of surprises. We do not guess to-day the mood, the pleasure, the power of to-morrow, when we are building up our being. Of lower states,—of acts of routine and sense, we can tell somewhat, but the masterpieces of God, the total growths, and universal movements of the soul, he hideth; they are incalculable. I can know that truth is divine and helpful, but how it shall help me, I can have no guess, for, *so to be* is the sole inlet of *so to know.* The new position of the advancing man has all the powers of the old, yet has them all new. It carries in its bosom all the energies of the past, yet is itself an exhalation of the morning. I cast away in this new moment all my once hoarded knowledge, as vacant and vain. Now, for the first time, seem I to know any thing rightly. The simplest words,—we do not know what they mean, except when we love and aspire.

The difference between talents and character is adroitness to keep the old and trodden round, and power and courage to make a new road to new and better goals. Character makes an overpowering present, a cheerful, determined hour, which fortifies all the company, by making them see that much is possible and excellent, that was not thought of. Character dulls the impression of particular events. When we see the conqueror, we do not think much of any one battle or success. We see that we had exaggerated the difficulty. It was easy to him. The great man is not convulsible or tormentable. He is so much, that events pass over him without much impression. People say sometimes, 'See what I have overcome; see how cheerful I am; see how completely I have triumphed over these black events.' Not if they still remind me of the black event,—they have not yet conquered. Is it conquest to be a gay and decorated sepulchre, or a half-crazed widow hysterically laughing? True conquest is the causing the black event to fade and disappear as an early cloud of insignificant result in a history so large and advancing.

32   The one thing which we seek with insatiable desire, is to forget ourselves, to be surprised out of our propriety, to lose our sempiternal memory, and to do something without knowing how or why; in short, to draw a new circle. Nothing great was ever achieved without enthusiasm.[14] The way of life is wonderful. It is by abandonment. The great moments of history are the facilities of performance through the strength of ideas, as the works of genius and religion. "A man," said Oliver Cromwell, "never rises so high as when he knows not whither he is going."[15] Dreams and drunkenness, the use of opium and alcohol are the semblance and counterfeit of this oracular genius, and hence their dangerous attraction for men. For the like reason, they ask the aid of wild passions, as in gaming and war, to ape in some manner these flames and generosities of the heart.

Notes

1. In the 1847 edition of *Essays* (titled *Essays: First Series*), this essay was preceded by the poem "Circles"; see *CW, 9:662.*

2. The early Christian church father and philosopher Saint Augustine (354–430) wrote at length about the nature of God and about circles, but he seems not to have used this metaphor. Emerson's source is John Norris, *An Essay Towards the Theory of the Ideal or Intelligible World,* 1:389 (*JMN,* 5:57).

3. With "another dawn risen on mid-noon," cf. Milton, *Paradise Lost,* V, 308–311.

4. With "raise himself above . . . man's relations," cf. Epistle *"To the Lady Margaret, Countess of Cumberland,"* ll. 98–99, by Samuel Daniel (1562–1619), English poet and historian.

5. Beginning with the three previous sentences, with "the spirit they partake . . . cloven flame," cf. Acts 2:1–4 and "Self-Reliance," para 46, above. Pentecost is both a Christian ceremony, celebrating the descent of the Holy Spirit to the apostles, held the seventh Sunday after Easter (Whitsunday), and the Jewish festival of Shavuoth (Feast of Weeks), commemorating God's presentation of the Ten Commandments to Moses.

6. The term "hodiernal" means "belonging to this day."

7. Punic refers to Carthage, an ancient city-state on the Bay of Tunis in northern Africa.

8. For parallax, see the note to "Self-Reliance," para 24, above.

9. The Italian poets Petrarch (1304–1374) and Ludovico Ariosto (1474–1533).

10. With "brave text of Paul's . . . all in all,'" cf. 1 Corinthians 15:28.

11. *The Complaint; or, Night Thoughts,* IX, ll. 2316–2317, by Edward Young (1683–1765), English poet and critic.

12. Pyrrhonism is a doctrine espoused by Pyrrho (ca. 360–ca. 270 BCE), Greek sceptic philosopher, that all knowledge is uncertain. With "lively stones out . . . true God," cf. 1 Peter 2:5.

13. Emerson attributed this belief about hell to Swedenborg (*JMN,* 7:521).

14. Popularly attributed to Emerson, the source for this statement is Samuel Taylor Coleridge, *The Statesman's Manual; A Lay Sermon . . .* (Burlington, Vt., 1832), p. 30 (*JMN,* 5:15).

15. Oliver Cromwell (1599–1658), English revolutionary who became Lord Protector of the Realm. Emerson's source for the quotation is Bishop William Warburton's annotation to the Earl of Clarendon's *History of the Rebellion and Civil Wars in England* (Boston ed., 1827), VIII, 1831 (*JMN,* 6:93).

The Transcendentalist

The first thing we have to say respecting what are called *new views* here in New England, at the present time, is, that they are not new, but the very oldest of thoughts cast into the mould of these new times. The light is always identical in its composition, but it falls on a great variety of objects, and by so falling is first revealed to us, not in its own form, for it is formless, but in theirs; in like manner, thought only appears in the objects it classifies. What is popularly called Transcendentalism among us, is Idealism; Idealism as it appears in 1842. As thinkers, mankind have ever divided into two sects, Materialists and Idealists; the first class founding on experience, the second on consciousness; the first class beginning to think from the data of the senses, the second class perceive that the senses are not final, and say, the senses give us representations of things, but what are the things themselves, they cannot tell. The materialist insists on facts, on history, on the force of circumstances, and the animal wants of man; the idealist on the power of Thought and of Will, on inspiration, on miracle, on individual culture. These two modes of thinking are both natural, but the idealist contends that his way of thinking is in higher nature. He concedes all that the other affirms, admits the impressions of sense, admits their coherency, their use and beauty, and then asks the materialist for his grounds of assurance that things are as his senses represent them. But I, he says, affirm facts not affected by the illusions of sense, facts which are of the same nature as the faculty which reports them, and not liable to doubt; facts which in their first appearance to us assume a native superiority to material facts, degrading these into a language by which the first are to be spoken; facts which it only needs a retirement from the senses to discern. Every materialist will be an idealist; but an idealist can never go backward to be a materialist.

The idealist, in speaking of events, sees them as spirits. He does not deny the sensuous fact; by no means; but he will not see that alone. He does not deny the presence of this table, this chair, and the walls of this room, but he looks at these things as the reverse side of the tapestry, as the *other end,* each being a sequel or completion of a spiritual fact which nearly concerns him. This manner of looking at things, transfers every object in nature from an independent and anomalous position without there, into the consciousness. Even the materialist Condillac, perhaps the most logical expounder of materialism, was constrained to say, "Though we should soar into the heavens, though we should sink into the abyss, we never go out of ourselves; it is always our own thought that we perceive."[1] What more could an idealist say? 2

The materialist, secure in the certainty of sensation, mocks at fine-spun theories, at star-gazers and dreamers, and believes that his life is solid, that he at least takes nothing for granted, but knows where he stands, and what he does. Yet how easy it is to show him, that he also is a phantom walking and working amid phantoms, and that he need only ask a question or two beyond his daily questions, to find his solid universe growing dim and impalpable before his sense. The sturdy capitalist, no matter how deep and square on blocks of Quincy granite he lays the foundations of his banking-house or Exchange,[2] must set it, at last, not on a cube corresponding to the angles of his structure, but on a mass of unknown materials and solidity, red-hot or white-hot, perhaps at the core, which rounds off to an almost perfect sphericity, and lies floating in soft air, and goes spinning away, dragging bank and banker with it at a rate of thousands of miles the hour, he knows not whither,—a bit of bullet, now glimmering, now darkling through a small cubic space on the edge of an unimaginable pit of emptiness. And this wild balloon, in which his whole venture is embarked, is a just symbol of his whole state and faculty. One thing, at least, he says is certain, and does not give me the headache, that figures do not lie; the multiplication table has been hitherto found unimpeachable truth; and, moreover, if I put a gold eagle in my safe, I find it again 3 to-morrow;³—but for these thoughts, I know not whence they are. They change and pass away. But ask him why he believes that an uniform experience will continue uniform, or on what grounds he founds his faith in his figures, and he will perceive that his mental fabric is built up on just as strange and quaking foundations as his proud edifice of stone.

4   In the order of thought, the materialist takes his departure from the external world, and esteems a man as one product of that. The idealist takes his departure from his consciousness, and reckons the world as an appearance. The materialist respects sensible masses, Society, Government, social art, and luxury, every establishment, every mass, whether majority of numbers, or extent of space, or amount of objects, every social action. The idealist has another measure, which is metaphysical, namely, the *rank* which things themselves take in his consciousness; not at all, the size or appearance. Mind is the only reality, of which men and all other natures are better or worse reflectors. Nature, literature, history, are only subjective phenomena. Although in his action overpowered by the laws of action, and so, warmly cooperating with men, even preferring them to himself, yet when he speaks scientifically, or after the order of thought, he is constrained to degrade persons into representatives of truths. He does not respect labor, or the products of labor, namely, property, otherwise than as a manifold symbol, illustrating with wonderful fidelity of details the laws of being; he does not respect government, except as far as it reiterates the law of his mind; nor the church; nor charities; nor arts, for themselves; but hears, as at a vast distance, what they say, as if his consciousness would speak to him through a pantomimic scene. His thought, —that is the Universe. His experience inclines him to behold the procession of facts you call the world, as flowing perpetually outward from an invisible, unsounded centre in himself, centre alike of him and of them, and necessitating him to regard all things as having a subjective or relative existence, relative to that aforesaid Unknown Centre of him.

5   From this transfer of the world into the consciousness, this beholding of all things in the mind, follows easily his whole ethics. It is simpler to be self-dependent. The height, the deity of man is to be self-sustained, to need no gift, no foreign force. Society is good when it does not violate me; but best when it is likest to solitude. Everything real is self-existent. Everything divine shares the self-existence of Deity. All that you call the world is the shadow of that substance which you are, the perpetual creation of the powers of thought, of those that are dependent and of those that are independent of

your will. Do not cumber yourself with fruitless pains to mend and remedy remote effects; let the soul be erect, and all things will go well. You think me the child of my circumstances: I make my circumstance. Let any thought or motive of mine be different from that they are, the difference will transform my whole condition and economy. I—this thought which is called I,—is the mould into which the world is poured like melted wax. The mould is invisible, but the world betrays the shape of the mould. You call it the power of circumstance, but it is the power of me. Am I in harmony with myself? my position will seem to you just and commanding. Am I vicious and insane? my fortunes will seem to you obscure and descending. As I am, so shall I associate; as I am, so shall I act; Cæsar's history will paint out Cæsar. Jesus acted so, because he thought so. I do not wish to overlook or to gainsay any reality; I say, I make my circumstance: but if you ask me, Whence am I? I feel like other men my relation to that Fact which cannot be spoken, or defined, nor even thought, but which exists, and will exist.

The Transcendentalist adopts the whole connexion of spiritual doctrine. He believes in miracle, in the perpetual openness of the human mind to new influx of light and power; he believes in inspiration, and in ecstasy. He wishes that the spiritual principle should be suffered to demonstrate itself to the end, in all possible applications to the state of man, without the admission of anything unspiritual; that is, anything positive, dogmatic, personal. Thus, the spiritual measure of inspiration is the depth of the thought, and never, *who* said it? And so he resists all attempts to palm other rules and measures on the spirit than its own.

In action, he easily incurs the charge of antinomianism by his avowal that he, who has the Lawgiver, may with safety not only neglect, but even contravene every written commandment.[4] In the play of Othello, the expiring Desdemona absolves her husband of the murder, to her attendant Emilia. Afterwards, when Emilia charges him with the crime, Othello exclaims,

> "You heard her say herself it was not I."

Emilia replies,

> "The more angel she, and thou the blacker devil."[5]

Of this fine incident, Jacobi, the Transcendental moralist, makes use, with other parallel instances, in his reply to Fichte.[6] Jacobi, refusing all measure of right and wrong except the determinations of the private spirit, remarks that there is no crime but has sometimes been a virtue. "I," he says, "am that atheist, that godless person who, in opposition to an imaginary doctrine of calculation, would lie as the dying Desdemona lied; would lie and deceive as Pylades when he personated Orestes; would assassinate like Timoleon; would perjure myself like Epaminondas, and John de Witt; I would resolve on suicide like Cato; I would commit sacrilege with David; yea, and pluck ears of corn on the Sabbath, for no other reason than that I was fainting for lack of food. For, I have assurance in myself that in pardoning these faults according to the letter, man exerts the sovereign right which the majesty of his being confers on him; he sets the seal of his divine nature to the grace he accords."[7]

9   In like manner, if there is anything grand and daring in human thought or virtue, any reliance on the vast, the unknown; any presentiment; any extravagance of faith, the spiritualist adopts it as most in nature. The oriental mind has always tended to this largeness. Buddhism is an expression of it. The Buddhist who thanks no man, who says, "do not flatter your benefactors," but who in his conviction that every good deed can by no possibility escape its reward, will not deceive the benefactor by pretending that he has done more than he should, is a Transcendentalist.

10   You will see by this sketch that there is no such thing as a Transcendental *party;* that there is no pure Transcendentalist; that we know of none but the prophets and heralds of such a philosophy; that all who by strong bias of nature have leaned to the spiritual side in doctrine, have stopped short of their goal. We have had many harbingers and forerunners; but of a purely spiritual life, history has yet afforded no example. I mean, we have yet no man who has leaned entirely on his character, and eaten angels' food; who, trusting to his sentiments, found life made of miracles; who, working for universal aims, found himself fed, he knew not how; clothed, sheltered, and weaponed, he knew not how, and yet it was done by his own hands. Only in the instinct of the lower animals we find the suggestion of the methods of it, and something higher than our understanding. The squirrel hoards nuts, and the bee gathers honey, without knowing what they do, and they are thus provided for without selfishness or disgrace.

11   Shall we say, then, that Transcendentalism is the Saturnalia or excess of Faith; the presentiment of a faith proper to man in his integrity, excessive only when his imperfect obedience hinders the satisfaction of his wish. Na-

ture is transcendental, exists primarily, necessarily, ever works and advances, yet takes no thought for the morrow.[8] Man owns the dignity of the life which throbs around him in chemistry, and tree, and animal, and in the involuntary functions of his own body; yet he is baulked when he tries to fling himself into this enchanted circle, where all is done without degradation. Yet genius and virtue predict in man the same absence of private ends, and of condescension to circumstances, united with every trait and talent of beauty and power.

This way of thinking, falling on Roman times, made Stoic philosophers; falling on despotic times, made patriot Catos and Brutuses;[9] falling on superstitious times, made prophets and apostles; on popish times, made protestants and ascetic monks, preachers of Faith against the preachers of Works; on prelatical times, made Puritans and Quakers; and falling on Unitarian and conservative times, makes the peculiar shades of Idealism which we know.

It is well known to most of my audience, that the Idealism of the present day acquired the name of Transcendental, from the use of that term by Immanuel Kant, of Konigsberg, who replied to the skeptical philosophy of Locke, which insisted that there was nothing in the intellect which was not previously in the experience of the senses, by showing that there was a very important class of ideas, or imperative forms, which did not come by experience, but through which experience was acquired;[10] that these were intuitions of the mind itself; and he denominated them *Transcendental* forms. The extraordinary profoundness and precision of that man's thinking have given vogue to his nomenclature, in Europe and America, to that extent, that whatever belongs to the class of intuitive thought, is popularly called at the present day *Transcendental*.

Although, as we have said, there is no pure transcendentalist, yet the tendency to respect the intuitions, and to give them, at least in our creed, all authority over our experience, has deeply colored the conversation and poetry of the present day; and the history of genius and of religion in these times, though impure, and as yet not incarnated in any powerful individual, will be the history of this tendency.

It is a sign of our times, conspicuous to the coarsest observer, that many intelligent and religious persons withdraw themselves from the common labors and competitions of the market and the caucus, and betake themselves to a certain solitary and critical way of living, from which no solid fruit has

12

13

14

15

yet appeared to justify their separation. They hold themselves aloof: they feel the disproportion between their faculties and the work offered them, and they prefer to ramble in the country and perish of ennui, to the degradation of such charities and such ambitions as the city can propose to them. They are striking work, and crying out for somewhat worthy to do! What they do, is done only because they are overpowered by the humanities that speak on all sides; and they consent to such labor as is open to them, though to their lofty dream the writing of Iliads or Hamlets, or the building of cities or empires seems drudgery.

16   Now every one must do after his kind, be he asp or angel, and these must. The question, which a wise man and a student of modern history will ask, is, what that kind is? And truly, as in ecclesiastical history we take so much pains to know what the Gnostics, what the Essenes, what the Manichees, and what the Reformers believed,[11] it would not misbecome us to inquire nearer home, what these companions and contemporaries of ours think and do, at least so far as these thoughts and actions appear to be not accidental and personal, but common to many, and so the inevitable flower of the Tree of Time. Our American literature and spiritual history are, we confess, in the optative mood; but whoso knows these seething brains, these admirable radicals, these unsocial worshippers, these talkers who talk the sun and moon away, will believe that this heresy cannot pass away without leaving its mark.

17   They are lonely; the spirit of their writing and conversation is lonely; they shed influences; they shun general society; they incline to shut themselves in their chamber in the house, to live in the country rather than in the town, and to find their tasks and amusements in solitude. Society, to be sure, does not like this very well; it saith, Whoso goes to walk alone, accuses the whole world; he declareth all to be unfit to be his companions; it is very uncivil, nay, insulting; Society will retaliate. Meantime, this retirement does not proceed from any whim on the part of these separators; but if any one will take pains to talk with them, he will find that this part is chosen both from temperament and from principle; with some unwillingness, too, and as a choice of the less of two evils; for these persons are not by nature melancholy, sour, and unsocial,—they are not stockish or brute,—but joyous, susceptible, affectionate; they have even more than others a great wish to be loved. Like the young Mozart, they are rather ready to cry ten times a day, "But are you sure you love me?"[12] Nay, if they tell you their whole thought, they will own that

love seems to them the last and highest gift of nature; that there are persons whom in their hearts they daily thank for existing,—persons whose faces are perhaps unknown to them, but whose fame and spirit have penetrated their solitude,—and for whose sake they wish to exist. To behold the beauty of another character, which inspires a new interest in our own; to behold the beauty lodged in a human being, with such vivacity of apprehension, that I am instantly forced home to inquire if I am not deformity itself; to behold in another the expression of a love so high that it assures itself,—assures itself also to me against every possible casualty except my unworthiness;—these are degrees on the scale of human happiness, to which they have ascended; and it is a fidelity to this sentiment which has made common association distasteful to them. They wish a just and even fellowship, or none. They cannot gossip with you, and they do not wish, as they are sincere and religious, to gratify any mere curiosity which you may entertain. Like fairies, they do not wish to be spoken of. Love me, they say, but do not ask who is my cousin and my uncle. If you do not need to hear my thought, because you can read it in my face and behavior, then I will tell it you from sunrise to sunset. If you cannot divine it, you would not understand what I say. I will not molest myself for you. I do not wish to be profaned.

And yet, when you see them near, it seems as if this loneliness, and not this love, would prevail in their circumstances, because of the extravagant demand they make on human nature. That, indeed, constitutes a new feature in their portrait, that they are the most exacting and extortionate critics. Their quarrel with every man they meet, is not with his kind, but with his degree. There is not enough of him,—that is the only fault. They prolong their privilege of childhood in this wise, of doing nothing,—but making immense demands on all the gladiators in the lists of action and fame. They make us feel the strange disappointment which overcasts every human youth. So many promising youths, and never a finished man! The profound nature will have a savage rudeness; the delicate one will be shallow, or the victim of sensibility; the richly accomplished will have some capital absurdity; and so every piece has a crack. 'T is strange, but this masterpiece is a result of such an extreme delicacy, that the most unobserved flaw in the boy will neutralize the most aspiring genius, and spoil the work. Talk with a seaman of the hazards to life in his profession, and he will ask you, "Where are the old sailors? do you not see that all are young men?" And we, on this sea of human

18

thought, in like manner inquire, Where are the old idealists? where are they who represented to the last generation that extravagant hope, which a few happy aspirants suggest to ours? In looking at the class of counsel, and power, and wealth, and at the matronage of the land, amidst all the prudence and all the triviality, one asks, Where are they who represented genius, virtue, the invisible and heavenly world, to these? Are they dead,—taken in early ripeness to the gods,—as ancient wisdom foretold their fate? Or did the high idea die out of them, and leave their unperfumed body as its tomb and tablet, announcing to all that the celestial inhabitant, who once gave them beauty, had departed? Will it be better with the new generation? We easily predict a fair future to each new candidate who enters the lists, but we are frivolous and volatile, and by low aims and ill example do what we can to defeat this hope. Then these youths bring us a rough but effectual aid. By their unconcealed dissatisfaction, they expose our poverty, and the insignificance of man to man. A man is a poor limitary benefactor. He ought to be a shower of benefits—a great influence, which should never let his brother go, but should refresh old merits continually with new ones; so that, though absent, he should never be out of my mind, his name never far from my lips; but if the earth should open at my side, or my last hour were come, his name should be the prayer I should utter to the Universe. But in our experience, man is cheap, and friendship wants its deep sense. We affect to dwell with our friends in their absence, but we do not; when deed, word, or letter comes not, they let us go. These exacting children advertise us of our wants. There is no compliment, no smooth speech with them; they pay you only this one compliment, of insatiable expectation; they aspire, they severely exact, and if they only stand fast in this watch-tower, and persist in demanding unto the end, and without end, then are they terrible friends, whereof poet and priest cannot choose but stand in awe; and what if they eat clouds, and drink wind, they have not been without service to the race of man.

19   With this passion for what is great and extraordinary, it cannot be wondered at, that they are repelled by vulgarity and frivolity in people. They say to themselves, It is better to be alone than in bad company. And it is really a wish to be met,—the wish to find society for their hope and religion,—which prompts them to shun what is called society. They feel that they are never so fit for friendship, as when they have quit mankind, and taken themselves to friend. A picture, a book, a favorite spot in the hills or the woods, which they

can people with the fair and worthy creation of the fancy, can give them often forms so vivid, that these for the time shall seem real, and society the illusion.

But their solitary and fastidious manners not only withdraw them from the conversation, but from the labors of the world; they are not good citizens, not good members of society; unwillingly they bear their part of the public and private burdens; they do not willingly share in the public charities, in the public religious rites, in the enterprizes of education, of missions foreign or domestic, in the abolition of the slave-trade, or in the temperance-society. They are inactive; they do not even like to vote. The philanthropists inquire whether Transcendentalism does not mean sloth. They had as lief hear that their friend was dead as that he was a Transcendentalist; for then is he paralyzed, and can never do anything for humanity. What right, cries the good world, has the man of genius to retreat from work, and indulge himself? The popular literary creed seems to be, 'I am a sublime genius; I ought not therefore to labor.' But genius is the power to labor better and more availably than others. Deserve thy genius: exalt it. The good, the illuminated, sit apart from the rest, censuring their dulness and vices, as if they thought that, by sitting very grand in their chairs, the very brokers, attorneys, and congressmen would see the error of their ways, and flock to them. But the good and wise must learn to act, and carry salvation to the combatants and demagogues in the dusty arena below.

On the part of these children, it is replied, that life and their faculty seem to them gifts too rich to be squandered on such trifles as you propose to them. What you call your fundamental institutions, your great and holy causes, seem to them great abuses, and, when nearly seen, paltry matters. Each 'Cause,' as it is called,—say Abolition, Temperance, say Calvinism, or Unitarianism,—becomes speedily a little shop, where the article, let it have been at first never so subtle and ethereal, is now made up into portable and convenient cakes, and retailed in small quantities to suit purchasers. You make very free use of these words "great and holy," but few things appear to them such. Few persons have any magnificence of nature to inspire enthusiasm, and the philanthropies and charities have a certain air of quackery. As to the general course of living, and the daily employments of men, they cannot see much virtue in these, since they are parts of this vicious circle; and, as no great ends are answered by the men, there is nothing noble in the arts by which they are maintained. Nay, they have made the experiment, and found that, from the liberal professions to the coarsest manual labor, and from the courtesies of the academy and the college to the conventions of the cotillon-room and the morning call, there is a spirit of cowardly compromise and seeming, which intimates a frightful skepticism, a life without love, and an activity without an aim.

22   Unless the action is necessary, unless it is adequate, I do not wish to per-form it. I do not wish to do one thing but once. I do not love routine. Once possessed of the principle, it is equally easy to make four or forty thousand applications of it. A great man will be content to have indicated in any the slightest manner his perception of the reigning Idea of his time, and will leave to those who like it the multiplication of examples. When he has hit the white, the rest may shatter the target. Every thing admonishes us how need-lessly long life is. Every moment of a hero so raises and cheers us, that a twelve-month is an age. All that the brave Xanthus brings home from his wars, is the recollection that, at the storming of Samos, "in the heat of the battle, Pericles smiled on me, and passed on to another detachment."[13] It is the quality of the moment, not the number of days, of events, or of actors, that imports.

23   New, we confess, and by no means happy, is our condition: if you want the aid of our labor, we ourselves stand in greater want of the labor. We are miserable with inaction. We perish of rest and rust. But we do not like your work.

24   'Then,' says the world, 'show me your own.'

25   'We have none.'

26   'What will you do, then?' cries the world.

27   'We will wait.'

28   'How long?'

29   'Until the Universe rises up and calls us to work.'

30   'But whilst you wait, you grow old and useless.'

31   'Be it so: I can sit in a corner and *perish,* (as you call it,) but I will not move until I have the highest command. If no call should come for years, for centu-ries, then I know that the want of the Universe is the attestation of faith by this my abstinence. Your virtuous projects, so called, do not cheer me. I know that which shall come will cheer me. If I cannot work, at least I need not lie. All that is clearly due to-day is not to lie. In other places, other men have en-

countered sharp trials, and have behaved themselves well. The martyrs were sawn asunder, or hung alive on meat-hooks. Cannot we screw our courage to patience and truth, and without complaint, or even with good-humor, await our turn of action in the Infinite Counsels?'

But, to come a little closer to the secret of these persons, we must say, that to them it seems a very easy matter to answer the objections of the man of the world, but not so easy to dispose of the doubts and objections that occur to themselves. They are exercised in their own spirit with queries, which acquaint them with all adversity, and with the trials of the bravest heroes. When I asked them concerning their private experience, they answered somewhat in this wise: It is not to be denied that there must be some wide difference between my faith and other faith; and mine is a certain brief experience, which surprised me in the highway or in the market, in some place, at some time,—whether in the body or out of the body, God knoweth,—[14] and made me aware that I had played the fool with fools all this time, but that law existed for me and for all; that to me belonged trust, a child's trust and obedience, and the worship of ideas, and I should never be fool more. Well, in the space of an hour, probably, I was let down from this height; I was at my old tricks, the selfish member of a selfish society. My life is superficial, takes no root in the deep world; I ask, When shall I die, and be relieved of the responsibility of seeing an Universe which I do not use? I wish to exchange this flash-of-lightning faith for continuous daylight, this fever-glow for a benign climate.

These two states of thought diverge every moment, and stand in wild contrast. To him who looks at his life from these moments of illumination, it will seem that he skulks and plays a mean, shiftless, and subaltern part in the world. That is to be done which he has not skill to do, or to be said which others can say better, and he lies by, or occupies his hands with some plaything, until his hour comes again.[15] Much of our reading, much of our labor, seems mere waiting: it was not that we were born for.[16] Any other could do it as well, or better. So little skill enters into these works, so little do they mix with the divine life, that it really signifies little what we do, whether we turn a grindstone, or ride, or run, or make fortunes, or govern the state. The worst feature of this double consciousness is, that the two lives, of the understanding and of the soul, which we lead, really show very little relation to each other, never meet and measure each other: one prevails now, all buzz and din; and the other prevails then, all infinitude and paradise; and, with the progress of life, the two discover no greater disposition to reconcile themselves. Yet, what is my faith? What am I? What but a thought of serenity and independence, an abode in the deep blue sky? Presently the clouds shut down again; yet we retain the belief that this petty web we weave will at last be overshot and reticulated with veins of the blue, and that the moments will characterize the days. Patience, then, is for us, is it not? Patience, and still patience. When we pass, as presently we shall, into some new infinitude, out of this Iceland of negations, it will please us to reflect that, though we had few virtues or consolations, we bore with our indigence, nor once strove to repair it with hypocrisy or false heat of any kind.

34 　But this class are not sufficiently characterized, if we omit to add that they are lovers and worshippers of Beauty.[17] In the eternal trinity of Truth, Goodness, and Beauty, each in its perfection including the three, they prefer to make Beauty the sign and head. Something of the same taste is observable in all the moral movements of the time, in the religious and benevolent enterprises. They have a liberal, even an æsthetic spirit. A reference to Beauty in action sounds, to be sure, a little hollow and ridiculous in the ears of the old church. In politics, it has often sufficed, when they treated of justice, if they kept the bounds of selfish calculation. If they granted restitution, it was prudence which granted it. But the justice which is now claimed for the black, and the pauper, and the drunkard, is for Beauty—is for a necessity to the soul of the agent, not of the beneficiary. I say this is the tendency, not yet the realization. Our virtue totters and trips, does not yet walk firmly. Its representatives are austere; they preach and denounce; their rectitude is not yet a grace. They are still liable to that slight taint of burlesque which, in our strange world, attaches to the zealot. A saint should be as dear as the apple of the eye. Yet we are tempted to smile, and we flee from the working to the speculative reformer, to escape that same slight ridicule. Alas for these days of derision and criticism! We call the Beautiful the highest, because it appears to us the golden mean, escaping the dowdiness of the good, and the heartlessness of the true.—They are lovers of nature also, and find an indemnity in the inviolable order of the world for the violated order and grace of man.

35 　There is, no doubt, a great deal of well-founded objection to be spoken or felt against the sayings and doings of this class, some of whose traits we have selected; no doubt, they will lay themselves open to criticism and to lampoons, and as ridiculous stories will be to be told of them as of any. There

will be cant and pretension; there will be subtilty and moonshine. These persons are of unequal strength, and do not all prosper. They complain that everything around them must be denied; and if feeble, it takes all their strength to deny, before they can begin to lead their own life. Grave seniors insist on their respect to this institution, and that usage; to an obsolete history; to some vocation, or college, or etiquette, or beneficiary, or charity, or morning or evening call, which they resist, as what does not concern them. But it costs such sleepless nights, and alienations and misgivings,—they have so many moods about it;—these old guardians never change *their* minds; they have but one mood on the subject, namely, that Antony is very perverse,—that it is quite as much as Antony can do, to assert his rights, abstain from what he thinks foolish, and keep his temper. He cannot help the reaction of this injustice in his own mind. He is braced-up and stilted; all freedom and flowing genius, all sallies of wit and frolic nature are quite out of the question; it is well if he can keep from lying, injustice, and suicide. This is no time for gayety and grace. His strength and spirits are wasted in rejection. But the strong spirits overpower those around them without effort. Their thought and emotion comes in like a flood, quite withdraws them from all notice of these carping critics; they surrender themselves with glad heart to the heavenly guide, and only by implication reject the clamorous nonsense of the hour. Grave seniors talk to the deaf,—church and old book mumble and ritualize to an unheeding, preöccupied and advancing mind, and thus they by happiness of greater momentum lose no time, but take the right road at first.

But all these of whom I speak are not proficients, they are novices; they only show the road in which man should travel, when the soul has greater health and prowess. Yet let them feel the dignity of their charge, and deserve a larger power. Their heart is the ark in which the fire is concealed, which shall burn in a broader and universal flame. Let them obey the Genius then most when his impulse is wildest; then most when he seems to lead to uninhabitable desarts of thought and life; for the path which the hero travels alone is the highway of health and benefit to mankind. What is the privilege and nobility of our nature, but its persistency, through its power to attach itself to what is permanent?

Society also has its duties in reference to this class, and must behold them with what charity it can. Possibly some benefit may yet accrue from them to the state. In our Mechanics' Fair, there must be not only bridges, ploughs,

carpenters' planes, and baking troughs, but also some few finer instruments,
—raingauges, thermometers, and telescopes; and in society, besides farmers,
sailors, and weavers, there must be a few persons of purer fire kept specially
as gauges and meters of character; persons of a fine, detecting instinct, who
betray the smallest accumulations of wit and feeling in the bystander. Perhaps too there might be room for the exciters and monitors;[18] collectors of
the heavenly spark with power to convey the electricity to others. Or, as the
storm-tossed vessel at sea speaks the frigate or 'line packet' to learn its longitude, so it may not be without its advantage that we should now and then
encounter rare and gifted men, to compare the points of our spiritual compass, and verify our bearings from superior chronometers.[19]

Amidst the downward tendency and proneness of things, when every
voice is raised for a new road or another statute, or a subscription of stock,
for an improvement in dress, or in dentistry, for a new house or a larger business, for a political party, or the division of an estate,—will you not tolerate
one or two solitary voices in the land, speaking for thoughts and principles
not marketable or perishable? Soon these improvements and mechanical inventions will be superseded; these modes of living lost out of memory; these
cities rotted, ruined by war, by new inventions, by new seats of trade, or
the geologic changes:—all gone, like the shells which sprinkle the seabeach
with a white colony to-day, forever renewed to be forever destroyed. But the
thoughts which these few hermits strove to proclaim by silence, as well as by
speech, not only by what they did, but by what they forbore to do, shall abide
in beauty and strength, to reorganize themselves in nature, to invest themselves anew in other, perhaps higher endowed and happier mixed clay than
ours, in fuller union with the surrounding system.

Notes

1. Étienne Bonnot de Condillac (1715–1780), French philosopher and exponent of
   sensationalism.
2. Quincy granite is an exceptionally hard rock quarried in Quincy, Massachusetts,
   among other places.
3. A "gold eagle" was a gold coin of the United States, valued at ten dollars.
4. For "antinomianism," see the note to "Self-Reliance," para 34, above.

5. Shakespeare, *Othello*, V, ii, 129–133.

6. Friedrich Heinrich Jacobi (1743–1819), German philosopher and novelist, published *Sendschreiben an Fichte* in 1799; Johann Gottlieb Fichte (1762–1814), German philosopher and a major proponent for German Idealism.

7. Coleridge's Translation. (Emerson's note.) The quotation is an adaptation by Coleridge in *The Friend*, 3 vols. (London, 1818), 2:216–217. References in the quotation are to Pylades, a figure in Greek mythology and a friend of Orestes, the son of Agamemnon, who assisted him in obtaining revenge against his mother for contriving to kill his father; Timoleon (d. ca. 337 BCE), a Corinthian who so hated tyranny that he murdered his own brother after he attempted to become dictator; Johan de Witt (1625–1672), Dutch statesman involved in writing the Treaty of Westminister (1654); Cato the Younger, first-century BCE Roman military man and philosopher, who committed suicide after his unsuccessful opposition to Caesar; and the biblical King David, who was guilty of murdering Bathsheba's husband, Uriah, in order to marry her.

8. With "takes no thought for the morrow," cf. Matthew 6:34.

9. Marcus Junius Brutus, first-century BCE Roman politician, assassinated Julius Caesar for what he claimed was the good of the republic.

10. Immanuel Kant (1724–1804), German philosopher, wrote, "I call knowledge transcendental which is occupied not so much with objects, as with our *a priori* concepts of objects" (*Critique of Pure Reason*, 1871 ed., p. 10; first published 1781).

11. Gnostics were an early Christian sect that taught that knowledge, as opposed to mere faith, is the true key to salvation. Essenes, an ascetic Jewish sect, flourished around the time of Christ. Manicheans, originally an Iranian sect, believed in a dualistic universe, in which good and evil are always present and in which knowledge is the way to salvation.

12. Wolfgang Amadeus Mozart (1756–1791), Austrian composer, achieved his greatest success as a boy and young man. The quotation is from "Lives of the Great Composers," *Dial* 2 (October 1841): 168, by Margaret Fuller (1810–1850), writer, feminist, and friend of Emerson's.

13. Emerson's source is *Pericles and Aspasia*, 2 vols. (London, 1836), 1:266 (*JMN*, 7:335, 8:48), by Walter Savage Landor (1775–1864), English Romantic poet.

14. With "whether in the . . . God knoweth," cf. 2 Corinthians 12:2.

15. The phrase "his hour comes again" is used frequently with slight variations by St. John.

16. With "it was not . . . born for," cf. John 18:37.

17. Emerson's line from "The Rhodora," "Beauty is its own excuse for being" (*CW*, 9:79), as well as this passage, should be interpreted in the light of his own identification of Beauty with the Greek "Cosmos," or universal harmony, a moral rather than a sensuous reading of the word.

18. In referencing "exciters and monitors," Emerson borrows two technical terms from the science of static electricity.

19. Here, Emerson is using "speaks" in the nautical sense of hailing another ship's captain and "line packet" as a vessel employed by the government to convey dispatches, or mail.

New England: Genius, Manners, and Customs

In my last lecture, I attempted to sketch some of the historical manifestations of the spirit of commerce which so strongly characterizes the English race in both hemispheres, and I enumerated the good results
with their limitations which have flowed therefrom in New England.[1] In the
present lecture, I proceed to add some details that may still farther fill up the
portrait of this race. Many of my remarks are of a miscellaneous character. I
am not careful that they are not. A principal object with me is to name, (in
any order), if I can, the chief facts in the recent literary and spiritual history
of New England, believing that if we can rightly select those, we write the
history of history: for it is to these that the mere recorder of facts must come
at last. Neither is it to me of any importance to confine my sketches to a geographical section, for I am well aware that as soon as we say anything deep
and true, it keeps no territorial limits. The heart is the citizen of every country, and so is strength of character. National characteristics, as soon as a man
is well awake, give way to individual ones: as physicians say that fever in every
new constitution is a new malady.

The national traits which have for ages distinguished the English race are
for the most part very obvious in the New England character, only qualified

by the new circumstances of a wide land, a sparse population, and a democratic government. The traits of the Englishman are found throughout America, so that to foreign nations it very naturally appears only an extension of the same people. In New England, where the population is most homogeneous and most English, they are very purely preserved, so as to give rise to the remark, that the Yankee is double distilled English. The British family is expanded, but not altered. The national traits are the same for centuries. We see at this moment only the demonstration of the thoughts which were already ripe in the beginning of the seventeenth century, when the Religious War drove the Puritans to America. The two main points by which the English nation was then distinguished, the two points by which they attached themselves to the heavens and the earth, to the mind and to matter, namely, Conscience and Common Sense, or, in view of their objects, the love of Religion and the love of Commerce,—Religion and Trade,—are still the two hands by which they hold the dominion of the globe.

3   I have elsewhere had occasion to speak at length of these two topics, the Religion and the Trade of New England; I shall not engage in their development this evening. My aim is to attempt some sketches of some remarkable particulars in the character and tendencies of the New England Man.

4   He is the old England man in a new place and new duties; and it is very easy to see the influence of his geographical position as a native of the seashore, and of a high latitude, in the modification of his character, distinguishing him not only from the European, but also from his fellow citizen of the interior and of the southern states.

5   A person of strong understanding, working to surround himself with defences against an extreme climate and a niggard soil, and gaining his victories over nature by successive expedients, as, by clothing, by warm building, by stove and furnace, and improved husbandry, his behaviour does not bely him. The Indian who puts out his fire, and hunts, eats, and sleeps in the snow; or the emigrant who quits a northern parallel and takes up his abode in a warmer clime,—these may be said each *at a single stroke* to relieve themselves of the long war with the elements, which the northern white man sustains. He, on the other hand, contests the field by inches, and his mind acquires the habit of detail, and his strength is that of caution, of forecast, of arithmetic, which accomplishes wonders, at last, by means of aggregation; builds a city, for example,—a noble and dazzling result, by a continual repetition of very

easy acts. But the Indian who flings himself into the snow, or the Southerner who resigns himself to the grand influences of nature with boundless leisure to enjoy them, becomes more easily the home of great and generous sentiments. He is not accustomed to check his charitable or his romantic purpose by too narrow a computation of the methods, and he is a much more natural, graceful, and heroic actor, inasmuch as he is more impulsive. This contrast of character is exhibited very strongly every day wherever the Northerner and Southerner meet; not only in results—tabulated results of trade, manufactures, of civil and criminal legislation,—but especially where the races face each other, as in the northern colleges, where young men from different sections often meet; and, most of all, in the city of Washington, where they face each other full-grown, and these contrasts are seen in full breadth. The Southerner lives for the moment, relies on himself, and conquers by personal address. He is wholly there in that thing which is now to be done. The Northerner lives for the year, and does not rely on himself, but on the whole apparatus of means he is wont to employ, and is only half-present when he comes in person: he has a great reserved force which is coming up. The result corresponds. The Southerner is haughty, wilful, generous, unscrupulous,— who will have his way, and has it. The Northerner must think the thing over, and his conscience and his commonsense throw a thousand obstacles between him and his wishes, which perplex his decision and unsettle his behaviour. The Northerner always has the advantage of the Southerner at the end of ten years; and the Southerner always has the advantage today.

I am far from wishing to exaggerate the peculiarities of districts of the country; the grand principles of probity and of beauty are far deeper in man than that a line or two of latitude or a difference of employment will make any important change. They underlie the differences of habit I have spoken of, and the great ideas of modern times are equally honoured with slight differences of costume throughout the Republic. 6

The traits which I prefer to consider are those moral agents which have been of importance in the history of our people as restraints on the spirit of economy and commerce, which their position generated. The flagrant feature in our history down to a quite recent period, was its religious character, as indeed the planting of New England was the work of the most religious nation in their most religious epoch. 7

Beside the direct culture of the conscience and the general probity which 8 this hereditary religious sentiment generates, I trace to this strong Calvinism other great and salutary results to the character of the New England people. First, namely, the culture of the intellect, which has always been found in the Calvinistic Church. The religious are always disposed to give to their children a more liberal discipline of books, of schools, and of liberal conversation, a fact borne out by all history—but especially by the history of New England. The Colony was planted in 1620: In 1636, Harvard College was founded.

9   The General Court of Massachusetts in 1647, "To the end that learning may not perish in the graves of our forefathers, *Ordered;* that every township after the Lord had increased them to the number of fifty householders shall appoint one to teach all children to write and read; and where any town shall increase to the number of one hundred families, they shall set up a grammar school, the masters thereof being able to instruct youth so far as they may be fitted for the university." Many and rich are the fruits of that simple statute. The universality of an elementary education in New England is her praise and her power in the whole world.

10   To the school succeeds the village Lyceum, now very general throughout the country towns, where every week through the winter lectures are read and debates sustained which prove a college for the young farmer. Hence, it happens that young farmers and mechanics who work all summer in the field or shop, in the winter often go into a neighbouring town to teach the district school arithmetic and grammar. As you know, New England supplies annually a large detachment of preachers, and schoolmasters, and private tutors to the interior of the South and West. Great numbers less critically instructed, yet still with some smattering of letters, are employed by the Connecticut bookdealers as book agents to travel in the interior and vend their editions. And it sometimes happens that a poor man's son in Connecticut, whose intellect is superior, who would fain go to college, but has not money, escapes from hard labour for which his finer organization unfits him, finds someone to trust him with wares, and goes as a pedlar into Virginia and Carolina that so he may, at a small expense, see the world, converse with men, and by intercourse with more polished persons than his native village can exhibit, supply the defects of his limited and humble training. One of the most intellectual men I have ever seen had his training so.[2]

11   It is a remark frequently made by those who are conversant with New England that such is the high value universally attached to a superior educa-

tion, that no political or religious prejudices are suffered to stand in its way. If the Catholics have a good school, or if the Unitarians have a good college, the most devoted adherents of other and conflicting sects will send their daughters or sons to these seminaries. It only needs a confidence that a superior culture is really to be had there, to bring as many pupils as are desired.

This is precisely the most agreeable picture which the Northern portion of the country has to show, the universality of a good elementary culture. If you ask me for the best result in this region, compared with the best advantages of other nations, I shall point you to a very common but always affecting spectacle,—the poor but educated family. Who can see unmoved the eager blushing boys discharging, as they can, their household chores, and hastening into the sitting-room to the study of tomorrow's merciless lesson: yet stealing time to read a novel hardly smuggled into the tolerance of father and mother: atoning for the same by some pages of Plutarch or Goldsmith; the warm sympathy with which they kindle each other in schoolyard or in barn and wood-shed. 12

If in New England the climate and the commerce powerfully tended to generate that spirit of detail which is not grand and enlarging, but which goes rather to pinch the features and degrade the character, the religious spirit, always enlarging, firing man, prompting the pursuit of the vast, the beautiful, the unattainable, was especially necessary as an antidote. In the midst of our laborious, and economical, and rude, and awkward population, where is little elegance and no facility, with great accuracy in details, little spirit of society, or knowledge of the world, you shall yet not unfrequently meet that refinement which no education and no habit of society can confer, which makes the elegance of wealth look stupid, and which unites itself by natural affinity to the highest minds of the world, and nourishes itself on Plato and Dante, Michel Angelo and Milton; on whatever is pure and sublime in art, and I may say, which gave a hospitality in that country to the spirit of Coleridge and Wordsworth, and now to the music of Beethoven, before yet their genius had found a hearty welcome in Great Britain.[3] 13

I pass now to a topic not remotely related to the last,—to consider, namely, the taste for eloquence, native to every people, and in which every man is a competitor, but always favoured by the institutions of republics. 14

The thirst of our people for eloquence is often remarked, and in the cities of New England it finds every year more opportunities of gratification. Fa- 15 neuil Hall is one of our best schools. Join the dark and closing groups that gather in the old house when fate hangs on the vote of the morrow. As the crowd grows and the hall fills, behold that solid block of life,—few old men, mostly young and middle aged, with shining heads and swollen veins. Much of the speaking shall no doubt be slovenly and tiresome. Then, the excited multitude predominates, is all the time interlocutor, and the air grows electric, and the multitude appear or disappear according to the success of the speaker. The pinched, wedged, elbowed, sweltering assembly, as soon as the speaker loses their ear, by the tameness of his harangue, feel sorely how ill accommodated they are, forget all politics and patriotism, and attend only to themselves and the coarse outcries which are made all around them. They back, push, resist, and fill the hall with cries of tumult. The speaker stops; the moderator persuades, commands, entreats; the speaker at length gives way. At last, the chosen man rises, the soul of the people, in whose bosom beats audibly the common heart. With his first words he strikes a note which all know. As he catches the light spirit of the occasion, his voice alters, vibrates, pierces the private ear of everyone: the mob quiets itself somehow,—everyone being magnetized, and the house hangs waiting on the lips of one man. Each man whilst he hears, thinks he too can speak, and, in the pauses of the orator, bursts forth the splendid voice of four or five thousand men in full cry,—the grandest sound in nature. If a dull speaker come again, instantly our poor wedges begin to feel their pains, and strive and cry.

16

New England is faithfully represented in her orators. The person most dear to the Yankees, of course, must be a person of very commanding understanding with every talent for its adequate expression. 'The American,' foreigners say, 'always reasons,' and their orator is the most American of the Americans. He should be a man of great good sense, always pertinent to time and place, with an eye to the simple facts of nature, the hour of the day, the neighborhood of the mountains or the sea, yet with sparing notice of these things, whilst he clings closely to the business-part of his speech; a man of gravity who trusts to his plain strength of statement for the attention of his assembly; a man of great fairness in debate, and who deserves his success by always carrying his points from his adversary by really taking higher ground than he: "I do not inflame, I do not exaggerate, I avoid all incendiary allusion."[4] He is one who is not at all magnetic, but the strongest intellect applied to business—intellect applied to affairs; the greatest of lawyers, and one who should rather carry points with the bench than with the jury or the caucus, and, therefore, carries points with a New England caucus. He shall have no puerilities, no tricks, no academical play in any of his speeches, but as it was said of the orations of Demosthenes that they were soldiers, so the speeches of the Yankee orator should all be men of business.[5] No following shall this man have, no troop of friends except those whose intellect he fires. No sweaty mob will carry him on their shoulders. And, yet, all New England to the remotest farmhouse or lumberer's camp in the woods of Maine delights to tell and hear anecdotes of his forensic power.

But a new field for eloquence has been opened in the Lyceum, an institution not a quarter of a century old, yet singularly agreeable to the taste and habits of the New England people, and extending every year to the south and west. It is of so recent origin, that, although it is beginning already like the invention of railways, to make a new profession, we have most of us seen all the steps of its progress. In New England it had its origin in as marked a manner as such things admit of being marked, from the genius of one distinguished person, who, after his connexion with the University, read public courses of literary lectures in Boston. And as this was an epoch of much note in the recent literary history of all that portion of the country, I shall ask leave to pause a little on the recollection. That individual has passed long since into new employments, so that the influence he then exerted and which was a capital fact in the literary annals of the country, now fairly belongs to the past; and one of his old scholars will be indulged in recalling an image so pleasing.[6]

There was an influence on the young people from the genius of this eminent scholar which was almost comparable to that of Pericles in Athens.[7] He had an inspiration which did not go beyond his head, but which made him the master of elegance. If any of my audience were at that period in Boston or Cambridge, they will easily remember, his radiant beauty of person, of a classic style; his heavy, large eye; marble lids, which gave the impression of mass which the slightness of his form needed; sculptured lips; a voice of such rich tones, such precise and perfect utterance, that, although slightly nasal, it was the most mellow, and beautiful, and correct of all the instruments of the time. The word that he spoke, in the manner in which he spoke it, became current and classical in New England.

He had in common with other distinguished members of his family, a

17

18

19

great talent for collecting facts, and for bringing those he had to bear with in-genious felicity on the topic of the moment. Let him rise to speak on what occasion soever, a fact had always just transpired which composed with some other fact well known to the audience the most pregnant and happy coinci-dence. It was remarked that for a man who threw out so many facts, he was seldom convicted of a blunder.

20   He had a good deal of special learning, and all his learning was available for purposes of the hour. It was all new learning, that wonderfully took and stimulated the young men. It was so coldly and weightily communicated from so commanding a platform,—as if in the consciousness and consider-ation of all history and all learning,—adorned with so many simple and aus-tere beauties of expression, and enriched with so many excellent digressions and significant quotations, that, though nothing could be conceived before-hand less attractive or, indeed, less fit for green boys from Connecticut, New Hampshire, and Massachusetts, with their unripe Latin and Greek reading, than exegetical discourses in the style of Hug, and Wolf, and Ruhnken on the Orphic and Ante-Homeric remains, yet this learning instantly took the high-est place to our imagination in our unoccupied American Parnassus.[8] All his auditors felt the extreme beauty and dignity of the manner, and even the coarsest were contented to go punctually to listen for the manner, when they had found out that the subject matter was not for them. In the lecture room, he abstained from all ornament and pleased himself with the play of detail-ing erudition in a style of perfect simplicity. In the pulpit, for he was then a clergyman, he made amends to himself and his auditor for the self-denial of the professor's chair, and with an infantine simplicity still of manner, he gave the reins to his florid, quaint, and affluent fancy.

21   Then was exhibited all the richness of a rhetoric which we have never seen rivalled in this country. Wonderful, how memorable were words made which were only pleasing pictures, and covered no new or valid thoughts. He abounded in sentences, in wit, in satire, in splendid allusion, in quotation im-possible to forget, in daring imagery, in parable, and even in a sort of defying experiment of his own wit and skill in giving an oracular weight to Hebrew or Rabbinical words, as *Selah, Ichabod, Tekel, Mene, Upharsin,* and the like— feats which no man could better accomplish, such was his self-command and the security of his manner. All his speech was music, and with such variety and invention, that the ear was never tired. Especially beautiful were his po-

etic quotations. He delighted in Milton, more rarely in Byron, and sometimes in a verse from Watts, and with such sweet modulation, that he seemed to give as much beauty as he borrowed; and whatever he has quoted will be remembered by any who heard him with inseparable association with his voice and genius.[9] This eminently beautiful person was followed from church to church, wherever the fame that he would preach led, by all the most cultivated and intelligent youths with grateful admiration. He had nothing in common with vulgarity and infirmity, but speaking, walking, sitting was as much aloof and uncommon as a star. The smallest anecdote of his behaviour or conversation was eagerly caught and repeated; and every young scholar could recite brilliant sentences from his sermons with mimicry good or bad of his voice. This influence went much farther; for he who was heard with such throbbing hearts and sparkling eyes, in the lighted and crowded churches, did not let go his hearer when the church was dismissed; but the bright image of that eloquent form followed the boy home to his bed chamber; and not a sentence was written in academic exercises, not a declamation attempted in the college chapel, but showed omnipresence of his genius to youthful heads. He thus raised the standard of writing and speaking in New England. This made every youth his defender, and boys filled their mouths with arguments to prove that the orator had a heart.

This was a triumph of Rhetoric. It was not the intellectual or the moral principles which he had to teach. It was not thoughts. When Massachusetts was full of his fame, it was not contended that he had thrown any truths into circulation. But his power lay in the magic of form; it was in the graces of manner, in a new perception of Grecian Beauty to which he had opened our eyes. And it was commonly said that he would be willing that every hearer should have a copy of his speech in his pocket: he would still be just as secure of their attention. 22

There was that finish about this person which is about women, and which distinguishes every piece of genius from the works of talent: that these last are more or less matured in every degree of completeness according to the time bestowed on them, but works of genius in their first and slightest form are still wholes. In every public discourse, there was nothing left for the indulgence of his hearer, no marks of late hours and anxious unfinished study, but the goddess of grace had breathed on the work a last fragrancy and glitter. 23

By a series of lectures largely and fashionably attended for two winters in 24

Boston, this individual made a beginning of popular literary and miscellaneous lectures which in that region, at least, had important results. It is acquiring greater importance every day and becoming a national institution.

25   But a field for eloquence higher and deeper seems to me already opened
in the Lyceum, an institution now in its infancy, yet growing every year into
use and favor in the Atlantic cities, as our present meeting bears witness. It
answers the purpose of a social meeting for both sexes in a very convenient
manner, involving no expense, and no dissipation, and especially of giving an
evening occupation to young men in the counting house, and so supplants
the theatre and the ballroom. It gives an hour's discourse on some topic not
far from the ordinary range, and by continually introducing new speakers,
furnishes new topics to conversation with new means of comparison, every
week. But these are the beginnings of its use. I set a higher value on it than
amusement or the statement of valuable facts. I look upon it as a vent for
new and higher communications than any to which we have been wont to
listen. I see with pleasure that the first men in the country are put under contribution by this institution, for services which they cheerfully render, led, as I
believe, by an instinct of its importance.

26   For this is precisely the most elastic and capacious theatre of eloquence,
—absolutely unrestricted. Is it not plain that not in senates and courts, which
only treat of a very narrow range of external rights, but in the depths of philosophy and poetry, the eloquence must be found that can agitate, convict,
inspire, and possess us and guide men to a true peace? I look on the Lecture
Room as the true Church of the coming time, and as the home of a richer
eloquence than Faneuil Hall or the Capitol ever knew. For here is all that the
true orator will ask, namely, a convertible audience,—an audience coming up
to the house, not knowing what shall befall them there, but uncommitted
and willing victims to reason and love. There is no topic that may not be
treated, and no method excluded. *Here,* everything is admissible, philosophy,
ethics, divinity, criticism, poetry, humor, anecdote, mimicry,—ventriloquism
almost,—all the breadth and versatility of the most liberal conversation, and
of the highest, lowest, personal, and local topics—all are permitted, and all
may be combined in one speech. It is a panharmonicon combining every
note on the longest gamut, from the explosion of cannon to the tinkle of a
guitar.

27   It deserves the attention of such as have any truth to offer to men and will

soon draw the best powers of the country to its aid. Let us, if we have any thought in our mind, try if Folly, Custom, Convention, and Phlegm cannot hear our sharp artillery. Here is a pulpit that makes the other chairs of instruction cold and ineffectual with their customary preparation for a delivery: the most decorous with fine things, pretty things, wise things, but no arrows, no axes, no nectar, no transpiercing, no loving, no enchantment. Here, the American orator shall find the theatre he needs; here, he may lay himself out utterly large, prodigal, enormous, on the subject of the hour. Here, he may dare to hope for the higher inspiration and a total transfusion of himself into the minds of men.

I please myself with the thought that this may yet be an organ of unparalleled power for the elevation of sentiment and enlargement of knowledge. Why should it not be capable of all the range whereof music is capable, and, as other nations have each their favorite instrument, as Spain her guitar, and Scotland her pibroch, and Italy a viol, and as we go eastward, cymbals and song, let the reasoning, fact loving, and moral American, not by nature a musician, yet with a hunger for eloquence, find his national music in halls opened for discourse and debate, the one leading to the other?[10] Will you let me say that I think the country will so give hospitality and hearing to its men of thought; and, as in former periods, the poet travelled as a harper from town to town, and from castle to castle, the bearer of thought and exhilaration, so now, in a manner fitting the habit of our institutions, the man of ideas and lover of beauty shall find a ready ear from his countrymen for those secrets which in the solitudes of nature the muse whispered in his walks? The lover of men shall find his office foreshown by the master of English song:

> Before the starry threshold of Jove's Court
> My mansion is, where those immortal shapes
> Of bright aerial spirits live insphered
> In regions mild of calm and serene air,
> Above the smoke and stir of this dim spot
> Which men call Earth, and with low thoughted care
> Confined and pestered in this pinfold here
> Strive to keep up a frail and feverish being,
> Unmindful of the crown that virtue gives,
> After this mortal change, to her true servants

28

Amongst the enthroned gods on sainted seats.

Yet some there be, that by due steps aspire

To lay their just hands on the golden key

That opes the palace of eternity;

To such my errand is.[11]

It will use less strict conventions than other assemblies or pulpits,—and invite, perhaps a bolder exercise of thought; for, with all deference to the lovers of precision and method, I think that the best method will always be a new one, new with each speaker, and proper to that which he has to say. There are, as I think, greatly higher merits than easiness of being reported. The great merit is power to excite the slumbering intellect, make it a party to the speaker's thought, and by hints and whispers even, if no more can be, from a great interior world, leave it with a renewed assurance that that world exists—and for him.

29   This institution, as a school of thought and reason, has vast importance as a check on the vices and insanities of the time. I have said that from the planting of New England down to a recent period, this country has been tinged with a religious spirit. But the boundless opportunity of labor and the rewards of labor opened before us have rapidly changed the genius of the people.

30   There is in the Anglo-Saxon race a great power of labor, and no country exhibits more results of incessant labor than New England. But is it climate, or is it hereditary temperament—the love of labour becomes usually in our people a certain fury, a storm of activity, and a necessity of excitement. Unhappily, the feature of the times seems to be a great sensualism, a headlong devotion to trade and to the conquest of the continent, and to each man as large a share of the same as he can carve for himself, and an extravagant confidence in our gregarious activity which becomes, whilst successful, a scornful materialism, but with the fatal fault of that habitude, of course, that it has no depth, no reserved force whereon to fall back when a reverse comes.

31   Our countrymen love intoxication of some sort. There is no repose in their character. All foreigners and we ourselves observe the sort of hunger, the voracity for excitement, which haunts us. Is it for food? Is it for news? Is it for money? Is it for stimulation in any form? One is drunk with rum, and one with politics, and one with barter, and one with impossible projects. Our

trade is wild and incalculable. Our people are wide travellers; our steamboats explode; our ships are known at sea by the quantity of canvass they carry; our people eat fast; our houses tumble; our enterprizes are rash; our legislation fluctuating. The cases of insanity in this country are said greatly to outnumber the patients in Europe. The last President could not stand the excitement of seventeen millions of people, but died of the presidency in one month.[12] A man should have a heart and a trunk vascular and on the scale of the Croton Aqueducts or the Cloaca Maxima at Rome to bear the friction of such a Mississippi stream.[13]

We want steadiness and repose. We are too rash and sanguine to the verge of insanity. We are all resting our confidence on new arts which have been invented: on new machinery, on steam, on the glimpses of mechanical power to be derived from electricity or galvanism; on photogenic drawing, on india-rubber clothing, on lamps that shine without shadow, on stoves that burn without fuel; on clocks to be wound by the tide; on iron boats; and cast steel tools; on steam batteries, life-preservers, and diving bells. 32

This fury is heated by the peculiar skill and genius of the time. The great achievements that distinguish this age are its mechanical inventions. It is the age of tools. *Now,* the standing topic in all stage coaches and railroad cars, is the improved means of conveyance; and continual impatience is expressed at the slow rate of travelling; twenty five miles the hour is mere creeping; the travelling public will not long submit to such baggage-wagon pace, and wonderful are the plans of the projectors which fill the columns of the daily press. 33

The men and women shall be galvanically conveyed, or may be put in large quills and propelled across the Atlantic by the pressure of the atmosphere; or dressed in diving-suits manufactured (No. 6 Tremont Street, Boston) by the Roxbury Company, and conveyed by submarine siphons, and come up near Liverpool in fountains spouting men and women; or a tunnel may run under the sea, and they may go dry-shod. In order to avoid the danger of submarine volcanoes, strenuous measures are to be adopted by the countries abutting on the two ends of the canal. It is disgraceful that every few years an earthquake should be allowed from mere want of proper ventilation to swallow a town like a custard. It only needs timely and vigorous attention from the Congress of Nations. Every boy can take out the pulp and seeds of a pumpkin and make a useful lanthorn of the same. The earth should be properly bored with an artesian well of five hundred miles diame- 34 ter at the mouth and running down to the depth of three thousand, then by means of steam excavator, the mephitic gases and whatever combustibles, should be brought to the surface and sold to the gas company. And a wholesome and agreeable circulation of air should be kept up.

35   It may hereafter be found best, when the structure of the human body is better understood and the science of anatomy is perfect, to take passengers to pieces and transport them in the air or under the sea *in parts* chemically packed to be put together by the Transportation Company on the other side at the depot, and the greatest care given to keep the packages *identical.* These marvellous expedients are but a specimen or symbol. In like manner, a certain hurry and impatience leads our people to short ways in every department of life: in short ways to science, to religion, to literature. The race of scholars, of laborious investigators will come to an end. Our people are insatiable readers of newspapers. What acres of these sheets they run through and spend several months of the year in that pastime. And so in their intellectual and scientific training. The vice of the American is that he is too easily pleased. A curious fact in the last ten or twelve years has been the dedication of this country to the study of phrenology, proved by its modification of the language and introduction into general use of as many words as the use of steam by land and water has added. I do not think this is to be wholly attributed to the facility of our people and their deceivability, but partly to the fact that the system, however rudely and coarsely, was a return to a natural instinct; it brought observation to a noble and fit object, to which too much study cannot be given. It betrayed the instinctive belief that under all these dismal masks of men, masks which we wear and which we meet, the form of man was something sacred and beautiful which should yet appear; and it showed the thirst of men for a teaching nearer to their business and bosom than any they enjoyed. Had it confined itself to a reverent accumulation of the facts, it would have been a good hint, but would have had no world's renown; but now with its speedy ascent by one jump into the chair of science, it has become a symbol of the times. Is it that we have found quicker than others the real poverty at the bottom of all this seeming affluence of life; the headlong speed with which each seeing soul comes straight through all the thin masquerade on the old fact; is it the disgust at this indigence of nature which makes these raging livers drive their steeds so hard, in the fury of living to forget the soup maigre of life?[14]

Phrenology especially seems to have been invented for the American people with its swift and shallow mode of disposing of the sacred secrets of nature: a man shall be a mystery no more; let me put my hand on his forehead and his hindhead; give me a pair of dividers and a foot rule, and nature cannot hide his genius where I cannot find it by inches and seconds; the recesses of human power and probity are laid open to my fingers. Character is as easily read as a placard, and the fortunes of a man are reduced to an arithmetic problem. Genius is an inflammation of the brain and conscience, a secretion of the left lobe of the heart.

Yet phrenology was modest compared with the pretensions of mesmerism.[15] The ignorant are always on the watch how to cheat nature, and, if all the stories are true, here seemed a chance to occur. Mankind were no longer to labor to come at their ends, nor to abridge their labor by dexterous physical combinations, nor to overpower physical opposition by moral force, but by a third power, by gentle touching of the knuckles, and by persuasive passes, and by coaxing, beckoning, and ogling of fingers, we could hope to raise the state of man to rare and transcendant degrees. The most stupid and perverse man when awake, once get him fast asleep in his chair, shall become an angel of light, a learned physician, a surpassing astronomer, and a telegraph so subtle and swift that he is the Paul Pry of the universe.[16]

And this is the way we will outwit the laws of Nature. With unwashed hands, and our whole day's task unattempted before us, we are grasping after new powers like some Aesop's dog snatching at the shadow of our bone.[17] We would be magians and somnambulists and see with elbows, and know the architecture in Orion, and tunnel the earth to come into pagodas of Pekin. And on the first hint of such powers being attained, we will enter heaven and enter hell, go to the poles and the antipodes so, and dodge the laws and the Fates, the powers of perseverence, the graces, the virtues, all angels, all heroes, all qualities, all gods, and pierce to the courts of power and light by this dull trick. The wise gods must needs laugh heartily this once.

That nature should have subtile compensations for infirmity, and morbid actions of natural organs, and even from all this profuse treasure house of power and organization some overflowings of light and vitality into crevices and chinks, is not to be doubted; but for men to choose these exceptions and anomalies instead of the law, and prefer these haloes and meteors to the sun and moon, does not do them much honor. By Lake Winnepesaukee, a man

36

37

38

39

lost his feet and learned to walk on his thumbs, and now all New Hampshire is learning to walk on its thumbs, and it will presently take a great genius to convince men that feet were made to walk with.

40   What is most noticeable is that men who never wondered at anything, who had thought it the most natural thing in the world that they should exist in this orderly and replenished world, have been unable to suppress their amazement at the disclosures of the somnambulist. The peculiarity of mesmerism is that it drew in as inquirers and students a class of persons never on any other occasion known as students and inquirers. Of course, the inquiry is pursued on low principles. Mesmerism peeps. It becomes a black art. The uses of the thing, the commodity, the power, at once come to mind and direct the course of inquiry. It seemed to open again that door which was open to the fancy of childhood: of magicians, and faeries, and lamps of Aladdin and travelling cloaks that were to satisfy the utmost wish of the senses without danger or one drop of sweat.[18] But as Nature can never be outwitted, as no man was ever known to get a cent's worth without paying in some form or other the cent, so this prodigious promiser ends always, and always will, as sorcery and alchemy have done before, in very small and smoky performance.

41   It is so wonderful that a man can see without his eyes, that it never occurs to the adept that it is just as wonderful that he should see with them. And that is ever the difference between the wise and the unwise: the latter wonders at what is unusual; the wise man wonders at the usual. Well, these things are only symptomatic of the disease of the people. That repose which is the ornament and the ripeness of man is not in New England, is not in America, but hurry, and partiality, and impatience are in its room.

42   The whole generation is discontented with the tardy rate of growth which contents every European community. America is, therefore, the country of small adventures, of short plans, of daring risks—not of patience, not of great combinations, not of long, persistent, close-woven schemes demanding the utmost fortitude, temper, faith, and poverty. Our books are fast changing to newspapers; our reformers are slight and wearisome talkers, not man-subduing, immutable—all attracting their own task, and so charming the eye with dread and persuading without knowing that they do so. We have no Duke Wellingtons, no George Washingtons, no Miltons, Bentleys, or Seldens among our rapid and dashing race, but abundance of Murats, of

Rienzis, of Wallers, and that slight race who put their whole stake on the first die they cast.[19] The great men bequeath never their projects to their sons to finish. These eat too much pound cake. Wordsworth said,

'Tis the most difficult of tasks to keep
Heights which the soul is competent to gain,[20]

and these lines are a sort of elegy on these times, and hardly less in the clerisy or scholastic class than in the practical. If we read in the books of one of the great masters of thought, in Plato, in Aristotle, or in the great thinkers of the age of Elizabeth, we are astonished at the vigor and breadth of the performance.[21] Here is no short breath and short flight, but an Atlantic strength which is everywhere equal to itself and dares great attempts because of the life with which it feels itself filled.

See the impatience of our people to rush into the lists without enduring the training. The Americans are too easily pleased and remind us of what was said of the Empire of Russia: that it was a fine fruit spoiled before it had ripened. Our people are too slight and vain. They are easily elated and easily depressed. See how fast they extend the fleeting fabric of their trade, not at all considering the remote reaction and bankruptcy, but with the same abandonment to the moment and the facts of the hour as the Esquimaux when he offers to sell his bed in the morning. An old merchant said to me that he had learned that he could not learn by experience; for, ten times he had been taught by hard times not to extend himself again, yet always a new crisis took him by surprise, and he was as unprepared as ever. They act on the moment and from external impulse. They all lean on some other, and this superstitiously and not from insight of his merit. They follow a fact, they follow success, and not skill. Therefore, as soon as the success stops, fails, and the admirable man blunders, they quit him; already they remember that long ago they suspected his judgment, and they transfer the repute of judgment to the next prosperous person who has not yet blundered. Of course, this levity makes them as easily despond. It seems as if history gave no account of any society in which despondency came so readily to heart as we see it and feel it in ours. Young men at thirty, and even earlier, lose all spring and vivacity, and if they fail in their first enterprize, throw up the game.

I think we have no worse trait, as far as it is a national one, than this levity, than this idolatry of success, this fear to fail. We shall never have heroes, until

43

44

we have learned that it is impossible to fail. Of course, this timidity about reputation, this terror of a disaster comes of looking at opinion as the measure of character, instead of seeing that character judges opinion. In the brave West, I rejoice to see symptoms of a more man-like sentiment than this timid asking leave to live of other men. The frank Kentuckian has a way of thinking concerning his reception by his friend that makes him whole: Here I am. If you do not appreciate me, the worse for you. And the great Indian sages had a lesson for the Bramin which every day returns to mind: "All that depends on another gives pain. All that depends on himself gives pleasure. In these few words is the definition of pleasure and of pain."[22] We must learn, too, failure is a part of success. Prosperity and pound cake are for very young gentlemen whom such things content: but a hero's, a man's success is made up of failures, because he experiments and ventures every day, and the more falls he gets, moves faster on: defeated all the time, and yet to victory born. I have heard that in horsemanship he is not the good rider who never was thrown, but that, rather, a man never will be a good rider until he is thrown; then, he will not be haunted any longer by the terror that he shall tumble, and *will ride,*—that is his business, *to ride,* whether with falls, or whether with none, *to ride unto the place whither he is bound.*

45   The noble Phocion, him of whom it has been so truly said, that, "Phocion haranguing the Athenian *Demos* was as solitary as a ship on the stormy Atlantic," was afraid of applause. For a true man feels that he has quite another office than to tickle or flatter. He is here to bite and to stab, to inflict wounds on self-love and easy, prosperous falsehood, which shall not quickly heal. Demosthenes, when the people hissed him for his ragged and untuneable voice, cried out, "You are to judge players, indeed, by their sweet voices, but orators by the gravity and power of their sentences."

46   It would seem as if history were full of tributes to the unrivalled ascendency of personal qualities. He is the hero who conquers alone.

> "In that immense crowd which throngs the avenues to power in
> the United States, I found very few men who displayed any of
> that manly candor and that masculine independence of opinion
> which frequently distinguished the Americans in former times,
> and which constitute the leading feature in distinguished charac-
> ters wherever they may be found. It seems at first sight as if all the

minds of the Americans were formed on one model, so accurately do they correspond in their manner of judging.

A stranger does indeed sometimes meet with Americans who dissent from these rigorous formularies; with men who deplore the defects of the laws, the mutability and the ignorance of democracy; who even go so far as to observe the evil tendencies which impair the national character and to point out such remedies as it might be possible to apply: but no one is there to hear these things beside yourself, and you to whom these secret reflections are confided, are a stranger and a bird of passage."[23]

Is not this tragic in so far as it is true, that this great country, hospitable to all nations, opened for the experiment of new ideas, now in the decrepitude and downfall of the old mythologies of church and state in Asia and Europe,—should be a country of dwarfs; cities and nations of democrats, and never an upright man? That our famous Equality should be a fear of all men; and our famous Liberty should be a servitude to millions; a despicable, skipping expediency; a base availableness, ducking with servile cap to the lowest and worst? I do not wonder that the well-disposed but slow of faith begin to look with wishful eyes to the decorum and police of monarchy, as the poetic and imaginative but drowsy mind is driven by the cold disputation of the Protestant to the stability and veneration of the Roman Church. Some of the most intelligent and virtuous foreigners who have been among us, and those who have surveyed us from afar, have expressed the feeling that the antidote to our excessive spirit of socialism must be found in a class of gentlemen or men of honor,—which, yet, they thought, our institutions did not go to form.

47

Notes

1. "New England: Genius, Manners, and Customs," the third of five lectures associated with Emerson's *New England* series (1843–1844), was the most popular of the series.

2. In this and the previous sentence, Emerson describes Bronson Alcott.

3. Ludwig van Beethoven (1770–1827), German composer.

4. Emerson quotes Daniel Webster (1782–1852), American statesman and orator.

5. Demosthenes (384–322 BCE), Athenian statesman, regarded as the greatest Greek orator.

6. Emerson is referring to Dr. William Ellery Channing (1780–1842), New England's most eminent Unitarian minister, who had recently died.

7. Pericles (ca. 495–429 BCE), Athenian statesman and orator.

8. Johann Leonhard Hug (1765–1846), German biblical scholar; Friedrich August Wolf (1759–1824), German classicist, argued that the *Iliad* and the *Odyssey* are works by several authors; David Ruhnken (1723–1798), German classical scholar; Mount Parnassus in ancient Greece was sacred to Apollo and the Muses and thus was the seat of the arts.

9. George Gordon Byron, known as Lord Byron (1788–1824), English Romantic poet; Isaac Watts (1674–1748), English theologian and hymn writer.

10. A "pibroch" is a set of martial or solemn variations played on the Scottish Highland bagpipe.

11. Milton, "Comus," ll. 1–15.

12. William Henry Harrison (1773–1841), ninth president of the United States, died of complications from pneumonia within a month of taking office.

13. The Croton Aqueduct (built 1834–1842) extended from southeastern New York State into New York City and brought in approximately seventy million gallons of water daily; the Cloaca Maxima was the primary drainage system of ancient Rome.

14. *Soupe-maigre,* the French term for "soup-meagre," a broth made chiefly from vegetables or fish.

15. Mesmerism is a type of hypnotism.

16. Paul Pry, title character of a play (produced in 1825) by the English dramatist John Poole (ca. 1786–1872), whose name came to stand for a troublesome adventurer.

17. Aesop is a legendary Greek fabulist of the sixth century BCE. In his fable of the dog and the shadow, a dog crossed a bridge over a stream with a piece of meat in his mouth, saw his own shadow in the water, and thought it another dog with a piece of meat double his own in size. Letting go of his own piece of meat and fiercely attacking the other dog to get the larger piece from him, the dog thus lost both pieces, because the one in the water was a shadow and his own was swept away by the stream.

18. Aladdin and his lamp, which houses two genii, is the subject of a tale in *The Arabian Nights' Entertainment* or *A Thousand and One Nights.*

19. Arthur Wellesley, 1st Duke of Wellington (1769–1852), British general and statesman; Richard Bentley (1664–1742), English cleric and classical scholar; John Selden (1584–1654), English jurist, historian, and author; Joachim Murat (1771–1815), king of Naples; Cola di Rienzo (ca. 1313–1354), popular Italian patriot; Sir William Waller (ca. 1597–1668), English general in the Thirty Years' War.

20. Wordsworth, *The Excursion,* 4.138–139.

21. Elizabeth I (1533–1603) ruled England (1558–1603) during a golden age of politics and literature.

22. Attributed by Emerson to *The Laws of Menu* (or *Manu*), Indian commentaries on religious laws and social obligations compiled between 200 BCE and 200 CE (*TN,* 3:269).

23. Alexis de Tocqueville (1805–1859), French writer and politician, best known for his two-volume *De la démocratie en Amérique (Democracy in America)* (1835, 1840), written after a nine-month stay in the United States, from which Emerson quotes.

The Poet

The Poet.

1
A moody child and wildly wise
Pursued the game with joyful eyes,
Which chose, like meteors, their way,
And rived the dark with private ray:
They overleapt the horizon's edge,
Searched with Apollo's privilege;
Through man, and woman, and sea, and star,
Saw the dance of nature forward far;
Through worlds, and races, and terms, and times,
Saw musical order, and pairing rhymes.[1]

2
Olympian bards who sung
Divine ideas below,
Which always find us young,
And always keep us so.[2]

3
      Those who are esteemed umpires of taste, are often persons who have acquired some knowledge of admired pictures or sculptures, and have an inclination for whatever is elegant; but if you inquire whether they are beautiful souls, and whether their own acts are like fair pictures, you learn that they are selfish and sensual. Their cultivation is local, as if you should rub a log of dry wood in one spot to produce fire, all the rest remaining cold. Their knowledge of the fine arts is some study of rules and particulars, or some limited judgment of color or form, which is exercised for amusement or for show. It is a proof of the shallowness of the doctrine of beauty, as it lies in the minds of our amateurs, that men seem to have lost the perception of the instant dependence of form upon soul. There is no doctrine of forms in our philosophy. We were put into our bodies, as fire is put into a pan, to be carried about; but there is no accurate adjustment between

the spirit and the organ, much less is the latter the germination of the former. So in regard to other forms, the intellectual men do not believe in any essential dependence of the material world on thought and volition. Theologians think it a pretty air-castle to talk of the spiritual meaning of a ship or a cloud, of a city or a contract, but they prefer to come again to the solid ground of historical evidence; and even the poets are contented with a civil and conformed manner of living, and to write poems from the fancy, at a safe distance from their own experience. But the highest minds of the world have never ceased to explore the double meaning, or, shall I say, the quadruple, or the centuple, or much more manifold meaning, of every sensuous fact: Orpheus, Empedocles, Heraclitus, Plato, Plutarch, Dante, Swedenborg, and the masters of sculpture, picture, and poetry.[3] For we are not pans and barrows, nor even porters of the fire and torch-bearers, but children of the fire, made of it, and only the same divinity transmuted, and at two or three removes, when we know least about it. And this hidden truth, that the fountains when all this river of Time, and its creatures, floweth, are intrinsically ideal and beautiful, draws us to the consideration of the nature and functions of the Poet, or the man of Beauty, to the means and materials he uses, and to the general aspect of the art in the present time.

The breadth of the problem is great, for the poet is representative. He stands among partial men for the complete man, and apprises us not of his wealth, but of the commonwealth. The young man reveres men of genius, because, to speak truly, they are more himself than he is. They receive of the soul as he also receives, but they more. Nature enhances her beauty, to the eye of loving men, from their belief that the poet is beholding her shows at the same time. He is isolated among his contemporaries, by truth and by his art, but with this consolation in his pursuits, that they will draw all men sooner or later. For all men live by truth, and stand in need of expression. In love, in art, in avarice, in politics, in labor, in games, we study to utter our painful secret. The man is only half himself, the other half is his expression. 4

Notwithstanding this necessity to be published, adequate expression is rare. I know not how it is that we need an interpreter; but the great majority of men seem to be minors, who have not yet come into possession of their own, or mutes, who cannot report the conversation they have had with nature. There is no man who does not anticipate a supersensual utility in the sun, and stars, earth, and water. These stand and wait to render him a pecu- 5 liar service.[4] But there is some obstruction, or some excess of phlegm in our constitution, which does not suffer them to yield the due effect. Too feeble fall the impressions of nature on us to make us artists. Every touch should thrill. Every man should be so much an artist, that he could report in conversation what had befallen him. Yet, in our experience, the rays or appulses have sufficient force to arrive at the senses, but not enough to reach the quick, and compel the reproduction of themselves in speech. The poet is the person in whom these powers are in balance, the man without impediment, who sees and handles that which others dream of, traverses the whole scale of experience, and its representative of man, in virtue of being the largest power to receive and to impart.

6   For the Universe has three children, born at one time, which reappear, under different names, in every system of thought, whether they be called cause, operation, and effect; or, more poetically, Jove, Pluto, Neptune; or, theologically, the Father, the Spirit, and the Son; but which we will call here, the Knower, the Doer, and the Sayer. These stand respectively for the love of truth, for the love of good, and for the love of beauty. These three are equal. Each is that which he is essentially, so that he cannot be surmounted or analyzed, and each of these three has the power of the others latent in him, and his own patent.[5]

7   The poet is the sayer, the namer, and represents beauty. He is a sovereign, and stands on the centre. For the world is not painted, or adorned, but is from the beginning beautiful; and God has not made some beautiful things, but Beauty is the creator of the universe. Therefore the poet is not any permissive potentate, but is emperor in his own right. Criticism is infested with a cant of materialism, which assumes that manual skill and activity is the first merit of all men, and disparages such as say and do not, overlooking the fact, that some men, namely, poets, are natural sayers, sent into the world to the end of expression, and confounds them with those whose province is action, but who quit it to imitate the sayers. But Homer's words are as costly and admirable to Homer, as Agamemnon's victories are to Agamemnon.[6] The poet does not wait for the hero or the sage, but, as they act and think primarily, so he writes primarily what will and must be spoken, reckoning the others, though primaries also, yet, in respect to him, secondaries and servants; as sitters or models in the studio of a painter, or as assistants who bring building materials to an architect.

For poetry was all written before time was, and whenever we are so finely organized that we can penetrate into that region where the air is music, we hear those primal warblings, and attempt to write them down, but we lose ever and anon a word, or a verse, and substitute something of our own, and thus miswrite the poem. The men of more delicate ear write down these cadences more faithfully, and these transcripts, though imperfect, become the songs of the nations.[7] For nature is as truly beautiful as it is good, or as it is reasonable, and must as much appear, as it must be done, or be known. Words and deeds are quite indifferent modes of the divine energy.[8] Words are also actions, and actions are a kind of words.

The sign and credentials of the poet are, that he announces that which no man foretold. He is the true and only doctor; he knows and tells; he is the only teller of news, for he was present and privy to the appearance which he describes.[9] He is a beholder of ideas, and an utterer of the necessary and causal. For we do not speak now of men of poetical talents, or of industry and skill in metre, but of the true poet. I took part in a conversation the other day, concerning a recent writer of lyrics, a man of subtle mind, whose head appeared to be a music-box of delicate tunes and rhythms, and whose skill, and command of language, we could not sufficiently praise.[10] But when the question arose, whether he was not only a lyrist, but a poet, we were obliged to confess that he is plainly a contemporary, not an eternal man. He does not stand out of our low limitations, like a Chimborazo under the line, running up from the torrid base through all the climates of the globe, with belts of the herbage of every latitude on its high and mottled sides;[11] but this genius is the landscape-garden of a modern house, adorned with fountains and statues, with well-bred men and women standing and sitting in the walks and terraces.[12] We hear, through all the varied music, the ground-tone of conventional life. Our poets are men of talents who sing, and not the children of music. The argument is secondary, the finish of the verses is primary.

For it is not metres, but a metre-making argument, that makes a poem,— a thought so passionate and alive, that, like the spirit of a plant or an animal, it has an architecture of its own, and adorns nature with a new thing. The thought and the form are equal in the order of time, but in the order of genesis the thought is prior to the form. The poet has a new thought: he has a whole new experience to unfold; he will tell us how it was with him, and all men will be the richer in his fortune. For, the experience of each new age requires a new confession, and the world seems always waiting for its poet. I remember, when I was young, how much I was moved one morning by tidings that genius had appeared in a youth who sat near me at table. He had left his work, and gone rambling none knew whither, and had written hundreds of lines, but could not tell whether that which was in him was therein told: he could tell nothing but that all was changed,—man, beast, heaven, earth, and sea. How gladly we listened! how credulous! Society seemed to be compromised. We sat in the aurora of a sunrise which was to put out all the stars. Boston seemed to be at twice the distance it had the night before, or was much farther than that. Rome,—what was Rome? Plutarch and Shakspeare were in the yellow leaf, and Homer no more should be heard of.[13] It is much to know that poetry has been written this very day, under this very roof, by your side. What! that wonderful spirit has not expired! these stony moments are still sparkling and animated! I had fancied that the oracles were all silent,[14] and nature had spent her fires, and behold! all night, from every pore, these fine auroras have been streaming. Every one has some interest in the advent of the poet, and no one knows how much it may concern him. We know that the secret of the world is profound, but who or what shall be our interpreter, we know not. A mountain ramble, a new style of face, a new person, may put the key into our hands. Of course, the value of genius to us is in the veracity of its report. Talent may frolic and juggle; genius realizes and adds. Mankind, in good earnest, have arrived so far in understanding themselves and their work, that the foremost watchman on the peak announces his news. It is the truest word ever spoken, and the phrase will be the fittest, most musical, and the unerring voice of the world for that time.

II   All that we call sacred history attests that the birth of a poet is the principal event in chronology. Man, never so often deceived, still watches for the arrival of a brother who can hold him steady to a truth, until he has made it his own. With what joy I begin to read a poem, which I confide in as an inspiration! And now my chains are to be broken; I shall mount above these clouds and opaque airs in which I live,—opaque, though they seem transparent,— and from the heaven of truth I shall see and comprehend my relations. That will reconcile me to life, and renovate nature, to see trifles animated by a tendency, and to know what I am doing.[15] Life will no more be a noise; now I shall see men and women, and know the signs by which they may be discerned from fools and satans. This day shall be better than my birth-day: then I became an animal: now I am invited into the science of the real. Such is the hope, but the fruition is postponed. Oftener it falls, that this winged man, who will carry me into the heaven, whirls me into the clouds, then leaps and frisks about with me from cloud to cloud, still affirming that he is bound heavenward; and I, being myself a novice, am slow in perceiving that he does not know the way into the heavens, and is merely bent that I should admire his skill to rise, like a fowl or a flying fish, a little way from the ground or the water; but the all-piercing, all-feeding, and ocular air of heaven, that man shall never inhabit.[16] I tumble down again soon into my old nooks, and lead the life of exaggerations as before, and have lost some faith in the possibility of any guide who can lead me thither where I would be.

But leaving these victims of vanity, let us, with new hope, observe how nature, by worthier impulses, has ensured the poet's fidelity to his office of announcement and affirming, namely, by the beauty of things, which becomes a new, and higher beauty, when expressed. Nature offers all her creatures to him as a picture-language. Being used as a type, a second wonderful value appears in the object, far better than its old value, as the carpenter's stretched cord, if you hold your ear close enough, is musical in the breeze. "Things more excellent than every image," says Jamblichus, "are expressed through images."[17] Things admit of being used as symbols, because nature is a symbol, in the whole, and in every part. Every line we can draw in the sand, has expression; and there is no body without its spirit or genius. All form is an effect of character; all condition, of the quality of the life; all harmony, of health; (and, for this reason, a perception of beauty should be sympathetic, or proper only to the good.) The beautiful rests on the foundations of the necessary. The soul makes the body, as the wise Spenser teaches:—

> "So every spirit, as it is most pure,
> And hath in it the more of heavenly light,
> So it the fairer body doth procure
> To habit in, and it more fairly dight,
> With cheerful grace and amiable sight.
> For, of the soul, the body form doth take,
> For soul is form, and doth the body make."[18]

Here we find ourselves, suddenly, not in a critical speculation, but in a holy place, and should go very warily and reverently. We stand before the secret of the world, there where Being passes into Appearance, and Unity into Variety.

The Universe is the externisation of the soul. Wherever the life is, that bursts into appearance around it. Our science is sensual, and therefore superficial. The earth, and the heavenly bodies, physics, and chemistry, we sensually treat, as if they were self-existent; but these are the retinue of that Being we have. "The mighty heaven," said Proclus, "exhibits, in its transfigurations, clear images of the splendor of intellectual perceptions; being moved in conjunction with the unapparent periods of intellectual natures."[19] Therefore, science always goes abreast with the just elevation of the man, keeping step with religion and metaphysics; or, the state of science is an index of our self-knowledge. Since everything in nature answers to a moral power, if any phenomenon remains brute and dark, it is that the corresponding faculty in the observer is not yet active.

14   No wonder, then, if these waters be so deep, that we hover over them with a religious regard. The beauty of the fable proves the importance of the sense; to the poet, and to all others; or, if you please, every man is so far a poet as to be susceptible of these enchantments of nature: for all men have the thoughts whereof the universe is the celebration. I find that the fascination resides in the symbol. Who loves nature? Who does not? Is it only poets, and men of leisure and cultivation, who live with her? No; but also hunters, farmers, grooms, and butchers, though they express their affection in their choice of life, and not in their choice of words. The writer wonders what the coachman or the hunter values in riding, in horses, and dogs. It is not superficial qualities. When you talk with him, he holds these at as slight a rate as you. His worship is sympathetic; he has no definitions, but he is commanded in nature, by the living power which he feels to be there present. No imitation, or playing of these things, would content him; he loves the earnest of the northwind, of rain, of stone, and wood, and iron. A beauty not explicable, is dearer than a beauty which we can see to the end of. It is nature the symbol, nature certifying the supernatural, body overflowed by life, which he worships, with coarse, but sincere rites.

15   The inwardness, and mystery, of this attachment, drives men of every class to the use of emblems. The schools of poets, and philosophers, are not more intoxicated with their symbols, than the populace with theirs. In our political parties, compute the power of badges and emblems. See the great ball which they roll from Baltimore to Bunker hill! In the political processions, Lowell goes in a loom, and Lynn in a shoe, and Salem in a ship.[20] Witness the cider-barrel, the log-cabin, the hickory-stick, the palmetto, and all

the cognizances of party. See the power of national emblems.[21] Some stars, lilies, leopards, a crescent, a lion, an eagle, or other figure, which came into credit God knows how, on an old rag of bunting, blowing in the wind, on a fort, at the ends of the earth, shall make the blood tingle under the rudest, or the most conventional exterior. The people fancy they hate poetry, and they are all poets and mystics!

Beyond this universality of the symbolic language, we are apprised of the divineness of this superior use of things, whereby the world is a temple, whose walls are covered with emblems, pictures, and commandments of the Deity, in this, that there is no fact in nature which does not carry the whole sense of nature; and the distinctions which we make in events, and in affairs, of low and high, honest and base, disappear when nature is used as a symbol. Thought makes every thing fit for use. The vocabulary of an omniscient man would embrace words and images excluded from polite conversation. What would be base, or even obscene, to the obscene, becomes illustrious, spoken in a new connexion of thought. The piety of the Hebrew prophets purges their grossness. The circumcision is an example of the power of poetry to raise the low and offensive. Small and mean things serve as well as great symbols. The meaner the type by which a law is expressed, the more pungent it is, and the more lasting in the memories of men: just as we choose the smallest box, or case, in which any needful utensil can be carried. Bare lists of words are found suggestive, to an imaginative and excited mind; as it is related of Lord Chatham, that he was accustomed to read in Bailey's Dictionary, when he was preparing to speak in Parliament.[22] The poorest experience is rich enough for all the purposes of expressing thought. Why covet a knowledge of new facts? Day and night, house and garden, a few books, a few actions, serve us as well as would all trades and all spectacles. We are far from having exhausted the significance of the few symbols we use. We can come to use them yet with a terrible simplicity. It does not need that a poem should be long. Every word was once a poem. Every new relation is a new word. Also, we use defects and deformities to a sacred purpose, so expressing our sense that the evils of the world are such only to the evil eye. In the old mythology, mythologists observe, defects are ascribed to divine natures, as lameness to Vulcan, blindness to Cupid, and the like, to signify exuberances.[23]

For, as it is dislocation and detachment from the life of God, that makes things ugly, the poet, who re-attaches things to nature and the Whole,—reattaching even artificial things, and violations of nature, to nature, by a deeper insight,—disposes very easily of the most disagreeable facts. Readers of poetry see the factory-village, and the railway, and fancy that the poetry of the landscape is broken up by these; for these works of art are not yet conse-crated in their reading; but the poet sees them fall within the great Order not less than the bee-hive, or the spider's geometrical web.[24] Nature adopts them very fast into her vital circles, and the gliding train of cars she loves like her own. Besides, in a centred mind, it signifies nothing how many mechanical inventions you exhibit. Though you add millions, and never so surprising, the fact of mechanics has not gained a grain's weight. The spiritual fact remains unalterable, by many or by few particulars; as no mountain is of any appre-ciable height to break the curve of the sphere. A shrewd country-boy goes to the city for the first time, and the complacent citizen is not satisfied with his little wonder. It is not that he does not see all the fine houses, and know that he never saw such before, but he disposes of them as easily as the poet finds place for the railway. The chief value of the new fact, is to enhance the great and constant fact of Life, which can dwarf any and every circumstance, and to which the belt of wampum, and the commerce of America, are alike.

18   The world being thus put under the mind for verb and noun, the poet is he who can articulate it. For, though life is great, and fascinates, and ab-sorbs,—and though all men are intelligent of the symbols through which it is named,—yet they cannot originally use them. We are symbols, and inhabit symbols; workman, work, and tools, words and things, birth and death, all are emblems; but we sympathize with the symbols, and, being infatuated with the economical uses of things, we do not know that they are thoughts. The poet, by an ulterior intellectual perception, gives them a power which makes their old use forgotten, and puts eyes, and a tongue, into every dumb and inanimate object. He perceives the independence of the thought on the symbol, the stability of the thought, the accidency and fugacity of the sym-bol. As the eyes of Lyncæus were said to see through the earth, so the poet turns the world to glass, and shows us all things in their right series and pro-cession.[25] For, through that better perception, he stands one step nearer to things, and sees the flowing or metamorphosis; perceives that thought is mul-tiform; that within the form of every creature is a force impelling it to ascend into a higher form; and, following with his eyes the life, uses the forms which express that life, and so his speech flows with the flowing of nature. All the

facts of the animal economy, sex, nutriment, gestation, birth, growth, are symbols of the passage of the world into the soul of man, to suffer there a change, and reappear a new and higher fact. He uses forms according to the life, and not according to the form. This is true science. The poet alone knows astronomy, chemistry, vegetation, and animation, for he does not stop at these facts, but employs them as signs. He knows why the plain, or meadow of space, was strown with these flowers we call suns, and moons, and stars; why the great deep is adorned with animals, with men, and gods; for, in every word he speaks he rides on them as the horses of thought.

By virtue of this science the poet is the Namer, or Language-maker, naming things sometimes after their appearance, sometimes after their essence, and giving to every one its own name and not another's, thereby rejoicing the intellect, which delights in detachment or boundary. The poets made all the words, and therefore language is the archives of history, and, if we must say it, a sort of tomb of the muses. For, though the origin of most of our words is forgotten, each word was at first a stroke of genius, and obtained currency, because for the moment it symbolized the world to the first speaker and to the hearer. The etymologist finds the deadest word to have been once a brilliant picture. Language is fossil poetry. As the limestone of the continent consists of infinite masses of the shells of animalcules, so language is made up of images, or tropes, which now, in their secondary use, have long ceased to remind us of their poetic origin. But the poet names the thing because he sees it, or comes one step nearer to it than any other. This expression, or naming, is not art, but a second nature, grown out of the first, as a leaf out of a tree. What we call nature, is a certain self-regulated motion, or change; and nature does all things by her own hands, and does not leave another to baptise her, but baptises herself; and this through the metamorphosis again. I remember that a certain poet described it to me thus:

Genius is the activity which repairs the decays of things, whether wholly or partly of a material and finite kind. Nature, through all her kingdoms, insures herself. Nobody cares for planting the poor fungus: so she shakes down from the gills of one agaric countless spores, any one of which, being preserved, transmits new billions of spores to-morrow or next day. The new agaric of this hour has a chance which the old one had not. This atom of seed is thrown into a new place, not subject to the accidents which destroyed its parent two rods off. She makes a man; and having brought him to ripe age, she will no longer run the risk of losing this wonder at a blow, but she detaches from him a new self, that the kind may be safe from accidents to which the individual is exposed. So when the soul of the poet has come to ripeness of thought, she detaches and sends away from it its poems or songs,—a fearless, sleepless, deathless progeny, which is not exposed to the accidents of the weary kingdom of time: a fearless, vivacious offspring, clad with wings (such was the virtue of the soul out of which they came), which carry them fast and far, and infix them irrecoverably into the hearts of men. These wings are the beauty of the poet's soul. The songs, thus flying immortal from their mortal parent, are pursued by clamorous flights of censures, which swarm in far greater numbers, and threaten to devour them; but these last are not winged. At the end of a very short leap they fall plump down, and rot, having received from the souls out of which they came no beautiful wings. But the melodies of the poet ascend, and leap, and pierce into the deeps of infinite time.

21   So far the bard taught me, using his freer speech. But nature has a higher end, in the production of new individuals, than security, namely, *ascension,* or, the passage of the soul into higher forms. I knew, in my younger days, the sculptor who made the statue of the youth which stands in the public garden.[26] He was, as I remember, unable to tell directly, what made him happy, or unhappy, but by wonderful indirections he could tell. He rose one day, according to his habit, before the dawn, and saw the morning break, grand as the eternity out of which it came, and, for many days after, he strove to express this tranquillity, and, lo! his chisel had fashioned out of marble the form of a beautiful youth, Phosphor, whose aspect is such, that, it is said, all persons who look on it become silent.[27] The poet also resigns himself to his mood, and that thought which agitated him is expressed, but *alter idem,* in a manner totally new.[28] The expression is organic, or, the new type which things themselves take when liberated. As, in the sun, objects paint their images on the retina of the eye, so they, sharing the aspiration of the whole universe, tend to paint a far more delicate copy of their essence in his mind. Like the metamorphosis of things into higher organic forms, is their change into melodies. Over everything stands its dæmon, or soul, and, as the form of the thing is reflected by the eye, so the soul of the thing is reflected by a mel-

ody. The sea, the mountain-ridge, Niagara, and every flower-bed, pre-exist, or super-exist, in pre-cantations, which sail like odors in the air, and when any man goes by with an ear suficiently fine, he overhears them, and endeavors to write down the notes, without diluting or depraving them. And herein is the legitimation of criticism, in the mind's faith, that the poems are a corrupt version of some text in nature, with which they ought to be made to tally. A rhyme in one of our sonnets should not be less pleasing than the iterated nodes of a sea-shell, or the resembling difference of a group of flowers. The pairing of the birds is an idyl, not tedious as our idyls are;[29] a tempest is a rough ode, without falsehood or rant: a summer, with its harvest sown, reaped, and stored, is an epic song, subordinating how many admirably executed parts. Why should not the symmetry and truth that modulate these, glide into our spirits, and we participate the invention of nature?

This insight, which expresses itself by what is called Imagination, is a very high sort of seeing, which does not come by study, but by the intellect being where and what it sees, by sharing the path, or circuit of things through forms, and so making them translucid to others. The path of things is silent. Will they suffer a speaker to go with them? A spy they will not suffer; a lover, a poet, is the transcendency of their own nature,—him they will suffer. The condition of true naming, on the poet's part, is his resigning himself to the divine *aura* which breathes through forms, and accompanying that.[30]

It is a secret which every intellectual man quickly learns, that, beyond the energy of his possessed and conscious intellect, he is capable of a new energy (as of an intellect doubled on itself), by abandonment to the nature of things; that, beside his privacy of power as an individual man, there is a great public power, on which he can draw, by unlocking, at all risks, his human doors, and suffering the ethereal tides to roll and circulate through him: then he is caught up into the life of the Universe, his speech is thunder, his thought is law, and his words are universally intelligible as the plants and animals. The poet knows that he speaks adequately, then only when he speaks somewhat wildly, or, "with the flower of the mind;" not with the intellect, used as an organ, but with the intellect released from all service, and suffered to take its direction from its celestial life; or, as the ancients were wont to express themselves, not with intellect alone, but with the intellect inebriated by nectar.[31] As the traveller who has lost his way, throws his reins on his horse's neck, and trusts to the instinct of the animal to find his road, so must we do with the divine animal

22

23

who carries us through this world. For if in any manner we can stimulate this instinct, new passages are opened for us into nature, the mind flows into and through things hardest and highest, and the metamorphosis is possible.

This is the reason why bards love wine, mead, narcotics, coffee, tea, opium, the fumes of sandal-wood and tobacco, or whatever other species of animal exhilaration. All men avail themselves of such means as they can, to add this extraordinary power to their normal powers; and to this end they prize conversation, music, pictures, sculpture, dancing, theatres, travelling, war, mobs, fires, gaming, politics, or love, or science, or animal intoxication, which are several coarser or finer *quasi*-mechanical substitutes for the true nectar, which is the ravishment of the intellect by coming nearer to the fact. These are auxiliaries to the centrifugal tendency of a man, to his passage out into free space, and they help him to escape the custody of that body in which he is pent up, and of that jail-yard of individual relations in which he is enclosed. Hence a great number of such as were professionally expressors of Beauty, as painters, poets, musicians, and actors, have been more than others wont to lead a life of pleasure and indulgence; all but the few who received the true nectar; and, as it was a spurious mode of attaining freedom, as it was an emancipation not into the heavens, but into the freedom of baser places, they were punished for that advantage they won, by a dissipation and deterioration. But never can any advantage be taken of nature by a trick. The spirit of the world, the great calm presence of the creator, comes not forth to the sorceries of opium or of wine. The sublime vision comes to the pure and simple soul in a clean and chaste body. That is not an inspiration which we owe to narcotics, but some counterfeit excitement and fury. Milton says, that the lyric poet may drink wine and live generously, but the epic poet, he who shall sing of the gods, and their descent unto men, must drink water out of a wooden bowl.[32] For poetry is not 'Devil's wine,' but God's wine.[33] It is with this as it is with toys. We fill the hands and nurseries of our children with all manner of dolls, drums, and horses, withdrawing their eyes from the plain face and sufficing objects of nature, the sun, and moon, the animals, the water, and stones, which should be their toys. So the poet's habit of living should be set on a key so low and plain, that the common influences should delight him. His cheerfulness should be the gift of the sunlight; the air should suffice for his inspiration, and he should be tipsy with water. That spirit which suffices quiet hearts, which seems to come forth to such from every dry knoll of sere grass, from every pine-stump, and half-imbedded stone, on which the dull March sun shines, comes forth to the poor and hungry, and such as are of simple taste. If thou fill thy brain with Boston and New York, with fashion and covetousness, and wilt stimulate thy jaded senses with wine and French coffee, thou shalt find no radiance of wisdom in the lonely waste of the pine-woods.[34]

If the imagination intoxicates the poet, it is not inactive in other men. The metamorphosis excites in the beholder an emotion of joy. The use of symbols has a certain power of emancipation and exhilaration for all men. We seem to be touched by a wand, which makes us dance and run about happily, like children. We are like persons who come out of a cave or cellar into the open air. This is the effect on us of tropes, fables, oracles, and all poetic forms. Poets are thus liberating gods. Men have really got a new sense, and found within their world, another world, or nest of worlds; for, the metamorphosis once seen, we divine that it does not stop. I will not now consider how much this makes the charm of algebra and the mathematics, which also have their tropes, but it is felt in every definition; as, when Aristotle defines *space* to be an immovable vessel, in which things are contained;[35]—or, when Plato defines a *line* to be a flowing point; or, *figure* to be a bound of solid;[36] and many the like. What a joyful sense of freedom we have, when Vitruvius announces the old opinion of artists, that no architect can build any house well, who does not know something of anatomy.[37] When Socrates, in Charmides, tells us that the soul is cured of its maladies by certain incantations, and that these incantations are beautiful reasons, from which temperance is generated in souls; when Plato calls the world an animal; and Timæus affirms that the plants also are animals;[38] or affirms a man to be a heavenly tree, growing with his root, which is his head, upward;[39] and, as George Chapman, following him, writes,—

> "So in our tree of man, whose nervie root
> Springs in his top;"[40]

when Orpheus speaks of hoariness as "'that white flower which marks extreme old age;"[41] when Proclus calls the universe the statue of the intellect;[42] when Chaucer, in his praise of 'Gentilesse,' compares good blood in mean condition to fire, which, though carried to the darkest house betwixt this and the mount of Caucasus, will yet hold its natural office, and burn as bright as if twenty thousand men did it behold;[43] when John saw, in the apocalypse, the ruin of the world through evil, and the stars fall from heaven, as the figtree casteth her untimely fruit;[44] when Æsop reports the whole catalogue of common daily relations through the masquerade of birds and beasts;—we take the cheerful hint of the immortality of our essence, and its versatile habit and escapes, as when the gypsies say, "it is in vain to hang them, they cannot die."[45]

26   The poets are thus liberating gods. The ancient British bards had for the title of their order, "Those who are free throughout the world."[46] They are free, and they make free. An imaginative book renders us much more service at first, by stimulating us through its tropes, than afterward, when we arrive at the precise sense of the author. I think nothing is of any value in books, excepting the transcendental and extraordinary. If a man is inflamed and carried away by his thought, to that degree that he forgets the authors and the public, and heeds only this one dream, which holds him like an insanity, let me read his paper, and you may have all the arguments and histories and criticism. All the value which attaches to Pythagoras, Paracelsus, Cornelius Agrippa, Cardan, Kepler, Swedenborg, Schelling, Oken, or any other who introduces questionable facts into his cosmogony, as angels, devils, magic, astrology, palmistry, mesmerism, and so on, is the certificate we have of departure from routine, and that here is a new witness.[47] That also is the best success in conversation, the magic of liberty, which puts the world, like a ball, in our hands. How cheap even the liberty then seems; how mean to study, when an emotion communicates to the intellect the power to sap and upheave nature: how great the perspective! nations, times, systems, enter and disappear, like threads in tapestry of large figure and many colors; dream delivers us to dream, and, while the drunkenness lasts, we will sell our bed, our philosophy, our religion, in our opulence.

27   There is good reason why we should prize this liberation. The fate of the poor shepherd, who, blinded and lost in the snowstorm, perishes in a drift within a few feet of his cottage door, is an emblem of the state of man. On the brink of the waters of life and truth, we are miserably dying. The inaccessibleness of every thought but that we are in, is wonderful. What if you come near to it,—you are as remote, when you are nearest, as when you are farthest. Every thought is also a prison; every heaven is also a prison. Therefore we love the poet, the inventor, who in any form, whether in an ode, or in an

action, or in looks and behavior, has yielded us a new thought. He unlocks our chains, and admits us to a new scene.

This emancipation is dear to all men, and the power to impart it, as it must come from greater depth and scope of thought, is a measure of intellect. Therefore all books of the imagination endure, all which ascend to that truth, that the writer sees nature beneath him, and uses it as his exponent. Every verse or sentence, possessing this virtue, will take care of its own immortality. The religions of the world are the ejaculations of a few imaginative men. 28

But the quality of the imagination is to flow, and not to freeze. The poet did not stop at the color, or the form, but read their meaning; neither may he rest in this meaning, but he makes the same objects exponents of his new thought. Here is the difference betwixt the poet and the mystic, that the last nails a symbol to one sense, which was a true sense for a moment, but soon becomes old and false. For all symbols are fluxional; all language is vehicular and transitive, and is good, as ferries and horses are, for conveyance, not as farms and houses are, for homestead. Mysticism consists in the mistake of an accidental and individual symbol for an universal one. The morning-redness happens to be the favorite meteor to the eyes of Jacob Behmen, and comes to stand to him for truth and faith;[48] and he believes should stand for the same realities to every reader. But the first reader prefers as naturally the symbol of a mother and child, or a gardener and his bulb, or a jeweller polishing a gem. Either of these, or of a myriad more, are equally good to the person to whom they are significant. Only they must be held lightly, and be very willingly translated into the equivalent terms which others use. And the mystic must be steadily told,—All that you say is just as true without the tedious use of that symbol as with it. Let us have a little algebra, instead of this trite rhetoric,—universal signs, instead of these village symbols,—and we shall both be gainers. The history of hierarchies seems to show, that all religious error consisted in making the symbol too stark and solid, and, at last, nothing but an excess of the organ of language. 29

Swedenborg, of all men in the recent ages, stands eminently for the translator of nature into thought. I do not know the man in history to whom things stood so uniformly for words. Before him the metamorphosis continually plays. Everything on which his eye rests, obeys the impulses of moral nature. The figs become grapes whilst he eats them. When some of his angels 30 affirmed a truth, the laurel twig which they held blossomed in their hands. The noise which, at a distance, appeared like gnashing and thumping, on coming nearer was found to be the voice of disputants. The men, in one of his visions, seen in heavenly light, appeared like dragons, and seemed in darkness: but, to each other, they appeared as men, and, when the light from heaven shone into their cabin, they complained of the darkness, and were compelled to shut the window that they might see.

31   There was this perception in him, which makes the poet or seer, an object of awe and terror, namely, that the same man, or society of men, may wear one aspect to themselves and their companions, and a different aspect to higher intelligences. Certain priests, whom he describes as conversing very learnedly together, appeared to the children, who were at some distance, like dead horses: and many the like misappearances.[49] And instantly the mind inquires, whether these fishes under the bridge, yonder oxen in the pasture, those dogs in the yard, are immutably fishes, oxen, and dogs, or only so appear to me, and perchance to themselves appear upright men; and whether I appear as a man to all eyes. The Bramins and Pythagoras propounded the same question, and if any poet has witnessed the transformation, he doubtless found it in harmony with various experiences. We have all seen changes as considerable in wheat and caterpillars.[50] He is the poet, and shall draw us with love and terror, who sees, through the flowing vest, the firm nature, and can declare it.

32   I look in vain for the poet whom I describe. We do not, with sufficient plainness, or sufficient profoundness, address ourselves to life, nor dare we chaunt our own times and social circumstance. If we filled the day with bravery, we should not shrink from celebrating it. Time and nature yield us many gifts, but not yet the timely man, the new religion, the reconciler, whom all things await. Dante's praise is, that he dared to write his autobiography in colossal cipher, or into universality. We have yet had no genius in America, with tyrannous eye, which knew the value of our incomparable materials, and saw, in the barbarism and materialism of the times, another carnival of the same gods whose picture he so much admires in Homer; then in the middle age; then in Calvinism. Banks and tariffs, the newspaper and caucus, methodism and unitarianism, are flat and dull to dull people, but rest on the same foundations of wonder as the town of Troy, and the temple of Delphos, and are as swiftly passing away.[51] Our logrolling, our stumps and their poli-

tics, our fisheries, our Negroes, and Indians, our boasts, and our repudiations, the wrath of rogues, and the pusillanimity of honest men, the northern trade, the southern planting, the western clearing, Oregon, and Texas, are yet unsung.[52] Yet America is a poem in our eyes; its ample geography dazzles the imagination, and it will not wait long for metres. If I have not found that excellent combination of gifts in my countrymen which I seek, neither could I aid myself to fix the idea of the poet by reading now and then in Chalmers's collection of five centuries of English poets.[53] These are wits, more than poets, though there have been poets among them. But when we adhere to the ideal of the poet, we have our difficulties even with Milton and Homer. Milton is too literary, and Homer too literal and historical.

But I am not wise enough for a national criticism, and must use the old largeness a little longer, to discharge my errand from the muse to the poet concerning his art.   33

Art is the path of the creator to his work. The paths, or methods, are ideal   34
and eternal, though few men ever see them, not the artist himself for years, or for a lifetime, unless he come into the conditions. The painter, the sculptor, the composer, the epic rhapsodist, the orator, all partake one desire, namely, to express themselves symmetrically and abundantly, not dwarfishly and fragmentarily. They found or put themselves in certain conditions, as, the painter and sculptor before some impressive human figures; the orator, into the assembly of the people; and the others, in such scenes as each has found exciting to his intellect; and each presently feels the new desire. He hears a voice, he sees a beckoning. Then he is apprised, with wonder, what herds of dæmons hem him in. He can no more rest; he says, with the old painter, "By God, it is in me, and must go forth of me." He pursues a beauty, half seen, which flies before him. The poet pours out verses in every solitude. Most of the things he says are conventional, no doubt; but by and by he says something which is original and beautiful. That charms him. He would say nothing else but such things. In our way of talking, we say, 'That is yours, this is mine;' but the poet knows well that it is not his; that it is as strange and beautiful to him as to you; he would fain hear the like eloquence at length. Once having tasted this immortal ichor, he cannot have enough of it, and, as an admirable creative power exists in these intellections, it is of the last importance that these things get spoken. What a little of all we know is said! What drops of all the sea of our science are baled up![54] and by what accident it is that

these are exposed, when so many secrets sleep in nature! Hence the necessity of speech and song; hence these throbs and heart-beatings in the orator, at the door of the assembly, to the end, namely, that thought may be ejaculated as Logos, or Word.

35   Doubt not, O poet, but persist. Say, 'It is in me, and shall out.' Stand there, baulked and dumb, stuttering and stammering, hissed and hooted, stand and strive, until, at last, rage draw out of thee that *dream*-power which every night shows thee is thine own; a power transcending all limit and privacy, and by virtue of which a man is the conductor of the whole river of electricity. Nothing walks, or creeps, or grows, or exists, which must not in turn arise and walk before him as exponent of his meaning. Comes he to that power, his genius is no longer exhaustible. All the creatures, by pairs and by tribes, pour into his mind as into a Noah's ark, to come forth again to people a new world. This is like the stock of air for our respiration, or for the combustion of our fireplace, not a measure of gallons, but the entire atmosphere if wanted. And therefore the rich poets, as Homer, Chaucer, Shakspeare, and Raphael, have obviously no limits to their works, except the limits of their lifetime, and resemble a mirror carried through the street, ready to render an image of every created thing.

36   O poet! a new nobility is conferred in groves and pastures, and not in castles, or by the sword-blade, any longer. The conditions are hard, but equal. Thou shalt leave the world, and know the muse only. Thou shalt not know any longer the times, customs, graces, politics, or opinions of men, but shalt take all from the muse. For the time of towns is tolled from the world by funereal chimes, but in nature the universal hours are counted by succeeding tribes of animals and plants, and by growth of joy on joy. God wills also that thou abdicate a manifold and duplex life, and that thou be content that others speak for thee. Others shall be thy gentlemen, and shall represent all courtesy and worldly life for thee; others shall do the great and resounding actions also. Thou shalt lie close hid with nature, and canst not be afforded to the Capitol or the Exchange. The world is full of renunciations and apprenticeships, and this is thine; thou must pass for a fool and a churl for a long season. This is the screen and sheath in which Pan has protected his well-beloved flower, and thou shalt be known only to thine own, and they shall console thee with tenderest love. And thou shalt not be able to rehearse the names of thy friends in thy verse, for an old shame before the holy ideal. And this is the

reward: that the ideal shall be real to thee, and the impresions of the actual
world shall fall like summer rain, copious, but not troublesome, to thy invulnerable essence. Thou shalt have the whole land for thy park and manor, the
sea for thy bath and navigation, without tax and without envy; the woods and
the rivers thou shalt own; and thou shalt possess that wherein others are only
tenants and boarders. Thou true land-lord! sea-lord! air-lord! Wherever snow
falls, or water flows, or birds fly, wherever day and night meet in twilight,
wherever the blue heaven is hung by clouds, or sown with stars, wherever are
forms with transparent boundaries, wherever are outlets into celestial space,
wherever is danger, and awe, and love, there is Beauty, plenteous as rain, shed
for thee, and though thou shouldest walk the world over, thou shalt not be
able to find a condition inopportune or ignoble.[55]

Notes

1. Emerson, "The Poet," *CW,* 9:664.
2. Emerson, "Ode to Beauty," ll. 60–63, *CW,* 9:174.
3. Like others of his time, Emerson believed that Orpheus was a historic person and
   the actual author of the hymns and fragments attributed to him by the ancients.
   Empedocles, fourth-century BCE Roman philosopher of nature; Heraclitus, Greek
   philosopher active circa 500 BCE who believed that the material world is constantly
   changing, that there is a unity of opposites, and that fire is the basic material of
   the world.
4. With "These stand and . . . peculiar service," cf. Milton, Sonnet XIX, l. 14.
5. This paragraph grew out of Emerson's reading in Ralph Cudworth, *The True Intellectual System of the Universe,* ed. Thomas Birch, 4 vols. (London, 1820), 2:473–474;
   see *CW,* 3:172. Jupiter is the central deity of the Roman religious world; Neptune is
   the Roman god of the sea.
6. Agamemnon is probably a reference to *Agamemnon* by Aeschylus (525–456 BCE),
   Athenian tragic dramatist.
7. In his journal, Emerson developed this and the previous sentence after hearing
   Henry David Thoreau (1817–1862) read aloud some poems of his own, which he
   liked for their "honest truth" and "rude strength" but ultimately thought "drossy
   & crude" (*JMN,* 7:257); see "Thoreau," para 7, below.
8. Here, Emerson uses "indifferent" in the old sense of "not different," "similar."
9. Here, Emerson uses "doctor" in its biblical meaning of "teacher"; cf. Luke 2:46.
   The journal passage from which Emerson extracted this sentence was an evalua-

tion of his friend William Ellery Channing II (1818–1901), poet and essayist, as "a very imperfect artist" (*JMN*, 7:468–469).

10. The "recent writer of lyrics" was Alfred, Lord Tennyson (1809–1892), who, in 1850, was named poet laureate of England to succeed Wordsworth (*JMN*, 7:471).

11. "Chimborazo under the line" refers to Chimborazo, the highest mountain in Ecuador at the equator, which was believed in Emerson's day to be the highest of the Andes.

12. In 1844, owners of cottages and villas surrounded by five hundred acres or only half an acre were genuinely concerned about the style and propriety of their landscaping.

13. With "the yellow leaf," cf. Shakespeare, *Macbeth*, V, iii, 23.

14. With "the oracles were all silent," cf. Milton, "On the Morning of Christ's Nativity," l. 173.

15. Here, "tendency" is used in the old sense of "a making toward something."

16. With "ocular air of heaven," cf. Emerson's "transparent eye-ball" passage in *Nature*, para 9, above.

17. Iamblichus, or Jamblichus, fourth-century Syrian Neoplatonic philosopher.

18. "An Hymne in Honour of Beautie," ll. 127–133, by Edmund Spenser (ca. 1552–1599), English poet best known for *The Fairie Queene* (1590).

19. Emerson's source is *The Commentaries of Proclus on the Timæus of Plato*, trans. Thomas Taylor, 2 vols. (London, 1820), 1:72–73. Proclus Lycæus (412–485) was the last of the great Greek Neoplatonists.

20. Each of these Massachusetts towns had a single reason for fame: Lowell, for its textile mills; Lynn, as America's major center for making shoes; and Salem, for its sea trade.

21. All of these emblems had been prominent in recent political events: the palmetto of South Carolina; the hickory stick of Andrew Jackson (1767–1845), seventh president of the United States; and the plebeian log cabin and the hard-cider barrel that dominated the successful presidential campaign of William Henry Harrison against Martin Van Buren (1782–1862), the eighth president, in 1840, but the most imaginative were the huge balls of cowhide or tin over wood that Harrison's rowdy supporters rolled along even the remotest of country roads.

22. Nathaniel Bailey (d. 1742), English lexicographer, first published his *An Universal Entymological English Dictionary* in 1721; it became the most widely used of eighteenth-century English dictionaries. Emerson's source for the anecdote about William Pitt, 1st Earl of Chatham, is Francis Thackeray, *A History of the Right Honourable William Pitt*, 2 vols. (London, 1827), 2:399 (*JMN*, 6:165).

23. Emerson's source is *The Commentaries of Proclus on the Timæus of Plato*, 1820, 1:120n (*JMN*, 12:347); here, by "exuberances" Emerson means "superabundances."

24. The poet is likely Henry Thoreau and the village one of the riverside mill towns

he and John Thoreau, his brother, saw on their journey along the Concord and the Merrimack rivers in 1839; see *The Writings of Henry D. Thoreau, A Week on the Concord and Merrimack Rivers* (Princeton: Princeton University Press, 1980), p. 87.

25. "As the eyes . . . the earth" is a near translation of *Argonautica*, I, ll. 153–155, by Apollonius Rhodius, or Apollonius of Rhodes, third-century BCE Greek writer.

26. Horatio Greenough (1805–1852), American sculptor and proponent of the organic theory in art.

27. Phosphor (or Phosphorus), or Lucifer, the morning star, was sometimes personified as a "beautiful youth" carrying a torch.

28. *Alter idem* means "as another and the same."

29. Here, "pairing" means "mating," as in "pairing-time."

30. The metaphor and italics in "divine *aura* which . . . through forms" suggest that here *"aura"* has its Latin meaning of "breeze."

31. Emerson's source for "with the flower of the mind," a translation of a Greek phrase in the "Chaldean Oracles" attributed to Zoroaster, is Cudworth, *The True Intellectual System of the Universe*, 2:71 (*JMN*, 6:179); his source for "as the ancients . . . by nectar" is *The Six Books of Proclus . . . on the Theology of Plato*, trans. Thomas Taylor, 2 vols. (London, 1816), 1:46.

32. Milton, "Elegia Sexta," ll. 51–64.

33. In the *Edinburgh Review* for January 1841, the reviewer of J. G. Lockhart's *Ancient Spanish Ballads* wrote that "one of the old fathers" had called poetry "Devil's wine"; when he outlined "The Poet" in his journal, Emerson attributed the phrase to "the Church Fathers" and gave its Latin original as "vinum dæmonum" (*JMN*, 12:349).

34. Emerson had recently returned from a lecture trip to New York when he wrote this sentence in his journal in March 1842 (*JMN*, 8:205).

35. Emerson's source is Aristotle, *Physics*, IV, 4, 212, a, 14 (*JMN*, 8:14).

36. Emerson's source for the definition of *"line,"* actually a trope, is *The Six Books of Proclus . . . on the Theology of Plato* (1816), 2:172, and for the definition of *"figure"* is Plato, *Meno*, 76, where Socrates defines the term.

37. In *On Architecture* by Marcus Vitruvius Pollio, first-century BCE Roman architect, see I, i, 3; I, ii, 4; and especially III, i, 1. See also *JMN*, 4:367–368, and "Montaigne, or the Skeptic," *CW*, 4:91.

38. In Plato's *Charmides*, 157, Socrates speaks of cures using incantations; Plato calls the world an animal in *Timæus*, 31; and Timæus affirms that plants are animals in Plato, *Timæus*, 77.

39. Here, Emerson quotes without quotation marks John Philips's translation of Plutarch's essay "Wherefore the *Pythian* Priestess Now Ceases to Deliver her *Oracles in Verse*"; see *Plutarch's Morals: Translated from the Greek, By Several Hands*, 5 vols. (London, 1718), 3:100. Plato develops the tree metaphor in *Timæus*, 90.

40. Emerson's source is the English poet, translator of Homer, and dramatist George

Chapman (ca. 1559–1634), "Epistle Dedicatory," ll. 132–133, to his translation of *The Iliad*.

41. Emerson's source is *The Six Books of Proclus . . . on the Theology of Plato* (1816), 1:333.

42. Emerson altered and simplified the metaphor of Proclus, presumably his source, from *The Six Books of Proclus . . . on the Theology of Plato* (1816), 2:298.

43. With "Chaucer, in his . . . natural office," cf. "The Wife of Bath's Tale," ll. 1132–1145. The Caucasus Mountains are in a region at the border of Europe and Asia, located between the Black and the Caspian seas.

44. Revelation 6:13.

45. Emerson's source is *The Zincali; or, an Account of the Gypsies of Spain . . .* (1842), by George Borrow (1803–1881), English traveler and linguist; the gypsy saying expresses a belief in the transmigration of souls.

46. Emerson's source is a letter of 1823 by the English poet Felicia Dorothea Hemans (1793–1835) quoted in Henry F. Chorley, *Memorials of Mrs. Hemans*, 2 vols. (New York, 1836), 1:74–75 (*JMN*, 5:346–347).

47. Paracelsus (1493–1541), German-Swiss alchemist and physician; Heinrich Cornelius Agrippa (1486–1535), German philosopher interested in alchemy; Gerolamo Cardano (1501–1576), Italian physician, mathematician, and astrologer ("Cardan" is the French version of the name); Friedrich Wilhelm Joseph von Schelling (1775–1854), German philosopher; Lorenz Oken (1779–1851), German naturalist and philosopher.

48. Jacob Behmen, or Jakob Böhme (1575–1624), German mystic, from whom Emerson derives the use of the "meteor" as being an "atmospheric phenomenon."

49. Beginning with his introduction of Swedenborg in the previous paragraph, all of the illustrative metamorphoses and misappearances appear in Swedenborg's 1766 *Apocalypsis Revelata (The Apocalypse Revealed)* in the "Memorable Revelations" (or visions), usually Swedenborg's own experiences, which conclude each chapter of the book.

50. In *The History of Ancient Philosophy*, published in multiple volumes beginning in 1829 and a work Emerson was familiar with, by the German philosopher Heinrich Ritter (1791–1869), the word "Brahman" is used interchangeably with "Hindoo" and "Indian." The aspect of Hinduism Emerson had in mind was what Ritter called "the doctrine of the transmigration of souls," the vision of life as "the toil of unceasing transmutations." In Pythagorean philosophy there also was "the doctrine of metempsychosis," the belief that "separated souls could again enter into other bodies . . . animal or human."

51. Troy is the setting for Homer's *Iliad*; Delphos is the home of the oracle of Delphi.

52. For readers of 1844, Emerson's reference to Oregon and Texas was probably more political than geographical. The decades-old dispute with Great Britain over the northern boundary of the Oregon Country had recently reached such a degree of

intensity that "reoccupation of Oregon" was a plank in the Democratic Party's platform of that year's presidential campaign and "Fifty-Four Forty or Fight" its belligerent slogan. The same platform promised the annexation of Texas, an action hotly opposed by those who feared annexation would mean the extension of slavery.

53. Alexander Chalmers (1759–1834), Scottish biographer and anthologist, edited in twenty-one volumes *The Works of the English Poets, from Chaucer to Cowper* (1810).

54. Here, "baled" is a variant spelling of "bailed."

55. Pan is the Greek god of nature, the wild, shepherds and their flocks, and, as here, is typically associated with the creative impulse. With "shed for thee," cf. "The Blood of our Lord Jesus Christ, which was shed for thee, preserve thy body and soul unto everlasting life," from "The Order of the Administration of the Lord's Supper, or Holy Communion" in *The Book of Common Prayer;* see also Luke 22:20.

Experience

Experience.

1

The lords of life, the lords of life,—
I saw them pass,
In their own guise,
Like and unlike,
Portly and grim,
Use and Surprise,
Surface and Dream,
Succession swift, and spectral Wrong,
Temperament without a tongue,
And the inventor of the game
Omnipresent without name;—
Some to see, some to be guessed,
They marched from east to west:
Little man, least of all,
Among the legs of his guardians tall,
Walked about with puzzled look:—
Him by the hand dear nature took;
Dearest nature, strong and kind,
Whispered, 'Darling, never mind!
Tomorrow they will wear another face,
The founder thou! these are thy race!'[1]

2   Where do we find ourselves? In a series of which we do not know the extremes, and believe that it has none. We wake and find ourselves on a stair; there are stairs below us, which we seem to have ascended; there are stairs above us, many a one, which go upward and out of sight. But the Genius which, according to the old belief, stands at the door by which we enter, and gives us the lethe to drink, that we may tell no tales, mixed the cup too strongly, and we cannot shake off the lethargy now at noonday.[2] Sleep lingers all our lifetime about our eyes, as night hovers all day in the boughs of

the fir-tree. All things swim and glitter. Our life is not so much threatened as our perception. Ghostlike we glide through nature, and should not know our place again. Did our birth fall in some fit of indigence and frugality in nature, that she was so sparing of her fire and so liberal of her earth, that it appears to us that we lack the affirmative principle, and though we have health and reason, yet we have no superfluity of spirit for new creation? We have enough to live and bring the year about, but not an ounce to impart or to invest. Ah that our Genius were a little more of a genius! We are like millers on the lower levels of a stream, when the factories above them have exhausted the water. We too fancy that the upper people must have raised their dams.

If any of us knew what we were doing, or where we are going, then when we think we best know! We do not know today whether we are busy or idle. In times when we thought ourselves indolent, we have afterwards discovered, that much was accomplished, and much was begun in us. All our days are so unprofitable while they pass, that 'tis wonderful where or when we ever got anything of this which we call wisdom, poetry, virtue. We never got it on any dated calendar day. Some heavenly days must have been intercalated some-where, like those that Hermes won with dice of the Moon, that Osiris might be born.³ It is said, all martyrdoms looked mean when they were suffered.⁴ Every ship is a romantic object, except that we sail in. Embark, and the ro-mance quits our vessel, and hangs on every other sail in the horizon. Our life looks trivial, and we shun to record it. Men seem to have learned of the hori-zon the art of perpetual retreating and reference. 'Yonder uplands are rich pasturage, and my neighbor has fertile meadow, but my field,' says the queru-lous farmer, 'only holds the world together.'⁵ I quote another man's saying; unluckily, that other withdraws himself in the same way, and quotes me. 'Tis the trick of nature thus to degrade today; a good deal of buzz, and some-where a result slipped magically in. Every roof is agreeable to the eye, until it is lifted; then we find tragedy and moaning women, and hard-eyed husbands, and deluges of lethe, and the men ask, 'What's the news?' as if the old were so bad. How many individuals can we count in society? how many actions? how many opinions? So much of our time is preparation, so much is routine, and so much retrospect, that the pith of each man's genius contracts itself to a very few hours. The history of literature—take the net result of Tiraboschi, Warton, or Schlegel,—is a sum of very few ideas, and of very few original tales,—all the rest being variation of these.⁶ So in this great society wide lying

3

around us, a critical analysis would find very few spontaneous actions. It is almost all custom and gross sense. There are even few opinions, and these seem organic in the speakers, and do not disturb the universal necessity.

4   What opium is instilled into all disaster! It shows formidable as we approach it, but there is at last no rough rasping friction, but the most slippery sliding surfaces. We fall soft on a thought. *Ate Dea* is gentle,

> "Over men's heads walking aloft,
> With tender feet treading so soft."[7]

People give and bemoan themselves, but it is not half so bad with them as they say. There are moods in which we court suffering, in the hope that here, at least, we shall find reality, sharp peaks and edges of truth. But it turns out to be scene-painting and counterfeit. The only thing grief has taught me, is to know how shallow it is. That, like all the rest, plays about the surface, and never introduces me into the reality, for contact with which, we would even pay the costly price of sons and lovers.[8] Was it Boscovich who found out that bodies never come in contact? Well, souls never touch their objects. An innavigable sea washes with silent waves between us and the things we aim at and converse with. Grief too will make us idealists. In the death of my son, now more than two years ago, I seem to have lost a beautiful estate,—no more. I cannot get it nearer to me.[9] If tomorrow I should be informed of the bankruptcy of my principal debtors, the loss of my property would be a great inconvenience to me, perhaps, for many years; but it would leave me as it found me,—neither better nor worse. So is it with this calamity: it does not touch me: something which I fancied was a part of me, which could not be torn away without tearing me, nor enlarged without enriching me, falls off from me, and leaves no scar. It was caducous. I grieve that grief can teach me nothing, nor carry me one step into real nature. The Indian who was laid under a curse, that the wind should not blow on him, nor water flow to him, nor fire burn him, is a type of us all.[10] The dearest events are summer-rain, and we the Para coats that shed every drop.[11] Nothing is left us now but death. We look to that with a grim satisfaction, saying, there at least is reality that will not dodge us.

5   I take this evanescence and lubricity of all objects, which lets them slip through our fingers then when we clutch hardest, to be the most unhandsome part of our condition. Nature does not like to be observed, and likes that we should be her fools and playmates. We may have the sphere for our

cricket-ball, but not a berry for our philosophy. Direct strokes she never gave us power to make; all our blows glance, all our hits are accidents. Our relations to each other are oblique and casual.

Dream delivers us to dream, and there is no end to illusion. Life is a train of moods like a string of beads, and, as we pass through them, they prove to be many-colored lenses which paint the world their own hue, and each shows only what lies in its focus. From the mountain you see the mountain. We animate what we can, and we see only what we animate. Nature and books belong to the eyes that see them. It depends on the mood of the man, whether he shall see the sunset or the fine poem. There are always sunsets, and there is always genius; but only a few hours so serene that we can relish nature or criticism. The more or less depends on structure or temperament. Temperament is the iron wire on which the beads are strung. Of what use is fortune or talent to a cold and defective nature? Who cares what sensibility or discrimination a man has at some time shown, if he falls asleep in his chair? or if he laugh and giggle? or if he apologize? or is affected with egotism? or thinks of his dollar? or cannot go by food? or has gotten a child in his boyhood? Of what use is genius, if the organ is too convex or too concave, and cannot find a focal distance within the actual horizon of human life? Of what use, if the brain is too cold or too hot, and the man does not care enough for results, to stimulate him to experiment, and hold him up in it? or if the web is too finely woven, too irritable by pleasure and pain, so that life stagnates from too much reception, without due outlet? Of what use to make heroic vows of amendment, if the same old law-breaker is to keep them? What cheer can the religious sentiment yield, when that is suspected to be secretly dependent on the seasons of the year, and the state of the blood? I knew a witty physician who found theology in the biliary duct, and used to affirm that if there was disease in the liver, the man became a Calvinist, and if that organ was sound, he became a Unitarian.[12] Very mortifying is the reluctant experience that some unfriendly excess or imbecility neutralizes the promise of genius. We see young men who owe us a new world, so readily and lavishly they promise, but they never acquit the debt;[13] they die young and dodge the account: or if they live, they lose themselves in the crowd.

Temperament also enters fully into the system of illusions, and shuts us in a prison of glass which we cannot see. There is an optical illusion about every person we meet. In truth, they are all creatures of given temperament,

6

7

which will appear in a given character, whose boundaries they will never pass: but we look at them, they seem alive, and we presume there is impulse in them. In the moment it seems impulse; in the year, in the lifetime, it turns out to be a certain uniform tune which the revolving barrel of the music-box must play. Men resist the conclusion in the morning, but adopt it as the evening wears on, that temper prevails over everything of time, place, and condition, and is inconsumable in the flames of religion. Some modifications the moral sentiment avails to impose, but the individual texture holds its dominion, if not to bias the moral judgments, yet to fix the measure of activity and of enjoyment.

8   I thus express the law as it is read from the platform of ordinary life, but must not leave it without noticing the capital exception. For temperament is a power which no man willingly hears any one praise but himself. On the platform of physics, we cannot resist the contracting influences of so-called science. Temperament puts all divinity to rout. I know the mental proclivity of physicians. I hear the chuckle of the phrenologists. Theoretic kidnappers and slave-drivers, they esteem each man the victim of another, who winds him round his finger by knowing the law of his being, and by such cheap signboards as the color of his beard, or the slope of his occiput, reads the inventory of his fortunes and character.[14] The grossest ignorance does not disgust like this impudent knowingness. The physicians say, they are not materialists; but they are:—Spirit is matter reduced to an extreme thinness: O *so thin!*—But the definition of *spiritual* should be, *that which is its own evidence.*[15] What notions do they attach to love! what to religion! One would not willingly pronounce these words in their hearing, and give them the occasion to profane them. I saw a gracious gentleman who adapts his conversation to the form of the head of the man he talks with![16] I had fancied that the value of life lay in its inscrutable possibilities; in the fact that I never know, in addressing myself to a new individual, what may befall me. I carry the keys of my castle in my hand, ready to throw them at the feet of my lord, whenever and in what disguise soever he shall appear. I know he is in the neighborhood hidden among vagabonds. Shall I preclude my future, by taking a high seat, and kindly adapting my conversation to the shape of heads? When I come to that, the doctors shall buy me for a cent.—'But, sir, medical history; the report to the Institute; the proven facts!'—I distrust the facts and the inferences. Temperament is the veto or limitation-power in the constitution, very justly ap-

plied to restrain an opposite excess in the constitution, but absurdly offered as a bar to original equity. When virtue is in presence, all subordinate powers sleep. On its own level, or in view of nature, temperament is final. I see not, if one be once caught in this trap of so-called sciences, any escape for the man from the links of the chain of physical necessity. Given such an embryo, such a history must follow. On this platform, one lives in a sty of sensualism, and would soon come to suicide. But it is impossible that the creative power should exclude itself. Into every intelligence there is a door which is never closed, through which the creator passes. The intellect, seeker of absolute truth, or the heart, lover of absolute good, intervenes for our succor, and at one whisper of these high powers, we awake from ineffectual struggles with this nightmare. We hurl it into its own hell, and cannot again contract ourselves to so base a state.

The secret of the illusoriness is in the necessity of a succession of moods or objects. Gladly we would anchor, but the anchorage is quicksand. This onward trick of nature is too strong for us: *Pero si muove.*[17] When, at night, I look at the moon and stars, I seem stationary, and they to hurry. Our love of the real draws us to permanence, but health of body consists in circulation, and sanity of mind in variety or facility of association. We need change of objects. Dedication to one thought is quickly odious. We house with the insane, and must humor them; then conversation dies out. Once I took such delight in Montaigne, that I thought I should not need any other book;[18] before that, in Shakspeare; then in Plutarch; then in Plotinus; at one time in Bacon; afterwards in Goethe; even in Bettine;[19] but now I turn the pages of either of them languidly, whilst I still cherish their genius. So with pictures; each will bear an emphasis of attention once, which it cannot retain, though we fain would continue to be pleased in that manner. How strongly I have felt of pictures, that when you have seen one well, you must take your leave of it; you shall never see it again. I have had good lessons from pictures, which I have since seen without emotion or remark. A deduction must be made from the opinion, which even the wise express of a new book or occurrence. Their opinion gives me tidings of their mood, and some vague guess at the new fact, but is nowise to be trusted as the lasting relation between that intellect and that thing. The child asks, 'Mamma, why don't I like the story as well as when you told it me yesterday?' Alas, child, it is even so with the oldest cherubim of knowledge.[20] But will it answer thy question to say, Because thou wert born to a whole, and this story is a particular? The reason of the pain this discovery causes us (and we make it late in respect to works of art and intellect), is the plaint of tragedy which murmurs from it in regard to persons, to friendship and love.

10   That immobility and absence of elasticity which we find in the arts, we find with more pain in the artist. There is no power of expansion in men. Our friends early appear to us as representatives of certain ideas, which they never pass or exceed. They stand on the brink of the ocean of thought and power, but they never take the single step that would bring them there. A man is like a bit of Labrador spar, which has no lustre as you turn it in your hand, until you come to a particular angle;[21] then it shows deep and beautiful colors. There is no adaptation or universal applicability in men, but each has his special talent, and the mastery of successful men consists in adroitly keeping themselves where and when that turn shall be oftenest to be practised. We do what we must, and call it by the best names we can, and would fain have the praise of having intended the result which ensues. I cannot recall any form of man who is not superfluous sometimes. But is not this pitiful? Life is not worth the taking, to do tricks in.

11   Of course, it needs the whole society, to give the symmetry we seek. The parti-colored wheel must revolve very fast to appear white. Something is learned too by conversing with so much folly and defect. In fine, whoever loses, we are always of the gaining party. Divinity is behind our failures and follies also. The plays of children are nonsense, but very educative nonsense. So it is with the largest and solemnest things, with commerce, government, church, marriage, and so with the history of every man's bread, and the ways by which he is to come by it. Like a bird which alights nowhere, but hops perpetually from bough to bough, is the Power which abides in no man and in no woman, but for a moment speaks from this one, and for another moment from that one.

12   But what help from these fineries or pedantries? What help from thought? Life is not dialectics. We, I think, in these times, have had lessons enough of the futility of criticism. Our young people have thought and written much on labor and reform, and for all that they have written, neither the world nor themselves have got on a step. Intellectual tasting of life will not supersede

muscular activity. If a man should consider the nicety of the passage of a piece of bread down his throat, he would starve. At Education-Farm, the noblest theory of life sat on the noblest figures of young men and maidens, quite powerless and melancholy. It would not rake or pitch a ton of hay; it would not rub down a horse; and the men and maidens it left pale and hungry.[22] A political orator wittily compared our party promises to western roads, which opened stately enough, with planted trees on either side, to tempt the traveller, but soon became narrow and narrower, and ended in a squirrel-track, and ran up a tree. So does culture with us; it ends in headache. Unspeakably sad and barren does life look to those, who a few months ago were dazzled with the splendor of the promise of the times. "There is now no longer any right course of action, nor any self-devotion left among the Iranis."[23] Objections and criticism we have had our fill of. There are objections to every course of life and action, and the practical wisdom infers an indifferency, from the omnipresence of objection. The whole frame of things preaches indifferency. Do not craze yourself with thinking, but go about your business anywhere. Life is not intellectual or critical, but sturdy. Its chief good is for well-mixed people who can enjoy what they find, without question. Nature hates peeping, and our mothers speak her very sense when they say, "Children, eat your victuals, and say no more of it." To fill the hour,—that is happiness; to fill the hour, and leave no crevice for a repentance or an approval. We live amid surfaces, and the true art of life is to skate well on them. Under the oldest mouldiest conventions, a man of native force prospers just as well as in the newest world, and that by skill of handling and treatment. He can take hold anywhere. Life itself is a mixture of power and form, and will not bear the least excess of either. To finish the moment, to find the journey's end in every step of the road, to live the greatest number of good hours, is wisdom. It is not the part of men, but of fanatics, or of mathematicians, if you will, to say, that, the shortness of life considered, it is not worth caring whether for so short a duration we were sprawling in want, or sitting high. Since our office is with moments, let us husband them. Five minutes of today are worth as much to me, as five minutes in the next millennium. Let us be poised, and wise, and our own, today. Let us treat the men and women well: treat them as if they were real: perhaps they are. Men live in their fancy, like drunkards whose hands are too soft and tremulous for successful labor. It is a tempest of fancies, and the only ballast I know, is a respect to the present hour. Without any shadow of doubt, amidst this vertigo of shows and politics, I settle myself ever the firmer in the creed, that we should not postpone and refer and wish, but do broad justice where we are, by whomsoever we deal with, accepting our actual companions and circumstances, however humble or odious, as the mystic officials to whom the universe has delegated its whole pleasure for us. If these are mean and malignant, their contentment, which is the last victory of justice, is a more satisfying echo to the heart, than the voice of poets and the casual sympathy of admirable persons. I think that however a thoughtful man may suffer from the defects and absurdities of his company, he cannot without affectation deny to any set of men and women, a sensibility to extraordinary merit. The coarse and frivolous have an instinct of superiority, if they have not a sympathy, and honor it in their blind capricious way with sincere homage.

13   The fine young people despise life, but in me, and in such as with me are free from dyspepsia, and to whom a day is a sound and solid good, it is a great excess of politeness to look scornful and to cry for company. I am grown by sympathy a little eager and sentimental, but leave me alone, and I should relish every hour and what it brought me, the potluck of the day, as heartily as the oldest gossip in the bar-room.[24] I am thankful for small mercies. I compared notes with one of my friends who expects everything of the universe, and is disappointed when anything is less than the best, and I found that I begin at the other extreme, expecting nothing, and am always full of thanks for moderate goods. I accept the clangor and jangle of contrary tendencies. I find my account in sots and bores also. They give a reality to the circumjacent picture, which such a vanishing meteorous appearance can ill spare. In the morning I awake, and find the old world, wife, babes, and mother, Concord and Boston, the dear old spiritual world, and even the dear old devil not far off. If we will take the good we find, asking no questions, we shall have heaping measures. The great gifts are not got by analysis. Everything good is on the highway. The middle region of our being is the temperate zone. We may climb into the thin and cold realm of pure geometry and lifeless science, or sink into that of sensation. Between these extremes is the equator of life, of thought, of spirit, of poetry,—a narrow belt. Moreover, in popular experience, everything good is on the highway. A collector peeps into all the picture-shops of Europe, for a landscape of Poussin, a crayon-sketch of Salvator; but the Transfiguration, the Last Judgment, the Communion of St. Jerome, and

what are as transcendent as these, are on the walls of the Vatican, the Uffizi, or the Louvre, where every footman may see them;[25] to say nothing of nature's pictures in every street, of sunsets and sunrises every day, and the sculpture of the human body never absent. A collector recently bought at public auction, in London, for one hundred and fifty-seven guineas, an autograph of Shakspeare: but for nothing a school-boy can read Hamlet, and can detect secrets of highest concernment yet unpublished therein. I think I will never read any but the commonest books,—the Bible, Homer, Dante, Shakspeare, and Milton. Then we are impatient of so public a life and planet, and run hither and thither for nooks and secrets. The imagination delights in the wood-craft of Indians, trappers, and bee-hunters. We fancy that we are strangers, and not so intimately domesticated in the planet as the wild man, and the wild beast and bird. But the exclusion reaches them also; reaches the climbing, flying, gliding, feathered and four-footed man. Fox and woodchuck, hawk and snipe, and bittern, when nearly seen, have no more root in the deep world than man, and are just such superficial tenants of the globe. Then the new molecular philosophy shows astronomical interspaces betwixt atom and atom, shows that the world is all outside: it has no inside.

The mid-world is best. Nature, as we know her, is no saint. The lights of the church, the ascetics, Gentoos and Grahamites, she does not distinguish by any favor.[26] She comes eating and drinking and sinning. Her darlings, the great, the strong, the beautiful, are not children of our law, do not come out of the Sunday School, nor weigh their food, nor punctually keep the commandments. If we will be strong with her strength, we must not harbor such disconsolate consciences, borrowed too from the consciences of other nations. We must set up the strong present tense against all the rumors of wrath, past or to come. So many things are unsettled which it is of the first importance to settle,—and, pending their settlement, we will do as we do. Whilst the debate goes forward on the equity of commerce, and will not be closed for a century or two, New and Old England may keep shop. Law of copyright and international copyright is to be discussed, and, in the interim, we will sell our books for the most we can.[27] Expediency of literature, reason of literature, lawfulness of writing down a thought, is questioned; much is to say on both sides, and, while the fight waxes hot, thou, dearest scholar, stick to thy foolish task, add a line every hour, and between whiles add a line. Right to hold land, right of property, is disputed, and the conventions convene, and

14

before the vote is taken, dig away in your garden, and spend your earnings as a waif or godsend to all serene and beautiful purposes. Life itself is a bubble and a skepticism, and a sleep within a sleep.[28] Grant it, and as much more as they will,—but thou, God's darling! heed thy private dream: thou wilt not be missed in the scorning and skepticism: there are enough of them: stay there in thy closet, and toil, until the rest are agreed what to do about it. Thy sickness, they say, and thy puny habit, require that thou do this or avoid that, but know that thy life is a flitting state, a tent for a night, and do thou, sick or well, finish that stint. Thou art sick, but shalt not be worse, and the universe, which holds thee dear, shall be the better.

15   Human life is made up of the two elements, power and form, and the proportion must be invariably kept, if we would have it sweet and sound. Each of these elements in excess makes a mischief as hurtful as its defect. Everything runs to excess: every good quality is noxious, if unmixed, and, to carry the danger to the edge of ruin, nature causes each man's peculiarity to superabound. Here, among the farms, we adduce the scholars as examples of this treachery. They are nature's victims of expression. You who see the artist, the orator, the poet, too near, and find their life no more excellent than that of mechanics or farmers, and themselves victims of partiality, very hollow and haggard, and pronounce them failures,—not heroes, but quacks,—conclude very reasonably, that these arts are not for man, but are disease. Yet nature will not bear you out. Irresistible nature made men such, and makes legions more of such, every day. You love the boy reading in a book, gazing at a drawing, or a cast: yet what are these millions who read and behold, but incipient writers and sculptors? Add a little more of that quality which now reads and sees, and they will seize the pen and chisel. And if one remembers how innocently he began to be an artist, he perceives that nature joined with his enemy. A man is a golden impossibility. The line he must walk is a hair's breadth. The wise through excess of wisdom is made a fool.

16   How easily, if fate would suffer it, we might keep forever these beautiful limits, and adjust ourselves, once for all, to the perfect calculation of the kingdom of known cause and effect. In the street and in the newspapers, life appears so plain a business, that manly resolution and adherence to the multiplication-table through all weathers, will insure success. But ah! presently comes a day, or is it only a half-hour, with its angel-whispering,—which discomfits the conclusions of nations and of years! Tomorrow again, every-

thing looks real and angular, the habitual standards are reinstated, common sense is as rare as genius,—is the basis of genius, and experience is hands and feet to every enterprise;—and yet, he who should do his business on this understanding, would be quickly bankrupt. Power keeps quite another road than the turnpikes of choice and will, namely, the subterranean and invisible tunnels and channels of life. It is ridiculous that we are diplomatists, and doctors, and considerate people: there are no dupes like these. Life is a series of surprises, and would not be worth taking or keeping, if it were not. God delights to isolate us every day, and hide from us the past and the future. We would look about us, but with grand politeness he draws down before us an impenetrable screen of purest sky, and another behind us of purest sky. 'You will not remember,' he seems to say, 'and you will not expect.' All good conversation, manners, and action, come from a spontaneity which forgets usages, and makes the moment great. Nature hates calculators; her methods are saltatory and impulsive. Man lives by pulses; our organic movements are such; and the chemical and ethereal agents are undulatory and alternate; and the mind goes antagonizing on, and never prospers but by fits. We thrive by casualties. Our chief experiences have been casual. The most attractive class of people are those who are powerful obliquely, and not by the direct stroke: men of genius, but not yet accredited: one gets the cheer of their light, without paying too great a tax. Theirs is the beauty of the bird, or the morning light, and not of art. In the thought of genius there is always a surprise; and the moral sentiment is well called "the newness," for it is never other;[29] as new to the oldest intelligence as to the young child,—"the kingdom that cometh without observation."[30] In like manner, for practical success, there must not be too much design. A man will not be observed in doing that which he can do best. There is a certain magic about his properest action, which stupefies your powers of observation, so that though it is done before you, you wist not of it. The art of life has a pudency, and will not be exposed. Every man is an impossibility, until he is born; every thing impossible, until we see a success. The ardors of piety agree at last with the coldest skepticism,—that nothing is of us or our works,—that all is of God. Nature will not spare us the smallest leaf of laurel. All writing comes by the grace of God, and all doing and having. I would gladly be moral, and keep due metes and bounds, which I dearly love, and allow the most to the will of man, but I have set my heart on honesty in this chapter, and I can see nothing at last, in success or failure, than more or less of vital force supplied from the Eternal. The results of life are uncalculated and uncalculable. The years teach much which the days never know. The persons who compose our company, converse, and come and go, and design and execute many things, and somewhat comes of it all, but an unlooked for result. The individual is always mistaken. He designed many things, and drew in other persons as coadjutors, quarrelled with some or all, blundered much, and something is done; all are a little advanced, but the individual is always mistaken. It turns out somewhat new, and very unlike what he promised himself.

17   The ancients, struck with this irreducibleness of the elements of human life to calculation, exalted Chance into a divinity, but that is to stay too long at the spark,—which glitters truly at one point,—but the universe is warm with the latency of the same fire. The miracle of life which will not be expounded, but will remain a miracle, introduces a new element. In the growth of the embryo, Sir Everard Home, I think, noticed that the evolution was not from one central point, but coactive from three or more points.[31] Life has no memory. That which proceeds in succession might be remembered, but that which is coexistent, or ejaculated from a deeper cause, as yet far from being conscious, knows not its own tendency. So is it with us, now skeptical, or without unity, because immersed in forms and effects all seeming to be of equal yet hostile value, and now religious, whilst in the reception of spiritual law. Bear with these distractions, with this coetaneous growth of the parts: they will one day be *members,* and obey one will. On that one will, on that secret cause, they nail our attention and hope. Life is hereby melted into an expectation or a religion. Underneath the inharmonious and trivial particulars, is a musical perfection, the Ideal journeying always with us, the heaven without rent or seam. Do but observe the mode of our illumination. When I converse with a profound mind, or if at any time being alone I have good thoughts, I do not at once arrive at satisfactions, as when, being thirsty, I drink water, or go to the fire, being cold: no! but I am at first apprised of my vicinity to a new and excellent region of life. By persisting to read or to think, this region gives further sign of itself, as it were in flashes of light, in sudden discoveries of its profound beauty and repose, as if the clouds that covered it parted at intervals, and showed the approaching traveller the inland mountains, with the tranquil eternal meadows spread at their base, whereon flocks graze, and

shepherds pipe and dance. But every insight from this realm of thought is felt as initial, and promises a sequel. I do not make it; I arrive there, and behold what was there already. I make! O no! I clap my hands in infantine joy and amazement, before the first opening to me of this august magnificence, old with the love and homage of innumerable ages, young with the life of life, the sunbright Mecca of the desert. And what a future it opens! I feel a new heart beating with the love of the new beauty. I am ready to die out of nature, and be born again into this new yet unapproachable America I have found in the West.

> "Since neither now nor yesterday began
> These thoughts, which have been ever, nor yet can
> A man be found who their first entrance knew."[32]

If I have described life as a flux of moods, I must now add, that there is that in us which changes not, and which ranks all sensations and states of mind. The consciousness in each man is a sliding scale, which identifies him now with the First Cause, and now with the flesh of his body; life above life, in infinite degrees. The sentiment from which it sprung determines the dignity of any deed, and the question ever is, not, what you have done or forborne, but, at whose command you have done or forborne it.

Fortune, Minerva, Muse, Holy Ghost,—these are quaint names, too narrow to cover this unbounded substance.[33] The baffled intellect must still kneel before this cause, which refuses to be named,—ineffable cause, which every fine genius has essayed to represent by some emphatic symbol, as, Thales by water, Anaximenes by air, Anaxagoras by (Νοῦς) thought, Zoroaster by fire, Jesus and the moderns by love: and the metaphor of each has become a national religion.[34] The Chinese Mencius has not been the least successful in his generalization. "I fully understand language," he said, "and nourish well my vast-flowing vigor."—"I beg to ask what you call vast-flowing vigor?"—said his companion. "The explanation," replied Mencius, "is difficult. This vigor is supremely great, and in the highest degree unbending. Nourish it correctly, and do it no injury, and it will fill up the vacancy between heaven and earth. This vigor accords with and assists justice and reason, and leaves no hunger."[35]—In our more correct writing, we give to this generalization the name of Being, and thereby confess that we have arrived as far as we can go. Suffice it for the joy of the universe, that we have not arrived at a wall, but at intermi-

18

nable oceans. Our life seems not present, so much as prospective; not for the affairs on which it is wasted, but as a hint of this vast-flowing vigor. Most of life seems to be mere advertisement of faculty: information is given us not to sell ourselves cheap; that we are very great. So, in particulars, our greatness is always in a tendency or direction, not in an action. It is for us to believe in the rule, not in the exception. The noble are thus known from the ignoble. So in accepting the leading of the sentiments, it is not what we believe concerning the immortality of the soul, or the like, but *the universal impulse to believe,* that is the material circumstance, and is the principal fact in the history of the globe. Shall we describe this cause as that which works directly? The spirit is not helpless or needful of mediate organs. It has plentiful powers and direct effects. I am explained without explaining, I am felt without acting, and where I am not. Therefore all just persons are satisfied with their own praise. They refuse to explain themselves, and are content that new actions should do them that office. They believe that we communicate without speech, and above speech, and that no right action of ours is quite unaffecting to our friends, at whatever distance; for the influence of action is not to be measured by miles. Why should I fret myself, because a circumstance has occurred, which hinders my presence where I was expected? If I am not at the meeting, my presence where I am, should be as useful to the commonwealth of friendship and wisdom, as would be my presence in that place. I exert the same quality of power in all places. Thus journeys the mighty Ideal before us; it never was known to fall into the rear. No man ever came to an experience which was satiating, but his good is tidings of a better. Onward and onward! In liberated moments, we know that a new picture of life and duty is already possible; the elements already exist in many minds around you, of a doctrine of life which shall transcend any written record we have. The new statement will comprise the skepticisms, as well as the faiths of society, and out of unbeliefs a creed shall be formed. For, skepticisms are not gratuitous or lawless, but are limitations of the affirmative statement, and the new philosophy must take them in, and make affirmations outside of them, just as much as it must include the oldest beliefs.

19   It is very unhappy, but too late to be helped, the discovery we have made, that we exist. That discovery is called the Fall of Man. Ever afterwards, we suspect our instruments. We have learned that we do not see directly, but

mediately, and that we have no means of correcting these colored and distort-
ing lenses which we are, or of computing the amount of their errors. Perhaps
these subject-lenses have a creative power; perhaps there are no objects. Once
we lived in what we saw; now, the rapaciousness of this new power, which
threatens to absorb all things, engages us. Nature, art, persons, letters, religions,—objects, successively tumble in, and God is but one of its ideas. Nature and literature are subjective phenomena; every evil and every good thing
is a shadow which we cast. The street is full of humiliations to the proud. As
the fop contrived to dress his bailiffs in his livery, and make them wait on his
guests at table,[36] so the chagrins which the bad heart gives off as bubbles, at
once take form as ladies and gentlemen in the street, shopmen or bar-keepers
in hotels, and threaten or insult whatever is threatenable and insultable in us.
'Tis the same with our idolatries. People forget that it is the eye which makes
the horizon, and the rounding mind's eye which makes this or that man a
type or representative of humanity with the name of hero or saint. Jesus the
"providential man," is a good man on whom many people are agreed that
these optical laws shall take effect. By love on one part, and by forbearance to
press objection on the other part, it is for a time settled, that we will look at
him in the centre of the horizon, and ascribe to him the properties that will
attach to any man so seen. But the longest love or aversion has a speedy term.
The great and crescive self, rooted in absolute nature, supplants all relative
existence, and ruins the kingdom of mortal friendship and love.[37] Marriage
(in what is called the spiritual world) is impossible, because of the inequality
between every subject and every object. The subject is the receiver of Godhead, and at every comparison must feel his being enhanced by that cryptic
might. Though not in energy, yet by presence, this magazine of substance
cannot be otherwise than felt: nor can any force of intellect attribute to the
object the proper deity which sleeps or wakes forever in every subject. Never
can love make consciousness and ascription equal in force. There will be the
same gulf between every me and thee, as between the original and the picture. The universe is the bride of the soul. All private sympathy is partial.
Two human beings are like globes, which can touch only in a point, and,
whilst they remain in contact, all other points of each of the spheres are inert; their turn must also come, and the longer a particular union lasts, the
more energy of appetency the parts not in union acquire.[38]

Life will be imaged, but cannot be divided nor doubled. Any invasion of

20

its unity would be chaos. The soul is not twin-born, but the only begotten, and though revealing itself as child in time, child in appearance, is of a fatal and universal power, admitting no co-life. Every day, every act betrays the ill-concealed deity. We believe in ourselves, as we do not believe in others. We permit all things to ourselves, and that which we call sin in others, is experiment for us. It is an instance of our faith in ourselves, that men never speak of crime as lightly as they think: or, every man thinks a latitude safe for himself, which is nowise to be indulged to another. The act looks very differently on the inside, and on the outside; in its quality, and in its consequences. Murder in the murderer is no such ruinous thought as poets and romancers will have it; it does not unsettle him, or fright him from his ordinary notice of trifles: it is an act quite easy to be contemplated, but in its sequel, it turns out to be a horrible jangle and confounding of all relations. Especially the crimes that spring from love, seem right and fair from the actor's point of view, but, when acted, are found destructive of society. No man at last believes that he can be lost, nor that the crime in him is as black as in the felon. Because the intellect qualifies in our own case the moral judgments. For there is no crime to the intellect. That is antinomian or hypernomian, and judges law as well as fact. "It is worse than a crime, it is a blunder," said Napoleon, speaking the language of the intellect.[39] To it, the world is a problem in mathematics or the science of quantity, and it leaves out praise and blame, and all weak emotions. All stealing is comparative. If you come to absolutes, pray who does not steal? Saints are sad, because they behold sin, (even when they speculate,) from the point of view of the conscience, and not of the intellect; a confusion of thought. Sin seen from the thought, is a diminution or *less:* seen from the conscience or will, it is pravity or *bad.* The intellect names it shade, absence of light, and no essence. The conscience must feel it as essence, essential evil. This it is not: it has an objective existence, but no subjective.

21   Thus inevitably does the universe wear our color, and every object fall successively into the subject itself. The subject exists, the subject enlarges; all things sooner or later fall into place. As I am, so I see; use what language we will, we can never say anything but what we are; Hermes, Cadmus, Columbus, Newton, Buonaparte, are the mind's ministers.[40] Instead of feeling a poverty when we encounter a great man, let us treat the new comer like a travelling geologist, who passes through our estate, and shows us good slate, or limestone, or anthracite, in our brush pasture. The partial action of each

strong mind in one direction, is a telescope for the objects on which it is pointed. But every other part of knowledge is to be pushed to the same extravagance, ere the soul attains her due sphericity. Do you see that kitten chasing so prettily her own tail? If you could look with her eyes, you might see her surrounded with hundreds of figures performing complex dramas, with tragic and comic issues, long conversations, many characters, many ups and downs of fate,—and meantime it is only puss and her tail. How long before our masquerade will end its noise of tambourines, laughter, and shouting, and we shall find it was a solitary performance?—A subject and an object,—it takes so much to make the galvanic circuit complete, but magnitude adds nothing. What imports it whether it is Kepler and the sphere; Columbus and America; a reader and his book; or puss with her tail?[41]

It is true that all the muses and love and religion hate these developments, and will find a way to punish the chemist, who publishes in the parlor the secrets of the laboratory. And we cannot say too little of our constitutional necessity of seeing things under private aspects, or saturated with our humors. And yet is the God the native of these bleak rocks. That need makes in morals the capital virtue of self-trust. We must hold hard to this poverty, however scandalous, and by more vigorous self-recoveries, after the sallies of action, possess our axis more firmly. The life of truth is cold, and so far mournful; but it is not the slave of tears, contritions, and perturbations. It does not attempt another's work, nor adopt another's facts. It is a main lesson of wisdom to know your own from another's. I have learned that I cannot dispose of other people's facts; but I possess such a key to my own, as persuades me against all their denials, that they also have a key to theirs. A sympathetic person is placed in the dilemma of a swimmer among drowning men, who all catch at him, and if he give so much as a leg or a finger, they will drown him. They wish to be saved from the mischiefs of their vices, but not from their vices. Charity would be wasted on this poor waiting on the symptoms. A wise and hardy physician will say, *Come out of that,* as the first condition of advice.

In this our talking America, we are ruined by our good nature and listening on all sides. This compliance takes away the power of being greatly useful. A man should not be able to look other than directly and forthright. A preoccupied attention is the only answer to the importunate frivolity of other people: an attention, and to an aim which makes their wants frivolous. This is

22

23

a divine answer, and leaves no appeal, and no hard thoughts. In Flaxman's drawing of the Eumenides of Æschylus, Orestes supplicates Apollo, whilst the Furies sleep on the threshold. The face of the god expresses a shade of regret and compassion, but calm with the conviction of the irreconcilableness of the two spheres.[42] He is born into other politics, into the eternal and beautiful. The man at his feet asks for his interest in turmoils of the earth, into which his nature cannot enter. And the Eumenides there lying express pictorially this disparity.[43] The god is surcharged with his divine destiny.

24   Illusion, Temperament, Succession, Surface, Surprise, Reality, Subjectiveness,—these are threads on the loom of time, these are the lords of life. I dare not assume to give their order, but I name them as I find them in my way. I know better than to claim any completeness for my picture. I am a fragment, and this is a fragment of me. I can very confidently announce one or another law, which throws itself into relief and form, but I am too young yet by some ages to compile a code. I gossip for my hour concerning the eternal politics. I have seen many fair pictures not in vain. A wonderful time I have lived in. I am not the novice I was fourteen, nor yet seven years ago. Let who will ask, where is the fruit? I find a private fruit sufficient. This is a fruit,—that I should not ask for a rash effect from meditations, counsels, and the hiving of truths. I should feel it pitiful to demand a result on this town and county, an overt effect on the instant month and year. The effect is deep and secular as the cause.[44] It works on periods in which mortal lifetime is lost. All I know is reception; I am and I have: but I do not get, and when I have fancied I had gotten anything, I found I did not. I worship with wonder the great Fortune. My reception has been so large, that I am not annoyed by receiving this or that superabundantly. I say to the Genius, if he will pardon the proverb, *In for a mill, in for a million.* When I receive a new gift, I do not macerate my body to make the account square, for, if I should die, I could not make the account square.[45] The benefit overran the merit the first day, and has overran the merit ever since. The merit itself, so-called, I reckon part of the receiving.

25   Also, that hankering after an overt or practical effect seems to me an apostasy. In good earnest, I am willing to spare this most unnecessary deal of doing. Life wears to me a visionary face. Hardest, roughest action is visionary also. It is but a choice between soft and turbulent dreams. People disparage knowing and the intellectual life, and urge doing. I am very content with

knowing, if only I could know. That is an august entertainment, and would suffice me a great while. To know a little, would be worth the expense of this world. I hear always the law of Adrastia, "that every soul which had acquired any truth, should be safe from harm until another period."[46]

I know that the world I converse with in the city and in the farms, is not the world I *think*. I observe that difference, and shall observe it. One day, I shall know the value and law of this discrepance. But I have not found that much was gained by manipular attempts to realize the world of thought. Many eager persons successively make an experiment in this way, and make themselves ridiculous. They acquire democratic manners, they foam at the mouth, they hate and deny. Worse, I observe, that, in the history of mankind, there is never a solitary example of success,—taking their own tests of success. I say this polemically, or in reply to the inquiry, why not realize your world? But far be from me the despair which prejudges the law by a paltry empiricism,—since there never was a right endeavor, but it succeeded. Patience and patience, we shall win at the last. We must be very suspicious of the deceptions of the element of time. It takes a good deal of time to eat or to sleep, or to earn a hundred dollars, and a very little time to entertain a hope and an insight which becomes the light of our life. We dress our garden, eat our dinners, discuss the household with our wives, and these things make no impression, are forgotten next week; but in the solitude to which every man is always returning, he has a sanity and revelations, which in his passage into new worlds he will carry with him. Never mind the ridicule, never mind the defeat: up again, old heart!—it seems to say,—there is victory yet for all justice; and the true romance which the world exists to realize, will be the transformation of genius into practical power.[47]

26

Notes

1. Emerson, "Experience," *CW*, 9:482–483.
2. Emerson's source for "the Genius which, . . . too strongly," is the parable of Er in the conclusion to Plato's *Republic*, where the souls of the dead choose freely the lives, human or animal, they are to lead in their next incarnation. Then the daimon (or genius) leads them to the River of Lethe, where they are "all required to drink a measure of the water, and those who were not saved by their good

sense drank more than the measure, and each one as he drank forgot all things" (X, section xvi).

3. Emerson's source for this mythological tale is Plutarch, "Of Isis and Osiris," where the Sun, having discovered Rhea's infidelity with Saturn, "pronounced a solemn Curse against her . . . that she should not be delivered in any Month or Year." Hermes, also Rhea's lover, cast dice with the Moon and won "five new Days," which became the birthdays of the Egyptian gods. On "the first of these they say *Osiris* was born" (*Plutarch's Morals*, 1718, 4:68–69). The only intercalary day required by the modern calendar is 29 February. Hermes is the Greek god who conducted souls to the underworld; Osiris is the Egyptian god who served as lord of the underworld.

4. Emerson's source is *Deerbrook: A Novel,* 2 vols. (New York, 1839), 2:62, by Harriet Martineau (1802–1876), English novelist and religious and economic writer (*JMN,* 7:387, 418).

5. Two entries in his journal suggest that Emerson himself was the greedy and querulous farmer (*JMN,* 8:287, 397).

6. Girolamo Tiraboschi (1731–1794), Italian professor and librarian, published the first thorough and scholarly treatment of Italian literature. Thomas Warton (1728–1790), English poet, wrote the first history of his country's verse. Emerson intends either Friedrich von Schlegel (1772–1829), German author and critic, or his elder brother, August Wilhelm von Schlegel (1767–1845), also a major figure in German Romantic criticism and scholarship; both wrote histories of German literature.

7. "Homer's Goddess *Ate,*" as Robert Burton (1577–1640) called her in his literary, scientific, and philosophical study *The Anatomy of Melancholy* (1621), had among her offices the duty of tormenting mankind "with some misery or other" (I, 2, iii, 10); the couplet is Burton's translation from the comedy *Podagra,* or *Gout,* ll. 185–186, by Lucian, second-century Greek rhetorician and satirist (*JMN,* 6:346).

8. Emerson often used the word "lovers" in the old sense of "friends"; in his essay on "Friendship," he writes, "High thanks I owe you, excellent lovers" (*CW,* 2:115).

9. Long after the fact, the sudden death of Emerson's son Waldo (1836–1842) from scarlet fever continued to affect him greatly and is arguably the occasion for his having written "Experience."

10. A reference by Emerson, though an inaccurate reading of the text, to *The Curse of Kehama* (1810), a Hindu mythological romance in verse, by Robert Southey (1774–1843), English poet, historian, and critic; the poem had been in Emerson's mind shortly after his son's death (*L,* 3:9–10).

11. Para coats are rubber raincoats, so called after the Brazilian seaport Pará, which is now best known as Belém. The process of vulcanization, which made possible the manufacture of all-rubber coats, was discovered by the American inventor Charles Goodyear (1800–1860) in 1839.

12. Emerson refers here to Gamaliel Bradford (1795–1839), his teacher at the Boston Public Latin School and the superintendent of the Massachusetts General Hospital.

13. In the journal version of this passage, Thoreau appears as an example of such promising but disappointing young men (*JMN*, 8:375).

14. The "occiput" is the back part of the skull.

15. The definition is Emerson's; see *JMN*, 8:382.

16. The journal version of this sentence suggests that this may be George Combe (1788–1858), the Scottish phrenologist (*JMN*, 9:120).

17. *"Pero si muove"* translates as "Nevertheless it moves"; the original is a variation on Galileo's legendary "Eppur si muove."

18. Michel Eyquem Montaigné (1533–1592), French essayist and skeptical philosopher.

19. "Bettine" is Elisabeth (Bettina) Brentano von Arnim (1785–1859), German writer whose correspondence with Goethe and *Die Günderode* (1840) were eagerly read by the Transcendentalists.

20. Although Emerson's source for the popular tradition that considered cherubim the most learned of angels is unknown, the first to make the claim was Dionysius the Pseudo-Areopagite, a late fifth- to early sixth-century Christian theologian and philosopher, whose *Concerning the Celestial Hierarchy* became the foundation of medieval angelology; earlier, Emerson made the same claim in "Intellect," *CW*, 2:204.

21. Labrador spar, or Labradorite, is an iridescent feldspar.

22. This and the previous sentence refer to the utopian community at Brook Farm (1841–1847) in West Roxbury, Massachusetts, which, according to John Thomas Codman, had among its declared purposes "to substitute a system of brotherly coöperation for one of selfish competition; to secure to our children, and to those who may be entrusted to our care, the benefits of the highest physical, intellectual and moral education . . . and thus to impart a greater freedom, simplicity, truthfulness, refinement and moral dignity to our mode of life" (*Brook Farm* [Boston, 1894], pp. 11–12).

23. Emerson's source is *The Desâtir or Sacred Writings of the Ancient Persian Prophets*, trans. Jonathan Duncan, 2 vols. (Bombay, 1818), 2:193.

24. This and the previous sentence reflect Emerson's investment of time in recent years corresponding and conversing with the ardent, cultivated young men and women who read and had already contributed to the *Dial* or would soon do so, and about whom he wrote with sympathy and detachment in "The Transcendentalist," above; his use of "eager" and "sentimental" in this sentence seems to be in the archaic sense of "impatient" and "overrefined," respectively.

25. Emerson's references here are to Nicolas Poussin (1594–1665), French painter and founder of the French Classical tradition; Salvator Rosa (1615–1673), Italian Ba-

roque painter; Raphael's "Transfiguration of Christ"; Michelangelo's "Last Judgment"; "Communion of St. Jerome" by Domenichino (1581–1641), Italian painter of religious subjects and landscapes; the Uffizi Gallery, a museum in Florence, Italy; and the Musée du Louvre in Paris.

26. Throughout the nineteenth century and long before it, the word "lights" meant "luminaries" or "shining lights" and was used for eminent divines. Gentoos is an almost archaic synonym for "Hindus." Grahamites were disciples of Sylvester Graham (1794–1851), a New England reformer and the originator of the graham cracker, who believed in the physical and spiritual values of vegetarianism and especially the proper making of bread. In the 1847 edition, Emerson changed "Grahamites" to "corn-eaters" because the word was obsolescent.

27. During Emerson's entire literary career, the lack of an effective international copyright law had left both American and British writers vulnerable to piracy.

28. With this sentence, cf. Shakespeare, *The Tempest,* IV, i, 156–158.

29. Emerson had read the phrase "the newness" two or three years earlier in a letter about the English associationist, educator, and vegetarian James Pierrepont Greaves (1777–1842): "a great apostle of the Newness to many, even when neither he nor they knew very clearly what was going forward" (*Dial* 3 [October 1842]: 289). By 1855, Emerson adopted the phrase to describe, among other things, inspiration (*JMN,* 13:486).

30. With "the kingdom . . . without observation," cf. Luke 17:20–21.

31. Sir Everard Home (1756–1832), a British physician, believed that he was the first physician actually to see a human ovum.

32. Sophocles, *Antigone,* ll. 455–457.

33. Minerva is the Roman goddess of wisdom.

34. Thales (ca. 624–ca. 546 BCE), Greek philosopher, mathematician, and astronomer. Anaximenes of Miletus (585–528 BCE), Greek philosopher who argued that air is the source of all things.

35. Mencius (ca. 371–ca. 289 BCE), Chinese Confucian philosopher. Emerson's source for this wisdom of Mencius is the "Shang Mung," a book in *The Chinese Classical Work Commonly Called the Four Books,* trans. David Collie (Malacca, 1828), p. 39 (*JMN,* 8:354).

36. Emerson's source for this anecdote about Richard Brinsley Sheridan (1751–1816), English dramatist and statesman, is Sir N. W. Wraxall, *Posthumous Memoirs of His Own Time,* 3 vols. (London, 1836), 1:43 (*JMN,* 8:346).

37. Here, "crescive," an already obsolete word when Emerson used it, means "growing."

38. To define human relations through a scientific metaphor, Emerson here drew on current demonstrations in physics that showed the behavior of static electricity.

39. In 1804, anxious about invasion and assassination and believing that the refugee

Louis Antoine de Bourbon-Conde, duc d'Enghien (1772–1804) was in league with the English, Napoleon had him kidnapped and killed. As Sir Walter Scott wrote in his biography of Napoleon, "the murder of the young and gallant prince, in a way so secret and so savage, had a deep moral effect upon the European world, and excited hatred against Buonaparte wherever the tale was told. In the well-known words of Fouché, the duke's execution was worse than a moral crime—it was a political blunder" (*Life of Napoleon Bonaparte*, 9 vols. [Edinburgh, 1827], 4:331). Joseph Fouché, 1st duc d'Otrante (1759–1820) was Napoleon's minister of police.

40. In Greek mythology, Cadmus is the founder of Thebes.

41. Emerson's inclusion of "Kepler and the sphere" in this sentence possibly references the astronomer's great discovery, in 1604, that the planet Mars revolves about the sun in an elliptical orbit.

42. Emerson interpreted imaginatively and accurately the emotional tensions of the illustration by the English artist John Flaxman (1755–1826) referenced in this and the previous sentence; his source is *Compositions from the Tragedies of Aeschylus. Designed by John Flaxman. . . .* (London, 1795), p. 24.

43. The Eumenides, or Erinyes, are the Greek gods of vengeance.

44. Here, "secular" means "long-lasting," as it does in "Nature looks provokingly stable and secular," "Circles," para 4, above.

45. Here, Emerson probably uses "macerate" to mean "waste away."

46. Emerson's source is Plato, *Phaedrus*, 248c, as quoted in *The Six Books of Proclus . . . on the Theology of Plato* (1816), 1:260 (*JMN*, 8:350).

47. In the journal from which it is drawn, this sentence is followed by one that, if Emerson had used it, would have given a distinctly Carlylean tone to the conclusion of "Experience": "The symbol of this is the *working King* like Ulysses, Alfred, Czar Peter" (*JMN*, 9:53). Czar Peter is Peter the Great, or Peter I (1672–1725), of Russia.

Nominalist and Realist

1

In countless upward-striving waves
The moon-drawn tide-wave strives;
In thousand far-transplanted grafts
The parent fruit survives;
So, in the new-born millions,
The perfect Adam lives.
Not less are summer-mornings dear
To every child they wake,
And each with novel life his sphere
Fills for his proper sake.[1]

2

I cannot often enough say, that a man is only a relative and representative nature. Each is a hint of the truth, but far enough from being that truth, which yet he quite newly and inevitably suggests to us. If I seek it in him, I shall not find it. Could any man conduct into me the pure stream of that which he pretends to be! Long afterwards, I find that quality elsewhere which he promised me. The genius of the Platonists, is intoxicating to the student, yet how few particulars of it can I detach from all their books.[2] The man momentarily stands for the thought, but will not bear examination; and a society of men will cursorily represent well enough a certain quality and culture, for example, chivalry or beauty of manners, but separate them, and there is no gentleman and no lady in the group. The least hint sets us on the pursuit of a character, which no man realizes. We have such exorbitant eyes, that on seeing the smallest arc, we complete the curve, and when the curtain is lifted from the diagram which it seemed to veil, we are vexed to find that no more was drawn, than just that fragment of an arc which we first beheld. We are greatly too liberal in our construction of each other's faculty and promise. Exactly what the parties have already done, they shall do again; but that which we inferred from their nature and inception, they will not do.

That is in nature, but not in them. That happens in the world, which we often witness in a public debate. Each of the speakers expresses himself imperfectly: no one of them hears much that another says, such is the preoccupation of mind of each; and the audience, who have only to hear and not to speak, judge very wisely and superiorly how wrongheaded and unskilful is each of the debaters to his own affair. Great men or men of great gifts you shall easily find, but symmetrical men never. When I meet a pure intellectual force, or a generosity of affection, I believe, here then is man; and am presently mortified by the discovery, that this individual is no more available to his own or to the general ends, than his companions; because the power which drew my respect, is not supported by the total symphony of his talents. All persons exist to society by some shining trait of beauty or utility, which they have. We borrow the proportions of the man from that one fine feature, and finish the portrait symmetrically; which is false; for the rest of his body is small or deformed. I observe a person who makes a good public appearance, and conclude thence the perfection of his private character, on which this is based; but he has no private character. He is a graceful cloak or lay-figure for holidays.[3] All our poets, heroes, and saints, fail utterly in some one or in many parts to satisfy our idea, fail to draw our spontaneous interest, and so leave us without any hope of realization but in our own future. Our exaggeration of all fine characters arises from the fact, that we identify each in turn with the soul. But there are no such men as we fable; no Jesus, nor Pericles, nor Cæsar, nor Angelo, nor Washington, such as we have made.[4] We consecrate a great deal of nonsense, because it was allowed by great men. There is none without his foible. I verily believe if an angel should come to chaunt the chorus of the moral law, he would eat too much gingerbread, or take liberties with private letters, or do some precious atrocity.[5] It is bad enough, that our geniuses cannot do anything useful, but it is worse that no man is fit for society, who has fine traits. He is admired at a distance, but he cannot come near without appearing a cripple. The men of fine parts protect themselves by solitude, or by courtesy, or by satire, or by an acid worldly manner, each concealing, as he best can, his incapacity for useful association, but they want either love or self-reliance.

Our native love of reality joins with this experience to teach us a little reserve, and to dissuade a too sudden surrender to the brilliant qualities of persons. Young people admire talents or particular excellences; as we grow older, we value total powers and effects, as, the impression, the quality, the spirit of men and things. The genius is all. The man,—it is his system: we do not try a solitary word or act, but his habit. The acts which you praise, I praise not, since they are departures from his faith, and are mere compliances. The magnetism which arranges tribes and races in one polarity, is alone to be respected; the men are steel-filings. Yet we unjustly select a particle, and say, 'O steel-filing number one! what heart-drawings I feel to thee! what prodigious virtues are these of thine! how constitutional to thee, and incommunicable!' Whilst we speak, the loadstone is withdrawn; down falls our filing in a heap with the rest, and we continue our mummery to the wretched shaving. Let us go for universals; for the magnetism, not for the needles. Human life and its persons are poor empirical pretensions. A personal influence is an *ignis fatuus.*[6] If they say, it is great, it is great; if they say, it is small, it is small; you see it, and you see it not, by turns; it borrows all its size from the momentary estimation of the speakers: the Will-of-the-wisp vanishes, if you go too near, vanishes if you go too far, and only blazes at one angle. Who can tell if Washington be a great man, or no? Who can tell if Franklin be? Yes, or any but the twelve, or six, or three great gods of fame? And they, too, loom and fade before the eternal.

4   We are amphibious creatures, weaponed for two elements, having two sets of faculties, the particular and the catholic. We adjust our instrument for general observation, and sweep the heavens as easily as we pick out a single figure in the terrestrial landscape. We are practically skilful in detecting elements, for which we have no place in our theory, and no name. Thus we are very sensible of an atmospheric influence in men and in bodies of men, not accounted for in an arithmetical addition of all their measurable properties. There is a genius of a nation, which is not to be found in the numerical citizens, but which characterizes the society. England, strong, punctual, practical, well-spoken England, I should not find, if I should go to the island to seek it. In the parliament, in the playhouse, at dinner-tables, I might see a great number of rich, ignorant, book-read, conventional, proud men,—many old women,—and not anywhere the Englishman who made the good speeches, combined the accurate engines, and did the bold and nervous deeds.[7] It is even worse in America, where, from the intellectual quickness of the race, the genius of the country is more splendid in its promise, and more slight in its performance. Webster cannot do the work of Webster. We conceive dis-

tinctly enough the French, the Spanish, the German genius, and it is not the less real, that perhaps we should not meet in either of those nations, a single individual who corresponded with the type. We infer the spirit of the nation in great measure from the language, which is a sort of monument, to which each forcible individual in a course of many hundred years has contributed a stone. And, universally, a good example of this social force, is the veracity of language, which cannot be debauched. In any controversy concerning morals, an appeal may be made with safety to the sentiments, which the language of the people expresses. Proverbs, words, and grammar inflections convey the public sense with more purity and precision, than the wisest individual.

In the famous dispute with the Nominalists, the Realists had a good deal of reason.[8] General ideas are essences. They are our gods: they round and ennoble the most partial and sordid way of living. Our proclivity to details cannot quite degrade our life, and divest it of poetry. The day-laborer is reckoned as standing at the foot of the social scale, yet he is saturated with the laws of the world. His measures are the hours; morning and night, solstice and equinox, geometry, astronomy, and all the lovely accidents of nature play through his mind. Money, which represents the prose of life, and which is hardly spoken of in parlors without an apology, is, in its effects and laws, as beautiful as roses. Property keeps the accounts of the world, and is always moral. The property will be found where the labor, the wisdom, and the virtue have been in nations, in classes, and (the whole life-time considered, with the compensations) in the individual also. How wise the world appears, when the laws and usages of nations are largely detailed, and the completeness of the municipal system is considered! Nothing is left out. If you go into the markets, and the custom-houses, the insurers' and notaries' offices, the offices of sealers of weights and measures, of inspection of provisions,—it will appear as if one man had made it all. Wherever you go, a wit like your own has been before you, and has realized its thought. The Eleusinian mysteries, the Egyptian architecture, the Indian astronomy, the Greek sculpture, show that there always were seeing and knowing men in the planet.[9] The world is full of masonic ties, of guilds, of secret and public legions of honor; that of scholars, for example; and that of gentlemen fraternizing with the upper class of every country and every culture.

I am very much struck in literature by the appearance, that one person wrote all the books; as if the editor of a journal planted his body of reporters

5

6

in different parts of the field of action, and relieved some by others from time to time; but there is such equality and identity both of judgment and point of view in the narrative, that it is plainly the work of one all-seeing, all-hearing gentleman. I looked into Pope's Odyssey yesterday: it is as correct and elegant after our canon of today, as if it were newly written.[10] The modernness of all good books seems to give me an existence as wide as man. What is well done, I feel as if I did; what is ill-done, I reck not of. Shakspeare's passages of passion (for example, in Lear and Hamlet) are in the very dialect of the present year. I am faithful again to the whole over the members in my use of books. I find the most pleasure in reading a book in a manner least flattering to the author. I read Proclus, and sometimes Plato, as I might read a dictionary, for a mechanical help to the fancy and the imagination. I read for the lustres, as if one should use a fine picture in a chromatic experiment, for its rich colors.[11] 'Tis not Proclus, but a piece of nature and fate that I explore. It is a greater joy to see the author's author, than himself. A higher pleasure of the same kind I found lately at a concert, where I went to hear Handel's Messiah. As the master overpowered the littleness and incapableness of the performers, and made them conductors of his electricity, so it was easy to observe what efforts nature was making through so many hoarse, wooden, and imperfect persons, to produce beautiful voices, fluid and soul-guided men and women. The genius of nature was paramount at the oratorio.[12]

7   This preference of the genius to the parts is the secret of that deification of art, which is found in all superior minds. Art, in the artist, is proportion, or, a habitual respect to the whole by an eye loving beauty in details. And the wonder and charm of it is the sanity in insanity which it denotes. Proportion is almost impossible to human beings. There is no one who does not exaggerate. In conversation, men are encumbered with personality, and talk too much. In modern sculpture, picture, and poetry, the beauty is miscellaneous; the artist works here and there, and at all points, adding and adding, instead of unfolding the unit of his thought. Beautiful details we must have, or no artist: but they must be means and never other. The eye must not lose sight for a moment of the purpose. Lively boys write to their ear and eye, and the cool reader finds nothing but sweet jingles in it. When they grow older, they respect the argument.[13]

8   We obey the same intellectual integrity, when we study in exceptions the law of the world. Anomalous facts, as the never quite obsolete rumors of magic and demonology, and the new allegations of phrenologists and neu-

rologists, are of ideal use. They are good indications. Homœopathy is insignificant as an art of healing, but of great value as criticism on the hygeia or medical practice of the time.[14] So with Mesmerism, Swedenborgism, Fourierism, and the Millennial Church;[15] they are poor pretensions enough, but good criticism on the science, philosophy, and preaching of the day. For these abnormal insights of the adepts, ought to be normal, and things of course.

All things show us, that on every side we are very near to the best. It seems not worth while to execute with too much pains some one intellectual, or æsthetical, or civil feat, when presently the dream will scatter, and we shall burst into universal power. The reason of idleness and of crime is the deferring of our hopes. Whilst we are waiting, we beguile the time with jokes, with sleep, with eating, and with crimes.

Thus we settle it in our cool libraries, that all the agents with which we deal are subalterns, which we can well afford to let pass, and life will be simpler when we live at the centre, and flout the surfaces. I wish to speak with all respect of persons, but sometimes I must pinch myself to keep awake, and preserve the due decorum. They melt so fast into each other, that they are like grass and trees, and it needs an effort to treat them as individuals. Though the uninspired man certainly finds persons a conveniency in household matters, the divine man does not respect them: he sees them as a rack of clouds, or a fleet of ripples which the wind drives over the surface of the water. But this is flat rebellion. Nature will not be Buddhist: she resents generalizing, and insults the philosopher in every moment with a million of fresh particulars. It is all idle talking: as much as a man is a whole, so is he also a part; and it were partial not to see it. What you say in your pompous distribution only distributes you into your class and section.[16] You have not got rid of parts by denying them, but are the more partial. You are one thing, but nature is *one thing and the other thing,* in the same moment. She will not remain orbed in a thought, but rushes into persons; and when each person, inflamed to a fury of personality, would conquer all things to his poor crotchet, she raises up against him another person, and by many persons incarnates again a sort of whole. She will have all. Nick Bottom cannot play all the parts, work it how he may:[17] there will be somebody else, and the world will be round. Everything must have its flower or effort at the beautiful, coarser or finer according to its stuff. They relieve and recommend each other, and the sanity of society is a balance of a thousand insanities. She punishes abstractionists, and will only forgive an induction which is rare and casual. We like to come to a height of land and see the landscape, just as we value a general remark in conversation. But it is not the intention of nature that we should live by general views. We fetch fire and water, run about all day among the shops and markets, and get our clothes and shoes made and mended, and are the victims of these details, and once in a fortnight we arrive perhaps at a rational moment. If we were not thus infatuated, if we saw the real from hour to hour, we should not be here to write and to read, but should have been burned or frozen long ago. She would never get anything done, if she suffered admirable Crichtons, and universal geniuses.[18] She loves better a wheelwright who dreams all night of wheels, and a groom who is part of his horse: for she is full of work, and these are her hands. As the frugal farmer takes care that his cattle shall eat down the rowen,[19] and swine shall eat the waste of his house, and poultry shall pick the crumbs, so our economical mother despatches a new genius and habit of mind into every district and condition of existence, plants an eye wherever a new ray of light can fall, and gathering up into some man every property in the universe, establishes thousandfold occult mutual attractions among her offspring, that all this wash and waste of power may be imparted and exchanged.

11   Great dangers undoubtedly accrue from this incarnation and distribution of the godhead, and hence nature has her maligners, as if she were Circe; and Alphonso of Castille fancied he could have given useful advice.[20] But she does not go unprovided; she has hellebore at the bottom of the cup.[21] Solitude would ripen a plentiful crop of despots. The recluse thinks of men as having his manner, or as not having his manner; and as having degrees of it, more and less. But when he comes into a public assembly, he sees that men have very different manners from his own, and in their way admirable. In his childhood and youth, he has had many checks and censures, and thinks modestly enough of his own endowment. When afterwards he comes to unfold it in propitious circumstance, it seems the only talent: he is delighted with his success, and accounts himself already the fellow of the great. But he goes into a mob, into a banking-house, into a mechanic's shop, into a mill, into a laboratory, into a ship, into a camp, and in each new place he is no better than an idiot: other talents take place, and rule the hour. The rotation which whirls every leaf and pebble to the meridian, reaches to every gift of man, and we all take turns at the top.

For nature, who abhors mannerism, has set her heart on breaking up all styles and tricks, and it is so much easier to do what one has done before, than to do a new thing, that there is a perpetual tendency to a set mode. In every conversation, even the highest, there is a certain trick, which may be soon learned by an acute person, and then that particular style continued indefinitely. Each man, too, is a tyrant in tendency, because he would impose his idea on others; and their trick is their natural defence. Jesus would absorb the race; but Tom Paine or the coarsest blasphemer helps humanity by resisting this exuberance of power.[22] Hence the immense benefit of party in politics, as it reveals faults of character in a chief, which the intellectual force of the persons, with ordinary opportunity, and not hurled into aphelion by hatred, could not have seen.[23] Since we are all so stupid, what benefit that there should be two stupidities! It is like that brute advantage so essential to astronomy, of having the diameter of the earth's orbit for a base of its triangles.[24] Democracy is morose, and runs to anarchy, but in the state, and in the schools, it is indispensable to resist the consolidation of all men into a few men. If John was perfect, why are you and I alive? As long as any man exists, there is some need of him; let him fight for his own. A new poet has appeared; a new character approached us; why should we refuse to eat bread, until we have found his regiment and section in our old army-files? Why not a new man? Here is a new enterprise of Brook Farm, of Skeneateles, of Northampton: why so impatient to baptise them Essenes, or Port-Royalists, or Shakers, or by any known and effete name?[25] Let it be a new way of living. Why have only two or three ways of life, and not thousands? Every man is wanted, and no man is wanted much. We came this time for condiments, not for corn. We want the great genius only for joy; for one star more in our constellation, for one tree more in our grove. But he thinks we wish to belong to him, as he wishes to occupy us. He greatly mistakes us. I think I have done well, if I have acquired a new word from a good author; and my business with him is to find my own, though it were only to melt him down into an epithet or an image for daily use.

"Into paint will I grind thee, my bride!"[26]

To embroil the confusion, and make it impossible to arrive at any general statement, when we have insisted on the imperfection of individuals, our affections and our experience urge that every individual is entitled to honor, and a very generous treatment is sure to be repaid. A recluse sees only two or three persons, and allows them all their room; they spread themselves at large. The man of state looks at many, and compares the few habitually with others, and these look less. Yet are they not entitled to this generosity of reception? and is not munificence the means of insight? For though gamesters say, that the cards beat all the players, though they were never so skilful, yet in the contest we are now considering, the players are also the game, and share the power of the cards.[27] If you criticise a fine genius, the odds are that you are out of your reckoning, and, instead of the poet, are censuring your own caricature of him. For there is somewhat spheral and infinite in every man, especially in every genius, which, if you can come very near him, sports with all your limitations. For, rightly, every man is a channel through which heaven floweth, and, whilst I fancied I was criticising him, I was censuring or rather terminating my own soul. After taxing Goethe as a courtier, artificial, unbelieving, worldly,—I took up this book of Helena, and found him an Indian of the wilderness, a piece of pure nature like an apple or an oak, large as morning or night, and virtuous as a briar-rose.[28]

14 But care is taken that the whole tune shall be played. If we were not kept among surfaces, every thing would be large and universal: now the excluded attributes burst in on us with the more brightness, that they have been excluded. "Your turn now, my turn next," is the rule of the game. The universality being hindered in its primary form, comes in the secondary form of *all sides:* the points come in succession to the meridian, and by the speed of rotation, a new whole is formed. Nature keeps herself whole, and her representation complete in the experience of each mind. She suffers no seat to be vacant in her college. It is the secret of the world that all things subsist, and do not die, but only retire a little from sight, and afterwards return again. Whatever does not concern us, is concealed from us. As soon as a person is no longer related to our present well-being, he is concealed, or *dies,* as we say. Really, all things and persons are related to us, but according to our nature, they act on us not at once, but in succession, and we are made aware of their presence one at a time. All persons, all things which we have known, are here present, and many more than we see; the world is full. As the ancient said, the world is a *plenum* or solid; and if we saw all things that really surround us, we should be imprisoned and unable to move. For, though nothing is impassable to the soul, but all things are pervious to it, and like highways, yet this is

only whilst the soul does not see them. As soon as the soul sees any object, it stops before that object. Therefore, the divine Providence, which keeps the universe open in every direction to the soul, conceals all the furniture and all the persons that do not concern a particular soul, from the senses of that individual. Through solidest eternal things, the man finds his road, as if they did not subsist, and does not once suspect their being. As soon as he needs a new object, suddenly he beholds it, and no longer attempts to pass through it, but takes another way. When he has exhausted for the time the nourishment to be drawn from any one person or thing, that object is withdrawn from his observation, and though still in his immediate neighborhood, he does not suspect its presence.

Nothing is dead: men feign themselves dead, and endure mock funerals and mournful obituaries, and there they stand looking out of the window, sound and well, in some new and strange disguise. Jesus is not dead: he is very well alive: nor John, nor Paul, nor Mahomet, nor Aristotle; at times we believe we have seen them all, and could easily tell the names under which they go.[29] 15

If we cannot make voluntary and conscious steps in the admirable science of universals, let us see the parts wisely, and infer the genius of nature from the best particulars with a becoming charity. What is best in each kind is an index of what should be the average of that thing. Love shows me the opulence of nature, by disclosing to me in my friend a hidden wealth, and I infer an equal depth of good in every other direction. It is commonly said by farmers, that a good pear or apple costs no more time or pains to rear, than a poor one; so I would have no work of art, no speech, or action, or thought, or friend, but the best. 16

The end and the means, the gamester and the game,—life is made up of the intermixture and reaction of these two amicable powers, whose marriage appears beforehand monstrous, as each denies and tends to abolish the other. We must reconcile the contradictions as we can, but their discord and their concord introduce wild absurdities into our thinking and speech. No sentence will hold the whole truth, and the only way in which we can be just, is by giving ourselves the lie; Speech is better than silence; silence is better than speech;—All things are in contact; every atom has a sphere of repulsion;[30]— Things are, and are not, at the same time;—and the like. All the universe over, there is but one thing, this old Two-Face, creator-creature, mind-matter, 17 right-wrong, of which any proposition may be affirmed or denied.[31] Very fitly, therefore, I assert, that every man is a partialist, that nature secures him as an instrument by self-conceit, preventing the tendencies to religion and science; and now further assert, that, each man's genius being nearly and affectionately explored, he is justified in his individuality, as his nature is found to be immense; and now I add, that every man is a universalist also, and, as our earth, whilst it spins on its own axis, spins all the time around the sun through the celestial spaces, so the least of its rational children, the most dedicated to his private affair, works out, though as it were under a disguise, the universal problem. We fancy men are individuals; so are pumpkins; but every pumpkin in the field, goes through every point of pumpkin history. The rabid democrat, as soon as he is senator and rich man, has ripened beyond possibility of sincere radicalism, and unless he can resist the sun, he must be conservative the remainder of his days. Lord Eldon said in his old age, "that, if he were to begin life again, he would be damned but he would begin as agitator."[32]

18   We hide this universality, if we can, but it appears at all points. We are as ungrateful as children. There is nothing we cherish and strive to draw to us, but in some hour we turn and rend it. We keep a running fire of sarcasm at ignorance and the life of the senses; then goes by, perchance, a fair girl, a piece of life, gay and happy, and making the commonest offices beautiful, by the energy and heart with which she does them, and seeing this, we admire and love her and them, and say, "Lo! a genuine creature of the fair earth, not dissipated, or too early ripened by books, philosophy, religion, society, or care!" insinuating a treachery and contempt for all we had so long loved and wrought in ourselves and others.

19   If we could have any security against moods! If the profoundest prophet could be holden to his words, and the hearer who is ready to sell all and join the crusade, could have any certificate that tomorrow his prophet shall not unsay his testimony! But the Truth sits veiled there on the Bench, and never interposes an adamantine syllable; and the most sincere and revolutionary doctrine, put as if the ark of God were carried forward some furlongs,[33] and planted there for the succor of the world, shall in a few weeks be coldly set aside by the same speaker, as morbid; "I thought I was right, but I was not,"— and the same immeasurable credulity demanded for new audacities. If we were not of all opinions! if we did not in any moment shift the platform on which we stand, and look and speak from another! if there could be any regu-

lation, any 'one-hour-rule,' that a man should never leave his point of view, without sound of trumpet.[34] I am always insincere, as always knowing there are other moods.

How sincere and confidential we can be, saying all that lies in the mind, and yet go away feeling that all is yet unsaid, from the incapacity of the parties to know each other, although they use the same words! My companion assumes to know my mood and habit of thought, and we go on from explanation to explanation, until all is said which words can, and we leave matters just as they were at first, because of that vicious assumption. Is it that every man believes every other to be an incurable partialist, and himself an universalist? I talked yesterday with a pair of philosophers: I endeavored to show my good men that I love everything by turns, and nothing long; that I loved the centre, but doated on the superficies; that I loved man, if men seemed to me mice and rats; that I revered saints, but woke up glad that the old pagan world stood its ground, and died hard; that I was glad of men of every gift and nobility, but would not live in their arms.[35] Could they but once understand, that I loved to know that they existed, and heartily wished them Godspeed, yet, out of my poverty of life and thought, had no word or welcome for them when they came to see me, and could well consent to their living in Oregon, for any claim I felt on them, it would be a great satisfaction.[36]

20

Notes

1. Emerson, "Nominalist and Realist," *CW*, 9:667.
2. Emerson's point of reference is ambiguous. By "Platonists," Emerson probably meant the Neoplatonists, whom he called "My dazzling friends of Alexandria" (*L*, 3:50), and whose mystical, symbolic, cabalistic books he frequently read or browsed in. However, the journal version of this sentence uses "Plotinus" rather than "Platonists" and also mentions Swedenborg as one whose genius is intoxicating (*JMN*, 9:76). As his elaboration on the thought of Socrates, Porphyry, or Behmen as intoxicating throughout his writings suggests, Emerson may intend mystics such as they here too.
3. Emerson doubtless had seen gracefully cloaked lay figures in the artists' studios of Rome and Boston and in Italian religious processions.
4. Angelo, a reference to Michelangelo Buonarroti.
5. Here, "too much gingerbread" may be a family joke, for when Emerson and his

brothers were children in Boston, they were each given ninepence every Election Day to spend at the festival booths on the Common; mainly they bought ginger-bread.

6. The expression *"ignis fatuus"* refers to a light that appears over marshy ground, often indicating a false or misleading impression.

7. Here, "nervous deeds" refers to strong and vigorous deeds, from the old meaning of "nerve" as sinew or tendon.

8. At least from Plato's time, philosophers had been engaged with the question of universals: do general ideas, as distinct from individual things or persons, truly exist? During the later Middle Ages those who said Yes—they are essences, existing before things or within things, they are the truly real—became known as Realists; those who said No—universals exist only as names—were called Nominalists.

9. "Eleusinian mysteries" are the most well-known of the secret religious rites of ancient Greece.

10. Alexander Pope's translation of Homer's *Odyssey* appeared in 1726.

11. What Emerson meant by this much-referred-to sentence is clear enough; what was in his mind's eye is not. Usually when the word "luster" is plural, it refers to particular and concrete things, but when "luster" is used in a general or abstract sense, with reference to the sheen of stones or stars or minds, it is almost always singular, as if the phenomena were always the same. However, from the earliest days of mineralogy, scientists had differentiated and named the five "sorts" of lus-ter as *metallic, adamantine* (diamond), *pearly* (mica), *resinous* (or waxy), *vitreous* (or glassy), and the five degrees of lustrous intensity as *splendid, shining, glistening, glimmering,* and *dull*. Possibly such distinctions were what Emerson envisioned in his plural noun.

12. In Boston on Christmas Day 1843, Emerson had heard a performance of *Messiah*, completed in 1742 by George Frideric Handel (1685–1759), the German-born Brit-ish Baroque composer (*JMN*, 9:59–60).

13. This phrase echoes Napoleon's admonition to a haughty lady in St. Helena who had ordered servants carrying boxes to keep away: "Respect the burden, Madam" (*JMN*, 5:485; 7:416). The word "argument" appears to be used here in the old sense of "subject matter."

14. Homœopathy, founded by German physician Christian Friedrich Samuel Hahne-mann (1755–1843), was a method for treating illnesses with the administration of drugs in minute doses.

15. Fourierism is based on the ideas of François Marie Charles Fourier (1772–1837), French social thinker, who believed it possible to distribute the functions of daily life among a group of people, all of whom added up to a completed whole; these doctrines guided the later period of the Brook Farm community. By Millennial Church, Emerson means the Shakers.

16. Here, Emerson develops a botanical metaphor: "distribution" meant "classification," as in the Linnæn system; a class was the highest group within a kingdom, and a section was a subgenus.

17. Emerson's allusion is to Shakespeare's *Midsummer Night's Dream,* I, ii, the scene at the first rehearsal when Nick Bottom, the weaver, volunteers to play not just Pyramus but Thisby and the lion too.

18. The epithet "admirable" for James Crichton (1560–1582) first appeared in John Johnston's *Heroes Scoti* (1603); for the next two centuries, Crichton was considered a wonder, a marvelous boy, a prodigy of the martial arts and of the intellect, but by 1844, however, the luster of his name had worn off.

19. Here, "rowen" is an American term for a field left in stubble so that cattle may graze on it.

20. Circe is the Greek goddess who turns Ulysses's companions into swine in the *Odyssey.* Alfonso the Wise (1221–1284), patron of the sciences and a poet, was also renowned for his jest about Ptolemaic astronomy, for when this complex system was explained to him, he replied that "if God had consulted him at the creation, the universe would have been on a better and simpler plan"; William Whewell, *History of Inductive Sciences,* 3 vols. (London, 1837), 1:180. See also Emerson's poem "Alphonso of Castile" (*CW,* 9:45–48).

21. Hellebore, according to Pliny's *Natural History* (XXV, paragraph 60), "is curative of epilepsy . . . giddiness, melancholia, insanity, wild distraction," and other afflictions.

22. Thomas Paine (1737–1809), Revolutionary agitator and writer; here, Emerson uses "exuberance" in the old sense of "superabundance."

23. Here, "aphelion" refers to the point in the path of a celestial body that is farthest from the sun.

24. Here, astronomy's advantage is having a baseline of known length from the ends of which to measure the angles, and thus the distances, of stars or planets.

25. Two recent collectivist enterprises, the Skaneateles Community began its brief life in January 1844, two miles north of Skaneateles Lake, New York, and the Northampton Association of Education and Industry bought a silk factory in what is now Florence, Massachusetts, and operated it communally from 1842 until 1846. The only "known and effete name" that might have been applied to any of these new communities was that of Port-Royal-des-Champs, a seventeenth-century French experiment celebrated for its pedagogical innovations and the brilliance of the intellectuals who were drawn to it.

26. Washington Allston, "The Paint King," in *The Sylphs of the Seasons, with Other Poems* (Boston, 1813), p. 124.

27. In 1829 Emerson had copied "The cards beat everybody, but the best player is the winner at the end of the year" into his journal (*JMN,* 6:94) and attributed it to

Abraham Tucker (1705–1774), English country gentleman and utilitarian philosopher.

28. Emerson regularly referred to *Faust, Part II* as "Helena," the title that Goethe had given the Helen of Troy episode when it was published independently in 1827.

29. Mahomet, or Mohammed (570–632), founder of Islam.

30. One of the basic principles of Boscovich's physics; see "Experience," para 4, above.

31. "Two-Face" is an allusion to Janus, the Roman god of doorways.

32. In his journal, Emerson copied this statement of John Scott, 1st Earl of Eldon (1751–1838), English jurist, politician, Lord Chancellor, but without a source (*JMN*, 9:75). Throughout his career, Scott was one of the sturdiest enemies of reform and change.

33. For "ark of God," see 2 Chronicles 6:1–11.

34. Commonly used in New England legislatures and adopted by the United States House of Representatives in 1847, the "'one-hour-rule'" placed a limit on speeches in debate.

35. In his journal, Emerson identified Bronson Alcott and Charles Lane (1800–1870), English-born reformer who cofounded the Fruitlands community with Alcott, as the philosophers with whom he engaged in this exchange; he concludes the entry, saying, "And so I parted from the divine lotos-eaters" (*JMN*, 8:386–387).

36. Emerson's reference to Oregon is timely, for it was the site of the "Great Immigration" across the American plains in 1843 and 1844.

An Address Delivered in the Court-House in Concord, Massachusetts, on 1ST August, 1844, on the Anniversary of the Emancipation of the Negroes in the British West Indies

Friends and Fellow Citizens,

We are met to exchange congratulations on the anniversary of an event singular in the history of civilization; a day of reason; of the clear light; of that which makes us better than a flock of birds and beasts: a day, which gave the immense fortification of a fact,—of gross history,—to ethical abstractions.[1] It was the settlement, as far as a great Empire was concerned, of a question on which almost every leading citizen in it had taken care to record his vote; one which for many years absorbed the attention of the best and most eminent of mankind. I might well hesitate, coming from other studies, and without the smallest claim to be a special laborer in this work of humanity, to undertake to set this matter before you; which ought rather to be done by a strict coöperation of many well-advised persons; but I shall not apologize for my weakness. In this cause, no man's weakness is any prejudice; it has a thousand sons; if one man cannot speak, ten others can; and whether by the wisdom of its friends, or by the folly of the adversaries; by speech and by silence; by doing and by omitting to do, it goes forward. Therefore I will speak,—or, not I, but the might of liberty in my weakness. The subject is said to have the property of making dull men eloquent.

3   It has been in all men's experience a marked effect of the enterprise in behalf of the African, to generate an overbearing and defying spirit. The institution of slavery seems to its opponent to have but one side, and he feels that none but a stupid or a malignant person can hesitate on a view of the facts. Under such an impulse, I was about to say, If any cannot speak, or cannot hear the words of freedom, let him go hence,—I had almost said, Creep into your grave, the universe has no need of you! But I have thought better: let him not go. When we consider what remains to be done for this interest, in this country, the dictates of humanity make us tender of such as are not yet persuaded. The hardest selfishness is to be borne with. Let us withhold every reproachful, and, if we can, every indignant remark. In this cause, we must renounce our temper, and the risings of pride. If there be any man who thinks the ruin of a race of men a small matter, compared with the last decoration and completions of his own comfort,—who would not so much as part with his ice-cream, to save them from rapine and manacles, I think, I must not hesitate to satisfy that man, that also his cream and vanilla are safer and cheaper, by placing the negro nation on a fair footing, than by robbing them. If the Virginian piques himself on the picturesque luxury of his vassalage, on the heavy Ethiopian manners of his house-servants, their silent obedience, their hue of bronze, their turbaned heads, and would not exchange them for the more intelligent but precarious hired-service of whites, I shall not refuse to show him, that when their free-papers are made out, it will still be their interest to remain on his estate, and that the oldest planters of Jamaica are convinced, that it is cheaper to pay wages, than to own the slave.

4   The history of mankind interests us only as it exhibits a steady gain of truth and right, in the incessant conflict which it records, between the material and the moral nature. From the earliest monuments, it appears, that one race was victim, and served the other races. In the oldest temples of Egypt, negro captives are painted on the tombs of kings, in such attitudes as to show that they are on the point of being executed; and Herodotus, our oldest historian, relates that the Troglodytes hunted the Ethiopians in four-horse-chariots.[2] From the earliest time, the negro has been an article of luxury to the commercial nations. So has it been, down to the day that has just dawned on the world. Language must be raked, the secrets of slaughter-houses and infamous holes that cannot front the day, must be ransacked, to tell what negro-slavery has been. These men, our benefactors, as they are producers of

corn and wine, of coffee, of tobacco, of cotton, of sugar, of rum, and brandy, gentle and joyous themselves, and producers of comfort and luxury for the civilized world,—there seated in the finest climates of the globe, children of the sun,—I am heart-sick when I read how they came there, and how they are kept there. Their case was left out of the mind and out of the heart of their brothers. The prizes of society, the trumpet of fame, the privileges of learning, of culture, of religion, the decencies and joys of marriage, honor, obedience, personal authority, and a perpetual melioration into a finer civility, these were for all, but not for them. For the negro, was the slave-ship to begin with, in whose filthy hold he sat in irons, unable to lie down; bad food, and insufficiency of that; disfranchisement; no property in the rags that covered him; no marriage, no right in the poor black woman that cherished him in her bosom,—no right to the children of his body; no security from the humors, none from the crimes, none from the appetites of his master: toil, famine, insult, and flogging; and, when he sunk in the furrow, no wind of good fame blew over him, no priest of salvation visited him with glad tidings: but he went down to death, with dusky dreams of African shadow-catchers and Obeahs hunting him.[3] Very sad was the negro tradition, that the Great Spirit, in the beginning, offered the black man, whom he loved better than the buckra or white, his choice of two boxes, a big and a little one. The black man was greedy, and chose the largest. "The buckra box was full up with pen, paper, and whip, and the negro box with hoe and bill; and hoe and bill for negro to this day."[4]

But the crude element of good in human affairs must work and ripen, spite of whips, and plantation-laws, and West Indian interest. Conscience rolled on its pillow, and could not sleep. We sympathize very tenderly here with the poor aggrieved planter, of whom so many unpleasant things are said; but if we saw the whip applied to old men, to tender women; and, undeniably, though I shrink to say so,—pregnant women set in the treadmill for refusing to work, when, not they, but the eternal law of animal nature refused to work;—if we saw men's backs flayed with cowhides, and "hot rum poured on, superinduced with brine or pickle, rubbed in with a cornhusk, in the scorching heat of the sun;"[5]—if we saw the runaways hunted with bloodhounds into swamps and hills; and, in cases of passion, a planter throwing his negro into a copper of boiling cane-juice,—if we saw these things with eyes, we too should wince. They are not pleasant sights. The blood is moral: the

5

blood is anti-slavery: it runs cold in the veins: the stomach rises with disgust, and curses slavery. Well, so it happened; a good man or woman, a country-boy or girl, it would so fall out, once in a while saw these injuries, and had the indiscretion to tell of them. The horrid story ran and flew; the winds blew it all over the world. They who heard it, asked their rich and great friends, if it was true, or only missionary lies. The richest and greatest, the prime minister of England, the king's privy council were obliged to say, that it was too true. It became plain to all men, the more this business was looked into, that the crimes and cruelties of the slave-traders and slave-owners could not be over-stated. The more it was searched, the more shocking anecdotes came up,— things not to be spoken. Humane persons who were informed of the reports, insisted on proving them. Granville Sharp was accidentally made acquainted with the sufferings of a slave, whom a West Indian planter had brought with him to London, and had beaten with a pistol on his head so badly, that his whole body became diseased, and the man useless to his master, who left him to go whither he pleased. The man applied to Mr. William Sharp, a charitable surgeon, who attended the diseases of the poor. In process of time, he was healed. Granville Sharp found him at his brother's, and procured a place for him in an apothecary's shop. The master accidentally met his recovered slave, and instantly endeavored to get possession of him again. Sharp protected the slave. In consulting with the lawyers, they told Sharp the laws were against him. Sharp would not believe it; no prescription on earth could ever render such iniquities legal. 'But the decisions are against you, and Lord Mansfield, now chief justice of England, leans to the decisions.'[6] Sharp instantly sat down and gave himself to the study of English law for more than two years, until he had proved that the opinions relied on of Talbot and Yorke, were in-compatible with the former English decisions, and with the whole spirit of English law.[7] He published his book in 1769, and he so filled the heads and hearts of his advocates, that when he brought the case of George Somerset, another slave, before Lord Mansfield, the slavish decisions were set aside, and equity affirmed.[8] There is a sparkle of God's righteousness in Lord Mans-field's judgment, which does the heart good. Very unwilling had that great lawyer been to reverse the late decisions; he suggested twice from the bench, in the course of the trial, how the question might be got rid of: but the hint was not taken; the case was adjourned again and again, and judgment delayed. At last judgment was demanded, and on the 22d June, 1772, Lord Mansfield is reported to have decided in these words;

"Immemorial usage preserves the memory of *positive law,* long after all traces of the occasion, reason, authority, and time of its introduction, are lost; and in a case so odious as the condition of slaves, must be taken strictly; (tracing the subject to natural principles, the claim of slavery never can be supported.) The power claimed by this return never was in use here. We cannot say the cause set forth by this return is allowed or approved of by the laws of this kingdom; and therefore the man must be discharged."

This decision established the principle that the "air of England is too pure for any slave to breathe,"[9] but the wrongs in the islands were not thereby touched. Public attention, however, was drawn that way, and the methods of the stealing and the transportation from Africa, became noised abroad. The Quakers got the story. In their plain meeting-houses, and prim dwellings, this dismal agitation got entrance. They were rich: they owned for debt, or by inheritance, island property; they were religious, tender-hearted men and women; and they had to hear the news, and digest it as they could. Six Quakers met in London on the 6th July, 1783; William Dillwyn, Samuel Hoar, George Harrison, Thomas Knowles, John Lloyd, Joseph Woods, "to consider what step they should take for the relief and liberation of the negro slaves in the West Indies, and for the discouragement of the slave-trade on the coast of Africa."[10] They made friends and raised money for the slave; they interested their Yearly Meeting; and all English and all American Quakers. John Woolman of New Jersey, whilst yet an apprentice, was uneasy in his mind when he was set to write a bill of sale of a negro, for his master.[11] He gave his testimony against the traffic, in Maryland and Virginia. Thomas Clarkson was a youth at Cambridge, England, when the subject given out for a Latin prize dissertation, was, "Is it right to make slaves of others against their will?" He wrote an essay, and won the prize; but he wrote too well for his own peace; he began to ask himself, if these things could be true; and if they were, he could no longer rest. He left Cambridge; he fell in with the six Quakers. They engaged him to act for them. He himself interested Mr. Wilberforce in the matter.[12] The shipmasters in that trade were the greatest miscreants, and guilty of every barbarity to their own crews. Clarkson went to Bristol, made himself acquainted with the interior of the slaveships, and the details of the trade. The facts confirmed his sentiment, "that Providence had never made that to be wise, which was immoral, and that the slave-trade was as impolitic as it was unjust;" that it was found peculiarly fatal to those employed in it.[13] More seamen died in that trade, in one year, than in the whole remaining trade of the country in two. Mr. Pitt and Mr. Fox were drawn into the generous enterprise.[14] In 1788, the House of Commons voted Parliamentary inquiry. In 1791, a bill to abolish the trade was brought in by Wilberforce, and supported by him, and by Fox, and Burke, and Pitt, with the utmost ability and faithfulness; resisted by the planters, and the whole West Indian interest, and lost.[15] During the next sixteen years, ten times, year after year, the attempt was renewed by Mr. Wilberforce, and ten times defeated by the planters. The king, and all the royal family but one, were against it. These debates are instructive, as they show on what grounds the trade was assailed and defended. Every thing generous, wise, and sprightly is sure to come to the attack. On the other part, are found cold prudence, barefaced selfishness, and silent votes. But the nation was aroused to enthusiasm. Every horrid fact became known. In 1791, three hundred thousand persons in Britain pledged themselves to abstain from all articles of island produce. The planters were obliged to give way; and in 1807, on the 25th March, the bill passed, and the slave-trade was abolished.

8   The assailants of slavery had early agreed to limit their political action on this subject to the abolition of the trade, but Granville Sharp, as a matter of conscience, whilst he acted as chairman of the London Committee, felt constrained to record his protest against the limitation, declaring that slavery was as much a crime against the Divine law, as the slave-trade. The trade, under false flags, went on as before. In 1821, according to official documents presented to the American government by the Colonization Society, 200,000 slaves were deported from Africa.[16] Nearly 30,000 were landed in the port of Havana alone. In consequence of the dangers of the trade growing out of the act of abolition, ships were built sharp for swiftness, and with a frightful disregard of the comfort of the victims they were destined to transport. They carried five, six, even seven hundred stowed in a ship built so narrow as to be unsafe, being made just broad enough on the beam to keep the sea. In attempting to make its escape from the pursuit of a man-of-war, one ship flung five hundred slaves alive into the sea. These facts went into Parliament. In the islands, was an ominous state of cruel and licentious society; every house had

a dungeon attached to it; every slave was worked by the whip. There is no end to the tragic anecdotes in the municipal records of the colonies. The boy was set to strip and to flog his own mother to blood, for a small offence. Looking in the face of his master by the negro was held to be violence by the island courts. He was worked sixteen hours, and his ration by law, in some islands, was a pint of flour and one salt herring a day. He suffered insult, stripes, mutilation, at the humor of the master: iron collars were riveted on their necks with iron prongs ten inches long; capsicum pepper was rubbed in the eyes of the females; and they were done to death with the most shocking levity between the master and manager, without fine or inquiry. And when, at last, some Quakers, Moravians, and Wesleyan and Baptist missionaries, following in the steps of Carey and Ward in the East Indies, had been moved to come and cheer the poor victim with the hope of some reparation, in a future world, of the wrongs he suffered in this, these missionaries were persecuted by the planters, their lives threatened, their chapels burned, and the negroes furiously forbidden to go near them.[17] These outrages rekindled the flame of British indignation. Petitions poured into Parliament: a million persons signed their names to these; and in 1833, on the 14th May, Lord Stanley, minister of the colonies, introduced into the House of Commons his bill for the Emancipation.[18]

The scheme of the minister, with such modification as it received in the legislature, proposed gradual emancipation; that on 1st August, 1834, all persons now slaves should be entitled to be registered as apprenticed laborers, and to acquire thereby all the rights and privileges of freemen, subject to the restriction of laboring under certain conditions. These conditions were, that the prædials should owe three fourths of the profits of their labor to their masters for six years, and the nonprædials for four years.[19] The other fourth of the apprentice's time was to be his own, which he might sell to his master, or to other persons; and at the end of the term of years fixed, he should be free.

With these provisions and conditions, the bill proceeds, in the twelfth section, in the following terms. "Be it enacted, that all and every person who, on the 1st August, 1834, shall be holden in slavery within any such British colony as aforesaid, shall upon and from and after the said 1st August, become and be to all intents and purposes free, and discharged of and from all manner of slavery, and shall be absolutely and forever manumitted; and that the children

9

10

thereafter born to any such persons, and the offspring of such children, shall, in like manner, be free from their birth; and that from and after the 1st August, 1834, slavery shall be and is hereby utterly and forever abolished and declared unlawful throughout the British colonies, plantations, and possessions abroad."

11   The ministers, having estimated the slave products of the colonies in annual exports of sugar, rum, and coffee, at £1,500,000 *per annum,* estimated the total value of the slave-property at 30,000,000 pounds sterling, and proposed to give the planters, as a compensation for so much of the slaves' time as the act took from them, 20,000,000 pounds sterling, to be divided into nineteen shares for the nineteen colonies, and to be distributed to the owners of slaves by commissioners, whose appointment and duties were regulated by the Act. After much debate, the bill passed by large majorities. The apprenticeship system is understood to have proceeded from Lord Brougham, and was by him urged on his colleagues, who, it is said, were inclined to the policy of immediate emancipation.[20]

12   The colonial legislatures received the act of Parliament with various degrees of displeasure, and, of course, every provision of the bill was criticised with severity. The new relation between the master and the apprentice, it was feared, would be mischievous; for the bill required the appointment of magistrates, who should hear every complaint of the apprentice, and see that justice was done him. It was feared that the interest of the master and servant would now produce perpetual discord between them. In the island of Antigua, containing 37,000 people, 30,000 being negroes, these objections had such weight, that the legislature rejected the apprenticeship system, and adopted absolute emancipation. In the other islands the system of the ministry was accepted.

13   The reception of it by the negro population was equal in nobleness to the deed. The negroes were called together by the missionaries and by the planters, and the news explained to them. On the night of the 31st July, they met everywhere at their churches and chapels, and at midnight, when the clock struck twelve, on their knees, the silent, weeping assembly became men; they rose and embraced each other; they cried, they sung, they prayed, they were wild with joy, but there was no riot, no feasting. I have never read anything in history more touching than the moderation of the negroes. Some American captains left the shore and put to sea, anticipating insurrection and general

murder. With far different thoughts, the negroes spent the hour in their huts and chapels. I will not repeat to you the well-known paragraph, in which Messrs. Thome and Kimball, the commissioners sent out in the year 1837 by the American Anti-slavery Society, describe the occurrences of that night in the island of Antigua. It has been quoted in every newspaper, and Dr. Channing has given it additional fame.[21] But I must be indulged in quoting a few sentences from the pages that follow it, narrating the behavior of the emancipated people on the next day.

"The first of August came on Friday, and a release was proclaimed from all work until the next Monday. The day was chiefly spent by the great mass of the negroes in the churches and chapels. The clergy and missionaries throughout the island were actively engaged, seizing the opportunity to enlighten the people on all the duties and responsibilities of their new relation, and urging them to the attainment of that higher liberty with which Christ maketh his children free. In every quarter, we were assured, the day was like a sabbath. Work had ceased. The hum of business was still: tranquillity pervaded the towns and country. The planters informed us, that they went to the chapels where their own people were assembled, greeted them, shook hands with them, and exchanged the most hearty good wishes. At Grace Hill, there were at least a thousand persons around the Moravian Chapel who could not get in. For once the house of God suffered violence, and the violent took it by force. At Grace Bay, the people, all dressed in white, formed a procession, and walked arm in arm into the chapel. We were told that the dress of the negroes on that occasion was uncommonly simple and modest. There was not the least disposition to gaiety. Throughout the island, there was not a single dance known of, either day or night, nor so much as a fiddle played."[22]

On the next Monday morning, with very few exceptions, every negro on every plantation was in the field at his work. In some places, they waited to see their master, to know what bargain he would make; but, for the most part, throughout the islands, nothing painful occurred. In June, 1835, the ministers, Lord Aberdeen and Sir George Grey, declared to the Parliament, that the system worked well;[23] that now for ten months, from 1st August, 1834, no injury or violence had been offered to any white, and only one black had been hurt in 800,000 negroes: and, contrary to many sinister predictions, that the new crop of island produce would not fall short of that of the last year.

But the habit of oppression was not destroyed by a law and a day of jubi-

14

15

16

lee. It soon appeared in all the islands, that the planters were disposed to use their old privileges, and overwork the apprentices; to take from them, under various pretences, their fourth part of their time; and to exert the same licentious despotism as before. The negroes complained to the magistrates, and to the governor. In the island of Jamaica, this ill blood continually grew worse. The governors, Lord Belmore, the Earl of Sligo, and afterwards Sir Lionel Smith, (a governor of their own class, who had been sent out to gratify the planters,) threw themselves on the side of the oppressed, and are at constant quarrel with the angry and bilious island legislature.[24] Nothing can exceed the ill humor and sulkiness of the addresses of this assembly.

17   I may here express a general remark, which the history of slavery seems to justify, that it is not founded solely on the avarice of the planter. We sometimes say, the planter does not want slaves, he only wants the immunities and the luxuries which the slaves yield him; give him money, give him a machine that will yield him as much money as the slaves, and he will thankfully let them go. He has no love of slavery, he wants luxury, and he will pay even this price of crime and danger for it. But I think experience does not warrant this favorable distinction, but shows the existence, beside the covetousness, of a bitterer element, the love of power, the voluptuousness of holding a human being in his absolute control. We sometimes observe, that spoiled children contract a habit of annoying quite wantonly those who have charge of them, and seem to measure their own sense of well-being, not by what they do, but by the degree of reaction they can cause. It is vain to get rid of them by not minding them: if purring and humming is not noticed, they squeal and screech; then if you chide and console them, they find the experiment succeeds, and they begin again. The child will sit in your arms contented, provided you do nothing. If you take a book and read, he commences hostile operations. The planter is the spoiled child of his unnatural habits, and has contracted in his indolent and luxurious climate the need of excitement by irritating and tormenting his slave.

18   Sir Lionel Smith defended the poor negro girls, prey to the licentiousness of the planters; they shall not be whipped with tamarind rods, if they do not comply with their master's will; he defended the negro women; they should not be made to dig the cane-holes, (which is the very hardest of the field-work;) he defended the Baptist preachers and the stipendiary magistrates, who are the negroes' friends, from the power of the planter.[25] The power of

the planters, however, to oppress, was greater than the power of the apprentice and of his guardians to withstand. Lord Brougham and Mr. Buxton declared that the planter had not fulfilled his part in the contract, whilst the apprentices had fulfilled theirs; and demanded that the emancipation should be hastened, and the apprenticeship abolished.[26] Parliament was compelled to pass additional laws for the defence and security of the negro, and in ill humor at these acts, the great island of Jamaica, with a population of half a million, and 300,000 negroes, early in 1838, resolved to throw up the two remaining years of apprenticeship, and to emancipate absolutely on the 1st August, 1838. In British Guiana, in Dominica, the same resolution had been earlier taken with more good will; and the other islands fell into the measure; so that on the 1st August, 1838, the shackles dropped from every British slave. The accounts which we have from all parties, both from the planters, and those too who were originally most opposed to the measure, and from the new freemen, are of the most satisfactory kind. The manner in which the new festival was celebrated, brings tears to the eyes. The First of August, 1838, was observed in Jamaica as a day of thanksgiving and prayer. Sir Lionel Smith, the governor, writes to the British Ministry, "It is impossible for me to do justice to the good order, decorum, and gratitude, which the whole laboring population manifested on that happy occasion. Though joy beamed on every countenance, it was throughout tempered with solemn thankfulness to God, and the churches and chapels were everywhere filled with these happy people in humble offering of praise."[27]

The Queen, in her speech to the Lords and Commons, praised the conduct of the emancipated population: and, in 1840, Sir Charles Metcalfe, the new governor of Jamaica, in his address to the Assembly, expressed himself to that late exasperated body in these terms.[28] "All those who are acquainted with the state of the island, know that our emancipated population are as free, as independent in their conduct, as well-conditioned, as much in the enjoyment of abundance, and as strongly sensible of the blessings of liberty, as any that we know of in any country. All disqualifications and distinctions of color have ceased; men of all colors have equal rights in law, and an equal footing in society, and every man's position is settled by the same circumstances which regulate that point in other free countries, where no difference of color exists. It may be asserted, without fear of denial, that the former slaves of Jamaica are now as secure in all social rights, as freeborn Britons."

19

He further describes the erection of numerous churches, chapels, and schools, which the new population required, and adds that more are still demanded. The legislature, in their reply, echo the governor's statement, and say, "The peaceful demeanor of the emancipated population redounds to their own credit, and affords a proof of their continued comfort and prosperity."

20   I said, this event is signal in the history of civilization. There are many styles of civilization, and not one only. Ours is full of barbarities. There are many faculties in man, each of which takes its turn of activity, and that faculty which is paramount in any period, and exerts itself through the strongest nation, determines the civility of that age; and each age thinks its own the perfection of reason. Our culture is very cheap and intelligible. Unroof any house, and you shall find it. The well-being consists in having a sufficiency of coffee and toast, with a daily newspaper; a well-glazed parlor, with marbles, mirrors, and centre-table; and the excitement of a few parties and a few rides in a year. Such as one house, such are all. The owner of a New York manor imitates the mansion and equipage of the London nobleman; the Boston merchant rivals his brother of New York; and the villages copy Boston. There have been nations elevated by great sentiments. Such was the civility of Sparta and the Dorian race, whilst it was defective in some of the chief elements of ours.[29] That of Athens, again, lay in an intellect dedicated to beauty. That of Asia Minor in poetry, music, and arts; that of Palestine in piety; that of Rome in military arts and virtues, exalted by a prodigious magnanimity; that of China and Japan in the last exaggeration of decorum and etiquette. Our civility, England determines the style of, inasmuch as England is the strongest of the family of existing nations, and as we are the expansion of that people. It is that of a trading nation; it is a shopkeeping civility. The English lord is a retired shopkeeper, and has the prejudices and timidities of that profession. And we are shopkeepers, and have acquired the vices and virtues that belong to trade. We peddle, we truck, we sail, we row, we ride in cars, we creep in teams, we go in canals—to market, and for the sale of goods. The national aim and employment streams into our ways of thinking, our laws, our habits, and our manners. The customer is the immediate jewel of our souls.[30] Him we flatter, him we feast, compliment, vote for, and will not contradict. It was or it seemed the dictate of trade, to keep the negro down. We had found a race who were less warlike, and less energetic shopkeepers than

we; who had very little skill in trade. We found it very convenient to keep them at work, since, by the aid of a little whipping, we could get their work for nothing but their board and the cost of whips. What if it cost a few unpleasant scenes on the coast of Africa? That was a great way off; and the scenes could be endured by some sturdy, unscrupulous fellows, who could go for high wages and bring us the men, and need not trouble our ears with the disagreeable particulars. If any mention was made of homicide, madness, adultery, and intolerable tortures, we would let the church-bells ring louder, the church-organ swell its peal, and drown the hideous sound. The sugar they raised was excellent: nobody tasted blood in it. The coffee was fragrant; the tobacco was incense; the brandy made nations happy; the cotton clothed the world. What! all raised by these men, and no wages? Excellent! What a convenience! They seemed created by providence to bear the heat and the whipping, and make these fine articles.

But unhappily, most unhappily, gentlemen, man is born with intellect, as well as with a love of sugar, and with a sense of justice, as well as a taste for strong drink. These ripened, as well as those. You could not educate him, you could not get any poetry, any wisdom, any beauty in woman, any strong and commanding character in man, but these absurdities would still come flashing out,—these absurdities of a demand for justice, a generosity for the weak and oppressed. Unhappily too, for the planter, the laws of nature are in harmony with each other: that which the head and the heart demand, is found to be, in the long run, for what the grossest calculator calls his advantage. The moral sense is always supported by the permanent interest of the parties. Else, I know not how, in our world, any good would ever get done. It was shown to the planters that they, as well as the negroes, were slaves; that though they paid no wages, they got very poor work; that their estates were ruining them, under the finest climate; and that they needed the severest monopoly laws at home to keep them from bankruptcy. The oppression of the slave recoiled on them. They were full of vices; their children were lumps of pride, sloth, sensuality and rottenness. The position of woman was nearly as bad as it could be, and, like other robbers, they could not sleep in security. Many planters have said, since the emancipation, that, before that day, they were the greatest slaves on the estates. Slavery is no scholar, no improver; it does not love the whistle of the railroad; it does not love the newspaper, the mailbag, a college, a book, or a preacher who has the absurd whim of saying what he thinks; it does not increase the white population; it does not improve the soil; everything goes to decay. For these reasons, the islands proved bad customers to England. It was very easy for manufacturers less shrewd than those of Birmingham and Manchester to see, that if the state of things in the islands was altered, if the slaves had wages, the slaves would be clothed, would build houses, would fill them with tools, with pottery, with crockery, with hardware; and negro women love fine clothes as well as white women. In every naked negro of those thousands, they saw a future customer. Meantime, they saw further, that the slave-trade, by keeping in barbarism the whole coast of eastern Africa, deprives them of countries and nations of customers, if once freedom and civility, and European manners could get a foothold there. But the trade could not be abolished, whilst this hungry West Indian market, with an appetite like the grave, cried, "More, more, bring me a hundred a day;" they could not expect any mitigation in the madness of the poor African war-chiefs. These considerations opened the eyes of the dullest in Britain. More than this, the West Indian estate was owned or mortgaged in England, and the owner and the mortgagee had very plain intimations that the feeling of English liberty was gaining every hour new mass and velocity, and the hostility to such as resisted it, would be fatal. The House of Commons would destroy the protection of island produce, and interfere on English politics in the island legislation: so they hastened to make the best of their position, and accepted the bill.

22   These considerations, I doubt not, had their weight, the interest of trade, the interest of the revenue, and, moreover, the good fame of the action. It was inevitable that men should feel these motives. But they do not appear to have had an excessive or unreasonable weight. On reviewing this history, I think the whole transaction reflects infinite honor on the people and parliament of England. It was a stately spectacle, to see the cause of human rights argued with so much patience and generosity, and with such a mass of evidence before that powerful people. It is a creditable incident in the history, that when, in 1789, the first privy-council report of evidence on the trade, a bulky folio, (embodying all the facts which the London Committee had been engaged for years in collecting, and all the examinations before the council,) was presented to the House of Commons, a late day being named for the discussion, in order to give members time,—Mr. Wilberforce, Mr. Pitt, the prime minister, and other gentlemen, took advantage of the postponement,

to retire into the country, to read the report.[31] For months and years the bill was debated, with some consciousness of the extent of its relations by the first citizens of England, the foremost men of the earth; every argument was weighed, every particle of evidence was sifted, and laid in the scale; and, at last, the right triumphed, the poor man was vindicated, and the oppressor was flung out. I know that England has the advantage of trying the question at a wide distance from the spot where the nuisance exists: the planters are not, excepting in rare examples, members of the legislature. The extent of the empire, and the magnitude and number of other questions crowding into court, keep this one in balance, and prevent it from obtaining that ascendency, and being urged with that intemperance, which a question of property tends to acquire. There are causes in the composition of the British legislature, and the relation of its leaders to the country and to Europe, which exclude much that is pitiful and injurious in other legislative assemblies. From these reasons, the question was discussed with a rare independence and magnanimity. It was not narrowed down to a paltry electioneering trap, and, I must say, a delight in justice, an honest tenderness for the poor negro, for man suffering these wrongs, combined with the national pride, which refused to give the support of English soil, or the protection of the English flag, to these disgusting violations of nature.

Forgive me, fellow citizens, if I own to you, that in the last few days that my attention has been occupied with this history, I have not been able to read a page of it, without the most painful comparisons. Whilst I have read of England, I have thought of New England. Whilst I have meditated in my solitary walks on the magnanimity of the English Bench and Senate, reaching out the benefit of the law to the most helpless citizen in her world-wide realm, I have found myself oppressed by other thoughts. As I have walked in the pastures and along the edge of woods, I could not keep my imagination on those agreeable figures, for other images that intruded on me. I could not see the great vision of the patriots and senators who have adopted the slave's cause:—they turned their backs on me. No: I see other pictures—of mean men: I see very poor, very ill-clothed, very ignorant men, not surrounded by happy friends,—to be plain,—poor black men of obscure employment as mariners, cooks, or stewards, in ships, yet citizens of this our Commonwealth of Massachusetts,—freeborn as we,—whom the slave-laws of the States of South Carolina, Georgia, and Louisiana, have arrested in the vessels in which

23

they visited those ports, and shut up in jails so long as the vessel remained in port, with the stringent addition, that if the shipmaster fails to pay the costs of this official arrest, and the board in jail, these citizens are to be sold for slaves, to pay that expense.[32] This man, these men, I see, and no law to save them. Fellow citizens, this crime will not be hushed up any longer. I have learned that a citizen of Nantucket, walking in New Orleans, found a free-born citizen of Nantucket, a man, too, of great personal worth, and, as it happened, very dear to him, as having saved his own life, working chained in the streets of that city, kidnapped by such a process as this. In the sleep of the laws, the private interference of two excellent citizens of Boston has, I have ascertained, rescued several natives of this State from these southern prisons. Gentlemen, I thought the deck of a Massachusetts ship was as much the territory of Massachusetts, as the floor on which we stand. It should be as sacred as the temple of God. The poorest fishing-smack, that floats under the shadow of an iceberg in the northern seas, or hunts the whale in the southern ocean, should be encompassed by her laws with comfort and protection, as much as within the arms of Cape Ann and Cape Cod. And this kidnapping is suffered within our own land and federation, whilst the fourth article of the Constitution of the United States ordains in terms, that, "The citizens of each State shall be entitled to all privileges and immunities of citizens in the several States." If such a damnable outrage can be committed on the person of a citizen with impunity, let the Governor break the broad seal of the State; he bears the sword in vain.[33] The Governor of Massachusetts is a trifler: the State-house in Boston is a play-house: the General Court is a dishonored body: if they make laws which they cannot execute. The great-hearted Puritans have left no posterity. The rich men may walk in State-street, but they walk without honor; and the farmers may brag their democracy in the country, but they are disgraced men. If the State has no power to defend its own people in its own shipping, because it has delegated that power to the Federal Government, has it no representation in the Federal Government?[34] Are those men dumb? I am no lawyer, and cannot indicate the forms applicable to the case, but here is something which transcends all forms. Let the senators and representatives of the State, containing a population of a million freemen, go in a body before the Congress, and say, that they have a demand to make on them so imperative, that all functions of government must stop, until it is satisfied. If ordinary legislation cannot reach it, then extraordinary must be applied. The Congress should instruct the President to send to those ports of Charleston, Savannah, and New Orleans, such orders and such force, as should release, forthwith, all such citizens of Massachusetts as were holden in prison without the allegation of any crime, and should set on foot the strictest inquisition to discover where such persons, brought into slavery by these local laws, at any time heretofore, may now be. That first;—and then, let order be taken to indemnify all such as have been incarcerated. As for dangers to the Union, from such demands!—the Union is already at an end, when the first citizen of Massachusetts is thus outraged. Is it an union and covenant in which the State of Massachusetts agrees to be imprisoned, and the State of Carolina to imprison? Gentlemen, I am loath to say harsh things, and perhaps I know too little of politics for the smallest weight to attach to any censure of mine,—but I am at a loss how to characterize the tameness and silence of the two senators and the ten representatives of the State at Washington.[35] To what purpose, have we clothed each of those representatives with the power of seventy thousand persons, and each senator with near half a million, if they are to sit dumb at their desks, and see their constituents captured and sold;—perhaps to gentlemen sitting by them in the hall? There is a scandalous rumor that has been swelling louder of late years,—perhaps it is wholly false,—that members are bullied into silence by southern gentlemen. It is so easy to omit to speak, or even to be absent when delicate things are to be handled. I may as well say what all men feel, that whilst our very amiable and very innocent representatives and senators at Washington, are accomplished lawyers and merchants, and very eloquent at dinners and at caucuses, there is a disastrous want of *men* from New England. I would gladly make exceptions, and you will not suffer me to forget one eloquent old man, in whose veins the blood of Massachusetts rolls, and who singly has defended the freedom of speech, and the rights of the free, against the usurpation of the slave-holder.[36] But the reader of Congressional debates, in New England, is perplexed to see with what admirable sweetness and patience the majority of the free States, are schooled and ridden by the minority of slave-holders. What if we should send thither representatives who were a particle less amiable and less innocent? I entreat you, sirs, let not this stain attach, let not this misery accumulate any longer. If the managers of our political parties are too prudent and too cold;—if, most unhappily, the ambitious class of young men and political men have found out, that these neglected victims are poor and without weight; that they have no graceful hospitalities to offer; no valuable business to throw into any man's hands, no strong vote to cast at the elections; and therefore may with impunity be left in their chains or to the chance of chains, then let the citizens in their primary capacity take up their cause on this very ground, and say to the government of the State, and of the Union, that government exists to defend the weak and the poor and the injured party; the rich and the strong can better take care of themselves. And as an omen and assurance of success, I point you to the bright example which England set you, on this day, ten years ago.

24   There are other comparisons and other imperative duties which come sadly to mind,—but I do not wish to darken the hours of this day by crimination; I turn gladly to the rightful theme, to the bright aspects of the occasion.

25   This event was a moral revolution. The history of it is before you. Here was no prodigy, no fabulous hero, no Trojan horse, no bloody war, but all was achieved by plain means of plain men, working not under a leader, but under a sentiment. Other revolutions have been the insurrection of the oppressed; this was the repentance of the tyrant. It was the masters revolting from their mastery. The slave-holder said, I will not hold slaves. The end was noble, and the means were pure. Hence, the elevation and pathos of this chapter of history. The lives of the advocates are pages of greatness, and the connexion of the eminent senators with this question, constitutes the immortalizing moments of those men's lives. The bare enunciation of the theses, at which the lawyers and legislators arrived, gives a glow to the heart of the reader. Lord Chancellor Northington is the author of the famous sentence, "As soon as any man puts his foot on English ground, he becomes free."[37] "I was a slave," said the counsel of Somerset, speaking for his client, "for I was in America: I am now in a country, where the common rights of mankind are known and regarded."[38] Granville Sharp filled the ear of the judges with the sound principles, that had from time to time been affirmed by the legal authorities. "Derived power cannot be superior to the power from which it is derived." "The reasonableness of the law is the soul of the law." "It is better to suffer every evil, than to consent to any."[39] Out it would come, the God's truth, out it came, like a bolt from a cloud, for all the mumbling of the lawyers. One feels very sensibly in all this history that a great heart and soul are behind there, superior to any man, and making use of each, in turn, and infinitely attractive to every person according to the degree

of reason in his own mind, so that this cause has had the power to draw to it every particle of talent and of worth in England, from the beginning. All the great geniuses of the British senate, Fox, Pitt, Burke, Grenville, Sheridan, Grey, Canning, ranged themselves on its side; the poet Cowper wrote for it: Franklin, Jefferson, Washington, in this country, all recorded their votes.[40] All men remember the subtlety and the fire of indignation, which the Edinburgh Review contributed to the cause; and every liberal mind, poet, preacher, moralist, statesman, has had the fortune to appear somewhere for this cause. On the other part, appeared the reign of pounds and shillings, and all manner of rage and stupidity; a resistance which drew from Mr. Huddlestone in Parliament the observation, "That a curse attended this trade even in the mode of defending it. By a certain fatality, none but the vilest arguments were brought forward, which corrupted the very persons who used them. Every one of these was built on the narrow ground of interest, of pecuniary profit, of sordid gain, in opposition to every motive that had reference to humanity, justice, and religion, or to that great principle which comprehended them all."[41]—This moral force perpetually reinforces and dignifies the friends of this cause. It gave that tenacity to their point which has insured ultimate triumph; and it gave that superiority in reason, in imagery, in eloquence, which makes in all countries anti-slavery meetings so attractive to the people, and has made it a proverb in Massachusetts, that, "eloquence is dog-cheap at the anti-slavery chapel."

I will say further, that we are indebted mainly to this movement, and to the continuers of it, for the popular discussion of every point of practical ethics, and a reference of every question to the absolute standard. It is notorious, that the political, religious, and social schemes, with which the minds of men are now most occupied, have been matured, or at least broached, in the free and daring discussions of these assemblies. Men have become aware through the emancipation, and kindred events, of the presence of powers, which, in their days of darkness, they had overlooked. Virtuous men will not again rely on political agents. They have found out the deleterious effect of political association. Up to this day, we have allowed to statesmen a paramount social standing, and we bow low to them as to the great. We cannot extend this deference to them any longer. The secret cannot be kept, that the seats of power are filled by underlings, ignorant, timid, and selfish, to a degree to destroy all claim, excepting that on compassion, to the society of the just and

26

generous. What happened notoriously to an American ambassador in England, that he found himself compelled to palter, and to disguise the fact that he was a slave-breeder, happens to men of state.[42] Their vocation is a presumption against them, among well-meaning people. The superstition respecting power and office, is going to the ground. The stream of human affairs flows its own way, and is very little affected by the activity of legislators. What great masses of men wish done, will be done; and they do not wish it for a freak, but because it is their state and natural end. There are now other energies than force, other than political, which no man in future can allow himself to disregard. There is direct conversation and influence. A man is to make himself felt, by his proper force. The tendency of things runs steadily to this point, namely, to put every man on his merits, and to give him so much power as he naturally exerts—no more, no less. Of course, the timid and base persons, all who are conscious of no worth in themselves, and who owe all their place to the opportunities which the old order of things allowed them to deceive and defraud men, shudder at the change, and would fain silence every honest voice, and lock up every house where liberty and innovation can be pleaded for. They would raise mobs, for fear is very cruel. But the strong and healthy yeomen and husbands of the land, the self-sustaining class of inventive and industrious men, fear no competition or superiority. Come what will, their faculty cannot be spared.

27   The First of August marks the entrance of a new element into modern politics, namely, the civilization of the negro. A man is added to the human family. Not the least affecting part of this history of abolition, is, the annihilation of the old indecent nonsense about the nature of the negro. In the case of the ship Zong, in 1781, whose master had thrown one hundred and thirty-two slaves alive into the sea, to cheat the underwriters, the first jury gave a verdict in favor of the master and owners: they had a right to do what they had done. Lord Mansfield is reported to have said on the bench, "The matter left to the jury is,—Was it from necessity? For they had no doubt,—though it shocks one very much,—that the case of slaves was the same as if horses had been thrown overboard. It is a very shocking case."[43] But a more enlightened and humane opinion began to prevail. Mr. Clarkson, early in his career, made a collection of African productions and manufactures, as specimens of the arts and culture of the negro; comprising cloths and loom, weapons, polished stones and woods, leather, glass, dyes, ornaments, soap, pipe-bowls, and trin-

kets.[44] These he showed to Mr. Pitt, who saw and handled them with extreme interest. "On sight of these," says Clarkson, "many sublime thoughts seemed to rush at once into his mind, some of which he expressed;" and hence appeared to arise a project which was always dear to him, of the civilization of Africa,—a dream which forever elevates his fame. In 1791, Mr. Wilberforce announced to the House of Commons, "We have already gained one victory: we have obtained for these poor creatures the recognition of their human nature, which, for a time, was most shamefully denied them."[45] It was the sarcasm of Montesquieu, "it would not do to suppose that negroes were men, lest it should turn out that whites were not;" for, the white has, for ages, done what he could to keep the negro in that hoggish state.[46] His laws have been furies. It now appears, that the negro race is, more than any other, susceptible of rapid civilization. The emancipation is observed, in the islands, to have wrought for the negro a benefit as sudden as when a thermometer is brought out of the shade into the sun. It has given him eyes and ears. If, before, he was taxed with such stupidity, or such defective vision, that he could not set a table square to the walls of an apartment, he is now the principal, if not the only mechanic, in the West Indies; and is, besides, an architect, a physician, a lawyer, a magistrate, an editor, and a valued and increasing political power. The recent testimonies of Sturge, of Thome and Kimball, of Gurney, of Phillippo, are very explicit on this point, the capacity and the success of the colored and the black population in employments of skill, of profit, and of trust; and, best of all, is the testimony to their moderation.[47] They receive hints and advances from the whites, that they will be gladly received as subscribers to the Exchange, as members of this or that committee of trust. They hold back, and say to each other, that "social position is not to be gained by pushing."[48]

I have said that this event interests us because it came mainly from the concession of the whites; I add, that in part it is the earning of the blacks. They won the pity and respect which they have received, by their powers and native endowments. I think this a circumstance of the highest import. Their whole future is in it. Our planet, before the age of written history, had its races of savages, like the generations of sour paste, or the animalcules that wriggle and bite in a drop of putrid water. Who cares for these or for their wars? We do not wish a world of bugs or of birds; neither afterward of Scythians, Caraibs, or Feejees.[49] The grand style of nature, her great periods, is all

28

we observe in them. Who cares for oppressing whites, or oppressed blacks, twenty centuries ago, more than for bad dreams? Eaters and food are in the harmony of nature; and there too is the germ forever protected, unfolding gigantic leaf after leaf, a newer flower, a richer fruit, in every period, yet its next product is never to be guessed. It will only save what is worth saving; and it saves not by compassion, but by power. It appoints no police to guard the lion, but his teeth and claws; no fort or city for the bird, but his wings; no res-cue for flies and mites, but their spawning numbers, which no ravages can overcome. It deals with men after the same manner. If they are rude and fool-ish, down they must go. When at last in a race, a new principle appears, an idea,—*that* conserves it; ideas only save races. If the black man is feeble, and not important to the existing races, not on a parity with the best race, the black man must serve, and be exterminated. But if the black man carries in his bosom an indispensable element of a new and coming civilization, for the sake of that element, no wrong, nor strength, nor circumstance, can hurt him: he will survive and play his part. So now, the arrival in the world of such men as Toussaint, and the Haytian heroes, or of the leaders of their race in Barbadoes and Jamaica, outweighs in good omen all the English and Ameri-can humanity.[50] The anti-slavery of the whole world, is dust in the balance before this,—is a poor squeamishness and nervousness: the might and the right are here: here is the anti-slave: here is man: and if you have man, black or white is an insignificance. The intellect,—that is miraculous! Who has it, has the talisman: his skin and bones, though they were of the color of night, are transparent, and the everlasting stars shine through, with attractive beams. But a compassion for that which is not and cannot be useful or lovely, is degrading and futile. All the songs, and newspapers, and money-subscriptions, and vituperation of such as do not think with us, will avail nothing against a fact. I say to you, you must save yourself, black or white, man or woman; other help is none. I esteem the occasion of this jubilee to be the proud discovery, that the black race can contend with the white; that, in the great anthem which we call history, a piece of many parts and vast com-pass, after playing a long time a very low and subdued accompaniment, they perceive the time arrived when they can strike in with effect, and take a mas-ter's part in the music. The civility of the world has reached that pitch, that their more moral genius is becoming indispensable, and the quality of this race is to be honored for itself. For this, they have been preserved in sandy deserts, in rice-swamps, in kitchens and shoe-shops, so long: now let them emerge, clothed and in their own form.

There remains the very elevated consideration which the subject opens, but which belongs to more abstract views than we are now taking, this namely, that the civility of no race can be perfect whilst another race is degraded. It is a doctrine alike of the oldest, and of the newest philosophy, that, man is one, and that you cannot injure any member, without a sympathetic injury to all the members. America is not civil, whilst Africa is barbarous. 29

These considerations seem to leave no choice for the action of the intellect and the conscience of the country. There have been moments in this, as well as in every piece of moral history, when there seemed room for the infusions of a skeptical philosophy; when it seemed doubtful, whether brute force would not triumph in the eternal struggle. I doubt not, that sometimes a despairing negro, when jumping over the ship's sides to escape from the white devils who surrounded him, has believed there was no vindication of right; it is horrible to think of, but it seemed so. I doubt not, that sometimes the negro's friend, in the face of scornful and brutal hundreds of traders and drivers, has felt his heart sink. Especially, it seems to me, some degree of despondency is pardonable, when he observes the men of conscience and of intellect, his own natural allies and champions,—those whose attention should be nailed to the grand objects of this cause, so hotly offended by whatever incidental petulances or infirmities of indiscreet defenders of the negro, as to permit themselves to be ranged with the enemies of the human race; and names which should be the alarums of liberty and the watchwords of truth, are mixed up with all the rotten rabble of selfishness and tyranny.[51] I assure myself that this coldness and blindness will pass away. A single noble wind of sentiment will scatter them forever. I am sure that the good and wise elders, the ardent and generous youth will not permit what is incidental and exceptional to withdraw their devotion from the essential and permanent characters of the question. There have been moments, I said, when men might be forgiven, who doubted. Those moments are past. Seen in masses, it cannot be disputed, there is progress in human society. There is a blessed necessity by which the interest of men is always driving them to the right; and, again, making all crime mean and ugly. The genius of the Saxon race, friendly to liberty; the enterprise, the very muscular vigor of this nation, are inconsistent with slavery. The Intellect, with blazing eye, looking through history 30 from the beginning onward, gazes on this blot, and it disappears. The senti-ment of Right, once very low and indistinct, but ever more articulate, be-cause it is the voice of the universe, pronounces Freedom. The Power that built this fabric of things affirms it in the heart; and in the history of the First of August, has made a sign to the ages, of his will.

Notes

1. The British Emancipation Act of 1833 abolished slavery in most of the British Em-pire as of 1 August 1834. This tenth anniversary commemoration was organized by the Concord Female Anti-Slavery Society. Emerson was "orator of the day"; other speakers included Frederick Douglass (1818–1895), African American former slave, gifted orator, and a leader in the abolitionist movement.

2. Emerson's source is Arnold H. L. Heeren, *Historical Researches into the Politics, In-tercourse, and Trade of the Carthaginians, Ethiopians, and Egyptians,* 2 vols. (Oxford, 1832), 2:283; 1:223. Herodotus, fifth-century BCE Greek historian who traveled over most of the known world of his time; "Troglodytes" was the Greeks' name for various primitive tribes.

3. "African shadow-catchers and Obeahs" is an allusion to practitioners of sorcery and witchcraft.

4. Emerson's source is James M. Phillippo, *Jamaica: Its Past and Present State* (London, 1843), p. 189, where the story is told in dialect. Phillippo (1798–1879) is described as "twenty years a Baptist missionary in that island."

5. "hot rum poured on, . . . heat of the sun": Emerson's source is Charles Stuart, *A Memoir of Granville Sharp* (New York, 1836), p. 14. Sharp (1735–1813), an English phi-lanthropist, helped organize and chaired an antislavery committee in London in 1787.

6. William Murray Mansfield, 1st Earl of Mansfield (1705–1793), chief justice of Eng-land (1756–1788).

7. Charles Talbot (1685–1737) and Philip Yorke (1690–1764), English jurists, had ruled in 1729 that a slave did not become free by residence in England or by baptism, and that an owner could compel a slave to return to the West Indies.

8. Emerson's source for the lengthy discussion of the case of James (not George) Somerset in 1772 is Stuart, *Memoir of Granville Sharp,* pp. 11–17.

9. Paraphrased from Stuart, *Memoir of Granville Sharp,* p. 19.

10. Emerson's source is *History of the Rise, Progress, and Accomplishment of the Abolition of the African Slave Trade by the British Parliament,* 2 vols. (London, 1808), 1:124, by Thomas Clarkson (1760–1846), an English abolitionist.

11. John Woolman (1720–1772), prominent Quaker abolitionist.

12. William Wilberforce (1759–1833), British reformer and leader of the evangelical Christian antislavery group known as the Clapham Sect.

13. Emerson's source is Clarkson, *History . . . of the Abolition*, 1:249.

14. William Pitt the Younger (1759–1806), prime minister (1783–1801 and 1804–1806); Charles James Fox (1749–1806), British politician.

15. Edmund Burke (1729–1797), Irish politician and natural philosopher.

16. The objective of the American Colonization Society, founded in 1817, was to transport manumitted slaves to Africa.

17. William Carey (1761–1834) and William Ward (1769–1823) were Baptist missionaries. Among the Protestant religious groups mentioned here, the Moravian church developed from followers of Jan Hus (ca. 1370–1415) in Bohemia and Moravia; Wesleyans were named for John Wesley, a founder of Methodism.

18. Edward George Geoffrey Smith Stanley (1799–1869), 14th Earl of Derby and three-time prime minister of England.

19. A "prædial" was a slave attached to an estate.

20. Henry Peter Brougham, 1st Baron Brougham and Vaux (1778–1868), Whig parliamentary leader and a founder of the *Edinburgh Review* (1802).

21. Americans James A. Thome (1813–1873) and J. Horace Kimball (1813–1838) published *Emancipation in the West Indies* (1838), which Emerson quotes from in the next paragraph and cites in paragraph 27 below. The eminent Unitarian minister William Ellery Channing included their account of "watch-night" in Antigua, which precedes the passage that Emerson quotes, in his address on the anniversary of West Indian Emancipation in 1842; see *Works of William E. Channing, D. D.* (Boston, 1880), p. 914.

22. "Emancipation in the West Indies: a Six Months Tour in Antigua, Barbadoes, and Jamaica, in the year 1837. By J. A. Thome and J. H. Kimball. New York, 1838."— pp. 146, 147. (Emerson's note.)

23. George Hamilton-Gordon, 4th Earl of Aberdeen (1784–1860), foreign secretary and a future prime minister; Sir George Grey (1799–1882), colonial administrator and undersecretary for the colonies.

24. Somerset Lowry-Corry, 2nd Earl Belmore (1774–1841), governor of Jamaica (1828–1832); Howe Peter Browne, 2nd Marquess of Sligo (1788–1845), governor of Jamaica (1834–1836); Sir Lionel Smith (1778–1842), governor of Barbados (1833–1836) and of Jamaica (1836–1839).

25. Stipendiary magistrates, paid magistrates under British law, heard cases involving lesser criminal offenses in magistrates' courts.

26. Thomas Fowell Buxton, 1st Baronet (1786–1845), philanthropist and advocate for prison reform and antislavery champion.

27. Emerson's source is a report in *The Annual Register, or a View of the History and Politics of the Year 1838* (London, 1839), p. 348.

28. Charles T. Metcalfe, Baron Metcalfe (1785–1846), governor of Jamaica (1839–1842), whose address and the parliamentary reply that follow were reported in *The Annual Register . . . of the Year 1840* (London, 1841), pp. 239–240.

29. The ruling military class of Sparta descended from the ancient Greek people known as Dorians.

30. An ironic allusion to a speech by Iago in Shakespeare, *Othello,* III, iii, 156.

31. This report, instigated by William Wilberforce as part of a parliamentary investigation, led to his introduction of resolutions condemning the slave trade. "London Committee" refers to the Committee for the Abolition of the Slave Trade, founded by Thomas Clarkson, Granville Sharp, and others in May 1787; its members included the Quaker abolitionists named in paragraph 7 above. The British parliament voted in 1807 to abolish the slave trade.

32. A South Carolina law of 1822, allowing detention of black sailors, was the first of several Negro Seamen's Acts passed by coastal Southern states. See the note in this paragraph below on Samuel Hoar's 1844 mission to Charleston on behalf of Massachusetts black sailors.

33. With "he bears the sword in vain," cf. Romans 13:4.

34. Behind this statement lay events of December 1844, after Samuel Hoar (1778–1856) of Concord was appointed commissioner of Massachusetts to South Carolina to intervene legally in the detention of African American seamen. Reaction in Charleston was so hostile that Hoar and his daughter Elizabeth were forced to leave the city; for Emerson's comments on the event, see *JMN,* 9:161, and "Samuel Hoar" and "Character of Samuel Hoar" (*CW,* 10:376–380, 381–384).

35. At the time Emerson spoke, the United States senators from Massachusetts were Isaac C. Bates (1799–1845) and Rufus Choate (1799–1859); his statement obviously was not intended to include Representative John Quincy Adams, to whom he pays tribute below.

36. John Quincy Adams (1767–1848), former president of the United States, used parliamentary skill during his terms in the House of Representatives (1831–1848) to evade a "gag rule" against antislavery petitions.

37. Robert Henley, 1st Earl of Northington (1708–1772), Lord High Chancellor of Great Britain (1761–1766), made this statement in a slave case of 1762, *Shanley v. Harvey.*

38. A reference to the case of James Somerset, discussed above in paragraphs 5–6; see Stuart, *Memoir of Granville Sharp,* p. 15. The quoted counsel was Sir James Mansfield (1733–1821), speaking in the persona of his client.

39. The quotations appear in Stuart, *Memoir of Granville Sharp,* pp. 86, 87, 57, respectively.

40. Not previously identified are British politicians George Grenville (1712–1770); Charles Grey, 2nd Earl Grey (1764–1845); and George Canning (1770–1827). Thomas

Jefferson (1743–1786), third president of the United States (1801–1809) and founder of the University of Virginia.

41. Clarkson, *History . . . of the Abolition,* 1:495–496; Huddlestone is not further identified.

42. Emerson refers to the Virginian Andrew Stevenson (1784–1857), United States minister to Great Britain (1836–1841). Stevenson's public denial that any "slave-breeders" existed in his home state drew ridicule from American antislavery advocates.

43. Captain Luke Collingwood of the slave ship *Zong* cast 133 sick slaves into the sea; all but one died. The insurance arrangement provided that if the slaves had died natural deaths the loss would fall on the owners and captain, but if they had been thrown alive into the sea on any pretext involving safety of the ship, the underwriters would pay (*EAW,* p. 209). The trial and reaction to Lord Mansfield's statement are recounted in Stuart, *Memoir of Granville Sharp,* pp. 29–32.

44. Emerson's source is Clarkson, *History . . . of the Abolition,* 1:474.

45. Clarkson, *History . . . of the Abolition,* 2:204.

46. Translated, with alterations, from Charles-Louis de Secondat, baron de La Brède et de Montesquieu, *L'Esprit des Lois, Oeuvres,* 8 vols. (Paris, 1819), 2:54. Montesquieu (1689–1755), French political philosopher, is best known for the 1748 work quoted here.

47. Joseph Sturge (1793–1859), English Quaker abolitionist, campaigned against indentured apprenticeships that replaced slavery; Joseph John Gurney (1788–1847), English Quaker minister.

48. This phrase, apparently proverbial, appears in Pauline E. Hopkins's *Contending Forces: A Romance Illustrative of Negro Life North and South* (1900; repr., New York, 1988), p. 264.

49. Emerson's examples of savage races include Scythians, a nomadic Iranian people described by Herodotus; Caraibs, or Caribs, an Amerindian people for whom the Caribbean Sea is named; and Feejees, an older spelling for residents of the Fiji archipelago in the South Pacific.

50. François-Dominique Toussaint L'Ouverture (ca. 1743–1803) led the Haitian independence movement that resulted in emancipation of slaves in all French territories (1794). Although included in the emancipation of 1834, Barbados and Jamaica remained under British colonial rule into the twentieth century.

51. Emerson is referring to the tendency of liberal and moderate politicians to cite the supposed extremism of abolitionists as a justification for their own inaction on the slavery issue; see his comments on Massachusetts politicians in paragraph 23 above.

England

The traveller on arriving in England is struck at once with the cultivation. On every side, he sees the triumph of labor. Man has subdued and made everything. The country is a garden. Under that ash-coloured sky, the fields are so combed and rolled, that it seems as if they had been finished with a pencil instead of a plough.[1] The structures that compose the towns, have been piled by the wealth and skill of ages. Nothing is left as it was made. Rivers, hills, valleys, the sea all feel the hand of a master. The long habitation of a powerful and ingenious race has turned every rood of land to its best use, has found all the capabilities, all the short cuts, all the arable soil, all the quarriable rock, all the navigable waters; and the new arts of intercourse meet you everywhere, so that England itself is a huge mill, or hotel, or palais-royale, where all that man wants is provided within the precinct. Cushioned and comforted in every manner, the traveller rides everywhere, as on a cannon-ball, high and low, over rivers and towns, and through mountains, in tunnels of three miles and more, at twice the speed, and with half the shaking, of our trains, and reads quietly the *Times* newspaper, which, again, by its wonderful system of correspondence and reporting, seems to have machinized the world for his occasion.

If one remembers here Mr. Landor's exclamation, "Who would live in a   2
new country, that can live in an old?",—especially, he recalls, in the old cities,
where the question would find a more unanimous affirmative,—no familiarity or long residence can exhaust the advantages of London, because the past
as well as the present are always filling the basket faster than any diligence
can empty it. Every age since Julius Caesar has left some trace of itself in the
building of old King Lud's town, and a certain civility and conservative instinct has kept all in repair.[2] The railway excavations, within this very year,
have laid bare a Roman pavement. Fragments of the London wall of that age
are still to be found near Ludgate Hill; and so down: Saxon arches, Norman
windows, mediæval towers; Westminster Abbey; palaces of Inigo Jones; St.
Paul's Cathedral and fifty-four churches of Christopher Wren;[3] old colleges,
immemorial hospitals, immense accommodations which modern commerce
has provided for itself, and all the facilities which the wealth of all the mon-
archs of Europe could not buy, but which are yielded for his small subscription of a few pence or shillings to the private citizen of an old town; facilities
that belong to the living on the spot where the great agencies centre and
where the ruling men in every kind are found; whence all ships, expresses,
roads, and telegraphs radiate for all parts of the world, and where every service you require is rendered by the first masters in that kind. Rothschild or
the Barings are your bankers;[4] Stephenson and Brunel your engineers;[5] Pugin
and Barry build;[6] Chadwick makes the aqueduct, Wheatstone the telegraph,
Reid ventilates;[7] the military arrangements (and, in April last, they were serious,) are made by the Duke of Wellington; the mighty debate in Parliament by Peel, Russell, Cobden, Brougham, and Stanley;[8] Faraday, and Richard Owen, Sedgwick, and Buckland, are the lecturers in science;[9] Herschel,
Airy, and Adams, in the observatory;[10] the great heirs of fame are living and
talking in society: Turner and Landseer paint;[11] Wordsworth, Landor, Hallam, Tennyson, Dickens, write;[12] and for your entertainment, Rachel plays,
and Macready;[13] Lablache, Grisi, and Jenny Lind sing, Taglioni dances, and
Soyer cooks.[14]

Happy is the man who lives where the best is cheap! Life is here in ex-   3
tremes; the traveller goes from show to show; he can be pampered to the
highest point; he sits in a cloud of pictures; he eats from off porcelain and
plate; his rug is the skin of a lion. Science will quiddle for him: if he will, his
light is polarised, his water distilled, he sleeps with a puff of chloroform on

water-bed, and all his implements, garments, and trinkets are the work of artists, whose names have been familiar to him for years as the best makers.

4 But, more than all, the riches of a cultivated population one cannot exaggerate. Every day you may meet a new man who is the centre of a new circle of thought and practice, which, but for what seems an accident, you should never have heard of, in this mob of gifted and educated men. The inequalities of power have their consolation here,—that they are superficial. Everyone can do something. When I see the power that every human being possesses to make himself valued and beloved by making himself useful and necessary to those with whom he finds himself,—I pity him no longer.

5 Some of the causes of the historical importance of England, I shall enumerate. But I premise with this remark, that the praise of England is not that it has freed itself from the evils under which other countries labor, not that England has found out how to create wealth and power without the creation of poverty and crime,—No, for all have these griefs and England also; but, that England has with this evil produced, in the last five hundred years, a greater number of strong, wise, educated, and humane men,—a greater number of excellent and finished men, than any other nation.

6 England has the best working climate in the world. It is never hot or cold. There is no hour in the year when one cannot work. Here is no winter, but such days as we have in Massachusetts in November. A climate which makes no exhausting demand on human strength, but allows the fullest development of the form.

7 Then, England has all the materials of a working country,—all the materials except wood. The constant rain, a rain with every tide in some parts of the island, keeps its multitude of rivers full and swift. It has abundance of water, of stone, of coal, and iron. It is a working country, and everybody works in England. It is computed, that only three or four percent of the whole population are idle.

8 The only drawback on this advantage that I know is the darkness of its grey sky. The night and day are too nearly of a color. It strains the eyes to read or to write. Add, the smoke of the manufacturing towns, where the *blacks* darken the air, give white sheep precisely the color of black sheep, discolor the human saliva,—and you will know the want of daylight in Leeds and Manchester.

9 In this climate, (which, however, Ireland also enjoys,) the English appear

to possess the advantage of the best blood. Without going into the history,—we may say, the mixture of Britons and Saxons was a good cross. Afterwards, England yielded to the Danes and Northmen in the tenth, and eleventh, and twelfth centuries; and was the receptacle into which all mettle of that strenuous population was poured. It would seem, that, the perpetual supply of the best men in Norway, Sweden, and Denmark to the piratical expeditions of the ninth and tenth centuries, into England, gradually exhausted those countries, like a tree which bears much fruit when young,—and these have been second-rate powers, ever since. Konghelle, the famed town, where the kings of Norway, Sweden, and Denmark, were wont to meet, is now rented to a private English gentleman as a shooting ground.[15]

The English, at the present day, have great vigor of body and endurance. Other countrymen look slight and undersized beside them, and invalids. They are bigger men than the Americans; I suppose, a hundred English, taken at random out of the street, would weigh a fourth more than so many Americans. Yet, I am told, the skeleton is not larger. They are round, ruddy, and handsome; at least, the whole bust is well formed; and there is a tendency to make stout and powerful frames, like castles. This stoutness of shape particularly struck me, on my first landing at Liverpool;—porter, drayman, coachman, guard,—what substantial, respectable, grandfatherly figures, with costume and manners to suit. The American has really arrived at the old mansion-house, and finds himself among his Uncles, Aunts, and Grandmothers. The pictures on the chimney-tiles of his nursery were pictures of these people. Here they are in the identical costumes and air which so took him. 10

There are two styles of dress here which a traveller in the trains will soon take note of, the tortoise style, and the supple or becoming; the former, wherein the man seems to have obtained by time and pains a sort of house of cloth and buckram built up around him and speaks out of his building, suits English manners well enough. 11

It is the fault of their forms that they grow stocky, and the women seem to have that defect to their beauty;—few tall, slender persons of flowing shape, but stunted and thickset figures. But they are a very handsome race and always have been. The bronze monuments of Crusaders lying cross-legged in the Temple Church in London and those in Worcester Cathedral which are nine hundred years old are of the same type as the best youthful heads of men now in England, and please by beauty of the same character, 12

—a certain expression, namely, of good nature, refinement, and valor, and mainly with that uncorrupt youth in the face of manhood, which is daily seen in the streets of London. They have a vigorous health and last well into middle and old age. The old men are as red as roses, and still handsome. A clean skin, and a peach-bloom complexion, is found all over the island.

13   The English head is round, and the animal powers are in perfection. Their veins are full of blood, and the people hearty eaters, attaching great importance to a plentiful and nutricious diet. The cyclops operative of England cannot subsist on food less solid than beef, and his performance is not more amazing to the foreign laborer than his diet is. Good mutton, wheat bread, and malt liquors are universal among the first-class laborers. It is curious that Tacitus found the English beer already in use among the Germans: *"Potui humor ex hordeo aut frumento in quandam simililudi nem vini corruptus."*[16] Lord Chief Justice Fortescue, in Henry VI's time, says, "the inhabitants drink no water unless at certain times on a religious score and by way of penance."[17] The extremes of poverty and of ascetic temperance never reach cold water in England. Wood, the antiquary, in describing the poverty and maceration of Father Lacey, an English Jesuit, does not deny him beer.[18] He says, "His bed was under a thatching, and the way to it up a ladder: His face was coarse, his drink of a penny a gaun or gallon."

14   They have more constitutional energy, physical and moral, than any other people, and this is no whit abated, but in full play at this moment. I find the Englishman to be he of all men who stands firmest in his shoes. They have in themselves what they value in their horses: mettle and bottom. A gentleman on the day of my arrival, in describing the Lord Lieutenant of Ireland, said, "Lord Clarendon has pluck like a cock and will fight till he dies;"[19] and what I heard first, I heard last, and the one thing the English value is pluck. The cabmen have it; the merchants have it; the bishops have it; the women have it; the journals have it; the *Times* newspaper, they say, is the pluckiest thing in England; and little Lord John Russell, the minister, would take the command of the Channel Fleet tomorrow.

15   It requires, men say, a good constitution to travel in Spain. I say as much of England, simply on account of the vigor and brawn of the people. I know nothing but the most serious business that could give me any counter-weight to these Baresarks, though they were only to order eggs and muffins for their breakfast.[20] The Englishman speaks with all his body; his elocution is sto-

machic as the American's is labial. The Englishman is very petulant and precise about his accommodation at inns and on the roads; a quiddle about his toast and his chop, and every species of convenience; and loud and pungent in his expressions of impatience at any neglect. He has that *aplomb* which results only from a good adjustment of the moral and physical nature, and the obedience of all the powers to the will. The axes of his eyes are united to his backbone, and only move with the trunk.

When I landed, the times were disastrous, and the commercial and political sky full of gloom.[21] But it was evident, that, let who will fail, England will not. It is plain, from the security of their manners, that these people have sat here a thousand years, and here will continue to sit. They will not break up, or arrive at any strange, desperate revolution like their neighbors, for they have as much energy and as much continence of character as they ever had. The immense power and possession which surround them is their own creation, and they exert the same commanding industry at this moment. 16

In America, we fancy that we live in a new and forming country, but that England was finished long ago. But we find London and England in full growth. The towns are growing, some of them almost at the rate of American towns. Birkenhead, opposite Liverpool, was growing as fast as South Boston. The towns in Lancashire will by and by meet, and make a city, as big as, and bigger than, London. London itself is enlarging at a frightful rate, even to the filling up of Middlesex, and the decoration and repairs in every part of the old city go on day by day. Trafalgar Square was only new finished in April 1848. The British Museum is in full course of growth and activity and projected arrangement; the Vernon Gallery is just added to the National. The London University opens like our mushroom colleges at the West, and the Houses of Parliament are just sending up their proud Victoria tower, four hundred feet into the air. Everything in England bespeaks an immense and energetic population. The buildings are on a scale of size and wealth far beyond ours. The colossal masonry of the docks and of all public buildings attests the multitudes who are to be accommodated by them and who are to pay for them. England could not now build her old castles and abbeys, but what the nineteenth century wants,—club houses, vaults, docks, mills, canals, railways,—she builds fast and well. 17

A manly ability, a general sufficiency, is the genius of the English. The land and climate are favorable to the breeding of good men; and it was an 18 odd proof of it, that, in my lectures, I hesitated to read many a disparaging phrase which I have been accustomed to throw into my writing, about poor, thin, unable, unsatisfying bipeds,—so much had the fine physique and the personal vigor of this robust race worked on my imagination. This abundant life and vigor betrays itself, at all points, in their manners, in the respiration, and the inarticulate noises they make in clearing the throat, all significant of burly strength. They have stamina; they can take the initiative on all emergences. And the one rule for the traveller in England, is,—This is no country for fainthearted people. Do not creep about diffidently. Make up your mind, take your course, and you shall find respect and furtherance.

19   This vigour appears in the manners of the people in the complete incuriosity and stony neglect of each to every other. Each man walks, eats, drinks, shaves, dresses, gesticulates, and, in every manner, is, acts, suffers, without reference to the bystanders, and in his own fashion, only careful not to interfere with them, or annoy them. It is not that he is trained to neglect the eyes of his neighbors; he is really occupied with his own affair, and does not think of them. In the first-class carriage, a clergyman takes his stout shoes out of his carpet bag, and puts them on, instead of thin ones, on approaching the station. Every man in this polished country consults only his convenience, as much as a solitary pioneer in Wisconsin. I know not where any personal eccentricity is so freely allowed, and no man gives himself any concern with it. An Englishman walks in a pouring rain swinging his closed umbrella, like a walking stick; wears a wig, or a shawl, or a saddle; or stands on his head; and no remark is made. And, as he has been doing this for several generations, it is now in the blood.

20   In short, every one of these islanders is an island himself,—safe, tranquil, incommunicable. In a company of strangers, you would think him deaf; his eyes never wander from his own table and newspaper; he is never betrayed into any curiosity or unbecoming emotion. They seem all to have been trained in one severe school of manners, and never to put off this iron harness. He does not give his hand. He does not let you meet his eye. It is almost an affront to look a man in the face, before being introduced. In mixed, or in select companies, they do not introduce persons, so that a presentation is a circumstance as valid as a contract. Introductions are sacraments. He withholds his name. At the hotel, if they ask his name at the book office, he stoops, and gives it in a low voice. If he give you his private address on a card,

it is like an avowal of friendship; and his bearing, on being introduced, is studiously cold, even though he is seeking your acquaintance, and is studying how he shall serve you.

'Tis no wonder that this rigor astonishes their lively neighbors across the Channel, so strongly contrasted with the social genius of the French, and is the standing theme of French raillery. "The islanders of Albion," says a brilliant French writer, 21

> "carry with them a peculiar fluid, which I shall call the *Britannic fluid*, and, in the midst of which, they travel, as little accessible to the atmosphere of the regions which they traverse, as the mouse at the centre of the exhausted receiver. It is not only to the thousand precautions with which they go surrounded that they owe their eternal impassivity; it is not because they wear three pair of breeches one over the other that they arrive perfectly dry and clean in spite of rain and mud; it is not because they have woolen wigs that their stiff and wiry frisure defies moisture; it is not because they go loaded each with as much pommade, brushes, and soap as would serve to adonize a whole regiment of Bas Breton conscripts that they have always the beard smooth and the nails irreproachable. It is because the external air does not touch them; it is because they walk, drink, eat, and sleep, *in their fluid*, as in a glass bell of twenty feet diameter, and, across which they behold with pity the cavaliers whose hair the wind discomposes, and the foot passenger whose shoes the snow soils."[22]

'Tis very certain that the Englishman has a confidence in the power and performance of his nation, which makes him provokingly incurious about other nations. It is a very old remark,—some centuries old,—that he dislikes foreigners. Swedenborg, who visited England many times in the last century, remarks: "There is a similitude of minds among them, in consequence of which, they contract a familiarity with friends who are from their nation, and seldom with others. They are lovers of their country, and zealous for its glory, and they regard foreigners as one looking through a telescope from the top of his palace regards those who dwell or wander about out of the city." But in a much older traveller, the *Relation of England* by a Venetian in 1500, three 22 hundred and fifty years ago, I find a similar testimony: "The English are great lovers of themselves, and of everything belonging to them. They think that there are no other men than themselves, and no other world but England; and whenever they see a handsome foreigner, they say that he looks like an Englishman, and it is a great pity he should not be an Englishman: and when they partake of any delicacy with a foreigner, they ask him whether such a thing is made in *his* country."[23]

23   It is very certain that this arrogance is really in the true-born Englishman, and all the goodness of heart and studious courtesy that belong to him fail to conceal it. When he accumulates epithets of praise, his climax of commendation is, *"So English,"* and when he wishes to pay you the highest compliment, he says, "I should not know you from an Englishman."

24   At the same time, I know no national pride that is so easily forgiven and so much respected as his, and for the reason that it is so well-founded. The Englishman is proud,—Yes, but he is admirable; he knows all things, has all things, and can do all things. How can he not be proud? There is a certain general culture wherein he surpasses other nations. There is no man so equally and harmoniously developed, and hence his easy pride when he finds every other countryman inferior to him as a social man. His wide outlook, his birth and breeding in the commercial and political centre of the world, have accustomed his eye and mind to whatever is best in the planet and made him instantly perceptive of any meanness or fault. A certain liberality and catholicism, an air of having seen much and seen the best, appears in all men. They are bored by anything provincial and detect the smutch of native clay sticking to the clothes of a villager. They notice in the American speech a certain purism, the accent of a man who knows how the word is spelled, rather than the unrestrained expression of a man who is only eager to say what he means.

25   Besides, it is quite inevitable that this spoiled child of nature and fortune should have the fastidiousness which the habit generates. He talks of his politics and institutions, but the real thing which he values is his home and that which belongs to it,—that general culture and high polish, which, in his experience, no man but the Englishman possesses, and which, he naturally believes, have some essential connexion with his throne and laws.

26   In all culture, so much depends on sympathy, on a great number who keep each other up to a high point, that, 'tis a pleasure to the traveller in Eng-

land to know that there is all around him an infinite number of educated and thoughtful people, all quietly and calmly carrying forward every variety of profound and elegant study, with the best aids and materials, though rarely communicating, and, for the most part, each wholly independent and unacquainted with the rest.

And here comes in an element of decisive importance, the existence of a superior or model class, legalised by statute and usage, fostered and privileged from the beginning of the national history, with all the institutions of the country to secure them in their hereditary wealth, owners of all the soil, with the best education to develop and stamp these advantages, and placed in every manner on such high ground, that, whatever benefit the nation reaps with its million arms outstretched from pole to pole,—they more. The finest race of men in the friendliest climate, possessing every natural and accidental advantage and secured in the possession of these by the loyal affection of the people, they easily came to produce sound minds in sound bodies and exhibit more finished men than any other nation.

The favoured class seem to gain as much as they lose by their position. They survey all society as from the top of St. Paul's, and, if they never hear plain truth from men, as the poor do, they see the best of everything in every kind, and they see things so grouped and amassed, as to infer easily the sum and genius, instead of tedious particularities. Their good behaviour deserves all its fame; and they have, in the highest degree, that simplicity and that air of repose which are such chief ornaments of greatness.

It was inevitable that these people should have a controlling influence on the manners of the people. They naturally furnish the best models of manly behaviour to their country and the world. Moreover, it has come to be the ambition of the English system of education,—of their schools and of the universities,—to turn out gentlemen, rather than scholars or skilful masters in any art; and the like feeling runs into the middle and lower classes.

It is not to be disguised, however, that there is much in this English culture, so much prized at home, so much admired abroad, that will not bear analysis,—is by no means the best thing in the English state; is material; is built on wealth, built on trifles, and certainly has another less reputable face and name as the height of cockneyism. For, it rests on land and money, on birth, on diet, on excellence in horsemanship, on hunting, on dogs, on boxing, on boating, and on betting. The self-command and continuity of will are exerted in affairs,—the bribes of speculation, the panics of trade, the game of party, all powerless,—foiled by an insight which commands the law of the game better than any other player,—it is the guarantee of victory.

31   They have carried inoffensiveness to a very high point. They have applied their strong understanding and their love of animal comfort to a perfect organization of the details of a domestic day, studiously excluding everything annoying or discordant, and have become superstitiously neat and proper, and orderly, and respectable. Their hat, and shoes, and linen, their horse and gun, their egg, and toast, and soda water, and wine, and politics, and visiting-set, are irreproachable. It is a world of trifles, and seems to argue a mediocrity of intellect in the nation which allows it so much importance. Whilst we pay homage to the indisputable merits of the English people, we must not confound their immense regard to trifles, with their virtues.

32   Their good form and habit are much indebted to the manly exercises to which they are trained from earliest youth. They begin with cricket, archery, and skittles,—in each of which games they acquire some skill at school and at college. They learn the use of oars at Eton and Westminster schools: at Oxford and Cambridge, the boat clubs are in daily practice; and yachting and regattas are favorite amusements of gentlemen in every part of the island where there is water.

33   Still more universal is their attachment to horses, and to hounds, and to every form of hunting. They are always on horseback, centaurs. Every inn-room is lined with pictures of racers. And expresses bring, every hour, news to London, from Newmarket and Ascot.

34   The universal practice of betting, too, is not without its uses as it makes the knowledge of all men whom you meet singularly accurate in regard to all common facts. Every distance has been measured in miles, rods, and inches. They know the distance of their towns, the length of their boats, the speed of their horses, the numbers of their partisans, and complain of looseness in the information of other countrymen on these points.

35   But what I think is the secret of English success, is, a certain balance of qualities in their nature, corresponding to what we call temper in steel. The geographical position of England is excellent; but there are many countries with good seacoasts besides England,—many countries with good climate, which make no pretension to British influence. But here is the best average brain. Men found that this people had a faculty of doing, which others had

not. There is an incompatibility in the Italians, in the Spaniards, in the Turks, of dealing with other nations,—of treating with them. But the English brain is of the right temper. Neither too cold, nor too hot; neither too swift, nor too slow.—Calm, energetic, tenacious, just, and wise.

The English metal is not brittle, is not soft, not explosive, but tenacious, incorruptible, and admitting a good working edge: That happy adaptedness to things which makes the ordinary Englishman a skilful and thorough workman, and the higher classes good heads for the combining and arranging of labour. The fabulous St. George has never seemed to me the patron saint of England;[24] but the scholar, monk, soldier, engineer, lawgiver, Alfred,—working-king; often defeated, never discouraged; patient of defeat, of affront, of labor, and victorious by fortitude and wisdom,—he is the model Englishman. They have many such in their annals. Cromwell is one. One is William of Wykeham,—Bishop of Winchester in the reign of Edward II, Edward III, and Richard II,[25]—a poor boy of obscure parentage, who by study, and practical talent, and sound judgment, and a certain humble magnanimity, conceived and carried out great plans; built roads and causeys; built Windsor Castle; built the sublime Winchester Cathedral; and, observing the gross ignorance of the priesthood, in his times, and, attributing many public evils to that cause,—established a school at Winchester, and livings for seventy boys, to be there trained for the university, at his expense, forever; and then established at Oxford Winchester or New College, with livings for seventy fellows, at his expense forever. In May (1848) I visited Oxford, and Dr. Williams, the polite head of the College, showed me the halls, chapel, library, and common rooms and gardens,[26]—over every gate of which was written in stone William of Wykeham's motto, "Manners maketh man"—and assured me that now, after five hundred years, the seventy boys at Winchester school and the seventy fellows at Winchester College, are still maintained on the bounty of the founder.

One of the merits of Wykeham was the stern investigation which he instituted into the embezzlement and perversion of the religious and charitable foundations in his time; especially, the account which he demanded of the revenues of the "Hospital of Saint Cross," where, long before him, Henry of Blois, brother of King Stephen, had founded a charity for the support of a hundred poor, and, with a provision, that a measure of beer and a piece of bread should be given forever to every son of man who should ask for it.[27] As

36

37

I passed the Hospital of Saint-Cross, on my way from Stonehenge, in July, I knocked at the door, to see if William-of-Wykeham's word was sterling yet in England, and received my horn of beer and my piece of bread, gratuitously, from the charity of a founder who has been dead seven centuries. I hardly think it less honorable that the man whom the English of this age put forward as the type of their race is a man so proverbial for his veracity, perseverance, and moderation as the Duke of Wellington.

38   I fear, that, in many points, the English tenacity is in strong contrast to American facility. The facile American sheds his Puritanism, when he leaves Cape Cod, runs into all English and French vices, with great zest, and is neither Unitarian, nor Calvinist, nor Catholic, nor Quaker, nor stands for any thought or thing; all which is very distasteful to English honor.

39   I do not think the English quite capable of doing justice to our countrymen. He is annoyed by the free and easy pretension, the careless manners, and the neglect of certain points of decorum and respect, to which he is accustomed to attach importance; and he does not see, that, this is his own self-reliance transferred to a new theatre, where there is no such division of labor as exists in England, and where every man must help himself in every manner, like an Indian, and remember much which the European more gracefully abandons to his valet.

40   But the main advantage which the American possesses, is a certain versatility, and, as far as I know, a greater apprehensiveness of mind. He more readily and genially entertains new thoughts, new modes, new books, is more speculative, more contemplative, and is really related to the future, whilst the Englishman seems mortgaged to the past. Each countryman is qualified for the part assigned him in history to play.

41   In drawing these sketches, I am well aware there is a dark side of England, which, I have not wished to expose. The first effect of the extraordinary determination of the national mind for so many centuries on wealth has been, in developing colossal wealth, to develop hideous pauperism. These fair, ruddy, muscular, well-educated bodies go attended by poor, dwarfed, starved, short-lived skeletons. There are two Englands;—rich, Norman-Saxon, learned, social England,—seated in castles, halls, universities, and middle class houses of admirable completeness and comfort, and poor, Celtic, peasant, drudging, Chartist England, in hovels and workhouses,

cowed and hopeless. I only recognize this fact, in passing. It is important that it be stated. It will not help us now to dwell on it.

England is the country of the rich. The great poor man does not yet appear. Whenever he comes, England will fall like France. It would seem, that an organizing talent applied directly to the social problem,—to bring, for example, labor to market; to bring want and supply face to face; would not be so rare. A man like Hudson, like Trevylian, like Cobden, should know something about it.[28] The Reform Bill took in new partners, and Chartism again takes in more.[29]

They are "strange, neat-handed Titans, and, if wanting fire from heaven, make, at least, the cheapest and most polished patent lamps for receiving it, when it shall come." They have propriety and parliamentariness, propriety felt both in what they do not say, and in what they say. The schools and universities cling to them, and give a certain mechanical integrity to their manners and culture and make it impossible to them to make a mistake. In the educated English, one feels the advantage of thorough drill. Eton, and Harrow, and Rugby have done their work; they know prosody, and tread securely through all the humanities.

But the Englishman is the victim of this excellence. The practical and comfortable oppress him with inexorable claims, and the smallest fraction of power remains for heroism and poetry. My own feeling is, that the English have sacrificed their grandeur to their cleverness. They have vaunted their practicalness, until the brain serves the hand, which ought to serve the brain, and until the nobler traits, which, in former times, distinguished the British nation, are disappearing before the indispensable demand of wealth and convenience.

The English boast the grandeur of their national genius; but seem not to observe that a total revolution has taken place in their estimate of mental greatness. The age of their greatness was an ideal and Platonic age: all the great men of the Elizabethan period had that tendency. Now, the intellect of England plumes itself on its limitary and practical turn. Once there was mysticism in the British mind, a deep vein of religion. Once there was Platonism, a profound poetry, and daring sallies into the realm of thought on every side. Now, there is musty, self-conceited decorum,—life made up of fictions hating ideas: but not a breath of Olympian air dilates the collapsing lungs. *Now,* we

42

43

44

45

have clever mediocrity: the paragraph writers, the fashionable-romance writers, the elegant travellers, and dapper diners-out, with anecdote and bons mots,—made up men with made up manners,—varied and exact information; facts,—(facts the Englishman delights in all day long;)—humour too, and all that goes to animate conversation. "Conversational powers," says Campbell, "are so much the rage in London, that no reputation is higher than his, who exhibits them to advantage."[30]

46   We have plenty of derision and worldliness. The genius of the House of Commons is a sneer. "What delights the House," says Fowell Buxton, "is a mixture of good sense and joking." We have no plain-dealing, no abandonment, but every sentence in good society must have a twist,—something unexpected, something the reverse of the probable, is required. The day's Englishman must have his joke as duly as his bread. Bold is he and absolute in his narrow circle, versed in all his routine, sure and elegant, his stories are good, his sentences firm, and all his statesmen, lawyers, men of letters, and poets, finished and solid as the pavement. But a faith in the laws of the mind like that of Archimedes; belief like that of Euler and Kepler, that experience must follow and not lead the laws of the mind; a devotion to the theory of politics, like that of Hooker, Milton, and Harrington;—the modern English mind repudiates.[31]

47   I am forced to say that aristocracy requires an intellectual and moral basis, and that though all the accidents are very well, they indispensably involve real elevation at last. But, in England, one had to humour the society. "It was very well, *considering*,"—as our country people say. Very fine masters, very fine misses, charming saloons,—but where were the great? The Americans who should succeed in it were the well-bred rich, and not those who make America to me. I am wearied and inconvenienced by what are called fine people. The moment I meet a grand person, a man of sense and comprehension, I am emancipated. Such persons I did not find. One would say there was a plentiful sterility of such. One goes through England making believe that this is good society. It is so old, so much has been spent on it, the case is so costly, it has such a history around it,—effigies of a nation of ancestors,—or it has so neatly stepped into the history and place of the real prince, that one easily lets it pass for true, and, nine times out of ten, does not doubt its legitimacy. But such illusion leads to suicide.—If this is the height of life, let me die.

48   Plutarch tells us, "that Archimedes considered the being busied about

mechanics, and, in short, every art which is connected with the common purposes of life, illiberal and ignoble; and those things alone were objects of his
ambition, with which the beautiful and the excellent were present, unmin-
gled with the necessary." I have to say that the whole fabric is wonderful, but
has cost too much; that the higher faculties have been sacrificed. The English
mind is less contemplative, less religious, less open, than it was in former periods. Books of larger scope, as Wordsworth and Coleridge, must come to
this country for their fame, before they gain it in England.

My own impression is, the English mind has more breadth and cosmo-
politanism, but no ascending scale. He has not the least interest in speculation. No men in England are quite ideal, living in an ideal world, and working
in politics and social life, only from that. Her best writer is an earth-son mixed
up with politics of the day as a partisan. I suffered myself to be dazzled willingly by the various brilliancy of men of talent. But he who values his days by
the number of insights he gets, will as rarely find a good conversation, a solid
dealing, man with man, in England, as in any country.

The English are eminently prosaic or unpoetic. All the poetic persons
whom I saw, were deviations from the national type. The people have wide
range, but no ascending scale in their speculation. An American, like a German, has many platforms of thought. But an Englishman requires to be humored, or treated with tenderness, as an invalid, if you wish him to climb.

Herein England has but obeyed the law, which, in the order of the world,
assigns one office to one people. Nature does one thing at a time. If she will
have a perfect hand, she makes head and feet pay for it. So now that she is
making railroad and telegraph ages, she starves the *spirituel,* to stuff the *mate-
riel* and *industriel.*

But with all the deductions from the picture which truth requires, I find
the English to have a thorough good nature; they are a true, benign, gentle,
benevolent, hospitable, and pious race, fearing God, and loving man. There is
respect for truth, and there is milk of kindness in them; and this in all classes,
from the Chartist to the Duke. In the shops, the articles you buy are thoroughly made, and you learn to rely on the probity of the tradesman. Probity
is the rule. In the large transactions, it is not less. An eminent merchant, by
birth American, whose name is known through the world as partner in one
of the first houses in London, said to me, "I have been here thirty years, and
no man has ever attempted to cheat me."[32] If you stand at the door of the

49

50

51

52

House of Commons, and look at the faces of the members, as they go in, you will say, these are just, kind, and honorable men, who mean to do right. If you go to Englishmen, properly introduced,—which is indispensable in this dense population, with the multitude of strangers, too, from all parts of the earth,—if you go to their houses, I do not think there is in the world such sincerity and thoroughness of hospitality. They see you through. They give you real service: they give you their time: they introduce you cordially to their friends: until you ask yourself,—'if they do thus to every stranger, how many hours will be left to them in the day and the year?'

53   They are as gentle and peaceful, as they are brave and magnanimous. At Oxford, I was told, among twelve hundred young men, comprising the most noble and spirited in the aristocracy, a duel never occurs. In Cambridge, among seventeen hundred, the same is true. And there is a sentiment of justice and honor resident in the people, which is always sure to respond aright, when any private or public wrong has been attempted.

54   I trace the peculiarities of English manners and English fortune, then, to their working climate, their dense population, the presence of an aristocracy or model class for manners and speech, to their diet generous and orderly taken, to their force of constitution, to the tenacity or perseverance of their nature, and to their fine moral quality. And these are some of the reasons why England is England. When to this vivacious stock at home, yielding armies of young men, every year, for her business of commercial conquest, all over the globe, you add the steady policy of planting a clear-headed, generous, and energetic gentleman, at every important point, all along their immense colonial territory, in islands and on the main, in the shape of a military, or diplomatic, or, at least, a commercial agent, you have the secret of British history. These Clives, Hastingses, Brookes, Cannings, Ponsonbys, and Hardinges, carry the eye and heart of the best circles of London into the extremities of the earth, and the homes of almost bestial barbarism.[33]

55   It is common to augur evil of England's future and to forbode her sudden or gradual decline under the load of debt, and pauperism, and the unequal competition with new nations where land is cheap. Certainly, she has enormous burthens to carry and grave difficulties to contend with. And her wisest statesmen incline to call her home from her immense colonial system. But though she may yield to time and change, what a fate is hers! She has planted her banian roots in the ground, they have run under the sea, and the new

shoots have sprung in America, in India, in Australia, and she sees the spread of her language and laws over the most part of the world made certain for as distant a future as the science of man can explore.

Notes

1. This description is drawn from the writings of Count Vittorio Alfieri (1749–1803), Italian dramatist, according to Emerson's note in the manuscript.
2. Julius Caesar invaded Britain in 55 and 54 BCE; Lud, legendary king of England, re-built the walls of London.
3. Inigo Jones (1573–1652), English architect, designed the government buildings at Whitehall in London; Sir Christopher Wren (1632–1723), English architect, pro-posed designs for rebuilding London after the Great Fire of 1666, including for St. Paul's Cathedral.
4. The Baring Brothers and Company (along with the Rothschilds) was a major banking firm of the day.
5. Robert Stephenson (1803–1859), English inventor, constructed the first railway into London, completed in 1859; Sir Marc Isambard Brunel (1769–1849), British engi-neer and inventor born in France, and his son, Isambard Kingdom Brunel (1806–1859), designers of, respectively, the Thames Tunnel and the Great Western Rail-way.
6. Augustus Welby Northmore Pugin (1812–1852), English architect and designer; Sir Charles Barry (1795–1860), English architect, won the competition for the best de-signs for the Houses of Parliament and built them with Pugin.
7. Sir Edwin Chadwick (1800–1890), English reformer, active in the first sanitary commission of 1839; Sir Charles Wheatstone (1802–1875), English physicist and an inventor of the electric telegraph; Sir William Reid (1791–1858), British meteorolo-gist and colonial administrator.
8. Sir Robert Peel (1788–1850), English politician and prime minister; John Russell, 1st Earl Russell of Kingston Russell (1792–1878), English politician and prime minis-ter; Richard Cobden (1804–1865), English politician and advocate for free trade.
9. Richard Owen (1804–1892), English comparative anatomist and paleontologist; Adam Sedgwick (1785–1873), English geologist; William Buckland (1784–1856), English clergyman and geologist.
10. Sir John Frederick William Herschel (1792–1871), English astronomer; Sir George Biddell Airy (1801–1892), English astronomer, directed the Royal Observatory at Greenwich; John Couch Adams (1819–1892), English astronomer, directed the Cambridge Observatory.

11. Joseph Mallard William Turner (1775–1851), English landscape painter known for his experiments with light; Sir Edwin Henry Landseer (1802–1873), English painter, popular for his animal paintings.

12. Henry Hallam (1777–1859), English historian; Charles Dickens (1812–1870), popular English novelist.

13. Mlle. Rachel (1821–1858), stage name of Élisa Félix, French actress; William Charles Macready (1793–1873), English tragedian and theater manager.

14. Luigi Lablache (1794–1858), most famous Italian bass of his generation; Giulia Grisi (1811–1869), Italian opera singer; Jenny Lind (1820–1887), singer known as the Swedish Nightingale; Marie Taglioni (1804–1884), member of a celebrated Italian family of ballet dancers; Alexis Benoît Soyer (1809–1858), English chef.

15. Konghelle, on the Gotha River near Gothenburg, Sweden, was an important trading center when King Sigurd the Crusader (ca. 1090–1130) made it his permanent residence and built a fortress there.

16. Emerson's source is *Germania*, chapter 23, section 1, by Tacitus Cornelius (ca. 55–ca. 117), Roman historian and orator; "simililudi" should be "similitudinem."

17. Sir John Fortescue (ca. 1394–ca. 1476), English jurist, named chief justice of the king's bench in 1442; Henry VI (1421–1471), king of England (1422–1461, 1470–1471).

18. Anthony à Wood (1632–1695), English antiquary and historian, best known for his *Athenæ Oxoniensis* (1691–1692); William Lacey (1584–1673), English Jesuit (*CW*, 5:222n).

19. George William Frederick Villiers, 4th Earl of Clarendon (1800–1870), English statesmen, lord lieutenant of Ireland (1847–1852).

20. For "Baresarks," from berserkers, see "The American Scholar," para 15, above.

21. Emerson had arrived in England in October 1847 during a period of revolutionary fervor on the Continent; the overthrow of the monarchy in Paris occurred the next year.

22. Attributed to George Sand, pen name of Amandine-Aurore-Lucile Dudevant (1804–1876), in Emerson's note in the manuscript.

23. Emerson's source is *A Relation, or Rather a True Account, of the Island of England . . . about the Year 1500*, trans. by Charlotte Augusta Sneyd (London, 1847), p. 21 (*JMN*, 10:198).

24. St. George (d. 303), usually depicted slaying a dragon, became the patron saint of England in the fourteenth century.

25. William of Wykeham (1324–1404), English prelate and politician, bishop of Winchester from 1367 to his death; Edward II of Caernarvon (1284–1327), king of England (1307–1327); Edward III of Windsor (1312–1377), king of England (1327–1377); Richard II (1367–1400), king of England (1377–1400).

26. David Williams (1786–1860), warder of New College, showed Emerson the grounds of Oxford when he visited there.

27. Henry of Blois (ca. 1099–1171), English prelate, succeeded in having his brother, Stephen (ca. 1097–1154), named king of England in 1135.

28. In light of the context in which they are named, Emerson is likely referring to George Hudson (1800–1871), English railway financier; "Trevylian" is probably Sir Walter Calverley Trevelyan (1797–1879), English naturalist whom Emerson described as "a baronet noted for his income of £40,000" after meeting him in Edinburgh (*L*, 4:21); and Richard Cobden (*JMN*, 10:295n).

29. The Reform Bill of 1832.

30. Attributed to Thomas Campbell (1777–1844), Scottish-born British poet and critic, by Emerson (*JMN*, 11:305).

31. Richard Hooker (ca. 1553–1600), English theologian; James Harrington (1611–1697), English political theorist.

32. Attributed to Joshua Bates (1788–1864), a partner in the Baring Brothers banking firm, by Emerson (*JMN*, 10:331).

33. Each of these individuals was involved in the colonization of India: Robert Clive (1725–1774), British soldier; Warren Hastings (1732–1818), English colonial administrator; Sir James Brooke (1803–1868), English soldier born in India; George Canning; and Sir Henry Hardinge (1785–1856), governor general of India (1844–1848). The line of Ponsonbys, an English family in Ireland, included John (1713–1789), speaker of the Irish House of Commons for fifteen years; his son George (1755–1817), lord chancellor of Ireland; and his son Sir Frederick Cavendish (1783–1837), a soldier and a governor of Malta.

Uses of Great Men

1   It is natural to believe in great men. If the companions of our childhood should turn out to be heroes, and their condition regal, it would not surprise us. All mythology opens with demigods, and the circumstance is high and poetic, that is, their genius is paramount. In the legends of the Gautama, the first men ate the earth, and found it deliciously sweet.[1]

2   Nature seems to exist for the excellent. The world is upheld by the veracity of good men.[2] They make the earth wholesome. They who lived with them, found life glad and nutricious. Life is sweet and tolerable only in our belief in such society; and actually, or ideally, we manage to live with superiors. We call our children and our lands by their names, their names are wrought into the verbs of language, their works and effigies are in our houses, and every circumstance of the day recalls an anecdote of them.

3   The search after the great is the dream of youth, and the most serious occupation of manhood. We travel into foreign parts to find his works—if possible, to get a glimpse of him. But we are put off with fortune instead. You say, the English are practical, the Germans are hospitable, in Valencia, the climate is delicious; and in the hills of the Sacramento, there is gold for the gathering.[3] Yes, but I do not travel to find comfortable, rich, and hospitable

people, or clear sky, or ingots that cost too much. But if there were any magnet that would point to the countries and houses where are the persons who
are intrinsically rich and powerful,—I would sell all, and buy it, and put myself on the road today.

The race goes with us on their credit. The knowledge that in the city is a   4
man who invented the railroad, raises the credit of all the citizens. But enormous populations, if they be beggars, are disgusting, like moving cheese, like
hills of ants, or of fleas,—the more, the worse.

Our religion is the love and cherishing of these patrons. The gods of fable   5
are the shining moments of great men. We run all our vessels into one
mould. Our colossal theologies of Judaism, Christism, Buddhism, Mahome-
tism are the necessary and structural action of the human mind. The student
of history is like a man going into a warehouse to buy cloths or carpets: he
fancies he has a new article. If he go to the factory, he shall find that his new
stuff still repeats the scrolls and rosettes which are found on the interior walls
of the pyramids of Thebes. Our theism is the purification of the human
mind. Man can paint or make or think nothing but man. He believes that the
great material elements had their origin from his thought. And our philosophy finds one essence collected or distributed.

If now we proceed to enquire into the kinds of service we derive from   6
others, let us be warned of the danger of modern studies and begin low
enough. We must not contend against love, or deny the substantial existence of other people. I know not what would happen to us. We have social
strengths. Our affection toward others creates a sort of vantage or purchase
which nothing will supply. I can do that by another which I cannot do alone. I
can say to you what I cannot first say to myself. Other men are lenses through
which we read our own minds. Each man seeks those of different quality
from his own, and such as are good of their kind; that is, he seeks other men,
and *the otherest.* The stronger the nature, the more it is reactive. Let us have
the quality pure. A little genius let us leave alone. A main difference betwixt
men, is, whether they attend their own affair or not. Man is that noble endogenous plant, which grows, like the palm, from within outward. His own affair, though impossible to others, he can open with celerity and in sport. It is
easy to sugar to be sweet, and to nitre to be salt. We take a great deal of pains
to waylay and entrap that which of itself will fall into our hand. I count him a

great man who inhabits a higher sphere of thought, into which other men rise with labor and difficulty: he has but to open his eyes to see things in a true light and in large relations; whilst they must make painful corrections, and keep a vigilant eye on many sources of error. His service to us is of like sort. It costs a beautiful person no exertion to paint her image on our eyes: Yet how splendid is that benefit! It costs no more for a wise soul to convey his quality to other men. And every one can do his best thing easiest. *"Peu de moyens, beaucoup d'effet."*[4] He is great who is what he is from nature, and who never reminds us of others.

7   But he must be related to us, and our life receive from him some promise of explanation. I cannot tell what I would know, but I have observed that there are persons who in their characters and actions answer questions which I have not skill to put. One man answers some question which none of his contemporaries put, and is isolated. The past and passing religions and philosophies answer some other question. Certain men affect us as rich possibilities, but helpless to themselves and to their times,—the sport perhaps of some instinct that rules in the air; they do not speak to our want. But the great are near; we know them at sight. They satisfy expectation, and fall into place. What is good is effective, generative; makes for itself room, food, and allies. A sound apple produces seed,—a hybrid does not. Is a man in his place, he is constructive, fertile, magnetic, inundating armies with his purpose, which is thus executed. The river makes its own shores, and each legitimate idea makes its own channels and welcome; harvests for food, institutions for expression, weapons to fight with, and disciples to explain it. The true artist has the planet for his pedestal: the adventurer after years of strife has nothing broader than his own shoes.

8   Our common discourse respects two kinds of use or service from superior men. Direct giving is agreeable to the early belief of men; direct giving of material or metaphysical aid, as of health, eternal youth, fine senses, arts of healing, magical power and prophecy. The boy believes there is a teacher who can sell him wisdom. Churches believe in imputed merit. But, in strictness, we are not much cognisant of direct serving. Man is endogenous, and education is his unfolding. The aid we have from others is mechanical, compared with the discoveries of nature in us. What is thus learned is delightful in the doing, and the effect remains. Right ethics are central, and go from the soul outward. Gift is contrary to the law of the universe. Serving others is

serving us. I must absolve me to myself. 'Mind thy affair,' says the Spirit:—
'Coxcomb! would you meddle with the skies, or with other people?'—Indirect service is left. Men have a pictorial or representative quality, and serve us in the intellect. Behmen and Swedenborg saw that things were representative. Men are also representative; first, of things, and, secondly, of ideas.

As plants convert the minerals into food for animals, so each man converts some raw material in nature to human use. The inventors of fire, electricity, magnetism, iron, lead, glass, linen, silk, cotton; the makers of tools; the inventor of decimal notation, the geometer, the engineer, the musician, severally make an easy way for all through unknown and impossible confusions. Each man is, by secret liking, connected with some district of nature whose agent and interpreter he is, as Linnæus, of plants; Huber, of bees; Fries of lichens; Van Mons of pears; Dalton of atomic forms; Euclid of lines; Newton of fluxions.⁵

A man is a centre for nature, running out threads of relation through everything fluid and solid, material and elemental; the earth rolls, every clod and stone comes to the meridian. So every organ, function, acid, crystal, grain of dust, has its relation to the brain. It waits long, but its turn comes. Each plant has its parasite, and each created thing its lover and poet. Justice has already been done to steam, to iron, to wood, to coal, to loadstone, to iodine, to corn, and cotton; but how few materials are yet used by our arts! The mass of creatures and of qualities are still hid and expectant. It would seem as if each waited, like the enchanted princess in fairy tales, for a destined human deliverer. Each must be disenchanted, and walk forth to the day in human shape. In the history of discovery the ripe and latent truth seems to have fashioned a brain for itself. A magnet must be made man in some Gilbert, or Swedenborg, or Oersted, before the general mind can come to entertain its powers.⁶

If we limit ourselves to the first advantages,—a sober grace adheres to the mineral and botanic kingdoms, which, in the highest moments, comes up as the charm of nature,—the glitter of the spar, the sureness of affinity, the veracity of angles. Light and darkness, heat and cold, hunger and food, sweet and sour, solid, liquid, and gas, circle us round in a wreath of pleasures, and, by their agreeable quarrel, beguile the day of life. The eye repeats every day the first eulogy on things: He saw that they were good.⁷ We know where to find them: and these performers are relished all the more after a little experience of the pretending races. We are entitled also to higher advantages. Something is wanting to science until it has been humanized. The table of logarithms is one thing, and its vital play in botany, music, optics, and architecture, another. There are advancements to numbers, anatomy, architecture, astronomy, little suspected at first, when, by union with intellect and will, they ascend into the life, and reappear in conversation, character and politics.

12   But this comes later. We speak now only of our acquaintance with them in their own sphere, and the way in which they seem to fascinate and draw to them some genius who occupies himself with one thing all his life long. The possibility of interpretation lies in the identity of the observer with the observed. Each material thing has its celestial side; has its translation through humanity into the spiritual and necessary sphere, where it plays a part as indestructible as any other. And to these their ends all things continually ascend. The gases gather to the solid firmament: the chemic lump arrives at the plant, and grows; arrives at the quadruped, and walks; arrives at the man, and thinks. But also the constituency determines the vote of the representative. He is not only representative but participant. Like can only be known by like. The reason why he knows about them, is that he is of them: he has just come out of nature, or from being a part of that thing. Animated chlorine knows of chlorine, and incarnate zinc of zinc. Their quality makes his career, and he can variously publish their virtues, because they compose him. Man made of the dust of the world does not forget his origin: and all that is yet inanimate will one day speak and reason. Unpublished nature will have its whole secret told. Shall we say that quartz mountains will pulverize into innumerable Werners, Von Buchs, and Beaumonts, and the laboratory of the atmosphere holds in solution I know not what Berzeliuses and Davys?[8]

13   Thus we sit by the fire, and take hold on the poles of the earth. This *quasi* omnipresence supplies the imbecility of our condition. In one of those celestial days when heaven and earth meet and adorn each other, it seems a poverty that we can only spend it once. We wish for a thousand heads, a thousand bodies, that we might celebrate its immense beauty in many ways and places. Is this fancy? Well, in good faith, we are multiplied by our proxies. How easily we adopt their labours! Every ship that comes to America got its chart from Columbus. Every novel is a debtor to Homer. Every carpenter who shaves with a foreplane borrows the genius of a forgotten inventor. Life

is girt all round with a zodiack of sciences, the contribution of men who have perished to add their point of light to our sky. Engineer, broker, jurist, physician, moralist, theologian, and every man, inasmuch as he has any science, is a definer and map-maker of the latitudes and longitudes of our condition. These road-makers on every hand enrich us. We must extend the area of life, and multiply our relations. We are as much gainers by finding a new property in the old earth, as by acquiring a new planet.

We are too passive in the reception of these material or semi-material aids. We must not be sacks and stomachs. To ascend one step;—we are better served through our sympathy. Activity is contagious. Looking where others look, and conversing with the same things, we catch the charm which lured them. Napoleon said, "You must not fight too often with one enemy or you will teach him all your art of war."[9] Talk much with any man of vigorous mind, and we acquire very fast the habit of looking at things in the same light, and, on each occurrence, we anticipate his thought.

Men are helpful through the intellect and the affections. Other help I find a false appearance. If you affect to give me bread and fire, I perceive that I pay for it the full price, and at last it leaves me as it found me, neither better nor worse; but all mental and moral force is a positive good. It goes out from you, whether you will or not, and profits me whom you never thought of. I cannot even hear of personal vigour of any kind, great power of performance, without fresh resolution. We are emulous of all that man can do. Cecil's saying of Sir Walter Raleigh, "I know that he can toil terribly," is an electric touch.[10] So are Clarendon's portraits,—of Hampden; "who was of an industry and vigilance not to be tired out or wearied by the most laborious, and of parts not to be imposed on by the most subtle and sharp, and of a personal courage equal to his best parts."—Of Falkland;—"who was so severe an adorer of truth, that he could as easily have given himself leave to steal, as to dissemble."[11] We cannot read Plutarch without a tingling of the blood; and I accept the saying of the Chinese Mencius; "A sage is the instructer of a hundred ages. When the manners of Loo are heard of, the stupid become intelligent, and the wavering, determined."[12]

This is the moral of biography; yet it is hard for departed men to touch the quick like our own companions, whose names may not last as long. What is he whom I never think of? whilst in every solitude are those who succour our genius, and stimulate us in wonderful manners. There is a power in love to divine another's destiny better than that other can, and by heroic encouragements hold him to his task. What has friendship so signal as its sublime attraction to whatever virtue is in us? We will never more think cheaply of ourselves or of life. We are piqued to some purpose, and the industry of the diggers on the railroad will not again shame us.

17 Under this head, too, falls that homage, very pure, as I think, which all ranks pay to the hero of the day,—from Coriolanus and Gracchus, down to Pitt, Lafayette, Wellington, Webster, Lamartine: Hear the shouts in the street![13] The people cannot see him enough. They delight in a man. Here is a head and a trunk! What a front; what eyes; Atlantean shoulders; and the whole carriage heroic, with equal inward force to guide the great machine! This pleasure of full expression to that which in their private experience is usually cramped and obstructed, runs also much higher, and is the secret of the reader's joy in literary genius. Nothing is kept back: there is fire enough to fuse the mountain of ore. Shakspeare's principal merit may be conveyed in saying, that he of all men best understands the English language, and can say what he will. Yet these unchoked channels and floodgates of expression are only health or fortunate constitution. Shakspeare's name suggests other and purely intellectual benefits.

18 Senates and sovereigns have no compliment with their medals, swords, and armorial coats, like the addressing to a human being thoughts out of a certain height, and presupposing his intelligence. This honour, which is possible in personal intercourse scarcely twice in a lifetime, genius perpetually pays, contented if now and then in a century, the proffer is accepted. The indicators of the values of matter are degraded to a sort of cooks and confectioners on the appearance of the indicators of ideas. Genius is the naturalist or geographer of the supersensible regions, and draws their map; and, by acquainting us with new fields of activity, cools our affection for the old. These are at once accepted as the reality, of which the world we have conversed with is the show.

19 We go to the gymnasium and the swimming-school to see the power and beauty of the body: there is the like pleasure and a higher benefit from witnessing intellectual feats of all kinds, as feats of memory, of mathematical combination, great power of abstraction, the transmutings of the imagination, even versatility, and concentration, as these acts expose the invisible organs and members of the mind, which respond member for member to the

parts of the body. For we thus enter a new gymnasium and learn to choose men by their truest marks, taught, with Plato, "to choose those who can without aid from the eyes, or any other sense, proceed to truth and to Being."[14] Foremost among these activities are the summersaults, spells, and resurrections wrought by the imagination. When this wakes, a man seems to multiply ten times or a thousand times his force. It opens the delicious sense of indeterminate size, and inspires an audacious mental habit. We are as elastic as the gas of gunpowder, and a sentence in a book, or a word dropped in conversation, sets free our fancy, and instantly our heads are bathed with galaxies, and our feet tread the floor of the Pit.[15] And this benefit is real, because we are entitled to these enlargements, and, once having passed the bounds, shall never again be quite the miserable pedants we were.

The high functions of the intellect are so allied, that some imaginative power usually appears in all eminent minds: even in arithmeticians of the first class, but especially in meditative men of an intuitive habit of thought. This class serve us, so that they have the perception of identity and the perception of reaction. The eyes of Plato, Shakspeare, Swedenborg, Goethe, never shut on either of these laws. The perception of these laws is a kind of metre of the mind. Little minds are little through failure to see them. 20

Even these feasts have their surfeit. Our delight in Reason degenerates into idolatry of the herald. Especially when a mind of powerful method has instructed men, we find the examples of oppression. The dominion of Aristotle, the Ptolemaic astronomy, the credit of Luther; of Bacon; of Locke; in religion, the history of hierarchies, of saints, and the sects which have taken the name of each founder, are in point.[16] Alas, every man is such a victim. The imbecility of men is always inviting the impudence of power. It is the delight of vulgar talent to dazzle and to blind the beholder. But true genius seeks to defend us from itself. True genius will not impoverish, but will liberate, and add new senses. If a wise man should appear in our village, he would create in those who conversed with him a new consciousness of wealth, by opening their eyes to unobserved advantages: he would establish a sense of immoveable equality, calm us with assurances that we could not be cheated; as every one would discern the checks and guaranties of condition. The rich would see their mistakes and poverty; the poor, their escapes and their resources. 21

But nature brings all this about in due time. Rotation is her remedy. The 22 soul is impatient of masters, and eager for change. Housekeepers say of a domestic who has been valuable, "She had lived with me long enough." We are tendencies, or rather symptoms, and none of us complete. We touch and go, and sip the foam of many lives. Rotation is the law of nature. When Nature removes a great man, people explore the horizon for a successor; but none comes, and none will. His class is extinguished with him. In some other and quite different field, the next man will appear: not Jefferson, not Franklin, but now a great salesman; then a road-contractor; then a student of fishes; then a buffalo-hunting explorer; or a semi-savage Western general. Thus we make a stand against our rougher masters; but against the best there is a finer remedy. The power which they communicate is not theirs. When we are exalted by ideas, we do not owe this to Plato, but to the idea, to which also Plato was debtor.

23

I must not forget that we have a special debt to a single class. Life is a scale of degrees. Between rank and rank of our great men, are wide intervals. Mankind have, in all ages, attached themselves to a few persons, who, either by the quality of that idea they embodied, or by the largeness of their reception, were entitled to the position of leaders and lawgivers. These teach us the qualities of primary nature, admit us to the constitution of things. We swim, day by day, on a river of delusions, and are effectually amused with houses and towns in the air, of which the men about us are dupes. But life is a sincerity. In lucid intervals, we say, 'Let there be an entrance opened for me into realities; I have worn the fool's cap too long.' We will know the meaning of our economies and politics. Give us the cipher, and, if persons and things are scores of a celestial music, let us read off the strains. We have been cheated of our reason,—yet there have been sane men who enjoyed a rich and related existence. What they know, they know for us. With each new mind a new secret of nature transpires, nor can the bible be closed until the last great man is born. These men correct the delirium of the animal spirits, make us considerate, and engage us to new aims and powers. The veneration of mankind selects these for the highest place. Witness the multitude of statues, pictures, and memorials which recall their genius in every city, village, house, and ship.

> "Ever their phantoms arise before us,
> Our loftier brothers, but one in blood,

At bed and table they lord it o'er us,
With looks of beauty, and words of good."[17]

How to illustrate the distinctive benefit of ideas, the service rendered by those who introduce moral truths into the general mind?—I am plagued in all my living with a perpetual tariff of prices. If I work in my garden, and prune an appletree, I am well enough entertained, and could continue indefinitely in the like occupation. But it comes to mind that a day is gone, and I have got this precious nothing done. I go to Boston or New York, and run up and down on my affairs; they are sped, but so is the day. I am vexed by the recollection of this price I have paid for a trifling advantage. I remember the *peau d'âne*, on which whoso sat, should have his desire, but a piece of the skin was gone for every wish.[18] I go to a convention of philanthropists. Do what I can, I cannot keep my eyes off the clock. But if there should appear in the company some gentle soul who knows little of persons or parties, of Carolina or Cuba, but who announces a law that disposes these particulars, and so certifies me of the equity which checkmates every false player, bankrupts every selfseeker, and apprises me of my independence on any conditions of country, or time, or human body, that man liberates me; I forget the clock; I pass out of the sore relation to persons; I am healed of my hurts; I am made immortal by apprehending my possession of incorruptible goods. Here is great competition of rich and poor. We live in a market, where is only so much wheat, or wool, or land; and if I have so much more, every other must have so much less. I seem to have no good, without breach of good manners. Nobody is glad in the gladness of another, and our system is one of war, of an injurious superiority. Every child of the Saxon race is educated to wish to be first. It is our system: and a man comes to measure his greatness by the regrets, envies, and hatreds of his competitors. But in these new fields, there is room: here are no selfesteems, no exclusions.

I admire great men of all classes, those who stand for facts, and for thoughts; I like rough and smooth, "Scourges of God," and "Darlings of the human race;"[19] I like the first Cæsar; and Charles V of Spain; and Charles XII of Sweden; Richard Plantagenet; and Bonaparte in France.[20] I applaud a sufficient man, an officer equal to his office; captains, ministers, senators: I like a master standing firm on legs of iron; well born, rich, handsome, eloquent, loaded with advantages, drawing all men by fascination into tributaries and

24

supporters of his power. Sword and staff, or talents sword-like or staff-like, carry on the work of the world. But I find him greater, when he can abolish himself and all heroes, by letting in this element of reason, irrespective of persons, this subtilizer, and irresistible upward force, into our thought, destroying individualism;—the power so great, that the potentate is nothing. Then he is a monarch who gives a constitution to his people; a pontiff, who preaches the equality of souls, and releases his servants from their barbarous homages; an emperor, who can spare his empire.

25   But I intended to specify with a little minuteness two or three points of service. Nature never spares the opium or nepenthe, but wherever she mars her creature with some deformity or defect, lays her poppies plentifully on the bruise, and the sufferer goes joyfully through life, ignorant of the ruin, and incapable of seeing it, though all the world point their finger at it every day. The worthless and offensive members of society, whose existence is a social pest, invariably think themselves the most ill used people alive, and never get over their astonishment at the ingratitude and selfishness of their contemporaries. Our globe discovers its hidden virtues not only in heroes and archangels, but in gossips and nurses. Is it not a rare contrivance that lodged the due inertia in every creature, the conserving resisting energy, the anger at being waked or changed? Altogether independent of the intellectual force in each, is the pride of opinion, the security that we are right. Not the feeblest grandame, not the mowing ideot, but uses what spark of perception and faculty is left, to chuckle and triumph in his or her opinion over the absurdities of all the rest. Difference from me is the measure of absurdity. Not one has a misgiving of being wrong. Was it not a bright thought that made things cohere with this bitumen, fastest of cements? But in the midst of this chuckle of selfgratulation, some figure goes by, which Thersites too can love and admire.[21] This is he that should marshal us the way we were going. There is no end to his aid. Without Plato, we should almost lose our faith in the possibility of a reasonable book. We seem to want but one, but we want one. We love to associate with heroic persons, since our receptivity is unlimited, and, with the great, our thoughts and manners easily become great. We are all wise in capacity, though so few in energy. There needs but one wise man in a company, and all are wise,—so rapid is the contagion.

26   Great men are thus a collyrium to clear our eyes from egotism, and enable us to see other people and their works. But there are vices and follies in-

cident to whole populations and ages. Men resemble their contemporaries, even more than their progenitors.[22] It is observed in old couples, or in persons who have been housemates for a course of years, that they grow alike, and, if they should live long enough, we should not be able to know them apart. Nature abhors these complaisances, which threaten to melt the world into a lump, and hastens to break up such maudlin agglutinations. The like assimilation goes on between men of one town, of one sect, of one political party: and the ideas of the time are in the air, and infect all who breathe it. Viewed from any high point, this city of New York, yonder city of London, the western civilization would seem a bundle of insanities. We keep each other in countenance, and exasperate by emulation the frenzy of the time. The shield against the stingings of conscience, is, the universal practice, or our contemporaries. Again; it is very easy to be as wise and good as your companions. We learn of our contemporaries what they know, without effort, and almost through the pores of the skin. We catch it by sympathy, or, as a wife arrives at the intellectual and moral elevations of her husband. But we stop where they stop. Very hardly can we take another step. The great, or such as hold of nature, and transcend fashions, by their fidelity to universal ideas, are saviours from these federal errors, and defend us from our contemporaries. They are the exceptions which we want, where all grows alike. A foreign greatness is the antidote for cabalism.

Thus we feed on genius, and refresh ourselves from too much conversation with our mates, and exult in the depth of nature in that direction in which he leads us. What indemnification is one great man for populations of pigmies! Every mother wishes one son a genius, though all the rest should be mediocre. But a new danger appears in the excess of influence of the great man. His attractions warp us from our place. We have become underlings and intellectual suicides. Ah! yonder in the horizon is our help: other great men, new qualities, counterweights and checks on each other. We cloy of the honey of each peculiar greatness. Every hero becomes a bore at last. Perhaps Voltaire was not badhearted, yet he said of the good Jesus, even, "I pray you, let me never hear that man's name again."[23] They cry up the virtues of George Washington. "Damn George Washington!" is the poor Jacobin's whole speech and confutation. But it is human nature's indispensable defence. The centripetence augments the centrifugence. We balance one man with his opposite, and the health of the state depends on the see-saw.

There is however a speedy limit to the use of heroes. Every genius is de-

27

28

fended from approach by quantities of unavailableness. They are very attractive, and seem at a distance our own: but we are hindered on all sides from approach. The more we are drawn, the more we are repelled. There is something not solid in the good that is done for us. The best discovery the discoverer makes for himself. It has something unreal for his companion, until he too has substantiated it. It seems as if the Deity dressed each soul which he sends into nature in certain virtues and powers not communicable to other men, and, sending it to perform one more turn through the circle of beings, wrote *"Not Transferable,"* and *"Good for this trip only,"* on these garments of the soul. There is somewhat deceptive about the intercourse of minds. The boundaries are invisible, but they are never crossed. There is such goodwill to impart, and such goodwill to receive, that each threatens to become the other; but the law of individuality collects its secret strength; you are you, and I am I, and so we remain.

29   For nature wishes everything to remain itself, and, whilst every individual strives to grow and exclude, and to exclude and grow, to the extremities of the Universe, and to impose the law of its being on every other creature, nature steadily aims to protect each against every other. Each is selfdefended. Nothing is more marked than the power by which individuals are guarded from individuals, in a world where every benefactor becomes so easily a malefactor, only by continuation of his activity into places where it is not due: where children seem so much at the mercy of their foolish parents, and where almost all men are too social and interfering. We rightly speak of the guardian angels of children. How superior in their security from infusions of evil persons, from vulgarity, and second thought! They shed their own abundant beauty on the objects they behold. Therefore they are not at the mercy of such poor educators as we adults. If we huff and chide them, they soon come not to mind it, and get a selfreliance: and if we indulge them to folly, they learn the limitation elsewhere.

30   We need not fear excessive influence. A more generous trust is permitted. Serve the great. Stick at no humiliation. Grudge no office thou canst render. Be the limb of their body, the breath of their mouth. Compromise thy egotism: Who cares for that, so thou gain aught wider and nobler? Never mind the taunt of Boswellism: the devotion may easily be greater than the wretched pride which is guarding its own skirts.[24] Be another: not thyself, but a Platonist; not a soul, but a Christian; not a naturalist, but a Cartesian;[25] not a

poet, but a Shakspearian. In vain. The wheels of tendency will not stop, nor will all the forces of inertia, fear, or of love itself, hold thee there. On, and forever onward! The microscope observes a monad or wheel-insect among the infusories circulating in water. Presently, a dot appears on the animal, which enlarges to a slit, and it becomes two perfect animals.[26] The ever-proceeding detachment appears not less in all thought and in society. Children think they cannot live without their parents: But long before they are aware of it, the black dot has appeared, and the detachment taken place. Any accident will now reveal to them their independence.

But *great men:* the word is injurious. Is there caste? is there Fate? What becomes of the promise to Virtue? The thoughtful youth laments the superfœtation of nature. 'Generous and handsome,' he says, 'is your hero; but look at yonder poor paddy, whose country is his wheelbarrow: look at his whole nation of paddies.' Why are the masses, from the dawn of history down, food for knives and powder? The idea dignifies a few leaders, who have sentiment, opinion, love, selfdevotion, and they make war and death sacred;—but what for the wretches whom they hire and kill?—The cheapness of man is every day's tragedy. It is as real a loss that others should be low, as that we should be low:—for we must have society.

Is it a reply to these suggestions, to say, society is a Pestalozzian school: all are teachers and pupils in turn.[27] We are equally served by receiving and by imparting. Men who know the same things are not long the best company for each other. But bring to each an intelligent person of another experience, and it is as if you let off water from a lake by cutting a lower basin. It seems a mechanical advantage, and great benefit it is to each speaker, as he can now paint out his thought to himself. We pass very fast in our personal moods from dignity to dependence. And if any appear never to assume the chair, but always to stand and serve, it is because we do not see the company in a sufficiently long period for the whole rotation of parts to come about. As to what we call the masses, and common men;—there are no common men. All men are at last of a size, and true art is only possible on the conviction that every talent has its apotheosis somewhere. Fair play and an open field! and freshest laurels to all who have won them! But heaven reserves an equal scope for every creature. Each is uneasy until he has produced his private ray unto the concave sphere, and beheld his talent also in its last nobility and exaltation.

The heroes of the hour are relatively great; of a faster growth; or they are such in whom, at the moment of success, a quality is ripe which is then in request. Other days will demand other qualities. Some rays escape the common observer, and want a finely adapted eye. Ask the great man if there be none greater? His companions are: and not the less great, but the more, that society cannot see them. Nature never sends a great man into the planet, without confiding the secret to another soul.

33   One gracious fact emerges from these studies, that there is true ascension in our love. The reputations of the nineteenth century will one day be quoted to prove its barbarism. The genius of humanity is the real subject whose biography is written in our annals. We must infer much, and supply many chasms in the record. The history of the universe is symptomatic, and life is mnemonical. No man in all the procession of famous men is reason or illumination, or that essence we were looking for; but is an exhibition in some quarter of new possibilities. Could we one day complete the immense figure which these flagrant points compose!—The study of many individuals leads us to an elemental region wherein the individual is lost, or wherein all touch by their summits. Thought and feeling that break out there, cannot be impounded by any fence of personality. This is the key to the power of the greatest men,—their spirit diffuses itself. A new quality of mind travels by night and by day in concentric circles from its origin, and publishes itself by unknown methods; the union of all minds appears intimate; what gets admission to one, cannot be kept out of any other: the smallest acquisition of truth or of energy, in any quarter, is so much good to the commonwealth of souls. If the disparities of talent and position vanish, when the individuals are seen in the duration which is necessary to complete the career of each; even more swiftly the seeming injustice disappears, when we ascend to the central identity of all the individuals, and know that they are made of the substance which ordaineth and doeth.

34   The genius of humanity is the right point of view of history. The qualities abide; the men who exhibit them have now more, now less, and pass away; the qualities remain on another brow. No experience is more familiar. Once you saw phœnixes: they are gone: the world is not therefore disenchanted.[28] The vessels on which you read sacred emblems, turn out to be common pottery, but the sense of the pictures is sacred, and you may still read them transferred to the walls of the world. For a time our teachers serve

us personally, as metres or milestones of progress. Once they were angels of knowledge, and their figures touched the sky. Then we drew near, saw their means, culture, and limits; and they yielded their place to other geniuses. Happy, if a few names remain so high, that we have not been able to read them nearer, and age and comparison have not robbed them of a ray. But at last we shall cease to look in men for completeness, and shall content ourselves with their social and delegated quality. All that respects the individual is temporary and prospective, like the individual himself, who is ascending out of his limits into a catholic existence. We have never come at the true and best benefit of any genius, so long as we believe him an original force. In the moment when he ceases to help us as a cause, he begins to help us more as an effect. Then he appears as an exponent of a vaster mind and will. The opake self becomes transparent with the light of the First Cause.

Yet within the limits of human education and agency, we may say, great men exist that there may be greater men. The destiny of organized nature is amelioration, and who can tell its limits? It is for man to tame the chaos; on every side, whilst he lives, to scatter the seeds of science and of song, that climate, corn, animals, men, may be milder, and the germs of love and benefit may be multiplied.

35

Notes

1. Siddhartha Gautama, or Buddha, the sixth-century BCE founder of Buddhism.
2. Emerson's paraphrase of *The Vishnu Purana, a System of Hindu Mythology and Tradition,* trans. H. H. Wilson (London, 1840), p. 312 (*JMN,* 9:258).
3. An allusion to the gold rush of 1849 in the foothills of the Sierra Nevada along the tributaries of the Sacramento and the San Joaquin rivers.
4. Emerson's source for this aesthetic insight, typically applied to architectural detail, is George Sand, *Le Compagnon du Tour de France* (Paris, 1843), p. 208 (chapter 18) (*JMN,* 9:61).
5. Elias Magnus Fries (1794–1878), Swedish botanist; Jean Baptiste van Mons (1765–1842), Belgian chemist and horticulturist; John Dalton (1766–1844), English chemist and physicist, revived and adapted to modern science the ancient atomic theory; Euclid (fl. 300 BCE), Greek mathematician whose *Elements* is the foundation of geometry ("fluxions").
6. William Gilbert (1544–1603), English physician and physicist.

7. A close paraphrase of God's repeated observation on the stages of creation in Genesis 1.

8. Abraham Gottlob Werner (1750–1817), German mineralogist and geologist, developed a theory that all rocks were deposits of a primeval ocean (Neptunism); Christian Leopold Von Buch (1774–1853), Werner's student, rejected that theory, arguing in favor of volcanic processes (Vulcanism); Jean Baptiste Armand Louis Léonce Elie de Beaumont (1798–1874), French geologist who theorized the formation of mountain ranges; Jöns Jakob Berzelius (1779–1848), Swedish chemist, developed a method for determining atomic and molecular weights and isolated many elements.

9. Routinely cited in dictionaries of quotation as the sole source of the attribution to Napoleon, the only occurrence of a passage similar to this is in Emerson's journal (*JMN*, 9:252).

10. Emerson's source is "Sir Walter Raleigh," *The Edinburgh Review* 71 (April 1840): 55 (American ed.); Raleigh (1552–1618) was an English aristocrat, courtier, spy, and explorer. Sir Robert Cecil, 1st Earl of Salisbury (ca. 1563–1612), English statesman.

11. Emerson's source for the characterizations of John Hampden and Lucius Cary, 2nd Viscount Falkland (ca. 1610–1643), parliamentary leaders during the reign of Charles I, is Edward Hyde, 1st Earl of Clarendon, *The History of the Rebellion and Civil Wars in England*, Book VII, paragraph 84, and Book IV, paragraph 123.

12. Emerson's paraphrase of a quotation attributed to Mencius in "Hea Mung," *The Chinese Classical Work Commonly Called the Four Books* (1828), p. 130 (*JMN*, 9:8).

13. Gnaeus Marcius Coriolanus, an aloof fifth-century BCE Roman military hero, led his former enemies victoriously against Rome; when he spared the city, his new followers killed him. Tiberius Sempronius Gracchus (163–133 BCE) and his brother Caius Sempronius Gracchus (154–121 BCE), radical Roman social reformers, were killed in riots and their reforms were quickly undone.Alphonse Marie Louis de Lamartine (1790–1869), French Romantic writer and statesman.

14. Emerson's paraphrase of Plato, *Republic*, VII, 16, 537d.

15. In his journal Emerson wrote, "'It is an expression of Pindar, that we tread the dark bottom of hell with necessities as hard as iron'" (*JMN*, 5:370); cf. Pindar, *Fragment* 207.

16. Aristotle's philosophy, revived as medieval scholasticism, and his astronomy, elaborated by the Greco-Roman scientist Ptolemy (90–168), fell before the scientific and philosophical revolutions of the sixteenth and seventeenth centuries; similarly, the inductive method proposed by Francis Bacon, the liberating religious reformation of Martin Luther, and the philosophical empiricism of John Locke were, by the end of the eighteenth century, thought encumbrances from the past.

17. Cf. "Dædalus," stanza 6, by John Sterling (1806–1844), Scottish writer.

18. The philosophical novel *La Peau de chagrin* (1831), by the French writer Honoré de

Balzac (1799–1850), turns on a talismanic wild ass's skin that shrinks as its owner is granted every wish; when the skin ultimately disappears, life is ended.

19. Emerson's respective sources for these expressions are *Tamburlaine* (1587–1588), pt. II, V, iii, 248, by the English dramatist Christopher Marlowe (1564–1593), who refers to the historical Turkic world conqueror Tamburlaine (1336–1405) as "the Scourge of God," and, as he noted in his journal (*JMN*, 6:209), Titus (39–81), Roman emperor, who was eulogized as "Deliciæ humani generis" (Suetonius, *The Lives of the Caesars*, Book VIII, "The Deified Titus," i).

20. Charles V (1500–1558), Holy Roman Emperor and also King Charles I of Spain; Charles XII (1682–1718), king of Sweden; Richard Plantagenet (1157–1199), king of England as Richard I.

21. As represented in Greek mythology, Homer's *Iliad*, and Shakespeare's *Troilus and Cressida*, Thersites is the ugliest and most scurrilous of the Greeks at Troy.

22. Emerson's source is *Practical Philosophy of the Muhammadan People*, trans. W. F. Thompson (London, 1839), p. 381 (*JMN*, 9:286).

23. François Marie Arouet de Voltaire (1694–1778), French writer and deist who attacked the divinity of Jesus; however, Emerson's source here is Thomas Carlyle's letter to him of 3 November 1844: "I daresay you are a little bored occasionally with 'Jesus' &c, as I confess I myself am . . . and an impatient person may exclaim with Voltaire, in serious moments: '*Au nom de Dieu, ne me parlez plus de cet homme-là!*'" (*CEC*, p. 371).

24. An allusion drawn from mid-nineteenth-century critiques of James Boswell's idolizing of his subject in *Life of Samuel Johnson* (1791).

25. A reference to René Descartes (1596–1650), French philosopher and scientist, who undertook to replace Aristotelian and Scholastic philosophy by applying mathematical certainty to metaphysics and emphasizing the distinction between mind and matter.

26. "Wheel-insects," or "wheel-animalcules" as Emerson calls them (*JMN*, 9:300), are the chief class, rotifera, of the phylum Trochelminthes. The microscopic rotifera are named for their rotary organs used in swimming, and some propagate by division as Emerson describes here. He uses the words "monad" in its biological sense of any minute simple organism and "infusories" to mean *Infusoria* in the general sense of microscopic animal life.

27. Emerson is here celebrating the organic principles of education championed by Johann Heinrich Pestalozzi, whereby teaching and learning are mutual endeavors between instructors and their students.

28. The Phenix, or Phoenix, is a fabulous Oriental bird of great beauty, which after living five or six centuries builds a funeral pyre, upon which it expires by fanning the flames with its wings, only to rise again in fresh beauty from the ashes.

The Anglo-American

1   Everything in America is at a rapid rate. The next moment eats the last. Whatever we do, suffer, or propose, is for the immediate entertainment of the company. We have a newspaper published every hour of the day, and our whole existence and performance slides into it. When I went to Ohio, I was asked, When were you here before?—Three years ago.—O, that is just one age in Ohio: Let me introduce you to the new generation.

2   A gentleman in Cincinnati defended his immoveableness by saying, "Sir, I have held that opinion three weeks." There is no difference between boy and man. As soon as a boy is table high, he contradicts his father.

3   "American" means speedy in Europe, as if the ingenuity of this country were directed on nothing so much. The impediment on the western rivers is the low water, at certain seasons, so they must have light boats. They once had on the Mississippi a boat called *Skim*, drawing so little water that they said it would sail in a heavy dew, and when it got aground, the crew jumped out and put their shoulders under the boat, and lifted it over the bar. On the sea, the value of freight is the warrant of quick arrival at the market; and the American builds clipper ships which outrun all other craft so far, that they command a higher freight in foreign ports, and the East India Company send

home cargoes in American vessels, in preference to their own![1] The American challenge has not been accepted,—to build and run a freight ship to Canton and home, for a purse of ten thousand pounds to the quickest. Lord DeBlaquiere advertised his yacht to race with all yachts, *not American.*[2]

Everything is sacrificed for speed,—solidity and safety. They would sail in a steamer built of lucifer matches if it would go faster; with spars of the very largest jackstraws.[3] A stability is only to be found in this Country in a few isolated localities as, for example, in Essex, Massachusetts, a little town which builds fishing boats, and where ninety families bear the name of Burnham and all the rest are Cogswells or Choates. Perhaps there is an influence continental, climatic, to modify the race, and free certain forces that lay latent before. The sun of America, and its western wind, as they work on the frame, certainly add vivacity and speed.

This national trait stands in strange contrast with the habit of the land of our forefathers. The English have a Cummerian Conservatism.[4] It is called *the Old Country,* and everything in it is old. Its manufactures reach back beyond the memory of history. Fuller says, "The date of cloth and of civility is one in this island."[5] Sheffield has made knives for five hundred years and more. Staffordshire has made potteries, Cornwall dug its mines, Nottingham woven its laces, for centuries. The Spitalfield weavers still pursue their trade as at the revocation of the Edict of Nantes.[6]

The sun returning to the spring solstice finds each man in England sitting at the same workbench at which he left him on that day twelvemonth. The same tenacity is in families and fames. "The Duke of Buckingham was born," says Wotton, "at Brookely in Leicestershire, where his ancestors had chiefly continued about the space of four hundred years, rather without obscurity, than with any great lustre."[7]

The air and aspect of England are loaded with stability and reverence. Take a map, and read the names. In England, it has taken Cambridge between seven and eight hundred years since the monks of Croyland taught in a farm and in a barn to reach the present wealth of its University. Oxford goes back one thousand years to King Alfred for its charter, and much longer, if, as is pretended, the Druids had a school on the same spot. In Merton College Library I found books still chained to the shelves to which they were locked centuries ago when books were precious as gold.

But we have changed all that, and, in our new states, we extemporize an

4

5

6

7

8

University like a picnic. In 1851, I chanced to witness this rapid crystallization at Rochester, New York. There had been some negociation about removing into the city a college which was situated twenty miles off. But the negociations dragged; no satisfactory result was likely to come: So an enterprising citizen (Mr. Wilder) bought a cheap hotel, (once a railroad terminus-station,) turned the dining-room into a chapel, by putting up a pulpit on one side; made the barroom into a Pythologian society's hall; the drawing-room into a library; the chambers, into recitation rooms and professors' apartments; all for seven hundred dollars a year.[8] He called in a painter, sent him up a ladder to paint "University of Rochester," on the wall; sent an omnibus up to Madison, and brought the whole faculty of professors bodily down,—bag and baggage, Greek, Hebrew, Chaldee, Latin, *Belles Lettres,* Mathematics, and all sciences; sent runners out on all roads to catch students: One lad, they said, came in yesterday; another, this morning; "thought they should like it first-rate." Already, the guardians of the institution evidently thought themselves ill used, if they did not add a new student every day, and were confident of graduating a class of ten, by the time green peas were ripe. Well, the next year they graduated fifteen Bachelors of Arts; the Greek professor published a Greek grammar of good pretention. Last year, Neander's Library was offered for sale, at Berlin, in Prussia.[9] Various colleges and private collectors were in treaty for the purchase; but the wide-awake little University said to itself, in the phrase of the country, "the longest pole takes the persimmon,"—had a man on the spot, with his money in his pocket,—bought the library,—and it is now triumphantly mounted on the shelves at Rochester, to be explored, at leisure, as soon as they have learned enough to read it.[10]

9   In every part of the country this vigorous people have struck out some bold and effectual resource. In the north, the summers were short, the soil sterile, and the crop uncertain. Near the foggy island of Newfoundland is stretched a sandbank six hundred miles long, and the sea flowing over this vast submarine mountain contains an amount of human food which the nations of Europe and America have for several centuries labored indefatigably to collect with nets, lines, and every process that could be contrived or imagined, and yet not the smallest diminution of fruitfulness has ever been observed. Thither he went, and if one should go to the capes of Massachusetts, to Gloucester, to Plymouth, Barnstable, Provincetown, he would find, that poor men, without other capital than their arms, built a boat of sixty or sev-

enty tons,—all the owners went in her,—every man carrying his own little bag of provisions,—(a little salt, molasses, and meal, and pork;—) every man fished for himself; and hence the phrase *on his own hook.* This fishing led to the hunting of the whale by some bold Quakers who lived in Nantucket, and who planted their little shipyards at New Bedford, and built up that gigantic trade.

East of the Penobscot River, the climate changes, and the earth will no longer produce wheat, or corn, or apples.[11] Even the potato now is cut off. The agricultural societies resolved, that the hackmetach root was their best esculent, and the shingle-mill their best orchard.[12] At Bangor, where the summer is only a two months' thaw, they fill the forests of Maine with lumberers; buy and sell townships and all the timber on the St. John's River; keep up a brisk game of saw- and slitting-mills.[13] They drag a pine log to mill, turn a crank, and it comes out chairs, and tables, and pianos.

An American in this ardent climate gets up early some morning, buys a river, advertises for twelve or fifteen hundred Irishmen, digs a new channel for it, brings it to his mills, and has a head of twenty-five feet of water: to give him an appetite for his breakfast, he raises a house; then carves out, within-doors, a quarter township into streets and building lots, tavern, school, and Methodist meetinghouse; sends up an engineer into New Hampshire to see where his water comes from, and, after advising with him, sends a trusty man of business to buy of all the farmers such mill privileges as will serve him among their waste hill and pasture lots, and comes home with glee, announcing that he is now owner of the great Lake Winnepesaukee, as reservoir for his Lowell mills at midsummer. The Lowell people gave $200,000 for one hundred square miles of water. Now, they put up their flashboards when there is too much water; and let them down, when there is too little; and have a just supply all summer.[14]

Plenty of ability for this taming and subduing the land, and for expediting internal intercourse. There is many a man who has built his city with all needful aids of engineering, ship and boat building, surveying, and machine shops at their disposal. Go into each great capital; Go into Wall Street. See how well the city of New York is officered for its wants. What large brains, what forcible and persevering gentlemen: six or eight citizens have pioneered the short way to California, and the short way to Liverpool, and the short railway to the Pacific.

10

11

12

13   The English slow, sure finish has changed into the irresistibility of the American. The climate itself is in extremes. We get, in summer, the splendor of the equator and a touch of Syria, with enormous productiveness. Nature in this climate, ardent, rushing up, after a shower, into a mat of vegetation. Nature goes into the genius, as well as into the cucumbers, whilst the poor polar man only gets the last of it. The man's irresistibility is like nature's. Like nature, he has no conscience. His motto, like her's, is, Our country right or wrong. He builds shingle palaces, shingle cities, picnic universities; extemporizes a state in California; in an altered mood, I suppose, he will build stone cities, with equal celerity. Tall, restless Kentucky strength: good stock;—but, though an admirable fruit, you shall not find one good sound, well-developed apple on the tree. Nature herself was in a hurry with these racers, and never finished one.

14   If you travel in New England, you will find in each town some manufacture rooted, for which the place offered no special facilities. In one town, there is a whip factory; in another, jewelry; in a third, church-organs; in a fourth, accordions; in a fifth, shoepegs; in a sixth, planes and case knives; in a seventh, fountain pens, and when you inquire what caused this thriving work which feeds hundreds and thousands, to grow up here, Why, Mr. Driver moved into the place, and set up his lathe, and, after a time, one of his men set up another, and so on. It was not that the leather grew here, or the ivory, or the iron; It was not nearer to the market; It was not the water power; It was only that here grew Mr. Driver's brain.

15   All is hasty, and with the penalty that speed must pay. Time respects nothing but what himself has made. All is hasty, incomplete, cheap, much of it counterfeit. There is superficial finish, and want of solidity. His leather is not tanned; his white lead is whiting; his sulphuric acid has half-strength; in architecture, his pillars are drums; his stone is well-sanded pumpkin-pine; his mahogany is veneered; and, I am sorry to say, in Philadelphia itself, he has learned to build marble houses with veneers instead of blocks.

16   Our newspapers name it as a merit, that the steam engine of our sea steamers was first put together in the ship. That circumstance will not recommend the boat to the Englishman who knows that his countrymen do not venture to put the machine into the ship until it first has been kept a'going for months in the works. Instead of the grand old knees of oak which nature has been employed for seven centuries in the forest to knot and gnarl into rocky strength,—we have found out, by more dexterous fashion of our saws,

to saw, out of refuse sapling stuff, knees of any shape; if they will hold together till they are nailed, they will hold till they are screwed, and then covered up with boards and veneered with bird's-eye maple, and varnished with copal; Who will ever know the difference! Ah, nobody—Nobody but the ugly Ocean, and the rending and bursting of the Southwestern Gale, and the drowning passengers.

Rashness of adventure marks all their acts and professions. Their steam-marine outnumbers every other nation's, but it is frail, and recklessly hazarded, burned, snagged, run into, and raced to ruin, and proverbially unsafe. The safety-valve is fastened down with a billet of wood. No eastern man travels on the western rivers, without a life-preserver. And I found, that whilst, on the Mississippi, my companions, who were western merchants, did not take off their clothes or their boots,—until they entered the Ohio; then they undressed, and went to sleep. Forty-seven steamboats were burned at St. Louis in the year 1849–1850. 17

Another form in which this levity shows itself is a social and public action, in which the individuals composing the assembly do not feel themselves committed. They are fond of excitement, and like crowds; and will lend their hand and voice to swell the clapping and huzzas that applaud some person or sentiment, on whose merits they have by no means made up their minds. They have a superficial heat, a two-inch enthusiasm, a passing flush and are willing to cry for anything with a million. It is a sort of rose-influenza, epidemic for a day or two, far and wide, and then forgotten. And if some foreign celebrity passes by, as Lafayette, or Kossuth, or Dickens, or Lord Morpeth, or Meagher, or Gavazzi, or Thackeray, the shout of welcome, first from a few voices, is echoed about and caught from city to city, East, West, North, South, until it swells into an oriental superlative of adulation, and deceives the object of it into some belief that he is the man they all were waiting for.[15] And they are only humbugging each other. If Kossuth had received on his landing in England, such a welcome as he found at the city of New York, it might have been relied on, whereas the very actors in the New York scene knew it meant nothing. 18

"Haste," said Mahomet, "is of the devil; Delay is of the All-giving." The like incompleteness runs into education, into the schools, and the trades and professions: The like into manners and plans of life. Fine manners, fine intercourse, require time, and abhor hurry. 19

The climate adds vivacity, but exhausts. In this close competition, every 20 man is tasked beyond his strength, and grows early old. Life is a lottery, in which everyone may draw a fortune, or a blank. In California, insanity abounds. It frequently happens, that one man is getting out of his digging twenty dollars a day; another, in the very next beside him, is getting out a thousand dollars a day. Of course, 'tis vain to say, "Gentlemen, in Digging number one, Keep cool! There's plenty of time." No: They work like dogs, because they are expecting every hour that they will strike on the same shelf. How can brains or bodies stand such excitement? Yet what happens in the mines, happens throughout the Union.

21   The leading features of national character are less glaring in our large and old cities, which have kept much of the European spirit. In the new-planted territory of the West, it found free play, and is seen without disguise. It is said, if you would see the American, you must cross the Alleghanies.

22   There is a levity of social and public action. I think there is a reaction on the people from the extraordinary advantages and invitations of their condition. In proportion to the personal ability of each man, he feels the invitation and career which the country opens to him. He is easily fed with wheat and game, with Ohio wine; but his brain is also pampered by finer draughts, by political power and by the power in the railroad board, or the mills, or the banks. This elevates his spirits and gives, of course, an easy self-reliance that makes him self-willed and unscrupulous.

23   I think, when we are most disturbed by their rash and immoral voting, it is not malignity, but recklessness. The people are better than their votes. They are careless of politics, because they do not ever feel seriously threatened; they feel strong and irresistible; they can do and undo; what they have enacted, they can repeal; and they do not entertain the possibility of being seriously caught and endangered in their own legislation. They stay away from the polls, saying, that *one vote can do no good;* and then they take another step, and say, *one vote can do no harm,* and vote for something which they do not approve, because their party or set, votes for it not from malice, but from levity. Of course, this levity puts them in the power of any party which has a steady interest to promote, which does not conflict manifestly with the pecuniary interest of the voters. New England, it is said, on each new political event, resolves itself into a debating society, and is the Germany of the United States.

24   The men also are uncertain. It is agreed by those who have lived there,

that you can form no conclusion to depend upon, from what a man on the prairie says, he will do. He says, he will come on Monday. He will not come on Monday. He may arrive some days later. He says, he will bring twenty hands. Perhaps he will bring three. Entire want of punctuality and business-habit—a principle cause of which is the uncertainty of health. The miasma takes the labourers.[16]

Go to the states on the Mississippi. Your western romance fades into 25 reality of some grimness. Everything wears a raw and ordinary aspect. You find much coarseness in manners; much meanness in politics; much swag-ger, and vaporing, and low filibusterism; the men have not shed their canine teeth. Well; don't be disgusted: 'tis the work of this river,—this Mississippi River,—that warps the men, warps the nations, and dinges them all with its own mud.

I found a good many burly fellows, with dangerous eyes, on the banks, 26 everyone with his cigar.—What is that man doing? What is that other man's work? And what of this? And this?—"O, they are river-hands; They follow the river." Never was a truer word. I found it every day more deeply exact, and of thousands and millions. *They follow the river.* They must chop down its woods; kill the alligator; eat the deer; shoot the wolf; mind the boat; plant the Mis-souri corn; cure, save, and send down stream the wild foison harvest, tilth, and wealth of this huge mud-trough of the two thousand miles or ten thou-sand miles of river.[17] How can they have a day's leisure for anything but the work of the river? Everyone has the mud up to his knees, and the coal of the country dinges his shirt. How can he know letters, or arts, or sciences?

Centre of all the Valley, and Gate of California, is St. Louis, a little French 27 town when it came into American possession fifty years ago.[18] And I have seen various persons who remember it, when there was only one brick house in it. It has now nearly 100,000 inhabitants, and is a well-built city, with spa-cious squares, and ample room to grow. The people are fully aware of their advantages: they have long smelled the Pacific Ocean. Cincinnati is a *bagatelle,* and they do not speak with due respect of New York.[19] A certain largeness ap-pears in the designs and enterprise of the people and a generosity. They talk St. Louis in all companies, all day, and great fortunes have been made by such as were wise or lucky enough to hold on to their lands. Governor Edwards, an old pioneer, told me that he remembered when St. Louis consisted of nothing but old tumbledown French houses with their little piazzas, whose columns, rotted away at bottom, and suspended from the top, were swinging in the wind: and that nobody who came here then, would think of buying land, in such a dilapidated place.[20] But a few men had the wisdom to look rather on the map, than in the streets; and they discovered that the two enormous river axes of the Continent, the Mississippi running North and South, and the Ohio and Missouri running East and West, had their practical intersection at St. Louis, and that sixty thousand miles of navigable river were tributary to this town; that this town must come to be "the greatest crossroads the world ever saw."

28   I stood at St. Louis and saw the Father of Waters rolling his steady flotilla of cakes and islands of ice, four miles an hour; and, day by day, the stream grew more impressive as one grew better acquainted with it.[21] 'Tis the only divinity that is worshipped on its banks. It is a power not to be trifled with. Here the river is only half a mile wide; But in freshets, it extends from bluff to bluff, or here ten to fifteen miles, and is crossed in steamboats so far. The engineers think the river here unconquerable and that they must follow, not dictate to it. They who know it best, fear it most. If you drive piles into it, to build a dam or pier, you only stir the bottom, which dissolves like sugar, and is all gone. Very laborious and costly constructions have been carried off. Real estate on the shores of Missouri is very floating capital.

29   Go into the states which make its valley, to know the powers of the river, the insatiate craving for nations of men to reap and cure its harvests, and the conditions it imposes, for it yields to no engineering. The prairie exists to yield the greatest quantity of tallow. For corn makes swine; swine is the export of all the land; and St. Louis, furiously, like some Eblis, vociferates, "Men! Men! more men, for I have more pork to pack."[22]

30   Cotton has done its office in the South,—cotton and sugar,—but now pig plays his unctuous part, draws his larded sides, like modest Prosperity, through the streets of all cities; grunts softly to nations; grunts melodiously to all who are not preoccupied by the new glitter of California, and seems to say, "My dear men, henceforth owe your aristocracy and civility to me!"

31   'Tis ever so. What earldoms of Guienne, Champagne, and Bourgogne lay sleeping in the first grape-store that was carried by travelling man or flying bird into the country of the Rhine? What civilization and power in the first grain of wheat on the Nile; in the first orange of Spain; in the tea plant of China; in the coal of England; in the peach-store of New Jersey; in the sugar

cane for the shores of the Gulf of Mexico? Thrones, constitutions, cities, states, laws, learning, arts, all dependent on some one plant which they ripen and sell: and not less, in all this prairie, on this modest quadruped. For, though it cannot be disputed that telegraphs are beautiful triumphs of science and art, if you hold your ear close to the poetic wires, the lightning is whispering to the packers, "A penny more on lard! An eighth on candles!"

Such as the people, such is the hero. I asked, "Who was the great man of the prairie?", and was shown a field of corn containing within one fence one thousand acres. The owner of this was the hero: one of themselves, a man who owned forty thousand acres, a cattle dealer who raises three or four thousand head of cattle, who delights to stand in the gap when great droves of cattle are to be separated,—these for the market, and those to pasture. The man who stands in the gap is to choose, on the instant, by their looks, as they come up, which to let through the gate, and which to keep off the other way, and he must be of such a size and look that a buffalo would not run over him. He delights in fat steers. He hardly knows what a bed is, sleeps behind a door, while his horse is baited; lives in the saddle; never knows leisure; eats his mush and milk with two spoons; he laughs at politics, as long as he is absolute in the market towns and cattle yards, and nobody can make money out of him.

I tell this story, because I passed a field alleged to be of these dimensions; though it seems, it is something incredible on the Atlantic states. For Mr. Greene of Cincinnati told me he knew of a simple field on the Big Miami River, which contains one thousand acres, and yielded one hundred bushels of corn to the acre.[23] Yet, he says: When he told this story in New England, Gentlemen would always take wine with him.

Narrow views, the narrow trade enforces, and yet the poverty and the habits of the swineherds and cattle dealers are wholesome for liberty. A stern equality is guarded and enjoyed. These men are fierce. Most of them live in loghouses,—the whole family in one room; eat ham and corn cakes; are all day in the open air, and accustomed to serve themselves; their dress is plain, and they pay no regard to a fine coat. Every man alternates the most daring and vigorous exertion, with listless repose.

They are all alike, all in working clothes. The Governor of the state works with his hands, and all the dignitaries must harness their own teams. I called on the Governor of the state at the statehouse, and, whilst I was paying my respects, the Secretary of State came into the room. "Governor," said the Secretary, "Did you take my screwdriver out of my room?" The executive acknowledged the act. It stood confessed, that he had borrowed it for his own uses. Need enough there was to use it: the statehouse was all cracking to pieces. They are all poor country people and live hard. But the sense of freedom and equality is never interrupted. New England men and women said, "We never knew what it was to be free, till we came to Missouri." They affirm, that, after people have been out west, ten years, nothing would draw them back to the old states. An alumnus of Yale, whom I discovered in grey working dress, told me, that, though his eyes ached for the hills when he went back to Connecticut, he could not breathe there;—a man was nothing there,—could not make his mark.

36   The people are all kings,—if the sceptre is a cattledealer's driving-whip. I noticed an extraordinary firmness, even to ferocity, in the face of many a drover, an air of independence, and lips which expressed more pluck, and perseverance, and wo to all opponents, than could be crowded into a coat of arms.

37   The condition of the Western states is today what was the condition of all the states fifty or a hundred years ago. It is the country of poor men. Here is practical democracy;—not the old experiment, out of a prostrate humanity, as out of a bank or magazine, to draw materials of culture to a class, and to avenge the injured many by wonderful success in a few; but here is the human race poured out over the continent to do itself justice; all mankind in its shirt-sleeves; not grimacing, like poor rich men in cities, pretending to be rich, but unmistakably taking off its coat, as in California, to hard work, when labor is sure to pay. This through all the country. For, really, though you see wealth in the capitals, it is only a sprinkling of rich men in the cities and at sparse points: the bulk of the population is poor. In Maine, every man is a lumberer. In Massachusetts, every twelfth man is a shoemaker and the rest millers, farmers, sailors, or fishermen.

38   Well, the result is, instead of the doleful experience of the European economist who tells us, "In almost all countries the condition of the great body of the people is poor and miserable,"[24] here that same great body has arrived at a sloven plenty;—ham and corn cakes, tight roof and coals enough have been attained; an unbuttoned comfort—not clean, not thoughtful, far from polished, without dignity in his repose; the man awkward and restless if

he have not something to do; but honest and kind, for the most part; understanding his own rights, and stiff to maintain them; and disposed to give his children a better education than he received.

The Anglo-Saxon race are characterised by their universal interest in politics. The people of England are educated by political discussion. In America, the public topic is not less absorbing; it is the one topic which neither age, nor sex, nor profession can long keep out of any conversation. But in this country a prodigious stride has been taken in practice, through universal suffrage. The fact that everybody elects and everybody is eligible, exasperates the discussion. In England, politics is a monopoly of a few; it is with the people a very distant affair. It is a choice of somebody far above them, and few of them are the choosers. The people whom I saw, eminent people, some of them, had never voted in their lives. But here, it is *you,* and *me,* and *him,* that are immediately concerned. 39

It were fatal to the happiness of a young man to set out with ultra-conservative notions in this country. He must settle it in his mind that the human race have got possession, and, though they will make many blunders, and do some great wrongs, yet, on the whole, they will consult the interest of the whole. 40

Practically, the tendency among us, is, to elect middle class men, and, by no means, first class men. 41

It is certainly desireable that men of capacity and virtue, that the best and wisest, should be entrusted with the helm of power, and the tendency to promote to this charge young men of very imperfect training, is, I know, regretted, and is, on many accounts, a bad feature. But there are certain benefits which mitigate the folly. I said, the people were educated by politics. Well, after a young man of the humblest class has passed through the village school, if he has vivacity and a social talent, and interests himself on the street, and at the railroad station, in talking politics, he is chosen to the Legislature. There, to his great surprise, he finds himself, for a whole winter, in far better company than he ever kept before; subject to social attentions and opportunities such as he never knew; listening (every day) to debates, to which he must listen, because he is to vote, and to give a reason for his vote, at home; and entertaining in his mind, daily, a class of questions wholly new to him, and quite above his habit. If he have capacity, this ordeal cannot fail to work on him, and I have known (it is notorious) an ordinary tavern brawler lose all his pro- 42 fanity and a large part of his other nonsense, and come back at the end of a single winter at the legislature, at least as much improved, as his young townsman from two years at the University.

43   There was in the Illinois Legislature a member, to whom plainly all parties looked with interest as a man likely to take a leading part. A gentleman who followed him in debate, took occasion to commend his speech, and to congratulate the legislature that this self-made man, so lately retired from a mechanical trade, had forsaken an honorable toil to lend his powerful service to the state. The new member made haste to correct his colleague (who described him as formerly a working man,) by saying, that he was still a mason, had by no means relinquished his trowel, had laid twenty thousand feet of plaster this fall and valued his work as a mason more than his skill in politics.

44   The American, in view of these great powers, appears passively to yield to this superincumbent Fate. His task is, to educe the capabilities of the Continent,—to make the most of it.

45   It is the American discovery, that, it is as easy to occupy large space, and do much work, as, to occupy a small space, and do little. And his task is the easier for the wonderful tools he uses. Mr. Webster had a good head, and loved Union; but the telegraph and railroad are better unionists than ten thousand Websters. He has a finer invention. In this age of tools, one of the skilfullest of all machines is this governing machine, rude as it is yet, which the Americans have so far perfected;—the distributing of political electricity over a vast area to avoid explosion. Last November, we had an election day,—and a revolution,—for every election is a revolution,—went off with the quietness of a pic-nic, or a sermon.

46   Thanks to his telegraph, his Election day, and his newspaper, he looks with a public eye, he works in a public spirit. The young American must know the geography of his continent, as exactly as his father did the streets of his town; such proximity have steam, rails, and telegraphs wrought.

47   Indeed, he has a wilderness of capabilities. He is versatile; (πολυτροποσ Oδυσσευσ;) has a many-turning Ulyssean culture.[25] He is confident as Jove in his powers and triumph; has a prospering look. He is a good combiner. The stock companies, the mills of the North, owe everything to the good concert of skilful men. His eyes run up and down, here and out there, and nothing escapes them. He thinks of Cuba, he thinks of Japan, he thinks of annexing South America, in due course. Nothing is impossible. He is accustomed to see things mind him. He believes, if he should attach his clamps to a

granite mountain, and let on the steam, it would follow him like a spaniel round the globe.

The English are stiff to their own ways. As I showed you, the towns are stiff to their old crafts for five centuries. It is the remark of our people employing English workmen, that they show great reluctance to deviate from their own methods, or proper work; whilst an American will turn his hand to anything. The very existence of our manufactures is a proof of aptitude: The stone cutters become sculptors. The house painters take to landscape and portraits. We can make everything but music and poetry. But also he has chambers opened in his mind which the English have not. He is intellectual and speculative, an abstractionist. He has solitude of mind and fruitful dreams. See what good readers of dreamy Germans we are—books which the English cannot bear. Many and many a good thought of some inspired man floats about for a time among studious men, and, not long after, I have noticed it caught up by some of the gladiators at Washington; and, endorsed or, rather, usurped by them, it passes into the newspapers, and, becomes, under these base colours, the property of the million.   48

This Fate, this natural growth, is really the ground on which the shrewd men of the world fall back, as their remedy for all evils. Such men do not believe much in any special policy, as free trade, nor put much faith in any statute in our capricious and fluctuating legislation; nor are they wont to trust the honesty of people, or to lift their eyes to considerations so large as the self-avenging power that mixes in human affairs, under the name of morals. But analyse what they say, and they do believe in the natural growth of the Republic; and this Fate really involves, in their mind, melioration, or, the self-avenging moral power. Name any benefit; One way or another, they believe the nation arrives at the same thing, which this ingenious person would compass with his law. Thus a strong party is for free trade; and all the reason and humanity is on their side; all the conclusions of history. But the old man shakes his head, and says, Look, You have got free trade in substance, though not in form; free trade with thirty-one nations, reaching through all climates, some of them manufacturing nations; some agricultural; some seafaring; some mining; and some hunting and fishing; all varieties of production, and not a customhouse.[26] You wanted tariff to protect your iron. Well, you did not get it; but, instead of twenty thousand tons, a year ago you manufactured 800,000.   49

Peace you want. But Mr. Cobden and Mr. Burritt, however respectable,   50 do not seem to him to say much to the purpose.[27] But trade can't afford to make war, or to suffer war to be made, and every man who has land, or money, or goods is by them bound ever to keep the peace. You talk of annexing new territory. It only adds to your burdens. By reciprocity, or free trade with England, you annex England, without the taxation of England.

51   Here, gentlemen, is a grave interest, the future of a quarter of the world, and of a race as energetic and as able as any in it: and one cannot help asking, What is to come of it?

52   Everybody working all day and half the night, and no man in this country knows whither we are driving, or can chant the destiny of the Anglo-American. The solar system, astronomers say, is moving toward a star in the arm of the Constellation Hercules: but whither we are drifting, who can tell.

53   When a new question is before Congress, or in the Courts, the presumption in all men's minds is that it will not be decided as the man within the breast would decide it, and a verdict on grounds of natural equity gives all men the joy of surprise. On Education; on Temperance; on Copyright; on claims of injured parties, whether states or private citizens; the Anglo-American usually gives a selfish and electioneering verdict. What can be worse than our legislation on Slavery? If there be any worse, be sure we shall find it out, and make that law.

54   But is this the action of legislatures only? It is also the public opinion as expressed in what are called the respectable journals. The tone of the press is not lower on Slavery than on everything else. Criminal on that point, ready to be criminal on every other. It has no great men. Its able men are not patriots, but simply attorneys of gross sectional interests. Its politics are the politics of trade. It goes for wars, if they be profitable wars. Its argument at the elections, is, "Roast Beef and two dollars a day;" and our people will not go for liberty of other people, no, nor for their own, but for annexation of territory, or a tariff, or whatever promises new chances for young men, more money to men of business.

55   The gain of the means of living absorbs them to the exclusion of the ends. Nothing but the brandy of politics will wake them from brute life. No song of any muse will they hear.

56   I know we must speak very modestly of the political good sense of the country and of its virtue. Any action of the well-disposed and intelligent class in its affairs is uniformly reckoned an impertinence, and they are presently

whipped back into their libraries and churches and Sunday schools. But drive out nature with a fork, and she presently comes back again. The moral sense is still renewed, and every child that is born is of nature's party.

We lack repose. As soon as we stop working, or active thinking, we mope. There is no self-respect, no grand sense of sharing the Divine preference. We are restless, run out and back, talk past, and overdo. When that civilization of their Universities and men of science and thought enters into their politics, I shall think they have made a real advance.

57

But this perhaps is partial and ungenerous, when we remember the sturdy minority, often for an age the majority, that, in England itself, has striven for the right, and the largest justice, and won so many charters, and still strives there with the lovers of liberty here. Rather, it is right to esteem without regard to geography this industrious liberty-loving Saxon wherever he works,—the Saxon, the colossus who bestrides the narrow Atlantic,—with one foot on England, and one on America,—at home on all land,—at home on all seas, asking no leave to be of any other,—formidable, conquering and to conquer, with his nervous and sufficient civilization weaponed already far beyond his present performing. At least I infer that the decided preference of the Saxon on the whole for civil liberty is the security of the modern world. He is healthy;—nature's democrat, nature's worker;—his instincts and tendencies, sound and right. Only let high and sound counsels be given to these twin nations, admonishing, and holding them up to their highest aim. At present, one hears only the tinkle of preparation. At present, their commerce is but costly trifling belting the world for raisins, oranges, oil, wine, tobacco, gums and drugs, hides and silk. But what for thought? What for humanity? What for the interests of the human soul? Is science, is the head, is the heart, always to be postponed, and only endured or tolerated? And our politics are no better than our trade. Are legislatures convened, with upheaval of the peace of nations in the fury of elections, to any noble, humane purpose? No; but to the most selfish and paltry.

58

It is impossible that a race so gifted and historied as this, should not presently make good the wonderful education of so many centuries. It is not indiscriminate masses of Europe that are shipped hitherward,—but the Atlantic is a sieve, through which only, or chiefly, the liberal, bold, *America-loving* part of each city, clan, or family, pass. It is mainly the light complexion, the blue eyes of Europe, that come; the black eyes, (the black drop,) the Europe

59

of Europe is left. Still, a portion of both races come, and the old contest of feudalism and of democracy renews itself here on a new battlefield.

60   That makes sometimes, and, at this moment, the vast interest of American history. Which principle, which branch of this compound English race is here (and now) to triumph? The liberty-loving, the thought-loving, the godly and grand British race, that have fought so many battles, and made so many songs, and created so many reverend laws and charters, and exhibited so much moral grandeur in private and poor men;—or, the England of Kings and Lords; castles and primogeniture; enormous wealth and fierce exclusion? Which is to be planted here? It is wonderful with how much rancour and premeditation at this moment the fight is prepared. Of late years, as I said, England has been materialized by its wealth, and the noble air of other times is gone.

61   Again, mark the differences more marked in every generation between the English and the Americans. The great majority of the Americans are of pure English descent. In some parts of America, their pedigrees have been well kept in family Bibles and in the town-clerk's office: Yet differences appear in stature, weight, complexion, feature, voice, widening too, in national character. These spring from new conditions, from climate, from the occupancy of wide territory, inducing solitary labor and sloven cultivation; from new staples of tillage and trade, new laws, new enemies. Climate draws the teeth, emaciates the body, spends the constitution, unbuilds and recomposes the bulky compact Briton into the loose-jointed, spare, swaggering Kentuckian. The Englishman, well-made, and even fatted by his climate of clouded sunshine, walks and sits erect, and his chair rests squarely on its legs. The American lolls and leans, tips his chair, adds rockers to it to keep it tipped, but is capable of equal energy in action and the mental powers are not impaired. The difference of manners is marked. The American is demonstrative; the English, shy and reserved.

62   When Rome has arrived at Cicero and Caesar, it has no more that it can do, and retreats. When Italy has got out Dante and Raffael, all the rest will be rubbish. So that we ought to be thankful that our hero or poet does not hasten to be born in America, but still allows us others to live a little, and warm ourselves at the fire of the sun; for, when he comes, we others must pack our petty trunks and be gone.

63   'Tis said, that when the Sphinx's riddle is solved, the Sphinx rolls herself

off the precipice and falls into the sea.[28] 'Tis said, every race or age ends with the successful man who knots up into himself the genius or idea of his nation, and, that, when the Jews have flowered into their prophet, or cluster of prophets, there is the practical end of the nation. When Greece is complete in Plato, Phidias, Pericles, the race is spent, and rapidly takes itself away.

The Anglo-American is a pushing, versatile, victorious race. Then it has wonderful powers of absorption and appropriating. The Mississippi swallows the Illinois, the Missouri, Ohio, and Red rivers, and does not widen: And this Anglo-American race absorbs into itself thousands and millions of Germans, French, Irish, Norwegians, and Swedes, and remains unchanged. 64

Our young men went to the Rhine to find the German genius which had charmed them and it was not there. Lessing, Herder, Schiller, Goethe, Wieland were all dead.[29] They hunted for it in Heidelberg, in Gottingen, in Halle, in Berlin: no one knew where it was. From Vienna to the frontier, it was not found; and they slowly and mournfully learned, that really America possessed more of that expansive inquisitive spirit, and they must return and look for it in Boston and New York. 65

The convictions of multitudes are sometimes as well expressed by braggart lips or in jeers that sound blasphemous,—and that word "manifest destiny," often profanely used, yet signifies the sense all men have of the prodigious energy and opportunity lying dormant here. The poor Prussian, or Austrian, or Italian escaping hither discovers that he has been handcuffed, fettered all his early lifetime, with monopolies and duties at every tollgate on his little cart of corn, or wine, or wood, or straw, or on his cow or ox or donkey, and his own lips and mind padlocked. No country, no education, no vote,— but passports, police, monks, and foreign soldiers instead. 66

The wild, exuberant tone of society in California is only an exaggeration of the uniform present condition of America in the excessive attraction of the extraordinary natural wealth. 'Tis doubtful whether London, whether Paris, whether Berlin can answer the questions which now rise in the American mind. American geography and vast population must be considered in all arrangements of commerce and politics, and we are forced, therefore, to make our own precedents. The radiation of character and manners here, the boundless America, gives opportunity as wide as the morning; and the effect is to dig away the peak of the mountain, to change the peak into a vast tableland, where millions can share the privilege of a handful of patricians. 67

Notes

1. England, France, and Holland all had their own East India companies. Emerson is referring to the English East India Company, formed in 1600 for trade with East and Southeast Asia; by the nineteenth century it had become the chief agent for British imperialism in India and China.

2. On 22 August 1851 the legendary yacht *America*, a gaff schooner class ship, won a fifty-three-mile race around the Isle of Wight sponsored by England's Royal Yacht Squadron and received the Squadron's "One Hundred Guinea Cup," which was then renamed the "America's Cup." John de Blaquiere, 4th Baron de Blaquiere (1812–1871), purchased the *America* immediately after its win.

3. The fiery, sulphuric burning effect of matches led to their being called "lucifers," after Lucifer, Latin name for the planet Venus and for the fallen archangel who rules the *Inferno* in Dante's *Divina commedia*.

4. "Cummer" is a Scottish word for an old woman, godmother, midwife, or even witch; except for the last, each of these meanings is consistent with Emerson's characterization of English character, history, and politics in this lecture.

5. Attributed to Thomas Fuller by Emerson (*JMN*, 13:93).

6. The Edict of Nantes (1598), promulgated by Henry IV of France, granted religious and civil liberties to French Protestants (also known as Huguenots); it was revoked by Louis XIV in 1685. Fleeing France after the revocation, many Huguenots settled in Spitalfields, in London's East End, where they worked as silk weavers.

7. A paraphrase of a characterization of George Villiers, 1st Duke of Buckingham (1592–1628), by Sir Henry Wotton (1568–1639), English diplomat and author, collected in the posthumous *Reliquiæ Wottonianæ* (1651).

8. John Nichols Wilder (1814–1858), a founder of the University of Rochester in New York. "Pythologian societies" were popular collegiate literary societies in the nineteenth century.

9. Johann August Wilhelm Neander (1789–1850), German theologian and church historian.

10. The adage, "the longest pole takes the persimmon," implies that success comes to those who have the advantage; in this case, Neander's library was sold to the person at the sale and who had "his money in his pocket."

11. The Penobscot River, including all its branches, is the longest river entirely in Maine.

12. "Hackmetach" is another name for the tamarack tree; esculent means edible.

13. The St. John River, principally in the province of New Brunswick, Canada, flows through the forested regions of northern Maine.

14. The American entrepreneur described in this paragraph is Francis Cabot Lowell

(1775–1817), who gathered together like-minded businessmen to form an association that purchased the land to build a new factory town east of Boston and leased or purchased rights to water to drive its textile mills; when incorporated in 1823, the town was named for its visionary principal founder. Nearby Lake Winnipesaukee, New Hampshire's largest lake, contributed to the town's rapid success.

15. Lajos Kossuth (1802–1894), Hungarian patriot and statesman, led the Hungarian revolution of 1848–1849; George William Frederick Howard, Viscount Morpeth (1802–1864), English statesman and viceroy of Ireland; Thomas Francis Meagher (1823–1867), American politician and soldier born in Ireland; Alessandro Gavazzi (1809–1889), Italian patriot and religious reformer; William Makepeace Thackeray (1811–1863), English novelist.

16. "Miasma," a noxious vapor rising from putrescent organic matter in marshlands, which pollutes the atmosphere, was formerly believed to be the carrier of various infections, particularly malaria.

17. "Foison" is an archaic term for a rich harvest.

18. St. Louis was ceded to America by the French in 1804.

19. A *"bagatelle"* is a seeming trifle or a thing of little importance.

20. Here, Emerson confuses Ninian Wirt Edwards (1809–1889), first superintendent of instruction in Illinois, with his father, Ninian Edwards (1775–1833), governor of the Illinois Territory and, then, the state of Illinois, as he had earlier (*JMN*, 11:527).

21. "Father of Waters" is a loose translation of the Algonquin name for the Mississippi River.

22. Eblis, prince of the evil spirits in Islamic mythology, was condemned by God to haunt ruins and eat unblessed food.

23. William Greene (1797–1881), Cincinnati lawyer.

24. Attributed to John Stuart Mill (1806–1873), English philosopher and economist, by Emerson (*JMN*, 13:82).

25. That is, the young American is similar to Homer's Odysseus, who in the *Odyssey* is depicted as a man of many devices.

26. The "old man" quoted here is Thomas Wren Ward (1786–1858), Boston merchant, whose reference to "thirty-one nations" is to the thirty-one states of the Union at the time (*JMN*, 11:408n).

27. Elihu Burritt (1810–1879), called "the Learned Blacksmith," American linguist and social reformer.

28. See the note to *Nature*, para 44, above.

29. In Emerson's youth, many prominent Americans traveled to Germany to seek out the scenes of German literature and the country's major writers and theologians; one of them was Emerson's brother William (1801–1868). German authors mentioned here include Gotthold Ephraim Lessing (1729–1781), Johann Gottfried von Herder (1744–1803), and Christoph Martin Wieland (1733–1813).

American Slavery

1 *Gentlemen,*[1]

2   I approach the grave and bitter subject of American slavery with diffidence and pain. It has many men of ability and devotion who have consecrated their lives to it. I have not found in myself the right qualifications to serve this any more than other political questions by my speech, and have therefore usually left it in their honored hands. Still, there is somewhat exceptional in this question, which seems to require of every citizen at one time or other, to show his hand, and to cast his suffrage in such manner as he uses. And, whilst I confide that heaven, too, has a hand in these events, and will surely give the last shape to these ends which we hew very roughly, yet I remember that our will and obedience is one of its means.

3   The subject seems exhausted. An honest man is soon weary of crying, 'Thief!' Who can long continue to feel an interest in condemning homicide, or counterfeiting, or wife-beating? 'Tis said, endless negation is a flat affair.

4   One must write with a red hot iron to make any impression. I thought, therefore, the policy of those societies which have opened courses of instruction on the aspects of slavery, wise, when they invited southern planters, the patrons and fathers of the system, to come hither and speak for it. Nay, I

think it would not have been ill-advised had they asked only such, and put the whole duty of expressing it on the slaveholders. I am sure it would have surprised northern men to see how little was to say on its behalf. But a difficulty arose in inducing them to come. The inviting committee were hospitable and urgent; but, most unfortunately, all the persons invited, with one or two brave exceptions, were absolutely pre-engaged. No solicitations were of any avail. It was left to us to open the subject, each as he could. And it is for us to treat it not as a thing that stands by itself,—that quickly tires and cloys,—but as it stands in our system;—how it can consist with the advantages and superiorities we fondly ascribe to ourselves.

A high state of general health cannot co-exist with a mortal disease in any part. If one member suffers, all the members suffer. Then, again, we must find relief from the uniform gloom of the theme, in large considerations of history, whereinto slavery and war enter as necessary shadows in the vast picture of Providence.   5

We have to consider that, however strongly the tides of public sentiment have set or are setting towards freedom, the code of slavery in this country is at this hour more malignant than ever before. The recent action of Congress has brought it home to New England, and made it impossible to avoid complicity.[2]   6

The crying facts are these, that, in a Republic professing to base its laws on liberty, and on the doctrines of Christianity, slavery is suffered to subsist: and, when the poor people who are the victims of this crime, disliking the stripping and peeling process, run away into states where this practice is not permitted,—a law has been passed requiring us who sit here to seize these poor people, tell them they have not been plundered enough, and must go back to be stripped and peeled again, and as long as they live.   7

But this was not yet the present grief. It was shocking to hear of the sufferings of these men: But the district was three hundred, five hundred, and a thousand miles off, and, however leagued with ours, was yet independent. And, for the national law which enacted this complicity, and threw us into conspiracy with the thief, it was an old dead law,—which had been made in an hour of weakness and fear, and which we had guarded ourselves from executing,—now revived and made stringent. But there was no fear that it would be valid.   8

But the destitution was here. We found well-born, well-bred, well-grown   9 men among ourselves, not outcasts, not foreigners, not beggars, nor convicts, but baptised, vaccinated, schooled, high-placed, official men, who abetted this law. 'O, by all means, catch the slave, and drag him back.' And when we went to the courts, the interpreters of God's right between man and man said, 'Catch the slave, and force him back.'

10 Now this was disheartening. Slavery is an evil, as cholera or typhus is, that will be purged out by the health of the system. Being unnatural and violent, I know that it will yield at last, and go with cannibalism, tattooing, inquisition, duelling, and burking;[3] and as we cannot refuse to ride in the same planet with the New Zealander, so we must be content to go with the southern planter, and say, you are you, and I am I, and God send you an early conversion.

11 But to find it here in our sunlight, here in the heart of Puritan traditions in an intellectual country, in the land of schools, of sabbaths and sermons, under the shadow of the White Hills, of Katahdin and Hoosac, under the eye of the most ingenious, industrious, and self-helping men in the world,—staggers our faith in progress.[4]

12 It is an accident of a larger calamity. It rests on skepticism, which is not local, but universal. The tone of society and of the press on slavery is only an index of the moral pulse. And I call slavery and the tolerance it finds, worst in this,—the stupendous frivolity it betrays in the heart and head of a society without faith, without aims, dying of inanition. An impoverishing skepticism scatters poverty, disease, and cunning, through our opinions, then through practice. The Dark Ages did not know that they were dark; and what if it should turn out, that our material civilization has no sun, but only ghastly gas-lights?

13 I find this skepticism widely spread. Young men want object, want foundation. They would gladly have somewhat to do, adequate to the powers they feel, somewhat that calls them with trumpet note to be heroes, some foeman worthy of their steel, some love that would make them greater than they are, which, not finding, they take up some second-best ground, finding no first-best—they slip into some niche or crevice of the state, some counting-room or rail-road, or whatever creditable employment,—not the least of whose uses is the covert it affords. They are not supported by any sense of greatness, and this reputable office screens them from criticism.

14 We are led to cast shrewd glances into our society. Among intellectual

men, you will find a waiting for, an impatient quest for more satisfying knowledge. It is believed that ordinarily the mind grows with the body, that the moment of thought comes with the power of action, and, that, in nations, it is in the time of great external power, that their best minds have appeared. But, in America, a great imaginative soul, a broad cosmopolitan mind, has not accompanied the immense industrial energy. Among men of thought and education, the unbelief is found as it is in the laymen. A dreary superficiality,— critics instead of thinkers, punsters instead of poets. They think the age of poetry is past. They think the Imagination belongs to the savage era. Yes, and serious men are found who think our Christianity and religion itself effete;— forms and sentiments that belonged to the infancy of mankind. I say intellectual men; but are there such, if we see to what uses the Intellect is applied? I think the atheism as much shown in the absence of intellectual action, as in the absence of profound morals.

Go into the festooned and tempered brilliancy of the drawing rooms, and 15 see the fortunate youth of both sexes, the flower of our society, for whom every favor, every accomplishment, every facility has been secured. Will you find genius and courage expanding those fair and manly forms? Or is their beauty only a mask for an aged cunning? Have they already grown worldly-wise? No illusions for them. A few cherished their early dream, and resisted to contumacy the soft appliances of fashion. But they tired of resistance and ridicule; they fell into file, and great is the congratulation of the refined companions that these self-willed protestants had settled down into sensible opinions and practices. Time was when a heroic soul conversing with eternity disdained the trifles of hard or easy lot, enamoured of honor and right.

The same career invites us. The method of nature is ever the same. God 16 instructs men through the Imagination. But the opera-glasses of our young men do not reach to ideas and realities.

The ebb of thought drains the law, the religion, the education of the land. 17 We send our boys to the universities. But do those institutions inspire the hope and gratitude, which, at great moments, have filled them with enthusiastic crowds? men eager to impart the light which has kindled them, and to set the whole land on flame? The boy looks at the professor and the textbook, with frightful penetration, and says, 'Has not the professor read his own books? I do not see that he is better or stronger for it all.'—He looks into the stables at the horses, and, after a few trials, concludes that the horses can teach him the most. They give him health, courage, and address, with no false pretences. The horse is what he stands for: perhaps he will break the rider's neck, but he never prated of ethics or of humanity, whilst the presidents and professors of the colleges were in this very rabble that voted down the moral sentiments of mankind.

18   Look at our politics. The great parties coeval with the origin of the government,—do they inspire us with any exalted hope? Does the Democracy stand really for the good of the many? of the poor? for the elevation of entire humanity? Have they ever addressed themselves to the enterprize of relieving this country of the pest of slavery?

19   The Party of Property, of education, has resisted every progressive step. Did Free Trade come from them? Have they urged the abolition of Capital Punishment? Have they urged any of the prophetic action of the time? No. They would nail the stars to the sky. With their eyes over their shoulders, they adore their ancestors, the framers of the Constitution. Nolumus mutari.[5] We do not wish to touch the Constitution. They wish their age should be absolutely like the last. There is no confession of destitution like this fierce conservatism. Can anything proclaim so loudly the absence of all aim or principle? What means this desperate grasp on the past, if not that they find no genius, no hope, no future in their own mind? Some foundation we must have, and, if we can see nothing, we cling desperately to those whom we believe can see.

20   Our politics have run very low, and men of character will not willingly touch them. This is fast becoming, if it has not already become, discreditable work. Those who have gone to Congress were honest, well-meaning men. I heard congratulations from good men, their friends, in relation to certain recent members, that "these were honest and thoroughly trustworthy, obstinately honest." Yet they voted on the late criminal measures with the basest of the populace. They ate dirt, and saw not the sneer of the bullies who duped them with an alleged state-necessity; And all because they had no burning splendor of law in their own minds. Well, what refuge for them? They had honor enough left to feel degraded: they could leave a place in which they could not preserve appearances. They become apathized and indifferentists. We leave them in their retreats. They represented the property of their constituency. Our merchants do not believe in anything but their trade. They loll in republican chairs, they eat and drink in republican Astor,

Tremont, and Girard Houses.⁶ They roll in easy and swift trains, telegraphing their wishes before them. And the power of money is so obtrusive as to exclude the view of the larger powers that control it.

I am sorry to say, that, even our political reforms show the same desperation. What shall we think of the new movement? We are clear that the old parties could not lead us. They were plainly bankrupt, their machineries and politicians discredited. We will have none of them. Yes, but shall we therefore abdicate our commonsense? I employed false guides and they misled me; shall I therefore put my head in a bag?   21

The late revolution in Massachusetts, no man will wonder at who sees how far our politics had departed from the path of simple right. The reigning parties had forfeited the awe and reverence which always attaches to a wise and honest government. And as they inspired no respect, they were turned out by an immense frolic. But to persist in a joke;—I don't like joking with edge-tools, and there is no knife so sharp as legislation.⁷   22

An Indian Rajah, Yokasindra, had a poor porter in his gate who resembled him in person. He put his royal robes on him, and seated him on his throne: Then he put on his own head the porter's cap, and stood in the gate, and laughed to see his ministers deceived, bowing down before the porter. But Datto, the porter, said, "Who is that fellow there on the threshold, laughing in my face? Off with his head." They obeyed him, and decapitated the Rajah, and Datto the porter reigned in his stead.⁸   23

What happens after periods of extraordinary prosperity, happened now. They could not see beyond their eye-lids, they dwell in the senses;—cause being out of sight is out of mind:—They see meat and wine, steam and machinery, and the career of wealth. I should find the same ebb of thought from all the wells alike. I should find it in science; I should find it in the philosophy of France, of England, and everywhere alike: a want of faith in laws, a worship of success. Everywhere, dreary superficiality, ignorance and disbelief in principles, a civilization magnifying trifles.   24

I saw a man in a calico-printing-mill, who fancied there was no reason why this pattern should please, and that pattern should not. They were all jumbles of color, of which one had the luck to take, and the other had the luck not to take, and that was all. I asked him, if he had that blue jelly he called his eye, by chance?   25

But geometry survives, though we have forgotten it. Everything rests on   26 foundations, alike the globe of the world, the human mind, and the calico print. The calico print pleases, because the arrangement of colors and forms agrees with the imperative requirements of the human eye. Is the reputation of the Parthenon, of the Elgin Marbles, the Apollo, and the Torso, a caprice?[9] Greek architecture was made by men of correcter eyes than others, who obeyed the necessities of their work, namely, the use of the building, the necessary support, the best aspect, entrance, light, and so forth, and, having satisfied these conditions, pared away all that could be spared for strength,—and behold, beauty.

27   Is the arch of the rainbow, the beauty of stars and sunshine, the joy of love, a caprice and an opinion? Or does any man suppose the reputation of Jesus accidental: the saint whom in different forms and opinions, but with unanimity of veneration as to character, the whole race of man worships? Or is the reputation of Socrates, of the Stoics, of Alfred, of Luther, or of Washington whimsical and unfounded?

28   There are periods of occultation when the light of mind seems to be partially withdrawn from nations as well as from individuals. This devastation reached its crisis in the acquiescence in slavery in this country,—and in the political servitude of Europe, during the same age. And there are moments of greatest darkness, and of total eclipse. In the French Revolution, there was a day when the Parisians took a strumpet from the street, seated her in a chariot, and led her in procession, saying, "This is the Goddess of Reason."[10] And, in 1850, the American Congress passed a statute which ordained that justice and mercy should be subject to fine and imprisonment, and that there existed no higher law in the universe than the Constitution and this paper statute which uprooted the foundations of rectitude and denied the existence of God.

29   Thus, in society, in education, in political parties, in trade and labor, in expenditure, or in the direction of surplus capital, you may see the credence of men; how deeply they live, how much water the ship draws. In all these, it is the thought of men, what they think, which is the helm that turns them all about. When thus explored, instead of rich belief, of minds great and wise sounding the secrets of nature, announcing the laws of science, and glowing with zeal to act and serve, and life too short to read the revelations inscribed on earth and heaven, I fear you will find non-credence, which produces nothing, but leaves sterility and littleness.

This skepticism assails a vital part when it climbs into the Courts, which are the brain of the State. The idea of abstract right exists in the human mind, and lays itself out in the equilibrium of nature, in the equalities and periods of our system, in the level of seas, in the action and reaction of forces, that nothing is allowed to exceed or absorb the rest; if it do, it is disease, and is quickly destroyed.

Among men, this limitation of my liberty by yours,—allowing the largest liberty to each compatible with the liberty of all,—protection in seeking my benefit, as long as it does not interfere with your benefit,—is justice, which satisfies everybody.

It was an early discovery of the human mind—this beneficent rule. This law is: Render to each his own.[11] As thou doest, shall it be done to thee.[12] As thou sowest, thou shall reap.[13] Smite and thou shalt smart; serve, and thou shalt be served.[14] If you love and serve men, you cannot by any dodge or stratagem escape the remuneration. Secret retributions are always restoring the level, when disturbed, of the Divine justice. It is impossible to tilt the beam. All the tyrants, and proprietors, and monopolists of the world in vain set their shoulders to heave the bar:—Settles forevermore the ponderous equator to its line, and man, and mote, and star, and sun must range with it, or be pulverized by the recoil. Any attempt to violate it, is punished, and re-coils on you. If you treat a man nobly, though he be of a mean habit, he will make an exception in your behalf, and will aim to do you justice. You cannot use a man as an instrument, without being used by him as an instrument. If you take advantage and steal from him, he watches his opportunity to make accounts square with you. If he is not strong enough to resist, then he will be cunning, and cheat you. Lord Coke said, "Any departure from the established principles of law, although at the time wearing the specious appearance of advantage, never fails to bring along with it such a train of unforeseen incon-veniences, as to demonstrate their excellence, and the necessity of return to them."[15]

Nature is not so helpless but it can rid itself at last of every crime. An Eastern poet, in describing the Golden Age, said, that God had made justice so dear to the heart of Nature, that, if any injustice lurked anywhere un-der the sky, the blue vault would shrivel to a snake-skin and cast it out by spasms.[16]

The fathers, in July 1787, consented to adopt population as the basis of

30

31

32

33

34

representation, and to count only three-fifths of the slaves, and to concede the reclamation of fugitive slaves;—for the consideration, that there should be no slavery in the Northwest Territory. They agreed to this false basis of representation and to this criminal complicity of restoring fugitives: and the splendor of the bribe, namely, the magnificent prosperity of America from 1787, is their excuse for the crime. It was a fatal blunder. They should have refused it at the risk of making no Union. Many ways could have been taken. If the southern section had made a separate alliance with England, or gone back into colonies, the slaves would have been emancipated with the West Indians, and then the colonies could have been annexed to us. The bribe, if they foresaw the prosperity we have seen, was one to dazzle common men, and I do not wonder that common men excuse and applaud it. But always, so much crime brings so much ruin. A little crime, a minor penalty; a great crime, a great disaster.

35   If the south country thinks itself enriched by slavery, read the census, read the valuation tables, or weigh the men. I think it impoverished. Young men are born in that country, I suppose, of as much ability as elsewhere, and yet some blight is on their education: in the present generation is there one living son to make good the reputation of the Past? If the north think it a benefit, I find the north saddled with a load which has all the effect of a partnership in a crime, on a virtuous and prosperous youth. It stops his mouth, ties his hands, forces him to submit to every sort of humiliation, and now it is a fountain of poison which is felt in every transaction and every conversation in this country.

36   Well, certain men were glad perceivers of this Right, with more clearness and steadiness than others, and labored to establish the application of it to human affairs. They were Lawgivers or Judges. And all men hailed the Laws of Menu, the Laws of Lycurgus, the Laws of Moses, the Laws of Confucius, the Laws of Jesus, the Laws of Alfred, and of men of less fame, who in their place, believing in an ideal right, strove to make it practical,—the Code of Justinian, the famous jurists, Grotius, Vattel, Daguesseau, Blackstone, and Mansfield.[17] These were original judges, perceivers that this is no child's play, no egotistic opinion, but stands on the original law of the world. And the reputation of all the judges on earth stands on the real perception of these few natural or God-anointed judges.

37   All these men held that law was not an opinion, not an egotism of any

king or the will of any mob, but a transcript of natural right. The judge was there as its organ and expounder, and his first duty was to read the law in accordance with equity. And, if it jarred with equity, to disown the law. All the great lawgivers and jurists of the world have agreed in this, that an immoral law is void. So held Cicero, Selden, and Hooker; and Coke, Hobart, Holt, and Mansfield, chief justices of England.[18] Even the Canon Law says, "Neither allegiance nor oath can bind to obey that which is unlawful."[19] Grotius, Vattel, Daguesseau, and Blackstone teach the same. Of course they do. What else could they? You cannot enact a falsehood to be true, nor a wrong act to be right. And I name their names, not, of course, to add authority to a self-evident proposition, but only to show that black-letter lawyers, supposed to be more than others tied to precedent and statute, saw the exquisite absurdity of enacting a crime.

And yet, in America justice was poisoned at its fountain. In our northern states, no judge appeared of sufficient character and intellect to ask not whether it was constitutional, but whether it was right. This outrage of giving back a stolen and plundered man to his thieves was ordained, and under circumstances the most painful. There was enough law of the State of Massachusetts to resist the dishonor and the crime, but no judge had the heart to invoke it, and no governor was found to execute it. The judges feared collision of the State and the Federal Courts. The Governor was a most estimable man—we all knew his sterling virtues, but he fell in an era when Governors do not govern, when Judges do not judge, when Presidents do not preside, and when representatives do not represent.[20]

The Judges were skeptics too and shared the sickness of the time. The open secret of the world was hid from their eyes: the art of subliming a private soul with inspirations from the great, and public, and divine soul from which we live. A man is a little thing whilst he works by and for himself. A judge who gives voice, as a judge should, to the rules of love and justice, is godlike; his word is current in all countries. But a man sitting on the Bench servile to precedent, or a windy politician, or a dangler trying to give authority to the notions of his superiors or of his set, pipes, and squeaks, and cheeps ridiculously. Judges are rare, and must be born such. King James said, "O, ay, I can mak him a lord, but I canna mak him a gentleman."[21] And governors and presidents can give a commission to sit on the Bench, but only wisdom can make a judge.

40   When the city is on fire, you will make but a feeble spray with your engine whilst you draw from your buckets. But once get your pipe screwed to a hose which is dipped in the river, or in the harbor, and you can pump as long as the Atlantic Ocean holds out.

41   This was the hiding of the light. But the light shone, if it was intercepted from us. Truth exists, though all men should deny it. There is a sound, healthy universe, whatever fires, or plagues, or desolation transpire in diseased corners. The sky has not lost its azure because your eyes are inflamed. Seas and waters, lime and oxygen, magnesia and iron, salts and metals, are not wasted: their virtues are safe, if an individual or a species sicken. And there's a healthy interior universe as well, and men are great and powerful as they conform to, or become recipient of, the great, equal general laws.

42   Now what is the effect of this evil government? To discredit government. When the public fails in its duty, private men take its place. When the British ministry is weak, the Times' editor governs the realm. When the American government and courts are false to their trust, men disobey the government, and put it in the wrong; the government is forced into all manner of false and ridiculous attitudes. Men hear reason and truth from private men who have brave hearts and great minds. This is the compensation of bad governments, —the field it affords for illustrious men. And we have a great debt to the brave and faithful men who, in the hour and place of the evil act, made their protest for themselves and their countrymen by word and deed. They are justified, and the law is condemned.

43   It is not to societies that the secrets of nature are revealed, but to private persons, to each man in his organization, in his thoughts. A serious man who has used his opportunities will early discover that he only works and thinks securely when he is acting on his own experience. All forcible men will agree that books and learned societies could not supply what their own good sense taught them.

44   It is common to say that the invention of gunpowder has equalized the strong and the weak. Never believe it. It has not made any deep difference, and Lord Wellington's weighing the soldiers proves it. Audacity and good sense have their old superiority, whatever weapons they wield. My political economy is very short: a man's capital must be in him.

45   'Tis a maxim in our politics that a man cannot be formidable in Congress, unless he is strong at home. I am glad to hear that confession, but I say

more,—that he must have his own support. 'Tis only what strength he carries with him everywhere, that can serve him anywhere. Paper money is good only as far as it represents real labor. A member who "walks into the chamber attended only by his own insignificance, cannot get any strength by the distant shouts of electors." All the British batteries cannot give comfort to the coward. If he knows there is weakness in his heart, tear off his epaulettes, break his sword, hoot him out of the camp.

But whilst I insist on the doctrine of the independence and the inspiration of the individual, I do not cripple but exalt the social action. Patriotism, public opinion, have a real meaning, though there is so much counterfeit rag money abroad under it, that the name is apt to disgust. A wise man delights in the powers of many people. Charles Fourier, noting that each man had a different talent, computed that you must collect eighteen hundred or two thousand souls to make one complete man. We shall need to call them all out.

Certainly, "the social state," "patriotism," "law," and "government," all did cover ideas, though the words have wandered from the things. The King or head of the state was god-like in the eyes of the people, whilst he was the foremost man of all the tribe, exponent of the laws, and the genius and the future of the tribe. It was so once in this country, when Washington, Adams, and Jefferson really embodied the ideas of Americans. But now we put obscure persons into the chairs, without character or representative force of any kind, and get a figure awful to office hunters.

And as the state is a reality, so it is certain that societies of men, a race, a people, have a public function, a part to play in the history of humanity. Thus, the theory of our government is Liberty. The thought and experience of Europe had got thus far, a century ago, to believe, that, as soon as favorable circumstances permitted, the experiment of self-government should be made. America afforded the circumstances, and the new order began. All the mind in America was possessed by that idea. The Declaration of Independence, the Constitution of the States; the parties; the newspapers, the songs, *The Star-spangled Banner*—land of the brave and home of the free—the very manners of the Americans, all showed them as the receivers and propagandists of this lesson to the world. "For this cause were they born and for this cause came they into the world: Liberty."[22] To each man the largest liberty compatible with the liberty of every other man.

[361]

49 It was not a sect, it was not a private opinion, but a gradual and irresistible growth of the human mind. That is the meaning of our national pride. That is at the bottom of all our brag about the star-spangled banner. It is a noble office. For liberty is a very serious thing. It is the severest test by which a government can be tried. All history goes to show, that it is the measure of all national success. Religion, arts, science, material production are as is the degree of liberty. Montesquieu said, "Countries are not cultivated in proportion to their population, but in proportion to their freedom."[23]

50 Most unhappily, this universally accepted duty and feeling have been antagonized by the calamity of southern slavery. And that institution, in its perpetual encroachment, has had, through the stronger personality, shall I say, of the southern people, and through their systematic devotion to politics, the art so to league itself with the government, as to check and pervert the natural sentiment of the people by their respect for law and statute.

51 And this country exhibits an abject regard to the forms, whilst we are swindled out of the liberty. Now this respect for forms, whilst the substance is filched away, is an insanity which nothing will cure but great outrages, such as the Boston Port Bill and Stamp Act, in 1770, and the Fugitive Slave Bill and Nebraska Bill.[24] These startle the common sense, and make us feel that we must put the Tea overboard, and hunt the slavehunter,—must destroy the law before the principle.[25]

52 Lord Nelson was a man of sterling English sense, and knowing himself to mean rightly, and being a rough, plain man much annoyed by the pedantic rules of the service, he went back to first principles, and once for all made up his mind.[26] "To obey orders," he said, "is thought to be all perfection, but the great order of all is to serve your country, and down with the French; and, whenever any statute militates with that, I go back," he said, "to the great order of all, out of which the little orders spring." And he was careful to explain to his officers, that, in case of no signals, or, in case of not understanding signals, no captain could go wrong who brought his ship close alongside an enemy's ship.

53 So every wise American will say, 'In the collision of statutes, or in the doubtful interpretation, liberty is the great order which all lesser orders are to promote.' That is the right meaning of the statute, which extirpates crime, and obtains to every man the largest liberty compatible with the liberty of every other man. No citizen will go wrong who on every question leans to

the side of general liberty. And whilst thus the society is no fiction, but has real rank—he who represents the ideas of the society being the head—it has a real function: That of our race is to liberty. So it has public actions which it performs with electric energy.

Men inspire each other. The affections are Muses. Hope is a muse, Love is, Despair is not, and selfishness drives away the angels. It is so delicious to act with great masses to great aims. For instance, the summary or gradual abolition of slavery. Why in the name of common sense and the peace of mankind is not this made the subject of instant negociation and settlement? Why do not the men of administrative ability in whose brain the prosperity of Philadelphia is rooted;—the multitude of able men who lead each enter-prize in the City of New York; in Boston; in Baltimore; why not the strong and courageous leaders of the south; join their heads and hearts to form some basis of negociation to settle this dangerous dispute on some ground of fair compensation, on one side, and of satisfaction, on the other, to the con-science of the Free States? Is it impossible to speak of it with reason and good nature? Why? Because it is property? Why, then it has a price. Because it is political? Well then, it intimately concerns us, threatens us, and there will never be a better time than the present time. It is really the great task fit for this country to accomplish, to buy that property of the planters, as the British nation bought the West Indian slaves. I say *buy*,—never conceding the right of the planter to own, but that we may acknowledge the calamity of his posi-tion, and bear a countryman's share in relieving him, and because it is the only practicable course, and is innocent.

Well, here is a right social or public function which one man cannot do, which all men must do. We shall one day bring the states shoulder to shoul-der, and the citizens man to man, to exterminate slavery. It is said, it will cost two thousand millions of dollars. Was there ever any contribution levied that was so enthusiastically paid as this will be? The United States shall give every inch of the public lands. The states shall give their surplus revenues, their unsold lands. The citizen, his private contribution. We will have a chimney-tax. We will give up our coaches, and wine, and watches. The churches will melt their plate. The Father of his country shall wait well-pleased a little longer for his monument: Franklin for his; the Pilgrim Fathers for theirs.[27] We will call on those rich benefactors who found Asylums, Hospitals, Athe-naeums, Lowell Institutes, Peabody Institutes, and Bates, and Astor, and City

54

55

libraries, and on wealthy bachelors and wealthy maidens to make the State their heir as they were wont in Rome.[28] The merchant will give his best voyage. The mechanic will give his fabric. The needlewomen will give. Children will have cent societies. If really the matter could come to negociation and a price were named, I do not think any price founded on an estimate that figures could tell would be quite unmanageable. Every man in the land would give a week's work to dig away this accursed mountain of sorrow once and forever out of the world.

Notes

1. After the Fugitive Slave Law passed in the United States Congress in September 1850 as part of the Compromise of 1850 between Southern slave-holding interests and Northern Free Soilers, Massachusetts, in 1851, famously resisted the new law that required the return of fugitive slaves found in the North to their owners, when the escaped slave Shadrach Minkins was rescued by Boston abolitionists. Abolitionist resistance was short-lived, however, for in 1854 the escaped slave Anthony Burns was arrested in Boston and returned to bondage. Emerson responded by preparing this lecture, which he delivered before the Massachusetts Anti-Slavery Society in Boston on 25 January 1855 and reprised five times before other anti-slavery societies over the next month.

2. An allusion to the Kansas-Nebraska Act of 1854, which Emerson sarcastically critiques, for in creating the territories of Kansas and Nebraska, the law allowed settlers in the territories to determine through the doctrine of "Popular Sovereignty" whether slavery would be allowed in each territory.

3. "Burking" is the crime of murdering a person without leaving telltale marks on the victim in order to sell the corpse.

4. The White Mountains of New Hampshire; Mount Katahdin in Maine; Hoosac Mountain in the Berkshires of western Massachusetts.

5. "We are unwilling to be changed."

6. Popular hotels of the day noted for their opulence: the Astor in New York, the Tremont in Boston, and the Girard in Philadelphia.

7. Emerson's thinly veiled attack on and outrage at the effectiveness of the Fugitive Slave Law in the recent case of Anthony Burns; see the note to paragraph 1 above and, for further details, Albert J. von Frank, *The Trials of Anthony Burns: Freedom and Slavery in Emerson's Boston* (Cambridge, Mass.: Harvard University Press, 1998).

8. Emerson's source is the Buddhist text, *The Mahâwanso*, ed. George Turnour (Ceylon: Cotta Church Mission Press, 1837), pp. 219–220 (*TN*, 3:321–322).

9. Between 1801 and 1803, Thomas Bruce (1766–1841), 7th Earl of Elgin, brought most of the marble frieze of the Parthenon—a temple of Athena on the Acropolis in Athens—back to England, where it is now in the British Museum. The sculptures of Apollo and the Torso Belvedere (an Athenian statue of Hercules in a sitting position) are in the Vatican.

10. A "strumpet" is a prostitute or a promiscuous woman.

11. Ezekiel 18:5.

12. Matthew 7:12.

13. Epistle to the Galatians 6:7.

14. Matthew 26:52 and John 13:14–16, respectively.

15. Edward Coke (1552–1634), English lawyer and lord chief justice of England and Wales.

16. The Eastern poet is not identified (*JMN*, 14:410).

17. According to tradition, Lycurgus was the ninth-century BCE lawgiver who imposed codes on Sparta designed to produce tough and able warriors; the Laws of Moses are the Ten Commandments; the Laws of Confucius refers to the *Analects*, a collection of moral and civic expressions written between 475 BCE and 221 BCE and traditionally believed to have been preserved by followers of the Chinese philosopher. Code of Justinian refers to the *Corpus Juris Civilis* (529–534) promulgated by Justinian I (ca. 482–565), emperor of Byzantium. Hugo Grotius (1583–1645), Dutch jurist; Emmerich de Vattel (1714–1767), Swiss jurist; Henri François d'Aguesseau (1668–1751), French jurist, whose surname was originally Daguesseau; William Blackstone (1723–1780), English lawyer and author of *Commentaries on the Laws of England* (1765–1769).

18. Sir Henry Hobart (ca. 1560–1625), 1st Baronet, English jurist and chief justice of the Court of Common Pleas; Sir John Holt (1642–1710), English jurist and lord chief justice of England.

19. Canon Law refers to the body of officially established regulations that govern the beliefs and practices of a Christian church.

20. Emerson is likely referring to one of the four governors of Massachusetts during this period: George N. Briggs (1796–1861), governor 1844–1851; George S. Boutell (1818–1905), governor 1851–1853; John H. Clifford (1809–1876), governor 1853–1854; and Emory Washburn (1800–1877), governor 1854–1855.

21. Emerson quotes this anecdote about the Scottish king James I (1566–1625) in his journal, but without a source (*JMN*, 13:170).

22. With "'For this cause . . . world: Liberty,'" cf. John 18:37.

23. Emerson's translation from Montesquieu, *L'esprit des lois, Oeuvres* (1819), 2:111 (*JMN*, 14:415).

24. The Boston Port Act passed by the British Parliament in 1774 outlawed the use of the Port of Boston to set up a blockade in fomenting "Rebellion"; the Stamp Act passed by the Parliament in 1765 imposed a direct tax on Britain's American colo-

nies and required that most printed materials in them be produced on stamped paper produced in London that carried an embossed revenue stamp.

25. "Tea overboard" is an allusion to the Boston Tea Party of 16 December 1773, when, as an act of civil protest against the tax policy of the British government and the East India Company, which controlled all the tea imported by the colonies, Boston's "Sons of Liberty" boarded three ships and threw their cargoes of taxed tea into Boston Harbor.

26. Horatio Nelson (1758–1805), 1st Viscount Nelson, English admiral.

27. The "Father of his country" is George Washington; the cornerstone for an obelisk-shaped monument honoring him in Washington, D.C., was laid in 1848, but the structure was not dedicated until 1885. Although today major American cities have established memorials that recognize Benjamin Franklin's contributions as a "Founding Father," the first formal memorial, a statue at the Old Post Office in Washington, D.C., was not dedicated until 1889. The Pilgrims had arrived at Plymouth in December 1620; the Pilgrim Fathers Memorial, a 252-foot tower in Provincetown, Massachusetts, was dedicated in 1910.

28. John Lowell, Jr. (1799–1836), helped Boston fund a free public lecture series; George Peabody (1795–1869) founded the Peabody Institute in Baltimore in 1857 with an endowment of $1.4 million; Joshua Bates (1788–1864) gave $50,000 to establish the Boston Public Library in 1852 and 30,000 volumes for its collections afterward; John Jacob Astor (1763–1848) helped to form the New York Public Library. All were merchants or bankers.

Address at the Woman's Rights Convention

Woman is the power of civilization. Man is a bear in colleges, in mines, in ships, because there are no women. Let good women sail in the ship, the manners at once are altered and mended; in a college, in California, the same remedy serves. Well, now in this country we are getting a little rough and reckless in voting. Here, at the right moment, when the land is full of committees examining election frauds and misdeeds, woman asks for her vote. It is the remedy at the moment of need. She is to civilize the voting as she has the sailors, the collegians, the miners. For now you must build noble houses proper to the State.

I suppose women feel in relation to men as geniuses feel among energetic workers, that though overlooked and thrust aside in the press, they outsee all these noisy masters. And we feel overlooked,—judged,—and sentenced. In that race, which is now predominant over all the other races of men, it was a cherished belief, that women had an oracular nature. They are more delicate than men, and, as thus more impressionable, they are the best index of the coming hour. I share this belief. I think their words are to be weighed,—but 'tis their inconsiderate words, according to the rule,—"Take their first advice, not their second." As Coleridge was wont to apply to a lady for her judgment in question of taste, and accept it, but, when she added, "I think so, because"

—"Pardon me, madam," he said, "leave me to find out the reasons for my-self." In this sense, then, as more delicate mercuries of the imponderable and immaterial influences, what they say and think are the shadows of coming events. Their very dolls are indicative. Frigg was the Norse goddess of women: "Weirdes all Frigg knoweth, though she telleth them never," said the *Edda*; that is to say, "All wisdoms woman knoweth, though she takes them for granted, and does not explain them as discoveries, like the understanding of man."[1] Men remark always the figure, they catch always the expression. They inspire by a look, and pass with us not so much by what they say or do, as by their presence. They learn so fast, and convey the result so fast, as to outrun the logic of their slow brother, and make his acquisitions poor. A woman of genius said, "I will forgive you that you do so much, and you me that I do nothing."[2] 'Tis their mood or tone that is important. Does their mind misgive them? or are they firm and cheerful? 'Tis a true report that things are going ill or well. And any remarkable opinion or movement shared by women will be the first sign of revolution.

3   Her strength is of her own kind. Plato said, "Women are the same as men in faculty, only less in degree." But the general voice of mankind has agreed that they have their own strength; that women are strong by sentiment; that the same mental height which their husbands attained by toil, they attain by sympathy with their husbands.

4   Man is the will, and woman the sentiment. In this ship of humanity, will is the rudder, and sentiment the sail. When woman affects to steer, the rud-der is only a masked sail. When women engage in any art or trade, 'tis usually as a resource, not a primary object. So with their schools and education of others' children. The life of the affections is primary to them, so that there is usually no employment or career which they will not, with their own ap-plause and that of society, quit for a suitable marriage. And they give entirely to their affections; set their whole fortune on the die; lose themselves eagerly in the glory of their husbands and children. Man stands astonished at a mag-nanimity that he cannot pretend to.

5   Mrs. Lucy Hutchinson, one of the heroines of the English Common-wealth, who wrote the life of her husband, the governor of Nottingham, says, "If he esteemed her at a higher rate than she in herself could have de-served, he was the author of that virtue he doted on, whilst she only reflected his own glories upon him. All that she was, was *him*, while he was here, and all that she is now, at best, but his pale shade."[3]

For Plato's opinion that "they are the same as men in faculty, only in less   6
degree": it is perhaps true that in no art or science, not in painting, poetry, or
music, have women produced a masterpiece. But there is an art which is better than poetry, painting, or music, or architecture, better than botany, geology, or any science, namely, conversation: wise, cultivated, genial conversation. Conversation is the last flower of civility, and the best result which life
has to offer us; a cup for gods, which has no repentance. It is our account of
ourselves. All we have, all we can do, all we know, is brought into play, and is
the reproduction in finer form of all our havings.

The part which women play in education, in the care of young, and the   7
tuition of older children, is their organic office in the world. So much sympathy as they have makes them inestimable as mediators between those
who have knowledge, and those who want it. Besides, their fine organization,
their taste and love of details, makes the knowledge better in their hands.

Coleridge esteems cultivated women to be the depositories and guard-   8
ians of English undefiled: and Luther commends that accomplishment of
pure German speech in his wife. Women are the civilizers. 'Tis difficult to
define. What is civilization? I call it the power of good women. It was Burns's
remark, "when he first came to Edinburgh, that between the men of rustic
life, and the polite world, he observed little difference; that, in the former,
though unpolished by fashion, and unenlightened by science, he had found
much observation, and much intelligence; but a refined and accomplished
woman was a being almost new to him, and of which he had formed a very
inadequate idea."[4]

Lucy Percy, Countess of Carlisle, the friend of Strafford and Pym, is thus   9
described by Sir Toby Matthew.[5]

> "She is of too high a mind and dignity not only to seek, but al-
> most to wish the friendship of any creature; they whom she is
> pleased to choose, are such as are of the most eminent condition,
> both for power and employment; not with any design towards
> her own particular, but her nature values fortunate persons. She
> prefers the conversation of men to that of women; not but she
> can talk on the fashions with her female friends, but she is too
> soon sensible that she can set them as she wills: that preeminence
> shortens all equality. She converses with those who are most dis-
> tinguished for their conversational powers. Of love freely will she

discourse, listen to all its faults, and mark all its power, . . . and will take a deep interest for persons of condition and celebrity."

10   "I like women, they are so finished," said a man of the world.[6] They finish society, manners, language. Form and ceremony are their realm. They embellish trifles; and these ceremonies that hedge our life around are not to be despised, and, when we have become habituated to them, cannot be dispensed with. Certainly, no woman can despise them with impunity. Then, genius delights, in ceremonies, in forms, in decorating life with manners, with proprieties, with order and grace. They are in their nature more relative. The circumstance must always be fit. Out of place they are disfranchised.

11   "Position," Sir Christopher Wren said, "is essential to the perfecting of beauty." A fine building is lost in a dark lane, and statues should stand in the air. So we commonly say, that easy circumstances seem necessary to the finish of the female character. But they make these with all their might.

12   The spiritual force of man is as much shown in taste, in his fancy and imagination attaching deep meanings to things and to arbitrary inventions of no real value, as in his perception of truth. He is as much raised above the beast by this creative faculty, as by any other. The horse or ox use no delays: they run to the river, when thirsty, to the corn, when hungry, and say, no thanks, and fight down whatever opposes their appetite. But man invents and adorns all he does with delays and degrees; paints it all over with forms, to please himself better; he invented majesty, and the etiquette of courts, and of drawing rooms; invented architecture, curtains, dress, and the elegance of privacy, to increase the joy of society; invented marriage, and surrounded by religion and comeliness, by all manner of dignities and renunciations, the union of the sexes.

13   And how should we better measure the gulf between the best intercourse of men in old Athens, in London, or in our American capitals,—between this, and the hedgehog existence of diggers of worms and the eaters of clay and offal, than by signalizing just this department of Taste or Comeliness? Yet herein woman is the prime genius and ordainer. There is no grace that is taught by the dancing master, no style adopted into the etiquette of courts, but was first the whim and action of some brilliant woman, who charmed beholders by this new expression, and made it remembered and copied.

14   They should be found in fit surroundings, with fair approaches, with

agreeable architecture. This convention should be holden in the sculpture gallery. And I think they should magnify their ritual of manners. Society, conversation, decorum, music, flowers, dances, colours, forms, are her homes and attendants.

> "The farfetched diamond finds its home
> Flashing and smouldering in her hair.
> For her, the seas their pearls reveal,
> Art and strange lands her pomp supply,
> With purple, chrome, and cochineal,
> Ochre, and lapis lazuli.
> The worm its golden woof presents,
> Whatever runs, flies, dives, or delves,
> All doff for her their ornaments
> Which suit her better than themselves."[7]

There is no gift of nature without some drawback; if we are here, we cannot be there; if we have day, we must forego night. And every extraordinary strength or possession that is added, usually lames the receiver on some part. So to woman this exquisite structure could not exist, without its own penalty: More vulnerable, more infirm, more mortal than men.

They could not be such excellent artists in this element of fancy, if they did not lend and give themselves to it. They are poets who believe their own poetry. They dwell more than men in the element and kingdom of illusion. They see only through Claude Lorraine glass.[8] They emit from all their pores a coloured atmosphere, one would say, wave upon wave of coloured light, in which they walk evermore, and see all objects through this warm tinted mist which envelopes them. And how dare any,—I dare not,—pluck away the coulisses, the roses, the stage effects,—shall I call them?—and routine, ceremonies, with which nature taught them to adorn and to console their life. "Yet fear not," says Mignon, "I shall dance blindfold the egg-dance, and shall not break an egg."[9]

But the starry crown of woman is in the power of her affection and sentiment, and the infinite enlargements to which they lead. Beautiful is the passion of love, painter and adorner of youth and early life; but none suspects in its blushes and tremors what tragedies and immortalities are beyond it. The passion with all its grace and poetry is profane to that which follows it. A few

15

16

17

years have changed the coy, haughty maiden into a matron existing for her children, a pelican feeding her young with her life. And these affections are only introductory to that which is sublime.

18   We men have no right to say it, 'tis very ungracious in man, but the omnipotence of Eve is in humility. The instincts of mankind have drawn the Virgin Mother,

> "Created beings all in lowliness
> Surpassing as in height above them."[10]

This is the divine person whom Dante and Milton saw in vision: this the victory of Griselda:[11] And it is when love has reached this height, that all our pretty rhetoric begins to have meaning, when we say, that it adds to the soul a new soul: it is honey in the mouth, music in the ear, and balsam in the heart.

> "Far have I clambered in my mind
> But nought so great as Love.
> 'What is thy tent? where dost thou dwell?'
> 'My mansion is Humility,
> Heaven's vastest capability;
> The further it doth downward tend,
> The higher up it doth ascend.'"[12]

19   The first thing men think of, when they love, is, to exhibit their usefulness and advantages. Women make light of these, asking only love. They wish it to be an exchange of nobleness. There is much in their nature, much in their social position, which gives them a divining power. Women know at first sight the characters of those with whom they converse. There is much that tends to give them a religious height which men do not attain. Their sequestration from affairs, and from the injury to the moral sense which affairs often inflict, aids them.

> "I use the Lord of the Kaaba, what is the Kaaba to me?" said Rabia. "I am so near to God, that, his word, 'whoso nears me by a span, to him come I a mile,' is true for me."
>
> Hassan Bassŏ, a famed Mahametan theologian, asked, "how she had lifted herself to this degree of the love of God?"
>
> She replied, "Hereby, that all things which I had found, I have lost in him."

The other said, "In what way or method hast thou known him?"
She answered, "O Hassan! Thou knowest after a certain art and
way, but I without art and way."

When once she was sick, three famed theologians came to her,
Hassan Vasri, Malek, and Balchi. Hassan said, "He is not upright
in his prayer who does not endure the blows of his Lord." Balchi
said, "He is not upright in his prayer, who does not rejoice in the
blows of his Lord." But Rabia, who, in these words, detected
some trace of egoism, said, "He is not upright in his prayer, who,
when he beholds his Lord, forgets not that he is stricken."[13]

I have known one bred in poverty and solitude, who realized to our expe-   20
rience the life of the saints of the convent, and religious houses. She was no
statute book of practical rules, nor orderly digest of any system of philosophy divine or human, but a Bible, miscellaneous in its parts, but one in Spirit,
wherein are sentences of condemnation, chapters of prophecy, promises,
and covenants of love, that make foolish the wisdom of the world with the
power of God.[14]

"When a daughter is born," said the Sheking, "she sleeps on the ground;   21
she is clothed with a wrapper; she plays with a tile; she is incapable of evil or
of good."[15] With the advancements of society, the position and fortunes of
women have changed, of course, as events brought her strength or her faults
into light. In modern times, three or four conspicuous instrumentalities may
be marked. After the deification of woman in the Catholic Church, the religious ages came again in the sixteenth and seventeenth centuries, when her
religious nature gave her, of course, new importance. The *Quakers* have the
honor of first having established in their discipline an equality in the sexes. It
is even more perfect in the later sect of *Shakers*. An epoch for Woman was
in France the building of the Hotel Rambouillet.[16] I think another step was
made by the doctrine of Swedenborg; a sublime genius who gave a scientific
exposition of the part played severally by man, and by woman, in the world;
and showed the difference of sex to run through nature and through thought.
Of all Christian sects, this is, at this moment, the most vital and aggressive.

Another step was the effect of the action of the age on the antagonism   22
to slavery. It was easy to enlist woman in this; it was impossible not to enlist
her. But that cause turned out, as you know, to be a great scholar: he was a
terrible metaphysician; he was a jurist, a poet, a divine. Was never a Univer-

sity of Oxford or Göttingen that made such students. It took a man from the plough, and made him acute, and eloquent, and wise to the silencing of the doctors. There was nothing it did not pry into, no right it did not explore, no wrong it did not expose, and it has, among its other effects, given woman a feeling of public duty, and an added self-respect.

23   One truth leads in another by the hand; one right is an accession of strength to take more. And the times are marked by the new attitude of woman urging, by argument and by association, her rights of all kinds, in short, to one half of the world: the right to education; to avenues of employment; to equal rights of property; to equal rights in marriage; to the exercise of the professions; to suffrage.

24   Of course, this conspicuousness had its inconveniences. 'Tis very cheap wit that has been spent on the subject, from Aristophanes, in whose comedies I confess my dulness to find good joke, to Rabelais in whom it is monstrous exaggeration of temperament and not borne out by anything in nature, down to the English comedy, and, in our day, Tennyson, and the American newspapers.[17] The body of the joke is all one, to charge them with temperament—victims of temperament—and is identical with Mahomet's opinion, that they have not a sufficient moral or intellectual force to control the perturbations of their physical structure. These were all drawings of morbid anatomy and such satire as might be written on the tenants of a hospital or an asylum for idiots.

25   Of course, it would be easy for women to retaliate in kind, by painting men from the dogs and orangs that have worn our shape: and the fact that they have not, is an eulogy on the taste and self-respect of women.

26   The good, easy world took the joke which it liked. There is always want of thought, always credulity. There are plenty of people who believe women to be incapable of anything but to cook; incapable of interest in affairs. There are plenty of people who believe that the world is only governed by men of dark complexion; that affairs are only directed by such; and do not see the use of contemplative men or how ignoble is the world that wanted them, and so without the affection of woman.

27   But for the general charge: No doubt the charge is well-founded. They are victims of their finer temperament. They have tears, and gaieties, and faintings, and glooms, and devotion to trifles. Nature's end of maternity,— maternity for twenty years,—was of so supreme importance, that it was to be secured at all events, even to the sacrifice of the highest beauty. They are

more personal. Men taunt them, that, whatever they do, say, read, or write, they are thinking of themselves and their set. Men are not to the same degree temperamented, for there are multitudes of men who live to objects quite out of them, as, to politics, to trade, to letters, or an art, unhindered by any influence of constitution.

The answer that, silent or spoken, lies in the mind of well meaning persons, to the new claims, is this: that, though their mathematical justice is not to be denied, yet the best women do not wish these things. These are asked for by people who intellectually seek them, but have not the support or sympathy of the truest women: and that if the laws and customs were modified in the manner proposed, it would embarrass and pain gentle and lovely persons, with duties which they would find irksome and distasteful.   28

Very likely. Providence is always surprising us with new and unlikely instruments. But perhaps it is because these persons have been deprived of education, fine companions, opportunities, such as they wished; because they feel the same rudeness and disadvantage which offends you,—that they have been stung to say, It is too late for us to be polished and fashioned into beauty; but at least we will see that the whole race of women shall not suffer as we have suffered.   29

Our marriages are bad enough, but that falls from the defects of the partners; but marriage, as it exists in America, England, and Germany, is the best solution that has been offered of the woman's problem. Orientalism, or Fourierism, or Mormonism, or the New York Socialism, are not solutions that any high woman will accept as even approximate to her ideas of well-being.[18] They have an unquestionable right to their own property. And, if the woman demand votes, offices, and political equality with men, as, among the Shakers, an Elder and Eldress are of equal power, and among the Quakers, it must not be refused.   30

'Tis very cheap wit that finds it so droll that a woman should vote. Educate and refine society to the highest point; bring together cultivated society of both sexes, in a drawing room, to consult and decide by voices on a question of taste, or a question of right,—and is there any absurdity, or any practical difficulty in obtaining their authentic opinions? If not, then there need be none in a hundred companies, if you educate them and accustom them to judge. And for the effect of it, I can say for one, that certainly all my points would be sooner carried in the state, if women voted.   31

On the questions that are important: Whether the government shall be in   32 one person, or whether representative, or whether democratic; whether men shall be holden in bondage, or shall be roasted alive and eaten as in *Typee,* or hunted with bloodhounds as in this country;[19] whether men shall be hanged for stealing, or hanged at all; whether the unlimited sale of cheap liquors shall be allowed; they would give, I suppose, as intelligent a vote as the five thousand Irish voters of Boston or New York.

33   Why need you vote? If new power is here, if a character which solves old tough questions, which puts me and all the rest in the wrong, tries and condemns our religion, customs, laws, and opens new career to young receptive men and women, you can well leave voting to the old dead people. Those whom you teach, and those whom you half-teach, will fast enough make themselves considered and strong with their new insight, and votes will follow from all the drill.

34   The objection to their voting is the same that is urged in the lobbies of legislatures against clergymen who take an active part in politics, that, if they are good clergymen, they are unacquainted with the expediences of politics, and if they become good politicians, they are the worse clergymen: so of women, that they cannot enter this arena without being contaminated and unsexed.

35   Here are two or three other objections to their voting: first, a want of practical wisdom; second, a too purely ideal view; and third, a danger of contamination.

36   For their want of intimate knowledge of affairs, I do not think this should disqualify them from voting at any town meeting which I ever attended. I could heartily wish the objection were sound. But if any man will take the trouble to see how our people vote—how many gentlemen are willing to take on themselves the trouble of thinking and determining for you, and, standing at the doors of the polls, give every innocent citizen his ticket as he comes in, informing him, that this is the vote of his party; and the innocent citizen, without further demur, carries it to the ballot box; I cannot but think that most women might vote as wisely.

37   For the other point, of their not knowing the world, and aiming at abstract right, without allowance for circumstances;—that is not a disqualification, but a qualification. Human society is made up of partialities. Each citizen has an interest and a view of his own, which, if followed out to the extreme, would leave no room for any other citizen. One man is timid, and

another rash; one would change nothing, and the other is pleased with nothing; one wishes, schools another armies; one gunboats, another public gardens.

Bring all these biases together, and something is done in favor of them all. Every one is a half vote; but the next elector behind him brings the other or corresponding half in his hand. A reasonable result is had. Now there is no lack, I am sure, of the expediency, or of the interest of trade, or of imperative class interests being neglected. There is no lack of votes representing the physical wants; and if, in your city, the uneducated emigrant vote by the thousands representing a brutal ignorance and mere animal wants, it is to be corrected by an educated and religious vote representing the desires of honest and refined persons.

38

If the wants, the passions, the vices are allowed a full vote, through the hands of a half-brutal, intemperate population, I think it but fair that the virtues, the aspirations, should be allowed a full vote as an offset, through the purest part of the people. As for the unsexing and contamination, that only accuses our existing politics, shows how barbarous we are, that our policies are so crooked, made up of things not to be spoken, to be understood only by wink and nudge, this man is to be coaxed, and that man to be bought, and that other to be duped. 'Tis easy to see there is contamination enough, but it rots the men now and fills the air with stench come out of that. 'Tis like a dance-cellar. The fairest names in this country in literature, in law, have gone into Congress and come out dishonored.

39

'Tis easy to see that many steps must be taken; an education of society; a purging of bullies out of the state; and a purging of the elegant cowards who have politely and elegantly betrayed us to them. And when I read the list of men of intellect, of refined pursuits, giants in law, or eminent scholars, or of social distinction, leading men of wealth and enterprise in the commercial community, and see what they voted for, or suffered to be voted for, I think no community was ever so politely and elegantly betrayed.

40

I do not think it yet appears that women wish this equal share in public affairs. But it is they, and not we, that are to determine it. Let the laws be purged of every barbarous remainder, every barbarous impediment to women. Let the public donation for education be equally shared by them. Let them enter a school, as freely as a church. Let them have, and hold, and give their property, as men do theirs. And, in a few years, it will easily appear

41

whether they wish a voice in making the laws that are to govern them. If you do refuse them a vote, you will also refuse to tax them according to our Teutonic principle: no representation, no tax.

42   'Tis idle to refuse them a vote on the ground of incompetency. I wish our masculine voting were so good that we had any right to doubt their equal discretion. They could not give worse vote, I think, than we do. Besides, it certainly is no new thing to see women interest themselves in politics. In English, French, German, Italian, and Russian history, you shall often find some Duchess of Marlborough or de Longueville or Madame Roland the centre of political power and intrigue.[20] See the experience of our Quakers, and of the Shakers, and of the Antislavery Society, in taking women as men into the council and government, and the women often possess superior administrative capacity.

43   All events of history are to be regarded as growths and off-shoots of the expanding mind of the race: and this appearance of new opinions, and their currency and force in many minds, is itself the wonderful fact. Whatever is popular, is important, and shows the spontaneous sense of the hour. The aspiration of this century will be the code of the next. It holds of high and distant causes, of the same influences that make the sun and moon. When new opinions appear, they will be entertained and respected by every fair mind according to their reasonableness, and not according to their convenience, or their fitness to shock our customs.

44   But let us deal with them greatly: let them make their way by the upper road, not by the way of manufacturing public opinion, which lapses continually into expediency, and makes charlatans. All that is spontaneous is irresistible: and forever it is individual force that interests. I need not repeat to you, —your own solitude will suggest it,—that a masculine woman is not strong, but a lady is. The loneliest thought, the purest prayer, is rushing to be the history of a thousand years. Let us have the true woman, the adorner, the hospitable, the religious heart, and no lawyer need be called in to write stipulations, the cunning clauses of provision, the strong investments; for woman moulds the lawgiver, and writes the law.

45   But I ought to say, I think it impossible to separate the education and interests of the sexes. Improve and refine the men, and you do the same by the women, whether you will or no. Every woman, being the wife, daughter, sister, or mother of a man, she can never be very far from his ear, never not of

his counsel, if she has something to urge that is good in itself and agreeable to nature. The slavery of women happened when the men were slaves of kings. The melioration of manners has brought their melioration, of course. It could not otherwise, and hence this new desire of better laws. For there are always a certain number of passionately loving fathers, brothers, husbands, and sons who put their might into the endeavor to make a daughter, a wife, or a mother happy in the way that suits best.

Woman should find in man her guardian. Silently she looks for that; and when she finds, as she instantly will, if he is not, she betakes her to her own defences, and does the best she can. But when he is her guardian,—fulfilled with all nobleness,—knows and accepts his duties as her brother, all goes well for both. The new movement is only a tide shared by the spirits of man and woman, and you may proceed in a faith, that, whatever the woman's heart is prompted to desire, the man's mind is simultaneously prompted to accomplish.

46

Notes

1. The Eddas, a collection of early Icelandic poetry.
2. Attributed to Caroline Sturgis Tappan (1819–1888), American author and longtime friend of Emerson and Margaret Fuller, by Emerson (*JMN*, 11:428).
3. Emerson's source is *Memoirs of the Life of Colonel Hutchinson, . . . written by his widow Lucy* (London, 1848), p. 30, by Lucy Hutchinson (1620–ca. 1680), English Puritan. Colonel John Hutchinson (1615–1664), an English soldier, signed the death warrant of King Charles I.
4. Attributed to *Reliques of [Robert] Burns* (1808), by Robert Hartley Cromek (1770–1812), English engraver, in Emerson's note in the manuscript.
5. Lucy Percy Hay, Countess of Carlisle (1599–1660), courtier; Sir Thomas Wentworth, 1st Earl of Strafford (1593–1641), statesman; John Pym (1584–1643), parliamentarian; and Sir Toby Matthew (1577–1655), writer and courtier, were politicians or activists during the English Civil War.
6. Attributed to Samuel Gray Ward (1817–1907), American poet, banker, and friend of Emerson, by Emerson (*JMN*, 7:465).
7. *The Angel in the House* (1854–1862), pt. 2, *The Espousals*, ll. 7–16, by Conventry Patmore (1823–1896), English poet.
8. Claude Gellée, known as Claude Lorrain, or Lorraine (1600–1682), French land-

scape painter. A Claude Lorraine glass is a convex hand mirror of dark or colored glass that reflects an image of diminished size and subdued color.

9. Mignon, a young Italian dancing girl, is a character in Goethe's *Wilhelm Miesters Lehrjahre (Wilhelm Miester's Apprenticeship)* (1795–1796).

10. Dante Alighieri, *Paradiso*, 33.2–3.

11. Griselda is a character in the *Decameron*, by Giovanni Boccaccio (1313–1375), who typifies patience as a wife and a mother subjected to many trials by her husband.

12. "Love and Humility," ll. 1–2, 7–11, by Henry More (1614–1687), English philosopher and poet.

13. Rābiah of Basra, Arab mystic and poetess, described as a "Mahometan saint" by Emerson (*JMN*, 15:42).

14. A portrait of Emerson's aunt Mary Moody Emerson (1774–1863), drawn from a letter of 1835 by Charles Chauncy Emerson (*JMN*, 5:158).

15. Quoted from *Shi King (Shih Ching),* a collection of poems attributed to Confucius.

16. Catherine d'Angennes, marquise de Rambouillet (1588–1665), French hostess, established a famous salon at her townhouse, the Hôtel de Rambouillet.

17. Aristophanes (ca. 450–ca. 380 BCE), Athenian writer of Greek comedies; François Rabelais (ca. 1494–1553), French satirist.

18. Orientalism is a term routinely used by art and literary historians in reference to Western authors' and artists' depiction or imitation of aspects of Middle Eastern or East Asian cultures. Mormonism (Church of Jesus Christ of the Latter-day Saints) is the predominant religious tradition of the American Latter Day Saint movement of Restorationist Christianity, founded by Joseph Smith, Jr. (1805–1844); Smith was succeeded by Brigham Young (1801–1877). The New York Socialists, led by Horace Greeley (1811–1872), political leader and editor of the *New-York Tribune,* and Parke Godwin (1816–1904), an editor of the *New York Evening Post,* generally followed the doctrines of Fourier.

19. *Typee: A Peep at Polynesian Life* (1846), a novel by Herman Melville (1819–1891), American writer.

20. Sarah Churchill, Duchess of Marlborough (1660–1744), was a member of Queen Anne's inner circle; Anne-Geneviève de Bourbon, duchesse de Longueville (1619–1679), was a French political activist; and Jeanne-Marie Roland de La Platière (1754–1793), known as Mme Roland, was a French revolutionary who fell to the guillotine.

Mr. R. W. Emerson's Remarks at the Kansas Relief Meeting in Cambridge

I regret with all this company the absence of Mr. Whitman   1
of Kansas, whose narrative was to constitute the interest of this meeting.[1]
Mr. Whitman is not here; but knowing, as we all do, why he is not, what duties kept him at home, he is more than present. His vacant chair speaks for
him. For quite other reasons, I had been wiser to have stayed at home, un-
skilled as I am to address a political meeting, but it is impossible for the most
recluse to extricate himself from the questions of the times.

There is this peculiarity about the case of Kansas, that all the right is on   2
one side. We hear the screams of hunted wives and children answered by the
howl of the butchers. The testimony of the telegraphs from St. Louis and the
border confirm the worst details. The printed letters of the Border ruffians
avow the facts.[2] When pressed to look at the cause of the mischief in the Kansas laws, the President falters and declines the discussion; but his supporters
in the senate, Mr. Cass, Mr. Geyer, Mr. Hunter, speak out, and declare the intolerable atrocity of the code.[3] It is a maxim that all party spirit produces the
incapacity to receive natural impressions from facts;[4] and our recent political history has abundantly borne out the maxim. But these details that have
come from Kansas are so horrible, that the hostile press have but one word

in reply, namely, that tis all exaggeration, 'tis an 'abolition lie'. Do the Committee of Investigation say, that the outrages have been overstated?[5] Does their dismal catalogue of private tragedies show it? Do the private letters? Is it an exaggeration, that Mr. Hoppe of Somerville, Mr. Hoyt of Deerfield, Mr. Jennison of Groton, Mr. Phillips of Berkshire, have been murdered? that Mr. Robinson of Fitchburg has been imprisoned, Rev. Mr. Nute of Springfield seized, and up to this time we have no tidings of his fate?[6]

3   In these calamities under which they suffer, and the worse which threaten them, the people of Kansas ask for bread, clothes, arms, and men to save them alive, and enable them to stand against these enemies of the human race. They have a right to be helped for they have helped themselves.

4   This aid must be sent, and this is not to be doled out as an ordinary charity, but bestowed up to the magnitude of the want, and, as has been elsewhere said, "on the scale of a national action." I think we are to give largely, lavishly to these men. And we must prepare to do it. We must learn to do with less, live in a smaller tenement, sell our appletrees, our acres, our pleasant houses. I know people who are making haste to reduce their expenses, and pay their debts, not with a view to new accumulations, but in preparation to save and earn for the benefit of the Kansas emigrants.

5   We must have aid from individuals;—we must also have aid from the State. I know that the last Legislature refused that aid. I know that lawyers hesitate on technical grounds, and wonder what method of relief the legislature will apply. But I submit, that, in a case like this, where citizens of Massachusetts, legal voters here, have emigrated to national territory, under the sanction of every law, and are then set on by highwaymen, driven from their new homes, pillaged, and numbers of them killed and scalped, and the whole world knows that this is no accidental brawl, but a systematic war to the knife, and in loud defiance of all laws and liberties, I submit that the governor and legislature should neither slumber nor sleep till they have found out how to send effectual aid and comfort to these poor farmers, or else, should resign their seats to those who can.[7] But first let them hang the halls of the State-house with black crape, and order funeral service to be said there for the citizens whom they were unable to defend.

6   We stick at the technical difficulties. I think there never was a people so choked and stultified by forms. We adore the forms of law instead of making them vehicles of wisdom and justice. I like the primary assembly. I own I have

little esteem for governments. I esteem them only good in the moment when they are established. I set the private man first. He only who is able to stand alone, is qualified to be a citizen. Next to the private man, I value the primary assembly, met to watch the government and to correct it. That is the theory of the American State, that it exists to execute the will of the citizens, is always responsible to them, and is always to be changed when it does not. First, the private citizen; then the primary assembly; and the government last.

In this country for the last few years the government has been the chief   7
obstruction to the common weal. Who doubts that Kansas would have been very well settled, if the United States had let it alone? The government armed and led the ruffians against the poor farmers. I do not know any story so gloomy as the politics of this county for the last twenty years, centralizing ever more manifestly round one spring, and that a vast crime, and ever more plainly, until it is notorious, that all promotion, power, and policy are dictated from one source—illustrating the fatal effects of a false position to demoralize legislation, and put the best people always at a disadvantage;—one crime always present,—always to be varnished over, to find fine names for, and we free-statesmen, as accomplices to the guilt, ever in the power of the grand offender.

Language has lost its meaning in the universal cant. *Representative Govern-*   8
ment is really misrepresentative; *Union* is a conspiracy against the northern states which the northern states are to have the privilege of paying for; the *adding of* Cuba and Central America to the slave-marts is *enlarging the area of Freedom. Manifest Destiny, Democracy, Freedom,* fine names for an ugly thing.[8] They call it otto of rose and lavender,—I call it bilge water.[9] It is called Chivalry and Freedom; I call it the taking all the earnings of a poor man and the earnings of his little girl and boy, and the earnings of all that shall come from him, his children's children forever.

But this is Union, and this is Democracy; and our poor people, led by the   9
nose by these fine words, dance and sing, ring bells, and fire cannon, with every new link of the chain which is forged for their limbs by the plotters in the capitol.

What are the results of law and union? There is no Union. Can any citi-   10
zen of Massachusetts travel in honor through Kentucky and Alabama and speak his mind? Or can any citizen of the southern country who happens to think kidnapping a bad thing, say so? Let Mr. Underwood of Virginia an-

swer.[10] Is it to be supposed that there are no men in Carolina who dissent from the popular sentiment now reigning there? It must happen, in the variety of human opinions, that there are dissenters. They are silent as the grave. Are there no women in that country,—women, who always carry the conscience of a people? Yet we have not heard one discordant whisper.

11   In the free states, we have a snivelling support to slavery. The judges give cowardly interpretations to the law, in direct opposition to the known foundation of all law, that *every immoral statute is void.*[11] And here of Kansas, the President says, "Let the complainants go to the courts"; though he knows, that, when the poor plundered farmer comes to the court, he finds the ringleader, who has robbed him, dismounting from his own horse, unbuckling his knife to sit as his judge.[12]

12   The President told the Kansas Committee, that the whole difficulty grew from "the factious spirit of the Kansas people, respecting institutions which they need not have concerned themselves about."[13] A very remarkable speech from a democratic president to his fellow citizens, that they are not to concern themselves with institutions which they alone are to create and determine. The President is a lawyer, and should know the statutes of the land. But I borrow the language of an eminent man used long since with far less occasion, "If that be law, let the ploughshare be run under the foundations of the Capitol;"—and if that be government, extirpation is the only cure.[14]

13   I am glad to see that the terror at disunion and anarchy is disappearing. Massachusetts, in its heroic day, had no government, was an anarchy. Every man stood on his own feet, was his own governor; and there was no breach of peace from Cape Cod to Mount Hoosac. California, a few years ago, by the testimony of all people at that time in the country, had the best government that ever existed.[15] Pans of gold lay drying outside of every man's tent, in perfect security. The land was measured into little strips of a few feet wide, all side by side. A bit of ground that your hand could cover was worth one or two hundred dollars, on the edge of your strip; and there was no dispute. Every man throughout the country was armed with knife and revolver, and it was known that instant justice would be administered to each offence: and perfect peace reigned. For, the Saxon man, when he is well awake, is not a pirate, but a citizen, all made of hooks and eyes, and links himself naturally to his brothers, as bees hook themselves to one another, and to their queen, in a loyal swarm.

But the hour is coming when the strongest will not be strong enough. A 14
harder task will the new revolution of the nineteenth century be, than was
the revolution of the eighteenth century. I think the American Revolution
bought its glory cheap. If the problem was new, it was simple. If there were
few people, they were united, and the enemy, 3,000 miles off. But now, vast
property, gigantic interests, family connections, webs of party, cover the land
with a network that immensely multiplies the dangers of war.

Fellow citizens, in these times full of the fate of the Republic, I think the 15
towns should hold town meetings, and resolve themselves into Committees
of Safety, go into permanent session, adjourning from week to week, from
month to month. I wish we could send the Sergeant-at-Arms to stop every
American who is about to leave the country. Send home every one who is
abroad, lest they should find no country to return to. Come home and stay at
home, while there is a country to save. When it is lost it will be time enough
then for any who are luckless enough to remain alive to gather their clothes
and depart to some land where freedom exists.

Notes

1. Edmund B. Whitman (1812–1873), friend and correspondent of John Brown, had
   moved to Lawrence, Kansas, in 1855 as an agent of the Massachusetts Kansas
   Committee.
2. Emerson's opening of this paragraph directly addresses the escalation of violence
   in "Bleeding Kansas" and the conflict between antislavery settlers, many of them
   emigrants from New England, and proslavery forces that often crossed over the
   border from Missouri.
3. Franklin Pierce (1804–1869), fourteenth president of the United States, was sympathetic to proslavery interests, including those of the United States senators
   named here: Lewis Cass (1782–1866) of Michigan, Henry Sheffie Geyer (1790–1859)
   of Missouri, and Robert M. Hunter (1808–1887) of Virginia. The "code" is the "Topeka constitution" (December 1855), designed to secure admission of Kansas as a
   free state and elections held under its auspices.
4. Emerson's source is *The Life and Letters of Barthold Georg Niebuhr,* trans. Susanna
   Winkworth, 3 vols. (London, 1852), 3:204. Niebuhr (1776–1831) was a German historian and critic.
5. The United States House of Representatives sent a committee of three members

to Kansas in March 1856; their extensive but ineffective *Report of the Special Committee Appointed to Investigate the Troubles in Kansas* was issued in July.

6. Mr. Hoppe, a brother-in-law of Ephraim Nute (see below), was shot and scalped by a proslavery ruffian near Lawrence, Kansas, on 19 August 1856. Mr. Hoyt may be Major S. D. Hoyt, murdered near Fort Saunders, Kansas, on 11 August 1856. William Phillips, an antislavery attorney, was murdered at Leavenworth, Kansas, on 1 September 1856. Charles Robinson (1818–1894), born in Hardwick, Massachusetts, was elected governor of Kansas in January 1856 under the Topeka constitution; for several months later in the year, he was held on a charge of treason at Camp Sackett. Ephraim Nute, Jr. (1819–1897) was a Unitarian clergyman and antislavery native of Massachusetts sent to Kansas in May 1855.

7. The expression "war to the knife" was the battle cry of Spanish general José de Palafox (1776–1847) at the defense of Zaragoza in 1808. The phrase occurs four years later in Byron's *Childe Harold's Pilgrimage,* Canto I, stanza 86, l. 9, and was revived by David R. Atchison (1807–1886), former senator from Missouri, in his newspaper, *The* (Atchison, Kansas) *Squatter Sovereign,* on 6 May 1856: "In a fight, let our motto be, 'War to the knife, and knife to the hilt.'" Extending his comments on the responsibility of elected officials here, Emerson joined Thoreau and others on 4 July 1856 in writing to Massachusetts governor Henry J. Gardner to intervene immediately on behalf of Massachusetts citizens who were victims of proslavery agitators in Kansas (*L,* 8:493).

8. Annexation of Cuba was a contentious possibility throughout the antebellum period. In 1848, President James K. Polk (1795–1849) authorized money to purchase Cuba, an idea revived by President Pierce. The Ostend Manifesto of October 1854 advocated conquest of Cuba in the interest of national security should efforts to purchase it failed. First expressed by John L. O'Sullivan (1813–1895), editor of the *United States Magazine and Democratic Review,* in 1845, "Manifest Destiny" registered the belief that the United States was destined to expand from the Atlantic to the Pacific and was thereafter invoked to justify national expansionist policies and actions.

9. This statement originally appears in Emerson's journal in reaction to remarks by Massachusetts politicians Daniel Webster and Rufus Choate in support of the Fugitive Slave Law (*JMN,* 13:339–340).

10. John Curtiss Underwood (1809–1873), a Republican lawyer, received threats due to his antislavery views and would leave Virginia in 1857 as a result.

11. This point is forcefully made in Emerson's "Address to the Citizens of Concord on the Fugitive Slave Law, 3 May 1851"; see *LL,* 1:263, and "American Slavery," para 37.

12. Here, through the first three sentences of the next paragraph, Emerson expresses his low opinion of "paltry" President Pierce (see *JMN,* 15:60).

13. Pierce's contemptuous statement about Kansans was reported in newspapers on

4 September 1856 (H. von Holst, *Constitutional and Political History of the United States, 1856–1859*, trans. John J. Lalor [Chicago, 1885], pp. 433–434).

14. Daniel Webster, "The Murder of John White," *Works*, 6 vols. (Boston, 1851), 6:76; Emerson chose not to name Webster here because of the late statesman's support for the Compromise of 1850, including the Fugitive Slave Law.

15. Emerson's source for this claim was the personal impressions of Albert Sands Southworth (1811–1894), the Boston daguerreotypist (*JMN*, 13:49).

The Natural Method of Mental Philosophy

1   Knowing is the measure of the man. By how much we know, so much we are. It is the measure of the man, because it is the measure of God. In all men, the first notion of God, is, the Omniscient. Homer says of his gods, "But Jove is the eldest, and knows the most." I quoted Plato as saying, "it is the law of Adrastia, that he who has known any truth shall be safe from harm until another period."[1] The Buddhists, in the East, say, "he who has well made Bana, (truths,) shall never be born into any hell."[2]

2   We are to each other as our perception is. It is the distinction of man to think and know. Otherwise, how can a man compare with a steam engine, or a self-acting mule, which stands up all day to work, never tires, and makes no fault?

3   We are getting to be proud of our Scandinavian descent, and the more, as we learn more of that race, and find they were always a sensible family. They thought, that he who could answer a question so as not to admit of any further answer, was the best man. In the Edda, the gods and heroes test their divinity by propounding questions to each other; and the one who cannot answer loses his life to the other. 'Tis like the riddles of the Sphinx, and on the same conditions; the heads of the speakers are at stake. So Thor is put to his wit at Asgard; Odin, in the Wastbrudius Hall; and Svend Vonved is a terrible

champion who rides up and down, putting conundrums, and killing such as take time to guess them.

It is very easy to see, that this game goes on in all societies of men, from the prize questions of Academies and Institutes; to the rivalries of the senate and the bar; the polished competition of wits at the dinner table; and the boisterous sally and retort of the swaggerers in the bar-room. We are to each other as our perception is. The nobility of a company, or of a period, is to be estimated by the depth of the ideas from which they live, and to which they appeal.

In that pure glory, what geometer can come with his angles? What astronomer can enter and plant his instruments, and take some instant measurement and inventory of this dome, in whose light forms, and substances, and sciences are dissolved? What chemist analyse these subtle elements, or find the metre of mind, whereon readily, as on our thermometer, we may say, this one had ten degrees, twenty degrees, one hundred degrees of intellect?

Now the method, the metaphysician, who can best help us, is, natural science. The German Steffens said, "The view of nature generally prevailing, at any determined time, in a nation, is the foundation of their whole Science; and its influence spreads over every department of life. It has an important influence on all social order, on morals, nay even on religion. 'Tis the peculiar mode of viewing nature which imparts a marked peculiarity to certain periods."[3]

We are always finding language wiser than we; and our best thought is already anticipated by the popular use of some word which covers it. After a man has made great progress, and fancies he has come to heights hitherto unscaled, the common words still fit his thought: Nay, he only now finds how wise they were:—for instance, 'Reason,' 'Conscience,' 'Substance,' 'Relation,' 'Nature,' 'Fortune,' 'Fate,' 'Person.'

After the student has waked all night, speculating on his relations to the world, and to the starry heaven, perhaps the first words he meets in the book he opens in the morning, are, macrocosm and microcosm; that is, the great world of nature, and the miniature world in man, showing him that some old thinker or nations of thinkers have thought his thoughts ages ago; that wherever he goes, men have been before him. What has Carlyle written about heroism, which the word hero did not already say to a gentle soul? The word Genius still is better than any definition of it.

The Greeks were the subtlest makers of words. It was a characteristic of

4

5

6

7

8

9

the Athenians, that they were anticipators of what the orator would say. And of these, the most eminent is Plato, who gave us many important words. Poet or Maker was one. And what a step was taken by the word Analogy, which he defined, "identity of ratio, the most beautiful of all bonds."[4] Not of facts, or of results, but of method. That was a perception of a few laws, of one law, streaming though nature, variously effecting a like result.

10   "There is a certain common bond that unites all the sciences together," said Cicero. The highest value of natural history, and, mainly, of the new results of geology, and the discovery of parallax, and the resolution of nebulae, is its translation into an universal cipher applicable to the Intellect. "All the languages should be studied abreast," said Kraitser.[5] And all the sciences should be, and all illuminate each other. Teach me the laws of Music, said Fourier, and I can tell you any secret in any part of the Universe,—in anatomy, for instance, or in astronomy. Kepler thought as much.

11   We are intent on Meteorology, and wish to find the law of the variable winds, and not get our hay wet. Winds and Tides, to be sure! I wish an Almanac for my farm. Tides indeed! What ebb and flow of power! as if life were a thunderstorm wherein we could now see by a flash the whole horizon, and then cannot see your hand. I wish to predict these, and not waste my time in attempting work which the soul today refuses.

12   Intellect; 'Tis a finer vegetation. It has, like that, germination, maturation, crossing, blight, and parasite. Reminiscence is only the perception of identity. Imagination is the being guided to the true symbol, by sharing the circulations of the universe. The intellect also finds its analogon in the atoms of chemistry, of electricity. Solitude is the father,—conversation the mother of thought.

13   Nature works after the same method as the human Imagination. Organic matter and mind go from the same law, and so correspond. Metaphysics might anticipate Jussieu.

14   And in the impenetrable mystery which hides (through absolute transparency) the mental nature, I await the insight which our advancing knowledge of material laws shall furnish. Thus, the laws of fluids, of the atmosphere, of light, heat, electricity, and galvanism, the law of undulation and polarity, are symbolical statements of the laws of memory and of thinking.

15   A physiologist told me, when he was at a loss in his study of embryos, he would go and talk with astronomers about the nebular theory, and what occurred in such and such conditions of the forming planet; and presently he

got the analogic hint he wanted.[6] Homology is the great gain of modern science.[7] And it reaches much wider, not only through matter, but through mind. He who enunciates a law of nature, enunciates a law of the mind.

The game of intellect is the perception that whatever befals (or can be stated,) is a universal proposition; and, contrariwise, that every general statement is poetical again, by being particularized or impersonated. Napoleon sees the same law running through all things. "Whatever they may tell you, believe that one fights with cannon as with fists." And J. Kemble said, steam carriages, Scythe chariots, Macedonian Phalanx, nay squadrons of horse are only larger bullets.[8] The scholar can easily translate all of Bonaparte's technics into all of his, and Carnot's and Maupertuis' laws of dynamics, and the laws of architecture and the rest.[9] Every breath of air is a carrier of the Universal Mind. So it is that every natural law enunciates a law of the mind. For all difference is quantitative. The quality is one.

All thought analogizes. Mental faculties are the transcendency of the physical. All above, as below, is organized. The symbolism of nature exists, because the mental series exactly tallies with the material series. And who enunciates a law of nature, enunciates a law of the mind.

Carnot added a new theorem to Dynamics, which was, in sum, that sudden alterations of speed are to be avoided in machinery, because all the power that, in the moment of stoppage, is taken from the legitimate action of the machine, goes to tear the machine asunder. When he was counselled to break up the French Directory, he replied, "No," for "sudden losses of speed are damaging." He too was a poet, and universalized his propositions, not only applied them to engines, but carried the hint up into higher planes of life.

Maupertuis taught, "that the quantity of action employed in nature to produce a change in the movement of bodies, is always a minimum."[10] And I have heard it announced as a thesis in zoology, that in nature there is a minimum of pain; that the bird of prey seizes its victim in the manner that kills with the least suffering.

In reference to men, we learn this lesson early. We have an instinct, that in spite of seeming difference, men are all of one pattern. We readily assume this, with our mates, with those with whom we talk and deal, and are disappointed and angry, if we find we are premature, and that their watches are slower than ours. In fact, the only sin which we never forgive in each other, is difference of opinion.

If we extend this identification, as we must,—beyond man, to the system

16

17

18

19

20

21

of animals,—we trace, on a lower plane, or in accommodation to some tyrannic circumstance, a repetition of our own properties and powers. Thus, if
man has organs for breathing, for sight, for locomotion, for taking food, for
digesting, for protection by house building, by attack and defence, for reproduction, and love, and care of his young, you shall find all the same in the
brute. You shall find all the same in the muskrat.

22   There is perfect correspondence, or, 'tis, only man modified to live in a
mud-bank. A fish, in like manner, is man furnished to live in the sea; a thrush,
to fly in the air; and a mollusk is a cheap edition, with a suppression of the
costlier illustrations, designed for dingy circulation or shelving in an oyster
bank, or among the seaweed.

23   And as man and man are superficially unlike, but radically identical,—
leaves of one tree,—and men and animals are modifications of one idea, so,
in a larger generalization, the animal creation and the globe on which they
live, or,—to take man as the representative,—man and his planet: these have
great common relations, the man being only a sort of compend of the globe
with its centrifugence and centripetence, with its chemistry, with its polarity,
with its undulation. And, lastly, as man and men, man and animals, man and
planet, are analogous, so, the same laws which these obey and express, run up
into the invisible world of the mind, namely, chemistry, polarity, undulation,
gravity, centrifugence, periodicity, and, that, hereby we acquire a key to these
sublimities which skulk and hide in the caverns of human consciousness;
namely; by the solar microscope of *Analogy*. 'Tis the key that opens the Universe. Nature shows every thing once,—shows every thing in coarse or colossal lines somewhere; and here, by extending into our dreams the same law by
which tides ebb and flow, moons wax and wane, trees grow, and stones fall.

24   All difference is quantitative: quality one. However we may conceive of
the wonderful little bricks of which the world is builded, we must suppose
similarity, and fitting, in their make. We must believe, that every hose in nature fits every hydrant, every atom screws to every atom. So only is chemistry, vegetation, animation, intellection, possible. Without identity at base,
chaos must be forever. In the initial forms or forces, be they what they may,
we must have already all the properties, which, in any combination, they afterwards exhibit.

25   Wonderful pranks this identity plays with us. It is because of this, that
nothing comes quite strange to us: As we knew our friends, before we were

introduced to them, and, at first sight distinguished them as ours; so to know, is to re-know, or to recognize. We hail each discovery of science as the most natural thing in the world.

"All things she knoweth are herself, and she is all that she knoweth."[11] All knowledge is assimilation to the object of knowledge. "The understanding transforms itself into the image of the thing understood.—The very under-standingness of a thing is nothing but a coming to and immediate approach of the unity of the understanding, and of the thing understood; So as the things themselves seem to talk with us without words."[12]

An angel who was present at the Creation saw, that from each man, as he was formed, a piece of the clay whereof he was made was taken, and set apart for him, as goods, or property; and it was allowed him to receive this in whatever form he desired, whether as wife, friend, son, daughter, or as house, land, warehouses, merchandize, horses, libraries, gardens, ships; also, he might have it now in one of these forms, and, at his will, it was converted into another. But, because it was one and the same lump, out of which all these were fashioned, and, as that was the clay of his own body, all these things had one and the same taste and quality to him, and he died at last of *ennui*.

We have shown that our help must be in that identity of ratio or design, which through all the variety of structure and element appears. What we see once, we see again; what is here, that is there: And it makes little difference what I learn; learn one thing thoroughly, and I have the key to all existences. This is that which the Indian sages, that which Plato, and Plotinus found. And we say, that, in the mind, all the laws of each department of nature, whether Botany, Anatomy, Chemistry, or Cosmology, are duly found repeated on a higher plane.

Thus, the first quality we know in matter, is, Centrality, which we commonly call gravity, and which holds the Universe together; which remains pure, and entire, and indestructible in each mote, as in masses and planets, and from each atom rays out illimitable influence. To this central essence answers Truth, in the intellectual world, Truth, whose centre is everywhere and its circumference nowhere, whose existence we cannot disimagine; Truth, the soundness and health of things against which no blow can be struck, but it recoils on the striker, and no fraud can prosper. Liars also are true. Let a man begin where he will, and work in whatever direction, he is sure to be

26

27

28

29

found instantly afterwards arriving at a right result! Truth, which we cannot wound; on whose side we always heartily are.

30   The mind is always true. Though the premises are false, the conclusions are right. And the self-reliance which belongs to every healthy human being is proof of it; proof that not he, but the soul of the world is in him; and, in proportion as it penetrates his crust of partiality, saith, 'Here am I; here is the whole.' Therefore, we require absoluteness in every man, absoluteness in the orator, in the poet, in the hero, in all manners; and if they have it not, they simulate it.

31   And if we are looking for intellectual metres, the first measure of a mind is its centrality, its veracity, its capacity of truth and its adhesion to the same. Every man is strong and mighty in proportion to his penetration of the facts of nature. And it would be easy to show, in intellectual action, the analogon of the momentum of falling bodies. The power of the mind, and its pace, increases as it approaches the end of its task.

32   How obvious is the momentum in our mental history! The momentum, which increases by exact law in falling bodies, increases by the like rate in intellectual action. Every scholar knows, that he applies coldly and slowly, at first, to his task; but, with the progress of the work, the mind becomes heated, and sees far and wide, as it approaches the end of the task, so that, it is the common remark of the student, 'Could I only have begun with the same fire I had on the last day, I should have done something.' Then, to do something well we must have done it often.

33   When we have *Gravity* or *Centrality* in Nature, then we have *Polarity*. As one is the principle of rest and permanence, so is this the principle of *difference, of generation, of change*. In the imponderable fluids, it shows itself in circulation, in undulation, in fits of easy transmission and reflection: In chemistry it appears in the affinities: In organized matter, in sex.

34   Well, this property is also the essential property of mental life,—the flowing, the generation, the melioration. The advance, everlasting. All things flow, said the Ancient; all flows; Πάντα ῥεῖ.[13] The Universe is only in transit, or, we behold it shooting the gulf from past to future: And this the mind shares. Transition is the attitude of power, and the essential act of life. The whole history of the mind is passage, pulsation, dark and light, preparation and arrival; and again, preparation and arrival. And as we only truly possess

what we mentally possess, that is, what we understand, we are passing into new earths and new heavens,—into new earths, by chemistry; into new heavens, in fact, by the movement of our solar system, and, in thought, by our better knowledge. The habit of saliency, of not pausing, but going on, is a sort of importation and domestication of the Divine effort into a man.

It is true, that, whilst it is the distinction of man to think, few men think truly. But there are in every society of well-born men, souls which apprehend things so correctly, that they seem to have been in the counsel of Nature. Their understanding seems to transform itself into the image of the thing understood, and that, not as a passive mirror, but as a living cause, so that they can not only describe the thing as it is, but can follow its genesis as a creator. They have the generalizing and ascending effort, which, even in chemistry, finds not atoms, at last, but spherules of force,—which measures and differences minds as they can take strides of advancing, as if one mind could only take one step, another could take two or three, another many. And there are minds which do not sit down in any finality, which neither gold, nor love of antiquity, nor old age, can tame or clip the wings of, but which, like Ulysses, sail the sea, and discover and project as long as they remain in our sight.

For man does not love fences. Each farmer covets the land that joins his own. And in mind there is always a better thought awaiting for us. What we call bounds of nature are only the limits of our organs. The microscope detects the eye of an invisible infusory, but it cannot reach to what the infusory sees. The microscope saw far; the infusory sees farther. There are no finalities in nature. The Torricellian tube was thought to make a vacuum. But no, over the mercury is the vapor of mercury.[14] The pores of glass, the pores of gold, are as wide to the mysterious ether and the elemental forces, as the chimney of a volcano. Our Arctic voyagers, as if obeying the laws of the mind, are now seeking beyond the polar barrier a Polynia, or open sea, north of the north. And, in mind, every thought leads in another thought by the hand. Every generalization shows the way to a larger; and every reform is only a cover, under which a larger reform, that dares not yet name itself, advances.

Transition, shooting the gulf, becoming somewhat else, is the whole game of nature: and death, the penalty of standing still. 'Tis not less in thought. I cannot conceive of any good in a thought which ends and stag-

35

36

37

nates. Liberty is the power to flow. To continue is to flow. Life is unceasing parturition.

"His very flight is presence in disguise."[15]

Inspiration is power to carry on and complete the metamorphosis, which, in the imperfect kinds is arrested for ages, and in the perfecter proceeds rapidly in the same individual.

38 Power of generalizing differences men, and it shows the rudeness of our metaphysics, though this is not down in the books. The number of successive saltations the nimble thought can make, measures the difference between the highest and lowest of mankind.

39 The nearness with which a man deals with his experiences, ranks him. If he go to antiquity, or to Europe for his subject, he avows incapacity. Therefore, I think that the poet consults his ease rather than his ability when he takes an ancient or a foreign subject.

40 The commonest remark, if the man could extend it a little, would make him a genius; but the thought is prematurely checked. All masters are distinguished by the power to add a second, a third, and perhaps, a fourth step, in a continuous line. Many a man had taken the first: with every additional step, you enhance immensely the value of the first.

41 So one would say of the force exerted at any one time in the works of nature, all depends on the battery. If it can give one shock, we shall get to the fish-form, and there stop; if two shocks, to the bird; if three, to the quadruped; if four, to the man. A great word was that which John Hunter introduced into Zoology,—*"arrested development,"* and which is now the commonplace of savans. And the measure of a mind is its fluidity, its sharing of the circulations,—of generalization,—of passing to interior and intimate thought, of watching the metamorphosis, the ascension into new forms, which is so dear a law of outward and inward nature.

42 See how the organism of mind corresponds to that of the body. There is the same hunger for food,—we call it curiosity; there is the same swiftness of seizing it,—we call it perception. The same assimilation of food to the eater, we call it culture; for simple recipiency is the virtue of space, not of a man.

43 The phenomena of sex reappear,—as, creation, in one mind, apprehension, in the other;—though I may remark, the sex of the mind does by no

means always follow the sex of the body, or, we often meet masculine minds in many women, and feminine minds in men. But as it is a law that, "Two great sexes animate the world," we note that a powerful mind impresses itself on a whole nation of minds; and is the parent of an innumerable spiritual progeny. What do you suppose is the census of the Platonists? or of the Aristotelian minds? What of the followers of St. Paul? or of Luther? or of Descartes? or of Voltaire? or of Swedenborg? or Goethe? Nature loves to cross her stocks, and does the variety and blending of talents less appear in new minds that have been bred under varied and antagonistic influence, under Napoleon and under Goethe?[16] Composite minds, like Burke, which blend two tendencies or streams of thought, give a rich result; And, usually, every mind of remarkable efficiency owes it to new combination of traits.

The gestation or bringing forth of the mind is seen in the act of detachment. Life is incessant parturition. There are viviparous and oviparous minds, minds that produce their thoughts complete men, like armed soldiers, ready and swift to go out to resist and conquer all the armies of error; and others, that deposit their dangerous, unripe thoughts here and there to lie still, for a time, and be brooded in other minds, and the shell shall not be broken until the next age, for them to begin, as new individuals, their career.

Some minds suffocate from too much store, too little vent. Kvasir, in the Norse legend, was a man so wise that none asked him any things which he knew not how to answer; but the dwarves said, that he had choked in his wisdom, there being none wise enow to ask him enough about learning. Health consists in the balance between knowing and expression; in keeping the channels open. Some minds choke from too much, some pine from too little communion. Some discharge their thought in volleys; and some would be invaluable, if you could attach to them a self-acting siphon, that would tap and draw them off, as now they carry about with them a perilous wisdom which they have no talent to impart. These are all related to the law of sex.

All natural functions are attended by their own pleasure: so are metaphysical. Perception gives pleasure; classification gives a keen pleasure; memory does; imagination intoxicates.

See how nature has secured the communication of knowledge. 'Tis certain that money does not more burn in a boy's pocket, than a piece of news burns in our memory, until we can tell it. And, in higher activity of the mind,

44

45

46

47

every new perception is attended with a thrill of pleasure; and the imparting of it to others is also attended with pleasure. Thought is the child of the intellect; and the child is conceived with joy, and born with joy.

48   Conversation is the laboratory and workshop of the student. The affection or sympathy helps. The wish to speak to the want of another mind,—assists to clear your own. A certain truth possesses us, which we in all ways labor to utter. Every time we say a thing in conversation, we get a certain mechanical advantage in detaching it well and deliverly. I value the mechanics of conversation. 'Tis pulley, and lever, and screw. To fairly disengage the mass, and find it jingling down, a good boulder, a block of quartz and gold, to be worked up at leisure in the useful arts.

49   Porosity is the best quality of matter. Every material possession must pass into the intellect, to become of real value. Until we have intellectual property, in a thing, we can have no right property in it. So works the poor little blockhead manikin. He must arrange and dignify his shop or farm, the best he can. At last, he must be able to tell you it, or write it, or to himself translate it all clumsily enough into the new sky-language he calls thought. Say not, 'tis bungling; he can't help it. The irresistible meliorations bear him forward; the fermentations go on, saccharine and vinous now; acetous by and by; upward to gas, and the imponderables at last.

50   Intellectual activity is contagious like the superinductions of chemistry. The boy becomes the hero of whom he reads: the man assimilates to the master he admires. Napoleon Napoleonizes and Plato Platonizes you. It is sufficient to set one in the mood of writing verses, at any time, to read any original poetry. And it is only necessary to look at the current literature, to see how one masterpiece brings into vogue a whole catalogue of books in the same style. What an impulse Cuvier, or Davy, or Liebig, or de Candolle, or Fresnel, or von Buch, has given to science![17]

51   The spectacle of vigor of any kind recruits us. In like manner, a blockhead makes a blockhead of you. In unfit company, the finest powers are benumbed; and no aids avail to resist the palsy of mis-association.

52   What's the use of telegraphs, what of newspapers? To know how men feel in Wisconsin, in Illinois, in Minnesota, I wait for no mails, no telegraphs. I ask my own heart. My interest tells me how their selfishness works; my honor what their honor dictates.

53   And this endless passing of one element into new forms, this incessant

metamorphosis, explains the importance which the Imagination holds in all our catalogue of mental powers. The Imagination is the reader of these forms; the Imagination accounts all productions and changes of nature as the nouns of language. The Imagination uses all the objects of nature representatively, too well pleased with their ulterior meaning to value their primary meaning much.

Now what is the drift of all this? What, but this:—that, Nature in every part is one,—that, in every particle is a hint of every mass, and of the Universe; every atom, a miniature of the world. That, the progress of all recent science has been, in the closet of each student, a tying together,—a study of one detail, under concentrating lamps of all the sciences and histories, and the total experience of a million observers.

54

I know there is a wisdom and love outside of all the liberty and vice of man, which redresses the disturbed balance. It is observed, that, as there are times of famine, of pest, and cholera, in races; so there are epochs of decline of genius, and destitution of thought. It has been noticed that these times precede as a cause such national calamities. It is a hybernation or sleep of the mind. But it appears also that the same periodicity which governs the ebb and flow of seas, and the astronomical motion, reaches also into the laws of thought. Each produces the other: the mind now retires inward; sheds her plumes; hoards by coarse activity; to be freed again for new power in science and art. And this alternation of animal and of intellectual eras follows one the other.

55

Not less large, not less exact, are the mysterious circulations in the realm we are exploring. The perceptions of a soul, its wondrous progeny, are born by the conversation, the marriage of Souls, so nourished, so enlarged. They are detached from their parent, they pass into other minds; ripened and unfolded by many, they hasten to incarnate themselves in action to take body, only to carry forward the will which sent them out: they take to them wood, and stone, and iron, and ships, and cities, and armies, and nations of men, and ages of duration, and the pomps of religion; the armaments of war, the codes and heraldry of states; agriculture, trade, colonies,—these are the ponderous instrumentalities, into which these nimble thoughts pass; and which they animate and alter. And, presently, antagonized by other thoughts which they first aroused, or by thoughts which are sons and daughters of these, the thought buries itself only in the new thought of larger scope which sprung

56

from it—its new creations and forwarder triumphs, whilst the old instrumentalities and incarnations are decomposed and recomposed into new.

57   The first illusion that is put upon us in the world is the amusing miscellany of colors, forms, and properties. Our education is through surfaces and particulars. Nature masks, under ostentatious subdivisions and manifold particulars, the poverty of her elements, and the rigid economy of her rules. Each has its enemy: brewer, sour fermentation; iron, rust; furrier, moths; orchardists, insects; farmer, frost; ice-man, heat. And as infants and children are occupied wholly with surface differences, so multitudes of people remain in the infant or animal estate, and never see or know more. They pass their whole existence in devotion to some huckster of fusty details; haberdasher in tape; fisher with his fish; grocer in candles; Cincinnati man in corn and bacon; Southern planter in short-staple and sea-island, and the rise and fall of a farthing or half-penny in cotton; towns of people live by shoes, or pails, or combs, or buttons, and so with countless trades, and tradesmen, and tradeswomen, all occupied in making much of small differences, to see which is nowise exhilarating to the student of man.

58   But in the measure in which there is wit, men leave looking at these trivial differences in things, and come to see that one ware is like another ware; nor at the difference between themselves and their customers and neighbors, friends and enemies, but perceive, that they are alike, that a fundamental unity or agreement exists, without which there could be neither marriage, nor conversation, politics, trade, literature, nor science.

59   And, lastly, Nature speaks to the imagination. Nature provides us in her changes and her productions with words to express every experience and thought of our own. The impressions made on our imagination make the great days in our life,—the book, poem, person, walk, which did not stay on the surface of the eye or ear, but penetrated to the inward senses, sets the whole man in movement, and is not forgotten. The imagination gives value to the day. Walking, working, or talking,—it is, how many strokes vibrate on the mystic string,—how many diameters are drawn quite through from matter to spirit; for, whenever you enunciate a natural law, you enunciate a law of the mind.

60   The spiritual crises are periods of as certain recurrence in some form to every mind as are dentition and puberty. The moment of early consciousness, when the young child first finds himself, as we say; the great day in

youth, when the mind begins to render account to itself; when it assumes its own vows; when its religious convictions befall; the day of love, when it joins itself to its kind; and the day of reason, when it sees all its partial and fiery experiences as elements of genius and destiny;—The *va et vient,* the ebb and flow, the pendulum, the alternation, the sleep and waking, the fits of easy transmission and reflection, the pulsation, the undulation, which shows itself as a fundamental secret of nature, exists in intellect.

The circulation of the waters: the rain falls, the brook runs into the river; the river into the sea; the sea exhales all day its mighty stream into the air; the universal vegetation sucks the stream, and gives it again to the atmosphere. It gathers into clouds, and drifts to mountains, and falls in rain, to renew its round. 61

The circulation of the gas locked up in blocks of basalt, in globe-crusts of granite, in beds of coal that floor counties and states, then heaved, in new ages, and unlocked by chemic affinities, and the joyful vesicle, with all its eternal properties safe and sound, there is no tear or wear to it,—through all its changes indestructible;—millions of years old, but as good as new,—sails away to enter into new combining; to make part of the plant, then part of the animal that feeds on it; then part of the man that feeds on the animal; then, by and by, buried once more in stone; inundated by new seas, for more millions of years; to wait for new fires to lift it again, to repeat the like circulation. 62

The circulation of the blood in the little world of man, food into chyme, chyme into chyle, chyle into blood, hurled from the heart in endless spasm, to rush through the system, carrying nutriment to every organ and every extremity. 63

Every discovery in any part gets recorded. It makes new instruments at the mathematical and philosophical shop: it requires and obtains a new modification in the construction of the observatory, in the coast-survey. It lets in some new light for the reading of ancient observations. Then the eyes of analogy bring it to the students of other sciences. Animal and vegetable structures correspond, and any new light on one is sure to suggest and to find some parallel provision by which analogous function in the other is worked. Even embryology, I have learned from its students, is served by the results of astronomy. Thus the most delicate and perishable improvement, gets recorded. 64

65   'Tis indifferent whether you say, All is matter, or, All is Spirit, and 'tis plain, there is a tendency in the times to an identity-philosophy. Once, we were timorous at allowing any dignity to matter. Matter was the principle of evil. Let there be no commerce between that Gentile and these Jews. Now, we are reconciling them in phrenology, the new German physiology, and in the new unproven sciences.

66   You do not degrade man by saying, Spirit is only finer body; nor exalt him by saying, Matter is phenomenal merely; all rests on the affection of the theorist, on the question whether his aim is noble. You will observe that it makes no difference herein whether you call yourself materialist or spiritualist. If there be but one substance or reality, and that is body, and it has the quality of creating the sublime astronomy, of converting itself into brain, and geometry, and reason; if it can reason in Newton, and sing in Homer and Shakspeare, and love and serve as saints and angels, then I have no objection to transfer to body all my wonder and allegiance.

Notes

1. Emerson first delivered "The Natural Method of Mental Philosophy" in Boston on 24 March 1858 as the fourth lecture of six in a series of the same title. In "The Powers of the Mind," the third lecture in the series, he quoted this passage from Plato's *Phaedrus*, 248c, from a version he drew from *Six Books of Proclus . . . on the Theology of Plato* (1816).
2. Quoted without a source in *JMN*, 14:115, and *TN*, 1:133.
3. Heinrich Steffens (1773–1845), German scientific philosopher born in Norway.
4. Emerson's paraphrase of a passage in Plato's *Timæus, The Works of Plato . . .*, trans. Floyer Sydenham and Thomas Taylor, 2 vols. (London, 1804), 2:479–480; see *JMN*, 14:216, and *TN*, 1:179 and 2:226.
5. Charles V. Kraitser (1840–1860), Hungarian-born linguist.
6. In the manuscript, Emerson identifies Louis Agassiz as the physiologist and Benjamin Peirce (1809–1880), English mathematician and astronomer, as one of the astronomers.
7. Homology is the observation of likeness in structure between parts of different organisms (e.g., the wing of a bat and the human arm) due to evolutionary differentiation from a corresponding part in a common ancestor, or the correspondence in structure between series of parts (e.g., vertebrae) in the same organism.

8. John Mitchell Kemble (1807–1857), English philologist and historian.

9. Lazare Nicholas Marguerite Carnot (1753–1853), French statesman and scientist who was Napoleon's geometer; Pierre Louis Morneau de Maupertuis (1698–1759), French mathematician and astronomer.

10. The following note by Emerson in the manuscript is keyed to the word "action" in the text: "action = mass × velocity + space thro wh. it passes."

11. Attributed to Sir Kenhelm Digby (1603–1665), English religious writer, in Emerson's note in the manuscript.

12. Emerson's source is *Oriatrike or, Physick Refined* . . . , trans. J[ohn] C[handler] (London, 1662), pp. 23, 25, by Jan Baptista van Helmont (1577–1644), Flemish physician and chemist (*TN*, 1:176).

13. This concept, expressed by the Greek phrase and elaborated on in English by Emerson, is attributed to Heraclitus and is a core principle underlying Emersonian organicism.

14. A Torricellian tube is a glass tube thirty or more inches in length, open at the lower end and sealed at the upper; it is named for Evangelista Torricelli (1608–1647), Italian physicist and mathematician, who invented the barometer.

15. Emerson's source is *Practical Philosophy of the Muhammadan People* (*TN*, 1:156).

16. Emerson's translation of "La Nature aime les croisements," which he attributes to Fourier, but without a source; see *JMN*, 9:50, 296, and 300; 10:44 and 45; 14:176; 15:244; and "Works and Days," para 11, below. For the French original, see "Inspiration," *CW*, 8:162.

17. Justus von Liebig (1803–1873), German chemist; Augustin Jean Fresnel (1788–1827), French physicist.

Fate

1   Delicate omens traced in air
To the lone bard true witness bare;
Birds with auguries on their wings
Chanted undeceiving things
Him to beckon, him to warn;
Well might then the poet scorn
To learn of scribe or courier
Hints writ in vaster character;
And on his mind, at dawn of day,
Soft shadows of the evening lay.
For the prevision is allied
Unto the thing so signified;
Or say, the foresight that awaits
Is the same Genius that creates.[1]

2   It chanced during one winter, a few years ago, that our cities were bent on discussing the theory of the Age. By an odd coincidence, four or five noted men were each reading a discourse to the citizens of Boston or New York, on the Spirit of the Times.[2] It so happened that the subject had the same prominence in some remarkable pamphlets and journals issued in London in the same season. To me, however, the question of the times resolved itself into a practical question of the conduct of life. How shall I live? We are incompetent to solve the times. Our geometry cannot span the huge orbits of the prevailing ideas, behold their return, and reconcile their opposition. We can only obey our own polarity.[3] 'Tis fine for us to speculate and elect our course, if we must accept an irresistible dictation.

3   In our first steps to gain our wishes, we come upon immovable limitations. We are fired with the hope to reform men. After many experiments, we find that we must begin earlier,—at school. But the boys and girls are not docile; we can make nothing of them. We decide that they are not of good

stock. We must begin our reform earlier still,—at generation: that is to say, there is Fate, or laws of the world.

But if there be irresistible dictation, this dictation understands itself. If we must accept Fate, we are not less compelled to affirm liberty, the significance of the individual, the grandeur of duty, the power of character. This is true, and that other is true. But our geometry cannot span these extreme points, and reconcile them. What to do? By obeying each thought frankly, by harping, or, if you will, pounding on each string, we learn at last its power. By the same obedience to other thoughts, we learn theirs, and then comes some reasonable hope of harmonizing them. We are sure, that, though we know not how, necessity does comport with liberty, the individual with the world, my polarity with the spirit of the times. The riddle of the age has for each a private solution. If one would study his own time, it must be by this method of taking up in turn each of the leading topics which belong to our scheme of human life, and, by firmly stating all that is agreeable to experience on one, and doing the same justice to the opposing facts in the others, the true limitations will appear. Any excess of emphasis, on one part, would be corrected, and a just balance would be made.

But let us honestly state the facts. Our America has a bad name for superficialness. Great men, great nations, have not been boasters and buffoons, but perceivers of the terror of life, and have manned themselves to face it. The Spartan, embodying his religion in his country, dies before its majesty without a question. The Turk, who believes his doom is written on the iron leaf in the moment when he entered the world, rushes on the enemy's sabre with undivided will.[4] The Turk, the Arab, the Persian, accepts the foreordained fate.

> "On two days, it steads not to run from thy grave,
> The appointed, and the unappointed day;
> On the first, neither balm nor physician can save,
> Nor thee, on the second, the Universe slay."[5]

The Hindoo, under the wheel, is as firm.[6] Our Calvinists, in the last generation, had something of the same dignity. They felt that the weight of the Universe held them down to their place. What could *they* do? Wise men feel that there is something which cannot be talked or voted away,—a strap or belt which girds the world.

"The Destiny, minister general,
That executeth in the world o'er all,
The purveyance which God hath seen beforne,
So strong it is, that tho' the world had sworn
The contrary of a thing by yea or nay,
Yet sometime it shall fallen on a day
That falleth not oft in a thousand year;
For, certainly, our appetités here,
Be it of war, or peace, or hate, or love,
All this is ruléd by the sight above."

CHAUCER: *The Knight's Tale.*[7]

The Greek Tragedy expressed the same sense: "Whatever is fated, that will take place. The great immense mind of Jove is not to be transgressed."[8]

6   Savages cling to a local god of one tribe or town. The broad ethics of Jesus were quickly narrowed to village theologies, which preach an election or favoritism. And, now and then, an amiable parson, like Jung Stilling, or Robert Huntington, believes in a pistareen-Providence, which, whenever the good man wants a dinner, makes that somebody shall knock at his door, and leave a half-dollar.[9] But Nature is no sentimentalist,—does not cosset or pamper us. We must see that the world is rough and surly, and will not mind drowning a man or a woman; but swallows your ship like a grain of dust. The cold, inconsiderate of persons, tingles your blood, benumbs your feet, freezes a man like an apple. The diseases, the elements, fortune, gravity, lightning, respect no persons. The way of Providence is a little rude. The habit of snake and spider, the snap of the tiger and other leapers and bloody jumpers, the crackle of the bones of his prey in the coil of the anaconda,—these are in the system, and our habits are like theirs. You have just dined, and, however scrupulously the slaughter-house is concealed in the graceful distance of miles, there is complicity,—expensive races,—race living at the expense of race. The planet is liable to shocks from comets, perturbations from planets, rendings from earthquake and volcano, alterations of climate, precessions of equinoxes. Rivers dry up by opening of the forest. The sea changes its bed. Towns and counties fall into it. At Lisbon, an earthquake killed men like flies. At Naples, three years ago, ten thousand persons were crushed in a few min-

utes.[10] The scurvy at sea; the sword of the climate in the west of Africa, at Cayenne, at Panama, at New Orleans, cut off men like a massacre. Our western prairie shakes with fever and ague. The cholera, the small-pox, have proved as mortal to some tribes, as a frost to the crickets, which, having filled the summer with noise, are silenced by a fall of the temperature of one night. Without uncovering what does not concern us, or counting how many species of parasites hang on a bombyx; or groping after intestinal parasites, or infusory biters, or the obscurities of alternate generation;—the forms of the shark, the *labrus,* the jaw of the sea-wolf paved with crushing teeth, the weapons of the grampus, and other warriors hidden in the sea,—are hints of ferocity in the interiors of nature.[11] Let us not deny it up and down. Providence has a wild, rough, incalculable road to its end, and it is of no use to try to whitewash its huge, mixed instrumentalities, or to dress up that terrific benefactor in a clean shirt and white neckcloth of a student in divinity.

Will you say, the disasters which threaten mankind are exceptional, and one need not lay his account for cataclysms every day? Aye, but what happens once, may happen again, and so long as these strokes are not to be parried by us, they must be feared. 7

But these shocks and ruins are less destructive to us, than the stealthy power of other laws which act on us daily. An expense of ends to means is fate;—organization tyrannizing over character. The menagerie, or forms and powers of the spine, is a book of fate: the bill of the bird, the skull of the snake, determines tyrannically its limits. So is the scale of races, of temperaments; so is sex; so is climate; so is the reaction of talents imprisoning the vital power in certain directions. Every spirit makes its house; but afterwards the house confines the spirit.[12] 8

The gross lines are legible to the dull: the cabman is phrenologist so far: he looks in your face to see if his shilling is sure. A dome of brow denotes one thing; a pot-belly another; a squint, a pug-nose, mats of hair, the pigment of the epidermis, betray character. People seem sheathed in their tough organization. Ask Spurzheim, ask the doctors, ask Quetelet, if temperaments decide nothing?[13] or if there be anything they do not decide? Read the description in medical books of the four temperaments, and you will think you are reading your own thoughts which you had not yet told.[14] Find the part which black eyes, and which blue eyes, play severally in the company. How shall a man escape from his ancestors, or draw off from his veins the black drop 9 which he drew from his father's or his mother's life?[15] It often appears in a family, as if all the qualities of the progenitors were potted in several jars,—some ruling quality in each son or daughter of the house,—and sometimes the unmixed temperament, the rank unmitigated elixir, the family vice, is drawn off in a separate individual, and the others are proportionally relieved. We sometimes see a change of expression in our companion, and say, his father, or his mother, comes to the windows of his eyes, and sometimes a remote relative. In different hours, a man represents each of several of his ancestors, as if there were seven or eight of us rolled up in each man's skin,—seven or eight ancestors at least,—and they constitute the variety of notes for that new piece of music which his life is. At the corner of the street, you read the possibility of each passenger, in the facial angle, in the complexion, in the depth of his eye. His parentage determines it. Men are what their mothers made them.[16] You may as well ask a loom which weaves huckaback, why it does not make cashmere, as expect poetry from this engineer, or a chemical discovery from that jobber. Ask the digger in the ditch to explain Newton's laws: the fine organs of his brain have been pinched by overwork and squalid poverty from father to son, for a hundred years. When each comes forth from his mother's womb, the gate of gifts closes behind him. Let him value his hands and feet, he has but one pair. So he has but one future, and that is already predetermined in his lobes, and described in that little fatty face, pig-eye, and squat form. All the privilege and all the legislation of the world cannot meddle or help to make a poet or a prince of him.

10   Jesus said, "When he looketh on her, he hath committed adultery."[17] But he is an adulterer before he has yet looked on the woman, by the superfluity of animal, and the defect of thought, in his constitution. Who meets him, or who meets her, in the street, sees that they are ripe to be each other's victim.

11   In certain men, digestion and sex absorb the vital force, and the stronger these are, the individual is so much weaker. The more of these drones perish, the better for the hive. If, later, they give birth to some superior individual, with force enough to add to this animal a new aim, and a complete apparatus to work it out, all the ancestors are gladly forgotten. Most men and most women are merely one couple more. Now and then, one has a new cell or camarilla opened in his brain,[18]—an architectural, a musical, or a philological knack, some stray taste or talent for flowers, or chemistry, or pigments, or story-telling, a good hand for drawing, a good foot for dancing, an athletic

frame for wide journeying, &c.—which skill nowise alters rank in the scale of nature, but serves to pass the time, the life of sensation going on as before. At last, these hints and tendencies are fixed in one, or in a succession. Each absorbs so much food and force, as to become itself a new centre. The new talent draws off so rapidly the vital force, that not enough remains for the animal functions, hardly enough for health; so that, in the second generation, if the like genius appear, the health is visibly deteriorated, and the generative force impaired.

People are born with the moral or with the material bias;—uterine brothers with this diverging destination: and I suppose, with high magnifiers, Mr. Frauenhofer or Dr. Carpenter might come to distinguish in the embryo at the fourth day, this is a Whig, and that a Free-soiler.[19]

It was a poetic attempt to lift this mountain of Fate, to reconcile this despotism of race with liberty, which led the Hindoos to say, "Fate is nothing but the deeds committed in a prior state of existence."[20] I find the coincidence of the extremes of eastern and western speculation in the daring statement of Schelling, "there is in every man a certain feeling, that he has been what he is from all eternity, and by no means became such in time."[21] To say it less sublimely,—in the history of the individual is always an account of his condition, and he knows himself to be a party to his present estate.

A good deal of our politics is physiological. Now and then, a man of wealth in the heyday of youth adopts the tenet of broadest freedom. In England, there is always some man of wealth and large connection planting himself, during all his years of health, on the side of progress, who, as soon as he begins to die, checks his forward play, calls in his troops, and becomes conservative. All conservatives are such from personal defects. They have been effeminated by position or nature, born halt and blind, through luxury of their parents, and can only, like invalids, act on the defensive. But strong natures, backwoodsmen, New Hampshire giants, Napoleons, Burkes, Broughams, Websters, Kossuths, are inevitable patriots, until their life ebbs, and their defects and gout, palsy and money, warp them.[22]

The strongest idea incarnates itself in majorities and nations, in the healthiest and strongest. Probably, the election goes by avoirdupois weight, and, if you could weigh bodily the tonnage of any hundred of the Whig and the Democratic party in a town, on the Dearborn balance, as they passed the hayscales, you could predict with certainty which party would carry it.[23] On

12

13

14

15

the whole, it would be rather the speediest way of deciding the vote, to put the selectmen or the mayor and aldermen at the hayscales.

16   In science, we have to consider two things: power and circumstance. All we know of the egg, from each successive discovery, is, *another vesicle;* and if, after five hundred years, you get a better observer, or a better glass, he finds within the last observed another. In vegetable and animal tissue, it is just alike, and all that the primary power or spasm operates, is, still, vesicles, vesicles. Yes,—but the tyrannical Circumstance! A vesicle in new circumstances, a vesicle lodged in darkness, Oken thought, became animal; in light, a plant. Lodged in the parent animal, it suffers changes, which end in unsheathing miraculous capability in the unaltered vesicle, and it unlocks itself to fish, bird, or quadruped, head and foot, eye and claw. The Circumstance is Nature. Nature is, what you may do. There is much you may not. We have two things,—the circumstance, and the life. Once we thought, positive power was all. Now we learn, that negative power, or circumstance, is half. Nature is the tyrannous circumstance, the thick skull, the sheathed snake, the ponderous, rock-like jaw; necessitated activity; violent direction; the conditions of a tool, like the locomotive, strong enough on its track, but which can do nothing but mischief off of it; or skates, which are wings on the ice, but fetters on the ground.

17   The book of Nature is the book of Fate. She turns the gigantic pages,—leaf after leaf,—never re-turning one. One leaf she lays down, a floor of granite; then a thousand ages, and a bed of slate; a thousand ages, and a measure of coal; a thousand ages, and a layer of marl and mud: vegetable forms appear; her first misshapen animals, zoophyte, trilobium, fish; then, saurians,—rude forms, in which she has only blocked her future statue, concealing under these unwieldy monsters the fine type of her coming king.[24] The face of the planet cools and dries, the races meliorate, and man is born. But when a race has lived its term, it comes no more again.

18   The population of the world is a conditional population; not the best, but the best that could live now; and the scale of tribes, and the steadiness with which victory adheres to one tribe, and defeat to another, is as uniform as the superposition of strata. We know in history what weight belongs to race. We see the English, French, and Germans planting themselves on every shore and market of America and Australia, and monopolizing the commerce of these countries. We like the nervous and victorious habit of our own branch

of the family. We follow the step of the Jew, of the Indian, of the Negro. We see how much will has been expended to extinguish the Jew, in vain. Look at the unpalatable conclusions of Knox, in his "Fragment of Races,"—a rash and unsatisfactory writer, but charged with pungent and unforgetable truths.[25] "Nature respects race, and not hybrids." "Every race has its own *habitat*." "Detach a colony from the race, and it deteriorates to the crab." See the shades of the picture. The German and Irish millions, like the Negro, have a great deal of guano in their destiny. They are ferried over the Atlantic, and carted over America, to ditch and to drudge, to make corn cheap, and then to lie down prematurely to make a spot of green grass on the prairie.

One more fagot of these adamantine bandages, is, the new science of Statistics. It is a rule, that the most casual and extraordinary events—if the basis of population is broad enough—become matter of fixed calculation.[26] It would not be safe to say when a captain like Bonaparte, a singer like Jenny Lind, or a navigator like Bowditch, would be born in Boston:[27] but, on a population of twenty or two hundred millions, something like accuracy may be had.[28]

'Tis frivolous to fix pedantically the date of particular inventions. They have all been invented over and over fifty times. Man is the arch machine, of which all these shifts drawn from himself are toy models. He helps himself on each emergency by copying or duplicating his own structure, just so far as the need is. 'Tis hard to find the right Homer, Zoroaster, or Menu; harder still to find the Tubal Cain, or Vulcan, or Cadmus, or Copernicus, or Fust, or Fulton, the indisputable inventor.[29] There are scores and centuries of them. "The air is full of men."[30] This kind of talent so abounds, this constructive tool-making efficiency, as if it adhered to the chemic atoms, as if the air he breathes were made of Vaucansons, Franklins, and Watts.[31]

Doubtless, in every million there will be an astronomer, a mathematician, a comic poet, a mystic. No one can read the history of astronomy, without perceiving that Copernicus, Newton, Laplace, are not new men, or a new kind of men, but that Thales, Anaximenes, Hipparchus, Empedocles, Aristarchus, Pythagoras, Œnopides, had anticipated them; each had the same tense geometrical brain, apt for the same vigorous computation and logic, a mind parallel to the movement of the world.[32] The Roman mile probably rested on a measure of a degree of the meridian.[33] Mahometan and Chinese know what we know of leap-year, of the Gregorian calendar, and of the precession of the equinoxes. As, in every barrel of cowries, brought to New Bedford, there shall be one *orangia,* so there will, in a dozen million of Malays and Mahometans, be one or two astronomical skulls.[34] In a large city, the most casual things, and things whose beauty lies in their casualty, are produced as punctually and to order as the baker's muffin for breakfast. Punch makes exactly one capital joke a week; and the journals contrive to furnish one good piece of news every day.

22   And not less work the laws of repression, the penalties of violated functions. Famine, typhus, frost, war, suicide, and effete races, must be reckoned calculable parts of the system of the world.

23   These are pebbles from the mountain, hints of the terms by which our life is walled up, and which show a kind of mechanical exactness, as of a loom or mill, in what we call casual or fortuitous events.

24   The force with which we resist these torrents of tendency looks so ridiculously inadequate, that it amounts to little more than a criticism or a protest made by a minority of one, under compulsion of millions.[35] I seemed, in the height of a tempest, to see men overboard struggling in the waves, and driven about here and there. They glanced intelligently at each other, but 'twas little they could do for one another; 'twas much if each could keep afloat alone. Well, they had a right to their eyebeams, and all the rest was Fate.

25   We cannot trifle with this reality, this cropping-out in our planted gardens of the core of the world. No picture of life can have any veracity that does not admit the odious facts. A man's power is hooped in by a necessity, which, by many experiments, he touches on every side, until he learns its arc.

26   The element running through entire nature, which we popularly call Fate, is known to us as limitation. Whatever limits us, we call Fate. If we are brute and barbarous, the fate takes a brute and dreadful shape. As we refine, our checks become finer. If we rise to spiritual culture, the antagonism takes a spiritual form. In the Hindoo fables, Vishnu follows Maya through all her ascending changes, from insect and crawfish up to elephant; whatever form she took, he took the male form of that kind, until she became at last woman and goddess, and he a man and a god. The limitations refine as the soul purifies, but the ring of necessity is always perched at the top.

27   When the gods in the Norse heaven were unable to bind the Fenris Wolf with steel or with weight of mountains,—the one he snapped and the other

he spurned with his heel,—they put round his foot a limp band softer than silk or cobweb, and this held him: the more he spurned it, the stiffer it drew.[36] So soft and so stanch is the ring of Fate. Neither brandy, nor nectar, nor sulphuric ether, nor hell-fire, nor ichor, nor poetry, nor genius, can get rid of this limp band. For if we give it the high sense in which the poets use it, even thought itself is not above Fate: that too must act according to eternal laws, and all that is wilful and fantastic in it is in opposition to its fundamental essence.

And, last of all, high over thought, in the world of morals, Fate appears as vindicator, levelling the high, lifting the low, requiring justice in man, and always striking soon or late, when justice is not done. What is useful will last; what is hurtful will sink. "The doer must suffer," said the Greeks: "you would soothe a Deity not to be soothed."[37] "God himself cannot procure good for the wicked," said the Welsh triad.[38] "God may consent, but only for a time," said the bard of Spain.[39] The limitation is impassable by any insight of man. In its last and loftiest ascensions, insight itself, and the freedom of the will, is one of its obedient members. But we must not run into generalizations too large, but show the natural bounds or essential distinctions, and seek to do justice to the other elements as well. 28

Thus we trace Fate, in matter, mind, and morals,—in race, in retardations of strata, and in thought and character as well. It is everywhere bound or limitation. But Fate has its lord; limitation its limits; is different seen from above and from below; from within and from without. For, though Fate is immense, so is power, which is the other fact in the dual world, immense. If Fate follows and limits power, power attends and antagonizes Fate. We must respect Fate as natural history, but there is more than natural history. For who and what is this criticism that pries into the matter? Man is not order of nature, sack and sack, belly and members, link in a chain, nor any ignominious baggage, but a stupendous antagonism, a dragging together of the poles of the Universe. He betrays his relation to what is below him,—thick-skulled, small-brained, fishy, quadrumanous,—quadruped ill-disguised, hardly escaped into biped, and has paid for the new powers by loss of some of the old ones. But the lightning which explodes and fashions planets, maker of planets and suns, is in him. On one side, elemental order, sandstone and granite, rock-ledges, peat-bog, forest, sea and shore; and, on the other part, thought, 29 the spirit which composes and decomposes nature,—here they are, side by side, god and devil, mind and matter, king and conspirator, belt and spasm, riding peacefully together in the eye and brain of every man.

30 Nor can he blink the freewill. To hazard the contradiction,—freedom is necessary. If you please to plant yourself on the side of Fate, and say, Fate is all; then we say, a part of Fate is the freedom of man. Forever wells up the impulse of choosing and acting in the soul. Intellect annuls Fate. So far as a man thinks, he is free. And though nothing is more disgusting than the crowing about liberty by slaves, as most men are, and the flippant mistaking for freedom of some paper preamble like a "Declaration of Independence," or the statute right to vote, by those who have never dared to think or to act, yet it is wholesome to man to look not at Fate, but the other way: the practical view is the other. His sound relation to these facts is to use and command, not to cringe to them. "Look not on nature, for her name is fatal," said the oracle.[40] The too much contemplation of these limits induces meanness. They who talk much of destiny, their birth-star, &c., are in a lower dangerous plane, and invite the evils they fear.

31 I cited the instinctive and heroic races as proud believers in Destiny. They conspire with it; a loving resignation is with the event. But the dogma makes a different impression, when it is held by the weak and lazy. 'Tis weak and vicious people who cast the blame on Fate. The right use of Fate is to bring up our conduct to the loftiness of nature. Rude and invincible except by themselves are the elements. So let man be. Let him empty his breast of his windy conceits, and show his lordship by manners and deeds on the scale of nature. Let him hold his purpose as with the tug of gravitation. No power, no persuasion, no bribe shall make him give up his point. A man ought to compare advantageously with a river, an oak, or a mountain. He shall have not less the flow, the expansion, and the resistance of these.

32 'Tis the best use of Fate to teach a fatal courage. Go face the fire at sea, or the cholera in your friend's house, or the burglar in your own, or what danger lies in the way of duty, knowing you are guarded by the cherubim of Destiny. If you believe in Fate to your harm, believe it, at least, for your good.

33 For, if Fate is so prevailing, man also is part of it, and can confront fate with fate. If the Universe have these savage accidents, our atoms are as savage in resistance. We should be crushed by the atmosphere, but for the reaction of the air within the body. A tube made of a film of glass can resist the shock

of the ocean, if filled with the same water. If there be omnipotence in the stroke, there is omnipotence of recoil.

1. But Fate against Fate is only parrying and defence: there are, also, the noble creative forces. The revelation of Thought takes man out of servitude into freedom. We rightly say of ourselves, we were born, and afterward we were born again, and many times. We have successive experiences so important, that the new forgets the old, and hence the mythology of the seven or the nine heavens.[41] The day of days, the great day of the feast of life, is that in which the inward eye opens to the Unity in things, to the omnipresence of law;—sees that what is must be, and ought to be, or is the best. This beatitude dips from on high down on us, and we see. It is not in us so much as we are in it. If the air come to our lungs, we breathe and live; if not, we die. If the light come to our eyes, we see; else not. And if truth come to our mind, we suddenly expand to its dimensions, as if we grew to worlds. We are as lawgivers; we speak for Nature; we prophesy and divine.

This insight throws us on the party and interest of the Universe, against all and sundry; against ourselves, as much as others. A man speaking from insight affirms of himself what is true of the mind: seeing its immortality, he says, I am immortal; seeing its invincibility, he says, I am strong. It is not in us, but we are in it. It is of the maker, not of what is made. All things are touched and changed by it. This uses, and is not used. It distances those who share it, from those who share it not. Those who share it not are flocks and herds. It dates from itself;—not from former men or better men,—gospel, or constitution, or college, or custom. Where it shines, Nature is no longer intrusive, but all things make a musical or pictorial impression. The world of men show like a comedy without laughter:—populations, interests, government, history;—'tis all toy figures in a toy house. It does not overvalue particular truths. We hear eagerly every thought and word quoted from an intellectual man. But, in his presence, our own mind is roused to activity, and we forget very fast what he says, much more interested in the new play of our own thought, than in any thought of his. 'Tis the majesty into which we have suddenly mounted, the impersonality, the scorn of egotisms, the sphere of laws, that engage us. Once we were stepping a little this way, and a little that way; now, we are as men in a balloon, and do not think so much of the point we have left, or the point we would make, as of the liberty and glory of the way.

Just as much intellect as you add, so much organic power. He who sees through the design, presides over it, and must will that which must be. We sit and rule, and, though we sleep, our dream will come to pass. Our thought, though it were only an hour old, affirms an oldest necessity, not to be separated from thought, and not to be separated from will. They must always have coëxisted. It apprises us of its sovereignty and godhead, which refuse to be severed from it. It is not mine or thine, but the will of all mind. It is poured into the souls of all men, as the soul itself which constitutes them men. I know not whether there be, as is alleged, in the upper region of our atmosphere, a permanent westerly current, which carries with it all atoms which rise to that height, but I see, that when souls reach a certain clearness of perception, they accept a knowledge and motive above selfishness. A breath of will blows eternally through the universe of souls in the direction of the Right and Necessary. It is the air which all intellects inhale and exhale, and it is the wind which blows the worlds into order and orbit.

37   Thought dissolves the material universe, by carrying the mind up into a sphere where all is plastic. Of two men, each obeying his own thought, he whose thought is deepest will be the strongest character. Always one man more than another represents the will of Divine Providence to the period.

38   2. If thought makes free, so does the moral sentiment.[42] The mixtures of spiritual chemistry refuse to be analyzed. Yet we can see that with the perception of truth is joined the desire that it shall prevail. That affection is essential to will. Moreover, when a strong will appears, it usually results from a certain unity of organization, as if the whole energy of body and mind flowed in one direction. All great force is real and elemental. There is no manufacturing a strong will. There must be a pound to balance a pound. Where power is shown in will, it must rest on the universal force. Alaric and Bonaparte must believe they rest on a truth, or their will can be bought or bent.[43] There is a bribe possible for any finite will. But the pure sympathy with universal ends is an infinite force, and cannot be bribed or bent. Whoever has had experience of the moral sentiment cannot choose but believe in unlimited power. Each pulse from that heart is an oath from the Most High. I know not what the word *sublime* means, if it be not the intimations in this infant of a terrific force. A text of heroism, a name and anecdote of courage, are not arguments, but sallies of freedom. One of these is the verse of the Persian Hafiz, "'Tis written on the gate of Heaven, 'Wo unto him who suffers himself to be betrayed by Fate!'"[44] Does the reading of history make us fatalists? What cour-

age does not the opposite opinion show! A little whim of will to be free gallantly contending against the universe of chemistry.

But insight is not will, nor is affection will. Perception is cold, and goodness dies in wishes; as Voltaire said, 'tis the misfortune of worthy people that they are cowards; *"un des plus grands malheurs des honnêtes gens c'est qu'ils sont des lâches."* There must be a fusion of these two to generate the energy of will. There can be no driving force, except through the conversion of the man into his will, making him the will, and the will him. And one may say boldly, that no man has a right perception of any truth, who has not been reacted on by it, so as to be ready to be its martyr.

39

The one serious and formidable thing in nature is a will. Society is servile from want of will, and therefore the world wants saviours and religions. One way is right to go: the hero sees it, and moves on that aim, and has the world under him for root and support. He is to others as the world. His approbation is honor; his dissent, infamy. The glance of his eye has the force of sunbeams. A personal influence towers up in memory only worthy, and we gladly forget numbers, money, climate, gravitation, and the rest of Fate.

40

We can afford to allow the limitation, if we know it is the meter of the growing man. We stand against Fate, as children stand up against the wall in their father's house, and notch their height from year to year. But when the boy grows to man, and is master of the house, he pulls down that wall, and builds a new and bigger. 'Tis only a question of time. Every brave youth is in training to ride and rule this dragon. His science is to make weapons and wings of these passions and retarding forces. Now whether, seeing these two things, fate and power, we are permitted to believe in unity? The bulk of mankind believe in two gods. They are under one dominion here in the house, as friend and parent, in social circles, in letters, in art, in love, in religion: but in mechanics, in dealing with steam and climate, in trade, in politics, they think they come under another; and that it would be a practical blunder to transfer the method and way of working of one sphere, into the other. What good, honest, generous men at home, will be wolves and foxes on change![45] What pious men in the parlor will vote for what reprobates at the polls! To a certain point, they believe themselves the care of a Providence. But, in a steamboat, in an epidemic, in war, they believe a malignant energy rules.

41

42   But relation and connection are not somewhere and sometimes, but everywhere and always. The divine order does not stop where their sight stops. The friendly power works on the same rules, in the next farm, and the next planet. But, where they have not experience, they run against it, and hurt themselves. Fate, then, is a name for facts not yet passed under the fire of thought;—for causes which are unpenetrated.

43   But every jet of chaos which threatens to exterminate us, is convertible by intellect into wholesome force. Fate is unpenetrated causes. The water drowns ship and sailor, like a grain of dust. But learn to swim, trim your bark, and the wave which drowned it, will be cloven by it, and carry it, like its own foam, a plume and a power. The cold is inconsiderate of persons, tingles your blood, freezes a man like a dew-drop. But learn to skate, and the ice will give you a graceful, sweet, and poetic motion. The cold will brace your limbs and brain to genius, and make you foremost men of time. Cold and sea will train an imperial Saxon race, which nature cannot bear to lose, and, after cooping it up for a thousand years in yonder England, gives a hundred Englands a hundred Mexicos. All the bloods it shall absorb and domineer: and more than Mexicos,—the secrets of water and steam, the spasms of electricity, the ductility of metals, the chariot of the air, the ruddered balloon are awaiting you.[46]

44   The annual slaughter from typhus far exceeds that of war; but right drainage destroys typhus. The plague in the sea-service from scurvy is healed by lemon juice and other diets portable or procurable: the depopulation by cholera and small-pox is ended by drainage and vaccination; and every other pest is not less in the chain of cause and effect, and may be fought off. And, whilst art draws out the venom, it commonly extorts some benefit from the vanquished enemy. The mischievous torrent is taught to drudge for man: the wild beasts he makes useful for food, or dress, or labor; the chemic explosions are controlled like his watch. These are now the steeds on which he rides. Man moves in all modes, by legs of horses, by wings of wind, by steam, by gas of balloon, by electricity, and stands on tiptoe threatening to hunt the eagle in his own element. There's nothing he will not make his carrier.

45   Steam was, till the other day, the devil which we dreaded. Every pot made by any human potter or brazier had a hole in its cover, to let off the enemy, lest he should lift pot and roof, and carry the house away. But the Marquis of Worcester, Watt, and Fulton bethought themselves, that, where was power, was not devil, but was God; that it must be availed of, and not by any means

let off and wasted.[47] Could he lift pots and roofs and houses so handily? he was the workman they were in search of. He could be used to lift away, chain, and compel other devils, far more reluctant and dangerous, namely, cubic miles of earth, mountains, weight or resistance of water, machinery, and the labors of all men in the world; and time he shall lengthen, and shorten space.

It has not fared much otherwise with higher kinds of steam. The opinion of the million was the terror of the world, and it was attempted, either to dissipate it, by amusing nations, or to pile it over with strata of society,—a layer of soldiers; over that, a layer of lords; and a king on the top; with clamps and hoops of castles, garrisons, and police. But, sometimes, the religious principle would get in, and burst the hoops, and rive every mountain laid on top of it. The Fultons and Watts of politics, believing in unity, saw that it was a power, and, by satisfying it, (as justice satisfies everybody,) through a different disposition of society,—grouping it on a level, instead of piling it into a mountain,—they have contrived to make of this terror the most harmless and energetic form of a State. [46]

Very odious, I confess, are the lessons of Fate. Who likes to have a dapper phrenologist pronouncing on his fortunes? Who likes to believe that he has hidden in his skull, spine, and pelvis, all the vices of a Saxon or Celtic race, which will be sure to pull him down,—with what grandeur of hope and resolve he is fired,—into a selfish, huckstering, servile, dodging animal? A learned physician tells us, the fact is invariable with the Neapolitan, that, when mature, he assumes the forms of the unmistakable scoundrel.[48] That is a little overstated,—but may pass. [47]

But these are magazines and arsenals. A man must thank his defects, and stand in some terror of his talents. A transcendent talent draws so largely on his forces, as to lame him; a defect pays him revenues on the other side. The sufferance, which is the badge of the Jew, has made him, in these days, the ruler of the rulers of the earth.[49] If Fate is ore and quarry, if evil is good in the making, if limitation is power that shall be, if calamities, oppositions, and weights are wings and means,—we are reconciled. [48]

Fate involves the melioration. No statement of the Universe can have any soundness, which does not admit its ascending effort. The direction of the whole, and of the parts, is toward benefit, and in proportion to the health. Behind every individual, closes organization: before him, opens liberty,—the Better, the Best. The first and worst races are dead. The second and imperfect [49] races are dying out, or remain for the maturing of higher. In the latest race, in man, every generosity, every new perception, the love and praise he extorts from his fellows, are certificates of advance out of fate into freedom. Liberation of the will from the sheaths and clogs of organization which he has outgrown, is the end and aim of this world. Every calamity is a spur and valuable hint; and where his endeavors do not yet fully avail, they tell as tendency. The whole circle of animal life,—tooth against tooth,—devouring war, war for food, a yelp of pain and a grunt of triumph, until, at last, the whole menagerie, the whole chemical mass is mellowed and refined for higher use,— pleases at a sufficient perspective.

50 But to see how fate slides into freedom, and freedom into fate, observe how far the roots of every creature run, or find, if you can, a point where there is no thread of connection. Our life is consentaneous and far-related. This knot of nature is so well tied, that nobody was ever cunning enough to find the two ends. Nature is intricate, overlapped, interweaved, and endless. Christopher Wren said of the beautiful King's College chapel, "that, if anybody would tell him where to lay the first stone, he would build such another." But where shall we find the first atom in this house of man, which is all consent, inosculation, and balance of parts?[50]

51 The web of relation is shown in *habitat,* shown in hybernation. When hybernation was observed, it was found, that, whilst some animals became torpid in winter, others were torpid in summer: hybernation then was a false name. The *long sleep* is not an effect of cold, but is regulated by the supply of food proper to the animal.[51] It becomes torpid when the fruit or prey it lives on is not in season, and regains its activity when its food is ready.

52 Eyes are found in light; ears in auricular air; feet on land; fins in water; wings in air; and, each creature where it was meant to be, with a mutual fitness. Every zone has its own *Fauna.* There is adjustment between the animal and its food, its parasite, its enemy. Balances are kept. It is not allowed to diminish in numbers, nor to exceed. The like adjustments exist for man. His food is cooked, when he arrives; his coal in the pit; the house ventilated; the mud of the deluge dried; his companions arrived at the same hour, and awaiting him with love, concert, laughter, and tears. These are coarse adjustments, but the invisible are not less. There are more belongings to every creature than his lair and his food. His instincts must be met, and he has predisposing power that bends and fits what is near him to his use. He is not possible until

the invisible things are right for him, as well as the visible. Of what changes, then, in sky and earth, and in finer skies and earth, does the appearance of some Dante or Columbus apprise us!

How is this effected? Nature is no spendthrift, but takes the shortest way to her ends. As the general says to his soldiers, "if you want a fort, build a fort," so nature makes every creature do its own work and get its living,—is it planet, animal, or tree.[52] The planet makes itself. The animal cell makes itself;—then, what it wants. Every creature,—wren or dragon,—shall make its own lair. As soon as there is life, there is self-direction, and absorbing and using of material. Life is freedom,—life in the direct ratio of its amount. You may be sure, the new-born man is not inert. Life works both voluntarily and supernaturally in its neighborhood. Do you suppose, he can be estimated by his weight in pounds, or, that he is contained in his skin,—this reaching, radiating, jaculating fellow? The smallest candle fills a mile with its rays, and the papillæ of a man run out to every star.

When there is something to be done, the world knows how to get it done. The vegetable eye makes leaf, pericarp, root, bark, or thorn, as the need is; the first cell converts itself into stomach, mouth, nose, or nail, according to the want: the world throws its life into a hero or a shepherd; and puts him where he is wanted. Dante and Columbus were Italians, in their time: they would be Russians or Americans to-day. Things ripen, new men come. The adaptation is not capricious. The ulterior aim, the purpose beyond itself, the correlation by which planets subside and crystallize, then animate beasts and men, will not stop, but will work into finer particulars, and from finer to finest.

The secret of the world is, the tie between person and event. Person makes event, and event person. The "times," "the age," what is that, but a few profound persons and a few active persons who epitomize the times?—Goethe, Hegel, Metternich, Adams, Calhoun, Guizot, Peel, Cobden, Kossuth, Rothschild, Astor, Brunel, and the rest.[53] The same fitness must be presumed between a man and the time and event, as between the sexes, or between a race of animals and the food it eats, or the inferior races it uses. He thinks his fate alien, because the copula is hidden. But the soul contains the event that shall befall it, for the event is only the actualization of its thoughts; and what we pray to ourselves for is always granted. The event is the print of your form. It fits you like your skin. What each does is proper to him. Events

53

54

55

are the children of his body and mind. We learn that the soul of Fate is the soul of us, as Hafiz sings,

> "Alas! till now I had not known,
> My guide and fortune's guide are one."[54]

All the toys that infatuate men, and which they play for,—houses, land, money, luxury, power, fame, are the selfsame thing, with a new gauze or two of illusion overlaid. And of all the drums and rattles by which men are made willing to have their heads broke, and are led out solemnly every morning to parade,—the most admirable is this by which we are brought to believe that events are arbitrary, and independent of actions. At the conjuror's, we detect the hair by which he moves his puppet, but we have not eyes sharp enough to descry the thread that ties cause and effect.

56   Nature magically suits the man to his fortunes, by making these the fruit of his character. Ducks take to the water, eagles to the sky, waders to the sea margin, hunters to the forest, clerks to counting-rooms, soldiers to the frontier. Thus events grow on the same stem with persons; are sub-persons. The pleasure of life is according to the man that lives it, and not according to the work or the place. Life is an ecstasy. We know what madness belongs to love, —what power to paint a vile object in hues of heaven. As insane persons are indifferent to their dress, diet, and other accommodations, and, as we do in dreams, with equanimity, the most absurd acts, so, a drop more of wine in our cup of life will reconcile us to strange company and work. Each creature puts forth from itself its own condition and sphere, as the slug sweats out its slimy house on the pear-leaf, and the woolly aphides on the apple perspire their own bed, and the fish its shell. In youth, we clothe ourselves with rainbows, and go as brave as the zodiac. In age, we put out another sort of perspiration,—gout, fever, rheumatism, caprice, doubt, fretting, and avarice.

57   A man's fortunes are the fruit of his character. A man's friends are his magnetisms. We go to Herodotus and Plutarch for examples of Fate; but we are examples. *"Quisque suos patimur manes."*[55] The tendency of every man to enact all that is in his constitution is expressed in the old belief, that the efforts which we make to escape from our destiny only serve to lead us into it: and I have noticed, a man likes better to be complimented on his position, as the proof of the last or total excellence, than on his merits.

A man will see his character emitted in the events that seem to meet, but which exude from and accompany him. Events expand with the character. As once he found himself among toys, so now he plays a part in colossal systems, and his growth is declared in his ambition, his companions, and his performance. He looks like a piece of luck, but is a piece of causation;—the mosaic, angulated and ground to fit into the gap he fills. Hence in each town there is some man who is, in his brain and performance, an explanation of the tillage, production, factories, banks, churches, ways of living, and society, of that town. If you do not chance to meet him, all that you see will leave you a little puzzled: if you see him, it will become plain. We know in Massachusetts who built New Bedford, who built Lynn, Lowell, Lawrence, Clinton, Fitchburg, Holyoke, Portland, and many another noisy mart. Each of these men, if they were transparent, would seem to you not so much men, as walking cities, and, wherever you put them, they would build one. [58]

History is the action and reaction of these two,—Nature and Thought;— two boys pushing each other on the curb-stone of the pavement. Everything is pusher or pushed: and matter and mind are in perpetual tilt and balance, so. Whilst the man is weak, the earth takes up him. He plants his brain and affections. By and by he will take up the earth, and have his gardens and vineyards in the beautiful order and productiveness of his thought. Every solid in the universe is ready to become fluid on the approach of the mind, and the power to flux it is the measure of the mind.[56] If the wall remain adamant, it accuses the want of thought. To a subtler force, it will stream into new forms, expressive of the character of the mind. What is the city in which we sit here, but an aggregate of incongruous materials, which have obeyed the will of some man? The granite was reluctant, but his hands were stronger, and it came. Iron was deep in the ground, and well combined with stone; but could not hide from his fires. Wood, lime, stuffs, fruit, gums, were dispersed over the earth and sea, in vain. Here they are, within reach of every man's day-labor,—what he wants of them. The whole world is the flux of matter over the wires of thought to the poles or points where it would build. The races of men rise out of the ground preoccupied with a thought which rules them, and divided into parties ready armed and angry to fight for this metaphysical abstraction. The quality of the thought differences the Egyptian and the Roman, the Austrian and the American. The men who come on the stage [59] at one period are all found to be related to each other. Certain ideas are in the air. We are all impressionable, for we are made of them; all impressionable, but some more than others, and these first express them. This explains the curious contemporaneousness of inventions and discoveries. The truth is in the air, and the most impressionable brain will announce it first, but all will announce it a few minutes later. So women, as most susceptible, are the best index of the coming hour. So the great man, that is, the man most imbued with the spirit of the time, is the impressionable man,—of a fibre irritable and delicate, like iodine to light. He feels the infinitesimal attractions. His mind is righter than others, because he yields to a current so feeble as can be felt only by a needle delicately poised.

60   The correlation is shown in defects. Moller, in his Essay on Architecture, taught that the building which was fitted accurately to answer its end, would turn out to be beautiful, though beauty had not been intended.[57] I find the like unity in human structures rather virulent and pervasive; that a crudity in the blood will appear in the argument; a hump in the shoulder will appear in the speech and handiwork. If his mind could be seen, the hump would be seen. If a man has a seesaw in his voice, it will run into his sentences, into his poem, into the structure of his fable, into his speculation, into his charity. And, as every man is hunted by his own dæmon, vexed by his own disease, this checks all his activity.

61   So each man, like each plant, has his parasites. A strong, astringent, bilious nature has more truculent enemies than the slugs and moths that fret my leaves. Such an one has curculios, borers, knife-worms: a swindler ate him first, then a client, then a quack, then smooth, plausible gentlemen, bitter and selfish as Moloch.[58]

62   This correlation really existing can be divined. If the threads are there, thought can follow and show them. Especially when a soul is quick and docile; as Chaucer sings,

> "Or if the soul of proper kind
> Be so perfect as men find,
> That it wot what is to come,
> And that he warneth all and some
> Of every of their aventures,
> By previsions or figures;

But that our flesh hath not might
It to understand aright
For it is warned too darkly."[59]

Some people are made up of rhyme, coincidence, omen, periodicity, and presage: they meet the person they seek; what their companion prepares to say to them, they first say to him; and a hundred signs apprise them of what is about to befall.

Wonderful intricacy in the web, wonderful constancy in the design this vagabond life admits. We wonder how the fly finds its mate, and yet year after year we find two men, two women, without legal or carnal tie, spend a great part of their best time within a few feet of each other. And the moral is, that what we seek we shall find;[60] what we flee from flees from us; as Goethe said, "what we wish for in youth, comes in heaps on us in old age,"[61] too often cursed with the granting of our prayer:[62] and hence the high caution, that, since we are sure of having what we wish, we beware to ask only for high things.[63]

One key, one solution to the mysteries of human condition, one solution to the old knots of fate, freedom, and foreknowledge, exists, the propounding, namely, of the double consciousness.[64] A man must ride alternately on the horses of his private and his public nature, as the equestrians in the circus throw themselves nimbly from horse to horse, or plant one foot on the back of one, and the other foot on the back of the other. So when a man is the victim of his fate, has sciatica in his loins, and cramp in his mind; a club-foot and a club in his wit; a sour face, and a selfish temper; a strut in his gait, and a conceit in his affection; or is ground to powder by the vice of his race; he is to rally on his relation to the Universe, which his ruin benefits. Leaving the dæmon who suffers, he is to take sides with the Deity who secures universal benefit by his pain.

To offset the drag of temperament and race, which pulls down, learn this lesson, namely, that by the cunning co-presence of two elements, which is throughout nature, whatever lames or paralyzes you, draws in with it the divinity, in some form, to repay. A good intention clothes itself with sudden power. When a god wishes to ride, any chip or pebble will bud and shoot out winged feet, and serve him for a horse.

Let us build altars to the Blessed Unity which holds nature and souls in perfect solution, and compels every atom to serve an universal end. I do not wonder at a snow-flake, a shell, a summer landscape, or the glory of the stars; but at the necessity of beauty under which the universe lies; that all is and must be pictorial; that the rainbow, and the curve of the horizon, and the arch of the blue vault are only results from the organism of the eye. There is no need for foolish amateurs to fetch me to admire a garden of flowers, or a sun-gilt cloud, or a waterfall, when I cannot look without seeing splendor and grace. How idle to choose a random sparkle here or there, when the indwelling necessity plants the rose of beauty on the brow of chaos, and discloses the central intention of Nature to be harmony and joy.

67   Let us build altars to the Beautiful Necessity. If we thought men were free in the sense, that, in a single exception one fantastical will could prevail over the law of things, it were all one as if a child's hand could pull down the sun. If, in the least particular, one could derange the order of nature,—who would accept the gift of life?

68   Let us build altars to the Beautiful Necessity, which secures that all is made of one piece; that plaintiff and defendant, friend and enemy, animal and planet, food and eater, are of one kind. In astronomy, is vast space, but no foreign system; in geology, vast time, but the same laws as to-day. Why should we be afraid of Nature, which is no other than "philosophy and theology embodied"?[65] Why should we fear to be crushed by savage elements, we who are made up of the same elements? Let us build to the Beautiful Necessity, which makes man brave in believing that he cannot shun a danger that is appointed, nor incur one that is not; to the Necessity which rudely or softly educates him to the perception that there are no contingences; that Law rules throughout existence, a Law which is not intelligent but intelligence,—not personal nor impersonal,—it disdains words and passes understanding; it dissolves persons; it vivifies nature; yet solicits the pure in heart to draw on all its omnipotence.

Notes

1. For details on the origin of this poem, which Emerson titles "Fate," see *CW*, 9:669–670.

2. In the winter of 1850, Emerson twice delivered "The Spirit of the Times" (*LL*,

1:101). Unitarian ministers George Putnam (1807–1878), Orville Dewey (1794–1882), and William Henry Channing (1810–1884), and the American essayist Edwin Percy Whipple (1819–1886), also lectured on the topic (*JMN*, 11:228).

3. In the journal version of this passage, "polarity" is followed by three clarifying clauses: "every mind has a polarity,—. . . that will finally guide us to the sea. I see no choice" (*JMN*, 9:218). The polarity Emerson intends is that of a compass needle.

4. The use of "Turk" to mean "Muslim" was still familiar in the nineteenth century. Emerson first encountered the predestinating "iron leaf" in John Dryden's *Tyrannic Love* (1669) (*JMN*, 2:273).

5. Emerson's translation of a quatrain by a Persian poet he identified as "Pindar of Rei in Cuhistan" from Joseph, Freiherr von Hammer-Purgstall, *Geschichte der schönen Redekünst Persiens* (Vienna, 1818), p. 43 (*JMN*, 11:103).

6. This Hindu here is likely a soul bound on the metaphorical wheel of birth, death, and reincarnation.

7. Chaucer, *The Canterbury Tales*, ll. 1663–1672 (I–A), slightly modernized.

8. Emerson's source is Aeschylus, *The Suppliants*, in *The Seven Tragedies of Aeschylus, Literally Translated . . .* , 3rd ed. (Oxford, 1843), p. 280 (*TN*, 1:64–65).

9. Emerson refers to Johann Heinrich Jung, or Jung-Stilling, (1740–1817), German physician whose *Heinrich Stillings Leben* (1806), an autobiographical romance, was so widely read that the fictional name became combined with Jung's real one; and, most likely, William, not Robert, Huntington (1714–1813), popular English providentialist preacher (see *W*, 6:338). A pistareen was a coin of the Spanish West Indies valued at about twenty cents.

10. Approximately forty thousand people died in the Lisbon earthquake of 1 November 1755; the Neapolitan earthquake of 19 December 1857 lasted three minutes.

11. A "bombyx" was a silkworm afflicted by diseases thought caused by protozoan parasites; "infusory biters" are minute creatures seen only by the use of a microscope. In his translation of A. Mouquin-Tandon's *Elements of Medical Zoology* (London, 1861), p. 49, Robert Thomas Hulme defined "alternate generation" as "the existence of two modes of reproduction in the same species." There is a fish called *Labrus*, but Emerson was likely thinking of the *Labrax*, which among ancient Greeks and Romans was notorious for its ferocity. In the nineteenth century, the grampus was thought to be the "killer whale."

12. In his journal version of this sentence, Emerson compares the spirit to a merchant "who ruins himself to live on Beacon St," a fashionable Boston address (*JMN*, 11:417).

13. Lambert Adolphe Jacques Quételet (1796–1874), Belgian astronomer and mathematician who applied statistical methods to studies of society.

14. In the nineteenth century, "the four temperaments" (sanguine, phlegmatic, cho-

leric, melancholic), based on classifications by Galen of Pergamon (129–ca. 216), were still taken seriously.

15. A "black drop" was an elixir of opium used for medical purposes; however, given his treatment of the four temperaments here, Emerson is referring to hereditary darkness associated with melancholy.

16. Emerson's source is *The History of the Manners and Customs of Ancient Greece,* 3 vols. (London, 1842), 1:xv, by the English traveler James Augustus St. John (1801–1875) (*JMN,* 11:212).

17. Matthew 6:28.

18. In both Spanish and English, a "camarilla" is literally a small room, metaphorically a cabal.

19. In this context "high magnifiers" refers to microscopes. Joseph von Fraunhofer [*sic*] (1787–1826), German optical physicist; William Benjamin Carpenter (1813–1885), English physician and physiologist.

20. Emerson's source is *The Hĕĕtōpădēs of Vĕĕshnŏŏ-Sărmā,* . . . , trans. Charles Wilkens (Bath, 1787), p. 6 (*JMN,* 8:489).

21. Emerson's source is an unpublished manuscript: Schelling, *Philosophische Untersuchungen über des Wesen der menschlichen Freiheit,* trans. James Elliot Cabot (*JMN,* 9:101; *TN,* 3:129, 336).

22. Emerson thought of New Hampshire as a wild land whence political activists such as Parker Pillsbury (1809–1898) entered Massachusetts as a one-man mob, out-shouting the mobs he encountered (*JMN,* 9:204, 426).

23. For the journal version of Emerson's fantasy, see *JMN,* 11:379; American Benjamin Dearborn (1754–1838) invented the spring scales.

24. A zoophyte is an invertebrate, plant-like animal, such as a coral. By "trilobium" Emerson meant the trilobite, an extinct, three-lobed creature whose fossil remains are present in shale quarried in Braintree, Massachusetts. The saurian is a form of sentient lizard.

25. In the preface to his *The Races of Men: A Fragment* (London, 1850), Scottish physician Robert Knox (1791–1862) argued that "Race is everything," "literature, science, art—in a word, civilization, depends on it." Knox believed that human hybridity led to degeneration and cultural, if not biological, sterility, but he never asserted the superiority of any single unmixed race. The quotations that follow are Emerson's own illustrations of "Knox's law of races" (*JMN,* 11:392).

26. The first part of this construction recalls the "adamantine chains" that bind fallen angels in fire in Milton's *Paradise Lost,* I, 47–48; the publication of Carl G. A. Knies's *Die Statistik als selbstständig Wissenschaft* (1850) may have signaled to Emerson the new science of statistics.

27. In addition to being a mathematical wizard, Nathaniel Bowditch spent his youth at sea and was a ship captain.

28. "Everything which pertains to the human species, considered as a whole, belongs to the order of physical facts. The greater the number of individuals, the more does the influence of the individual will disappear, leaving predominance to a series of general facts dependent on causes by which society exists, and is preserved."—QUETELET. (Emerson's footnote.)

29. In the list of persons mentioned here, Emerson is raising the question, Had each individual done the deeds history or legend attributes to them? Tubal-cain was the teacher "of every artificer in brass and iron"; see Genesis 4:22. Vulcan is the Roman god of fire. Johann Fust (ca. 1400–1466), was the partner and successor of German engraver and printer Johannes Gutenberg (ca. 1395–1468).

30. William Ellery Channing II, "Death," l. 13.

31. Jacques de Vaucanson (1709–1782), French mechanical engineer.

32. Hipparchus of Nicaea (190–120 BCE), Greek astronomer and mathematician; Aristarchus of Samos (310–230 BCE), Greek astronomer who first argued that the sun was the center of the universe and earth revolved around it; Œnopides of Chios (fl. 475 BCE), Greek geometrician and astronomer who measured the inclination of the earth's axis.

33. The Roman mile was a distance of a thousand double (or five-foot) paces.

34. Cowry shells were brought to New England from the South Pacific because of their beauty; brilliant orange cowries were highly prized. By "astronomical skulls," Emerson alludes to the findings of phrenologists that the organ through which the intellectual faculty was exercised lay just above the frontal sinuses and was documented as protrusive in the heads of Sir Walter Scott, Columbus, Galileo, and Newton; see George Combe, *A System of Phrenology* (Boston, 1839), p. 390.

35. With "torrents of tendency," cf. Wordsworth, "the mighty stream of tendency," in *The Excursion*, IX, 87, where "tendency" is also used in its old meaning of "going forward."

36. Emerson's source is *The Prose or Younger Edda . . . Ascribed to Snorri Sturluson*, trans. George Webbe Dasent (London, 1842), pp. 35–36 (*JMN*, 10:108).

37. Emerson drew "The doer must suffer" from his translation of a line in Aeschylus, *The Libation Bearers*, in *Tragoediae* (Leipzig, 1819), p. 307, as "Doer must suffer" (*TN*, 1:63); his source for "'you would soothe . . . be soothed'" is Aeschylus, *The Suppliants* (1843), p. 280 (*TN*, 1:65).

38. Emerson's source is Edward Davies, *The Mythology and Rites of the British Druids* (London, 1809), p. 79 (*JMN*, 13:150; 14:381).

39. A "Spanish proverb" (*JMN*, 13:82), also used in "Seventh of March Speech on the Fugitive Slave Law, 7 March 1854" (*LL*, 1:344).

40. Emerson's source is "The Oracles of Zoroaster," *The Phenix; A Collection of Old and Rare Fragments* (New York, 1835), p. 158 (*JMN*, 7:389).

41. Concentric or successive heavens have long served to express degrees of bliss; St.

Paul alludes to them in 2 Corinthians 12:2, the Koran speaks of seven heavens, and Ptolemaic astronomers counted as many as eleven.

42. With "thought makes free," cf. John 8:31–32.

43. Alaric (370–410), king of the Visigoths (395–410), sacked Rome in 410.

44. Hafiz was a fourteenth-century Shi'ite Muslim, a dervish, and a Sufi, who lived most of his life in the city of Shiraz; his nom de plume means that he knew the Koran by heart. The quotation here is Emerson's translation of two lines from Joseph, Freiherr von Hammer-Purgstall, *Der Diwan von Mohammed Schemsed-din Hafis*, 2 vols. (Stuttgart, 1812–1813), 2:386 (*JMN*, 10:55).

45. That is, "at the Stock Exchange."

46. An allusion to the ability of aeronauts to steer balloons in flight, which would be finally accomplished in 1872, by Henri Dupuy de Lôme (1816–1885).

47. Edward Somerset, 2nd Marquess of Worcester (ca. 1601–1667), claimed to have invented the steam engine when, imprisoned in the Tower of London (1653–1654), he watched the lid of a steaming saucepan rise and fall.

48. In 1860, physiognomy, the pseudoscience of reading the mind's construction in the face, was approaching its fullest development; although Emerson never names the "learned physician," given his sympathy with ideas of caste, type, and psychosomatic determinism, Bostonian Oliver Wendell Holmes (1809–1894) is a possibility.

49. With "sufferance, . . . of the Jew," cf. Shylock's speech to Antonio in Shakespeare, *The Merchant of Venice*, I, iii, 110–111.

50. "Inosculation" is a physiological term formerly used for the way blood vessels flow into one another.

51. Charles Darwin, in *The Voyage of the Beagle* (1839), chapter V, paragraph 25, complained about the inaccuracy of the word "hybernation" when applied to the summer-sleep of animals: "within the tropics, the hybernation, or more properly aestivation, of animals is determined not by the temperature, but by the times of drought."

52. Emerson never identified this general, but the meaning of his words is clear in their journal context: "In youth we go for freedom" (*JMN*, 10:117).

53. Georg Wilhelm Friedrich Hegel (1770–1831), German philosopher and proponent for German Idealism; Klemens von Metternich (1773–1859), Austrian statesman; John C. Calhoun (1782–1850), American politician and political theorist who defended slavery; François Pierre Guillaime Guizot (1787–1874), French historian; Lionel Nathan de Rothschild (1808–1879), English politician and head of the Rothschild banking family.

54. Emerson's source for the original in German is Hammer-Purgstall, *Der Diwan von Mohammed Schemsed-din Hafis*, 2:118; his translation was included in "Persian Poetry" (*CW*, 8:130).

55. *Æneid*, VI, 743, by Virgil (or Vergil) (70–19 BCE), Roman epic poet; the gist of the quotation is that humans each suffer the effects of their personal demons or fears.

56. The transitive form of the verb "flux," no longer used by chemists and metallurgists, meant to melt, fuse, or make fluid.

57. Georg Möller (1784–1852), German architect.

58. In Emerson's journal, the man of a "bilious" (i.e., belligerent) nature was his brother-in-law, Charles T. Jackson (1805–1880), a physician, chemist, geologist, and one of the first scientists to experiment with nitrous oxide (laughing gas) as an anesthetic; Jackson's "enemies" included Nathaniel Bowditch and Francis Bowen (1811–1890), an American philosopher. The fretted leaves were those on Emerson's pear trees (*JMN*, 11:111–112); the "knife-worm" is a voracious nocturnal caterpillar.

59. Emerson's modernization of Chaucer, *The House of Fame*, ll. 43–51.

60. With "what we seek we shall find," cf. Luke 11:9.

61. Goethe, *The Auto-biography* . . . , trans. John Oxenford, 2 vols. (1848–1849), 2:181 (*JMN*, 11:388).

62. An allusion to Alexander Pope's "curs'd with ev'ry granted prayer," *Moral Essays*, Epistle II, l. 147 (*JMN*, 11:388).

63. In his journal, Emerson attributes "ask only for high things" to Charles King Newcomb (1820–1894), a Brook Farmer and a contributor to the *Dial* (*JMN*, 9:338; 11:388).

64. With "fate, freedom, and foreknowledge," cf. Milton, *Paradise Lost*, II, 559–560.

65. Emerson's source is James John Garth Wilkinson's introduction to Emanuel Swedenborg, *The Economy of the Animal Kingdom*, trans. Augustus Clissold, 2 vols. (London, 1845–1846), 2:lxxvii (*JMN*, 10:26).

American Civilization

1   A certain degree of progress from the rudest state in which man is found,—a dweller in caves, or on trees, like an ape, a cannibal, an eater of pounded snails, worms, and offal,—a certain degree from this extreme is called Civilization. It is a vague, complex name, of many degrees. Nobody has attempted a definition. Mr. Guizot writing a book on the subject, does not.[1] It implies the evolution of a highly organized man, brought to supreme delicacy of sentiment, as in practical power, religion, liberty, sense of honor, and taste. In the hesitation to define what it is, we usually suggest it by negations. A nation that has no clothing, no alphabet, no iron, no marriage, no arts of peace, no abstract thought, we call barbarous. And after many arts are invented or imported, as among the Turks and Moorish nations, it is often a little complaisant to call them civilized.

2   Each nation grows after its own genius, and has civilization of its own. The Chinese and Japanese, though each complete in his way, is different from the man of Madrid or the man of New York. The term imports a mysterious progress. In the brutes is none; and in mankind, the savage tribes do not advance. The Indians of this country have not learned the white man's work; and in Africa, the negro of today is the negro of Herodotus.[2] But in other

races the growth is not arrested; but the like progress that is made by a boy, "when he cuts his eye-teeth," as we say,—childish illusions passing daily away, and he seeing things really and comprehensively,—is made by tribes. It is the learning the secret of cumulative power, of advancing on oneself. It implies a facility of association, power to compare, the ceasing from fixed ideas. The Indian is gloomy and distressed when urged to depart from his habits and traditions. He is overpowered by the gaze of the white, and his eye sinks. The occasion of one of these starts of growth is always some novelty that astounds the mind, and provokes it to dare to change. Thus there is a Manco Capac at the beginning of each improvement, some superior foreigner importing new and wonderful arts, and teaching them.[3] Of course, he must not know too much, but must have the sympathy, language, and gods of those he would inform. But chiefly the sea-shore has been the point of departure to knowledge, as to commerce. The most advanced nations are always those who navigate the most. The power which the sea requires in the sailor makes a man of him very fast, and the change of shores and population clears his head of much nonsense of his wigwam.

Where shall we begin or end the list of those feats of liberty and wit, each of which feats made an epoch of history? Thus, the effect of a framed or stone house is immense on the tranquility, power, and refinement of the builder. A man in a cave, or in a camp, a nomad, will die with no more estate than the wolf or the horse leaves. But so simple a labor as a house being achieved, his chief enemies are kept at bay. He is safe from the teeth of wild animals, from frost, sunstroke, and weather; and fine faculties begin to yield their fine harvest. Invention and art are born, manners and social beauty and delight. 'Tis wonderful how soon a piano gets into a log-hut on the frontier.[4] You would think they found it under a pine-stump. With it comes a Latin grammar, and one of those tow-head boys has written a hymn on Sunday. Now let colleges, now let senates take heed! for here is one, who, opening these fine tastes on the basis of the pioneer's iron constitution, will gather all their laurels in his strong hands.

When the Indian trail gets widened, graded, and bridged to a good road, —there is a benefactor, there is a missionary, a pacificator, a wealth-bringer, a maker of markets, a vent for industry. The building three or four hundred miles of road in the Scotch highlands in 1726 to 1749 effectively tamed the ferocious clans, and established public order. Another step in civility is the

3

4

change from war, hunting, and pasturage, to agriculture. Our Scandinavian forefathers have left us a significant legend to convey their sense of the importance of this step. "There was once a giantess who had a daughter, and the child saw a husbandman ploughing in the field. Then she ran and picked him up with her finger and thumb, and put him and his plough and his oxen into her apron, and carried them to her mother, and said, 'Mother, what sort of a beetle is this that I found wriggling in the sand?' But the mother said, 'Put it away, my child; we must be gone out of this land, for these people will dwell in it.'"⁵ Another success is the post-office with its educating energy, augmented by cheapness, and guarded by a certain religious sentiment in mankind, so that the power of a wafer or a drop of wax or gluten to guard a letter, as it flies over sea, over land, and comes to its address as if a battalion of artillery brought it, I look upon as a fine metre of civilization.⁶

5   The division of labor, the multiplication of the arts of peace, which is nothing but a large allowance to each man to choose his work according to his faculty, to live by his better hand, fills the State with useful and happy laborers,—and they, creating demand by the very temptation of their productions, are rapidly and surely rewarded by good sale: and what a police and ten commandments their work thus becomes! So true is Dr. Johnson's remark, that "men are seldom more innocently employed, than when they are making money."⁷

6   The skilful combinations of civil government, though they usually follow natural leadings, as the lines of race, language, religion, and territory, yet require wisdom and conduct in the rulers, and in their result delight the imagination. "We see insurmountable multitudes obeying, in opposition to their strongest passions, the restraints of a power which they scarcely perceive, and the crimes of a single individual marked and punished at the distance of half the earth."⁸

7   Right position of woman in the State is another index. Poverty and industry with a healthy mind read very easily the laws of humanity, and love them: place the sexes in right relations of mutual respect, and a severe morality gives that essential charm to woman, which educates all that is delicate, poetic, and self-sacrificing, breeds courtesy and learning, conversation and wit, in her rough mate; so that I have thought it a sufficient definition of civilization to say, it is the influence of good women.

8   Another measure of culture is the diffusion of knowledge, overrunning

all the old barriers of caste, and, by the cheap press, bringing the university to every poor man's door in the newsboy's basket. Scraps of science, of thought, of poetry, are in the coarsest sheet, so that in every house we hesitate to burn a newspaper until we have looked it through.

The ship, in its latest complete equipment, is an abridgement and compend of a nation's arts: the ship steered by compass and chart, longitude reckoned by lunar observation, and, when the heavens are hid, by chronometer; driven by steam; and in wildest sea-mountains, at vast distances from home,

> "The pulses of her iron heart
> Go beating through the storm."[9]

No use can lessen the wonder of this control, by so weak a creature, of forces so prodigious. I remember I watched, in crossing the sea, the beautiful skill whereby the engine in its constant working was made to produce two hundred gallons of fresh water out of salt water, every hour,—thereby supplying all the ship's want.[10]

The skill that pervades complex details; the man that maintains himself; the chimney taught to burn its own smoke; the farm made to produce all that is consumed on it; the very prison compelled to maintain itself and yield a revenue, and, better still, made a reform school, and a manufactory of honest men out of rogues, as the steamer made fresh water out of salt: all these are examples of that tendency to combine antagonisms, and utilize evil, which is the index of high civilization.

Civilization is the result of highly complex organization. In the snake, all the organs are sheathed: no hands, no feet, no fins, no wings.[11] In bird and beast, the organs are released, and begin to play. In man, they are all unbound, and full of joyful action. With this unswaddling, he receives the absolute illumination we call Reason, and thereby true liberty.

Climate has much to do with this melioration. The highest civility has never loved the hot zones. Wherever snow falls, there is usually civil freedom. Where the banana grows, the animal system is indolent and pampered at the cost of higher qualities: the man is grasping, sensual, and cruel. But this scale is not invariable. For high degrees of moral sentiment control the unfavorable influences of climate; and some of our grandest examples of men and of races come from the equatorial regions,—as the genius of Egypt, of India, and of Arabia.

13   These feats are measures or traits of civility; and temperate climate is an important influence, though not quite indispensable, for there has been learning, philosophy, and art in Iceland, and in the tropics. But one condition is essential to the social education of man,—namely, morality. There can be no high civility without a deep morality, though it may not always call itself by that name, but sometimes the point of honor, as in the institution of chivalry; or patriotism, as in the Spartan and Roman republics; or the enthusiasm of some religious sect which imputes its virtue to its dogma; or the cabalism, or *esprit de corps,* of a masonic or other association of friends.

14   The evolution of a highly destined society must be moral; it must run in the grooves of the celestial wheels. It must be catholic in aims. What is moral? It is the respecting in action catholic or universal ends. Hear the definition which Kant gives of moral conduct: "Act always so that the immediate motive of thy will may become a universal rule for all intelligent beings."[12]

15   Civilization depends on morality. Everything good in man leans on what is higher. This rule holds in small as in great. Thus, all our strength and success in the work of our hands depends on our borrowing the aid of the elements. You have seen a carpenter on a ladder with a broad-axe chopping upward chips and slivers from a beam. How awkward! at what disadvantage he works! But see him on the ground, dressing his timber under him. Now, not his feeble muscles, but the force of gravity brings down the axe; that is to say, the planet itself splits his stick. The farmer had much ill-temper, laziness, and shirking to endure from his hand-sawyers, until, one day, he bethought him to put his saw-mill on the edge of a waterfall, and the river never tires of turning his wheel. The river is good-natured, and never hints an objection.

16   We had letters to send: couriers could not go fast enough, nor far enough; broke their wagons, foundered their horses; bad roads in spring, snowdrifts in winter, heats in summer; could not get the horses out of a walk. But we found out that the air and earth were full of electricity;[13] and it was always going our way,—just the way we wanted to send.—*Would he take a message?*—Just as lief as not; had nothing else to do; would carry it in no time. Only one doubt occurred, one staggering objection,—he had no carpet-bag, no visible pockets, no hands, not so much as a mouth, to carry a letter. But, after much thought and many experiments, we managed to meet the conditions, and to fold up the letter in such invisible compact form as he could carry in those

invisible pockets of his, never wrought by needle and thread,—and it went like a charm.

I admire still more than the saw-mill the skill which, on the sea-shore, makes the tides drive the wheels and grind corn, and which thus engages the assistance of the moon, like a hired hand, to grind, and wind, and pump, and saw, and split stone, and roll iron. 17

Now that is the wisdom of a man, in every instance of his labor, to hitch his wagon to a star, and see his chore done by the gods themselves. That is the way we are strong, by borrowing the might of the elements. The forces of steam, gravity, galvanism, light, magnets, wind, fire serve us day by day, and cost us nothing. 18

Our astronomy is full of examples of calling in the aid of these magnificent helpers. Thus, on a planet so small as ours, the want of an adequate base for astronomical measurements is early felt, as, for example, in detecting the parallax of a star. But the astronomer, having by an observation fixed the place of a star, by so simple an expedient as waiting six months, and then repeating his observation, contrived to put the diameter of the earth's orbit, say two hundred millions of miles, between his first observation and his second, and this line afforded him a respectable base for his triangle.[14] 19

All our arts aim to win this vantage. We cannot bring the heavenly powers to us, but, if we will only choose our jobs in directions in which they travel, they will undertake them with the greatest pleasure. It is a peremptory rule with them, that *they never go out of their road.* We are dapper little busybodies, and run this way and that way superserviceably,—but they swerve never from their foreordained paths,—neither the sun, nor the moon, nor a bubble of air, nor a mote of dust. 20

And as our handiworks borrow the elements, so all our social and political action leans on principles. To accomplish anything excellent, the will must work for catholic and universal ends. A puny creature walled in on every side, as Daniel wrote,— 21

> "Unless above himself he can
> Erect himself, how poor a thing is man!"[15]

but when his will leans on a principle, when he is the vehicle of ideas, he borrows their omnipotence. Gibraltar may be strong, but ideas are impregnable, and bestow on the hero their invincibility. "It was a great instruction," said a saint in Cromwell's war, "that the best courages are but beams of the Almighty."[16] Hitch your wagon to a star. Let us not fag in paltry works which serve our pot and bag alone. Let us not lie and steal. No god will help. We shall find all their teams going the other way,—Charles's Wain, Great Bear, Orion, Leo, Hercules:—every god will leave us.[17]

22   If we can thus ride in Olympian chariots by putting our works in the path of the celestial circuits, we can harness also evil agents, the powers of darkness, and force them to serve against their will the ends of wisdom and virtue. Thus, a wise Government puts fines and penalties on pleasant vices. What a benefit would the American Government, not yet relieved of its extreme need, render to itself, and to every city, village, and hamlet in the States, if it would tax whiskey and rum almost to the point of prohibition! Was it Bonaparte who said that he found vices very good patriots? He got five millions from the love of brandy, and he should be glad to know which of the virtues would pay him as much. Tobacco and opium have broad backs, and will cheerfully carry the load of armies, if you choose to make them pay high for such joy as they give and such harm as they do.

23   These are traits, and measures, and modes; and the true test of civilization is, not the census, nor the size of cities, nor the crops,—no, but the kind of man the country turns out. I see the vast advantages of this country, spanning the breadth of the temperate zone. I see the immense material prosperity,—towns on towns, states on states, and wealth piled in the massive architecture of cities, California quartz-mountains dumped down in New York to be re-piled architecturally along-shore from Canada to Cuba, and thence westward to California again.[18] But it is not New York streets built by the confluence of workmen and wealth of all nations, though stretching out towards Philadelphia until they touch it, and northward until they touch New Haven, Hartford, Springfield, Worcester, and Boston,—not these that make the real estimation. But, when I look over this constellation of cities which animate and illustrate the land, and see how little the Government has to do with their daily life, how self-helped and self-directed all families are,—knots of men in purely natural societies,—societies of trade, of kindred blood, of habitual hospitality, house and house, man acting on man by weight of opinion, of longer or better-directed industry, the refining influence of women, the invitation which experience and permanent causes open to youth and labor,

—when I see how much each virtuous and gifted person whom all men consider lives affectionately with scores of excellent people who are not known far from home, and perhaps with great reason reckons these people his superiors in virtue, and in the symmetry and force of their qualities, I see what cubic values America has, and in these a better certificate of civilization than great cities or enormous wealth.

In strictness, the vital refinements are the moral and intellectual steps. The appearance of the Hebrew Moses, of the Indian Buddh,—in Greece, of the Seven Wise Masters, of the acute and upright Socrates, and of the Stoic Zeno,—[19] in Judæa, the advent of Jesus,—and in modern Christendom, of the realists Huss, Savonarola, and Luther, are causal facts which carry forward races to new convictions, and elevate the rule of life.[20] In the presence of these agencies, it is frivolous to insist on the invention of printing or gunpowder, of steampower and gaslight, percussion caps, and rubber shoes, which are toys thrown off from that security, freedom, and exhilaration which a healthy morality creates in society. These arts add a comfort and smoothness to house and street life; but a purer morality, which kindles genius, civilizes civilization, casts backward all that we held sacred into the profane, as the flame of oil throws a shadow when shined upon by the flame of the Bude light.[21] Not the less the popular measures of progress will ever be the arts and the laws.

But if there be a country which cannot stand any one of these tests,—a country where knowledge cannot be diffused without perils of mob-law and statute-law,—where speech is not free,—where the post-office is violated, mail-bags opened, and letters tampered with,—where public debts and private debts outside of the State are repudiated,—where liberty is attacked in the primary institution of their social life,—where the position of the white woman is injuriously affected by the outlawry of the black woman,—where the arts, such as they have, are all imported, having no indigenous life,— where the laborer is not secured in the earnings of his own hands,—where suffrage is not free or equal,—that country is, in all these respects, not civil, but barbarous, and no advantages of soil, climate, or coast can resist these suicidal mischiefs.

Morality is essential, and all the incidents of morality,—as, justice to the subject, and personal liberty. Montesquieu says, "Countries are well cultivated, not as they are fertile, but as they are free;" and the remark holds not

24

25

26

less, but more, true of the culture of men than of the tillage of land.[22] And the highest proof of civility is that the whole public action of the state is directed on securing the greatest good of the greatest number.[23]

27 Our Southern states have introduced confusion into the moral sentiments of their people, by reversing this rule in theory and practice, and denying a man's right to his labor. The distinction and end of a soundly-constituted man is his labor. Use is inscribed on all his faculties. Use is the end to which he exists. As the tree exists for its fruit, so a man for his work. A fruitless plant, an idle animal, is not found in the universe. They are all toiling, however secretly or slowly, in the province assigned them, and to a use in the economy of the world: The higher and more complex organizations, to higher and more catholic service; and man seems to play a certain part that tells on the general face of the planet,—as if dressing the globe for happier races of his own kind, or, as we sometimes fancy, for beings of superior organization.

28 But thus use, labor of each for all, is the health and virtue of all beings. ICH DIEN, *I serve,* is a truly royal motto.[24] And it is the mark of nobleness to volunteer the lowest service,—the greatest spirit only attaining to humility. Nay, God is God, because he is the servant of all. Well, now comes this conspiracy of Slavery,—they call it an institution, I call it a destitution,—this stealing of men and setting them to work,—stealing their labor, and the thief sitting idle himself, and for two or three ages it has lasted, and has yielded a certain quantity of rice, cotton, and sugar. And standing on this doleful experience these people have endeavored to reverse the natural sentiments of mankind, and to pronounce labor disgraceful, and the well-being of a man to consist in eating the fruit of other men's labor. Labor: a man coins himself into his labor; turns his day, his strength, his thought, his affection, into some product which remains as the visible sign of his power; and to protect that, to secure that to him, to secure his past self to his future self, is the object of all government. There is no interest in any country so imperative as that of labor; it covers all, and constitutions and governments exist for that: to protect and ensure it to the laborer. All honest men are daily striving to earn their bread by their industry. And who is this who tosses his empty head at this blessing in disguise, the constitution of human nature, and calls labor vile, and insults the faithful workman at his daily toil? I see for such madness, no hellebore; for such calamity, no solution but servile war, and the Africanization of the country that permits it.[25]

At this moment in America, the aspects of political society absorb attention.[26] In every house, from Canada to the Gulf, the children ask the serious father, 'What is the news of the war today? and when will there be better times?' The boys have no new clothes, no gifts, no journeys; the girls must go without new bonnets; boys and girls find their education, this year, less liberal and complete. All the little hopes that heretofore have made the year pleasant are deferred. The state of the country fills us with anxiety and stern duties. We have attempted to hold together two states of civilization—a higher state, where labor and the tenure of land and the right of suffrage are democratical; and a lower state, in which the old military tenure of prisoners or slaves, and of power and land in a few hands, make an oligarchy;—we have attempted to hold these two states of society under one law. But the rude and early state of society does not work well with the later, nay, works badly, and has poisoned politics, public morals, and social intercourse in the Republic, now for many years.

30

The times put this question—Why cannot the best civilization be extended over the whole country, since the disorder of the less civilized portion menaces the existence of the country? Is this secular progress we have described, this evolution of man to the highest powers, only to give him sensibility, and not to bring duties with it? Is he not to make his knowledge practical? to stand and to withstand? Is not civilization heroic also? Is it not for action? has it not a will? "There are periods," said Niebuhr, "when something much better than happiness and security of life is attainable."[27] We live in a new and exceptional age. America is another word for opportunity. Our whole history appears like a last effort of the Divine Providence in behalf of the human race; and a literal slavish following of precedents, as by a justice of the peace, is not for those who at this hour lead the destinies of this people. The evil you contend with has taken alarming proportions, and you still content yourself with parrying the blows it aims, but, as if enchanted, abstain from striking at the cause.

If the American people hesitate, it is not for want of warning or advices. The telegraph has been swift enough to announce our disasters.[28] The journals have not suppressed the extent of the calamity. Neither was there any want of argument or of experience. If the war brought any surprise to the North, it was not the fault of sentinels on the watch-towers, who had furnished full details of the designs, the muster, and the means of the enemy.

Neither was anything concealed of the theory or practice of slavery. To what purpose make more big books of these statistics? There are already mountains of facts, if anyone wants them. But people do not want them. They bring their opinions into the world. If they have a comatose tendency in the brain, they are pro-slavery while they live; if of a nervous sanguineous temperament, they are abolitionists. Then interests were never persuaded. Can you convince the shoe interest or the iron interest or the cotton interest, by reading passages from Milton or Montesquieu? You wish to satisfy people that slavery is bad economy. Why, the Edinburgh Review pounded on that string, and made out its case forty years ago. A democratic statesman said to me, long since, that, if he owned the State of Kentucky, he would manumit all the slaves, and be a gainer by the transaction.[29] Is this new? No, everybody knows it. As a general economy it is admitted. But there is no one owner of the state, but a good many small owners. One man owns land and slaves; another owns slaves only. Here is a woman who has no other property, like a lady in Charleston I knew of, who owned fifteen chimneysweeps, and rode in her carriage. It is clearly a vast inconvenience to each of these to make any change, and they are fretful and talkative, and all their friends are, and those less interested are inert, and, from want of thought, averse to innovation. It is like free trade, certainly the interest of nations, but by no means the interest of certain towns and districts, which tariff feeds fat: and the eager interest of the few overpowers the apathetic general conviction of the many. Bank-notes rob the public, but are such a daily convenience, that we silence our scruples and make believe they are gold.[30] So imposts are the cheap and right taxation; but by the dislike of people to payout a direct tax, governments are forced to render life costly by making them pay twice as much, hidden in the price of tea and sugar.[31]

32   In this national crisis, it is not argument that we want, but that rare courage which dares commit itself to a principle, believing that Nature is its ally, and will create the instruments it requires, and more than make good any petty and injurious profit which it may disturb. There never was such a combination as this of ours, and the rules to meet it are not set down in any history. We want men of original perception and original action, who can open their eyes wider than to a nationality, namely, to considerations of benefit to the human race, can act in the interest of civilization. Government must not be a parish clerk, a justice of the peace. It has of necessity in any crisis of the

state the absolute powers of a Dictator. The existing Administration is entitled to the utmost candor. It is to be thanked for its angelic virtue, compared with any executive experiences with which we have been familiar.[32] But the times will not allow us to indulge in compliment. I wish I saw in the people that inspiration, which, if Government would not obey the same, it would leave the Government behind, and create on the moment, the means and executors it wanted. Better the war should more dangerously threaten us,—should threaten fracture in what is still whole, and punish us with burned capitals and slaughtered regiments, and so exasperate the people to energy,—exasperate our nationality. There are Scriptures written invisibly on men's hearts, whose letters do not come out until they are enraged. They can be read by war-fires, and by eyes in the last peril.

We cannot but remember that there have been days in American history, when, if the free states had done their duty, Slavery had been blocked by an immovable barrier, and our recent calamities forever precluded. The free states yielded, and every compromise was surrender, and invited new demands.[33] Here again is a new occasion which Heaven offers to sense and virtue. It looks as if we held the fate of the fairest portion of mankind in our hands, to be saved by our firmness or to be lost by hesitation.   33

The one power that has legs long enough and strong enough to cross the Potomac, offers itself at this hour;—the one strong enough to bring all the civility up to the height of that which is best,—prays now at the door of Congress for leave to move. Emancipation is the demand of civilization. That is a principle; everything else is an intrigue. This is a progressive policy, puts the whole people in healthy, productive, amiable position, puts every man in the South in just and natural relations with every man in the North, laborer with laborer.   34

We shall not attempt to unfold the details of the project of Emancipation. It has been stated with great ability by several of its leading advocates. I will only advert to some leading points of the argument, at the risk of repeating the reasons of others.[34]   35

The war is welcome to the Southerner: a chivalrous sport to him, like hunting, and suits his semi-civilized condition. On the climbing scale of progress, he is just up to war, and has never appeared to such advantage as in the last twelvemonth. It does not suit us. We are advanced some ages on the war-state,—to trade, art, and general cultivation. His laborer works for him at   36 home, so that he loses no labor by the war. All our soldiers are laborers; so that the South with its inferior numbers, is almost on a footing in effective war-population with the North. Again: as long as we fight without any affirmative step taken by the Government, any word intimating forfeiture in the rebel States of their old privileges under the law,—they and we fight on the same side, for Slavery. Again: if we conquer the enemy,—what then? We shall still have to keep him under, and it will cost as much to hold him down as it did to get him down. Then comes the summer, and fever will drive our soldiers home; next winter, we must begin at the beginning, and conquer him over again. What use, then, to take a fort, or a privateer, or get possession of an inlet, or to capture a regiment of rebels?

37   But one weapon we hold which is sure. Congress can, by edict, as a part of the military defence which it is the duty of Congress to provide, abolish slavery, and pay for such slaves as we ought to pay for.[35] Then, the slaves near our armies will come to us: those in the interior will know in a week what their rights are, and will, where opportunity offers, prepare to take them.[36] Instantly, the armies that now confront you must run home to protect their estates, and must stay there, and your enemies will disappear.

38   There can be no safety until this step is taken. We fancy that the endless debate, emphasized by the crime and by the cannons of this war, has brought the Free States to some conviction that it can never go well with us whilst this mischief of Slavery remains in our politics, and that by concert or by might we must put an end to it. But we have too much experience of the futility of an easy reliance on the momentary good dispositions of the public. There does exist perhaps a popular-will, that the Union shall not be broken; that our trade, and therefore our laws, must have the whole breadth of the continent, and from Canada to the Gulf. But, since this is the rooted belief and will of the people, so much the more are they in danger, when impatient of defeats, or impatient of taxes, to go with a rush for some peace, and what kind of peace shall, at that moment, be easiest attained: they will make concessions for it; will give up the slaves;—and the whole torment of the past half-century will come back to be endured anew.

39   Neither do I doubt, if such a composition should take place, that the Southerners will come back quietly and politely, leaving their haughty dictation. It will be an era of good feelings.[37] There will be a lull after so loud a storm: and, no doubt, there will be discreet men from that section who will

earnestly strive to inaugurate more moderate and fair administration of the Government, and the North will for a time have its full share and more, in place and counsel. But this will not last, not for want of sincere good will in sensible Southerners, but because Slavery will again speak through them its harsh necessity. It cannot live but by injustice, and it will be unjust and violent to the end of the world.

The power of Emancipation is this, that it alters the atomic social consti- 40
tution of the Southern people. Now their interest is in keeping out white la-
bor; then, when they must pay wages, their interest will be to let it in; to get the best labor, and, if they fear the blacks, to invite Irish, German, and Ameri-
can laborers. Thus, whilst Slavery makes and keeps disunion, emancipation removes the whole objection to Union. Emancipation at one stroke elevates the poor white of the South and identifies his interest with that of the northern laborer.

Now in the name of all that is simple and generous, why should not this 41
great right be done? Why should not America be capable of a second stroke for the well-being of the human race, as, eighty or ninety years ago, she was for the first? an affirmative step in the interests of human civility, urged on her, too, not by any romance of sentiment but by her own extreme perils? It is very certain that the statesman who shall break through the cobwebs of doubt, fear, and petty cavil that lie in the way, will be greeted by the unanimous thanks of mankind. Men reconcile themselves very fast to a bold and good measure, when once it is taken, though they condemned it, in advance. A week before the two captive commissioners were surrendered to England, everyone thought it could not be done: it would divide the North. It was done, and in two days, all agreed it was the right action.[38] And this action which costs so little, (the parties injured by it being such a handful, that they can very easily be indemnified,) rids the world, at one stroke, of this degrading nuisance, the cause of war and ruin to nations. This measure at once puts all parties right. This is borrowing, as I said, the omnipotence of a principle. What is so foolish as the terror lest the blacks should be made furious by freedom and wages? It is denying these, that is the outrage; and makes the danger from the blacks. But justice satisfies everybody, white man, red man, yellow man, and black man. All like wages, and the appetite grows by feeding.

But this measure to be effectual must come speedily. The weapon is slip- 42
ping out of our hands. "Time," say the Indian Scriptures, "drinketh up the

essence of every great and noble action which ought to be performed, and which is delayed in the execution."[39]

43   I hope it is not a fatal objection to this policy that it is simple and benefi- cent thoroughly, which is the attribute of a moral action. An unprecedented material prosperity has not tended to make us Stoics or Christians. But the laws by which the Universe is organized reappear at every point, and will rule it. The end of all political struggle is to establish morality as the basis of all legislation. It is not free institutions, 'tis not a republic, 'tis not a democracy, that is the end, no, but only the means. Morality is the object of government. We want a state of things in which crime shall not pay. This is the consolation on which we rest in the darkness of the future and the afflictions of today, that the government of the world is moral, and does forever destroy what is not.

44   It is the maxim of natural philosophers, that the natural forces wear out in time all obstacles, and take place: and 'tis the maxim of history, that, vic- tory always falls at last where it ought to fall; or, there is perpetual march and progress to ideas. But, in either case, no link of the chain can drop out. Na- ture works through her appointed elements; and ideas must work through the brains and arms of good and brave men, or they are no better than dreams.

45   Since the above pages were written, President Lincoln has proposed to Congress that the Government shall coöperate with any State that shall enact a gradual abolishment of Slavery.[40] In the recent series of national successes, this Message is the best. It marks the happiest day in the political year. The American Executive ranges itself for the first time on the side of freedom. If Congress has been backward, the President has advanced. This state-paper is the more interesting that it appears to be the President's individual act, done under a strong sense of duty. He speaks his own thought in his own style. All thanks and honor to the Head of the State! The Message has been received throughout the country with praise, and, we doubt not, with more pleasure than has been spoken. If Congress accords with the President, it is not yet too late to begin the emancipation; but we think it will always be too late to make it gradual. All experience agrees that it should be immediate. More and bet- ter than the President has spoken shall, perhaps, the effect of this message be,—but, we are sure, not more or better than he hoped in his heart, when,

thoughtful of all the complexities of his position, he penned these cautious words.

Notes

1. François Guizot, *Histoire de la civilisation en Europe*, 3 vols. (Paris, 1828).

2. Emerson is evidently suggesting that nineteenth-century Africans live much as they did at the time they were described by Herodotus in the fifth century BCE.

3. In Incan tradition, Manco Capac (fl. 1200) founded the Inca dynasty by consolidating the Indian tribes of the Peruvian highlands.

4. Margaret Fuller discussed this phenomenon in *Summer on the Lakes, in 1843* (Boston: Charles C. Little and James Brown, 1844), pp. 63–64.

5. Emerson drafted this tale from notes he entered in his journal, but without a source (*JMN*, 13:111).

6. Gluten is a mixture of plant proteins sometimes used as an adhesive; the "wafer" to which Emerson refers is a thin disk of dried paste or the like, which also serves to seal letters.

7. James Boswell, *The Life of Samuel Johnson,* report on 27 March 1775.

8. Emerson attributes this quotation to Dr. Thomas Brown in a note in the printed text.

9. "The Steamboat" (1840), ll. 27–28, by the American physician and author Oliver Wendell Holmes, misquoted.

10. The Atlantic crossing Emerson remembers is that of his second journey of three to Europe, in 1847–1848, when he sailed from Boston to Liverpool on the new clipper ship *The Washington Irving.* As Emerson attests in "Voyage to England" (*CW*, 5:13–17), such ships boasted every modern mechanical convenience, including the capacity to desalinate sea water through a process of reverse osmosis.

11. Translated by Emerson from Goethe, *Werke*, 55 vols. (Stuttgart, 1828–1833), 55:208; cf. *JMN*, 12:119.

12. Kant's definition of moral conduct, which is a direct application of his theory of the categorical imperative, appears in section I of *Grundlegen zur Metaphysik der Sitten* (1785). The English version Emerson prints may have been his own translation of Kant's original.

13. Emerson's alludes to the electrical telegraph, developed and patented in the United States in 1837 by the American inventor Samuel F. B. Morse (1791–1872).

14. As Emerson explains, the parallax of a star is the difference in its apparent position as seen from two different points on the earth's surface or from opposite points in the earth's orbit around the sun. Using powerful telescopes, the English astrono-

mers Sir William Herschel, his son Sir John Frederick William Herschel, and his sister Caroline Lucretia Herschel (1750–1848) made definitive calculations of planetary and star distances from the Earth.

15. *"To the Lady Margaret, Countess of Cumberland,"* ll. 95–96, by Samuel Daniel.

16. Emerson's source is Lucy Hutchinson, *Memoirs of the Life of Colonel Hutchinson . . .* , 2 vols. (London, 1822), 1:312.

17. Although "Hitch your wagon to a star" is one of Emerson's best known sayings, its meaning in this essay has to be understood in its Civil War context. In the journal in which he drafted this paragraph, Emerson promotes the justice of the Northern side in the conflict, while avoiding self-righteousness and favoring, instead, those virtues "the gods honor & promote" (*JMN*, 15:185). His argument is that if Northerners were to descend into self-righteousness, they would find the teams of the gods of fortune "going the other way," a point he underscores through reference to Charles's Wain (the Big Dipper), which as an image appears to be a wagon hitched to a star in the constellation *Ursa Major* ("Great Bear"), and the constellations Orion, Leo, and Hercules.

18. Emerson developed this and the previous two sentences out of a letter he wrote to Thomas Carlyle on 11 March 1854 (*CEC*, p. 499); cf. *JMN*, 14:227 and 15:181–182.

19. The "Seven Wise Masters" are normally credited to be seven sixth-century BCE Greeks noted for their maxims, but there are multiple candidates for the designation. The list drawn from the *Lives of Eminent Philosophers* by the third-century Greek writer Diogenes Laertius is the one most often cited and includes Bias ("Most men are bad"), Chilo ("Consider the end"), Cleobulos ("Avoid extremes"), Periander ("Nothing is impossible to industry"), Pittacos ("Know thy opportunity"), Solon ("Know thyself"), and Thales ("Suretyship is the forerunner of ruin"). Competing lists are found in Plato, *Protagoras*, 343a; Plutarch, "The Banquet of the Seven Wise Men," *Plutarch's Morals* (1718), 2:3–41; and Titus Flavius Clemens (ca. 150–ca. 211), better known as Clement of Alexandria, *Stromateis*, 1.14.59.

20. Girolamo Savonarola (1452–1498), Italian religious reformer, who, like Jan Hus, was martyred.

21. The "Bude" or "Gurney light" was devised by Sir Goldsworthy Gurney (1793–1875) of Bude, Cornwall, in which an intense light was produced by supplying the burner with a stream of oxygen.

22. See the note to "American Slavery," para 49, above.

23. Emerson understood the signature principle of utilitarianism as "The greatest happiness of the greatest number is the foundation of all morals and legislation" (Jeremy Bentham, *An Introduction to the Principles of Morals and Legislation*, ed. J. H. Burns and H. L. A. Hart [Oxford, UK, and New York, 1996], p. 11). Emerson restates the principle in "Character," para 2, below.

24. The motto of the Prince of Wales.

25. "Hellebore" refers to a number of plants used medicinally for their emetic effects.

26. When "American Civilization" was published in April 1862, the American Civil War was entering its second year.

27. Emerson's source is *Life and Letters of Barthold Georg Niebuhr* (1852), 2:361–362.

28. The most notable of these was the Confederate victory at the first Battle of Bull Run (21 July 1861).

29. Emerson attributes the statement to George Sewall Boutwell (1818–1905), governor of Massachusetts (1851–1852) (*JMN*, 15:162).

30. The United States government did not issue paper currency until 1862, although banknotes of the First and Second Banks of the United States were quasi-official until 1836. Banknotes issued by individual banks were often counterfeited and vulnerable to economic fluctuations.

31. Emerson's point is that customs duties (imposts) that raise the prices of imported goods are effectively a hidden tax.

32. Abolitionist-minded Northerners found the Lincoln administration frustratingly slow to engage slavery yet admirable by comparison to its predecessors.

33. A reference to the Missouri Compromise of 1820 and, particularly, to the Compromise of 1850, which strengthened fugitive slave laws.

34. "I refer mainly to a discourse by the Rev. M. D. Conway, delivered before the 'Emancipation League,' in Boston, in January last." (Emerson's note in the printed text.) Moncure D. Conway (1832–1907), a native of Virginia, left his Methodist pulpit, alienated his family by giving up his inheritance of slaves, and moved north, where he became a Unitarian minister. Emerson had known Conway since 1853 and was sympathetic to his views on emancipation, some of which he adopted. For Conway's account of his lecture and meetings with Emerson at the time, see *Autobiography: Memories and Experiences of Moncure Daniel Conway*, 2 vols. (Boston: Houghton, Mifflin, 1905), 2:344–348.

35. Ultimately, military necessity would be Lincoln's justification for emancipation by executive order. Compensated emancipation was another option but implemented only in the District of Columbia, in 1862.

36. The Confiscation Act, signed 6 August 1861, allowed for appropriation of property, including slaves, being used in the rebellion. Known as *contraband of war*, escaped slaves were welcomed behind Union lines and thus effectively freed themselves.

37. This phrase was originally applied to the period of weak political parties and an apparent lack of partisanship that characterized the administration of United States president James Monroe (1758–1831) from 1817 to 1825.

38. This and the previous sentence refer to the "Trent Affair" following the Union capture of two Confederate agents, James Mason and John Slidell, from a British

ship on 8 November 1861. After weeks of tension and the threat of war with Great Britain, the United States released Mason and Slidell. Of his decision to free the agents, Lincoln reputedly said, "One war at a time."

39. Emerson's source is *The Hĕĕtōpădēs of Vĕĕshnŏŏ-Sărmā*. . . (1787), p. 149. Printed in "Veeshnoo Sarma," the *Dial* 3 (July 1842): 84 (*JMN,* 8:485; 15:183).

40. This paragraph, not in the manuscript, was composed by Emerson after he submitted "American Civilization" for publication in the *Atlantic Monthly.*

Thoreau

Henry D. Thoreau was the last male descendant of a French ancestor who came to this country from the isle of Guernsey.[1] His character exhibited occasional traits drawn from this blood in singular combination with a very strong Saxon genius. 1

He was born in Concord, Massachusetts, on the 12th of July, 1817. He was graduated at Harvard College, in 1837, but without any literary distinction.[2] An iconoclast in literature, he seldom thanked colleges for their service to him, holding them in small esteem, whilst yet his debt to them was important.[3] After leaving the University, he joined his brother in teaching a private school, which he soon renounced.[4] His father was a manufacturer of lead pencils, and Henry applied himself for a time to this craft, believing he could make a better pencil than was then in use. After completing his experiments, he exhibited his work to chemists and artists in Boston, and having obtained their certificates to its excellence and to its equality with the best London manufacture, he returned home contented. His friends congratulated him that he had now opened his way to fortune. But he replied, that he should never make another pencil. "Why should I? I would not do again what I have done once." He resumed his endless walks, and miscellaneous studies, mak- 2 ing every day some new acquaintance with Nature, though as yet never speaking of zoology or botany, since, though very studious of natural facts, he was incurious of technical and textual science.

3   At this time, a strong, healthy youth fresh from college, whilst all his companions were choosing their profession, or eager to begin some lucrative employment, it was inevitable that his thoughts should be exercised on the same question, and it required rare decision to refuse all the accustomed paths, and keep his solitary freedom at the cost of disappointing the natural expectations of his family and friends. All the more difficult that he had a perfect probity, was exact in securing his own independence, and in holding every man to the like duty. But Thoreau never faltered. He was a born protestant. He declined to give up his large ambition of knowledge and action for any narrow craft or profession, aiming at a much more comprehensive calling, the art of living well. If he slighted and defied the opinions of others, it was only that he was more intent to reconcile his practice with his own belief. Never idle or self-indulgent, he preferred when he wanted money, earning it by some piece of manual labor agreeable to him, as building a boat or a fence, planting, grafting, surveying, or other short work, to any long engagements. With his hardy habits and few wants, his skill in wood-craft, and his powerful arithmetic, he was very competent to live in any part of the world. It would cost him less time to supply his wants than another. He was therefore secure of his leisure.

4   A natural skill for mensuration,[5] growing out of his mathematical knowledge, and his habit of ascertaining the measures and distances of objects which interested him, the size of trees, the depth and extent of ponds and rivers, the height of mountains and the air-line distance of his favorite summits,—this, and his intimate knowledge of the territory about Concord, made him drift into the profession of land-surveyor. It had the advantage for him that it led him continually into new and secluded grounds, and helped his studies of nature. His accuracy and skill in this work were readily appreciated, and he found all the employment he wanted.

5   He could easily solve the problems of the surveyor, but he was daily beset with graver questions which he manfully confronted. He interrogated every custom, and wished to settle all his practice on an ideal foundation. He was a protestant à l'outrance and few lives contain so many renunciations.[6] He was bred to no profession; he never married; he lived alone; he never went to

church; he never voted; he refused to pay a tax to the state; he ate no flesh, he drank no wine, he never knew the use of tobacco; and, though a naturalist, he used neither trap nor gun. He chose wisely, no doubt, for himself to be the bachelor of thought and nature. He had no talent for wealth, and knew how to be poor without the least hint of squalor or inelegance. Perhaps he fell into his way of living, without forecasting it much, but approved it with later wisdom. "I am often reminded," he wrote in his journal, "that, if I had bestowed on me the wealth of Crœsus, my aims must be still the same, and my means essentially the same."[7] He had no temptations to fight against; no appetites, no passions, no taste for elegant trifles. A fine house, dress, the manners and talk of highly cultivated people were all thrown away on him. He much preferred a good Indian, and considered these refinements as impediments to conversation, wishing to meet his companion on the simplest terms. He declined invitations to dinner-parties, because there each was in every one's way, and he could not meet the individuals to any purpose. "They make their pride," he said, "in making their dinner cost much: I make my pride in making my dinner cost little." When asked at table, what dish he preferred, he answered, "the nearest." He did not like the taste of wine, and never had a vice in his life. He said, "I have a faint recollection of pleasure derived from smoking dried lily stems, before I was a man. I had commonly a supply of these. I have never smoked any thing more noxious."[8]

He chose to be rich by making his wants few, and supplying them himself. In his travels, he used the railroad only to get over so much country as was unimportant to the present purpose, walking hundreds of miles, avoiding taverns, buying a lodging in farmers' and fishermen's houses, as cheaper, and more agreeable to him, and because there he could better find the men and the information he wanted.

There was somewhat military in his nature not to be subdued, always manly and able, but rarely tender, as if he did not feel himself except in opposition. He wanted a fallacy to expose, a blunder to pillory, I may say, required a little sense of victory, a roll of the drum, to call his powers into full exercise. It cost him nothing to say No; indeed he found it much easier than to say Yes. It seemed as if his first instinct on hearing a proposition was to controvert it, so impatient was he of the limitations of our daily thought. This habit of course is a little chilling to the social affections; and though the companion would in the end acquit him of any malice or untruth, yet it mars

6

7

conversation. Hence no equal companion stood in affectionate relations with one so pure and guileless. "I love Henry," said one of his friends, "but I cannot like him: and as for taking his arm, I should as soon think of taking the arm of an elm-tree."[9]

8   Yet hermit and stoic as he was, he was really fond of sympathy, and threw himself heartily and childlike into the company of young people whom he loved, and whom he delighted to entertain, as he only could, with the varied and endless anecdotes of his experiences by field and river. And he was always ready to lead a huckleberry party or a search for chestnuts or grapes. Talking one day of a public discourse, Henry remarked, that whatever succeeded with the audience, was bad. I said, "Who would not like to write something which all can read, like 'Robinson Crusoe'; and who does not see with regret that his page is not solid with a right materialistic treatment, which delights everybody." Henry objected, of course, and vaunted the better lectures which reached only a few persons. But, at supper, a young girl, understanding that he was to lecture at the Lyceum, sharply asked him, "whether his lecture would be a nice, interesting story such as she wished to hear, or whether it was one of those old philosophical things that she did not care about?" Henry turned to her, and bethought himself, and, I saw, was trying to believe that he had matter that might fit her and her brother, who were to sit up and go to the lecture, if it was a good one for them.[10]

9   He was a speaker and actor of the truth,—born such,—and was ever running into dramatic situations from this cause. In any circumstance, it interested all bystanders to know what part Henry would take, and what he would say: and he did not disappoint expectation, but used an original judgment on each emergency. In 1845, he built himself a small framed house on the shores of Walden Pond, and lived there two years alone, a life of labor and study. This action was quite native and fit for him. No one who knew him would tax him with affectation. He was more unlike his neighbors in his thought, than in his action. As soon as he had exhausted the advantages of that solitude, he abandoned it.[11] In 1847, not approving some uses to which the public expenditure was applied, he refused to pay his town-tax, and was put in jail. A friend paid the tax for him, and he was released.[12] The like annoyance was threatened the next year. But, as his friends paid the tax, notwithstanding his protest, I believe he ceased to resist. No opposition or ridicule had any weight with him. He coldly and fully stated his opinion without affecting to believe

that it was the opinion of the company. It was of no consequence if every one present held the opposite opinion. On one occasion he went to the University Library to procure some books. The Librarian refused to lend them. Mr. Thoreau repaired to the President, who stated to him the rules and usages which permitted the loan of books to resident graduates, to clergymen who were alumni, and to some others resident within a circle of ten miles' radius from the College. Mr. Thoreau explained to the President that the railroad had destroyed the old scale of distances,—that the library was useless, yes, and President and College useless, on the terms of his rules,—that the one benefit he owed to the College was its library,—that at this moment, not only his want of books was imperative, but he wanted a large number of books, and assured him that he Thoreau, and not the Librarian, was the proper custodian of these. In short, the President found the petitioner so formidable and the rules getting to look so ridiculous, that he ended by giving him a privilege which in his hands proved unlimited thereafter.[13]

No truer American existed than Thoreau. His preference of his country and condition was genuine, and his aversion from English and European manners and tastes almost reached contempt. He listened impatiently to news or bon mots gleaned from London circles; and, though he tried to be civil, these anecdotes fatigued him. The men were all imitating each other, and on a small mould. Why can they not live as far apart as possible, and each be a man by himself? What he sought was the most energetic nature, and he wished to go to Oregon, not to London. "In every part of Great Britain," he wrote in his diary, "are discovered traces of the Romans, their funereal urns, their camps, their roads, their dwellings. But New England, at least, is not based on any Roman ruins. We have not to lay the foundations of our houses on the ashes of a former civilization."[14]

But idealist as he was, standing for abolition of slavery, abolition of tariffs, almost for abolition of government, it is needless to say he found himself not only unrepresented in actual politics, but almost equally opposed to every class of reformers. Yet he paid the tribute of his uniform respect to the anti-slavery party. One man, whose personal acquaintance he had formed, he honored with exceptional regard. Before the first friendly word had been spoken for Captain John Brown, after the arrest, he sent notices to most houses in Concord, that he would speak in a public hall on the condition and character of John Brown, on Sunday Evening, and invited all people to come. The

Republican committee, the abolitionist committee, sent him word that it was premature and not advisable. He replied, "I did not send to you for advice but to announce that I am to speak." The hall was filled at an early hour by people of all parties, and his earnest eulogy of the hero was heard by all respectfully, by many with a sympathy that surprised themselves.[15]

12 It was said of Plotinus, that he was ashamed of his body, and 'tis very likely he had good reason for it;[16] that his body was a bad servant, and he had not skill in dealing with the material world, as happens often to men of abstract intellect. But Mr. Thoreau was equipped with a most adapted and serviceable body. He was of short stature, firmly built, of light complexion, with strong, serious blue eyes, and a grave aspect; his face covered in the late years with a becoming beard. His senses were acute, his frame well-knit and hardy, his hands strong and skilful in the use of tools. And there was a wonderful fitness of body and mind. He could pace sixteen rods more accurately than another man could measure them with rod and chain.[17] He could find his path in the woods at night, he said, better by his feet than his eyes. He could estimate the measure of a tree very well by his eye; he could estimate the weight of a calf or a pig, like a dealer. From a box containing a bushel or more of loose pencils, he could take up with his hands fast enough just a dozen pencils at every grasp. He was a good swimmer, runner, skater, boatman, and would probably out-walk most countrymen in a day's journey. And the relation of body to mind was still finer than we have indicated. He said, he wanted every stride his legs made. The length of his walk uniformly made the length of his writing. If shut up in the house, he did not write at all.

13 He had a strong common sense, like that which Rose Flammock, the weaver's daughter, in Scott's romance, commends in her father, as resembling a yardstick, which, whilst it measures dowlas and diaper, can equally well measure tapestry and cloth of gold.[18] He had always a new resource. When I was planting forest trees, and had procured half a peck of acorns, he said, that only a small portion of them would be sound, and proceeded to examine them, and select the sound ones. But finding this took time, he said, "I think, if you put them all into water, the good ones will sink," which experiment we tried with success. He could plan a garden, or a house, or a barn; would have been competent to lead a "Pacific Exploring Expedition";[19] could give judicious counsel in the gravest private or public affairs. He lived for the day, not cumbered and mortified by his memory. If he brought you yesterday

a new proposition, he would bring you to-day another not less revolutionary. A very industrious man, and setting, like all highly organized men, a high value on his time, he seemed the only man of leisure in town, always ready for any excursion that promised well, or for conversation prolonged into late hours. His trenchant sense was never stopped by his rules of daily prudence, but was always up to the new occasion. He liked and used the simplest food, yet, when some one urged a vegetable diet, Thoreau thought all diets a very small matter; saying, that "the man who shoots the buffalo lives better than the man who boards at the Graham house."[20] He said, "You can sleep near the railroad, and never be disturbed. Nature knows very well what sounds are worth attending to, and has made up her mind not to hear the railroad-whistle. But things respect the devout mind, and a mental ecstacy was never interrupted."

He noted what repeatedly befel him, that, after receiving from a distance a rare plant, he would presently find the same in his own haunts. And those pieces of luck which happen only to good players happened to him. One day walking with a stranger who inquired, where Indian arrowheads could be found, he replied, "Every where," and stooping forward, picked one on the instant from the ground. At Mount Washington, in Tuckerman's Ravine, Thoreau had a bad fall, and sprained his foot. As he was in the act of getting up from his fall, he saw for the first time, the leaves of the *Arnica mollis*.[21]   14

His robust common sense, armed with stout hands, keen perceptions, and strong will, cannot yet account for the superiority which shone in his simple and hidden life. I must add the cardinal fact that there was an excellent wisdom in him, proper to a rare class of men, which showed him the material world as a means and symbol. This discovery, which sometimes yields to poets a certain casual and interrupted light serving for the ornament of their writing, was in him an unsleeping insight; and, whatever faults or obstructions of temperament might cloud it, he was not disobedient to the heavenly vision. In his youth, he said, one day, "The other world is all my art: my pencils will draw no other; my jack-knife will cut nothing else; I do not use it as a means."[22] This was the muse and genius that ruled his opinions, conversation, studies, work, and course of life. This made him a searching judge of men. At first glance, he measured his companion, and, though insensible to some fine traits of culture, could very well report his weight and calibre. And this made the impression of genius which his conversation often gave.   15

16 He understood the matter in hand at a glance, and saw the limitations and poverty of those he talked with, so that nothing seemed concealed from such terrible eyes. I have repeatedly known young men of sensibility converted in a moment to the belief that this was the man they were in search of, the man of men, who could tell them all they should do. His own dealing with them was never affectionate, but superior, didactic; scorning their petty ways; very slowly conceding or not conceding at all the promise of his society at their houses or even at his own. "Would he not walk with them?"—He did not know. There was nothing so important to him as his walk; he had no walks to throw away on company. Visits were offered him from respectful parties, but he declined them. Admiring friends offered to carry him at their own cost to the Yellow Stone River; to the West Indies; to South America. But though nothing could be more grave or considered than his refusals, they remind one in quite new relations of that fop Brummel's reply to the gentleman who offered him his carriage in a shower, "But where will *you* ride then?"[23] And what accusing silences, and what searching and irresistible speeches battering down all defences, his companions can remember!

17 Mr. Thoreau dedicated his genius with such entire love to the fields, hills, and waters of his native town, that he made them known and interesting to all reading Americans, and to people over the sea. The river on whose banks he was born and died, he knew from its springs to its confluence with the Merrimack.[24] He had made summer and winter observations on it for many years, and at every hour of the day and the night. The result of the recent survey of the Water Commissioners appointed by the State of Massachusetts, he had reached by his private experiments, several years earlier. Every fact which occurs in the bed, on the banks, or in the air over it; the fishes, and their spawning and nests, their manners, their food; the shad-flies which fill the air on a certain evening once a year, and which are snapped at by the fishes so ravenously, that many of these die of repletion; the conical heaps of small stones on the river shallows, one of which heaps will sometimes overfill a cart,—these heaps the huge nests of small fishes;[25] the birds which frequent the stream, heron, duck, sheldrake, loon, osprey; the snake, muskrat, otter, woodchuck, and fox, on the banks; the turtle, frog, hyla, and cricket, which make the banks vocal,—were all known to him, and, as it were, townsmen and fellow-creatures:[26] so that he felt an absurdity or violence in any narrative of one of these by itself apart, and still more of its dimensions on an inch-

rule, or in the exhibition of its skeleton, or the specimen of a squirrel or a bird in brandy. He liked to speak of the manners of the river, as itself a lawful creature, yet with exactness, and always to an observed fact. As he knew the river, so the ponds in this region.

One of the weapons he used, more important than microscope or alcohol receiver, to other investigators, was a whim which grew on him by indulgence, yet appeared in gravest statement, namely, of extolling his own town and neighborhood as the most favored centre for natural observation.[27] He remarked that the Flora of Massachusetts embraced almost all the important plants of America,—most of the oaks, most of the willows, the best pines, the ash, the maple, the beech, the nuts. He returned Kane's "Arctic Voyage" to a friend of whom he had borrowed it with the remark, that "most of the phenomena noted might be observed in Concord."[28] He seemed a little envious of the Pole, for the coincident sunrise and sunset, or five minutes' day after six months. A splendid fact which Annursnuc had never afforded him.[29] He found red snow in one of his walks; and told me that he expected to find yet the *Victoria regia* in Concord.[30] He was the attorney of the indigenous plants, and owned to a preference of the weeds to the imported plants, as of the Indian to the civilized man: and noticed with pleasure that the willow bean-poles of his neighbor had grown more than his beans. "See these weeds," he said, "which have been hoed at by a million farmers all spring and summer, and yet have prevailed, and just now come out triumphant over all lanes, pastures, fields, and gardens, such is their vigor. We have insulted them with low names too, as pigweed, wormwood, chickweed, shad blossom." He says they have brave names too, ambrosia, stellaria, amelanchier, amaranth, etc.[31]

I think his fancy for referring every thing to the meridian of Concord, did not grow out of any ignorance or depreciation of other longitudes or latitudes, but was rather a playful expression of his conviction of the indifferency of all places, and that the best place for each is where he stands. He expressed it once in this wise: "I think nothing is to be hoped from you, if this bit of mould under your feet is not sweeter to you to eat, than any other in this world, or in any world."[32]

The other weapon with which he conquered all obstacles in science was patience. He knew how to sit immoveable, a part of the rock he rested on, until the bird, the reptile, the fish, which had retired from him, should come

18

19

20

back, and resume its habits, nay, moved by curiosity should come to him and watch him.

21   It was a pleasure and a privilege to walk with him. He knew the country like a fox or a bird, and passed through it as freely by paths of his own.[33] He knew every track in the snow, or on the ground, and what creature had taken this path before him. One must submit abjectly to such a guide, and the reward was great. Under his arm he carried an old music book to press plants; in his pocket, his diary and pencil, a spy-glass for birds, microscope, jack-knife, and twine. He wore straw hat, stout shoes, strong gray trowsers, to brave shrub-oaks and smilax, and to climb a tree for a hawk's or a squirrel's nest. He waded into the pool for the water-plants, and his strong legs were no insignificant part of his armour. On the day I speak of he looked for the menyanthes, detected it across the wide pool, and, on examination of the florets, decided that it had been in flower five days. He drew out of his breast-pocket his diary, and read the names of all the plants that should bloom on this day, whereof he kept account as a banker when his notes fall due. The cypripedium not due till tomorrow. He thought, that, if waked up from a trance, in this swamp, he could tell by the plants what time of the year it was within two days. The redstart was flying about and presently the fine grosbeaks, whose brilliant scarlet makes the rash gazer wipe his eye, and whose fine clear note Thoreau compared to that of a tanager which has got rid of its hoarseness.[34] Presently he heard a note which he called that of the night-warbler, a bird he had never identified, had been in search of twelve years, which always, when he saw it, was in the act of diving down into a tree or bush, and which it was vain to seek; the only bird that sings indifferently by night and by day.[35] I told him he must beware of finding and booking it, lest life should have nothing more to show him. He said, "What you seek in vain for, half your life, one day you come full upon all the family at dinner. You seek it like a dream, and, as soon as you find it, you become its prey."

22   His interest in the flower or the bird lay very deep in his mind, was connected with Nature,—and the meaning of Nature was never attempted to be defined by him. He would not offer a memoir of his observations to the Natural History Society. "Why should I? To detach the description from its connections in my mind, would make it no longer true or valuable to me: and they do not wish what belongs to it." His power of observation seemed to indicate additional senses. He saw as with microscope, heard as with ear-

trumpet, and his memory was a photographic register of all he saw and heard. And yet none knew better than he that it is not the fact that imports, but the impression or effect of the fact on your mind. Every fact lay in glory in his mind, a type of the order and beauty of the whole.

His determination on Natural History was organic.[36] He confessed that he sometimes felt like a hound or a panther, and, if born among Indians, would have been a fell hunter. But, restrained by his Massachusetts culture, he played out the game in this mild form of botany and ichthyology.[37] His intimacy with animals suggested what Thomas Fuller records of Butler the apiologist, that "either he had told the bees things or the bees had told him."[38] Snakes coiled round his leg; the fishes swam into his hand, and he took them out of the water; he pulled the woodchuck out of its hole by the tail, and took the foxes under his protection from the hunters. Our naturalist had perfect magnanimity; he had no secrets: he would carry you to the heron's haunt, or, even to his most prized botanical swamp;—possibly knowing that you could never find it again,—yet willing to take his risks. 23

No college ever offered him a diploma, or a professor's chair; no academy made him its corresponding secretary, its discoverer, or even its member. Whether these learned bodies feared the satire of his presence. Yet so much knowledge of nature's secret and genius few others possessed, none in a more large and religious synthesis. For not a particle of respect had he to the opinions of any man or body of men, but homage solely to the truth itself. And as he discovered everywhere among doctors some leaning of courtesy, it discredited them. He grew to be revered and admired by his townsmen, who had at first known him only as an oddity. The farmers who employed him as a surveyor soon discovered his rare accuracy and skill, his knowledge of their lands, of trees, of birds, of Indian remains, and the like, which enabled him to tell every farmer more than he knew before of his own farm. So that he began to feel as if Mr. Thoreau had better rights in his land than he. They felt, too, the superiority of character which addressed all men with a native authority. 24

Indian relics abound in Concord, arrowheads, stone chisels, pestles, and fragments of pottery; and, on the river bank, large heaps of clam-shells and ashes mark spots which the savages frequented. These, and every circumstance touching the Indian, were important in his eyes. His visits to Maine were chiefly for love of the Indian. He had the satisfaction of seeing the man- 25 ufacture of the bark-canoe, as well as of trying his hand in its management on the rapids. He was inquisitive about the making of the stone arrowhead, and, in his last days, charged a youth setting out for the Rocky Mountains, to find an Indian who could tell him that: "It was well worth a visit to California, to learn it."[39] Occasionally, a small party of Penobscot Indians would visit Concord, and pitch their tents for a few weeks in summer on the river bank. He failed not to make acquaintance with the best of them, though he well knew that asking questions of Indians is like catechizing beavers and rabbits. In his last visit to Maine, he had great satisfaction from Joseph Polis, an intelligent Indian of Oldtown, who was his guide for some weeks.[40]

26   He was equally interested in every natural fact. The depth of his perception found likeness of law throughout nature, and, I know not any genius who so swiftly inferred universal law from the single fact. He was no pedant of a department. His eye was open to beauty, and his ear to music. He found these, not in rare conditions, but wheresoever he went. He thought the best of music was in single strains;[41] and he found poetic suggestion in the humming of the telegraph wire.

27   His poetry might be bad or good; he no doubt wanted a lyric facility, and technical skill; but he had the source of poetry in his spiritual perception. He was a good reader and critic, and his judgment on poetry was to the ground of it. He could not be deceived as to the presence or absence of the poetic element in any composition, and his thirst for this made him negligent and perhaps scornful of superficial graces. He would pass by many delicate rhythms, but he would have detected every live stanza or line in a volume, and knew very well where to find an equal poetic charm in prose. He was so enamoured of the spiritual beauty, that he held all actual written poems in very light esteem in the comparison. He admired Æschylus and Pindar, but when some one was commending them, he said, that, "Æschylus and the Greeks, in describing Apollo and Orpheus, had given no song, or no good one. They ought not to have moved trees, but to have chaunted to the gods such a hymn as would have sung all their old ideas out of their heads, and new ones in." His own verses are often rude and defective. The gold does not yet run pure, is drossy and crude. The thyme and marjoram are not yet honey. But if he want lyric fineness, and technical merits, if he have not the poetic temperament, he never lacks the causal thought, showing that his genius was better than his talent. He knew the worth of the Imagination for the

uplifting and consolation of human life, and liked to throw every thought into a symbol. The fact you tell is of no value, but only the impression. For this reason his presence was poetic, always piqued the curiosity to know more deeply the secrets of his mind. He had many reserves,—an unwillingness to exhibit to profane eyes what was still sacred in his own, and knew well how to throw a poetic veil over his experience. All readers of "Walden" will remember his mythical record of his disappointments:—

> "I long ago lost a hound, a bay horse, and a turtle-dove, and am still on their trail. Many are the travellers I have spoken concerning them, describing their tracks, and what calls they answered to. I have met one or two who had heard the hound, and the tramp of the horse, and even seen the dove disappear behind a cloud, and they seemed as anxious to recover them as if they had lost them themselves."[42]

His riddles were worth the reading, and I confide that, if at any time I do not understand the expression, it is yet just. Such was the wealth of his truth, that it was not worth his while to use words in vain.

His poem entitled "Sympathy" reveals the tenderness under that triple steel of stoicism, and the intellectual subtlety it could animate. His classic poem on "Smoke" suggests Simonides, but is better than any poem of Simonides.[43] His biography is in his verses. His habitual thought makes all his poetry a hymn to the Cause of causes, the spirit which vivifies and controls his own.

> "I hearing get, who had but ears,
> And sight, who had but eyes before;
> I moments live, who lived but years,
> And truth discern, who knew but learning's lore."[44]

And still more in these religious lines:—

> "Now chiefly is my natal hour,
> And only now my prime of life;
> I will not doubt the love untold,
> Which not my worth or want hath bought,

Which wooed me young, and wooes me old,
And to this evening hath me brought."[45]

29   Whilst he used in his writings a certain petulance of remark in reference
to churches or churchmen, he was a person of a rare, tender, and absolute
religion, a person incapable of any profanation, by act or by thought. Of
course, the same isolation which belonged to his original thinking and living
detached him from the social religious forms. This is neither to be censured
nor regretted. Aristotle long ago explained it, when he said, "One who surpasses his fellow citizens in virtue, is no longer a part of the city. Their law is
not for him, since he is a law to himself."[46]

30   Thoreau was sincerity itself, and might fortify the convictions of prophets in the ethical laws, by his holy living. It was an affirmative experience
which refused to be set aside. A truth-speaker he, capable of the most deep
and strict conversation; a physician to the wounds of any soul; a friend knowing not only the secret of friendship, but almost worshipped by those few
persons who resorted to him as their confessor and prophet, and knew the
deep value of his mind and great heart. He thought that without religion or
devotion of some kind, nothing great was ever accomplished: and he thought
that the bigoted sectarian had better bear this in mind.

31   His virtues of course sometimes ran into extremes. It was easy to trace to
the inexorable demand on all for exact truth that austerity which made this
willing hermit more solitary even than he wished. Himself of a perfect probity, he required not less of others. He had a disgust at crime, and no worldly
success could cover it. He detected paltering as readily in dignified and prosperous persons as in beggars, and with equal scorn. Such dangerous frank-
ness was in his dealing, that his admirers called him "that terrible Thoreau,"
as if he spoke, when silent, and was still present when he had departed. I
think the severity of his ideal interfered to deprive him of a healthy sufficiency of human society.

32   The habit of a realist to find things the reverse of their appearance inclined him to put every statement in a paradox. A certain habit of antagonism
defaced his earlier writings, a trick of rhetoric not quite outgrown in his later,
of substituting for the obvious word and thought its diametrical opposite. He
praised wild mountains and winter forests for their domestic air; in snow and

ice, he would find sultriness; and commended the wilderness for resembling Rome and Paris.[47] "It was so dry, that you might call it wet."

The tendency to magnify the moment, to read all the laws of nature in 33 the one object or one combination under your eye, is of course comic to those who do not share the philosopher's perception of identity. To him there was no such thing as size. The pond was a small ocean; the Atlantic, a large Walden Pond. He referred every minute fact to cosmical laws. Though he meant to be just, he seemed haunted by a certain chronic assumption that the science of the day pretended completeness and he had just found out that the savans had neglected to discriminate a particular botanical variety, had failed to describe the seeds, or count the sepals. "That is to say," we replied, "the blockheads were not born in Concord, but who said they were? It was their unspeakable misfortune to be born in London, or Paris, or Rome; but, poor fellows, they did what they could, considering that they never saw Bateman Pond, or Nine-Acre-Corner, or Becky Stow's Swamp. Besides, what were you sent into the world for, but to add this observation?"[48]

Had his genius been only contemplative, he had been fitted to his life, but 34 with his energy and practical ability he seemed born for great enterprise and for command: and I so much regret the loss of his rare powers of action, that I cannot help counting it a fault in him that he had no ambition. Wanting this, instead of engineering for all America, he was the captain of a huckleberry party. Pounding beans is good to the end of pounding empires one of these days, but if, at the end of years, it is still only beans!—[49]

But these foibles, real or apparent, were fast vanishing in the incessant 35 growth of a spirit so robust and wise, and which effaced its defects with new triumphs. His study of nature was a perpetual ornament to him, and inspired his friends with curiosity to see the world through his eyes, and to hear his adventures. They possessed every kind of interest. He had many elegances of his own, whilst he scoffed at conventional elegance. Thus he could not bear to hear the sound of his own steps, the grit of gravel; and therefore never willingly walked in the road, but in the grass, on mountains, and in woods. His senses were acute, and he remarked that by night every dwelling-house gives out bad air, like a slaughter-house. He liked the pure fragrance of melilot.[50] He honored certain plants with special regard, and over all the pond-lily,—then the gentian, and the *Mikania scandens,* and "Life Everlasting,"[51] and a bass tree which he visited every year when it bloomed in the middle of July.[52] He thought the scent a more oracular inquisition than the sight,— more oracular and trustworthy. The scent, of course, reveals what is concealed from the other senses. By it he detected earthiness. He delighted in echoes, and said, they were almost the only kind of kindred voices that he heard. He loved nature so well, was so happy in her solitude, that he became very jealous of cities, and the sad work which their refinements and artifices made with man and his dwelling. The axe was always destroying his forest— "Thank God," he said, "they cannot cut down the clouds. All kinds of figures are drawn on the blue ground, with this fibrous white paint."[53]

36   I subjoin a few sentences taken from his unpublished manuscripts not only as records of his thought and feeling, but for their power of description and literary excellence.[54]

> "Some circumstantial evidence is very strong, as when you find a trout in the milk."
>
> "The chub is a soft fish, and tastes like boiled brown paper salted."
>
> "The youth gets together his materials to build a bridge to the moon, or, perchance, a palace or temple on the earth, and, at length, the middle-aged man concludes to build a woodshed with them."
>
> "The locust z-ing."
>
> "Devil's-needles zig-zagging along the Nut-Meadow brook."
>
> "Sugar is not so sweet to the palate, as sound to the healthy ear."
>
> "I put on some hemlock boughs, and the rich salt crackling of their leaves was like mustard to the ear, the crackling of uncountable regiments. Dead trees love the fire."
>
> "The blue-bird carries the sky on his back."
>
> "The tanager flies through the green foliage, as if it would ignite the leaves."
>
> "If I wish for a horse-hair for my compass-sight, I must go to the stable; but the hair-bird with her sharp eyes goes to the road."
>
> "Immortal water, alive even to the superficies."
>
> "Fire is the most tolerable third party."

"Nature made ferns for pure leaves, to show what she could do in that line."

"No tree has so fair a bole, and so handsome an instep as the beech."

"How did these beautiful rainbow tints get into the shell of the fresh-water clam, buried in the mud at the bottom of our dark river?"

"Hard are the times when the infant's shoes are second-foot."

"We are strictly confined to our men to whom we give liberty."

"Nothing is so much to be feared as fear. Atheism may comparatively be popular with God himself."

"Of what significance the things you can forget? A little thought is sexton to all the world."

"How can we expect a harvest of thought, who have not had a seed-time of character?"

"Only he can be trusted with gifts, who can present a face of bronze to expectations."

"I ask to be melted. You can only ask of the metals that they be tender to the fire that melts them. To nought else can they be tender."

There is a flower known to botanists, one of the same genus with our summer plant called "Life Everlasting," a *Gnaphalium* like that, which grows on the most inaccessible cliffs of the Tyrolese mountains, where the chamois dare hardly venture, and which the hunter, tempted by its beauty, and by his love, (for it is immensely valued by the Swiss maidens,) climbs the cliffs to gather, and is sometimes found dead at the foot, with the flower in his hand. It is called by botanists the *Gnaphalium leontopodium,* but by the Swiss, *Edelweisse,* which signifies, *Noble Purity.* Thoreau seemed to me living in the hope to gather this plant, which belonged to him of right. The scale on which his studies proceeded was so large as to require longevity, and we were the less prepared for his sudden disappearance. The country knows not yet, or in the least part, how great a son it has lost. It seems an injury that he should leave in the midst his broken task, which none else can finish,—a kind of indignity to so noble a soul, that it should depart out of nature before yet he has been really shown to his peers for what he is. But he, at least, is content. His soul was made for the noblest society; he had in a short life exhausted the capabilities of this world; wherever there is knowledge, wherever there is virtue, wherever there is beauty, he will find a home.

Notes

1. Jean Thoreau, Henry's grandfather, was not born on Guernsey but on Jersey, another English Channel island, where the family had lived since leaving mainland France during the persecution of Protestants in the late seventeenth century.
2. In fact, Thoreau's record at Harvard earned him a place in the commencement exercises in 1837.
3. When Emerson remarked that all branches of learning were taught at Harvard, Thoreau replied: "Yes, indeed, all the branches and none of the roots" (*CW*, 10:766).
4. Thoreau took over the Concord Academy in September 1838; his brother John Thoreau Jr. joined him the following February. The school closed in April 1841, due as much to John's declining health as to any lack of enthusiasm on Henry's part.
5. See paragraph 12 below for examples.
6. The expression *"à l'outrance"* means "to the utmost."
7. 29 January 1852, *Journal* (Princeton: Princeton University Press, 1981—), 4:301. Croesus, sixth-century BCE Greek king of Lydia, was fabled for his wealth, which nevertheless did not secure happiness.
8. 26 June 1852, *Journal*, 5:151.
9. Emerson attributed this statement to Elizabeth Sherman Hoar (*JMN*, 8:375).
10. This and the previous four sentences relate to Emerson's lecture "The Anglo-American" (printed above), which he delivered at the Concord Lyceum on 1 December 1853; the young girl and her brother are Edith (1841–1929) and Edward Waldo (1844–1930) Emerson, ages twelve and nine; the anticipated Thoreau lecture was "Journey to Moose Head Lake," delivered at the Lyceum on 14 December 1853 (see *JMN*, 13:270). *Robinson Crusoe* (1719), a novel by Daniel Defoe (1660–1731), English journalist and author.
11. This and the previous four sentences relate to Thoreau's two years at Walden Pond, the source of *Walden* (1854). Thoreau's "Conclusion" gives his reason for ending the experiment: ". . . it seemed to me that I had several more lives to live, and could not spare any more time for that one" (Princeton: Princeton University Press, 1971, p. 323).
12. Abolitionists encouraged nonpayment of the Massachusetts poll tax as a protest against slavery. Bronson Alcott and Charles Lane were arrested, though not jailed,

in 1843. Thoreau's arrest, which he wanted to be seen as a protest against the Mexican War, occurred in July 1846; the friend who paid his tax has never been conclusively identified. The incident forms the background to Thoreau's "Resistance to Civil Government" ("Civil Disobedience") (1849).

13. Actually, Thoreau twice went to Harvard presidents over library privileges: to Josiah Quincy (1772–1864) in 1841 and to Jared Sparks (1789–1866) in 1849. Emerson refers here to the later episode.

14. 3 August 1852, *Journal*, 5:272–273.

15. The abolitionist John Brown (1800–1859) was hanged for leading a raid on Harpers Ferry, Virginia, intended to spur a slave revolt. Thoreau's speech was "A Plea for Captain John Brown," delivered at Concord's Town Hall in October 1859 while Brown was on trial. This event is described in Sandra Harbert Petrulionis, *To Set This World Right: The Antislavery Movement in Thoreau's Concord* (Ithaca: Cornell University Press, 2006), pp. 136–137.

16. See the note to *Nature*, para 84, above.

17. Sixteen rods are equivalent to 228 feet. A rod (16.5 feet) was the unit of linear measurement most frequently employed by land surveyors in Thoreau's time.

18. Rose Flammock is a character in *The Betrothed* (1825), by Sir Walter Scott; "dowlas" is coarse linen or cotton cloth, while "diaper" is linen or cotton fabric with a woven pattern of small, repeated figures.

19. The North Pacific Exploring and Surveying Expedition (1853–1856) explored coastal areas from Southeast Asia north to the Bering Sea and Puget Sound.

20. "Graham house" was a Boston boardinghouse that followed the precepts of Sylvester Graham.

21. *"Arnica mollis,"* also known as "hairy arnica," is a perennial herb native to the United States.

22. Emerson dates this statement 1844, approximately when he recorded it in his journal (*JMN*, 9:103).

23. George Bryan Brummell (1778–1840), known as Beau Brummell, was an English dandy.

24. The Concord River, which begins at the confluence of the Sudbury and the Assabet rivers near Concord, flows into the Merrimack River approximately fifteen miles north. Thoreau published *A Week on the Concord and Merrimack Rivers* in 1849.

25. 12 July 1852, *Journal*, 5:217–218.

26. A "hyla" is a type of tree frog.

27. An "alcohol receiver" is the receptacle in which alcohol is collected after distillation.

28. The reference is to *Arctic Explorations* (1856), by United States Navy physician and explorer Elisha Kent Kane (1820–1857).

29. Annursnuc Hill is in Concord.

30. *Victoria regia* is a water lily native to South America.

31. Emerson summarized this conversation with Thoreau in his journal for 1851 (*JMN*, 13:70).

32. Recorded by Emerson, probably in January 1858, after he "found Henry T. yesterday in my woods" (*JMN*, 14:195).

33. See *JMN*, 13:187.

34. The expression "makes the rash gazer wipe his eye" occurs in "Virtue" (1633), l. 6, by George Herbert.

35. 20 May 1856; *JMN*, 14:90–91. In this and the previous five sentences, menyanthes, or bogbean, is a flowering plant that grows in marshy areas; cypripedium, best known as lady's slipper, is a wild orchid; the American redstart is a small warbler; grosbeaks encompass several species of songbirds; tanagers include the scarlet tanager, a songbird found throughout eastern North America; and "night-warbler" most commonly refers to the sedge-warbler, or night singer, a European bird not found in the United States.

36. In the nineteenth century, "natural history" was the common term encompassing systematic observation and description of plants, animals, and natural phenomena of particular places.

37. Ichthyology is the branch of zoology dealing with fish.

38. The reference is to Thomas Fuller's *History of the Worthies of England,* edited for publication by his son John Fuller, in 1662. Charles Butler (d. 1647) wrote *The Feminine Monarchie; or, A Treatise Concerning Bees, and the Due Ordering of Them* (1609).

39. The youth was Edward Waldo Emerson, who began a five-month Western journey for his health in 1862, three days after Thoreau's funeral.

40. Thoreau employed Polis during his trip to the Maine woods in July and August of 1857. Oldtown, or Old Town, is on an island in Penobscot County, Maine.

41. This was a matter of disagreement, as Emerson reports: "All the music, Henry T. says, is in the strain; the tune don't signify, 'tis all one vibration of the string. He says, people don't sing a song, or play a tune, only for one strain that is in it. I don't understand this, & remind him that collocation makes the force of a word, & that [Sir Christopher] Wren's rule, *'position essential to beauty,'* is universally true, but accept what I know of the doctrine of leasts" (*JMN*, 15:112).

42. *Walden,* p. 20. (Emerson's note.) See *Walden* (1971), p. 17; Emerson's page reference is to the first edition (Boston, 1854).

43. Simonides (ca. 556–ca. 468 BCE), lyric poet from the Greek island of Ceos.

44. The first four lines were published by Thoreau in the "Friday" chapter of *A Week on the Concord and Merrimack Rivers.* It is also stanza 4 (ll. 13–16) of his "Inspiration," which Emerson included in *Parnassus* (1875), a poetry collection.

45. "Inspiration," ll. 18–19 joined to ll. 25–28.

46. A paraphrase of *Politics*, 3.13, 1284a2 and following, in which Aristotle notes that democracies generally preserve equality by ostracizing such superior individuals.

47. Emerson originally made these observations to Thoreau about his essay "A Winter Walk" when it was submitted for publication in the October 1843 *Dial*; see *JMN*, 9:9, and *L*, 7:559.

48. Emerson found Thoreau's assumption "amusing" when he recorded these reflections in 1859 (*JMN*, 14:278).

49. In Emerson's journal, this observation is preceded by a comment on Thoreau: "He is a boy, & will be an old boy" (*JMN*, 11:404).

50. 11 July 1852, *Journal*, 5:216; melilot is sweet clover.

51. 18 July 1852, *Journal*, 5:229. *"Mikania scandens"* is hempweed, or climbing hempvine; "Life Everlasting" is cudweed, an herb with medicinal uses.

52. See, for example, 16 July 1852, *Journal*, 5:224.

53. Emerson's combination of two journal entries, 21 January 1852 and 20 January 1853 (*Journal*, 4:273; 5:445).

54. The sources of the following extracts are: "Some circumstantial evidence . . . ," 11 November 1850, *Journal*, 3:139 (that is, when the milk has been watered down); "The chub . . . ," after 12 May 1850 (3:71); "The youth . . . ," 14 July 1852 (5:223); "The locust z-ing," 15 June and 5 July 1852 (5:96, 184); "Devil's-needles . . . ," 1 July 1852 (5:169); "Sugar is not so sweet . . . ," 31 December 1853 (7:216); "I put on . . . ," 20 February 1854 (8:14); "The blue-bird . . . ," 3 April 1852 (4:423); "The tanager . . . ," 20 May 1853 (6:139); "If I wish . . . ," 25 June 1853 (6:243); "Immortal water . . . ," 8 May 1854 (8:106); "Fire is . . . ," 2 January 1853 (5:421); "Nature made ferns . . . ," 29 July 1853 (6:277); "No tree . . . ," 7 November 1851 (4:166); "How did these . . . ," 16 May 1852 (5:61); "Hard are the times . . . ," 7 February 1852 (4:332); "We are strictly . . . ," 13 January 1852 (4:251); "Nothing is . . . ," 7 September 1851 (4:51); "Of what significance . . . ," 4 May 1852 (5:25); "How can we expect . . . ," 7 August 1854 (8:256–257); "Only he . . . ," 16 April 1852 (4:453); "I ask . . . ," 11 April 1852 (4:434).

The President's Proclamation

In so many arid forms which states incrust themselves with,—once in a century, if so often, a poetic act and record occur. These are the jets of thought into affairs, when roused by danger or inspired by genius, the political leaders of the day break the else insurmountable routine of class and local legislation and take a step forward in the direction of catholic and universal interests. Every step in the history of political liberty is a sally of the human mind into the untried future, and has the interest of genius and is fruitful in heroic anecdotes. Liberty is a slow fruit. It comes, like religion, for short periods and in rare conditions, as if awaiting a culture of the race which shall make it organic and permanent. Such moments of expansion in modern history were, the Confession of Augsburg; the plantation of America; the English Commonwealth of 1648; the Declaration of American Independence in 1776; the British emancipation of slaves in the West Indies; the passage of the Reform Bill; the repeal of the Corn-Laws; the Magnetic Ocean Telegraph, though yet imperfect; the passage of the Homestead Bill in the last Congress; and now, eminently, President Lincoln's Proclamation on the twenty-second of September.[1] These are acts of great scope, working on a long future, and on permanent interests, and honoring alike those who initiate and those who receive them. These measures provoke no noisy joy, but are received into a sympathy so deep as to apprise us that mankind are greater and better than we know. At such times, it appears as if a new public were created to greet the new event. It is as when an orator, having ended the compliments and pleasantries with which he conciliated attention, and having run over the superficial fitness and commodities of the measure he urges, suddenly lending himself to some happy inspiration, announces with vibrating voice the grand human principles involved,—the bravoes and wits who greeted him loudly thus far, are surprised and overawed, a new audience is found in the heart of the assembly, an audience hitherto passive and unconcerned, now at last so searched and kindled, that they come forward every one a representative of mankind, standing for all nationalities.

The extreme moderation with which the President advanced to his design; his long avowed expectant policy, as if he chose to be strictly the executive of the best public sentiment of the country, waiting only till it should be unmistakably pronounced;—so fair a mind, that none ever listened so patiently to such extreme varieties of opinion; so reticent, that his decision has taken all parties by surprise, whilst yet it is the just sequel of his prior acts;[2]— the firm tone in which he announces it, without inflation, or surplusage,—all these have bespoken such favor to the act, that great as the popularity of the President has been, we are beginning to think that we have underestimated the capacity and virtue which the Divine Providence has made an instrument of benefit so vast. He has been permitted to do more for America than any other American man. He is well entitled to the most indulgent construction. Forget all that we thought shortcomings, every mistake, every delay. In the extreme embarrassments of his part, call these endurance, wisdom, magnanimity, illuminated, as they now are, by this dazzling success.

When we consider the immense opposition that has been neutralized or converted by the progress of the war, (for it is not long since the President anticipated the resignation of a large number of officers in the army, and the secession of three States, on the promulgation of this policy);[3] when we see how the great stake which foreign nations hold in our affairs has recently brought every European power as a client into this court, and it became every day more apparent what gigantic and what remote interests were to be affected by the decision of the President;—one can hardly say the deliberation was too long. Against all timorous counsels he had the courage to seize the moment; and such was his position, and such the felicity attending the action, that he has replaced Government in the good graces of mankind. "Better is virtue in the sovereign, than plenty in the season," say the Chinese.[4]

4 'T is wonderful what power is, and how ill it is used, and how its ill use makes life mean, and the sunshine dark. Life in America had lost much of its attraction in the later years. The virtues of a good magistrate undo a world of mischief and, because nature works with rectitude, seem vastly more potent than the acts of bad governors, which are ever tempered by the good nature in the people, and the incessant resistance which fraud and violence encounter. The acts of good governors work at a geometrical ratio as one midsummer day seems to repair the damage of a year of war.[5] A day which most of us dared not hope to see; an event worth the dreadful war, worth its costs and uncertainties, seems now to be close before us. October, November, December, will have passed over beating hearts and plotting brains: then the hour will strike, and all men of African descent who have faculty enough to find their way to our lines, are assured of the protection of American Law.[6]

5 It is by no means necessary that this measure should be suddenly marked by any signal results on the negroes or on the rebel masters. The force of the act is that it commits the country to this justice; that it compels the innumerable officers, civil, military, naval, of the Republic, to range themselves on the line of this equity. It draws the fashion to this side. It is not a measure that admits of being taken back. Done, it cannot be undone by a new administration. For slavery overpowers the disgust of the moral sentiment only through immemorial usage. It cannot be introduced as an improvement of the nineteenth century. This act makes that the lives of our heroes have not been sacrificed in vain. It makes a victory of our defeats. Our hurts are healed; the health of the nation is repaired. With a victory like this, we can stand many disasters. It does not promise the redemption of the black race: that lies not with us: but it relieves it of our opposition. The President by this act has paroled all the slaves in America; they will no more fight against us; and it relieves our race once for all of its crime and false position.[7] The first condition of success is secured in putting ourselves right. We have recovered ourselves from our false position and planted ourselves on a law of nature.

"If that fail
The pillared firmament is rottenness,
And earth's base built on stubble."[8]

The Government has assured itself of the best constituency in the world; every spark of intellect, every virtuous feeling, every religious heart, every man of honor, every poet, every philosopher, the generosity of the cities, the health of the country, the strong arms of the mechanics, the endurance of farmers, the passionate conscience of women, the sympathy of distant nations,—all rally to its support.

6

Of course, we are assuming the firmness of the policy thus declared. It must not be a paper proclamation. We confide that Mr. Lincoln is in earnest, and, as he has been slow in making up his mind, has resisted the importunacy of parties and of events to the latest moment, he will be as absolute in his adhesion. Not only will he repeat and follow up his stroke, but the nation will add its irresistible strength. If the ruler has duties, so has the citizen. In times like these, when the nation is imperilled, what man can, without shame, receive good news from day to day, without giving good news of himself? What right has any one to read in the journals tidings of victories, if he has not bought them by his own valor, treasure, personal sacrifice, or by service as good in his own department? With this blot removed from our national honor, this heavy load lifted off the national heart, we shall not fear henceforward to show our faces among mankind. We shall cease to be hypocrites and pretenders, but what we have styled our free institutions will be such. In the light of this event the public distress begins to be removed. What if the brokers' quotations show our stocks discredited and the gold dollar costs one hundred and twenty-seven cents. These tables are fallacious. Every acre in the Free States gained substantial value on the twenty-second of September. The cause of disunion and war has been reached, and begun to be removed. Every man's house-lot and garden are relieved of the malaria which the purest winds and the strongest sunshine could not penetrate and purge. The territory of the Union shines to-day with a lustre, which every European emigrant can discern from far; a sign of inmost security and permanence.

7

Is it feared that taxes will check immigration? That depends on what the taxes are spent for. If they go to fill up this yawning Dismal Swamp which

8

engulfed armies and populations, and created plague, and neutralized hitherto all the vast capabilities of this continent,—then this taxation, which makes the land wholesome and habitable, and will draw all men unto it,—is the best investment in which property-holder ever lodged his earnings.

9   Whilst we have pointed out the opportuneness of the Proclamation, it remains to be said that the President had no choice. He might look wistfully for what variety of courses lay open to him. Every line but one was closed up with fire. This one too bristled with danger, but through it was the sole safety. The measure he has adopted was imperative. It is wonderful to see the unseasonable senility of what is called the Peace party through all its masks blinding their eyes to the main feature of the war, namely, its inevitableness. The war existed long before the cannonade of Sumter and could not be postponed. It might have begun otherwise or elsewhere, but war was in the minds and bones of the combatants, it was written on the iron leaf, and you might as easily dodge gravitation. If we had consented to a peaceable secession of the rebels, the divided sentiment of the border states made peaceable secession impossible, the insatiable temper of the South made it impossible, and the slaves on the border, wherever the border might be, were an incessant fuel to rekindle the fire.[9] Give the Confederacy New Orleans, Charleston, and Richmond, and they would have demanded St. Louis and Baltimore. Give them these, and they would have insisted on Washington.[10] Give them Washington, and they would have assumed the Army and Navy, and, through these, Philadelphia, New York, and Boston. It looks as if the battlefield would have been at least as large in that event as it is now. The war was formidable, but could not be avoided. The war was and is an immense mischief, but brought with it the immense benefit of drawing a line, and rallying the Free States to fix it impassably; preventing the whole force of Southern connection and influence throughout the North from distracting every city with endless confusion, detaching that force and reducing it to handfuls, and, in the progress of hostilities, dis-infecting us of our habitual proclivity through the affection of trade, and the traditions of the Democratic Party to follow Southern leading.[11]

10   These necessities which have dictated the conduct of the Federal Government are overlooked especially by our foreign critics. The popular statement of the opponents of the war abroad is the impossibility of our success. 'If you could add,' say they, 'to your strength the whole army of England, of France,

and of Austria, you could not coerce eight millions of people to come under this government against their will.' This is an odd thing for an Englishman, a Frenchman, or an Austrian to say, who remembers the Europe of the last seventy years,—the condition of Italy, until 1859; of Poland, since 1793; of France, of French Algiers; of British Ireland, and British India.[12] But, granting the truth, rightly read, of the historical aphorism, that "the people always conquer," it is to be noted, that, in the Southern States, the tenure of land, and the local laws, with slavery, give the social system not a democratic, but an aristocratic complexion; and those States have shown every year a more hostile and aggressive temper, until the instinct of self-preservation forced us into the war. And the aim of the war on our part is indicated by the aim of the President's Proclamation, namely, to break up the false combination of Southern society, to destroy the piratic feature in it which makes it our enemy only as it is the enemy of the human race and so allow its reconstruction on a just and healthful basis. Then new affinities will act, the old repulsions will cease, and, the cause of war being removed, nature and trade may be trusted to establish a lasting peace.

We think we cannot overstate the wisdom and benefit of this act of the Government. The malignant cry of the Secession press within the Free States, and the recent action of the Confederate Congress are decisive as to its efficiency and correctness of aim.[13] Not less so is the silent joy which has greeted it in all generous hearts, and the new hope it has breathed into the world. It was well to delay the steamers at the wharves, until this edict could be put on board. It will be an insurance to the ship as it goes plunging through the sea with glad tidings to all people. Happy are the young who find the pestilence cleansed out of the earth, leaving open to them an honest career. Happy the old, who see Nature purified before they depart. Do not let the dying die: hold them back to this world, until you have charged their ear and heart with this message to other spiritual societies, announcing the melioration of our planet.

> "Incertainties now crown themselves assured,
> And Peace proclaims olives of endless age."[14]

Meantime, that ill-fated, much-injured race which the Proclamation respects will lose somewhat of the dejection sculptured for ages in their bronzed countenance, uttered in the wailing of their plaintive music, a race naturally benevolent, joyous, docile, industrious, and whose very miseries sprang from their great talent for usefulness, which, in a more moral age will not only defend their independence, but will give them a rank among nations.

Notes

1. Among these events not previously identified, the Augsburg Confession (1530) was a key document of the Lutheran Reformation in Germany; the "plantation of America" refers to the founding of Plymouth Plantation (1620) by English Separatist Puritans (Pilgrims); the "English Commonwealth" refers to the Protectorate under Oliver and Richard Cromwell that ruled England (1649–1659); the British "Corn-Laws" tariffs were repealed by Parliament in 1846; the "Magnetic Ocean Telegraph" refers to an Atlantic telegraph cable that had worked briefly in 1857–1858; the "Homestead Bill" refers to the American Homestead Act (1862), which provided free land to settlers who improved it; President Lincoln's "Proclamation on the twenty-second of September" was a preliminary emancipation proclamation, in which he announced his intention to free all slaves in areas remaining in rebellion against the United States on 1 January 1863.
2. Unknown to Emerson, Lincoln had discussed the proclamation with his cabinet in July 1862 but decided to withhold it until after a military victory, which came at Antietam on 17 September.
3. The slave states of Maryland, Kentucky, and Missouri (along with Delaware) had remained in the Union. Slaves in these loyal border states were not included in the emancipation of 1863.
4. Emerson's source is the *Practical Philosophy of the Muhammadan People . . .*, p. 457.
5. Emerson attributes this statement, likely a paraphrase, to Goethe: "This field has been reaped for a thousand years, but lo! A little sun & rain and all is green again" (*JMN*, 15:274).
6. The final Emancipation Proclamation would be signed on 1 January 1863.
7. Lincoln justified emancipation as a military measure, encouraging slaves to desert their masters and thus deprive the Confederacy of their labor. "Parole" is the agreement of a prisoner of war not to take up arms again if released.
8. Milton, *Comus, A Mask,* ll. 597–599.
9. In this and previous sentences, Emerson elaborates his image of the Civil War as a "yawning [Great] Dismal Swamp" in paragraph 8, above. The recalcitrance of Southern slave culture is a major concern in "American Civilization," above; see also *JMN*, 15:266–267. On 12 April 1861 Confederate batteries fired on Fort Sumter in Charleston harbor, initiating hostilities in the Civil War.

10. St. Louis and Baltimore were the leading cities of slave states that did not secede; slavery existed in Washington, D.C., until 16 April 1862.

11. Although Northerners, the two Democratic presidents of the 1850s, Franklin Pierce and James Buchanan, supported slavery; the issue divided the Democratic Party in 1860, making possible the election of Lincoln.

12. Much of Italy was effectively controlled by the Austrian Habsburg Empire prior to the Second Italian War of Independence in 1858. Poland lost its independence and was partitioned in 1793–1795, a state of affairs that lasted until 1918. Since 1789, France had experienced revolution, the Napoleonic Empire, constitutional monarchy, and the Second Empire; in 1830, France captured Algiers and began a century-long effort to assert political and cultural control over this part of North Africa. Protestant Britain had controlled Catholic Ireland for centuries and brought India under direct rule in 1858.

13. Copperhead (anti-war and anti-abolition) Northern newspapers, the most strident of which was the *Chicago Times,* made the proclamation an issue in the congressional election of 1862. Confederate reaction to the proclamation was vehement and included measures threatened against black Union soldiers and their officers, which led Lincoln to widen conscription laws on 27 September 1862 and issue an Order of Retaliation in July 1863.

14. Shakespeare, Sonnet CVII, ll. 7–8.

The Scholar

1 *Gentlemen of the Literary Societies,*[1]

2   The anniversaries of the College never lose their interest. You have wisely united your anniversary to the academical holiday, so to add your tribute to the literary excitement of the season, and to borrow from the interest which a graduating class is sure to awaken, a share for all the College. Some of you are today saying your farewells to each other, and tomorrow will receive the parting honors of the College. You go to be teachers, to become physicians, lawyers, divines; in due course, statesmen, naturalists, philanthropists; I hope, some of you, to be the men of letters, critics and philosophers; perhaps the rare gift of poetry already sparkles, and may yet burn. At all events, before the shadows of these times darken over your youthful sensibility and candor, let me use the occasion which your kind request gives me, to offer you some counsels which an old scholar may without pretension bring to youth in regard to the career of letters, the power and joy that belong to it, and its high office in evil times.

3   They are the minority to stand fast for eternal truth, and say, cannons and bayonets for such as already know nothing stronger. But we are here for immortal resistance to wrong. We are they who make the essence and stability of society.

I offer perpetual congratulation to the scholar—he has drawn the white [4]
lot in life. The very disadvantages of his condition point at superiorities. He is
too good for the world, is in advance of his race, his function is prophetic. He
belongs to a superior society and is born one or two centuries too early for
the rough and sensual population into which he is thrown. But the Heaven
which sent him hither knew that well enough, and sent him as a leader
to lead.

Are men perplexed with evil times? The inviolate soul is in perpetual tele- [5]
graphic communication with the source of events. He has earlier information, a private dispatch which relieves him of the terror which presses on
the rest of the community. He is a learner of the laws of nature and the experiences of history; an ear to hear; an organ to receive and impart; a prophet
surrendered with self-abandoning sincerity to the Heaven which pours
through him its will to mankind.

This is the theory. But you know how far this is from the fact:—that noth- [6]
ing has been able to resist the tide with which the material prosperity of
America in years past has beat down the hope of youth, the piety of learning.

The country was full of activity, with its land, wheat, coal, iron, cotton;— [7]
the wealth of the globe was here,—too much work, and not men enough to
do it. Britain, France, Germany, Scandinavia, sent millions of laborers;—still
the need was more. Every kind of skill was in demand, and the bribe came to
men of intellectual culture; Come, drudge in our mill, and you shall have
wealth soon to go back to your own libraries again.

America at large exhibited such a confusion as California showed in 1849, [8]
when the cry of gold was first raised. All the distinctions of profession and
habit ended at the mines. All the world took off their coats, and worked in
shirt-sleeves. Lawyers went and came with pick and wheelbarrow; doctors of
medicine turned teamsters; stray clergymen kept the bar in saloons; professors of colleges sold mince pies, matches, cigars, and so on.

It is the perpetual tendency of wealth to draw on the spiritual class, not in [9]
this coarse way, but in a plausible and covert way. Here is ease, here is refinement, here is elegance of living. Do not denounce me. Don't be such a
cynic. The bribe to many proves irresistible. "We are men of like passions
with you," and the sequel might be told in the old story of the preacher on
the seacoast, when a wreck was seen from the church windows: "Stop, brethren, till I come down from the pulpit, and let us start fair."

Now this, as medicine to a sick scholar, or as necessity to a starved one, [10] might be a manly part;—but, in any other plight, it was profanation. It was not for this that this costly culture was given. The provision of Nature is to keep the balance of matter by the infusion of mind. As certainly as water falls in rain on the tops of mountains, and runs down into valleys, plains, and pits,—so does thought fall first on the best minds, and run down, from class to class, until it reaches the masses, and works revolutions.

11   It is charged that all vigorous nations except ourselves have balanced their labor by mental activity, and especially by the Imagination, the cardinal human power, the Angel of earnest and believing ages. The subtle Hindoo, who carried religion to ecstasy, and philosophy to idealism, produced the wonderful *Epic of the Mahābārat,* of which in the present century the translations have added new regions to thought.[2] The Egyptian built Thebes and Karnak on a scale which dwarfs our art, and by the paintings on the interior walls of the pyramids, invited us into the secret of the religious belief whence he drew such power. The Hebrew nation compensated the insignificance of its numbers and territory by its religious genius, its tenacious belief; and its poems and histories cling to the soil of this globe like the primitive rocks. The Greek was so perfect in action and in imagination, his poems, from Homer to Euripides, so charming in form, and so true to the human mind, that we cannot forget or outgrow their mythology.[3] On the south and east shore of the Mediterranean, Mahomet impressed his fierce genius how deeply into the manners, language, and poetry of Arabia and Persia.

12   See the activity of the imagination in the Crusades. The front of morn was full of fiery shapes; the chasm was bridged over; heaven walked on earth, and earth could see with eyes the *Paradiso* and the *Inferno.*[4] Dramatic "Mysteries" were the entertainment of the people.[5] Parliaments of love and poesy served them, instead of the House of Commons, Congress, and the newspaper. In Puritanism, how the whole Jewish history became flesh and blood in those men,—let Bunyan show.[6]

13   Now it is agreed that we are utilitarian, that we are skeptical, frivolous; that with universal, cheap education, we have stringent theology, comparable in power to the severe doctrine of the monastic orders, Franciscan, Dominican, and Jesuit, but religion is low. There is much criticism, not on deep grounds; but an affirmative philosophy is wanting.

14   Our profoundest philosophy, (if it were not contradiction in terms,) is Skepticism. The great poem of the age is the disagreeable poem of *Faust,* of

which the "Festus" of Bailey and the "Paracelcus" of Browning are English variations.[7] We have superficial sciences: restless, gossiping, aimless activity. We run to Paris, to London, to Rome, to mesmeric spiritualism, to Pusey, to the Catholic Church, as if for the want of thought.[8] And those who would check and guide them have a dreary feeling that in the change and decay of the old creeds and motives, there was no offset to supply their place. Our industrial skill and arts, ministering to convenience and luxury, have made life expensive, and therefore greedy, careful, and anxious, and turned the eyes downward to the earth, not upward to thought.

Ernest Renan finds, that Europe has twice assembled for exhibitions of industry, at the Crystal Palace in London, in 1851, and at Paris in 1855, and not a poem graced the occasion, and nobody remarked the defect.[9] A French prophet of our age, Fourier, predicted, that, one day, instead of by battles and Oecumenical Councils, the rival portions of humanity would dispute to each other excellence in the manufacture of little cakes. So Coleridge of improved breeds in Highlands.

"In my youth," said a Scotch mountaineer, "A highland gentleman measured his importance by the number of men his domain could support. After some time, the question was, to know how many great cattle it would feed. Today we are come to count the number of sheep—I suppose posterity will ask, how many rats and mice it will feed."[10]

Dickens complained in America that, as soon as he arrived in the western towns, the committees waited on him, and invited him to deliver a Temperance Lecture.[11] Bowditch translated Laplace, and, when he removed to Boston, the Hospital Life Assurance Company insisted that he should make their tables of annuities. Napoleon knows the art of war, but should not be put on picket duty. Linnaeus or Robert Brown must not be set to raise gooseberries and cucumbers, though they be excellent botanists.[12] A shrewd broker out of State Street visited a quiet countryman possessed of all the virtues, and in his glib talk said, "With your character, now, I could raise all this money at once, and make an excellent thing of it."[13]

There is an oracle current in the world that nations die by suicide: And the sign of it is the decay of thought. Niebuhr has given striking examples of that fatal portent, as in the loss of power of thought that followed the disasters of the Athenians in Sicily. The country complains loudly of the inefficiency of the army. It was badly led. But before this, it was not the army

15

16

17

18

alone,—it was the population that was badly led. The clerisy, the spiritual guides, the scholars, the seers, have been false to their trust.

19   My point is, that the movement of the whole machine, the motive force of life, and of every particular life, is moral. The world stands on thoughts, and not on iron nor on cotton: And, the iron of iron, the fire of fire, the ether and source of all the elements, is, moral forces.

20   I cannot forgive a homeless scholar his despondency. The worst times only show him how independent he is of times,—only relieve and bring out the splendor of his privilege. Disease alarms the family,—but the physician sees in it a temporary mischief, which he can check and expel.

21   The fears and agitations of men who watch the markets, the crops, the plenty or scarcity of money, or other superficial events are not for him even more serious disasters. He knows that the world is always equal to itself; that the forces which uphold and pervade it are eternal. Air, water, fire, iron, gold, wheat, electricity, animal fibre have not lost any particle of power, and no decay has crept on the spiritual force which gives bias and period to boundless nature.

22   Bad times! What are bad times?

23   The world is always equal to itself. Nature is rich, exuberant, and mocks at the puny forces of destruction: Man makes no more impression on her wealth, than the caterpillar or the cankerworm, whose petty ravage, though noticed in an orchard or a village, is insignificant in the vast exuberance of the summer. The world shines with works of men: towns, railroads, forts, and fleets. War comes, and they are annihilated;—gone like the last year's snow—and caring Nature cannot pause. Weeks, months, pass,—a new harvest;—trade springs up, and there stand new cities, new homes, all rebuilt, and sleepy with permanence. Italy, France: a hundred times the soils of those countries have been trampled with armies, and burned over: a few summers, and they smile with plenty, and yield new men and new revenues to the state.

24   Great is Nature, who cunningly hides every wrinkle of her inconceivable antiquity under roses, and violets, and morning dew. Every inch of the mountain is scarred by horrible convulsions, yet the new day is purple with the bloom of youth and love. Look out into this August night, and see the broad silver flame which flashes up the half of heaven fresh and delicate as the bonfires of the meadow flies. Yet the powers of numbers cannot compute its enormous age,—embosomed in Time and Space. What are they? Our first

problems, which we ponder all our lives through, and leave where we found them; whose outrunning immensity, the ancients believed, astonished the gods themselves; on whose dizzy vastitudes all the worlds of God are a mere dot on the margin, impossible to deny, impossible to believe.

Stand by your order, but the first lesson and the first power of the scholar is that he is not stubborn, but docile. He does not begin with brag, but sets himself accurately, acquaints himself with his duties. Nature is rich and strong. We brag our arts; that is, we have learned two or three of her secrets; but our knowledge is a drop of the sea. Roger Bacon, and Monk Schwartz, invented gunpowder: and today the whole art of war, all fortifications by land and sea, all our drill and military education,—all our arms, are founded on that,—one chemic compound.[14] All are an extension of a gunbarrel, as if the gases, the earth, water, lightning, and caloric, had not a million energies, the discovery of any one of which will change the art of war again, and put an end to war, by the exterminating forces man can apply.

Our modern wealth stands on a few staples. And the interest nations take in our war is exasperated by the importance of cotton trade. And, what is cotton? One plant in 200,000 plants known to the botanist, vastly the largest part of which are reckoned weeds; that is to say, because their virtues are not yet discovered; and every one of them probably yet to be of utility in the arts. As Bacchus was of the vine, as Arkwright and Whitney were the gods of cotton,—so, prolific Time will yet bring an inventor to every plant.[15] There is not a property in Nature but a mind is born to accost it.

There is no unemployed force in nature: All decomposition is recomposition. War disorganizes, but it is to reorganize. If churches are effete, it is because the new heaven forms. If men are sensible of the decay, it must be that the new birth is far on its way. For a new population is incessantly arriving, to whom the utmost stability and supreme benefit of natural and social order is due, and by them will be claimed.

You are here as the carriers of the power of Nature, as Roger Bacon with his secret of gunpowder, with his secret of the balloon, and of steam. As Copernicus with his secret of the true astronomy, as Columbus with America in his log-book. As Newton with his gravity; Harvey with his circulation; Smith with his law of trade.[16] Franklin with lightning; Adams with independance; Kant with pure reason; Swedenborg with his spiritual world. You are the carrier of ideas which are to fashion the mind and so the history of this breathing world, so as they shall be and not otherwise. Steward of Power, Doctor of Laws, interpreter of secrets, Poet, Master,—Every man is a scholar potentially, and does not need any one good so much as this of right thought.

"Calm pleasures here abide, majestic pains."[17]

29   Coleridge traces "three silent revolutions," and the first occurred "when the clerisy fell from the church."[18] A scholar was once a priest. But the church clung to ritual, and the scholar clung to joy, low as well as high, and thus the separation was a mutual fault. But I think it a schism which must be healed. The true Scholar is the Church. Only the duties of Intellect must be owned.

30   Down with these dapper trimmers and sycophants! and let us have masculine and divine men, formidable lawgivers, Pythagoras, Plato, Aristotle, who warp the churches of the world from their traditions, and penetrate them through and through with original perception. Intellectual man lives in perpetual victory. So let his habits be formed, and all his economies heroic; no spoiled child, no drone, no epicure, but a stoic, formidable and athletic, knowing how to be poor, loving labor, and not flogging his youthful wit with tobacco and wine;—treasuring his youth.—

31   The ambassador is held to maintain the dignity of the Republic which he represents. But what does the scholar represent? The organ of ideas, the subtle force which creates nature, and men, and states,—consoler, upholder, imparting pulses of light, and shocks of electricity,—guidance and courage. Let his manners and breeding accord. I wish the youth to be an armed and complete man; no helpless angel to be slapped in the face, but a man dipped in the river Styx of human experience, and knowing good and evil, and made invulnerable so; and self-helping.[19]

32   A redeeming trait of the Sophists of Athens, Hippias and Gorgias, is that they made their own clothes and shoes.[20] Learn to harness a horse, to row a boat, to camp down in the woods, to cook your supper. I chanced lately to be at West Point, and after hearing examination in scientific classes, I went into the barracks. The chamber was in perfect order, the mattress on the iron campbed rolled up, as if ready for removal. I asked the first cadet, Who makes your bed? "I do." Who fetches your water? "I do." Who blacks your shoes? "I do." It was so in every room.[21]

33   These are first steps to power. Learn of Samuel Johnson that it is a primary duty of the man of letters to secure his independence. These times of

ours are serious—full of calamity. But all times are essentially alike. As soon
as there is life, there is danger. Aplomb rules,—he whose word or deed you
cannot predict, who answers you without any supplication in his eye, who
draws his determination from within and instantly—that man rules.

It will always be so. Every principle is a war-note. Whoever attempts to 34
carry out the rule of right, and love, and freedom, must take his life in his
hand. Stand by your order. 'Tis some thirty years since the days of the Reform Bill in England, when on the walls in London you read everywhere plac-
ards, "Down with the Lords."—At that time, Earl Grey, who was a leader of
Reform, was asked in the Parliament his policy on the measures of the radicals; he replied, "I shall stand by my order."[22]

What I would say to you is: Where there is no vision, the people perish. 35
The fault lies with the educated class, the men of study and thought. There is
a very low feeling of duty; the merchant is true to the merchant; the noble in
England and Europe stands by his order; the politician believes in his arts and
combinations, but the scholar does not stand by his order, but defers to the
men of this world.

Pythias of Aegina was victor in the Pancratium of the boys, in the Isth- 36
mian games. He came to the poet Pindar and wished him to write an ode in
his praise, and inquired what was the price of a poem. Pindar replied that he
should give him one talent, about a thousand dollars of our money. "A talent!" cried Pythias, "Why for so much money I can erect a statue of bronze in
the Temple." "Very likely." On second thought, he returned and paid for the
poem. And now not only all the statues of bronze or marble in the temples of
Aegina are destroyed, but the temples themselves and the very walls of the
city are utterly gone, whilst the Ode of Pindar in praise of Pythias remains
entire.[23]

Education itself is on trial. And war seems at first to make it an imperti- 37
nence, and shoulders it aside, as rich men and kings have done before. Stand
by your order, and show these upstarts their place.

There is a proverb that Napoleon, when the Mameluke Cavalry ap- 38
proached the French lines, ordered the grenadiers to the front, the asses and
the savans to fall into the hollow square. It made a good story, and circulated
in that day. But how stands it now? The military expedition was a failure,
Bonaparte deserted himself, and the army got home as it could,—all fruitless,—not a trace of it remains. All that is left of it, is, the researches of those

savans on the antiquities of Egypt, including the great work of Denon, which led the way to all the subsequent studies of Wilkinson and the English and German scholars, who, on that foundation, France, least of all, should disparage the intellect.[24] It is her sons who have made war a science. Napoleon came to know, or, I may say, never did not know his debt to it. Carnot was his geometer, who, by his warlike mathematics, organized victory. Bonaparte was accustomed to say that, "the Ecole Polytechnique was the hen that laid him all the golden eggs." And as compared with France in the distinction given to intellect in the state and in society, England is Chinese in her servility to wealth and old wealth.[25]

39   Gentlemen, I am here to commend your art and profession as thinkers to you. It is real. It is the secret of power. It is the art of command. Greek gods, Norse Gods, and Yankee Gods are well agreed in this matter. All superiority is this, or related to this; for I conceive morals and mind to be in eternal solidarity.

40   "All that the world admires comes from within."[26] Thought makes us men; ranks us; distributes society; distributes the work of the world; is the prolific source of all arts, of all wealth, of all delight, of all grandeur. Men are as they believe. Men are as they think. A certain quantity of power belongs to a certain quantity of truth, and the man who knows any truth not yet discerned by other men is master of all other men so far as that truth and its wide relations are concerned.

41   Stand by his order. He represents intellectual or spiritual force. I wish him to rely on the spiritual arm; to live by his strength, not by his weakness. Swedenborg and Behmen were great men because they knew that a spiritual force was greater than any material force. Swedenborg knew that a text of Scripture would make men black in the face,—drive them out of their houses,—pull down towns and states;—or, build up new, on despised or unthought of foundations.

42   Intellect measures itself by its counteraction to any accumulation of material force. There is no mass which it cannot surmount and dispose. The exertions of this force are the eminent experiences—out of a long life all that is worth remembering. These are the moments that balance years. Does anyone doubt between the strength of a thought and that of an institution? Does anyone doubt that a good general is better than a park of artillery? See a political revolution dogging a book. See armies, institutions, literatures, appearing

in the train of some wild Arabian's dream. See the ponderous instrumentalities which follow a speech in parliament, or a vote in congress.

Scholars are idealists, and should stand for freedom, justice, and public good. They are bound to stand for all the virtues, and all the liberties,—liberty of trade, liberty of press, liberty of religion, and they should open all the prizes of success, and all the roads of Nature to free competition. Scholars are they who make the essence and stability of society. We stand for truth and immortal resistance to wrong. 43

Gird up the loins of your mind. Every principle is a war-note. See on which side you are. A scholar defending the cause of slavery, of arbitrary government, of monopoly, of the oppressor, is a traitor to his profession. He has ceased to be a scholar. He is not company for clean people. 44

We have many revivals of religion. We have had once what was called the revival of letters. I wish to see a revival of the human mind; to see man's sense of duty extend to the cherishing and use of their intellectual powers; their religion should go with their thought and hallow it. Is thought to be confined to a class? No more than goodness. The immortality is as truly preached from the mind as from morals. 45

All that is urged by the saint for the superiority of faith over works, is as truly urged for the higher state of intellectual perception or beholding over any intellectual performance, such as the creation of algebra, or of the *Iliad*. The conscience of the coming age will put its surveillance on the intellect. We accuse ourselves that we have been useless; we ought to accuse ourselves that we have been thoughtless. It is the Law of Adrastia, that whatever soul has perceived any truth shall be safe from harm. 46

The English nation have the common credit of being more individual, more outspoken, and downright, than we are. Each man of them is, very likely, narrow and committed to opinions of no great liberality or dignity, but, such as they are, he heartily stands for them; silent or loud, he is content to be known to all the world as their champion; they grow to him; he is enraged, he curses and swears for them. In the House of Lords, the patrician states his opinion, very clumsily and drearily perhaps, but at least not looking for your ballot and approbation, rather with an air that says, such is my opinion, and who the devil are you? 47

Our people have this levity and complaisance, fear to offend, do not wish to be misunderstood, do not wish of all things to be in the minority. 48

49   God and nature are altogether sincere, and art should be as sincere. It is not enough that the work should show a skilful hand, ingenious contrivance, and admirable polish and finish: it should have a commanding motive in the time and condition in which it was made. We should see in it the great belief of the artist which caused him to make it so as he did, and not otherwise; nothing frivolous, nothing that he might do or not do, as he chose, but somewhat that must be done then and there by him; he could not take his neck out of that yoke, and save his soul, and this design must shine through the whole performance.

50   Never was anything great accomplished but under a religious impulse. The same law holds for the intellect, as for the will. When the will is absolutely surrendered to the moral sentiment,—that is virtue; when the wit is totally surrendered to intellectual truth,—that is genius. Talent for talent's sake is a bauble and a show. Talent working in rapture in the cause of universal truth, lifts the possessor to new power as a benefactor.

51   Sincerity is, in dangerous times, discovered to be an immeasurable advantage. Bishop Latimer tells us, that his father taught him, when a boy, not to shoot with his arms, but to lay his body to the bow.[27] For sincerity is the test of truth, of talent, of genius. True genius is always moral: "Show me a wicked man who has written poetry, and I will show you where his poetry is not poetry; or rather, I will show you in his poetry no poetry at all."[28]—

52   I distrust all the legends of great accomplishments or performance of unprincipled men. Very little reliance must be put on the common stories that circulate of this great senator's or that great barrister's learning, their Greek, their varied literature. That ice won't bear. Reading! Do you mean that this senator or this lawyer who stood by, and allowed the passage of infamous laws, was a reader of Greek books? That is not the question—but, to what purpose did they read? I allow them the merit of that reading which appears in their opinions, tastes, beliefs, and practice. They read that they might know, did they not? Well, these men did not know. They blundered. They were utterly ignorant of that which every boy or girl of fifteen knows perfectly,—the rights of men and women. And this big-mouthed talker, among his dictionaries and Leipsic editions of Lysias, had lost his knowledge.[29] But the President of the Bank nods to the President of the Insurance Office, and relates, that, at Virginia Springs, this idol of the forum exhausted a trunk full of classic authors.

There is always the previous question, How came you on that side? Your argument is ingenious, your language copious, your illustrations brilliant, but your major proposition palpably absurd. Will you establish a lie? You are a very elegant writer;—but you can't write up what gravitates down.

Stand by your order. Stand by yourself. Stay at home in your mind. Aplomb is power in all companies. Sit silent, and hearkening, and docile, not like the vulgar who say whatever occurs to them, but as the liege of truth. In your study of great books, I should say, read a little proudly; as if one should say to the author, 'tis of no account what your reputation is abroad: You have now to convince *Me,* or I leave you.

Rely on yourself. There is respect due to your teachers exactly in proportion to their faithful labors, but every age is new, and has problems to solve insoluble by the last age. Men over forty are no judges of a book written in a new spirit. Neither your teachers, nor the universal teachers, the laws, the customs or dogmas of nations, neither saint nor sage, can compare with that counsel which is open to you. "No angel in his heart acknowledges anyone superior to himself, but the Lord alone."[30]

But I shall be told it is of no use for one to resist a thousand, for a solitary scholar to waste his breath in protesting against tendencies of the continent. Not literary history alone, but all history, is a record of the power of minorities—and of minorities of one. Every book is written with a constant secret reference to the few intelligent persons whom the writer knows or believes to exist in the million. The artist has always the masters in his eye, though he affect to flout them. Michel Angelo is thinking of Da Vinci, and Raffaelle is thinking of Michel Angelo.[31] Tennyson would give his fame for a verdict in his favor from Wordsworth.

In the recovery of the antique marbles in the last century, what were the marbles till Winckelmann could see and pronounce?[32] When the Elgin Marbles came to England, the cry of voices went against them; but Haydon and Fuseli asserted their genuineness to Parliament and people, until the whole world came and saw them through their wiser eyes.[33] Agassiz, and Owen, and Huxley affect to address the American and the English people, but are really writing to each other.[34] Everett dreamed of Webster; McKay, the shipbuilder, thinks of George Steers, and Steers thinks of Pook, the naval constructor.[35] The names of the masters at the head of each department of science, art, or quality, are often little known to the world, but are always known to the ad-

53

54

55

56

57

epts; as Robert Brown in Botany, and Gauss in Mathematics.[36] Often, the master is a hidden man, but not to the true student. Invisible to all the rest, but resplendent to him. All his own work and culture forms the eye to see the master.

58   See in politics the importance of minorities of one, as of Socrates, of Phocion, Cato, Lafayette, Arago.[37] The importance of the one person who has the truth, over nations who have it not, is because power obeys reality, and not appearance: power is according to quality, and not quantity.

59   Let me recall your own experience, when I say that every generous youth capable of thought and action,—with however bold a front and stoical demeanor,—dwells in a little heaven of his own with the images of a few men and a few women,—perhaps with two or one. There was a time when Christianity existed in one child. If the child had been killed by Herod, would the element have been lost?[38] God sends his message, if not by one, then quite as well by another, or could have made every heart preach his commandment. When the Master of the Universe has ends to fulfil, he impresses his will on the structure of single minds.

60   Whoever looks with heed into his thoughts will find our science of the mind has not got far. We divide the mind into faculties of Perception, Conception, Understanding, Imagination, Reason, and Memory, and we attempt some education of these faculties. But who looks with his own eyes will find that there is somebody within him that knows more than he does; (that this education of the Understanding is not always wise: a low and limitary power which works to short ends, to the senses, to daily life in house and street;) a certain dumb life in life; a simple wisdom behind all acquired wisdom; somewhat not educated, or educable, not altered or alterable; a motherwit, which does not learn by experience or by books, but knew it all already; makes no progress,—but was wise in youth as in age.

61   More or less clouded, it yet resides the same in all, saying *Aye, Aye,* or *No, No,* to every proposition: Yet its grand *Aye* and its grand *No,* are more musical than all eloquence. Nobody has found the limits of its knowledge. Whatever object is brought before it is already well known to it.

62   It is impossible to extricate oneself from the questions in which our age is involved. I am not insensible to the stern benefits wrought by the War. War always exalts an age, speaks to slumbering virtue, makes of quiet, plain men unexpected heroes; out of a territory which was hitherto vulgar farm and

market, makes a country, and of people whom we did not know, and only counted in the census, or, as producers and customers, makes countrymen.

All of us have shared the new enthusiasm of country and of liberty, which swept like whirlwind through all souls at the outbreak of war; and brought, by ennobling us, already an offset for its calamity. I learn with joy and with deep respect, that this College has sent its full quota to the field. I learn with grief, but with honoring pain, that you have had your sufferers in the battle, and the noble youth have returned wounded and maimed. 63

The War uplifted us into generous sentiments: War ennobles the age. We do not often have a moment of grandeur in these hurried, slipshod lives. But the behaviour of the young men has taught us much. The solemnity of action of those who had been gay and thoughtless until now. We will not again disparage America, now that we have seen what men it will bear. Battle with his sword has cut many a Gordian knot in twain, which all the wit of East and West, of Northern and Border statesmen, could not untie.[39] We have abandoned ourselves to the current, and the current has known the way. The War floated us into Emancipation, which we dared not enact; into arming the blacks; into treating an enemy as an enemy. 64

The mind always responds to any just demand. It is the nobility of the mind, its military armament, Nature's Home-Guard,—that danger brings its own concentration and added activity, and, if even to gentle natures, a grim joy which the sense of power always gives, and which many private experiences in the present war, told in army letters, abundantly confirm. Tender youths who have passed from every luxury to every hardship, say, "Do not pity me. I assure you I have never spent a year so happily." 65

The times are dark, but heroic. The times develop the strength they need. Boys are heroes. Women have shown a tender patriotism and inexhaustible charity: and, on each new threat of faction, the ballot of the people has been unexpectedly right and decisive. But the issues already appearing overpay the cost. The slavery is broken, and, we use our advantage,—irretrievably. For such a gain,—to end once for all that pest of all free institutions, one generation might well be sacrificed—perhaps it will,—that this continent be purged and a new era of equal rights dawn on the universe. 66

Who would not?—If it could be made certain that the new morning of universal liberty should rise on our race, by the perishing of one generation,—who would not consent to die? The War is a new glass through which 67 to see things. It has undeceived us about European states. They had exhibited a great dislike of America in France and in England on account of our slavery. And we gave England credit for sincerity. She had at least achieved the emancipation of slaves in the West Indies.[40] But deeper than in freedom was her interest in her trade, and naval superiority, and superiority of all kinds, which we threatened. Her joy was great at seeing our nation broken, and her interest in the success of the rebellion undisguised. Money, law, tacit protection, aid of the press; loud advocacy by nobility and Parliament; were freely given to the rebellion. And when challenged on the point of all this protection to slavery, they affected to think that the North was not emancipating, and they talked through their noses. War, seeking for the roots of strength, comes upon the moral aspects at once. In quiet times, custom stifles this discussion as sentimental, and brings in the brazen devil, as by immemorial right.

68   When the course of events goes amiss, there is always a spiritual cause. Have we Despondency, Luxury, Avarice, Slavery, War?—Why these are as natural as eating. Every man is an animal. It was said of the precocity of Siberian civilization, "Skin a Russian, and you have a Tartar"; and Hobbes said, "Man is to man a wolf."[41] Wolf and tiger tear and slay to eat, and slay a great deal more than they eat; and man in his savage state does the same. But why did he not know and do better? Was there no Bible? Was there no tamer? no Von Amburg among the lions? Manco Capac among the cannibals? No scholar? no college? no clerisy? no missionary? no reason? A Mexico of wild horses, and no Rarey; a Rocky Mountain of grizzly bears, and no Grizzly Bear Adams?[42] An America full of cotton, land, and money, and no literature? Slave-hunters, and slave commissioners, and truckling merchants, and politicians,—and no hero to befriend the friendless, no redeemer with a whip of cord to drive away the profaners of temple?[43]

69   Gentlemen, I hold the Scholars, when they are truly such, to be the first-class in the state. I shall treat them so, and speak to their interest as the first. Now the War, which, while it afflicts, ennobles this country, has this inconvenience,—that it absorbs all conversation, and displaces everything but itself. But in the precinct of the College, let us be severely just. Let us indulge ourselves with defying for this day the political and military interest and indulge ourselves with topics proper to the place at the risk of disgusting the popular ear. I please myself with the belief that you, members of this literary association, have kept your ear and heart open to the voice of wise men, to the voice of poets,—still better, to the great hope and lofty counsels of perfect solitude;

that you have not been pained when fashion and frivolity did not smile on you, while you had a better ambition, and were seeking selecter companions.

It is an ever ascending profession. You cannot go back to your childish books. Every step you make disqualifies you for the lower plane of thought you leave behind. He who has learned to read Plato, and once tasted the true joy of that book, does not care much for *Sinbad, the Sailor.*[44] Every piece of new knowledge refines you, and you can never be again the savage you were.

70

Notes

1. Emerson delivered this discourse on 22 July 1863 before the United Literary Societies of Dartmouth College in Hanover, New Hampshire, and repeated it on 11 August before the Erosophian Society of Waterville (now Colby) College in Waterville, Maine. Invitations to speak at college exercises were familiar to Emerson between the 1830s and 1860s.
2. *"Epic of the Mahābārat"* is a reference to the *Mahābhārata,* a collection of legendary and didactic Indian poetry.
3. Euripides (480–406 BCE), Athenian playwright.
4. An allusion to the paradise and hell segments, respectively, of Dante's *Divina commedia.*
5. During the Middle Ages, mystery (or morality) plays represented biblical subjects and were often performed from the backs of wagons.
6. John Bunyan (1628–1688), English cleric and author of *The Pilgrim's Progress from This World to That Which Is to Come* (1678).
7. *Faust, the First Part of the Tragedy* (1808) by Goethe is the story of an old scholar, Faust, who promised his soul to Mephistopheles in return for all knowledge and experience; *Festus* (1839) by Philip James Bailey (1816–1902), English poet; *Paracelsus* (1835) by Robert Browning (1812–1889), English poet.
8. Edward Bouverie Pusey (1800–1882), English theologian.
9. Joseph-Ernest Renan (1823–1892), French philosopher, philologist, and historian.
10. Possibly by Samuel Taylor Coleridge, to whom the quotation is attributed by Emerson (*JMN,* 15:334–335; *TN,* 3:277).
11. Charles Dickens first toured America in 1842 and would again in 1867–1868.
12. Robert Brown (1773–1858), English botanist and physicist.
13. State Street, the main commercial center of Boston.
14. Both Roger Bacon and Berthold Schwartz, a fourteenth-century German monk and alchemist, were reputed inventors of gunpowder.
15. Bacchus, the Roman name for Dionysus, Greek god of nature and divine ecstasy;

Sir Richard Arkwright (1732–1792), English inventor of the spinning frame for producing cotton warp thread; Eli Whitney (1765–1825), inventor of the cotton gin,
which separated the fiber from the seed.

16. William Harvey (1578–1657), English anatomist and physiologist known for his
work detailing how the blood circulates.

17. Wordsworth, "Laodamia" (1815), l. 72.

18. Emerson's source is *Specimens of the Table-Talk of the Late Samuel Taylor Coleridge*
(1835) (*JMN*, 5:52; *TN*, 3:120).

19. The Styx is the mythical river crossed by the dead into Hades.

20. Hippias (d. ca. 490 BCE), Athenian ruler; Gorgias (ca. 485–380 BCE), Greek rhetorician and Sophist philosopher.

21. On 6 May 1863, Edward McMasters Stanton (1814–1869), secretary of war, appointed Emerson a member of a visiting board of eighteen citizens charged to
conduct examinations of all the classes of West Point cadets in June 1863; Emerson may have been instrumental in having the board's final report explicitly recommend the study of ethics in any revised curriculum (*L*, 5:328n).

22. Charles Grey, 2nd Earl Grey, conceived of the Reform Bill of 1832 while he was
prime minister.

23. A reference to Nemean Ode 5 by Pindar.

24. Baron Dominique-Vivant Denon (1747–1825), French archeologist and illustra-
tor who published a book about Egypt; Sir John Gardner Wilkinson (1797–1875),
Egyptologist and author of numerous books on the subject.

25. Attributed to Francis Lieber (1800–1872), American political economist and professor at South Carolina College, in Emerson's note in the manuscript.

26. "An Inquisition Upon Fame and Honour" (1633), l. 512, by Fulke Greville, 1st Baron
Brooke (1554–1628), English poet and statesman.

27. Hugh Latimer (ca. 1485–1555), English Catholic priest who converted to Reformist
doctrine.

28. Quoted from *Counterparts* (1854) by Elizabeth Sara Sheppard (ca. 1830–1862), English novelist (*TN*, 2:207).

29. Lysias (ca. 450–ca. 380 BCE), Athenian orator.

30. Attributed to Emanuel Swedenborg by Emerson (*JMN*, 15:25).

31. Leonardo da Vinci (1452–1519), Italian painter, sculptor, architect, engineer, and
scientist.

32. Johann Joachim Winckelmann (1717–1768), German antiquities expert.

33. Benjamin Robert Haydon (1786–1846), English painter of historical and biblical
scenes; John Henry Fuseli (1741–1825), Swiss-born English painter and art critic.

34. Thomas Henry Huxley (1825–1895), English biologist.

35. Edward Everett (1794–1865), American Unitarian minister, Harvard professor, and
politician; Donald McKay (1810–1880), naval architect and shipbuilder, best known

for his fast clipper ships; George Steers (1820–1856), yacht builder; Samuel Hartt Pook (1827–1901), designer of the first New England clipper ship, in 1850.

36. Karl Friedrich Gauss (1777–1855), German mathematician and astronomer.

37. François Arago (1786–1853), French astronomer and physicist.

38. Herod I (73–4 BCE), king of Judea, massacred the infants of Bethlehem out of fear that a rival Jewish king was among them; see Matthew 2.

39. Gordius, king of Phrygia, tied a knot that could be untied only by the future ruler of Asia; Alexander the Great cut it with his sword.

40. The British emancipation of slaves in the West Indies was enacted by the British Slavery Abolition Act of 1833, which took effect on 1 August 1834; see Emerson's *Address . . . on the Anniversary of the Emancipation of the Negroes in the British West Indies* (1844) above.

41. Thomas Hobbes (1588–1679), English materialist philosopher.

42. Isaac H. Von Amburg (1811–1865), German animal trainer and the first man to put his head in the mouth of a lion; John Solomon Rarey (1827–1866), American horse trainer; Grizzly Adams (1812–1860), American frontiersman and hunter.

43. See, for example, Matthew 21:12–13 and Mark 11:15–17.

44. "Sinbad the Sailor" is a tale collected in *The Arabian Nights' Entertainments*.

Character

1   Morals respects what men call goodness, that which all men agree to honor as justice, truth-speaking, good-will, and good works. Morals respects the source or motive of this action. It is the science of substances, not of shows. It is the *what,* and not the *how.* It is that which all men profess to regard, and by their real respect for which recommend themselves to each other.

2   There is this eternal advantage to morals, that, in the question between truth and goodness, the moral cause of the world lies behind all else in the mind. It was for good, it is to good, that all works. Surely it is not to prove or show the truth of things,—that sounds a little cold and scholastic,—no, it is for benefit, that all subsists.[1] As we say in our modern politics, catching at last the language of morals, that the object of the state is the greatest good of the greatest number,—so, the reason we must give for the existence of the world is, that it is for the benefit of all being.[2]

3   Morals implies freedom and will. The will constitutes the man. He has his life in Nature, like a beast, but choice is born in him; here is he that chooses; here is the Declaration of Independence, the July Fourth of zoölogy and astronomy. He chooses,—as the rest of the creation does not. But will,

pure and perceiving, is not wilfulness. When a man, through stubbornness, insists to do this or that, something absurd or whimsical, only because he will, he is weak; he blows with his lips against the tempest, he dams the incoming ocean with his cane. It were an unspeakable calamity, if anyone should think he had the right to impose a private will on others. That is the part of a striker, an assassin. All violence, all that is dreary and repels, is not power, but the absence of power.

Morals is the direction of the will on universal ends. He is immoral who is acting to any private end. He is moral,—we say it with Marcus Aurelius and with Kant,—whose aim or motive may become a universal rule, binding on all intelligent beings; and with Vauvenargues, "the mercenary sacrifice of the public good to a private interest is the eternal stamp of vice."[3]   4

All the virtues are special directions of this motive: justice is the application of this good of the whole to the affairs of each one: courage is contempt of danger in the determination to see this good of the whole enacted; love is delight in the preference of that benefit redounding to another over the securing of our own share; humility is a sentiment of our insignificance, when the benefit of the universe is considered.   5

If from these external statements we seek to come a little nearer to the fact, our first experiences in moral as in intellectual nature force us to discriminate a universal mind, identical in all men. Certain biases, talents, executive skills, are special to each individual; but the high, contemplative, all-commanding vision, the sense of Right and Wrong, is alike in all. Its attributes are self-existence, eternity, intuition, and command. It is the mind of the mind. We belong to it, not it to us. It is in all men, and constitutes them men. In bad men it is dormant, as health is in men entranced or drunken; but, however inoperative, it exists underneath whatever vices and errors. The extreme simplicity of this intuition embarrasses every attempt at analysis. We can only mark, one by one, the perfections which it combines in every act. It admits of no appeal, looks to no superior essence. It is the reason of things.   6

The antagonist nature is the individual, formed into a finite body of exact dimensions, with appetites which take from everybody else what they appropriate to themselves, and would enlist the entire spiritual faculty of the individual, if it were possible, in catering for them. On the perpetual conflict between the dictate of this universal mind and the wishes and interests of the individual, the moral discipline of life is built. The one craves a private bene-   7 fit, which the moral nature requires him to renounce out of respect to the absolute good. Every hour puts the individual in a position where his wishes aim at something which the sentiment of duty forbids him to seek. He that speaks the truth executes no private function of an individual will, but the world utters a sound by his lips. He who doth a just action seeth therein nothing of his own, but an inconceivable nobleness attaches to it, because it is a dictate of the general mind. We have no idea of power so simple and so entire as this. It is the basis of thought, it is the basis of being. Compare all that we call ourselves, all our private and personal venture in the world, with this deep of moral nature in which we lie, and our private good becomes an impertinence, and we take part with hasty shame against ourselves.

> "High instincts, before which our mortal nature
> Did tremble like a guilty thing surprised. . . .
> Which, be they what they may,
> Are yet the fountain-light of all our day,
> Are yet the master-light of all our seeing,—
> Uphold us, cherish, and have power to make
> Our noisy years seem moments in the being
> Of the eternal silence,—truths that wake
> To perish never."[4]

8   The moral element invites man to great enlargements, to find his satisfaction, not in particulars or events, but in the purpose and tendency; not in bread, but in his right to his bread; not in much corn or wool, but in its communication. No one is accomplished whilst anyone is incomplete. Weal does not exist for one, with the woe of any other.

9   Not by adding, then, does the moral sentiment help us; no, but in quite another manner. It puts us in place. It centres, it concentrates us. It puts us at the heart of Nature, where we belong, in the cabinet of science and of causes,—there where all the wires terminate which hold the world in magnetic unity,—and so converts us into universal beings.

10   This wonderful sentiment, which endears itself as it is obeyed, seems to be the fountain of intellect; for no talent gives the impression of sanity, if wanting this; nay, it absorbs everything into itself. Truth, Power, Goodness, Beauty, are its varied names,—faces of one substance. Before it, what are persons, prophets, or seraphim, but its passing agents, momentary rays of its light?

The moral sentiment is alone omnipotent. There is no labor or sacrifice   11
to which it will not bring a man, and which it will not make easy. Thus, there
is no man who will bargain to sell his life, say at the end of a year, for a million or ten millions of gold dollars in hand, or for any temporary pleasures,
or for any rank, as of peer or prince; but many a man who does not hesitate
to lay down his life for the sake of a truth, or in the cause of his country, or to
save his son or his friend. And under the action of this sentiment of the Right,
his heart and mind expand above himself, and above Nature.

> Though Love repine, and Reason chafe,
> There came a voice without reply,—
> "'Tis man's perdition to be safe,
> When for the truth he ought to die."[5]

Such is the difference of the action of the heart within and of the senses without. One is enthusiasm, and the other more or less amounts of horse-power.

Devout men, in the endeavor to express their convictions, have used dif-   12
ferent images to suggest this latent force; as, the light, the seed, the Spirit, the
Holy Ghost, the Comforter, the Dæmon, the still, small voice, etc.,—all indicating its power and its latency.[6] It refuses to appear, it is too small to be seen,
too obscure to be spoken of; but, such as it is, it creates a faith which the contradiction of all mankind cannot shake, and which the consent of all mankind cannot confirm.

It is serenely above all mediation. In all ages, to all men, it saith, *I am;* and   13
he who hears it feels the impiety of wandering from this revelation to any
record or to any rival.[7] The poor Jews of the wilderness cried: "Let not the
Lord speak to us; let Moses speak to us."[8] But the simple and sincere soul
makes the contrary prayer: "Let no intruder come between thee and me; deal
Thou with me; let me know it is thy will, and I ask no more." The excellence
of Jesus, and of every true teacher, is, that he affirms the Divinity in him and
in us,—not thrusts himself between it and us. It would instantly indispose us
to any person claiming to speak for the Author of Nature, the setting forth
any fact or law which we did not find in our consciousness. We should say
with Heraclitus: "Come into this smoky cabin; God is here also; approve
yourself to him."[9]

We affirm that in all men is this majestic perception and command; that it   14
is the presence of the Eternal in each perishing man; that it distances and degrades all statements of whatever saints, heroes, poets, as obscure and con-

fused stammerings before its silent revelation. *They* report the truth. *It* is the truth. When I think of Reason, of Truth, of Virtue, I cannot conceive them as lodged in your soul and lodged in my soul, but that you and I and all souls are lodged in that; and I may easily speak of that adorable nature, there where only I behold it, in my dim experiences, in such terms as shall seem to the frivolous, who dare not fathom their consciousness, as profane. How is a man a man? How can he exist to weave relations of joy and virtue with other souls, but because he is inviolable, anchored at the centre of Truth and Being? In the ever-returning hour of reflection, he says: 'I stand here glad at heart of all the sympathies I can awaken and share, clothing myself with them as with a garment of shelter and beauty, and yet knowing that it is not in the power of all who surround me to take from me the smallest thread I call mine. If all things are taken away, I have still all things in my relation to the Eternal.'

15   We pretend not to define the way of its access to the private heart. It passes understanding. The soul of God is poured into the world through the thoughts of men. There was a time when Christianity existed in one child. But if the child had been killed by Herod, would the element have been lost? God sends his message, if not by one, then quite as well by another. When the Master of the Universe has ends to fulfil, he impresses his will on the structure of minds.

16   The Divine Mind imparts itself to the single person: his whole duty is to this rule and teaching. The aid which others give is like that of the mother to the child,—temporary, gestative, a short period of lactation, a nurse's or a governess's care; but on his arrival at a certain maturity, it ceases, and would be hurtful and ridiculous if prolonged. Slowly the body comes to the use of its organs; slowly the soul unfolds itself in the new man. It is partial at first, and honors only some one or some few truths. In its companions it sees other truths honored, and successively finds their foundation also in itself. Then it cuts the cord, and no longer believes "because of thy saying," but because it has recognized them in itself.[10]

17   The Divine Mind imparts itself to the single person: but it is also true that men act powerfully on us. There are men who astonish and delight, men who instruct and guide. Some men's words I remember so well that I must often use them to express my thought. Yes, because I perceive that we have heard the same truth, but they have heard it better. That is only to say, there is degree and gradation throughout Nature; and the Deity does not break his

firm laws in respect to imparting truth, more than in imparting material heat
and light. Men appear from time to time who receive with more purity and
fulness these high communications. But it is only as fast as this hearing from
another is authorized by its consent with his own, that it is pure and safe to
each; and all receiving from abroad must be controlled by this immense res-
ervation.

It happens now and then, in the ages, that a soul is born which has no   18
weakness of self,—which offers no impediment to the Divine Spirit,—which
comes down into nature as if only for the benefit of souls, and all its thoughts
are perceptions of things as they are, without any infirmity of earth. Such
souls are as the apparition of gods among men, and simply by their presence
pass judgment on them. Men are forced by their own self-respect to give
them a certain attention. Evil men shrink and pay involuntary homage by
hiding or apologizing for their action.

When a man is born with a profound moral sentiment, preferring truth,   19
justice, and the serving of all men to any honors or any gain, men readily feel
the superiority. They who deal with him are elevated with joy and hope; he
lights up the house or the landscape in which he stands. His actions are poetic
and miraculous in their eyes. In his presence, or within his influence, everyone believes in the immortality of the soul. They feel that the invisible world
sympathizes with him. The Arabians delight in expressing the sympathy of
the unseen world with holy men.

> "When Omar prayed and loved,
>   Where Syrian waters roll,
>   Aloft the ninth heaven glowed and moved
>   To the tread of the jubilant soul."[11]

A chief event of life is the day in which we have encountered a mind that   20
startled us by its large scope. I am in the habit of thinking,—not, I hope, out
of a partial experience, but confirmed by what I notice in many lives,—that
to every serious mind Providence sends from time to time five or six or seven
teachers who are of the first importance to him in the lessons they have to
impart. The highest of these not so much give particular knowledge as they
elevate by sentiment and by their habitual grandeur of view.

Great men serve us as insurrections do in bad governments. The world   21
would run into endless routine, and forms incrust forms, till the life was

gone. But the perpetual supply of new genius shocks us with thrills of life, and recalls us to principles. Lucifer's wager in the old drama was, "There is no steadfast man on earth."[12] He is very rare. "A man is already of consequence in the world when it is known that we can implicitly rely on him."[13] See how one noble person dwarfs a whole nation of underlings. This steadfastness we indicate when we praise character.

22   Character denotes habitual self-possession, habitual regard to interior and constitutional motives, a balance not to be overset or easily disturbed by outward events and opinion, and by implication points to the source of right motive. We sometimes employ the word to express the strong and consistent will of men of mixed motive, but, when used with emphasis, it points to what no events can change, that is, a will built on the reason of things. Such souls do not come in troops: oftenest appear solitary, like a general without his command, because those who can understand and uphold such appear rarely, not many, perhaps not one, in a generation. And the memory and tradition of such leader is preserved in some strange way by those who only half understand him, until a true disciple comes, who apprehends and interprets every word.

23   The sentiment never stops in pure vision, but will be enacted. It affirms not only its truth, but its supremacy. It is not only insight, as science, as fancy, as imagination are;—or an entertainment, as friendship and poetry are, but it is a sovereign rule; and the acts which it suggests—as when it impels a man to go forth and impart it to other men, or sets him on some asceticism or some practice of self-examination to hold him to obedience, or some zeal to unite men to abate some nuisance, or establish together some reform or charity which it commands—are the homage we render to this sentiment, as compared with the lower regard we pay to other thoughts: and the private or social practices we establish in its honor we call religion.

24   The sentiment, of course, is the judge and measure of every expression of it,—measures Judaism, Stoicism, Christianity, Buddhism, or whatever philanthropy, or politics, or saint, or seer pretends to speak in its name. The religions we call false were once true. They also were affirmations of the conscience correcting the evil customs of their times. The populace drag down the gods to their own level, and give them their egotism; whilst in Nature is none at all, God keeping out of sight, and known only as pure law, though resistless. Châteaubriand said, with some irreverence of phrase, If God made

man in his image, man has paid him well back. *"Si Dieu a fait l'homme à son image, l'homme l'a bien rendu."*[14] Every nation is degraded by the goblins it worships instead of this Deity. The Dionysia and Saturnalia of Greece and Rome, the human sacrifice of the Druids, the Sradda of Hindoos, the Purgatory, the Indulgences, and the Inquisition of Popery, the vindictive mythology of Calvinism, are examples of this perversion.[15]

Every particular instruction is speedily embodied in a ritual, is accommodated to humble and gross minds, and corrupted. The moral sentiment is the perpetual critic on these forms, thundering its protest, sometimes in earnest and lofty rebuke, but sometimes also it is the source, in natures less pure, of sneers and flippant jokes of common people, who feel that the forms and dogmas are not true for them, though they do not see where the error lies. 25

The religion of one age is the literary entertainment of the next. We use in our idlest poetry and discourse the words Jove, Neptune, Mercury, as mere colors, and can hardly believe that they had to the lively Greek the anxious meaning, which, in our towns, is given and received in churches, when our religious names are used.[16] And we read with surprise the horror of Athens, when, one morning, the statues of Mercury, in the temples, were found broken, and the like consternation was in the agora, as if, in Boston, all the orthodox churches should be burned in one night.[17] 26

The greatest dominion will be to the deepest thought. The establishment of Christianity in the world does not rest on any miracle, but the miracle of being the broadest and most humane doctrine. Christianity was once a schism and protest against the impieties of the time, which had originally been protests against earlier impieties, but had lost their truth. Varnhagen von Ense, writing, in Prussia, in 1848, says: "The Gospels belong to the most aggressive writings. No leaf thereof could attain the liberty of being printed (in Berlin today). What Mirabeaus, Rousseaus, Diderots, Fichtes, Heines, and many another heretic, one can detect therein!"[18] 27

But before it was yet a national religion, it was alloyed, and, in the hands of hot Africans, of luxurious Byzantines, of fierce Gauls, its creeds were tainted with their barbarism. In Holland, in England, in Scotland, it felt the national narrowness. How unlike our habitual turn of thought was that of the last century in this country! Our ancestors spoke continually of angels and archangels with the same good faith as they would have spoken of their own parents or their late minister.[19] Now the words pale, are rhetoric, and all 28 credence is gone. Our horizon is not far, say one generation, or thirty years: we all see so much. The older see two generations, or sixty years. But what has been running on through three horizons, or ninety years, looks to all the world like a law of nature, and 'tis an impiety to doubt.

29   Thus, 'tis incredible to us, if we look into the religious books of our grandfathers, how they held themselves in such a pinfold.[20] But why not? As far as they could see, through two or three horizons, nothing but ministers, ministers, ministers. Calvinism was one and the same thing in Geneva, in Scotland, in Old and New England. If there was a wedding, they had a sermon; if a funeral, then a sermon; if a war, or small-pox, or a comet, or canker-worms,—or a deacon died,—still a sermon. Nature was a pulpit.[21] The church-warden or tithing-man was a petty persecutor; the presbytery, a tyrant; and in many a house, in country places, the poor children found seven sabbaths in a week. Fifty or a hundred years ago, prayers were said, morning and evening, in all families; grace was said at table; an exact observance of the Sunday was kept in the houses of laymen as of clergymen. And one sees with some pain the disuse of rites so charged with humanity and aspiration. But it by no means follows, because those offices are much disused, that the men and women are irreligious; certainly not that they have less integrity or sentiment, but only, let us hope, that they see that they can omit the form without loss of real ground; perhaps that they find some violence, some cramping of their freedom of thought, in the constant recurrence of the form.

30   So of the changed position and manners of the clergy. They have dropped, with the sacerdotal garb and manners of the last century, many doctrines and practices once esteemed indispensable to their order. But the distinctions of the true clergyman are not less decisive. Men ask now, Is he serious? Is he a sincere man, who lives as he teaches? Is he a benefactor? So far the religion is now where it should be. Persons are discriminated as honest, as veracious, as illuminated, as helpful, as having public and universal regards, or otherwise,—are discriminated according to their aims, and not by these ritualities.

31   The changes are inevitable; the new age cannot see with the eyes of the last. But the change is in what is superficial; the principles are immortal, and the rally on the principle must arrive as people become intellectual. I consider theology to be the rhetoric of morals. The mind of this age has fallen away from theology to morals. I conceive it an advance. I suspect, that, when the

theology was most florid and dogmatic, it was the barbarism of the people, and that, in that very time, the best men also fell away from theology, and rested in morals. I think that all the dogmas rest on morals, and that it is only a question of youth or maturity, of more or less fancy in the recipient; that the stern determination to do justly, to speak the truth, to be chaste and humble, was substantially the same, whether under a self-respect, or under a vow made on the knees at the shrine of Madonna.

When once Selden had said that the priests seemed to him to be baptizing their own fingers, the rite of baptism was getting late in the world.[22] Or when once it is perceived that the English missionaries in India put obstacles in the way of schools, (as is alleged,)—do not wish to enlighten, but to Christianize the Hindoos,—it is seen at once how wide of Christ is English Christianity.

Mankind at large always resemble frivolous children: they are impatient of thought, and wish to be amused. Truth is too simple for us; we do not like those who unmask our illusions. Fontenelle said: "If the Deity should lay bare to the eyes of men the secret system of Nature, the causes by which all the astronomic results are effected, and they, finding no magic, no mystic numbers, no fatalities, but the greatest simplicity,—I am persuaded they would not be able to suppress a feeling of mortification, and would exclaim, with disappointment, 'Is that all?'"[23] And so we paint over the bareness of ethics with the quaint grotesques of theology.

We boast the triumph of Christianity over Paganism, meaning the victory of the spirit over the senses, but Paganism hides itself in the uniform of the Church. Paganism has only taken the oath of allegiance, taken the cross, but is Paganism still, outvotes the true men by millions of majority, carries the bag, spends the treasure, writes the tracts, elects the minister, and persecutes the true believer.

There is a certain secular progress of opinion, which, in civil countries, reaches everybody. One service which this age has rendered is, to make the life and wisdom of every past man accessible and available to all. Socrates and Marcus Aurelius are allowed to be saints, a Mahomet is no longer accursed.[24] Voltaire is no longer a scarecrow. Spinoza has come to be revered.[25] "The time will come," says Varnhagen von Ense, "when we shall treat the jokes and sallies against the myths and church-rituals of Christianity—say the sarcasms of Voltaire, Frederic the Great, and D'Alembert—good-naturedly and without offence: since, at bottom, those men mean honestly, their polemics proceed out of a religious striving, and what Christ meant and willed is in essence more with them than with their opponents, who only wear and misrepresent the *name* of Christ. Voltaire was an apostle of Christian ideas; only the names were hostile to him, and he never knew it otherwise. He was like the son of the vine-dresser in the Gospel, who said No, and went; the other said, Yea, and went not. These men preached the true God,—Him whom men serve by justice and uprightness; but they called themselves atheists."[26]

36   When the highest conceptions, the lessons of religion, are imported, the nation is not culminating, has not genius, but is servile. A true nation loves its vernacular tongue. A completed nation will not import its religion. Duty grows everywhere, like children, like grass; and we need not go to Europe or to Asia to learn it. I am not sure that the English religion is not all quoted. Even the Jeremy Taylors, Fullers, George Herberts, steeped, all of them, in the Church traditions, are only using their fine fancy to emblazon their memory.[27] 'Tis Judæa, not England, which is the ground. So with the mordant Calvinism of Scotland and America. But this quoting distances and disables them: since with every repeater something of creative force is lost, as we feel when we go back to each original moralist. Pythagoras, Socrates, the Stoics, the Hindoo, Behmen, George Fox,—these speak originally; and how many sentences and books we owe to unknown authors,—to writers who were not careful to set down name or date or titles or cities or postmarks in these illuminations!

37   We, in our turn, want power to drive the ponderous State. The constitution and law in America must be written on ethical principles, so that the entire power of the spiritual world can be enlisted to hold the loyalty of the citizen, and to repel every enemy as by force of Nature. The laws of old empires stood on the religious convictions. Now that their religions are outgrown, the empires lack strength. Romanism in Europe does not represent the real opinion of enlightened men. The Lutheran Church does not represent in Germany the opinions of the universities. In England, the gentlemen, the journals, and now, at last, churchmen and bishops, have fallen away from the Anglican Church. And in America, where are no legal ties to churches, the looseness appears dangerous.

38   Our religion has got on as far as Unitarianism. But all the forms grow pale. The walls of the temple are wasted and thin, and, at last, only a film of

whitewash, because the mind of our culture has already left our liturgies behind.[28] "Every age," says Varnhagen, "has another sieve for the religious tradition, and will sift it out again. Something is continually lost by this treatment, which posterity cannot recover."[29]

But it is a capital truth, that Nature, moral as well as material, is always
equal to herself. Ideas always generate enthusiasm. The creed, the legend,
forms of worship, swiftly decay. Morals is the incorruptible essence, very
heedless in its richness of any past teacher or witness, heedless of their lives
and fortunes. It does not ask whether you are wrong or right in your anecdotes of them; but it is all in all how you stand to your own tribunal.

The lines of the religious sects are very shifting; their platforms unstable;
the whole science of theology of great uncertainty, and resting very much on
the opinions of who may chance to be the leading doctors of Oxford or Edinburgh, of Princeton or Cambridge, today. No man can tell what religious
revolutions await us in the next years; and the education in the divinity colleges may well hesitate and vary. But the science of ethics has no mutation;
and whoever feels any love or skill for ethical studies may safely lay out all his
strength and genius in working in that mine. The pulpit may shake, but this
platform will not. All the victories of religion belong to the moral sentiment.
Some poor soul beheld the Law blazing through such impediments as he had,
and yielded himself to humility and joy. What was gained by being told that
it was justification by faith?

The Church, in its ardor for beloved persons, clings to the miraculous, in
the vulgar sense, which has even an immoral tendency, as one sees in Greek,
Indian, and Catholic legends, which are used to gloze every crime.[30] The soul,
penetrated with the beatitude which pours into it on all sides, asks no inter-
positions, no new laws,—the old are good enough for it,—finds in every cart-
path of labor ways to heaven, and the humblest lot exalted. Men will learn to
put back the emphasis peremptorily on pure morals, always the same, not
subject to doubtful interpretation, with no sale of indulgences, no massacre
of heretics, no female slaves, no disfranchisement of woman, no stigma on
race; to make morals the absolute test, and so uncover and drive out the false
religions. There is no vice that has not skulked behind them. It is only yesterday that our American churches, so long silent on Slavery, and notoriously
hostile to the Abolitionist, wheeled into line for Emancipation.

I am far from accepting the opinion that the revelations of the moral sentiment are insufficient, as if it furnished a rule only, and not the spirit by which the rule is animated. For I include in these, of course, the history of Jesus, as well as those of every divine soul which in any place or time delivered any grand lesson to humanity; and I find in the eminent experiences in all times a substantial agreement. The sentiment itself teaches unity of source, and disowns every superiority other than of deeper truth. Jesus has immense claims on the gratitude of mankind, and knew how to guard the integrity of his brother's soul from himself also; but, in his disciples, admiration of him runs away with their reverence for the human soul, and they hamper us with limitations of person and text. Every exaggeration of these is a violation of the soul's right, and inclines the manly reader to lay down the New Testament, to take up the Pagan philosophers. It is not that the Upanishads or the Maxims of Antoninus are better, but that they do not invade his freedom;[31] because they are only suggestions, whilst the other adds the inadmissible claim of positive authority,—of an external command, where command cannot be. This is the secret of the mischievous result, that, in every period of intellectual expansion, the Church ceases to draw into its clergy those who best belong there, the largest and freest minds, and that in its most liberal forms, when such minds enter it, they are coldly received, and find themselves out of place. This charm in the Pagan moralists, of suggestion, the charm of poetry, of mere truth, (easily eliminated from their historical accidents, which nobody wishes to force on us,) the New Testament loses by its connection with a church. Mankind cannot long suffer this loss, and the office of this age is to put all these writings on the eternal footing of equality of origin in the instincts of the human mind. It is certain that each inspired master will gain instantly by the separation from the idolatry of ages.

43   To their great honor, the simple and free minds among our clergy have not resisted the voice of Nature and the advanced perceptions of the mind; and every church divides itself into a liberal and expectant class, on one side, and an unwilling and conservative class, on the other. As it stands with us now, a few clergymen, with a more theological cast of mind, retain the traditions, but they carry them quietly. In general discourse, they are never obtruded. If the clergyman should travel in France, in England, in Italy, he might leave them locked up in the same closet with his "occasional sermons" at home, and, if he did not return, would never think to send for them. The orthodox clergymen hold a little firmer to theirs, as Calvinism has a more te-

nacious vitality; but that is doomed also, and will only die last; for Calvinism rushes to be Unitarianism, as Unitarianism rushes to be pure Theism.[32]

But the inspirations are never withdrawn. In the worst times, men of or- ganic virtue are born,—men and women of native integrity, and indifferently in high and low conditions. There will always be a class of imaginative youths, whom poetry, whom the love of beauty, lead to the adoration of the moral sentiment, and these will provide it with new historic forms and songs. Religion is as inexpugnable as the use of lamps, or of wells, or of chimneys. We must have days and temples and teachers. The Sunday is the core of our civilization, dedicated to thought and reverence. It invites to the noblest soli- tude and the noblest society, to whatever means and aids of spiritual refresh- ment. Men may well come together to kindle each other to virtuous living. Confucius said, "If in the morning I hear of the right way, and in the evening die, I can be happy."[33]

The churches already indicate the new spirit, in adding, to the peren- nial office of teaching, beneficent activities,—as in creating hospitals, ragged schools, offices of employment for the poor, appointing almoners to the helpless, guardians of foundlings and orphans.[34] The power that in other times inspired crusades, or the colonization of New England, or the modern revivals, flies to the help of the deaf-mute and the blind, to the education of the sailor and the vagabond boy, to the reform of convicts and harlots,—as the war has created the Hilton Head and Charleston missions, the Sanitary Commission, the nurses and teachers at Washington.[35]

In the present tendency of our society, in the new importance of the indi- vidual, when thrones are crumbling, and presidents and governors are forced every moment to remember their constituencies,—when counties and towns are resisting centralization, and the individual voter his party,—society is threatened with actual granulation, religious as well as political. How many people are there in Boston? Some two hundred thousand. Well, then so many sects. Of course, each poor soul loses all his old stays. No bishop watches him; no confessor reports that he has neglected the confessional; no class- leader admonishes him of absences. No fagot, no penance, no fine, no re- buke. Is not this wrong? Is not this dangerous? 'Tis not wrong, but the law of growth. It is not dangerous, any more than the mother's withdrawing her hands from the tottering babe, at his first walk across the nursery-floor: the

44

45

46

child fears and cries, but achieves the feat, instantly tries it again, and never wishes to be assisted more. And this infant soul must learn to walk alone. At first he is forlorn, homeless; but this rude stripping him of all support drives him inward, and he finds himself unhurt; he finds himself face to face with the majestic Presence, reads the original of the Ten Commandments, the original of Gospels and Epistles; nay, his narrow chapel expands to the blue cathedral of the sky, where he

> "Looks in and sees each blissful deity,
> Where he before the thunderous throne doth lie."[36]

47   To nations or to individuals the progress of opinion is not a loss of moral restraint, but simply a change from coarser to finer checks. No evil can come from reform which a deeper thought will not correct. If there is any tendency in national expansion to form character, religion will not be a loser. There is a fear that pure truth, pure morals, will not make a religion for the affections. Whenever the sublimities of character shall be incarnated in a man, we may rely that awe and love and insatiable curiosity will follow his steps. Character is the habit of action from the permanent vision of truth. It carries a superiority to all the accidents of life. It compels right relation to every other man,—domesticates itself with strangers and enemies. "But I, father," says the wise Prahlada, in the Vishnu Purana, "know neither friends nor foes, for I behold Kesava in all beings as in my own soul."[37] It confers perpetual insight. It sees that a man's friends and his foes are of his own household, of his own person; that he himself strikes the stroke which he imputes to fortune. Man is always throwing his praise or blame on events, and fails to see that he only is real, and the world is his mirror and echo. What would it avail me, if I could destroy my enemies? There would be as many tomorrow. That which I hate and fear is really in myself, and no knife is long enough to reach to its heart. Confucius said one day to Ke Kang: "Sir, in carrying on your government, why should you use killing at all? Let your evinced desires be for what is good, and the people will be good. The grass must bend, when the wind blows across it." Ke Kang, distressed about the number of thieves in the state, inquired of Confucius how to do away with them. Confucius said, "If you, sir, were not covetous, although you should reward them to do it, they would not steal."[38]

48   Its methods are subtle, it works without means. It indulges no enmity

against any, knowing, with Prahlada, that "the suppression of malignant feeling is itself a reward."[39] The more reason, the less government. In a sensible family, nobody ever hears the words "shall" and "sha'n't"; nobody commands, and nobody obeys, but all conspire and joyfully coöperate. Take off the roofs of hundreds of happy houses, and you shall see this order without ruler, and the like in every intelligent and moral society. Command is exceptional, and marks some break in the link of reason; as the electricity goes round the world without a spark or a sound, until there is a break in the wire or the water chain. Swedenborg said, that, "in the spiritual world, when one wishes to rule, or despises others, he is thrust out of doors."[40] Goethe, in discussing the characters in "Wilhelm Meister," maintained his belief, "that pure loveliness and right good-will are the highest manly prerogatives, before which all energetic heroism, with its lustre and renown, must recede."[41] In perfect accord with this, Henry James affirms, that "to give the feminine element in life its hard-earned but eternal supremacy over the masculine has been the secret inspiration of all past history."[42]

There is no end to the sufficiency of character. It can afford to wait; it can do without what is called success; it cannot but succeed. To a well-principled man existence is victory. He defends himself against failure in his main design by making every inch of the road to it pleasant. There is no trifle, and no obscurity to him: he feels the immensity of the chain whose last link he holds in his hand, and is led by it. Having nothing, this spirit hath all. It asks, with Marcus Aurelius, "What matter by whom the good is done?"[43] It extols humility,—by every self-abasement lifted higher in the scale of being. It makes no stipulations for earthly felicity,—does not ask, in the absoluteness of its trust, even for the assurance of continued life. 49

Notes

1. The scholastic method, developed by medieval philosophy, is characterized by exhaustive thoroughness; Emerson's characterization of the method as "cold" is the equivalent of saying it is "pedantic."
2. The signature principle of utilitarianism, "the greatest good of the greatest number" also appears in "American Civilization," para 26, above.
3. Luc de Clapiers, marquis de Vauvenargues (1715–1747), French essayist; Emerson

is translating from Charles Augustine Sainte-Beuve, *Causeries du Lundi,* 15 vols. (Paris, 1851–1862), 3:104.

4. Wordsworth, "Ode: Intimations of Immortality Recollected from Early Childhood," ll. 146–156.

5. This quotation derives from *Calebs [sic] Integrity in Following the Lord Fully, . . . A Sermon* (1642) by Richard Vines (ca. 1600–1656), English clergyman; Emerson also used the quotation as his poem "Sacrifice," *CW,* 9:540–541.

6. For "the still, small voice," see 1 Kings 19:12.

7. With "it saith, *I am,*" cf. Exodus 2:14.

8. A paraphrase of Exodus 20:19.

9. Emerson's source is Cudworth, *The True Intellectual System of the Universe* (1820), 2:243.

10. For "because of thy saying," see John 4:42.

11. This quatrain appears (with "Ali" for "Omar") as the last stanza of a poem with the nonauthorial title "The Waterfall" in *W,* 9:370; see also *PN,* p. 892.

12. The allusion is to the book of Job.

13. In his journal Emerson attributes this statement to Edward Bulwer-Lytton, 1st Baron Lytton (1803–1873), English novelist and politician (*JMN,* 14:65); *The Friends' Intelligencer* (Philadelphia), 17 (1861): 703, identifies it as part of Bulwer-Lytton's 1856 inaugural address as rector of Glasgow University.

14. The quotation is actually by Voltaire, *Candide: Le Sottisier,* XXXII, *Faits detaches,* not François-René, Vicomte de Châteaubriand (1768–1848), French writer, politician, and historian.

15. The Dionysia was an Athenian religious festival honoring Dionysius, god of wine and ecstatic experience; Saturnalia was a Roman celebration honoring Saturn, the god of agriculture; Sradda is a Hindu rite honoring a deceased ancestor; in Roman Catholicism the concept of purgatory as the site of temporal punishment for a period of time that could be lessened by the procurement of "indulgences" served as one of the impetuses to the Protestant Reformation; the Inquisition denotes Catholic repressions of heresy, especially during the late Medieval and Renaissance periods.

16. Mercury is the Roman god of commerce and eloquence as well as the messenger of the gods and the guide of those consigned to the underworld.

17. The "horror of Athens" is recounted in Book VI of the fifth- century BCE historian and Athenian general Thucydides, *History of the Peloponnesian War,* 2 vols. (New York, 1836), 1:153–154.

18. Emerson's source is Karl August Ludwig Philipp Varnhagen von Ense, *Tagebücher,* 14 vols. (Leipzig, 1861–1870), 1:170. The "heretic" writers named here include Comte de Mirabeau (1749–1791), statesman and orator of the French Revolution; Jean Jacques Rousseau (1712–1778), French philosopher and a founder of Romanti-

cism; Denis Diderot (1713–1784), French encyclopedist; and Heinrich Heine (1797–1856), German poet.

19. The journal version of this and the previous sentence specify Mary Moody Emerson and her contemporaries as the "ancestors" (*JMN*, 15:442).

20. A "pinfold" is an early name for a "pound," the place where animals are confined.

21. Emerson attributed this metaphor to Mary Moody Emerson (*JMN*, 15:121).

22. Emerson's source is *Table-Talk of John Selden*, ed. S. W. Singer (London, 1847), p. 5.

23. Emerson's source is Thomas Brown, *Lectures on the Philosophy of the Human Mind*, 3 vols. (Philadelphia, 1824), 1:92.

24. Marcus Aurelius Antoninus (121–180), Roman emperor, Stoic philosopher, and author of the *Meditations*.

25. Baruch Spinoza (1632–1677), Dutch-born rationalist philosopher.

26. Emerson merged several quotations from different sources into this seeming one quotation: "The time will . . . *name* of Christ" and "Voltaire was an . . . it otherwise" are drawn from Varnhagen von Ense, *Tagebücher*, 1:80 (*JMN*, 15:286); for "He was like . . . went not," see Matthew 21:28–30; "These men preached . . . athiests" is drawn from *Essais de Morale et de Critique* (Paris, 1860), p. 62, by Joseph-Ernest Renan. Frederick II (1712–1786), known also as Frederick the Great, king of Prussia (1740–1786) and military genius.

27. An allusion to Jeremy Taylor (1613–1667), English clergyman noted for his prose style.

28. Trained as a Unitarian minister, Emerson wrote the following in June 1832, a few months before he resigned from his pulpit: "I have sometimes thought that in order to be a good minister it was necessary to leave the ministry. The profession is antiquated. In an altered age, we worship in the dead forms of our forefathers" (*JMN*, 4:27).

29. Varnhagen von Ense, *Tagebücher*, 1:55.

30. "Gloze" means to "gloss over" or "explain away."

31. The Upanishads are Hindu scriptures; "the Maxims of Antoninus" refers to the *Meditations* by Marcus Aurelius Antoninus.

32. In his journal Emerson identifies Unitarians Frederic Henry Hedge (1805–1890) and James Freeman Clarke (1810–1888) among the clergy who quietly retain traditions in this paragraph, and Henry Ward Beecher (1813–1887), Jacob Merrill Manning (1824–1882), and Horace Bushnell (1802–1876) among those more tenacious of orthodoxy (*JMN*, 15:228).

33. Emerson's source is *The Works of Confucius; Containing the Original Text, with a Translation . . . by Joshua Marshman* (Serampore, 1809), p. 226.

34. Originating in England in the 1840s, "ragged schools" were charity educational institutions; an "almoner" was a church official who distributed alms to the poor.

35. The missions that Emerson refers to are better known as the Port Royal Experi-

ment, a program begun during the early days of the Civil War that relocated former slaves onto abandoned plantations along the coastal islands of South Carolina; the United States Sanitary Commission was formed in 1861 to raise money
and supervise medical and relief work during the war.

36. Milton, ll. 35–36, in a work variously known as "Anno Aetatis 19," "Address to His
    Native Language," and "Vacation Exercise."

37. Emerson's source is *The Vishnu Purana* (1840), p. 139.

38. Emerson's source for the passage beginning "Confucius said one day" is James
    Legge, *The Chinese Classics,* 5 vols. (Hong Kong, 1861–1870), 1:122–123.

39. *The Vishnu Purana,* p. 132.

40. In his journal, Emerson attributes this statement to Henry James Sr. (1811–1882),
    American theologian and adherent of Swedenborgianism (*JMN,* 15:91).

41. Varnhagen von Ense, *Tagebücher,* 1:84.

42. Henry James Sr., *Substance and Shadow* (Boston, 1863), p. 243.

43. Most likely a paraphrase of Marcus Aurelius Antoninus, *Meditations,* X, 13, this
    saying was a favorite of Mary Moody Emerson; see "Greatness," *CW,* 8:173, 290.

Works and Days

This shining moment is an edifice
Which the Omnipotent cannot rebuild.[1]

Our nineteenth century is the age of tools. They grow out of our structure. "Man is the metre of all things," said Aristotle; "the hand is the instrument of instruments, and the mind is the form of forms."[2] The human body is the magazine of inventions, the patent-office, where are the models from which every hint was taken. All the tools and engines on earth are only extensions of its limbs and senses. One definition of man is "an intelligence served by organs."[3] Machines can only second, not supply, his unaided senses. The body is a metre. The eye appreciates finer differences than art can expose. The apprentice clings to his foot-rule, a practised mechanic will measure by his thumb and arm with equal precision; and a good surveyor will pace sixteen rods more accurately than another man can measure them by tape.[4] The sympathy of eye and hand by which an Indian or a practised slinger hits the mark with a stone, or a wood-chopper or a carpenter swings his axe to a hair-line on his log, are examples; and there is no sense or organ which is not capable of exquisite performance.

Men love to wonder, and that is the seed of our science; and such is the mechanical determination of our age, and so recent are our best contrivances, that use has not dulled our joy and pride in them; and we pity our fathers for dying before steam and galvanism, sulphuric ether and ocean tele-graphs, photograph and spectograph arrived, as cheated out of half their human estate.[5] These arts open great gates of a future, promising to make the world plastic and to lift human life out of its beggary to a godlike ease and power.

4   Our century, to be sure, had inherited a tolerable apparatus. We had the compass, the printing-press, watches, the spiral spring, the barometer, the telescope. Yet so many inventions have been added, that life seems almost made over new; and as Leibnitz said of Newton, "that if he reckoned all that had been done by mathematicians from the beginning of the world down to Newton, and what had been done by him, his would be the better half,"[6] so one might say that the inventions of the last fifty years counterpoise those of the fifty centuries before them. For the vast production and manifold application of iron is new; and our common and indispensable utensils of house and farm are new; the sewing-machine, the power-loom, the McCor-mick reaper, the mowing-machines, gas-light, lucifer matches, and the im-mense productions of the laboratory, are new in this century, and one franc's worth of coal does the work of a laborer for twenty days.[7]

5   Why need I speak of steam, the enemy of space and time, with its enor-mous strength and delicate applicability, which is made in hospitals to bring a bowl of gruel to a sick man's bed, and can twist beams of iron like candy-braids, and vies with the forces which upheaved and doubled over the geo-logic strata? Steam is an apt scholar and a strong-shouldered fellow, but it has not yet done all its work. It already walks about the field like a man, and will do anything required of it. It irrigates crops, and drags away a mountain. It must sew our shirts, it must drive our gigs; taught by Mr. Babbage, it must calculate interest and logarithms.[8] Lord Chancellor Thurlow thought it might be made to draw bills and answers in chancery.[9] If that were satire, it is yet coming to render many higher services of a mechanico-intellectual kind, and will leave the satire short of the fact.

6   How excellent are the mechanical aids we have applied to the human body, as in dentistry, in vaccination, in the rhinoplastic treatment; in the beau-tiful aid of ether, like a finer sleep; and in the boldest promiser of all,—the transfusion of the blood,—which, in Paris, it was claimed, enables a man to change his blood as often as his linen![10]

7   What of this dapper caoutchouc and gutta-percha, which make water-

pipes and stomach-pumps, belting for mill-wheels, and diving bells, and rain-proof coats for all climates, which teach us to defy the wet, and put every man on a footing with the beaver and the crocodile?[11] What of the grand tools with which we engineer, like kobolds and enchanters,—tunnelling Alps, canalling the American Isthmus, piercing the Arabian desert?[12] In Massachusetts, we fight the sea successfully with beach-grass and broom,—and the blowing sand-barrens with pine plantations. The soil of Holland, once the most populous in Europe, is below the level of the sea. Egypt, where no rain fell for three thousand years, now, it is said, thanks Mehemet Ali's irrigations and planted forests for late-returning showers.[13] The old Hebrew king said, "He makes the wrath of man to praise him."[14] And there is no argument of theism better than the grandeur of ends brought about by paltry means. The chain of western railroads from Chicago to the Pacific has planted cities and civilization in less time than it costs to bring an orchard into bearing.[15]

What shall we say of the ocean telegraph, that extension of the eye and ear, whose sudden performance astonished mankind as if the intellect were taking the brute earth itself into training, and shooting the first thrills of life and thought through the unwilling brain?[16]   8

There does not seem any limit to these new informations of the same Spirit that made the elements at first, and now, through man, works them. Art and power will go on as they have done,—will make day out of night, time out of space, and space out of time.   9

Invention breeds invention. No sooner is the electric telegraph devised, than gutta-percha, the very material it requires, is found. The aeronaut is provided with gun-cotton, the very fuel he wants for his balloon.[17] When commerce is vastly enlarged, California and Australia expose the gold it needs. When Europe is over-populated, America and Australia crave to be peopled; and so, throughout, every chance is timed, as if Nature, who made the lock, knew where to find the key.   10

Another result of our arts is the new intercourse which is surprising us with new solutions of the embarrassing political problems. The intercourse is not new, but the scale is new. Our selfishness would have held slaves, or would have excluded from a quarter of the planet all that are not born on the soil of that quarter. Our politics are disgusting; but what can they help or hinder when from time to time the primal instincts are impressed on masses of mankind, when the nations are in exodus and flux? Nature loves to cross her   11 stocks,—and German, Chinese, Turk, Russ, and Kanaka were putting out to sea, and intermarrying race with race;[18] and commerce took the hint, and ships were built capacious enough to carry the people of a county.

12   This thousand-handed art has introduced a new element into the state. The science of power is forced to remember the power of science. Civilization mounts and climbs. Malthus, when he stated that the mouths went on multiplying geometrically, and the food only arithmetically, forgot to say that the human mind was also a factor in political economy, and that the augmenting wants of society would be met by an augmenting power of invention.[19]

13   Yes, we have a pretty artillery of tools now in our social arrangements: we ride four times as fast as our fathers did; travel, grind, weave, forge, plant, till, and excavate better. We have new shoes, gloves, glasses, and gimlets; we have the calculus; we have the newspaper, which does its best to make every square acre of land and sea give an account of itself at your breakfast-table; we have money, and paper money; we have language,—the finest tool of all, and nearest to the mind. Much will have more. Man flatters himself that his command over nature must increase. Things begin to obey him. We are to have the balloon yet, and the next war will be fought in the air. We may yet find a rose-water that will wash the negro white. He sees the skull of the English race changing from its Saxon type under the exigences of American life.

14   Tantalus, who in old times was seen vainly trying to quench his thirst with a flowing stream, which ebbed whenever he approached it, has been seen again lately.[20] He is in Paris, in New York, in Boston. He is now in great spirits; thinks he shall reach it yet; thinks he shall bottle the wave. It is, however, getting a little doubtful. Things have an ugly look still. No matter how many centuries of culture have preceded, the new man always finds himself standing on the brink of chaos, always in a crisis. Can anybody remember when the times were not hard, and money not scarce? Can anybody remember when sensible men, and the right sort of women, were plentiful? Tantalus begins to think steam a delusion, and galvanism no better than it should be.

15   Many facts concur to show that we must look deeper for our salvation than to steam, photographs, balloons, or astronomy. These tools have some questionable properties. They are reagents. Machinery is aggressive. The weaver becomes a web, the machinist a machine. If you do not use the

tools, they use you. All tools are in one sense edge-tools, and dangerous. A man builds a fine house; and now he has a master, and a task for life: he is to furnish, watch, show it, and keep it in repair, the rest of his days. A man has a reputation, and is no longer free, but must respect that. A man makes a picture or a book, and, if it succeeds, 'tis often the worse for him. I saw a brave man the other day, hitherto as free as the hawk or the fox of the wilderness, constructing his cabinet of drawers for shells, eggs, minerals, and mounted birds. It was easy to see that he was amusing himself with making pretty links for his own limbs.

Then the political economist thinks "'tis doubtful if all the mechanical inventions that ever existed have lightened the day's toil of one human being."[21] The machine unmakes the man. Now that the machine is so perfect, the engineer is nobody. Every new step in improving the engine restricts one more act of the engineer,—unteaches him. Once it took Archimedes; now it only needs a fireman, and a boy to know the coppers, to pull up the handles or mind the water-tank. But when the engine breaks, they can do nothing. 16

What sickening details in the daily journals! I believe they have ceased to publish the "Newgate Calendar" and the "Pirate's Own Book" since the family newspapers, namely, the New York Tribune and the London Times, have quite superseded them in the freshness, as well as the horror, of their records of crime.[22] Politics were never more corrupt and brutal; and Trade, that pride and darling of our ocean, that educator of nations, that benefactor in spite of itself, ends in shameful defaulting, bubble, and bankruptcy, all over the world. 17

Of course, we resort to the enumeration of his arts and inventions as a measure of the worth of man. But if, with all his arts, he is a felon, we cannot assume the mechanical skill or chemical resources as the measure of worth. Let us try another gauge. 18

What have these arts done for the character, for the worth of mankind? Are men better? 'Tis sometimes questioned whether morals have not declined as the arts have ascended. Here are great arts and little men. Here is greatness begotten of paltriness. We cannot trace the triumphs of civilization to such benefactors as we wish. The greatest meliorator of the world is selfish, huckstering Trade. Every victory over matter ought to recommend to man the worth of his nature. But now one wonders who did all this good. Look up the inventors. Each has his own knack; his genius is in veins and spots. But the great, equal, symmetrical brain, fed from a great heart, you 19 shall not find. Every one has more to hide than he has to show, or is lamed by his excellence. 'Tis too plain that with the material power the moral progress has not kept pace. It appears that we have not made a judicious investment. Works and days were offered us, and we took works.

20   The new study of the Sanskrit has shown us the origin of the old names of God,—Dyaus, Deus, Zeus, Zeu Pater, Jupiter,—names of the sun, still recognizable through the modifications of our vernacular words, importing that the Day is the Divine Power and Manifestation, and indicating that those ancient men, in their attempts to express the Supreme Power of the universe, called him the Day, and that this name was accepted by all the tribes.

21   Hesiod wrote a poem which he called "Works and Days," in which he marked the changes of the Greek year, instructing the husbandman at the rising of what constellation he might safely sow, when to reap, when to gather wood, when the sailor might launch his boat in security from storms, and what admonitions of the planets he must heed. It is full of economies for Grecian life, noting the proper age for marriage, the rules of household thrift, and of hospitality. The poem is full of piety as well as prudence, and is adapted to all meridians, by adding the ethics of works and of days. But he has not pushed his study of days into such inquiry and analysis as they invite.

22   A farmer said "he should like to have all the land that joined his own." Bonaparte, who had the same appetite, endeavored to make the Mediterranean a French lake.[23] Czar Alexander was more expansive, and wished to call the Pacific *my ocean;* and the Americans were obliged to resist his attempts to make it a close sea.[24] But if he had the earth for his pasture, and the sea for his pond, he would be a pauper still. He only is rich who owns the day. There is no king, rich man, fairy, or demon who possesses such power as that. The days are ever divine as to the first Aryans. They are of the least pretension, and of the greatest capacity, of anything that exists. They come and go like muffled and veiled figures, sent from a distant friendly party; but they say nothing; and if we do not use the gifts they bring, they carry them as silently away.[25]

23   How the day fits itself to the mind, winds itself round it like a fine drapery, clothing all its fancies! Any holiday communicates to us its color. We wear its cockade and favors in our humor. Remember what boys think in the morning of "Election Day," of the Fourth of July, of Thanksgiving or Christmas. The very stars in their courses wink to them of nuts and cakes, bon-

bons, presents, and fireworks. Cannot memory still descry the old school-house and its porch, somewhat hacked by jack-knives, where you spun tops and snapped marbles; and do you not recall that life was then calendared by moments, threw itself into nervous knots or glittering hours, even as now, and not spread itself abroad in equable felicity? In college terms, and in years that followed, the young graduate, when the Commencement anniversary returned, though he were in a swamp, would see a festive light, and find the air faintly echoing with plausive academic thunders. In solitude and in the country, what dignity distinguishes the holy time! The old Sabbath, or Seventh Day, white with the religions of unknown thousands of years, when this hallowed hour dawns out of the deep,—a clean page, which the wise may inscribe with truth, whilst the savage scrawls it with fetishes,—the cathedral music of history breathes through it a psalm to our solitude.

So, in the common experience of the scholar, the weathers fit his moods. 24 A thousand tunes the variable wind plays, a thousand spectacles it brings, and each is the frame or dwelling of a new spirit. I used formerly to choose my time with some nicety for each favorite book. One author is good for winter, and one for the dog-days. The scholar must look long for the right hour for Plato's Timæus. At last the elect morning arrives, the early dawn,—a few lights conspicuous in the heaven, as of a world just created and still becoming,—and in its wide leisures we dare open that book.

There are days when the great are near us, when there is no frown on 25 their brow, no condescension even; when they take us by the hand, and we share their thought. There are days which are the carnival of the year. The angels assume flesh, and repeatedly become visible. The imagination of the gods is excited, and rushes on every side into forms. Yesterday not a bird peeped; the world was barren, peaked, and pining; to-day 'tis inconceivably populous; creation swarms and meliorates.

The days are made on a loom whereof the warp and woof are past and 26 future time. They are majestically dressed, as if every god brought a thread to the skyey web. 'Tis pitiful the things by which we are rich or poor,—a matter of coins, coats, and carpets, a little more or less stone, or wood, or paint, the fashion of a cloak or hat; like the luck of naked Indians, of whom one is proud in the possession of a glass bead or a red feather, and the rest miserable in the want of it. But the treasures which Nature spent itself to amass,—the secular, refined, composite anatomy of man,—which all strata go to form, which the prior races, from infusory and saurian, existed to ripen; the surrounding plastic natures; the earth with its foods; the intellectual, temperamenting air; the sea with its invitations; the heaven deep with worlds; and the answering brain and nervous structure replying to these; the eye that looketh into the deeps, which again look back to the eye,—abyss to abyss;—these, not like a glass bead, or the coins or carpets, are given immeasurably to all.

27   This miracle is hurled into every beggar's hands. The blue sky is a covering for a market, and for the cherubim and seraphim. The sky is the varnish or glory with which the Artist has washed the whole work,—the verge or confines of matter and spirit. Nature could no farther go. Could our happiest dream come to pass in solid fact,—could a power open our eyes to behold "millions of spiritual creatures walk the earth,"[26]—I believe I should find that mid-plain on which they moved floored beneath and arched above with the same web of blue depth which weaves itself over me now, as I trudge the streets on my affairs.

28   'Tis singular that our rich English language should have no word to denote the face of the world. *Kinde* was the old English term, which, however, filled only half the range of our fine Latin word, with its delicate future tense,—*natura, about to be born,* or what German philosophy denotes as a *becoming.* But nothing expresses that power which seems to work for beauty alone.[27] The Greek *Kosmos* did; and therefore, with great propriety, Humboldt entitles his book, which recounts the last results of science, *Cosmos.*[28]

29   Such are the days,—the earth is the cup, the sky is the cover, of the immense bounty of nature which is offered us for our daily aliment; but what a force of *illusion* begins life with us, and attends us to the end! We are coaxed, flattered, and duped, from morn to eve, from birth to death; and where is the old eye that ever saw through the deception? The Hindoos represent Maia, the illusory energy of Vishnu, as one of his principal attributes.[29] As if, in this gale of warring elements, which life is, it was necessary to bind souls to human life as mariners in a tempest lash themselves to the mast and bulwarks of a ship, and Nature employed certain illusions as her ties and straps,—a rattle, a doll, an apple, for a child; skates, a river, a boat, a horse, a gun, for the growing boy;—and I will not begin to name those of the youth and adult, for they are numberless. Seldom and slowly the mask falls, and the pupil is permitted to see that all is one stuff, cooked and painted under many counterfeit appearances. Hume's doctrine was that the circumstances vary, the amount of

happiness does not; that the beggar cracking fleas in the sunshine under a hedge, and the duke rolling by in his chariot, the girl equipped for her first ball, and the orator returning triumphant from the debate, had different means, but the same quantity of pleasant excitement.[30]

This element of illusion lends all its force to hide the values of present time. Who is he that does not always find himself doing something less than his best task? "What are you doing?" "O, nothing; I have been doing thus, or I shall do so or so, but now I am only——" Ah! poor dupe, will you never slip out of the web of the master juggler,—never learn that, as soon as the irrecoverable years have woven their blue glory between to-day and us, these passing hours shall glitter and draw us, as the wildest romance and the homes of beauty and poetry? How difficult to deal erect with them! The events they bring, their trade, entertainments, and gossip, their urgent work, all throw dust in the eyes and distract attention. He is a strong man who can look them in the eye, see through this juggle, feel their identity, and keep his own; who can know surely that one will be like another to the end of the world, nor permit love, or death, or politics, or money, war, or pleasure, to draw him from his task.

The world is always equal to itself, and every man in moments of deeper thought is apprised that he is repeating the experiences of the people in the streets of Thebes or Byzantium. An everlasting Now reigns in nature, which hangs the same roses on our bushes which charmed the Roman and the Chaldæan in their hanging gardens. 'To what end, then,' he asks, 'should I study languages, and traverse countries, to learn so simple truths?'

History of ancient art, excavated cities, recovery of books and inscriptions,—yes, the works were beautiful, and the history worth knowing; and academies convene to settle the claims of the old schools. What journeys and measurements,—Niebuhr and Müller and Layard,—to identify the plain of Troy and Nimroud town![31] And your homage to Dante costs you so much sailing; and to ascertain the discoverers of America needs as much voyaging as the discovery cost. Poor child! that flexile clay of which these old brothers moulded their admirable symbols was not Persian, nor Memphian, nor Teutonic, nor local at all, but was common lime and silex and water, and sunlight, the heat of the blood, and the heaving of the lungs; it was that clay which thou heldest but now in thy foolish hands, and threwest away to go and seek in vain in sepulchres, mummy-pits, and old book-shops of Asia Mi-

30

31

32

nor, Egypt, and England. It was the deep to-day which all men scorn; the rich poverty, which men hate; the populous, all-loving solitude, which men quit for the tattle of towns. HE lurks, *he* hides,—*he* who is success, reality, joy, and power. One of the illusions is that the present hour is not the critical, decisive hour. Write it on your heart that every day is the best day in the year. No man has learned anything rightly, until he knows that every day is Doomsday. 'Tis the old secret of the gods that they come in low disguises. 'Tis the vulgar great who come dizened with gold and jewels. Real kings hide away their crowns in their wardrobes, and affect a plain and poor exterior. In the Norse legend of our ancestors, Odin dwells in a fisher's hut, and patches a boat. In the Hindoo legends, Hari dwells a peasant among peasants. In the Greek legend, Apollo lodges with the shepherds of Admetus; and Jove liked to rusticate among the poor Ethiopians. So, in our history, Jesus is born in a barn, and his twelve peers are fishermen. 'Tis the very principle of science that Nature shows herself best in leasts; 'twas the maxim of Aristotle and Lucretius; and, in modern times, of Swedenborg and of Hahnemann.[32] The order of changes in the egg determines the age of fossil strata. So it was the rule of our poets, in the legends of fairy lore, that the fairies largest in power were the least in size.[33] In the Christian graces, humility stands highest of all, in the form of the Madonna; and in life, this is the secret of the wise. We owe to genius always the same debt, of lifting the curtain from the common, and showing us that divinities are sitting disguised in the seeming gang of gypsies and pedlers. In daily life, what distinguishes the master is the using those materials he has, instead of looking about for what are more renowned, or what others have used well. "A general," said Bonaparte, "always has troops enough, if he only knows how to employ those he has, and bivouacs with them."[34] Do not refuse the employment which the hour brings you, for one more ambitious. The highest heaven of wisdom is alike near from every point, and thou must find it, if at all, by methods native to thyself alone.

33   That work is ever the more pleasant to the imagination which is not now required. How wistfully, when we have promised to attend the working committee, we look at the distant hills and their seductions!

34   The use of history is to give value to the present hour and its duty. That is good which commends to me my country, my climate, my means and materials, my associates. I knew a man in a certain religious exaltation, who

"thought it an honor to wash his own face." He seemed to me more sane than those who hold themselves cheap.[35]

Zoölogists may deny that horse-hairs in the water change to worms; but I find that whatever is old corrupts, and the past turns to snakes. The reverence for the deeds of our ancestors is a treacherous sentiment. Their merit was not to reverence the old, but to honor the present moment; and we falsely make them excuses of the very habit which they hated and defied.

Another illusion is, that there is not time enough for our work. Yet we might reflect that though many creatures eat from one dish, each, according to its constitution, assimilates from the elements what belongs to it, whether time, or space, or light, or water, or food. A snake converts whatever prey the meadow yields him into snake; a fox, into fox; and Peter and John are working up all existence into Peter and John. A poor Indian chief of the Six Nations of New York made a wiser reply than any philosopher, to some one complaining that he had not enough time. "Well," said Red Jacket, "I suppose you have all there is."[36]

A third illusion haunts us, that a long duration, as a year, a decade, a century, is valuable. But an old French sentence says, "God works in moments," —"En peu d'heure Dieu labeure."[37] We ask for long life, but 'tis deep life, or grand moments, that signify. Let the measure of time be spiritual, not mechanical. Life is unnecessarily long. Moments of insight, of fine personal relation, a smile, a glance,—what ample borrowers of eternity they are! Life culminates and concentrates; and Homer said, "The gods ever give to mortals their apportioned share of reason only on one day."[38]

I am of the opinion of the poet Wordsworth, "that there is no real happiness in this life, but in intellect and virtue."[39] I am of the opinion of Pliny, "that, whilst we are musing on these things, we are adding to the length of our lives."[40] I am of the opinion of Glauco, who said, "The measure of life, O Socrates, is, with the wise, the speaking and hearing such discourses as yours."[41]

He only can enrich me who can recommend to me the space between sun and sun. 'Tis the measure of a man,—his apprehension of a day. For we do not listen with the best regard to the verses of a man who is only a poet, nor to his problems, if he is only an algebraist; but if a man is at once acquainted with the geometric foundations of things and with their festal

35

36

37

38

39

splendor, his poetry is exact and his arithmetic musical. And him I reckon the most learned scholar, not who can unearth for me the buried dynasties of Sesostris and Ptolemy, the Sothiac era, the Olympiads and consulships, but who can unfold the theory of this particular Wednesday.[42] Can he uncover the ligaments concealed from all but piety, which attach the dull men and things we know to the First Cause? These passing fifteen minutes, men think, are time, not eternity; are low and subaltern, are but hope or memory, that is, the way *to* or the way *from* welfare, but not welfare. Can he show their tie? That interpreter shall guide us from a menial and eleemosynary existence into riches and stability.[43] He dignifies the place where he is. This mendicant America, this curious, peering, itinerant, imitative America, studious of Greece and Rome, of England and Germany, will take off its dusty shoes, will take off its glazed traveller's-cap, and sit at home with repose and deep joy on its face. The world has no such landscape, the æons of history no such hour, the future no equal second opportunity. Now let poets sing! now let arts unfold!

40   One more view remains. But life is good only when it is magical and musical, a perfect timing and consent, and when we do not anatomize it. You must treat the days respectfully, you must be a day yourself, and not interrogate it like a college professor. The world is enigmatical,—everything said, and everything known or done,—and must not be taken literally, but genially.[44] We must be at the top of our condition to understand anything rightly. You must hear the bird's song without attempting to render it into nouns and verbs. Cannot we be a little abstemious and obedient? Cannot we let the morning be?

41   Everything in the universe goes by indirection. There are no straight lines.[45] I remember well the foreign scholar who made a week of my youth happy by his visit. "The savages in the islands," he said, "delight to play with the surf, coming in on the top of the rollers, then swimming out again, and repeat the delicious manœuvre for hours. Well, human life is made up of such transits. There can be no greatness without abandonment. But here your very astronomy is an espionage. I dare not go out of doors and see the moon and stars, but they seem to measure my tasks, to ask how many lines or pages are finished since I saw them last. Not so, as I told you, was it in Belleisle. The days at Belleisle were all different, and only joined by a perfect love

of the same object. Just to fill the hour,—that is happiness. Fill my hour, ye gods, so that I shall not say, whilst I have done this, 'Behold, also, an hour of my life is gone,'—but rather, 'I have lived an hour.'"[46]

We do not want factitious men, who can do any literary or professional feat, as, to write poems, or advocate a cause, or carry a measure, for money; or turn their ability indifferently in any particular direction by the strong effort of will. No, what has been best done in the world,—the works of genius,—cost nothing. There is no painful effort, but it is the spontaneous flowing of the thought. Shakspeare made his Hamlet as a bird weaves its nest.[47] Poems have been written between sleeping and waking, irresponsibly. Fancy defines herself:

> "Forms that men spy
> With the half-shut eye
> In the beams of the setting sun, am I."[48]

The masters painted for joy, and knew not that virtue had gone out of them. They could not paint the like in cold blood. The masters of English lyric wrote their songs so. It was a fine efflorescence of fine powers; as was said of the letters of the Frenchwomen,—"the charming accident of their more charming existence."[49] Then the poet is never the poorer for his song. A song is no song unless the circumstance is free and fine. If the singer sing from a sense of duty or from seeing no way of escape, I had rather have none. Those only can sleep who do not care to sleep; and those only write or speak best who do not too much respect the writing or the speaking.

The same rule holds in science. The savant is often an amateur. His performance is a memoir to the Academy on fish-worms, tadpoles, or spiders' legs; he observes as other academicians observe; he is on stilts at a microscope, and,—his memoir finished and read and printed,—he retreats into his routinary existence, which is quite separate from his scientific. But in Newton, science was as easy as breathing; he used the same wit to weigh the moon that he used to buckle his shoes; and all his life was simple, wise, and majestic. So was it in Archimedes,—always self-same, like the sky. In Linnæus, in Franklin, the like sweetness and equality,—no stilts, no tiptoe;—and their results are wholesome and memorable to all men.

In stripping time of its illusions, in seeking to find what is the heart of the

42

43

44

day, we come to the quality of the moment, and drop the duration altogether. It is the depth at which we live, and not at all the surface extension, that imports. We pierce to the eternity, of which time is the flitting surface; and, really, the least acceleration of thought, and the least increase of power of thought, make life to seem and to be of vast duration. We call it time; but when that acceleration and that deepening take effect, it acquires another and a higher name.

45   There are people who do not need much experimenting; who, after years of activity, say, we knew all this before; who love at first sight and hate at first sight; discern the affinities and repulsions; who do not care so much for conditions as others, for they are always in one condition, and enjoy themselves; who dictate to others, and are not dictated to; who in their consciousness of deserving success constantly slight the ordinary means of attaining it; who have self-existence and self-help; who are suffered to be themselves in society; who are great in the present; who have no talents, or care not to have them, —being that which was before talent, and shall be after it, and of which talent seems only a tool;—this is character, the highest name at which philosophy has arrived.

46   'Tis not important how the hero does this or this, but what he is. What he is will appear in every gesture and syllable. In this way the moment and the character are one.

47   'Tis a fine fable for the advantage of character over talent, the Greek legend of the strife of Jove and Phœbus. Phœbus challenged the gods, and said, "Who will outshoot the far-darting Apollo?" Zeus said, "I will." Mars shook the lots in his helmet, and that of Apollo leaped out first. Apollo stretched his bow and shot his arrow into the extreme west. Then Zeus arose, and with one stride cleared the whole distance, and said, "Where shall I shoot? there is no space left."[50] So the bowman's prize was adjudged to him who drew no bow.

48   And this is the progress of every earnest mind; from the works of man and the activity of the hands to a delight in the faculties which rule them; from a respect to the works to a wise wonder at this mystic element of time in which he is conditioned; from local skills and the economy which reckons the amount of production *per* hour to the finer economy which respects the quality of what is done, and the right we have to the work, or the fidelity with which it flows from ourselves; then to the depth of thought it betrays, look-

ing to its universality, or, that its roots are in eternity, not in time. Then it flows from character, that sublime health which values one moment as another, and makes us great in all conditions, and is the only definition we have of freedom and power.

Notes

1. For Emerson's drafts of this epigraph, see *JMN*, 14:56, 124, 211. Emerson drew the title for this essay from the Greek poet Hesiod (fl. ca. 800 BCE), whose *Works and Days* treats his everyday experiences with precepts drawn from various sources interspersed throughout.

2. Emerson devised this sentence out of three sources, none of which is by Aristotle. For "Man is the metre [that is, measure] of all things," attributed to the Greek Sophist Protagoras (ca. 481–411 BCE), see Plato, *Cratylus*, 386a, and *Theætetus*, 160d; the source of "the hand is . . . of forms," is Francis Bacon, *The Advancement of Learning*, Book V, in *The Works of Francis Bacon*, ed. James Spedding, R. L. Ellis, and D. D. Heath, 15 vols. (Boston, 1860–1864), 9:63 (*JMN*, 6:186).

3. Although Emerson places this definition of man within quotation marks, those dictionaries of quotation that print it cite Emerson as its lone source.

4. Emerson drew this illustration from Thoreau's reputation as an accurate surveyor; he observed in his journal, "I admire Thoreau . . . with his powerful arithmetic, & his whole body co-working. He can pace sixteen rods more accurately than another man can measure it by tape" (*JMN*, 11:438).

5. These new discoveries or nineteenth-century applications of older ones include steam, especially the steam engine, invented in 1698 by the English military engineer Thomas Savery (ca. 1650–1715), then improved on in the 1760s by James Watt; sulphuric ether, formed by the catalytic action of sulphuric acid on alcohol, was first used in 1844 as an anesthesia in dentistry by Americans Horace Wells (1815–1848) and Gardner Q. Colton (1814–1898); an Atlantic telegraph cable, completed with the assistance of American financier Cyrus West Field (1819–1892) and under the direction of English engineers Samuel Canning (1823–1908) and Daniel Gooch (1816–1889), worked briefly in 1857–1858, but a successful installation occurred in 1865–1866 under Canning's direction and was put into service in 1869; the photograph, which grew out of collaborative experiments between French physicist Joseph Nicéphore Niepce (1765–1833) and French painter Louis Jacques Mandé Daguerre (1789–1851), led Daguerre to a process for creating photographs as daguerreotypes in 1839, which French physicist Claude Félix Abel Niepce de Saint-

Victor (1805–1870) extended to fix images on glass; and the spectograph, or spectography, by which Emerson refers to either nineteenth-century experiments in the frequency (or wavelength) in a spectrum or studies of the colored bands into which a beam of light is decomposed by means of a prism.

6. Emerson's source is Sir David Brewster, *Memoirs of the Life, Writings and Discoveries of Sir Isaac Newton*, 2 vols. (Edinburgh, 1855), 2:406 (*JMN*, 13:429). Leibnitz invented new calculus notations before Newton's (first developed in 1665–1666) appeared in print and published them in 1684.

7. Americans Elias Howe (1819–1867) invented the sewing machine in 1846, Cyrus Hall McCormick (1809–1884) the reaping machine in 1831, and Peter Gaillard (dates uncertain) the horse-drawn mowing machine in 1810. Edmund Cartwright (1743–1823), a British subject, invented the power loom in 1787 and Charles Sauria (1812–1895) of France "lucifer" (or friction) matches in 1830. William Murdock (1754–1839), English engineer, in 1802 lighted the exterior of a factory in Soho with coal gas produced by a process he invented.

8. Charles Babbage (1791–1871), English mathematician, developed a programmable calculating machine and, in 1827, a table of logarithms from 1 to 108,000.

9. Emerson's source for this anecdote of Edward Thurlow, 1st Baron Thurlow (1731–1806), English jurist and lord chancellor (1778–1783), is Horace Twiss, *The Public and Private Life of Lord Chancellor Eldon*, 2 vols. (Philadelphia, 1844), 2:166–167 (*JMN*, 13:195).

10. Advancements in nineteenth-century medicine that Emerson mentions include the increased use of smallpox vaccination and new rhinoplastic treatments that aided in the restoration of noses lost by disease or external injury; for the connection between dentistry and ether, see note 5 above. Transfusions of the blood of a person or an animal into the veins of another were in the experimental stage when Emerson wrote "Works and Days." William Paley (1743–1805), English theologian, attested in his *Natural Theology* (1802) that experiments in transfusion proved that the blood of one animal could serve for that of another, but since blood groups were not identified until 1901 by the Austrian pathologist Karl Landsteiner (1868–1943), transfusions of the sort that Paley and Emerson describe were a dangerous proposition.

11. Caoutchouc is pure rubber; gutta-percha is a durable plastic substance derived from the latex of several Malaysian trees. Discovered in 1845, rubber was introduced to the European market in 1858 and used for either waterproofing or pencil erasers; by 1876, rubber began to be used as a coating for telegraph wires.

12. The first Alpine tunnel was opened in 1848 by the Semmering Railway. In 1849 Cornelius Vanderbilt (1794–1877), American capitalist, contracted with the Nicaraguan government to build a canal connecting the Pacific and the Atlantic oceans, which was begun but not completed; the first international attempt to build a ca-

nal across Central America under the Clayton-Bulwer Treaty (1850) signed by the United States and Britain was also unsuccessful. The dream persisted, and, after a failed attempt by the French, the Panama Canal was completed by the United States in 1913. Using a system of qanats—well-like vertical shafts—water had been drawn from the deserts of Arabia since the fifth century BCE.

13. Emerson's source is Alphonse Toussenel, *Passional Zoology; or, Spirit of the Beasts of France,* trans. M. Edgeworth Lazarus (New York, 1852), p. 23 (*JMN*, 13:209, 331). Also known as Mohammed Ali, Mehemet Ali (1769–1849), viceroy of Egypt (1805–1848), laid the foundations of Khartoum in 1823 at the junction of the White and the Blue Nile rivers, where he encouraged rain through the scientific planting of trees.

14. Cf. Psalm 76:10.

15. The Transcontinental Railroad, constructed between 1863 and 1869, linked the eastern United States rail system that ended at Council Bluffs, Iowa, to San Francisco.

16. For the Atlantic telegraph cable, see note 5 above.

17. Because gun-cotton (cellulose nitrate) is a highly explosive material used in smokeless powder, Emerson overstates its use as fuel for an aeronaut's balloon. The first practical hot air balloon was invented by the French brothers Joseph Michel (1740–1810) and Jacques Étienne (1745–1799) Montgolfier and carried them aloft near Paris on 5 June 1783.

18. For the expression "Nature loves to cross her stocks," see the note to "The Natural Method of Mental Philosophy," para 43, above.

19. Thomas Robert Malthus (1766–1834), English economist.

20. In Greek mythology, Tantalus, a Phrygian king thought to be a son of Zeus, was condemned for his crimes against the gods to remain standing, hungry and thirsty, in water with fruit-laden branches hanging above his head, but whenever he tried to drink or eat, the fruit and water receded out of his reach.

21. Emerson's source is John Stuart Mill as quoted in William Johnston, *England As It Is . . . in the Middle of the Nineteenth Century,* 2 vols. (London, 1851), 1:82 (*JMN*, 13:81).

22. *The Newgate Calendar,* which printed accounts of prisoners in London's Newgate Prison, first appeared in 1773; Charles Ellms's popular *The Pirates Own Book[:] Authentic Narratives of the Most Celebrated Sea Robbers* was first printed in Portland, Maine, in 1837. The *New York Tribune* was published between 1841 and 1924; *The Daily Universal Register,* founded in 1785, was renamed the London *Times* in 1788.

23. In Emerson's journal construction of this passage, Napoleon and his ambitions are the subjects of this and the previous sentence (*JMN*, 8:287 and 9:141).

24. Emerson's historical perspective here is the result of his compression of two separate historical events. The ambition of Russian Czar Nicholas I (1796–1855) to reduce the Balkan and Mediterranean worlds to a "close[d] sea" led to the Crimean

War (1854–1856) and Russia's defeat to an alliance that included Great Britain, France, and Turkey; then, under Czar Alexander II (1818–1881), Nicholas's son, after purchasing Alaska from Russia in 1867, the United States effectively controlled both the northern Pacific and southern Arctic oceans and the Bering Sea.

25. Cf. Emerson, "Days," *CW*, 9:427.

26. Milton, *Paradise Lost*, IV, 677.

27. In his journal Emerson attributes the combined observation of this and the previous sentence to William Ellery Channing II (*JMN*, 10:167–168).

28. In *Kosmos* (1845–1862), Humboldt sought to combine the vague ideals of the eighteenth century with the exacting scientific requirements of the nineteenth century in order to formulate a concept of unity amid the complexity of nature.

29. Emerson's source is *The Vishnu Purana* (1840), p. 498 (*JMN*, 9:322). Vishnu is the chief god of Hindu mythology; Maya (or Maia in Emerson's source) is Vishnu's consort and the mother of the world.

30. David Hume (1711–1776), Scottish writer known for his philosophical skepticism and restriction of human knowledge to experience and impressions.

31. Carsten Niebuhr (1733–1815), German explorer, traveled through the Middle East and Asia Minor; Karl Otfried Müller (1797–1840), German philologist and archaeologist, wrote on the ancient Greeks, Macedonians, and Etruscans; Sir Austen Henry Layard (1817–1894) began excavations in 1845 near the site of ancient Nineveh, where he found artifacts later identified as from the Assyrian city of Calah, the biblical name of Nimroud (or, as it is now known, Nimrod), near Mosul in Iraq.

32. Emerson quotes Francis Bacon, who quotes Aristotle in *The Advancement of Learning* ("Aristotle noteth well, 'that the nature of every thing is best seen in its smallest portions'") from *The Works of Francis Bacon,* ed. Basil Montagu, 3 vols. (Philadelphia, 1850), 1:188. Emerson attributed the concept that "Nature shows herself best in leasts" variously to Aristotle, the Roman poet and author of *De Rerum Natura* Titus Lucretius Carus (ca. 94–55 BCE), and Swedenborg.

33. In a list of *"Leasts"* Emerson wrote, "Faeries the greater in power they are, the less in size," and gave examples drawn from the Editor's Preface to Thomas Warton, *The History of English Poetry,* 4 vols. (London, 1824), 1:50–51 (*TN*, 3:211).

34. Emerson's source is *The Confidential Correspondence of Napoleon Bonaparte with his Brother Joseph . . .* , 2 vols. (New York, 1856), 1:151 (*JMN*, 14:48).

35. The complimentary anecdote related in this and the previous sentence concerns Jones Very (1813–1880), Transcendentalist poet and mystic; see *JMN*, 7:123.

36. Seneca Chief "Red Jacket" (ca. 1750–1830), whose youthful name, Otetiani, was changed to Sagoyewatha at manhood, received his English name from the British, on whose side he fought during the American Revolution; see *JMN*, 14:15.

37. "God works in moments" is Emerson's translation of the sentence in French that

he quoted from Goethe, *Dichtung und Wahrheit*, IV, in *Werke* (1828–1833), 48:49 (*JMN*, 5:191); see "Prudence," *EL*, 2:323.

38. Cf. Homer, *Odyssey*, XVIII, 136–137.

39. Emerson's source is Christopher Wordsworth, *Memoirs of William Wordsworth . . .* , ed. Henry Reed, 2 vols. (Boston, 1851), 1:269 (*JMN*, 11:384).

40. Emerson's source is Gaius Plinius Secundus, *The Natural History of Pliny*, trans. John Bostock and H. T. Riley, 6 vols. (London, 1855–1857), 1:6 (*JMN*, 13:418–419).

41. Emerson's source is *The Works of Plato . . .* (1804), 1:289 (*JMN*, 10:476; 13:419); see Plato's *Republic*, 450b, and "Plato, or the Philosopher," *CW*, 4:36. The name of Plato's brother, one of the interlocutors in *Republic*, is usually translated as Glaucon.

42. Sesostris, a Greek corruption of the Egyptian Senusret, or Senusrit, was the name of three kings of ancient Egypt of the twelfth (Theban) dynasty: Sesostris I (ca. 1980–1935 BCE), Sesostris II (ca. 1906–1887 BCE), and Sesostris III (ca. 1887–1849 BCE). Ptolemy was the name of fifteen (some say more, some less) Egyptian kings who comprised the thirty-first (Ptolemaic) dynasty (304–30 BCE). By the "Sothiac era" Emerson is alluding to a "Sothic" era, a period of 1,461 years averaging 365 days each in the ancient Egyptian calendar. The Olympiads, by which the Greeks computed time from 776 BCE, were a period of four years reckoned from one celebration of the Olympic games to the next.

43. An "eleemosynary existence" is one supported by the charity of others.

44. By "genially" Emerson likely intends "innately."

45. Cf. Emerson, "Uriel," *CW*, 9:33–35, ll. 15–24.

46. Emerson creates here an anecdote in which he disguises the context of his meeting with an unnamed "foreign scholar" and that person's gender. According to passages in his journals from the 1840s, Emerson's scholar appears to be Margaret Fuller. For a more detailed commentary, see *CW*, 7:217–218.

47. This and the previous two sentences comprise Emerson's translation and adaptation to Shakespeare of an assessment of the artistry of French playwright Pierre Corneille (1606–1684) (see *TN*, 2:282; cf. *TN*, 1:176).

48. Emerson's source is the song of the White Lady of Avenel in Sir Walter Scott, *The Monastery* (1820), chapter 9; cf. *TN*, 2:282.

49. Emerson's source is "Woman in France: Madame de Sablé," *Westminster Review* [English edition] 62 (October 1854): 449 (*JMN*, 13:337).

50. Emerson's source is *The Works of Plato: A New and Literal Version . . .* , 6 vols. (London, 1848–1854), 6:107. Jove is the Roman king of the gods and god of sky and thunder, Phœbus Apollo the Greek god of light, and Mars the Roman god of war.

Credits

bridge, Wednesday Evening, Sept. 10 (1856)," "American Civilization (*Atlantic Monthly,* April 1862)," "Thoreau (*Atlantic Monthly,* August 1862)," "The President's Proclamation (*Atlantic Monthly,* November 1862)," and "Character (*North American Review,* April 1866)." Reprinted by permission of the publisher from COLLECTED WORKS OF RALPH WALDO EMERSON, VOLUME X: UNCOLLECTED PROSE WRITINGS: ADDRESSES, ESSAYS, AND REVIEWS, Historical Introduction, Textual Introduction, Text Established, and Textual Apparatus by Ronald A. Bosco and Joel Myerson, Notes and Parallel Passages by Glen M. Johnson, Cambridge, Mass.: The Belknap Press of Harvard University Press, Copyright © 2013 by the President and Fellows of Harvard College.

The following lectures by Emerson are reprinted by permission of the publisher from *The Later Lectures of Ralph Waldo Emerson,* edited by Ronald A. Bosco and Joel Myerson, 2 vols., Athens, Ga.: The University of Georgia Press, Copyright © 2001 by The University of Georgia Press: "New England: Genius, Manners, and Customs," "England," "The Anglo-American," "American Slavery," "Address at the Woman's Rights Convention," "The Natural Method of Mental Philosophy," and "The Scholar." Additionally, the following early lectures by Emerson are reprinted by permission of the publisher from *The Selected Lectures of Ralph Waldo Emerson,* edited by Ronald A. Bosco and Joel Myerson, Athens, Ga.: The University of Georgia Press, Copyright © 2005 by The University of Georgia Press: "The Uses of Natural History" and "Humanity of Science."

"Sermon CLXII ['The Lord's Supper']" [MS Am 120.215 (162A)]. Reprinted with permission from Ralph Waldo Emerson Memorial Association deposit, Houghton Library, Harvard University.

Index

In this Index, endnotes are keyed to page and endnote number. Typically, numbered endnotes identify the full name of persons, the authors and titles of works of prose, dramatic writing, or poetry, and the significance of major events the first time they occur in Emerson's writings printed in this volume or in the endnotes.